Mastering™

PRAISE FROM OUR READERS

Mastering HTML 4

"This is THE book!! If you can't find what you are looking for or learn HTML from this book, then there is no hope. This is the most comprehensive HTML book I have ever seen! Well worth the money and time to read it!"
Martha Rich, Arkansas

"Fantastic, Comprehensive, Easy-to-Read! I've thumbed through, and read thoroughly, many HTML books, but this one just grabs your brain, rattles out your neurons and implants the goodies you need to slam-dunk a great Web site. The authors provide an easy-to-read format with just the right amount of examples and details that won't leave you asking more questions or bore you with too many arcane details."
Sabrina Hanley, North Carolina

Mastering FrontPage 98

"Best of the 9 FrontPage 98 books I own. Sybex does it again! I have been reading computer books for the last 10 years and Sybex has been a great publisher—putting out excellent books. After reading 3/4 of the book so far, I know that the publisher and the authors take pride in their product. It's a wonderful book!"
Mike Perry, New Jersey

"This is THE book for mastering FrontPage 98! I skimmed through 4 other books before deciding to buy this one. Every other book seemed like a larger version of the weak documentation that comes with the software. This book provided the insight on advanced subjects necessary for administering a web. A must buy for FrontPage users."
Richard Hartsell, Utah

Mastering CorelDraw 8

"I'm a computer graphics instructor (college level) and the 'Mastering' books have long been on my Highly Recommended list for students. As for Rick Altman, I've been using his Corel books for the last four versions. This is a reference book, and a beautifully complete one. This is for the artist who needs to truly understand an effect or feature and get back to work. It's also readable. Students can work through chapters, or even the entire book, and they certainly won't get bored. I love following an Altman book from start to finish."
Christine C. Frey, Maryland

SYBEX
www.sybex.com

MASTERING
MICROSOFT

FRONTPAGE 2000

PREMIUM EDITION

MASTERING™
MICROSOFT®
FRONTPAGE® 2000
PREMIUM EDITION

Daniel A. Tauber
Brenda Kienan
Molly E. Holzschlag

SYBEX®

San Francisco • Paris • Düsseldorf • Soest • London

Associate Publisher: Amy Romanoff
Contracts & Licensing Manager: Kristine O'Callaghan
Acquisitions & Developmental Editors: Kim Crowder
and Cheryl Applewood
Editor: Emily K. Wolman
Technical Editor: Rebecca Horakh
Book Designers: Patrick Dintino and Catalin Dulfu
Graphic Illustrator: Tony Jonick
Electronic Publishing Specialist: Nila Nichols
Project Team Leader: Lisa Reardon
Proofreaders: Catherine Morris, Richard Ganis, and
Blythe Woolston
Indexer: Matthew Spence
Cover Designer: Design Site
Cover Illustrator: Jack D. Myers

Library of Congress Card Number: 99-62863
ISBN: 0-7821-2456-9

Manufactured in the United States of America

10 9 8 7 6 5 4 3 2 1

To Claire,

who was born with the first edition,

walked with the second, and with this

one, has learned to say "No."

—Brenda Kienan and Dan Tauber

For Larry S,

Though lost to the years, your influence

helped get me where I am today.

—Molly E. Holzschlag

ACKNOWLEDGMENTS

A big book on a short schedule is never a solitary venture. Our thanks go to the many people involved in making this one a reality.

At Sybex, thanks as always to the home team of Barbara Gordon, Chris Meredith, and Kristine O'Callaghan; many thanks also to Amy Romanoff, Cheryl Applewood, Kim Crowder, and Emily Wolman for keeping the project on track; to production players Lisa Reardon, Nila Nichols, and Tony Jonick, and to proofreaders Catherine Morris, Richard Ganis, and Blythe Woolston for pulling manuscript and screen shots together into an actual book; to Becky Horakh for reviewing technical details; and to Matthew Spence for plucking and categorizing references into an index.

Continued thanks to those who worked so hard on *Mastering FrontPage 98*, including Sybex's Dan Brodnitz and Anamary Ehlen; our esteemed colleague J. Tarin Towers; contributing writers E. Stephen Mack, Ann Navarro, Wendy Van Wazer, Dave Kearns, and LANwrights; and to Rael and Asha Dornfest.

From Dan and Brenda, many thanks once again to the Studio B literary agency, especially to David Rogelberg and Sherry Rogelberg, for good counsel and a sense of humor as well as perspective.

We also remain grateful for the support and caring of family and friends: Joani and Jessica Buehrle; Sharon Crawford and Charlie Russel; the Cunningham family; Rion Dugan; Femmes Who Feast (Dana Dubinsky, Janice Berman, and Sofia Marchant); Fred Frumberg; Jessica, Martin, and Lori Grant; Caroline Heller; Mai Le Bazner, Katri Foster, and Peter Bazner; the McArdle and Undercoffer families; Carolyn Miller; Lonnie Moseley and Cordell Sloan; Wynn Moseley and her family; Freeman Ng; Margaret Tauber; Ron and Frances Tauber; Judy Tauber; Savitha Varadan; and Robert E. Williams III. Thanks also to Barbara Cohen, Kent Gerard, Ana Ortiz, and Charlie Wright for their contributions to family, home, and hearth.

From Molly, a hearty thanks to Waterside Productions and especially, David Fugate for his friendship, wisdom, and constancy. Thank you, Julie Ciamporcero, for your able assistance and enthusiastic, warm friendship. To all my family, friends, readers, and students, I thank you most gratefully. You keep me happy, challenged, fulfilled, and, most of all, appreciated and loved.

CONTENTS AT A GLANCE

TABLE OF CONTENTS

PART II · CREATING SOPHISTICATED DESIGNS

12 Fantastic Frames   339

13 Getting in Style with Cascading Style Sheets   377

PART VI • STEP-BY-STEP FRONTPAGE SITES

APPENDICES

INTRODUCTION

FrontPage 2000 is no mere HTML editor. It offers an interface that places both the novice and professional at the helm of a powerful tool. Whether your goal is easy creation of single Web pages or the planning, building, and maintenance of a big site that will be tended by a whole team of Webmasters, FrontPage 2000 can meet your needs, and *Mastering FrontPage 2000 Premium Edition* is your indispensable guide to maximizing FrontPage 2000's potential.

What's New in FrontPage 2000

FrontPage 2000 has improved on its predecessor, FrontPage 98, in several important ways:

- Complete integration of the Explorer and Editor into a singular interface, resulting in even greater usability.

- FrontPage 2000 works seamlessly with its fellow Office 2000 application mates. This integration allows users—especially companies—to increase productivity dramatically.

- Hands-off HTML and scripting means that if you have a customized piece of HTML or a script that you want to add to any FrontPage document, you can do so without FrontPage altering that code. This gives designers a lot more flexibility in how they use FrontPage to create Web sites.

FrontPage 2000 also allows you to:

- Create and edit HTML with the ease of word processing. You can also switch from editing to previewing the page or viewing the HTML source code in a snap.

- Design tables using true drag-and-drop features. You can also resize rows and columns quickly, making page layout much easier.

- Use dialog boxes to create handy, informative forms. You can set preferences such that when users fill out these forms, the data they provide will be routed via e-mail or saved to a server.

- Establish a consistent look for the whole site or portions of the site using Cascading Style Sheets.

- Produce text animation and other special effects using Dynamic HTML as well as Image Composer's sophisticated graphics and animation tools.

- Assign permission to view or to change various parts of the site to specified site reviewers or members of your Web development team.

- Create navigation bars, hover buttons, hit counters, and more, all automatically, without any need for actual programming.

- Find, repair, and update outdated content or broken links on your site. You can also assign these and other tasks to Web development team members to be done now or later, and you can even track whether assigned tasks have been completed, when, and by whom.

All of these features make FrontPage 2000 an impressive Web site management package; it lets you move seamlessly from building an effective site to maintaining the site, and because of FrontPage's *What-You-See-Is-What-You-Get* (*WYSIWYG*) interface, you can do so without having to overcome a steep learning curve. Whether your site is large or small, and whether you are an HTML novice or an old pro, you'll find out why FrontPage is just the application you need to manage your site.

Is This Book for You?

This book is an excellent choice for novices and intermediate readers alike. Written in plain English and filled with practical examples and step-by-step exercises, *Mastering FrontPage 2000 Premium Edition* will take you where you want to go with Web site development—and quickly! It will get you started in no time using all of the features of FrontPage 2000. You'll rapidly be able to create dazzling effects just using FrontPage's basic tools, its themes (prepackaged looks), and a selection of FrontPage components, which can add function to your site with no programming whatsoever.

If you already have the basics under your belt, you'll find that this book will help you produce and maintain a powerful Web site presence in no time flat, with insider tips that might otherwise take you forever to stumble onto. *Mastering FrontPage 2000 Premium Edition* offers strategic advice on designing a successful site, making the most of typography, assigning and managing site creation and maintenance tasks, and even promoting your site and measuring its success.

This special, premium edition includes a variety of advanced chapters that will help bring you to the domain of the professional developer. With advanced graphics techniques, you'll learn how to create graphics like the best designers in the business.

Back-end and project management information will give you a solid conceptual foundation for what, beyond software, is necessary for Web developers to know. Finally, we walk you step-by-step through the production of Web sites, so you can see how FrontPage 2000 really works.

Throughout this book, you'll find pointers to handpicked Web sites of all kinds that we know will provide you with additional information on every topic in this book. We'll tell you where to find Web-friendly color palettes, images, animations, sound files, and ActiveX controls you can use, as well as more tips on publishing a terrific Web site and announcing it to the world.

How This Book Is Organized

This book is organized into six parts containing 32 chapters. Part I, *Building Basic FrontPage Webs*, sets the stage for future work by introducing sound Web design principles and then leading you through the FrontPage interface. It teaches you how to create basic pages with FrontPage, introduces you to working with text and type, and gears you up to manage tasks and then publish a site right to the Web.

Part II, *Creating Sophisticated Designs*, introduces how to incorporate design elements and media like graphics, animation, image maps, sound, video, and music into your site. It covers using FrontPage's Cascading Style Sheets features to apply a consistent look to your site, and discusses how to implement effective forms and use frames well. You'll be introduced to special effects, and address perhaps the most important design concern of all: Browsers are not equal! Chapter 16 shows you how to take into consideration the ins and outs of designing for multiple browsers using FrontPage 2000.

Part III, *Advanced Web Graphic Design*, hones in on various aspects of graphic production for the Web. You'll get situated with an understanding of important design concepts, move on to a wealth of information about today's hottest design software that will complement the work you do in FrontPage, and finish up with production techniques that will get and keep you organized and your sites moving along admirably.

Part IV, *Taking Your Webs to the Top*, shows you how to integrate Microsoft Office into your sites, and how to take advantage of FrontPage's handy components—which let you incorporate effects that typically require programming know-how, even if you have no programming experience at all. Then you'll learn how FrontPage manages important programming elements such as JavaScript, Dynamic HTML (DHTML), and databases. The section finishes up with a tutorial on how to maintain and promote your sites for the long term.

Part V, *Back-End Applications and Professional Management*, helps you put on the Web developer cap. In this section of the book, you'll learn about back-end technologies such as CGI and Perl, take an in-depth look at Active Server Pages and databases, and read about another software application that's akin to FrontPage: Microsoft's Visual InterDev.

Part VI, *Step-By-Step FrontPage Sites*, wraps up the book by putting the learning to the literal test. This section's four chapters walk you through the actual creation of four types of sites, a personal Web page, a small business site, a community site, and a large-scale site. Each of these chapters has plenty of professional tips and provides visual references throughout the process.

You'll also find five appendices at the back of the book. Appendix A steps you through customizing FrontPage, Appendix B guides you in choosing and installing the correct server software so your installation of FrontPage will go smoothly, Appendix C describes the FrontPage Server Extensions, Appendix D demystifies installing and troubleshooting TCP/IP, and Appendix E offers a comprehensive HTML reference. Finally, the What's on the CD page at the back of the book will guide you through the software we've made available on this book's accompanying CD-ROM.

 MASTERING WHAT'S ONLINE

A Complete, Updated HTML Reference

At www.htmlreference.com, you'll find a complete, easy-to-use online reference to HTML 4 including the Netscape and Internet Explorer extensions and style sheet attributes.

Conventions Used in This Book

Mastering FrontPage 2000 Premium Edition uses various conventions to help you find the information you need quickly and effortlessly. Tips, Notes, and Warnings, shown here, are placed strategically throughout the book to help you zero in on important information in a snap.

 TIP Here you'll find insider tips and shortcuts—quick information meant to help you use FrontPage more adeptly.

NOTE Here you'll find reminders, asides, and bits of important information that should be especially noted.

 WARNING Here you'll find cautionary information describing trouble spots you may encounter when using the software.

A simple kind of shorthand used in this book helps to save space so more crucial matters can be discussed. For example, directions to "pull down the File menu and choose Save" appear as "select File ➢ Save."

Long but important or interesting digressions are set aside as boxed text, called *sidebars*.

These Are Called Sidebars

In boxed text like this, you'll find background information and side issues—anything that merits attention or adds to your knowledge base, but can be skipped in a real pinch. There are three particular types of sidebars that you'll see repeated throughout the book.

 MASTERING THE OPPORTUNITIES

Make the Most of FrontPage 2000

Distinctive *Mastering the Opportunities* sidebars highlight ways you can use Front-Page 2000 to its best advantage. These sidebars provide you with more than just tips—they provide solutions.

MASTERING TROUBLESHOOTING

Sidestep Trouble

Mastering Troubleshooting sidebars show you how to stay out of potentially serious trouble or how to find your way to a problem-solving fix or workaround should you need one.

MASTERING WHAT'S ONLINE

Web Resources for Just About Everything!

Special *Mastering What's Online* sidebars tell you exactly where on the World Wide Web you can find out more about the topic at hand or where to find the home page being described. The URL for the home page of interest at the moment appears in a special font: www.tauberkienan.com.

Let's Get Started!

Enough about what's in the book—we're sure you want to get going! It's just a turn of the page and you'll be off to a great start learning how to create Web sites with FrontPage 2000.

 NOTE VIsit the Microsoft FrontPage Web site, www.microsoft.com/frontpage/.

PART 1

Building Basic FrontPage Webs

LEARN TO:

- **Understand the basics of creating great sites**

- **Explore FrontPage 2000's new interface**

- **Work with text and typography**

- **Manage tasks**

- **Publish your pages to the Web**

CHAPTER 1

Introduction to Web Design

We know you're itching to get busy using FrontPage 2000, but before you do, let's spend a little time learning how to plan your site, develop its *look and feel* (visual presence), and get a sense of what successful sites look like. Yes, this process will demand some of your time before you jump in and learn FrontPage, but take our advice—spending this time now will save you many hours (maybe even days) in the long run.

This chapter will teach you how to go about planning your Web site. It will also provide a number of Web site do's and don'ts that will ensure that your site looks great and works well, too. Finally, it will point out some sites that demonstrate high quality design, and introduce some ways FrontPage and the tools that come with it can help you along the way. After reading this chapter, you'll be ready to create your own successful Web site.

Planning Your Site

The importance of planning your site cannot be stressed enough. It is a step that many people don't know about, or don't understand the importance of. Planning a Web site is akin to planning a home. Some might just jump in and begin building, but inevitably they will find they have to do things over again, or that they don't have the right tools or enough materials, and so forth. Of course, even the most careful planners will encounter the need to make changes or modify an approach along the way. However, proper planning is going to reduce and even possibly eliminate the frustrations that will *definitely* occur without going through this important process.

These basic steps will help you plan your site:

1. Define your target audience.

2. Organize your concepts and materials.

3. Create a directory structure (also known as *site mapping*).

4. Create a *storyboard* (sketch) of the page(s) you intend to create.

5. Design and refine the look and feel of the site.

If all this sounds complicated, don't worry! Rest assured that these steps are well worth the time you take. The next sections will go into detail on each of these steps, walking you through the concepts as well as providing tips on how to make the planning process a success.

Step 1: Define Your Target Audience

Your Web site will be accessed by dozens if not hundreds or thousands of people every day. You'll want your site to clearly convey the message you intend, whether that's promoting your wonder widgets, publishing the results of research, showing off your resume, or describing what's happening at the local soda pop machine.

But how do Web sites—or any media for that matter—convey this message? This is done by first understanding who you want to convey this message to. Without this information, you'll miss the intended mark and message—the critical foundation upon which your Web site will operate.

Therefore, the first essential step in any design project is to define the target audience. You need to consider the viewers' backgrounds and previous experiences, their interests, their tastes, and why they're visiting your site. You will also do well to know what their general ages are, what geographical locations they live in, and what they want out of their Web experience.

WARNING If your Web site exists solely as a personal statement or creative exercise, you may think you can ignore this step and design your site based upon your own tastes and preferences. Should you choose to do this, you are actually limiting yourself because you haven't defined who your site is really for. If you want to reach beyond that limitation, it's better to walk through the planning steps discussed in this chapter.

How do you figure out information about your audience? Well, if you're working in a professional environment, it's highly likely someone has collected information about the current users of your product or services. Find out if any demographic studies have been done that reflect your client base.

If you don't have this information available, or you're in a more casual environment, you can use the following list as a guide.

Demographic Survey

Describe your current and intended future audience in detail. Be sure to include information on:

- Age
- Gender
- Financial status
- Educational background

Continued

CONTINUED

- Geographical location
- Marital status

What else do you know about your audience? Are they friends? Relatives? Business buddies or clients? Write several paragraphs about who your site is intended to reach now, as well as who you'd like it to reach down the road.

It's important to think this step out. Missing your target audience can result in your Web site missing the opportunity to provide those individuals with an experience they might really want or need.

Think of it this way: A lot of gadgets that make a Web site fun might be fine for an entertainment-oriented audience, but could annoy and distract a serious researcher or technical professional looking for information or solutions. Lots of graphics and multimedia effects might add excitement to a Web publication on a corporate intranet, where everyone accesses the site via a speedy *local area network (LAN)*, but in that setting, the snappy graphics and active media also might be distracting.

The keys to successfully communicating with your audience are first to identify who they are and then anticipate their reaction to the various elements of your Web site. You can tailor almost every aspect of your Web site to your target audience— from the way you organize information to the kinds of fonts and images you use.

MASTERING WHAT'S ONLINE

You can learn a lot about demographics and how to get good demographic information for your site by visiting the following sites:

- Facts on File—Most of the information in Facts on File is found in real-time libraries. However, they have good information to get you started at their Web site: www.lib.us.edu/facts.htm.

- Census Information—If you live outside the United States, you can search for census information using your favorite search engine; census information for the U.S. can be found at www.census.gov.

- The Internet Advertising Resource Guide—This guide will help you understand more about the importance of planning and knowing your audience: www.admedia .org/internet/planning.html.

Continued

MASTERING WHAT'S ONLINE CONTINUED

- KnowX—This public records search can help you find all kinds of interesting information for free, or at a very low cost: www.knowx.com.
- Marketing tools and resources—Another advertising guide to help you with appropriately positioning your Web site: www.marketingpower.com/sources/default.htm.

Later in this chapter, we'll look at some specific examples of Web sites that use various design and navigational elements to accomplish their purposes; you can make your own tour of Web sites to investigate what works and what doesn't. As you do, notice the design decisions other Web site creators have made, and how they contribute to the effectiveness of the site. For example, sites offering quick technical solutions or easy software downloads may not always employ fancy graphics, and sites showcasing fine furniture that might be ordered by professional interior decorators probably do warrant high design.

 NOTE If your audience wants the newest gizmo, you may want to go the route of designing for the latest and greatest. If your audience is, for example, people in underfunded countries who may have slow connections and older browsers, you will want to take that into consideration. Whatever kinds of people make up your audience, consider their true browser capabilities and design your site accordingly. See Chapter 16, *Cross-Browser Design,* for more details.

Step 2: Set Goals and Get Organized

To start designing your Web page, you must first conceptualize. Think through what your site's goals and mission might be—to inform? Promote? Educate? Research and report? Or are you in this for entertainment? Make sure your site goals are clear to you, and if yours is a company site, make sure that its goals are in line with the company's values and mission. Most companies—indeed, many departments within bigger companies—have a mission statement from which they work. You can check in with those mission statements and even write one for the site.

What's Your Mission?

To write a mission statement for your site, consider:

- What product or service do you or your company offer, either generally or through the site?
- What three to five goals do you (or your company) plan to achieve? (Will the site inform, entertain, sell, promote, distribute, or research and report? Most sites are geared toward accomplishing some combination of these general goals.) Think both for the short- and long-term here, anticipating that the needs of today might be different from your longer-term plans.
- What few words or simple phrase can describe your image or the site's intended image?
- What audience or user base should the site reach?
- How will the site itself help to reach that audience or achieve those overall goals?
- What sorts of content or technologies are available for use in the site, given the boundaries of your budget and keeping in mind the appropriateness of that stuff for your audience and goals?
- How will you and/or your company recognize success in your Web site?

Go ahead and pull these thoughts together into a cohesive, written statement describing your site's mission. Keep it short—one paragraph or a few brief sentences will be fine. If one piece of information seems to conflict with another—for example, if the company's goal is to distribute server-side software but the site as envisioned is one that entertains via an online soap-opera style story—go back and prioritize. Always keep in mind what will serve your overall goals.

As you go on to actually plan your site, check and double-check to make sure your tactics suit your strategy and that your content and design fulfill the mission you've set out, whatever that may be. This is vital to getting and remaining organized as you plan and execute your site.

Organize!

Now, organize your assets. Pull together any existing documents and images you want to work with—for example, artwork and stuff you've written if it's a personal site. Or, if it's a company site, you may want to assemble logos, company information, and product descriptions. You may find that you need to create new content and write lots of copy. If so, just jot down a few ideas for now and do the writing later. You're just planning at this stage.

Think about the message you want to convey to fulfill your mission and which types of images or text might be appropriate. If your site's goal suggests fun and lightheartedness, then chatty, informal language and whimsical graphics may fit the bill. On the other hand, a seriously corporate site is more suited to formal, concise language and smooth, elegant graphics.

Do the Shuffle

Once you've got your mission and strategy clearly laid out, and you have your materials in hand, shuffle those materials around a bit. Put like things together into groupings, and eliminate any instances of repetition. You may want to get yourself to a big whiteboard, tape pages onto it, and shuffle them around further, forming the whole business into a giant chart. At this point, a site plan will begin to emerge, but don't get too attached to any aspect of it just yet. Instead, ponder that plan and fiddle with it. You may find that you need to create some new material to go with what already exists. Move things around until they look really organized. You can never do too much organizing and planning, and the bigger your site will be, the more of this you should do. In the next step, you can start to nail things down more formally.

MASTERING WHAT'S ONLINE

It's a common misconception that everything on the Web is "in the public domain." It isn't. Make sure you have the legal right to use any materials you find on the Web (or anywhere else) and plan to include in your Web site. Some copyright and legal resources include:

- A U.S. copyright law page published by Cornell University at www.law.cornell.edu/topics/copyright.html
- The Internet Legal Resource Guide at www.ilrg.com
- The Copyright Web Site at www.benedict.com
- The Nolo Press Self-Help Law Center at www.nolo.com

These last three include special focus on issues related to the Internet and online publishing.

Step 3: Create a Directory Structure

Once you've organized your thinking, it's time to arrange your content into a filing system of sorts. If your site will contain a small number of HTML and image files, you can store all the files in a single directory as you build the Web site. More complex sites require *file management*—you'll want to organize your files into directories and subdirectories to make identifying them and maintaining your site easier.

Setting up a directory structure for your Web site's files, also referred to as *site mapping*, is a piece of cake—provided you do it in advance. Developing a logical directory structure is an essential part of planning your Web site. It becomes even more important once you start adding links and images to your Web site, as you must specify the correct path for each file you reference in a Web page. If you later move files or change filenames, and specify an incorrect path, the references will no longer work.

 TIP FrontPage allows you to build "webs," which actually are somewhat like directories, in that they are a means of organizing content. When you build a site using FrontPage, you can either go the route of creating webs within the bigger web that is your site, or of creating directories within the big web. (Any web, by the way, can contain directories.) The advantage of using webs rather than just directories is that you can then set things up so that different people can author or update different parts of the site. For example, you can place all the Press Relations content in one web, giving the PR folks access to that web but not to the web with the Tech Support content in it.

You can use the information you gleaned from the last section, "Step 2: Set Goals and Get Organized," in this step. You'll need to organize your pages into a top-down directory structure, just as you might organize your hard disk or a filing cabinet.

To help visualize your directory structure, first draw a box (you can use a pen and paper, or work in the imaging software of your choice) to represent your home page. Below that, draw a horizontal line and sketch boxes under it to represent the directories that will contain major groupings of material. You can place smaller groupings within subdirectories at a deeper level.

 NOTE Much of this is an automatic process in FrontPage. However, we offer this information as a general primer to building a Web site.

As you do all of this, consider again which pages can be linked, and don't place two copies of the same page in two separate directories. Note, too, that every page and file that will make up your site must go in one directory or another; keep fooling with your directory structure until you can make that happen neatly. Keep the names you use for directories and subdirectories short and descriptive. For example, instead of /JOBLISTINGS, just go with /JOBS.

TIP On larger sites, you will want to create separate directories for elements other than the primary HTML. A common example of this is the subdirectory of /images. Most Web designers use this area to hold all of the site's images. You will also have subdirectories for specific content.

Step 4: Create a Storyboard

Now create a storyboard (sketch) of your home page and each page it will link to. Include in your storyboard all of the elements you're considering (text, images, buttons, hyperlinks), and don't be afraid to make adjustments. You needn't be an artist to do this, by the way—your goal is still organization, not final design. If your original concept doesn't flow nicely, axe it and start again. Better to find out now than when you're halfway through the actual design stage.

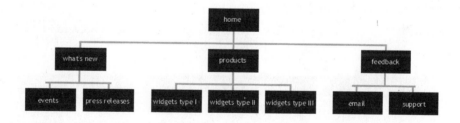

NOTE Having come up with a general site plan and directory structure, you may have noticed that your content falls into certain types. If so, it might be possible to work within various page templates into which you'll pour content so that you don't have to design the site page by time-consuming page. You can do this easily in FrontPage! Visit Chapter 3, *Working in Page View*, and Chapter 4, *Creating Basic Pages*.

Remember that the Web thrives on links and that Web users don't expect to read an entire Web site like a novel, moving from page to page in a linear fashion. They want to jump quickly to an item that interests them and then move on to something else. Viewers may enter your Web site at any point via a link from another site.

Users must be able to move around a Web site quickly and easily so they can find what they seek with a minimum of fuss and bother. If your Web site is difficult to navigate, folks will hike away in frustration and probably won't bother coming back. Provide people with aids to navigation—a navigation bar, for example, with simple text links or nice buttons. Provide one-click access to key sections of your Web site from the home page or from other key pages. There are all sorts of ways to do this; what's most important is that you make navigational elements clear to see and easy to use.

Keep in mind that the difference between an exciting Web site and a dull one usually has less to do with the complexity or technical sophistication of your design and more to do with the quality of the site's content *and* the success of its presentation. Design each page of your Web site so that it stands alone and yet is part of a larger whole. Consider what *palette*, or combination of colors, you might want to use, what sorts of fonts might work, and where you will place items such as these:

- Navigational elements such as a nav bar with buttons, or any text links to other pages
- Identifying banners, logos, and so on
- Illustrations and other types of artwork
- Text of all types
- Any notice of ownership or copyright you may want to include

MASTERING WHAT'S ONLINE

A great way to get a grip on what works is to look at what *not* to do.

- Cruise through Web Pages That Suck at www.webpagesthatsuck.com.
- To see some surprising examples of bad style, check out the Bad Style Page at www.earth.com/bad-style.
- Look (as long as you're able to) at Clay Shirky's Worst Page on the World Wide Web at www.panix.com/~clays/biff.
- For more finger-pointing fun, check out Yecch!!!, a great parody of Yahoo!, at www.yeeeoww.com/yecch/yecchhome.html.

Step 5: Develop a Look and Feel

The next step is to work on the look and feel of your Web site. What do we mean by *look and feel*? This is a design term that refers to the overall visual representation of your site. It is essentially the combination of color, graphics, type, and text that help to convey your meaning with style and impact.

You've already done your planning and created a storyboard that has the elements of your site. Now you want to work those elements into a sophisticated—and integrated—visual design.

FrontPage 2000 can help you do this because it provides a wide range of outstanding site templates (see Chapter 3). Figure 1.1 shows some of the FrontPage 2000 templates. However, you want to be able to have total flexibility and control over your site, and to do this, the ability to visualize the end product is important.

FIGURE 1.1

FrontPage 2000 offers a large variety of site templates.

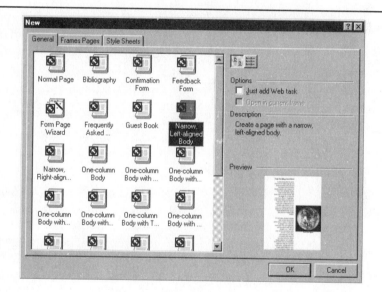

If you don't have a design background, one short section in a chapter of a software book isn't going to give you one. However, there are several important steps you can take to ensure that a consistent look and feel evolves. Furthermore, there are some terrific resources that can help you with gaining a more refined esthetic when it comes to matching your site's message with its design.

Here's a list of elements you'll want to be sure to take into consideration when developing your site's look and feel:

Space and Balance This is the amount of space the elements on your page take up, as well as the amount of empty, or "white" space—and how everything balances out. Typically, designers want to see plenty of white space along with elements. This balance improves readability and makes visitors feel as if they are relaxed instead of cluttered.

Color We'll look at Web color throughout this book—particularly when we study text, fonts, and tables. As a starting point, though, you should think about what colors mean, and how they will best work for your site. If you're doing a personal home page and are a splashy, bright person, then splashy, bright colors might well be in order. On the other hand, a serious Web site will do better with muted color.

Type Type, like color, adds personality and impact to a site. Type also must be appropriate for a site's message. And, like space, type must be balanced. In other words, you don't want to have 20 conflicting typefaces on a page—it will look unprofessional and confusing. We'll take a closer look at how to work with type in Chapter 6, *Fantastic Fonts*.

Shapes As you surf around the Web, you might notice that there are a lot of rectangles. Look at those common advertising banners—they are always rectangular! So are many page headers, buttons, and other page elements. Rectangles are okay, but because they are so common, you should think about other shapes for your site, too—like ovals and triangles. Shapes help make a site distinctive.

Texture You'll see texture showing up in background graphics, but this isn't the only place where you can add the look of stone, or recycled paper, or a silky sheen. Think about how your concept can best be represented by texture, and work that texture into your site if you feel it makes sense to do so. But be careful: texture can often conflict with readability. Be sure to select texture that is subtle enough that text on top of it is clear and easy to see.

Special Effects Is your site going to benefit from special effects, such as animations or mouseovers? If you think so, begin planning them now, but use a light hand! Special effect overkill is rampant on the Web, and you don't want to blow a good site by adding too many bouncing, jumping, and blinking elements. You'll learn more about special effects in Chapter 15.

Consistency Think about how your site will look from page to page. Using a single color scheme throughout is a good way to achieve consistency. Another way to achieve this is to use the same navigation aids on each page.

Variation Should every page be the exact same color? No! Depending upon your site map, you can make subtle changes at different levels while keeping the site consistent. You'll see an example of this later on in this chapter, when we take a visit to San Francisco's Exploratorium.

Developing a look and feel is a major part of design. Many people building Web pages are not necessarily designers, so they might not be aware of the kinds of concerns mentioned in the previous section. Study these issues well, and you'll have greater insight into how to create a visually interesting series of pages.

Believe it or not, you've just gotten a good taste of how to plan your site! It wasn't that painful at all, now was it? And you're sure to have better results in the long term, because you took the time to work through these concepts.

The following Web Designer's Toolbox sidebar can help you independently seek out more information on how to become a more refined creator of Web pages.

MASTERING WHAT'S ONLINE

Web Designer's Toolbox

Use these URLs and books to help you gain a better understanding of how to design Web sites:

- Builder.com. CNET's Developer site has vast resources and snappy articles to help you gain a better understanding of design as well as Web technology: www.builder.com.
- SiteBuilder Network. This Microsoft site is a power network with tutorials, articles, software, newsgroups, chats, and special events all geared around the joy of building Web sites. Lots of great stuff for designers, and particularly those using FrontPage and other Microsoft products such as the Internet Explorer browser. Membership is free: www.microsoft.com/sitebuilder.
- Netscape's DevEdge. Surf the edge of the Web's wave and learn how to design sites using Netscape's time-honored wisdom and technology: developer .netscape.com.
- Webreview.com is a great site for those with a real hunger for all that's new in the Web design and development world. Articles, departments, community, and live events: www.webreview.com.
- The Web Design Community: Molly's Web Answers for Everyone. Specializing in helping the novice get acquainted with the world of Web Design, this Microsoft Network community also offers articles, chats, events, and newsgroups for intermediate and advanced Web designers, too: communities.msn.com/webdesign.

Continued

MASTERING WHAT'S ONLINE CONTINUED

- The Web Design Group: Create sites accessible to *all* browsers. Tools, articles, links, and discussion: htmlhelp.inet.tele.dk.
- The Web Developer's Virtual Library is a constantly growing resource on every aspect of Web development and design: www.wdvl.com.
- If you enjoy reading your way to success, *web by design: The Complete Guide* by Molly E. Holzschlag (Sybex, 1998) is a must-have reference for all people interested in developing sophisticated visual sites. With lots of information on type, color, shape, space, and technology, this book is sure to be a big help as you work toward aesthetic excellence.
- Another book you'll want on your shelves is *Web Pages That Suck* (Sybex, 1998). This is a full-color, humorous look at learning good design by checking out designs that, well, suck! Written by Vince Flanders and Michael Willis.

Page Design Do's and Don'ts

Keep in mind when designing your Web site that you have about two seconds to grab your reader's attention. TWO seconds! That's common knowledge in advertising and publishing circles. You can't go wrong if you follow these basic tips for designing an eye-catching page with links that work:

- Make the title short, catchy, descriptive, and accurate. And whatever you do, fulfill its promise. If you call your page "Thousands of Yummy Recipes," it had better be that.
- Provide clues at the top of the page about what the page contains; don't expect anyone to scroll down.
- If your page is longer than three "screenfuls," break it up into more than one page.
- A sense of balance is key; don't let your page design get lopsided. Do balance white space, large and small images, different shapes, and blocks of text to give your page interest and variety.
- It isn't cool to overload your page with extraneous doo-dads.
- Use text and link colors that complement rather than clash with the background.

- Be sure that anything that looks like a button behaves like one.

- Don't create two links with the same name that go to two different places, or two links with different names that go to one place. Also, always offer a way back from one link to the originating page if the link is within your site.

- Make your links descriptive; avoid the generic. "Click Here!" isn't all that intriguing.

- Use well-compressed images.

- Use thumbnails as links to larger images.

- Remember that people will access your pages using different browsers that have different capabilities.

- Keep filenames short and make them consistent.

- Tell people the size of any downloadable files you include.

- Get permission to use text or images created by someone else.

- Create a link to the e-mail address of the Webmaster.

Follow these tips and you're off to a powerful, successful start. Now, let's look at how the pros do it.

A Quick Look at Successful Page Designs

The best way to get ideas and to create a winning Web page is to study examples, so we're going to take a look at a few especially well-designed pages, pointing out what makes them so terrific. Most of the pages we've selected use fairly basic HTML to achieve stunning results. We've also included a few pages that use more complex and challenging effects—like tables, frames, and forms (covered in Part II of this book)—to show you what you might one day aspire to.

 TIP If you want to see exactly what a Web designer did to create a specific page, launch your Web browser, load the page of interest, and from the browser's menu bar, select the option for viewing the HTML code behind the page. For example, in Navigator 4, select View ➤ Page Source, and in Internet Explorer, select View ➤ Source. The HTML code for the page you're looking at will appear in a separate window, baring any secret techniques to you.

MASTERING WHAT'S ONLINE

A great way to explore successful Web page design is to look at the sites of successful Web designers. You may find it useful to keep an eye on what's up with Organic at www.organic.com, Razorfish at www.razorfish.com, Brainbug at www.brainbug.com/, and Design inSites at designinsites.com. Be sure to check out the pages of their clients, which often get more attention from the designers than their own home pages.

Simple, Friendly, and Clear

Using simple HTML and colorful graphics scanned from original watercolor paintings, The Tea Shop (Figure 1.2) is a very friendly site with clear intent, well-organized content, and an appealing look and feel that supports the message of the site. Visitors are quickly inspired to relax, imagining they're in an exotic teashop, breathing in the lovely scents of different teas and herbs.

FIGURE 1.2

Relax and enjoy a cuppa in the warm and friendly atmosphere of The Tea Shop.

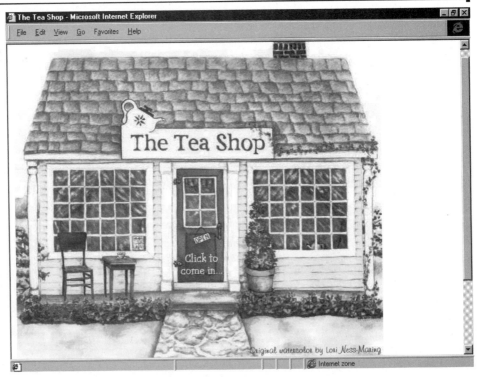

Visitors can learn about teas from around the world, including Ceylon, Japan, China, and India. Want to buy some tea? You can order right online. The Tea Shop also offers a selection of books, gifts, and accessories related to teas. And, if you want to get in touch, you can send tEa-mail!

The Tea Shop is a fine example of a from-the-heart design that emphasizes warmth and ease rather than focusing on the slick and complex.

MASTERING WHAT'S ONLINE

Take a break at The Tea Shop: www.theteashop.com/.

Terrifically Clickable

A stunning and visionary museum, San Francisco's Exploratorium has an excellent Web site, filled with online exhibits that are both beautiful to see and fun to navigate (see Figure 1.3). The Exploratorium Web site uses bars of color running down the left side of the page, with a field of color to the right. This effect is achieved using a background GIF—this popular technique (explained in Chapter 9, *Designing Graphics for the Web*) can be highly effective in adding color and intrigue to a page.

The page shown in Figure 1.4 is from the section of the Exploratorium site called the Learning Studio. Note that while the background graphic technique used here creates a sense of consistency, there's a distinct look and feel to this section of the site. There's splashy red color running down the left side of the page, and the right side of the page is a deep gold. The buttons also have plenty of eye appeal, and you can tell at a glance what lies behind them.

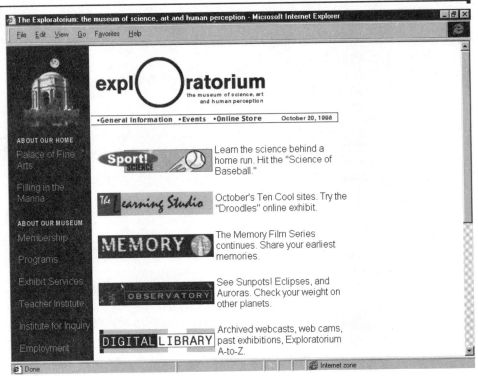

MASTERING WHAT'S ONLINE

Venture to the Exploratorium's home page at www.exploratorium.edu, and be sure to check out the Learning Studio section of the site, too, at www.exploratorium.edu/learning_studio.

FIGURE 1.4

The Learning Studio is consistent in layout with the parent site, but with a unique flare and feel.

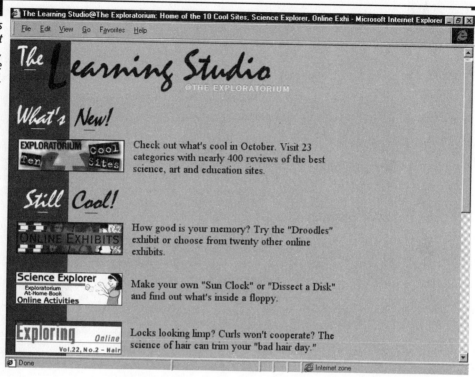

A Selective Color Palette

Ritual Objects is an astonishingly beautiful site that was built for a beginning Web design class by artist Sloane Haywood. Not only is the site built with precision in the HTML, but also in the look and feel. Using an intriguing mix of black, gold, and deep red, the artist lets the color palette support photos of her artwork (Figure 1.5). The black background creates the perfect backdrop for her art. White would be too bright, and the idea is to let the colors of the art itself be the point of visual interest. Because her work contains gold and deep red, Haywood has used these colors for text and other accents, but *very sparingly*! The result of such a specific use of color is that the pages are consistent, easy on the eyes, and never divert attention from the main focus of the site: the art within it.

To see the site in full color, be sure to visit Haywood's work in progress. You'll find more information within the sidebar in this section.

FIGURE 1.5

Ritual Objects uses a refined color palette to offset the beauty of the art within the site.

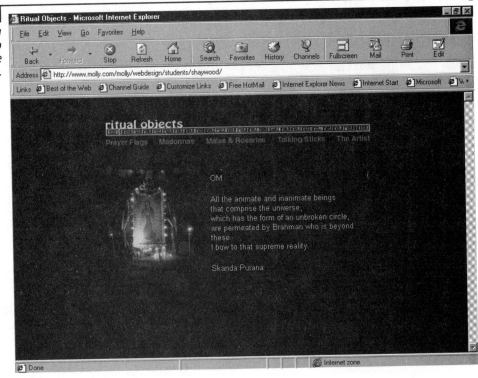

In addition to the intriguing color palette, another important lesson to be learned from Haywood's site is the well-researched and well-developed written content. No misspellings, no typos, no extraneous words—everything on this site has a reason for being.

MASTERING WHAT'S ONLINE

Visit artist Sloane Haywood's first attempt at Web site design at www.molly.com/molly/webdesign/students/shaywood. Remember that this is a work in progress—Haywood intends to eventually build a complete gallery representing her many artistic endeavors.

Clean Columns

Addicted 2: Stuff is a stylish and funny home page. The creators did not build the site for money, but it looks as good as or better than many big-budget commercial sites we know. The front page (Figure 1.6) is made up primarily of text, with a nice banner graphic and navigation aids beside columns of text. The columns are achieved through the use of tables with the borders turned off. (Chapter 11, *Using Tables for Advanced Layout*, tells you all about using tables.) You'll be using this technique a lot when creating pages in Front-Page—it's one of the best ways to get cross-platform, cross-browser layout that is stable and attractive.

MASTERING WHAT'S ONLINE

Addicted 2: Stuff can be found at `www.addicted2stuff.com`.

FIGURE 1.6

Addicted 2: Stuff uses borderless tables in this clever site that collects everything but dust.

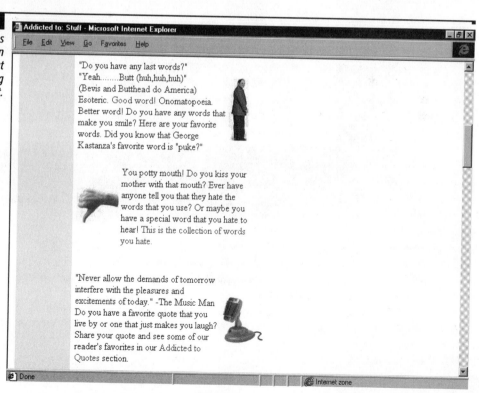

Fully Functional Frames

GroundZero, a Web design firm in New York City, uses *frames* quite wonderfully in its own site. Frames are an HTML feature that allows you to divide a browser window into smaller, separately scrollable windows or frames.

Frames were vastly overused when they were first introduced, but now that the novelty has worn off, people seem less inclined to junk pages up with too many frames. The GroundZero site uses frames well, both as a navigation aid, and to show users their portfolio while keeping them within the GroundZero site (Figure 1.7).

FIGURE 1.7

The most common and effective use of frames is to keep navigation links accessible at all times.

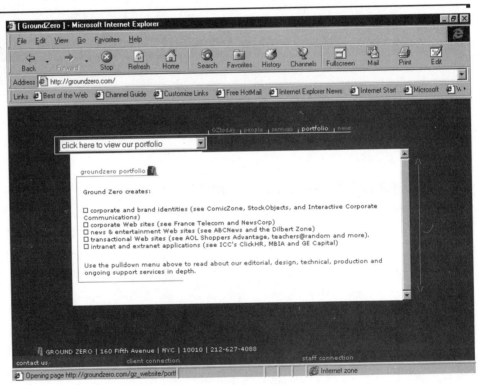

 TIP FrontPage 98 makes it a snap to create framed documents. It allows you to select the organization of the frames you'll use from a number of popular options. It also lets you choose the HTML documents that will appear in a given frame, and even provides the option of creating new blank HTML documents as placeholders until you create that part of your site. See Chapter 12, *Fantastic Frames,* for more details on frames.

MASTERING WHAT'S ONLINE

Blast by Ground Zero's site at groundzero.com to see frames put to good use. When you're ready to tackle frames yourself, visit Netscape's introduction at home.netscape .com/assist/net_sites/frames.html.

An Effective Button-Style Navigation Bar

Using a button bar may well be one of the best ways to provide your site's users a clear navigation scheme. The navigation bar you can see in Figure 1.8 is from the IRS's daily newsletter, a surprisingly non-stodgy piece of publishing from everybody's favorite government agency.

FIGURE 1.8

The button bar at the bottom of the IRS's page is clearly clickable.

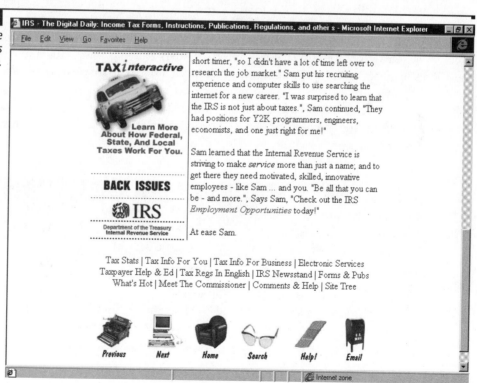

TIP You can use FrontPage's Navigation view to generate navigation bars for your site automatically. See Chapter 15 for more information.

 MASTERING WHAT'S ONLINE

There's nothing taxing about the design of the IRS site at www.irs.ustreas.gov/prod/cover.html.

The quality of the sites you've just seen should give you a great deal of inspiration toward designing your own site. Web design isn't an easy task, contrary to some people's opinions. It can and will challenge both your technological know-how as well as your sense of aesthetics. We like to think of this as an opportunity for personal growth!

One of the greatest things about FrontPage 2000 is that it will help make this growth process much easier on you. It offers a variety of ways for you to be creative on your own, and barring that, provides a full tool kit for those less creatively inclined.

Still, it's important to visit Web sites regularly. Your sense of what makes good design and bad design will become more refined, and you'll gain a clearer idea of what you want *your* site to be like!

 MASTERING WHAT'S ONLINE

David Siegel is a master Web designer whose site is jam-packed with tips, solid information, examples, and links to other sites you may find helpful in your Web designing adventures. His home page, www.dsiegel.com, is in itself an example of good design. Be sure to follow the Web Wonk and Fonts links for great advice on Web page design, and go to the Nine Act Structure for wonderful information on structuring content. Siegel bestows the High Five Awards for excellence in Web design and presentation; take a look at www.highfive.com to see winners of this selective award.

Up Next

Now that you have a sense of basic design and planning concepts, no doubt you're anxious to begin working with FrontPage itself. In Chapter 2, *Exploring FrontPage 2000*, we'll do exactly that.

Get ready to explore FrontPage's interface and actually step through some procedures that will help you familiarize yourself with the way the software works.

PART

I

Building Basic FrontPage Webs

CHAPTER <u>2</u>

Exploring FrontPage 2000

I n this chapter, we start by placing FrontPage in the context of the Web publishing process. We introduce you to the workings of FrontPage. Then, we get straight to the business of creating Web sites.

The Web sometimes seems like a vast and confusing place, and publishing a Web site within it may seem like a daunting task. Of course, the Web isn't really a "place" at all—it's actually separate sections of information stored on computers called *Web servers*, all of which are hooked together with phone lines and other types of network connections. When you surf the Web using a *Web browser* such as Netscape Navigator or Microsoft Internet Explorer, you can access the files stored on these servers.

Understanding Page Basics

The individual files you access with your browser are called *Web pages*. Web pages contain the text, pictures, and other elements that you see as you explore the Web. A *Web site* is simply a collection of linked Web pages that contain related information— you got a taste of these in Chapter 1, *Introduction to Web Design*, when we took a tour of some well-designed sites.

The first step in creating your own Web site is to create one or more Web pages. If you've followed the guidelines we discussed in the last chapter regarding site planning, look and feel, and general do's and don'ts, you should be mentally prepared to take on the task!

It's important to remember that until recently, Web page creation was mainly reserved for individuals with a bit of technical background. Why? Because underneath the text-and-picture pages you see lies the skeletal system of every Web page: the *Hypertext Markup Language*, or *HTML*.

HTML is made up of code consisting of *tags* that define how Web pages look and allow Web browsers to interpret them so you can see them. For example, one HTML tag (<B>) creates bold text, and another HTML tag (<IMG>) inserts an image onto a page. When you view a Web page using a Web browser, the browser translates the HTML tags (as shown in Figure 2.1) into attractive, clearly laid-out pages (as shown in Figure 2.2).

At its most basic, HTML is not difficult to learn, but developing HTML fluency and proficiency does take time. As we all know, time is always in short supply, especially when you've got an important project to finish by the end of the day. For that reason, many people have shied away from learning HTML, and have instead relied on other people to build Web pages for them.

If you spent time planning out your site, you undeniably want to begin to see it take shape. Fortunately, you won't need to contact a professional, because FrontPage will help you build a Web site with ease, even if you know nothing about HTML and never *want* to know a thing about it!

FIGURE 2.1

Behind every Web page is the skeletal system of the Web: HTML.

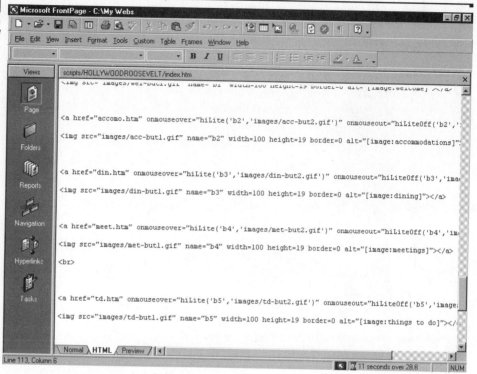

But for anyone interested in taking the general lessons of Chapter 1, combining them with the powerful tool that is FrontPage, and working toward a viable profession in the Web design industry, a knowledge of HTML is going to be a great asset. The reason for this lies in control and troubleshooting, which you can always do more of if you know how to "get under the hood" and correct potential problems.

MASTERING WHAT'S ONLINE

For a broad-spectrum introduction to HTML, visit the CNET HTML authoring site at builder.cnet.com/Authoring. For a good HTML authoring reference, see www.htmlhelp.com.

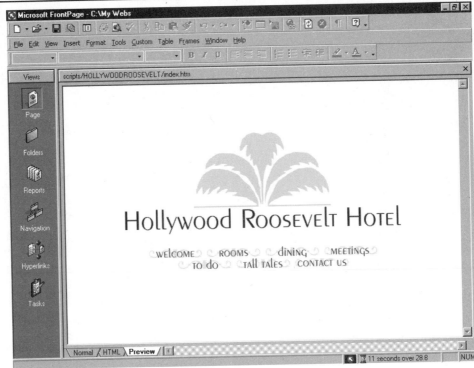

If you do decide to learn more about HTML, that won't stop you from creating a great Web site right now. You've got everything you need already—good concepts regarding design and an excellent tool to work with. You're ready to go to work! Soon, you'll have a complete Web site to call your very own.

After that Web site is complete, the site must be *published* on the Web so it is visible to the rest of the world. Publishing a site involves copying its pages and files from the computer on which the site was created to a Web server. For most people, gaining access to a Web server requires signing up for an account with an *Internet service provider* (*ISP*) or an online service. Some companies maintain their own Web servers and Internet connections in-house; some individuals do that, too, but for the most part, individuals have their sites hosted at ISPs. Chapter 8, *Publishing Your Pages*, goes into detail about the publishing process.

What Is FrontPage?

So, there's the Web, which is full of Web sites, which are made up of Web pages, which are created using HTML. Where does FrontPage fit in? FrontPage is one example of a breed of software called *Web authoring* or *Web publishing* programs. Web publishing programs put the power of Web site creation in everyone's hands—including those who don't want to or don't have the time to learn HTML.

FrontPage enables you to create Web pages using a familiar word-processing-like interface: You add and format text, pictures, and other page content using menus and toolbar buttons, and FrontPage generates the corresponding HTML tags in the background. This method is known as What-You-See-Is-What-You-Get (or *WYSIWYG*, pronounced *wiz-ee-wig*), which is another way you'll see FrontPage described. FrontPage not only helps you create Web pages; it also helps you maintain the constantly changing structure and content of your site as a whole.

One of the exciting additions to FrontPage 2000 from earlier versions is that it allows you to have all of the power of a WYSIWYG editor combined with full control over your editing needs. This means you can go into the HTML view and make any changes you like. In the past, FrontPage would alter your edits; now the control is in your hands. Other fantastic features are available in FrontPage 2000 that make it one of the best products for both newcomers and professionals to use. We'll be looking at these features throughout this chapter and the rest of this book.

It Builds Web Sites Big and Small

You can use FrontPage to build a variety of sites, including:

A Personal Web Site An extremely popular type of public Internet site, the personal Web site is all about *you*. It can include information on your interests, your friends, your family, and your favorite Web site links. Go on—be creative! A personal Web site is truly an experimental ground where many future Web professionals get their first taste at site design. FrontPage can help you build a great personal Web site—it's fast and user-friendly, making it a perfect choice for this small, but exciting type of Web site.

A Small Business Site If you have a home-based or small business with a limited advertising budget, a Web site is often a great way to get your product or services advertised to a large number of people. FrontPage can help you create a Web site for your small business. It's got terrific templates and will help you set up a professional storefront without having to spend years learning techniques and technologies.

A Corporate Web Site Larger companies require public Internet sites to provide product information, customer support, consumer relations information, and even online shopping. FrontPage is useful in a corporate setting because it has powerful tracking features—allowing more than one person to make changes and updates to Web site pages. Moreover, FrontPage's compatibility and integration with other software products make it a very powerful professional tool.

A Corporate Intranet A corporate *intranet* is an internal company network based on the same technology as the Internet. An intranet works like a Web site, except that it's available only to those users who can access the network. Because an intranet is protected from curious Web surfers, internal company information such as sales figures, human resources communications, and department resources can be transmitted company-wide. FrontPage has tools that allow you to create customized intranets. See the sidebar in this section for more information.

MASTERING WHAT'S ONLINE

Microsoft offers a 60-Minute Intranet Kit to help you use FrontPage and Office to build an Intranet site from scratch. You can download the kit from the FrontPage Web site at www.microsoft.com/office/intranet.

It's a Collaborative Software Program

FrontPage can shoulder small jobs as well as complex jobs because it divides the work among components. Not only does FrontPage provide many useful tools of its own; it also works in collaboration with a variety of other Microsoft applications, including:

Microsoft Office 2000 FrontPage 2000 shares menus and toolbars with Office, and allows for support and integration of many Office documents including those created in Word, Excel, and PowerPoint. Furthermore, users of Office products can export their work from other Office programs to a FrontPage web.

Visual Studio and Visual Source Safe (VSS) Visual Studio is a suite of software for network and database development professionals. VSS allows multiple users to manage large Web sites by checking in and checking out files. VSS also provides time, date, and name stamping pages for tracking purposes.

Visual InterDev Visual InterDev is a high-powered management and programming solution for database applications, often used on the "back end" of high-powered Web sites. High-end developers use Visual InterDev to manage sites by incorporating behind-the-scenes scripting, search, and interactive features. Chapter 28, *Using FrontPage with Microsoft's Visual InterDev*, reviews how Visual InterDev and FrontPage work together as a powerful team.

PhotoDraw Use this brand-new member of the Office suite of programs with FrontPage 2000 to create powerful, attractive graphics for the Web. You can read a bit more about PhotoDraw in Chapter 9, *Designing Graphics for the Web*.

Microsoft Internet Explorer Use this powerful Web browser to surf the Web and to preview your site before it goes live (we show you how to preview your pages in Chapter 3, *Working in Page View*).

The ability of FrontPage 2000 to integrate with other programs is one of its most powerful features. This integration sets FrontPage apart from "just" an HTML or Web site tool and puts it in the league of a professional, administrative application—if that's what you need it to do. This kind of flexibility and power are what make the software so appealing to such a broad range of individuals, whether novice or pro.

MASTERING WHAT'S ONLINE

You can find detailed information and news about the products discussed previously at the following Web sites:

- Microsoft Office: www.microsoft.com/office
- Visual Source Safe: msdn.microsoft.com/vstudio
- Visual Interdev: msdn.microsoft.com/vinterdev
- PhotoDraw: www.microsoft.com/office/photodraw
- Microsoft Internet Explorer: www.microsoft.com/ie

FrontPage Web-Building Basics

We believe that the best way to learn a new skill is to just do it! Since you already have a good idea of how the Web works, and you understand what a powerful tool FrontPage is, you are definitely ready to jump in feet-first.

We'll begin by revving up FrontPage and starting a new Web site. In the process, you'll become familiar with the FrontPage interface and learn how to add new pages to the site as you like.

Throughout this book, we'll often refer to Web sites created with or maintained using FrontPage as *FrontPage webs* (or simply *webs*, with a lowercase *w*). FrontPage webs are the same as other Web sites, in that they are made up of Web pages and are written using HTML. However, FrontPage can differentiate between its own webs and Web sites created by other programs (or hand-tagged using HTML). FrontPage simply "hides" the HTML behind an easy-to-use graphical interface. To take full advantage of FrontPage's powerful features, you can create webs using FrontPage, or update and maintain existing Web sites by *importing* them into the program.

So let's take the plunge and create a new FrontPage web. We'll make things easy by using one of FrontPage's pre-existing templates.

 NOTE If you haven't yet installed FrontPage on your computer, turn to the installation instructions in Appendix A.

Starting FrontPage

Starting FrontPage involves the same steps as starting most other Windows programs. To start FrontPage in one easy step, from the Windows Start menu, select Programs ➤ Microsoft FrontPage. FrontPage starts (see Figure 2.3).

If you've used earlier editions of FrontPage, you'll notice something quite different here—there's no opening dialog box! That's because FrontPage 2000 has integrated FrontPage 98's Explorer and Editor. The entire interface is now structured around a main editing window, known as *Page view*. This new interface makes using FrontPage very easy, but you'll need to read on to learn about new startup features. For newcomers to FrontPage 2000, all this means is that you have a little less to learn—and you will be able to jump in to the *making* of Web sites that much faster. In the following sections of this chapter, we'll step you through what you see on the screen and explain how to get started working on webs, including using site templates, using wizards, and building pages from scratch.

FIGURE 2.3

*The FrontPage inter-
face at startup*

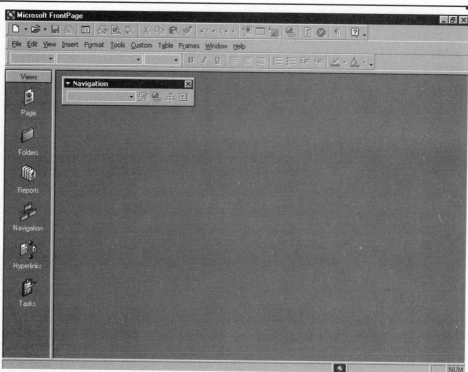

How to Get Help within FrontPage

For quick FrontPage assistance, turn to the FrontPage Help system. The Help system identifies unfamiliar menu items and toolbar buttons, and provides general overviews and step-by-step instructions for FrontPage operations. To access FrontPage Help, select Help ➢ Microsoft FrontPage Help. To get context-sensitive help, click the Help button available in many FrontPage dialog boxes, or press Shift+F11 and then click the item of interest.

Creating a Site with Templates

If you're not sure how to begin building your Web site, or you need a complete Web site fast, FrontPage gives you plenty of help in the form of templates. *Templates* are pre-set pages, where all that is required of you is to add text and, if you wish, modify graphics. FrontPage provides a variety of templates for typical Web sites: a Customer Support web, a Personal web, and a Project web. There's also a One Page web, which you can use to create a single page, and an empty Web, which sets up a Web structure but allows you more control over the content of the individual pages. You can also create your own templates by either modifying an existing template or creating one from scratch. You'll learn more about this in Chapter 3.

Templates generate a collection of linked pages containing boilerplate text. You can then customize those pages with your own content and design.

To create a Web site using a pre-existing template, follow these steps:

1. Start FrontPage as described in the previous section. From the menu bar, select File ➢ New ➢ Web, as shown in Figure 2.4.

FIGURE 2.4

Using the menu to start up a FrontPage web

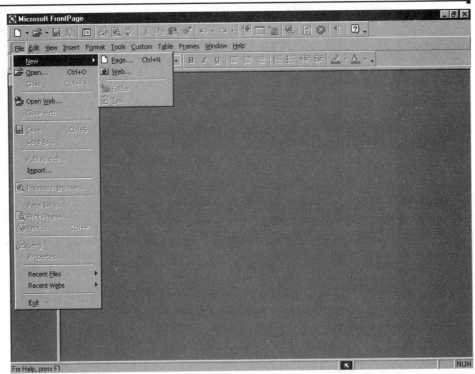

2. The New dialog box appears, showing the templates available (see Figure 2.5). You'll also see several wizards, but we'll get to those in a bit. For the sake of an example, Personal Web is a good choice. It will create a web designed to highlight your personal interests.

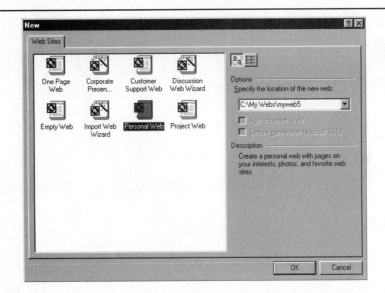

FIGURE 2.5

Templates and wizards in the New dialog box

3. Highlight the Personal Web icon. On the right side of the dialog box, you're asked to specify a location for the Web. You can choose one that is already set up in the FrontPage directory, or you can create a new directory on your hard drive to accommodate the files for the new web (see the following tip).

4. Click OK. FrontPage will now do some thinking, and it might take a minute or two before your new web is ready.

 TIP When you create a web, FrontPage generates a *local URL* for your web (URL stands for *Uniform Resource Locator*, another name for a Web site address). The URL points to an address on your computer. You can either use one of the predefined FrontPage addresses or create a new address (directory) on your hard drive. To do this, open Windows Explorer. Then, find an area where you want to put your new web. Highlight the name of the folder where your new subdirectory will be located. Select File ➢ New Folder. Name your new folder whatever you like, but it's best to keep it to one short word. Now you can go back to FrontPage and fill in that location, and the template or wizard will know where to put your web's files. You'll see that in FrontPage, the folder you created is now viewed as a location on a server and appears as a URL.

In the upcoming section called "FrontPage Views," we'll introduce you to Front-Page's views, each of which is meant to help you with a different aspect of site creation, management, and maintenance. For now, just look at the left pane of the editing window to see a list of the different views you can use—Folders, Reports, Navigation, and Hyperlinks. For example, select Navigation to see a hierarchical layout of your personal site (see Figure 2.6).

FIGURE 2.6

Navigation view of a personal site

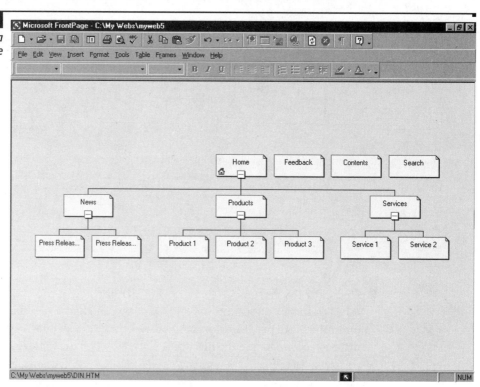

To view your new page, you can go to Folders, and then double-click the file named default.htm. Your page now loads into the main window (Figure 2.7).

NOTE   Notice that the filenames FrontPage generates have the extension .htm rather than the more familiar .html. In addition, FrontPage names the home page default.htm instead of the more familiar index.html. This is a convenience for the software; when you actually upload the files to the server that will make them public, the files will be renamed automatically to whatever is appropriate for that particular server.

FIGURE 2.7

A newborn, ready-to-edit Web page, based on the Personal Web template

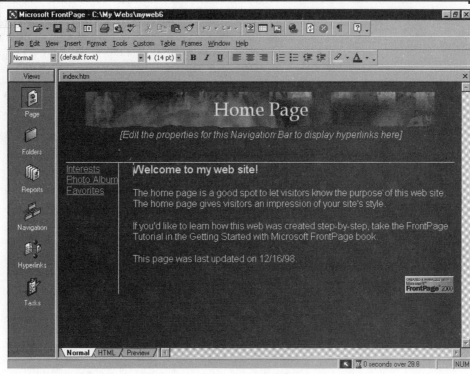

You'll be doing a whole lot more with this down the road, but let's move on to learning other ways to view and use webs within FrontPage 2000.

Creating a Site with Wizards

FrontPage provides wizards for its two most complex templates, the Corporate Presence web and the Discussion web. A *wizard* is a small program-within-a-program that takes you step-by-step through the process of creating the Web site that you need. The Corporate Presence Web Wizard takes you through the process of building an entire corporate site by asking you about the kind of information you want the site to contain. After you tell the wizard what you want, the wizard generates the Web site. The Discussion Web Wizard creates a FrontPage *discussion group* (a web that hosts a public forum where visitors can submit and respond to article postings—we discuss this in Chapter 15, *Special Effects*). There's also an Import Web Wizard, but we'll get to that later in this chapter.

NOTE This procedure introduces the general steps for using a wizard to create a site. If you'd like a more detailed view of using a wizard to create a specific site, turn to Chapter 7, *Managing Tasks*, where we dwell at length on the topic of working with the Corporate Presence Web Wizard.

To create a web using a wizard, follow these steps:

1. Start FrontPage as described previously in the section titled "Starting Front-Page." Then select File ➢ New ➢ Web.

2. When the New dialog box appears, choose either the Corporate Presence Web Wizard or the Discussion Web Wizard. Click OK. The Web Wizard appears (see Figure 2.8).

FIGURE 2.8

The Corporate Presence Web Wizard

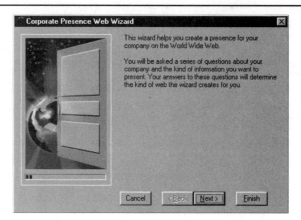

3. After reading the introduction, click Next to advance to the next panel, where you can specify which pages you'd like to have included in your web. Customize these by removing or adding a check next to the page description. When you're ready, click Next.

4. You'll now be asked for a descriptive title for your web. Make it a sensible title—something that relates to the subject you're working on.

5. In each subsequent panel, read and follow the wizard's directions. To proceed to the next panel, click Next. To go back to a previous panel, click Back .

6. When you reach the final panel, the Next button appears grayed out. To finish the web, click Finish. The wizard uses the information you provided to generate

the web. When the web is complete, you can open and view it in Page view by going to Folders and clicking `default.htm` (see Figure 2.9).

FIGURE 2.9

The wizard has created this page, all ready to be customized.

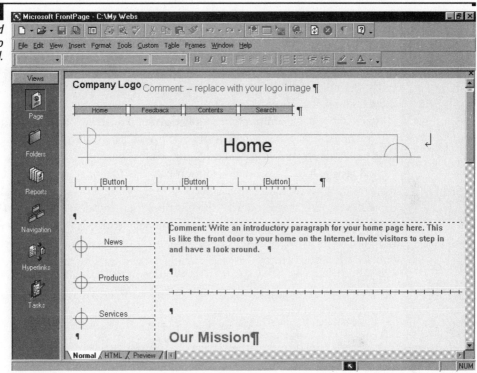

After the wizard creates your web, you can open the web's pages to customize their contents.

 WARNING Web sites created using FrontPage templates and wizards contain all sorts of unique FrontPage features. A few of these features—for example, keyword site searches and discussion groups—work only if the site is published on a Web server that supports the *FrontPage Server Extensions*. We talk about the FrontPage Server Extensions in Chapter 8, as well as in Appendix C.

Creating a New Page from Scratch

If you're not sure where to begin, or if you'd like to see examples of how typical Web sites are structured, FrontPage templates and wizards provide you with a helpful boost. However, if you already have a faint inkling about how you want your page to look, you may find it easier to build your site from scratch. In that case, you can start with a single blank Web page, to which you will add your own content. After that, you can tack more new pages onto your Web site, gradually filling in until the site is complete. (Well, as complete as a Web site can be—part of the beauty of the Web is that nothing there is chiseled in stone.)

To create a page from scratch, simply open up FrontPage. Make sure that under Views, the Page icon is selected. In the right pane, you'll have a blank page—the clean slate upon which you can begin designing your page.

Add text, graphics—whatever you want on this first page. Again, this is for those readers who already have enough know-how to begin putting their page together. For those new to FrontPage and Web site creation, look ahead to Chapter 4, *Creating Basic Pages,* for a great starting point on how to manage your page's design. Once the page is, in fact, together, simply select File ➢ Save As, and save your file to the desired directory as `default.htm`.

Now you can add more pages to your site. Base the pages you want to create on the site plan you developed in Chapter 1. Repeat the process described in this section until you have all the pages you want.

TIP You can also build your own FrontPage web by starting with the Empty Web template, although there is little reason to use this option when you start out. This template sets aside space for a new web, but contains no initial pages. Because your first step (presumably) would be to add a home page to the empty web, you may as well use the One Page Web template instead. You might, however, want to use the Empty Web template as a convenient spot into which you can import existing Web pages. See the section "Importing Existing Web Pages" later in this chapter.

Importing an Existing Web Site into FrontPage

To use FrontPage to update an existing Web site, you must first import that site into FrontPage (thereby transforming the site into a FrontPage web). You'll do this using the Import Web Wizard, which is able to import Web site files that are currently stored on your computer, on your local network, and/or on the World Wide Web itself.

NOTE When you import a Web site into FrontPage, the original Web site remains unchanged in its original location. Once it is imported, it is treated as a FrontPage web.

To import an existing Web site into FrontPage, follow these steps:

1. Start FrontPage as described in the section titled "Starting FrontPage." Select File ➢ New ➢ Web.

2. In the Web Sites dialog box, highlight the Import Web Wizard. Click OK. The Import Web Wizard appears, asking where you want to import the Web from (see Figure 2.10).

FIGURE 2.10

Here you'll specify the location from which a Web site will be imported.

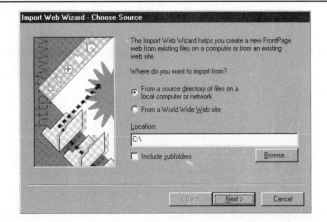

3. In this dialog box, specify the current location of the Web site you want to import. If the site is currently stored in a folder on your computer or local network, click the From A Source Directory Of Files On A Local Computer Or Network button. In the Location text box, type the path to that folder, or click the Browse button to select a folder from a list of folders on your computer and local network. To import files stored in the site's subfolders, click the Include Subfolders checkbox. If the site is available on the World Wide Web, click the button labeled From A World Wide Web Site, and in the Location text box, type the site's URL.

4. Click Next. Which dialog box appears next depends on the current location of the Web site files. If the site is stored on your computer or network, the Import Web Wizard - Edit File List dialog box appears. If the site is stored on the Web, the Import Web Wizard - Choose Download Amount dialog box appears.

5. In the Import Web Wizard - Edit File List dialog box, the Files list box lists all the Web site files contained in the location you specified. To exclude one or more files, press the Ctrl key while clicking the names of the file(s), and then click the Exclude button. To start over with a complete file list, click the Refresh button.

or

In the Import Web Wizard - Choose Download Amount dialog box, specify the download options you want the wizard to use. The dialog box enables you to control the number of *levels* (the successive depth of subfolders) to import and the total file size of the imported files. You can also choose to import only the site's Web pages and its image files.

6. In either dialog box, click Next. The Import Web Wizard - Finish dialog box appears.

7. Click the Finish button. The Import Web Wizard imports the selected files into the new FrontPage web (this may take a moment, especially if you're importing a big Web site). When the import process is finished, the Import Web Wizard closes, and you can now view the web using any number of views, described later in this chapter.

You can now use FrontPage to update and maintain the new web. When you're ready to start working on this web, turn to Chapter 3 to learn more.

Keep It Contained

For the Import Web Wizard to properly import a Web site, the site's files must be contained within a single main folder (it's okay if the main folder contains subfolders). If the site's pages are not contained in one folder, you'll need to import the folder's pages by using the Import Web Wizard, and then import the rest of the pages individually (we'll show you how in the section called "Importing Existing Web Pages" later in this chapter). Because the imported site's file system will no longer fit the site's original structure, importing a site in this manner risks creating *broken hyperlinks*. (*Hyperlinks* are bits of highlighted text or images in a Web page. You click these to jump to different locations.) You'll learn how hyperlinks work in Chapter 4, *Creating Basic Pages*. We'll show you how to detect and fix broken hyperlinks in Chapter 24, *Site Maintenance and Promotion*.

FrontPage Views

As with most standard application interfaces, FrontPage is designed with a standard top navigation bar that includes general file management commands as well as specific tools for editing and modifying pages. And, as with most standard applications, there's a status bar along the bottom of the interface that provides you with helpful information.

Once your web is open in the FrontPage interface, you can look at it using one of FrontPage's views, located along the left side of the screen. To activate a view, simply click its icon.

Each view shows different types of information about the web and enables you to work with the site in a variety of ways. In this section, we'll look carefully at each of these views and explain their individual uses.

Page View

You can think of *Page view* as the "editor" view. Page view displays the individual page you're working on (see Figure 2.11), allowing you to make changes or adjustments to the items on that page.

FIGURE 2.11

FrontPage's Page view in Normal mode, with a page to be edited in the editing panel

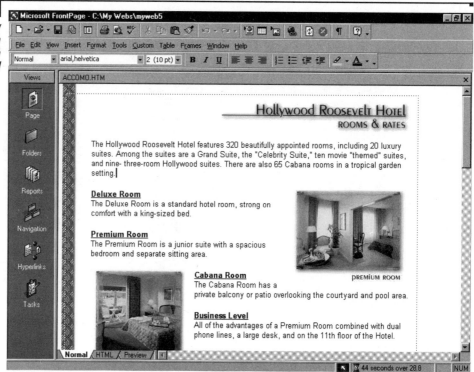

You can edit the page elements by right-clicking objects anywhere on the page while in Page view. You can also use the standard toolbars running along the top of the interface to add or alter formatting information.

One of the most powerful aspects of Page view is that you can use the tabs running along the bottom bar to switch between *editing panes*, or *modes*.

The editing panes are:

Normal This is your standard editing pane—it's the visual editor without the HTML showing. Figure 2.11 shows this view.

HTML In this pane, you can actually get to the meat of the matter: the HTML code. You can make changes directly to the code, or see how the code has been altered by changes made in the visual editor. (See Figure 2.12.)

FIGURE 2.12

FrontPage's Page view in HTML mode

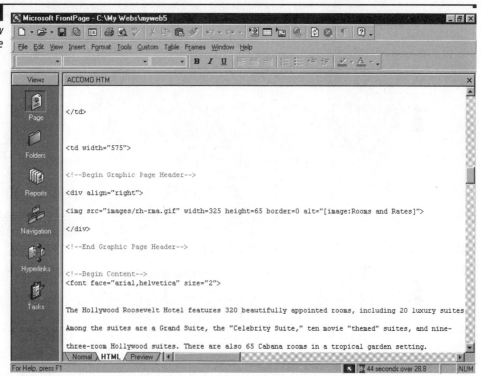

Preview Here's where you get to check out your page as it will look once published! It shows the final results of the page, with no code or editing marks. (See Figure 2.13.)

FIGURE 2.13

FrontPage's Page view
in Preview mode

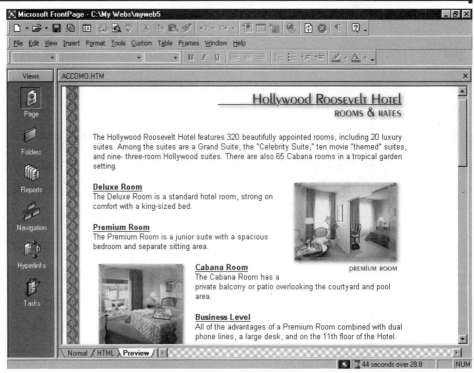

Page view is especially helpful because you can not only make visual alterations, but also work with the HTML directly, and then check out the way the page will look in Preview mode. It's also where you're going to spend most of your FrontPage time, so it's wise to get comfortable using this view.

Folders View

Folders view (shown in Figure 2.14) is split into two panes. The left pane contains a hierarchical list of folders inside the current web. The right pane contains a detailed list of pages and files contained inside the selected folder.

FIGURE 2.14

FrontPage's
Folders view

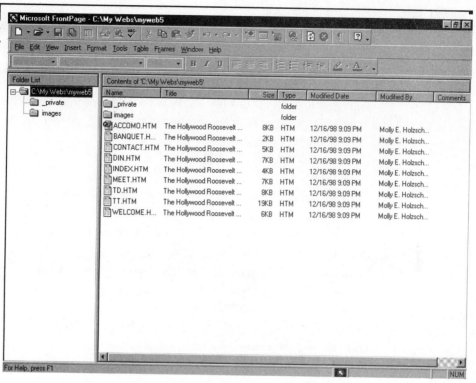

Use this view for file management tasks such as renaming files, creating new folders, and dragging pages into subfolders. When you change the name or location of any web file, FrontPage automatically updates that file's associated links throughout the site.

Each FrontPage web comes equipped with two standard folders: the Private folder and the Images folder. Once the site is published, pages stored in the Private folder remain hidden from Web browsers (making this folder a good storage location for pages you don't want other people to see—for example, in-progress work). You can also use the Private folder to shield pages from the FrontPage text-indexing system; this system works in conjunction with the Search Form *component* to create a keyword site search. (FrontPage components are prepackaged interactive elements you can add to your site without the need for programming. Find out more about them in Chapter 15.)

WARNING Pages in the Private folder are private only if the web is published on a Web server that supports the FrontPage Server Extensions. For more information about FrontPage Server Extensions, refer to Chapter 8 or Appendix C.

The Images folder is the best place to store your Web graphics. By keeping Web pages and graphic files in separate locations, you can more easily manage the elements of your site. We'll talk more about Web graphics in Chapter 9.

Here is a rundown of some of the file management tasks you're likely to do while using the Folders view:

To see the contents of a folder Double-click the folder name.

To rename a file In the right pane, right-click that file and from the menu bar, select Rename. Type a new name and then press Enter. Your file now bears its new name.

To create a new folder From the FrontPage menu bar, select File ➤ New ➤ Folder. A new folder appears in both panes, and the folder's name is highlighted in the right pane. Type the new folder name of your dreams and then press Enter. You now have a new folder with its very own name.

To move a page into a folder Click and drag the page to the target folder (in either pane), and then release the mouse button. The page moves to its new location.

To sort the file list in the right pane Click one of the header labels at the top of the pane. For example, to sort the list by name, click the Name label.

To delete a file Click the filename and press the Delete key. The Confirm Delete dialog box appears, asking you to verify the deletion. To do so, click Yes, and your file will be history.

To open a file Double-click the filename. The file opens in Page view (if it's an HTML file) or Image Composer (if it's a graphic).

To view a file's properties Right-click the filename, and from the menu that appears, select Properties. The Properties dialog box appears.

Reports View

Reports view is used to help you manage pages within your web. Remember, when working with webs, FrontPage sees the project as an individual entity (the web) made up of smaller parts (the files). Reports view gives you a wide range of information about files within the web (see Figure 2.15).

FIGURE 2.15

Reports view displays information about individual files within a web.

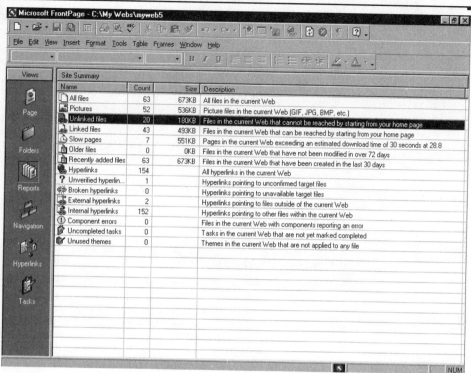

In Reports view, you can see a summary of information about each file in a web:

- Name: The type of files in question, such as Pictures, Linked Files, and Slow Pages.
- Count: The number of files that fall into a type of file (see Name).
- Size: The total size of the file, *including* any dependencies (such as graphics).
- Description: This item describes in detail the name, or type, of file(s) under scrutiny. In general Web—designer terminology, what FrontPage is referring to as size is also referred to as *page weight*—the size, in kilobytes, of Web-based files.

Navigation View

Navigation view (Figure 2.16) helps you chart how visitors will find their way through your site. By building a *navigational structure* in the view's top pane, you create the basis for *navigation bars* (rows of text hyperlinks or buttons that visitors click to move to a different page). The bottom pane contains a file list similar to what you encountered in the Folders view. In Chapter 15, you'll learn to build a navigational structure and use navigation bars.

FIGURE 2.16

Navigation view, also known as a site map

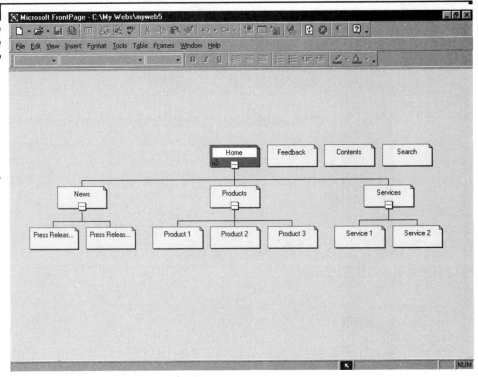

 NOTE If you're ever asked to create a *site map* for a client, you can use Navigation view to generate the map. Simply import the site into FrontPage using the Import Web Wizard and click Navigation View. You can print out your site map when in Navigation view mode by selecting File ➢ Print.

Hyperlinks View

Hyperlinks view (shown in Figure 2.17) offers you the eagle-eye view of all those handy hyperlinks in your web. Webs created using templates or wizards come equipped with hyperlinks that connect the site's pages to one another, and, in some cases, to other Web sites. When you build your own site from scratch, however, you must insert hyperlinks yourself (we show you how in Chapter 4).

FIGURE 2.17

Hyperlinks view

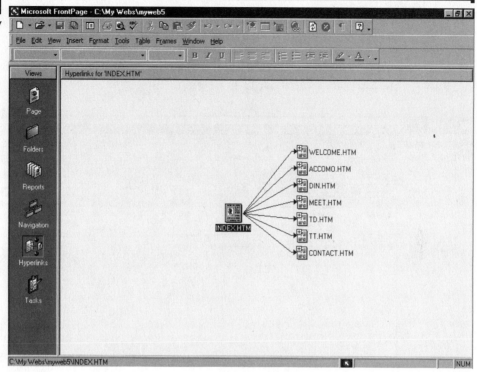

In Hyperlinks view, the left pane contains a site "outline" or "tree" of sorts, with any top-level page(s) (usually the home page) sitting at the top. The right pane shows a close-up diagram of the page that's selected in the left pane. Incoming hyperlinks are shown on the left, and outgoing hyperlinks are shown on the right.

To navigate around, just point and click. For example, click any page in the outline, and the pages linked to it appear listed below it. Click any other page in the outline, and that page's links appear in the right pane in place of the last one. Click the little plus sign attached to any page in the diagram, and the diagram expands from that page.

NOTE Don't be surprised if a page shows up more than once in the outline in the left pane. This outline reflects the *hyperlinks* in your web, not the number of pages. Some pages are linked to and from many other pages.

Tasks View

In *Tasks view* (shown in Figure 2.18), you can maintain an ongoing to-do list of items you need to complete as you build your site. Tasks view is especially useful if more than one author works on the site, because the entire web-building team can share the list. Learn more about Tasks view in Chapter 7.

FIGURE 2.18

Tasks view maintains a list of things to do.

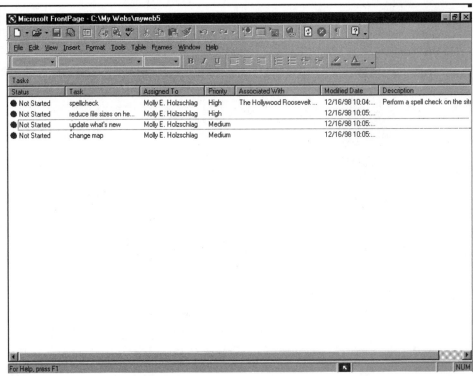

Adding Pages to a FrontPage Web

After you create a FrontPage web (especially if it's a one-page web), you're sure to want to add new pages to your site. You'll do most of your page building using Page view (see Chapter 3). However, if you simply want to tack on a blank page or two, or if you want to import an existing page into a Web site, you can accomplish these tasks quite easily.

Creating a New Web Page

FrontPage lets you add empty pages to your web that you can later open and fill with content. To create a new blank page in a FrontPage web, it's best to be in the Folders view.

1. With your web open in the Folders view, from the FrontPage menu bar select File ➤ New ➤ Page (or on the Standard toolbar, click the New Page button, or press Ctrl+N).

2. Type a filename for your new page. The filename should be short, descriptive, easy to remember, and have an extension of .htm or .html. Then press Enter. Presto! The file has a new name.

 TIP It's easy to create blank pages, but if you'd prefer some page layout assistance, use FrontPage's templates to create your new pages. We show you how in Chapter 4.

Importing Existing Web Pages

If you've already created (or have access to) finished Web pages, and you want to attach them to your FrontPage web, you can easily import them. You can import single files and complete folders that are stored on your computer, local network, or the World Wide Web.

 TIP You can actually import *any* type of file from a Web site into your FrontPage web—not just HTML files, but also graphics files, sound files, text files, and so on.

It's easy; just follow these steps:

1. Select File ➤ Import from the main tool bar. The Import File To FrontPage Web dialog box appears.

2. You can import individual files or an entire folder, either from a local source or the World Wide Web. To import one or more files that are stored on your computer or local network, in the Import File To FrontPage Web dialog box, click the Add File button. The Add File To Import List dialog box appears.

   or

To import an entire folder that's stored on your computer or local network, in the Import File To FrontPage Web dialog box, click the Add Folder button. The Browse For Folder dialog box appears.

or

To import a file or folder that is currently located on the World Wide Web, in the Import File To FrontPage Web dialog box, click the From Web button. The Import Web Wizard - Choose Source dialog box appears. (For help with using the Import Web Wizard, refer to the section in this chapter titled "Importing an Existing Web Site into FrontPage.")

3. If you are importing individual files, in the Add File To Import List dialog box, select the file(s) you want to import. Then click Open. The dialog box closes, and the selected file(s) appear in the import list in the Import File To FrontPage Web dialog box.

or

If you are importing a folder, in the Browse For Folder dialog box, select the folder you want to import, then click OK. The dialog box closes, and the file(s) contained in the selected folder appear in the import list in the Import File To FrontPage Web dialog box.

TIP In the import list, the imported file's local URL appears under the URL heading. To change where FrontPage stores the file, simply click the Edit URL button. The Edit URL dialog box appears. In the text box labeled FileLocation Within Your FrontPage Web, enter a new location. For example, if you are importing an image named face.gif and you want the image to be stored in the Images folder, type images/face.gif in the text box. Click OK to close the dialog box. The new URL appears in the import list.

4. In the Import File To FrontPage Web dialog box, click OK. FrontPage imports the file(s) you chose. When the import process is finished, the dialog box closes.

Opening an Existing FrontPage Web

You can use FrontPage to create and maintain many webs on the same computer, but you can open and work on only one at a time. To open an existing FrontPage web, follow these steps:

1. From the FrontPage menu bar, select File ➤ Open Web.

2. In the Open Web area's list of webs, click the one you want to open and then click Open.

If you've been working on a web recently, you can always select File ➤ Recent Webs, and then select the web you want from the available drop-down list.

 NOTE You can open only one FrontPage web at a time. If you open a FrontPage web while another web is currently open, the first web will automatically close.

The FrontPage Family Tree: Root and Child Webs

FrontPage comes installed with a default web called the *root web*. The root web is the Web server's top-level web. Each time you create a new FrontPage web, you create a *child web*, or a second-level web. You can link together the root web and child webs to create a network of webs, or each web can stand on its own.

To better understand the concept of root and child webs, think about a family tree. Most family trees begin with a couple (usually the oldest relatives the genealogist can find). That couple is the *root* of the family. As the couple has children and their family tree expands, each new family, while a distinct unit, remains connected to the family's root.

Many large Web sites are divided into root and child webs, which are then linked together to form a massive network of files. For example, the designers of a big corporate site may store the main Web site files in the root web, and then create independent webs devoted to a product catalog, company information, and so on.

Whether you divide your site into root and child webs is up to you. Should you decide to do so, begin your site by opening the FrontPage root web. This root web contains placeholder pages that you can either replace with your own pages or leave available for reference. To add a child web, simply create a new web following the steps outlined in this chapter, and then link the two sites together (we show you how in Chapter 4).

Deleting a FrontPage Web

If you're a prolific Web publisher, FrontPage will soon contain evidence of your work: many—perhaps too many—FrontPage webs. You can easily delete those that have become obsolete. To do so, follow these steps:

1. Open the condemned web in FrontPage and from the menu bar, select File ➢ Delete Web. The Confirm Delete dialog box appears, giving you two choices.

2. To delete the web but preserve the files, click the button next to Remove Only FrontPage Information From This Web, Preserving All Other Files And Folders, then click OK. The dialog box closes, and FrontPage removes FrontPage information from the files.

3. To completely erase the web from your hard disk, click the button next to Remove This Web Entirely By Deleting All Of Its Files And Folders. Click OK, and your web is completely deleted.

 WARNING Once you delete a web, it is gone for good. FrontPage does not include undelete or undo features to reverse the results of deleting a web. Obviously, you should use care when deleting a web. If you nix a web by mistake, you'll just have to start over.

Quitting FrontPage

To exit FrontPage, first close any open dialog boxes, and then do this:

1. From the FrontPage menu bar, select File ➢ Exit, or press Alt+F4.

 NOTE Before closing, FrontPage looks for any unsaved work sitting around. If it finds any, the Close Web dialog box appears, prompting you to save your files as needed.

2. FrontPage closes, and the Windows Desktop reappears.

Up Next

With all this interface exploration done and understood, you're ready to move on and actually edit pages. In Chapter 3, *Working in Page View*, we'll talk about how to work with Page view in order to create simple, but effective pages. Page view is where you'll be spending most of your FrontPage time, adding and modifying page elements, and testing your pages.

CHAPTER <u>3</u>

Working in Page View

I n Chapter 2, we showed you around the FrontPage interface, birthplace and home of the FrontPage web. We also lookd briefly at Page view. Now we'll take an in-depth look, as Page view is your central command post for almost all FrontPage 2000 tasks. It is where you'll create, modify, and preview the individual pages within your web.

In this chapter, you'll get acquainted with the basic features of Page view. In upcoming chapters, you'll find out how to use FrontPage's page-building tools.

Getting to Know Page View

You can think of FrontPage's Page view as a program within a program. The main program is FrontPage itself; it handles all of the tasks associated with FrontPage webs, such as creating them, importing them, displaying them, and so on. Page view works within the FrontPage application, concentrating on tasks associated with the individual pages that make up the site. You use Page view to add and format text, create hyperlinks, insert pictures, and work with all the other elements that go into a Web page.

The other FrontPage views that we introduced in Chapter 2—Folders, Reports, Navigation, Hyperlinks, and Tasks—work cleanly with Page view. As you edit and save a Web site's pages, you can switch between views to see how page changes affect the rest of the site. For example, after you create a hyperlink using Page view, you can switch to Hyperlinks view to see how that hyperlink fits into the rest of the site. (We show you how to create hyperlinks in Chapter 4, *Creating Basic Pages*.) By moving between views as you build the webs that make up your Web site, you can work on design details as you keep the site-wide perspective in view.

You'll find that you do the majority of your FrontPage web-building work in this way—using Page view to work on pages that are part of the web currently open in the main interface. Sometimes, however, you'll want to open a Web page that's *not* part of a FrontPage web. That's okay, too. FrontPage can accommodate a number of scenarios, as you'll soon see. And, for those of you who have used previous versions of FrontPage, you'll see that FrontPage 98's Editor and Explorer have been merged, making Page view the command center of your Web page work.

Getting Started

To begin working in Page view, follow these steps:

1. Start FrontPage. (If you don't know how to start FrontPage, refer to the section "Starting FrontPage" in Chapter 2.)

2. Start a new FrontPage web by selecting Tools ➤ New ➤ Web, or open an existing web (for instructions, refer to the Chapter 2 sections, "FrontPage Web-Building Basics" and "Opening an Existing FrontPage Web"). The FrontPage web appears in Page view.

To open a single file, make sure you are using Folders, Navigation, or Hyperlinks View. Double-click the icon for the page you want to open. FrontPage displays the contents of the selected page (see Figure 3.1).

PART

I

Building Basic
FrontPage Webs

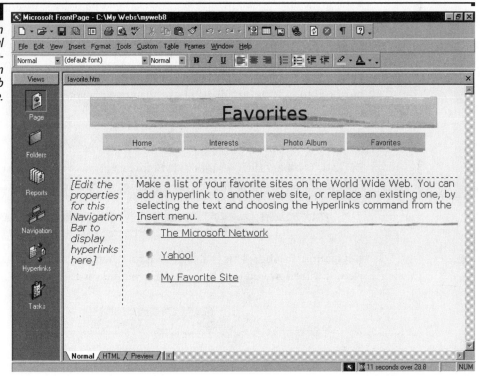

FIGURE 3.1

Use Page view to open and edit individual Web pages. This example was created from the Personal Web template.

If the current FrontPage web was created with a template or wizard, the page that opens will contain placeholder text, and possibly a few design elements such as a background graphic, a page banner, and a navigation bar. If you're building the Web site from scratch, the page will be empty.

Take a look at the interface. You are likely to recognize a few buttons and tools, especially if you're a Microsoft Office user. FrontPage works very much like a word-processing program, with the active page visible in Page view.

Two available toolbars, the Standard toolbar and the Formatting toolbar, are shown in Figure 3.1. There are six toolbars in all, most of which are relevant to the work you'll do in Page view. To make a toolbar visible, open the View menu, select Toolbars, and then select the name of the toolbar you want to display.

Here's a quick rundown of each toolbar:

Standard Toolbar This toolbar contains buttons for many standard program operations, including creating, opening, saving, and printing pages, in addition to tasks specific to Web publishing, such as creating hyperlinks and inserting images.

Formatting Toolbar This toolbar contains buttons and drop-down lists for the most common text-formatting tasks. Chapter 4 explains many of the tools on this toolbar.

DHTML Toolbar The Dynamic HTML toolbar allows you to add special effects such as *mouseovers* to your page. (See Chapter 15, *Special Effects*.)

Navigation Toolbar This toolbar is helpful when you switch to Navigation view. It will allow you to view and edit hyperlinks within the web.

Picture Toolbar This toolbar helps you control how images appear in your Web pages. It also enables you to transform images into image maps (images that contain several clickable hotspots). You'll work with Web graphics and image maps in Chapter 9, *Designing Graphics for the Web*.

Tables Toolbar The choices on this toolbar simplify using tables (rows and columns of content) in your Web page. We show you how to work with tables in Chapter 11, *Using Tables for Advanced Layout*.

How to Get Help within FrontPage 2000

The FrontPage Help system identifies unfamiliar menu items and toolbar buttons. To access FrontPage Help, select Help ➢ Microsoft FrontPage Help. For information about the role of a toolbar button or other on-screen item, on the Standard toolbar, click the Help button, and then click the item you don't recognize. A Help screen will appear containing information about the item you just clicked. Context-sensitive help is also available by clicking the Help button available in many FrontPage dialog boxes, or by pressing Shift+F11 and then clicking the item of interest.

Creating a New Page in Page View

In Chapter 2, we showed you how to tack new, blank pages onto the web currently open in FrontPage. You can also use Page view to create new pages. In fact, you may prefer to do so, because there are some helpful page templates available.

To create a new page using a template, follow these steps:

1. From the menu bar, select File ➢ New ➢ Page (or press Ctrl+N). The New dialog box will appear, as shown in Figure 3.2. This dialog box contains a list of all available page templates. (Note that the dialog box's General tab is selected. If

you select the Frames Pages or Style Sheets tab, you'll see a list of framed pages and style sheets that FrontPage can create. See Chapter 12, *Fantastic Frames*, and Chapter 13, *Getting in Style with Cascading Style Sheets*.)

FIGURE 3.2

The New dialog box lets you choose from several page templates.

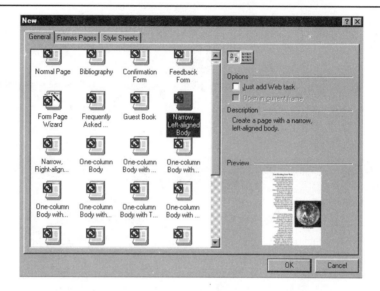

2. From the list, click a name that looks interesting. A brief description of that template appears in the Description area of the dialog box, and a miniature representation of the template appears in the Preview area.

3. When you find a template you like, click OK. The New dialog box closes, and the new page appears (see Figure 3.3).

As you can see in Figure 3.3, new pages based on templates contain placeholder text and, in some cases, sample graphics to give you an idea how the completed page will look (except for the Normal template, which creates an empty page). From here, you can replace the generic text with your own content, and make any other layout changes you see fit.

The dotted gridlines surrounding the text in most templates are the boundaries of *invisible tables* (tables without any border specifications). Invisible tables are the framework for the page's layout. You'll find out how to work with tables in Chapter 11.

Of course, you can also use Page view to create a new blank page. To do so, use the previous procedure, but select the Normal template. Or, on the Standard toolbar, click the New button.

FIGURE 3.3

A new page opened in Page view

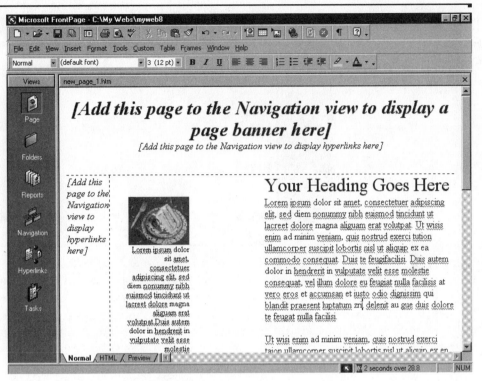

Opening a Web Page in Page View

Once FrontPage is running, you can open more than one page in Page view. Most often, you'll work on pages that are part of the current FrontPage web. You can also open Web pages that are stored on your computer or local network and *aren't* part of a FrontPage web, and you can even open pages directly from the World Wide Web.

If the Page Is Part of the Current FrontPage Web

If you created your Web site in FrontPage using a template or wizard (or if you added new pages to your one-page site), then your web already contains several pages. To open a page that's part of a web, follow these steps:

1. From the FrontPage menu bar, select File ➤ Open (or Ctrl+O). The Open dialog box appears (see Figure 3.4).

FIGURE 3.4

The Open dialog box
displays the current
FrontPage web's files
and folders.

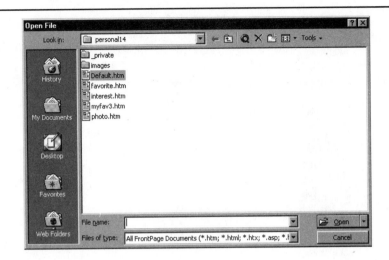

2. The Open dialog box lists the HTML files and folders that make up the web that is currently open. In the dialog box's file list, double-click the name of the file you want to open. (Or, double-click a folder to display its contents, and then double-click the filename.) The dialog box closes, and the selected file opens.

That's all there is to it!

If the Page Is Stored on Your Computer or Local Network

Even if a page isn't part of the current FrontPage web, you can open any page stored on your computer's file system or your local network in Page view.

To do so, follow these steps:

1. From the menu bar, select File ➢ Open (or on the Standard toolbar, click the Open button, or press Ctrl+O). The Open dialog box appears.

2. In the Open File dialog box, you can look inside the file system of your computer or network to find the file you want to open. (See the sidebar "Converting Other Documents into Web Pages" later in this chapter, or Chapter 20, *Integrating Sites with Microsoft Office*, for information about opening non-HTML files.)

3. Using this dialog box, find the Web page you want to open. When the file is visible, double-click the file's icon. The Select File dialog box and the Open dialog box close, and the selected file opens.

You can now edit the page just as if it were part of a FrontPage web.

MASTERING THE OPPORTUNITIES

Converting Other Documents into Web Pages

FrontPage can open several document formats, and, in so doing, convert copies of those documents into Web pages. This feature greatly simplifies transforming existing literature into content for your Web site.

FrontPage can convert the following document formats into Web pages:

- Microsoft Word documents (Word for Windows, versions 2.*x*, 6, Word 95, and Word 97 and Word 2000; and Word for Macintosh, versions 4 to 5.1 and 6)
- Microsoft Works documents (versions 3 and 4)
- WordPerfect documents (versions 5.*x* and 6.*x*)
- Microsoft Excel and Lotus 1-2-3 spreadsheets
- Rich Text Format (.rtf) files
- Text (ASCII) files

In Chapter 20, we talk more about integrating Office files into your FrontPage webs.

Understanding Properties

Each page you create or open in FrontPage contains general settings that govern how the page works and, in some cases, how it looks. FrontPage refers to these settings as *properties* and groups them together in the Page Properties dialog box (see Figure 3.5).

FIGURE 3.5

The Page Properties dialog box lets you control general page settings.

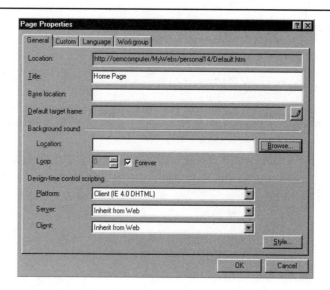

To access the Properties dialog box, from the menu bar, select File ➤ Properties. The Properties dialog box contains four tabs, each of which controls a different set of properties. Most of the properties are addressed in upcoming chapters, but we'll provide a brief overview of them here:

The General tab displays a panel containing general information about the page. This panel shows the page's current URL and lets you change the page's title (you'll learn how to title a new page in the upcoming section, "Saving a Page"). In this panel, you can also set the page's *default target frame* (these terms will make sense after you learn about frames in Chapter 12). You can use this panel to specify a *background sound* (adding background sound is covered in Chapter 10, *Adding Multimedia*). Other features include setting scripting controls.

WARNING While the background sound option may sound terrific, we have to point out the big caveat that it works only for users of Internet Explorer. Any user who accesses your site with Netscape Navigator or another Web browser will hear nothing. See Chapter 10 for more about sound, and Chapter 16, *Cross-Browser Design*, for information about which features work in all browsers.

The Custom tab displays a panel that controls the inclusion of *META tags* in the page. For more information about META tags, turn to Chapter 24, *Site Maintenance and Promotion.*

The Language tab displays a panel that determines which character will appear when the page is viewed in a Web browser. We talk more about selecting character sets for various languages in Chapter 24.

The Workgroup tab is an advanced feature of FrontPage 2000 that allows you to set the page up as part of a workgroup. You can name the workgroup yourself, or select from a list of pre-specified groups. Each group can be assigned to an individual by name, and you can set the status of each page. In this case, *status* refers to the development stage of a page. For example, if the page is fully coded, the next step in your defined process might be to have it copyedited. You can set this as the status.

Using the Text-Editing Tools

As much as graphics, multimedia, and interactive effects tend to grab the spotlight, text is what keeps the Web propped up and moving forward. FrontPage's Page view is essentially an editor, which means it contains all sorts of tools for manipulating and smoothing out text.

Like its Microsoft Office teammates, FrontPage has powerful text-editing features that include cutting and pasting, dragging and dropping, finding and replacing, spell checking, and the option to choose alternative words through a thesaurus. We'll look closely at each of these tools in this section.

Moving Text around the Page

Because so much of Web publishing is really plain old writing and document design, you'll surely want to rearrange your text as you build pages. FrontPage takes advantage of two Windows operations you probably already know and love: *cutting and pasting* and *dragging and dropping.*

You can cut and paste or drag and drop text inside a Web page, between open pages in Page view, and between applications. (For example, you can cut text from a Microsoft Word document and paste it directly into a Web page.)

To cut and paste text, follow these steps:

1. With a page open in Page view, highlight the text to be moved.

2. From the menu bar, select Edit ➤ Cut (to move the text to a different location) or Edit ➤ Copy (to place a copy of the selected text in a new location).

3. Place the cursor where you want the cut or copied text to appear.

4. From the menu bar, select Edit ➤ Paste. The text appears in the new location.

 NOTE To quickly cut, copy, and paste text, you can instead click the Cut, Copy, and Paste buttons on the Standard toolbar, or you can use the keyboard shortcuts Ctrl+X (Cut), Ctrl+C (Copy), and Ctrl+V (Paste). Or, click the right mouse button and select Cut, then Paste from the menu that appears.

To drag and drop text, follow these steps:

1. With a page open in Page view, highlight the text to be moved.

2. Click the highlighted area and hold down the mouse button. Drag the cursor to a new location, then release the mouse button. The text appears in the new location.

 TIP You can cut, copy, and paste (or drag and drop) any Web page element, including images, tables, and more.

Checking Spelling

To ensure that your site looks professional, always check your spelling. And with Front-Page's powerful spell checker, you have no excuse not to. It's easy, quick, and the right thing to do.

To check the spelling of text in your page, follow these steps:

1. With a page open in Page view, from the menu bar, select Tools ➤ Spelling, or press F7. The Spelling dialog box appears, showing the first instance of a misspelled or unrecognized word in its Not In Dictionary text box (see Figure 3.6).

 NOTE FrontPage automatically checks spelling starting at the top of the page, and ending at the bottom of the page, no matter where your cursor was placed.

FIGURE 3.6

The Spelling dialog box tells you what's wrong and how to fix it.

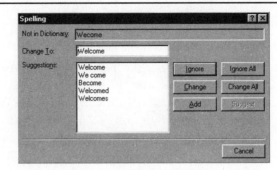

2. FrontPage suggests a correct spelling in the Change To text box and lists other close approximations in the Suggestions list box. To accept the spelling suggestion, click the Change button. To change all instances of the misspelled word at once, click the Change All button.

or

To ignore the supposedly misspelled word and move along, click the Ignore button. To ignore all instances of the same word, click the Ignore All button.

or

To add the word to the dictionary so FrontPage won't hassle you about it in the future, click the Add button.

3. After you click one of the buttons, the next misspelled or unrecognized word appears in the Not In Dictionary text box. Repeat step 2 until the spell check is complete.

4. Click OK to close the dialog box.

 NOTE The spell checker operates on the text in the active page. To check the spelling of all the text in your site, select Tools ➢ Spelling. See Chapter 24 for details.

Using the Thesaurus

FrontPage's thesaurus helps you identify synonyms for selected words or phrases in your Web page. Use this tool when you need a fresh word but can't think of another way to express a thought or concept.

To use the thesaurus, follow these steps:

1. With a page open in FrontPage, click inside the word or highlight the phrase you want to look up in the thesaurus.

2. From the menu bar, select Tools ➤ Thesaurus (or press Shift+F7). The Thesaurus dialog box appears, with the selected word or phrase visible in the Looked Up text box (see Figure 3.7). Different meanings for the selected word or phrase appear in the Meanings list box. FrontPage suggests the closest synonym and lists other alternatives in the accompanying list box.

FIGURE 3.7

FrontPage's thesaurus helps keep your text varied and interesting.

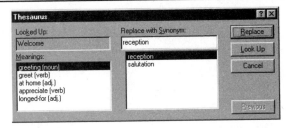

3. If the meaning you want is not already selected in the Meanings list box, click a more appropriate meaning. The synonyms in the list box to the right change to match the selected meaning.

4. If the synonym you want to use doesn't appear in the Replace With Synonym text box, click the synonym you want in the accompanying list box, and then click the Replace button. The Thesaurus dialog box closes, and the highlighted word or phrase in your page is replaced with the synonym you chose.

From here, you can continue working with your page as usual.

Finding Text

As you build your Web site, you'll sometimes need to change certain text. The Find and Replace feature makes wholesale text changes easy. You can instantly find all the instances of a character, word, or phrase in a page, and if you like, replace the found items with different text.

To find text, follow these steps:

1. With your page open in the Page view, place the cursor where you want the search to start. (Unlike a spell check, which always starts at the top of the page, this search starts where you tell it to start.)

2. From the menu bar, select Edit ➢ Find (or press Ctrl+F). The Find dialog box appears.

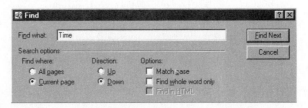

3. In the Find What text box, type the character, word, or phrase you want to find.

4. Click one of the Find Where buttons to specify whether you want to search just the selected page or the entire web.

5. If you want to find only instances of the whole word (for example, you want to find the word *he*, but you don't want to stop when you encounter *the*), click the checkbox labeled Find Whole Word Only.

6. If you want to pay attention to upper- and lowercase letters, select the checkbox labeled Match Case.

7. By default, FrontPage searches for text by moving down the page, starting at the current location of the cursor. If you want the search to move in the opposite direction, click the Up button.

8. Click the Find Next button. In the page, the cursor jumps to the first instance it finds of the specified search string, and highlights the found text (the Find dialog box remains visible). To change the selected text, click the page and make whatever change you like.

9. To find the next instance of the text, click the Find Next button in the Find dialog box. Or, if you're all done, click Cancel to close the Find dialog box. Any changes you made along the way will remain in place.

That was easy. But wouldn't it be even easier if you could automatically replace that text? Read on.

NOTE The FrontPage Search and Replace tool allows you to search for an item on one page or within an entire web.

Replacing Text

Replacing text works like finding text; the only difference is that FrontPage will automatically replace the found text with whatever you tell it to.

To find and replace text, follow these steps:

1. With a page open in Page view, place the cursor where you want the search to start.

2. From the menu bar, select Edit ➢ Replace (or press Ctrl+H). The Replace dialog box appears.

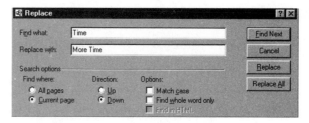

3. In the Find What text box, enter the character, word, or phrase you want to find.

4. In the Replace With text box, type the text you want to use to replace the found text.

5. If you want to find only instances of the whole word, click the checkbox labeled Find Whole Word Only.

6. If you want to pay attention to upper- and lowercase letters, click the Match Case checkbox.

7. Click the Find Next button. In the page, the cursor jumps to and highlights the next instance of the specified text.

8. To replace the text, click the Replace button. Voilà! The highlighted text is instantly replaced with the text you specified.

 TIP To replace text without asking permission, in step 7, click the Replace button. The next instance of the errant text will be replaced automatically. To replace all instances of the text in one step, click the Replace All button. If you make a mistake, you can undo the replace by selecting Edit ➢ Undo or using the key combination Ctrl+Z to undo each instance of the changed items.

---

9. Continue finding and replacing text until you are finished, then click Cancel to close the Replace dialog box.

You can now return to your regular page-building duties.

NOTE The Find and Replace feature operates on the text in the active page or an entire web. Simply select the appropriate Find Where button.

Saving Pages

Saving your work is, of course, the most important part of any computer project. After all, you want to preserve your creative efforts, right? Save your work often and you'll be glad you did, if and when your computer goes down with a "slipped disk."

NOTE How FrontPage saves a page depends on how the page was originally created or opened. Be sure to remember this when you're ready to save your work.

Saving a Page in the Current FrontPage Web

By default, FrontPage saves all new Web pages as part of the current web. (FrontPage considers pages opened directly from the World Wide Web or converted from other file types to be new Web pages.) If, however, the Web page was originally opened from your computer or local network, you must specifically tell FrontPage to save the page as part of the current web; the operation doesn't happen automatically, as it does with new Web pages.

To save a page as part of the current FrontPage web, have it open in Page view and follow these steps:

1. From the menu bar, select File ➤ Save As. The Save As dialog box appears (see Figure 3.8), showing the contents of the current FrontPage web. The URL text box displays the page's filename, and the Title text box displays the page's title.

NOTE FrontPage generates placeholder filenames and page titles based on the page's content. If the page is new, the filename and title will contain the words "New Page." If the page was originally opened from a location outside the FrontPage web, FrontPage will use text in the page's title or the first line of text content to create a filename.

2. If you haven't saved this page before, you'll have to type a filename into the URL text box. For the page's filename, you can use any combination of alphanumeric characters, but most punctuation marks are illegal. Use of lowercase letters or a name with only the first letter in uppercase is customary. But you must include the filename extension .htm or .html.

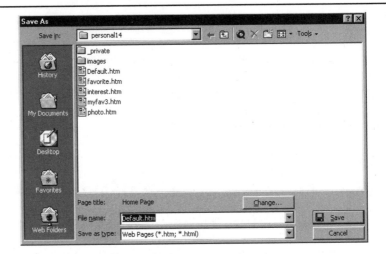

3. If the page has already been saved as part of a web, it will have a title. You can change the title by clicking the Change button next to the page title. In the Title text box, type a brief but descriptive title. Choose a title that reflects the page's content or purpose, not something generic such as "My Web Site." (We talk more about the importance of meaningful page titles in Chapter 24).

 TIP If you've saved your Web page before, you can save new changes in a jiffy by selecting from the menu bar File ➤ Save, or by clicking the Save button on the toolbar. This saves the file without prompting you for a filename—the current filename is used.

4. Click OK. The dialog box closes, and the page is saved as part of the current FrontPage web.

Now that your page is saved, you can continue working on it as usual. To save subsequent changes, simply click the Save button and your work will be saved, no questions asked.

Saving a Page That Contains Embedded Files

When you insert graphics and multimedia files into your Web page, FrontPage places a reference from the page to those files using their current locations. (You'll find out more about how this process works in Chapters 9 and 10.) When you save the page, to maintain these references, copies of all embedded files are saved in the same location as the Web page. Therefore, every time you save a page with embedded files, the Save Embedded Files dialog box appears.

The Embedded Files To Save area of the dialog box lists each embedded file in the file you are saving. The Folder column lists the location where each file will be saved (the same location as the current page being saved), and the Action column lists the action about to be taken on each file. (If the Folder column appears blank, the embedded file will be saved inside the main folder of the current FrontPage web.) You can do a few things using this dialog box:

- To rename one or more of the embedded files, click the file you want to rename, then click the Rename button. The filename appears highlighted. Type a new filename, and then press Enter.

Continued

PART

I

Building Basic FrontPage Webs

CONTINUED

- To change the folder the selected file is to be saved in, click the Change Folder button, and, in the dialog box that appears, select the folder you prefer. Click OK to close the dialog box and return to the Save Embedded Files dialog box.

- To control how the file is saved, click the Set Action button. The Set Action dialog box appears. In this dialog box, you can save the file (the default setting); not save the file, but maintain the reference in the Web page; or, if you're saving an edited version of the embedded file, overwrite the current version of the file. Choose an option by clicking the appropriate radio button, then click OK to close the dialog box and return to the Save Embedded Files dialog box. (These options will make more sense when you learn how to use graphic and multimedia files, as discussed in Chapter 9.)

- To save the embedded files along with the Web page, click OK. The Save Embedded Files dialog box closes, and the Editor saves your page and its embedded files as specified.

Saving a Page as a File

You can easily bypass the current FrontPage web, and instead save a page in a location on your computer or local network. Follow these steps:

1. With the page of interest open in Page view, if the page is new, click the Save button on the Standard toolbar.

   or

   If the page was originally opened from a location on your computer or local network, and you want to save the file in a different location, from the menu bar, select File ≻ Save As. (Clicking the Save button simply saves the page's changes in the original location.) The Save As dialog box appears.

2. In the Save As dialog box, browse through the file system of your computer or network to select the location where you want to save the file.

3. Click the Save button.

4. The Save As File dialog box and the Save As dialog box close, and FrontPage saves the file in the selected location.

Now that your page is saved, you can continue working on it as usual. To save subsequent changes to the same location, click the Save button on the toolbar.

Saving a Web Page as a Template

If you regularly add pages to your Web site using a standard look or standard elements (for example, the same copyright notice on every page), you can conserve your time and effort by saving the standard stuff as a page template. After you save a page as a template, the template will appear with the other FrontPage templates in the New dialog box (refer to the section titled "Creating a New Page in Page View" if you're not sure how to access the New dialog box).

To save a page as a template, follow these steps:

1. From the menu bar, select File ➤ Save As. The Save As dialog box appears.

2. In the dialog box, click the Save As Type arrow. Select the FrontPage Template (*.tem). Name the file. The Save As Template dialog box appears.

3. In the Title text box, type a descriptive title for the template. This title is used for presenting the template in the New dialog box, so if you specify a name that begins with an *A* or an underscore, the custom template will be listed at the top of the template list, making it easy to find.

4. In the Name text box, enter a short, one-word name (the filename is constructed out of the word you choose).

5. In the Description text box, briefly describe the template's layout or function. This will remind you and any other Web team members how to use the template.

6. Click OK. Both the Save As Template dialog box and the Save As dialog box close.

 NOTE   If the page contains images, the Save Embedded Files dialog box appears. Read "Saving a Page That Contains Embedded Files" for information on how to use the options in this dialog box. Or, if the page does not contain images, FrontPage simply saves the page as a template.

7. Change the template as necessary, and then click the Save button on the toolbar to save the changes. Or, from the menu bar, select File ➤ Close to close the newly saved template.

The next time you create a new page based on a template, the name of your custom template will be listed in the New dialog box.

Previewing a Page

As you build your web, the page you are currently working on will appear in the Editor window looking much as it will when a user sees it using a Web browser such as Microsoft Internet Explorer or Netscape Navigator. To see exactly what it will look like once it's published, however, you must *preview* your page.

You can preview your page by using the Preview tab, or by launching a separate Web browser to view the page. Let's take a look.

Viewing a Page with the Preview Tab

If Microsoft Internet Explorer (version 3 or later) is installed on your computer, a Preview tab appears in the lower-left corner of the Editor window. Click this tab from within the Editor, and you can see how the currently open page would look if a user viewed it with Internet Explorer. This option is handy for quick back-and-forth previewing.

Viewing a Page with a Web Browser

If you don't have a Preview tab, or if you want to see how your page will look to users who have Web browsers other than Internet Explorer, or if you just want an exact preview, you can launch a separate Web browser and have a look. We recommend using this method because you can (and should!) check out the page in both Netscape Navigator and Internet Explorer, as well as any other browsers your site's audience is likely to use. (For details about browser-specific features and considering which to include or not include, refer to Chapter 16.)

To preview your page using a Web browser, follow these steps:

1. From the menu bar select File ➢ Preview In Browser. The Preview In Browser dialog box appears, as shown in Figure 3.9. The Browser area of the dialog box lists the different browsers installed on your computer.

2. In the Browser list box, click the name of the browser you want to use. (You can add more browsers to the Browser list box; see Chapter 16.)

3. In the Window Size area, click the button next to the screen resolution that you want the browser window size to approximate.

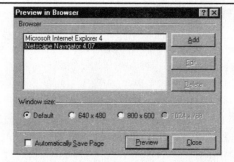

FIGURE 3.9

*Choose a browser to
preview your page.*

 TIP We recommend first previewing your page using the lowest possible resolution (640 × 480) to see how your page will look to Web surfers who use small or low-resolution monitors. Then you can check the page at other resolutions.

4. To have the Editor save page changes each time you preview the page, select the Automatically Save Page checkbox.

5. Click the Preview button. The dialog box closes, and your chosen Web browser starts up and displays the page.

If you want to make changes to the pages you're previewing, return to FrontPage. Make your changes, in Page view, save the page, then switch back to the Web browser. To see the updated page, you'll have to reload it (in the browser's toolbar, click the Reload or Refresh button). You can keep switching back and forth between the browser and FrontPage in this way as you build and fine-tune your page.

 TIP You can also switch between the Web browser and FrontPage by pressing Alt+Tab.

To quickly preview your page (using whichever settings you last specified in the Preview In Browser dialog box), on the Standard toolbar, click the Preview In Browser button.

Printing One or More Pages

If you want paper copies of your pages to distribute at a meeting or fax to a colleague, you can make quick printouts using FrontPage.

 TIP To see how your page will look before you commit it to paper, from the menu bar, select File ➢ Print Preview.

To print your page(s), follow these steps:

1. With the page you want to print open in Page view, from the menu bar, select File ➢ Print or press Ctrl+P. The Print dialog box appears.

2. If the name of the printer you want to use is not already visible in the Name list box, select it.

 NOTE FrontPage uses the printer's default settings to print the page. If you want to change the page's orientation (vertical or horizontal), specify a different paper size or source, or change the graphic resolution, click the Properties button. In the Properties dialog box that appears, change the necessary settings, then click OK to close the dialog box and return to the Print dialog box.

3. If you want to specify a print range (number of pages to print) in the Print Range area, click the Pages button, and in the accompanying text boxes, type the range. For example, if the current page fits on five pieces of paper, but you want to print only the first two pages, in the From text box, enter 1, and in the To text box, enter 2.

4. In the Number Of Copies text box, type the number of copies you want to print. If you want the copies to be collated, select the Collate checkbox.

5. Click OK. The dialog box closes, and your page(s) then print.

 NOTE FrontPage prints pages with the page title at the top of the page and page numbers at the bottom of the page. Each page prints with half-inch margins. To change the header, footer, or margins, from the menu bar, select File ➢ Page Setup. The Page Setup dialog box appears. In the dialog box, enter new header, footer, and margin values, and then click OK to close the dialog box. The new page setup properties take effect immediately.

WARNING Keep in mind that the changes you make here affect all future printouts of the current web *and* of any other webs. Also, make sure you have sensible information entered into these fields before you print your web. The last thing you want to do is put yesterday's client's name on the header for a printout of someone else's web you are working on today!

Exiting FrontPage

When you are satisfied with your work, you're ready to exit the program. To do so, simply save all open files as described earlier within the chapter. Then, from the menu bar, select File ➤ Exit to close FrontPage.

NOTE If you've left any files unsaved, FrontPage will let you know. When you attempt to exit the program, FrontPage queries you about any unsaved pages. You can then choose to save, or not save, any work you've left open during your editing session.

Up Next

At this point, you should be familiar with some basic Web design principles and the FrontPage 2000 interface. Now that you're comfortable using Page view, it's time to start actually creating Web pages! Chapter 4 teaches you how to do just this.

CHAPTER 4

Creating Basic Pages

Ready to have some *fun*? We hope so, because in this chapter, you'll see how easy it is to create a new page and then add text and images to it, along with jazzing up the formatting. We'll also show you how to set the title and colors of your page. This is where we move away from the foundational knowledge of sensible page design and into the activity of building the pages of a site.

 NOTE Although FrontPage includes buttons and menu options for most formatting we're going to tackle in this chapter, we are also going to use a few fancy HTML tricks that involve inserting pieces of code, called *tags*, into your documents. You can apply the things you learn about text and HTML in this chapter to nearly anything you want to do with your Web pages.

Getting Started

In Chapter 3, *Working in Page View*, you learned how to work with editing tools and create a new Web page. Now you're ready to put these basic skills into action and work with specific page features. As explained in Chapter 3, Page view is where you lay out a page and generate the HTML documents—the Web pages—that make up your site. This chapter explains how to add basic elements such as text and images to your pages, and how to format those elements. You'll also learn how to work with links—they're the essence of the Web.

Opening an Existing Web Page

You may have already started working on a page, either with a previous version of Front-Page, with another HTML editor, or with a plain text editor. If you want to start your FrontPage editing experience with a work-in-progress, just follow these steps:

1. Open or create a FrontPage web using Page view (see Chapter 3 if you need help with this).

2. From the menu bar, select File ➢ Open (or press Ctrl+O). The Open dialog box appears.

3. Browse through the list of files on your computer until you locate the file you want to work with (it will most likely end in either .htm or .html). Then click Open, and the Web page appears in Page view.

Depending on which you've selected, either a new blank page or one that has been started appears in the Page view window. That's all there is to opening a Web page. You're ready to start adding text and images to the page.

PART

I

> **TIP** You can edit any page in your FrontPage web simply by double-clicking that page's icon to automatically launch FrontPage and open the selected page.

Creating a New Page

If you want to create a Web page from scratch, follow these steps to create a new page in your FrontPage web:

1. To create a new file, select File ➢ New ➢ Page.

2. From the General page dialog box, choose a page that suits your fancy. I'm going to select the Three-Column Staggered page.

3. Click OK. The file will open up in the editing pane, with a default name of new-page1.htm (see Figure 4.1). You'll also see gridlines, "dummy" text (meaningless text that you can fill in with your own copy), and, depending upon the page you've selected, images.

Building Basic
FrontPage Webs

FIGURE 4.1

When you create a new web page, you might find that it's already decked out with images and a background.

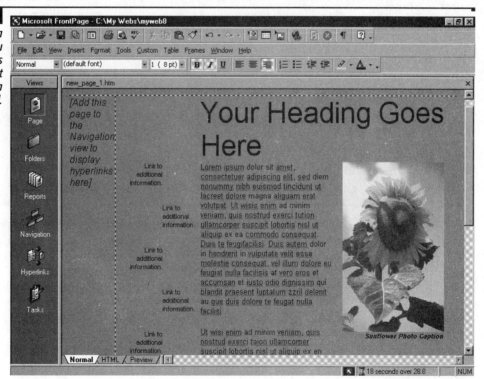

NOTE   If you are opening a page from a web you've already created (see Chapter 3), not only will the page you see have text and images in it, but several pages may already exist. For example, if you were to create a web using the Personal Web template, you'd find a home page (`default.htm`), a photo album page (`photo.htm`), a hobbies page (`myinterests.htm`), and a couple of versions of a favorite sites page (`favorite.htm` and `myfav3.htm`). You can open up any of these pages and modify them, as explained throughout this chapter, or you can delete them from your web if you like.

Viewing the HTML behind Your Page

So you have a web, or a Web page. You're ready to begin adding text and images, and eventually you'll be manipulating those images. But before we show you how to do those things, we feel you need to be able to view and understand the *way* your text and images are put on the page.

In addition to providing a WYSIWYG interface for editing Web pages, Page view allows you to work directly with the underlying HTML code—this is the code that tells the browser where to put your text, images, and other media. Using FrontPage, you can not only stick with Page view, as we described in Chapter 3, but also peek under the virtual hood and add code yourself. This means you can enter HTML code that is not directly supported by FrontPage, check your work, and even make changes to a page's code.

To view the HTML code and open it for editing, be sure you have the page you're interested in working with open in Page view. Then select the HTML tab. The contents of the window change to show the HTML source code for the document.

You can now make changes by typing new or modified HTML directly into the code shown in Page view. You can also delete any extraneous or unwanted HTML by highlighting the unwanted code and pressing the Delete key.

WARNING   Be careful: It is very easy to turn your functioning Web page into a non-functioning page by deleting necessary code. This can result from something as simple as removing just one tag that you don't realize is required by FrontPage. This is why it's good to get some background in HTML if you're interested in doing more "hands on" work. Check out *Mastering HTML 4* (Second Edition) from Sybex (1999).

When you are done and want to switch back to Normal view, simply click the Normal tab at the bottom of the Page view window. The contents of the window change to reflect your choice. You now see your page, with any modifications that you just made, in the WYSIWYG view.

Now that you know how to look under the hood and make adjustments, it's time to get back in the driver's seat. You're almost ready to add text and images, but first let's make sure you give your document a proper title.

Fixing Imported Files

You can use any one of a number of methods to import existing Web pages into FrontPage (see Chapter 2 for details). Importing existing Web pages is a great way to start using FrontPage's powerful tools for maintaining and expanding your existing Web pages and sites. But, sad to say, not all Web pages import into FrontPage flawlessly. FrontPage is much pickier about HTML than most Web browsers are. It requires that certain tags be there to enable your Web page to work properly. If you import a page and it does not appear correct in Page view (or if it appears as a blank page when you know there is supposed to be information on it), view the page's HTML source code by selecting the HTML tab at the bottom of the Page view window. The contents of the window change to show the HTML code behind the page. Look for these common issues:

- Verify that the first and last tags of the file are <HTML> and </HTML> respectively.
- Verify that the <TITLE> tag is between the <HEAD> and </HEAD> tags.
- Verify that the body of the page is between the <BODY> and </BODY> tags.

If you notice that any of these tags are missing or out of place, go ahead and make corrections. Then switch back to the Normal view and see if that fixes the problem.

Titling Your Document

The *title* of a document in this context is not text that appears on the page itself to say what the page is about, but rather the words that show up *in the title bar* of the browser window. This title also appears in the browser's menu bar, its Go or File menu, and its button on the Windows taskbar. It's generally also the title indexed by search engines, directories, and any hotlists that point fellow Web surfers to your page.

NOTE Giving your page a clear, descriptive title is *very* smart. Many search engines grant particular importance to words used in the title, so the accuracy of your title will help users to find you. The title also appears in the search engine's hit list (the index of search results a user gets), and even in bookmark lists. See the discussion of META tags in Chapter 24, *Site Maintenance and Promotion*, for tips on coaxing search engines into recognizing your site and titling the page effectively.

Giving your page a title is easiest to do when you save it. The first time you save your Web page, the Save As dialog box appears (see Figure 4.2), and you are prompted to give your document not just a filename, but a page title as well. At this point, simply type the title in the Save As dialog box's Set Page Title text box.

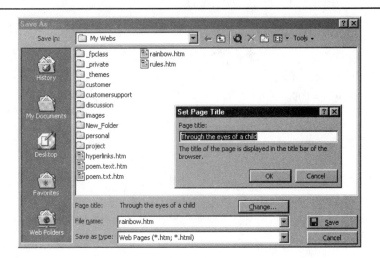

You can change the title of your page at any time. Just follow these steps:

1. With a page open in Page view, from the menu bar, select File ➢ Properties. The Page Properties dialog box appears, as shown in Figure 4.3.

2. In the Title text box, type a new title for your page.

3. Click OK to close the Properties dialog box and return to the Page view window.

Your page now has a distinguishable title.

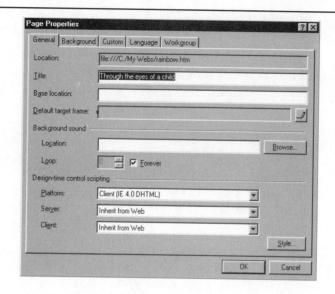

FIGURE 4.3

*Using the Page
Properties dialog
box, you can change
the title of the
current page.*

Adding Text

To add text to your page, just open a Web page and begin typing in Page view. You can also copy or cut text from a text file, a Microsoft Word file, an e-mail message, or another Web page, and then paste it into the page you're working on. Just follow these steps:

1. Open the document that has the content you want to use on your Web page.

2. Select the text you want, and from that program's menu bar, select Edit ➢ Copy (or press Ctrl+C).

3. Switch to the Page view window by using the taskbar or by pressing Alt+Tab. The screen updates to reflect your choice.

4. Click in the Page view window to place the insertion point, and from the menu bar, select Edit ➢ Paste (or press Ctrl+V). The text appears in the window.

That's all there is to that—it's just like copying text from one part of a document to another.

NOTE   It is very important to spend plenty of time getting familiar with how to add and manipulate text and navigate in Page view. You'll have ample opportunity to get fancy with stylizing text in Chapters 5 and 6.

Making Paragraphs Work

Paragraphs are used as a means of grouping text in all kinds of documents, and creating paragraphs isn't exactly complex. Page view wraps text just like most text editors and word-processing programs do. Just type the text, and it automatically wraps within the window. Press Enter to create a new paragraph.

 TIP The paragraphs you type in HTML automatically wrap in both FrontPage and the user's browser window, which means that if you want a line to break in a certain place, you have to specifically break the line (by pressing Enter, usually). Text that seems to occupy a certain amount of space on your screen may be seen differently by people who are using a different Web browser, or even people using the same browser who have changed the default font settings or browser window size.

In HTML, the language of the Web, paragraph breaks don't mean quite the same thing that they do in printed text. For instance, there's no standard tab or margin scheme to add indents like the one at the beginning of this paragraph. New paragraphs are generally indicated by a line of white space, although fastidious designers often find a way to create the illusion of indents and other conventions of printed text. You can find out some options for manipulating the way your paragraphs fit together in the upcoming sections of this chapter on paragraph alignment and nonbreaking spaces.

Inserting Paragraph Breaks

Paragraphs in HTML are a little different from the paragraphs used in text documents. They're not necessarily the standard units of "three cohesive sentences" you learned about in elementary school—they're basically just visual units of separate items on a page, whether those items are text, images, or whatever. You can even use paragraph breaks to separate sections of text *from* images, or images from other images.

While in Page view, inserting a paragraph break is as simple as pressing Enter. The default behavior of the Enter key in Page view is to create a paragraph break, which is then indicated in HTML by the <P> tag, which you'd see if you viewed the source code (we'll get more into that in a moment). This tag breaks a line wherever it is inserted, and also inserts a line of blank space between one page element and the next.

Breaking Lines

Line breaks, represented as <BR> in HTML, can be used to format text when you want to end one line and continue on the following line, without inserting a blank line between the items you're delineating. For example, if you're formatting text such as a poem, a recipe, a masthead, or a table of contents, you may want a break between lines but not a chasm of white space dividing them. Figure 4.4 shows a poem in Preview mode, formatted with paragraph breaks, and the same poem below it, formatted with line breaks.

FIGURE 4.4

Paragraph breaks insert a line of white space between units of text, while line breaks simply break lines.

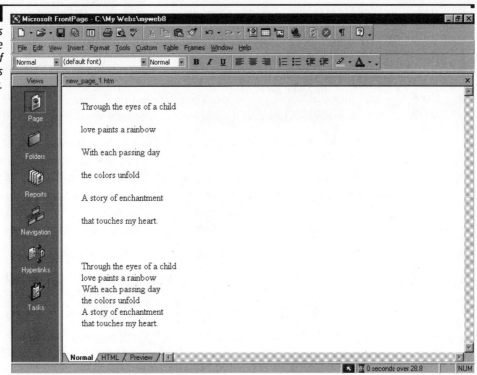

To insert a line break, follow these quick steps:

1. With the Page view window open and a page in view, place the cursor's insertion point at the exact spot on the page where you want the line break to appear.

2. From the menu bar, select Insert ➢ Break. The Break Properties dialog box appears, as shown in Figure 4.5.

TIP You can insert a line break quickly by holding down the Shift key and pressing Enter.

The Break Properties dialog box offers some options for aligning text with line breaks.

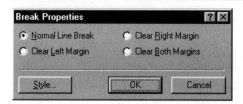

3. Click the Normal Line Break button, and then click OK. The Break Properties dialog box closes, and the Page view window reappears.

You'll now see the line break. You can apply a few different attributes to this break, if you want to use line breaks to format the placement of images. For instance, Figure 4.6 shows an image with a caption. The first example uses a normal line break, the second clears the left margin, the third clears the right margin, and the last example clears both margins. To format line breaks around images, follow steps 1 and 2 of the previous procedure, and then, in the Break Properties dialog box, select one of these options:

Select This...	To Do This...
Normal Line Break	Insert a regular line break between the image and the text
Clear Left Margin	Move the next line of text down until it clears the left margin of the image
Clear Right Margin	Move the next line of text down until it clears the right margin of the image
Clear Both Margins	Move the next line of text down until it clears both margins of the image

FIGURE 4.6

This page demonstrates different margin options when you're using line breaks.

Aligning Paragraphs

Text that you type or paste into Page view is aligned with the left edge of the window by default. If you want to center your text or align it with the right margin, follow these steps:

1. To align a single paragraph, in Page view, click in the paragraph. To align multiple consecutive paragraphs, highlight all of the paragraphs to be aligned.

2. Click one of the alignment buttons (left, right, or center) on the Formatting toolbar. The paragraphs move accordingly.

You can also realign images, headers, and horizontal rules this way. Just highlight the object whose alignment you want to change, and click the appropriate button.

 NOTE Another type of alignment, known as *justify*, is supported by most 4.*x* browsers. Justified alignment makes the left and right margins completely flush. This is commonly used in newspapers. You can justify a paragraph by first highlighting the paragraph, then selecting Format ➢ Paragraph. In the Indents And Spacing dialog box, select Justify from the Alignment drop-down menu. If a browser does not support Justify, the text will default to left alignment.

Indenting Paragraphs

As we mentioned in the beginning of this section, tabs (the indents produced when you press Tab on your keyboard) are not valid characters in HTML. You can use nonbreaking spaces, as described in the following section called "Using Nonbreaking Spaces," to create an artificial tab, or you can indent an entire paragraph to make it stand out from the rest of the text on a page.

This process is quite similar to adjusting the alignment of a paragraph. Just follow these steps:

1. To indent an entire paragraph along one margin of the page, highlight the paragraph (or other element) you want to indent.

2. On the Page view toolbar, click the Increase Indent button. The paragraph is indented from the margin to which it's aligned. For example, if your paragraph is left-aligned, it is indented toward the right, and if it's right-aligned, it is indented to the left.

NOTE Centered paragraphs can't be indented—how would you indent from the middle? If you want a paragraph to be off-center, change its alignment to either left- or right-aligned (see the previous section called "Aligning Paragraphs") and then indent it several times.

You can click the Increase Indent button several times over to indent an element further and further into a page. To remove an indent later, simply highlight the indented text and click the Decrease Indent toolbar button.

TIP Style sheets afford you much more control over the alignment and indentation of paragraphs. See Chapter 13 for more information on using style sheets with FrontPage.

Using Nonbreaking Spaces

A *nonbreaking space* is kind of what it sounds like: a space that doesn't break. What this means is that a particular kind of space (indicated by the code   in HTML) is particularly considered as a character unto itself, rather than just a space *between* characters. To be more specific, plain spaces that you get by pressing the spacebar are considered extraneous by most Web browsers; if you put in a bunch of blank spaces one after another to try to format text, only one will show up.

NOTE Just like word processors, Web browsers wrap text from one line to the next at spaces. They do not, however, wrap text at nonbreaking spaces; that's why they're called *nonbreaking*.

In comes the role of the nonbreaking space. Put together, a bunch of nonbreaking spaces in a row will all show up. (Some designers use nonbreaking spaces to create artificial tabular indents or to format text that requires shaping with space.)

Let's say your company's name is ABC Computers, and that company style is to not allow a break between "ABC" and "Computers." If you just use the text "ABC Computers" on a Web page, anybody's browser could and well might break up the two words to make the text fit on the page or even in a table cell. If instead you use

`ABC Computers`

then the text will not be broken between the words. In other examples, you might not want to allow a break between parts of a date (`February 13`), parts of a phone number (`((415) 555-1234`), or someone's initials (`e. e. cummings`).

To insert a nonbreaking space, you'll use the same Symbols dialog box you use to insert special characters. Just follow these steps:

1. In the Page view window, click to place the insertion point at the spot in the text where you want the nonbreaking space to be.

2. From the menu bar, select Insert ➤ Symbol. The Symbol dialog box appears, as shown in Figure 4.7.

FIGURE 4.7

The Symbol dialog box lets you insert special characters into your Web pages.

3. The very first symbol in that box, in the top-left corner, is a nonbreaking space (its little box looks empty). Click this space, then click Insert to insert it. The space appears on your page, although the dialog box may obscure your view of it.

4. Click OK to close the Symbol dialog box. Your page is visible, and you're all set.

 TIP You can click the nonbreaking space in the Symbol dialog box and then click Insert several times in a row to insert several nonbreaking spaces in a row. You can also press the Tab key on your keyboard to insert three nonbreaking spaces at a time.

Making Multiple Paragraph Breaks

Although you can stack line breaks (<br>), you can't stack paragraphs (<P>). Place several <P> tags in a row, and Web browers will ignore everything after the first single <P> tag. If you need to add blank space, you can use one of these methods:

- Combine one <P> tag and several <br> tags:

  <P>

- Stack as many <br> tags as you want:

- Press Enter several times in a row in Page view to produce code that looks like this:

  <P> </P>

  <P> </P>

  <P> </P>

  <P> </P>

- This code tells the Web browser to leave several lines of white space, by creating a paragraph whose only character is a nonbreaking space.

This last method is particular only to WYSIWYG editors like FrontPage.

Using Special Characters

A few symbols, known as *special characters*, are commonly used in day-to-day editing, but don't appear on your keyboard. Word processors generally provide these symbols within a special menu, or special symbol font. Unfortunately, HTML does not recognize these symbols, and they just plain won't show up on Web pages if you simply paste them in from a word-processed document. Often you'll find that you want to use the ® (registered symbol, to denote a type of trademark) or © (copyright symbol) to denote ownership; or you may want to use letters like *è* and *ñ* if you're working with languages other than English.

Just as HTML provides codes to control the formatting of text, it also provides special codes, called *escape characters,* which are used to generate special characters not found on your keyboard. These aren't tags, precisely, but bits of code that tell a Web browser it should display a special character. FrontPage makes it easy to insert these characters using a simple dialog box similar to Microsoft Word's Insert ➢ Symbol menu command. In fact, FrontPage has its own Insert ➢ Symbol menu command! Just follow these steps to use it:

1. From the Page view menu bar, select Insert ➢ Symbol, and the Symbol dialog box appears.

2. Locate the symbol you want to insert, click it, and then click Insert. The symbol appears in your document. (Sometimes it appears behind the Symbol dialog box, so have a good look before you decide it's not there.)

3. Click Close to close the dialog box and return to the Page view window when you're done.

While your text is really the meat of your Web page matter, the spice is going to be images. Images can be used to really express your message, and to give your page visual interest and make a memorable impression, too.

Working with Images

The Web is comprised of much more than just text. Today's Web site is designed to be graphical. To add impact to your Web pages, you can use an image you've stored in the FrontPage web, an image on your hard drive, or an image on the Internet. Or you can spruce up your pages with something from the FrontPage Clip Art Gallery, which we'll take a look at now.

NOTE Images must be in GIF or JPEG format to be viewed using most Web browsers. If the images you want to use aren't in one of these two formats, use your favorite image editor to convert them to GIF or JPEG files (see Chapter 9, *Designing Graphics for the Web*).

Using the FrontPage Clip Art Gallery

Clip art on the Web is just like clip art in those big books of stock images; it's named such because you could just buy a book and cut out pictures to use on flyers or in newsletters and the like. Not everyone is artistically inclined enough to create or scan and manipulate images to put on their pages, so having a library of digital clip art at your fingertips will save you time and energy and fill in blank spots on your pages. FrontPage includes a Clip Art Gallery of simple icons, buttons, lines, backgrounds, and animated graphics.

 NOTE You can find out more about clip art by reading Chapter 9.

Placing this clip art on your page is very straightforward. Just follow these steps:

1. In Page view, from the menu bar, select Insert ➤ Picture ➤ Clip Art (or click the Insert Picture button on the Standard toolbar). The Clip Art Gallery appears.

2. Click a category, such as Cartoons, Signs, or Web Buttons, and the images available in that category appear in the large panel of the dialog box (see Figure 4.8).

 NOTE The Clip Art Gallery contains a couple dozen categories of clip art, each of which contains from a few to a hundred images. There are more than 500 available images in all.

FIGURE 4.8

*You can use the
FrontPage Clip Art
Gallery to insert pre-
pared buttons and
icons into your pages.*

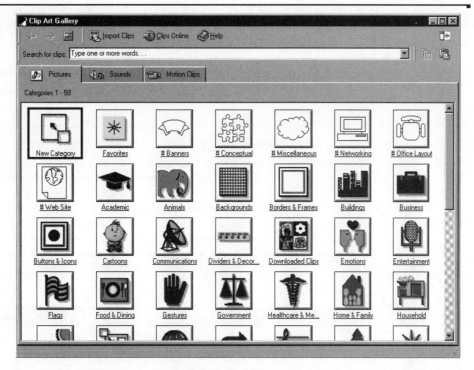

3. Once you've found something you like, click the image. A caption menu
appears, offering several options, including Insert Clip, Preview Clip, Add Clip
To Favorites, and Find Similar Clips.

 NOTE Previewing the clip allows you to get a closer look at clip details. If you really like
a piece of clip art and feel you'll be using it again, add it to your Favorites category, making
it easier to find in the future. Finding similar clips is a good option to help you create a consistent image style between pages.

4. To insert the clip, simply click the Insert Clip button on the caption menu, and FrontPage inserts the clip into the page.

5. The dialog box closes and Page view reappears, with the image you selected inserted into your document.

You can repeat this process as often as you wish to add as much clip art to your page as your heart desires.

TIP Once an image is safely on your page, you can highlight it with your mouse, then cut and paste to reposition it, or copy and paste to make multiple copies of the same image on your page. This technique is particularly handy and timesaving for buttons and other items that may be repeated on the page. You can also click and hold and then drag and drop an image to another part of the page, or even resize it using the little resizing marks, called *handles*, around the edge of the image.

MASTERING WHAT'S ONLINE

Get a whole plethora of clip art by connecting to the Web and using the Microsoft Clip Gallery Live. Just click the Web button in the Clip Art Gallery dialog box, or point your Web browser to www.microsoft.com/clipgallerylive/. Once you're there, just follow the instructions to download more art from the Web.

Importing Images into Your FrontPage Web

Importing an image is the process of taking an image that you have stored locally, or have found on a Web site, and moving it into your very own Web space.

When you import an image to your FrontPage web, it doesn't mean you're adding it to a Web page. Rather, it means you're getting the images onto your site so that you'll have easy access to the image files when you are ready to put them on the pages themselves. And when you publish your pages, your images will be safely in place.

Importing images is a simple process. Once you have your web opened up in FrontPage, just follow these steps:

1. From the Views menu, click the Folder View button. This displays the folders and files in your FrontPage web.

TIP   It's a good idea to keep all your images in the folder called Images on your Front-Page web (see Chapter 3 if you don't have an Images folder and want to create one). This way, if you want to use an image more than once on your site, all your images will be in a central location, and you won't have to move them around or keep multiple copies on hand.

2. Now you're going to import some images from your hard drive and into your FrontPage web. Using the Folders view, double-click the Images folder to display its contents (it may be empty right now, or it may contain pre-set images from a template or wizard).

 TIP   You're not limited to importing files into the Images directory—you can import files into *any* directory simply by selecting the desired directory in step 2.

3. From the File menu, select Import. The Import File To FrontPage Web dialog box appears (see Figure 4.9).

*The Import File
To FrontPage Web
dialog box helps you
get all your images
onto your site.*

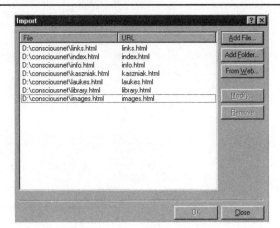

4. To add a single file to the Images folder, click Add File. The Add File To Import List dialog box appears. Use it just like any other Open dialog box you encounter in a Windows-based program to locate the image you want to add to your page, by browsing through folders until you've found the image file and selected it. When you're done, click Open to return to the Import File dialog box, where you'll see the name of the file you just selected.

or

To add the entire contents of a folder (assuming it's full of images) to your FrontPage web's Images folder, click Add Folder. The Browse For Folder dialog box appears, as shown in Figure 4.10. Locate the folder full of images on your hard drive or local network, then click its icon. When you're done, click OK to return to the Import File dialog box, where you'll see the names of all the files in the folder you just selected.

or

To add files from an existing Web site, click From Web. The Import Web Wizard appears. Simply follow the wizard through the necessary steps to import the file(s) you want right off the Web.

FIGURE 4.10

The Browse For Folder dialog box lets you import an entire folder full of images at once.

 NOTE If there are non-image files in your import folder, they'll be imported too; the Import File dialog box is for importing all kinds of documents, not just images. You can delete the extraneous files from your FrontPage web when you're done, or you can instead move only the images in, one at a time, as described above.

5. You can repeat step 4 as often as you like until you've selected all the images you'd like to add to your FrontPage web. When you're ready to copy these files to your FrontPage web, click OK. The files begin to load, and the Import File To FrontPage Web dialog box closes when the files have been copied.

Now that you've imported all your image files into your FrontPage web folder, putting the images on your pages will be a snap.

 TIP See Chapter 9 to learn how you can create original images for your Web page.

Placing Images on Your Web Page

Now that the images you want to use safely reside in your FrontPage web, you can use Page view to easily place them in your pages. To perform the basic task of dropping an image onto your page, just follow these steps:

1. With a Web page open in Page view, from the menu bar, select Insert ➢ Picture ➢ From File. The Image dialog box appears, as shown in Figure 4.11.

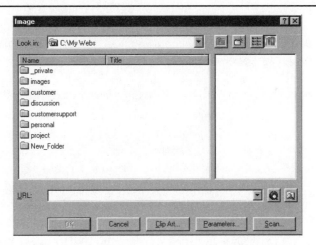

2. The Image dialog box displays the folders in your current FrontPage web. If the image is available on your current FrontPage web, click the folder that contains the image (probably the Images folder) to display the contents of that folder, and then click the name of the image. The image's location appears in the URL area of the dialog box.

3. Now that you've specified the location of the image you want to add, click OK to close the Image dialog box. Page view reappears.

Your image is there, displayed in the Page view window. You can leave it where it is, or cut and paste it to a new location on your page using the familiar Windows cut-and-paste techniques.

 NOTE Although it's easy to add images from other people's pages to your own works, the legal ramifications aren't so simple. If the images are clearly marked as being public domain, and you are very confident that this is true, you can feel free to use them as you like. Otherwise, the author of the image holds copyright on it—there are no exceptions to this rule of intellectual property. If you can't live without that image, write its owner an e-mail message asking permission to use it—and then respect his or her decision.

Adjusting Image Properties

Once an image is on your page, there could very well be something about the image you want to change. Maybe you'd like to change the size or the alignment, or add a border around the image. In Chapter 9 we talk about adjusting the quality and transparency of images, and about using an image editor to make big changes to an image. In this section, we're going to focus on image properties set within the document itself.

Once you have an image placed on your page, just follow these steps:

1. Right-click the image whose properties you want to adjust and, from the pop-up menu that appears, select Image Properties (or press Alt+Enter). The Image Properties dialog box appears, with the location (known as *image source*) and type of image already defined, as shown in Figure 4.12.

2. Next, you can specify that a low-resolution, black-and-white version of the image be loaded before the real image; many Web browsers will comply with this, and those that don't will simply load the image as usual instead. To specify that this feature be used, type the URL into the Low-Res text box. Note that this practice is being used less often on the Web these days, so you may choose to leave this area blank.

FIGURE 4.12

*The Image Properties
dialog box lets you
adjust your image to
fit your needs.*

Image Properties

General | Video | Appearance

Image Source:

lates/1033/Pages/4cstagl.tem/Sunflowr.jpg   Browse...   Edit...

Type

○ GIF □ Transparent   ⊙ JPEG Quality: 75

□ Interlaced   Progressive Passes: 0

○ PNG

Alternative representations

Low-Res: Browse...

Text:

Default hyperlink

Location: Browse...

Target
Frame:

Style...

OK   Cancel

3. In almost all cases of visible graphics, you will want to specify alternate text (also called ALT text) within the image code. This text helps people with auto image loading turned off, or people who are using text-only browsers. People with newer browsers will also see the alternate text as a tool tip when they mouse over an image. To add this handy text, just type a description or name for your image in the Text box.

WARNING It's very important to include alternate text for any image that will be visibly displayed. The reason for this is because many people accessing the Web cannot see images. There is a significant disabled population using the Internet, and many of those individuals must use text-based browsers to visit Web pages. Also, individuals in remote areas are often at the mercy of restricted bandwidth or older computer systems, necessitating text-only browsing, or browsing without images. Still others prefer fast access to information, so they will browse with the auto image-loading feature in their browser turned off.

4. You can modify any style sheet information included with the text by clicking the Style button. A new dialog box pops up, and you can make changes to the styles there (see Chapter 13 for more information on style sheets).

5. Click the Appearance tab of the Image Properties dialog box, and it changes to reflect your choice (see Figure 4.13).

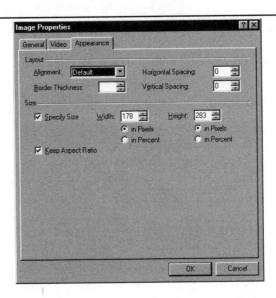

6. In the Layout area of the dialog box, you can choose alignment for your image. You can choose to have your image aligned according to the browser's default behavior (most browsers use baseline alignment as the default), in which case you'd leave the Default setting selected. To choose another alignment for your image, click the Alignment list box, and select an option from the following list.

Select This...	To Do This...
Left	Place the image on the left side of the browser window, with text or other elements wrapped around the right side of the image.
Right	Place the image on the right side of the browser window, with text or other elements wrapped around the left side of the image.
Top	Align the top of the image with the top of the tallest element on the same line.
Texttop	Align the top of the image with the top of the tallest character on the same line.

Select This...	To Do This...
Middle	Align the middle of the image with the middle of the surrounding text.
Absmiddle	Align the middle of the image with the middle of the largest item on the current line.
Baseline	Align the bottom of the image with the bottom of the surrounding text (this is another name for bottom).
Bottom	Align the bottom of the image with the bottom of the surrounding text (this is another name for baseline).
Absbottom	Align the bottom of the image with the bottom of the current line of text.
Center	Center the image horizontally in the browser window.

7. You can specify that the browser leave a margin of white space around your image. Type a number (in pixels) in the Horizontal and Vertical text boxes (10 is a good start; you can experiment from there).

NOTE If you're concerned about the visual appearance of your pages (as well you should be!), you'll want to be sure to have white space around your images. This is especially true when you have text wrapping around an image. If the text is too close to the image, the page will appear cramped and be difficult to read.

8. Specifying the size of an image allows the browser to load the page more efficiently, because it can draw a placeholder while it's fetching the image itself. FrontPage automatically sets the image size when you first insert it, but if you want to resize the image, you can change this.

WARNING It is unwise to change the size of the image using this feature. If you want the image to be larger or smaller, change the physical size of the image in an image editor before inserting it into your page. You can do this in almost any image editor. One of the rare exceptions to this good rule of thumb is when using single pixel GIFs to fix table widths or create visual rules. See Chapter 9 for more information.

9. You can have a solid border appear around an image. If you'd like your image to include a border, type a number (in pixels) in the Border Thickness text box.

Either leaving the text box empty or typing 0 will prevent the border from appearing at all. Since borders around images can make a page look tight and cluttered, leaving this setting empty or specifying 0 is the recommended way to go.

10. When you're all finished, click OK to close the Image Properties dialog box and return to Page view. The changes you made to the image properties are visible.

Using Images from the Web

If an image you want to use resides on an FTP or Web server somewhere on the Internet, you can use your Web browser to select it, then you can use the Image dialog box as described in "Placing Images on Your Web Page" to drop it onto your page. Or, if you're using Microsoft Internet Explorer, you can simply right-click an image and, from the pop-up menu that appears, select Copy Picture. You can then go to Page view and paste the image directly onto your page by pressing Ctrl+V. Note that this procedure does not incorporate the actual image file into your FrontPage web. It does place the image itself onto your page, using a URL that points to the remote server.

If you're using Netscape Navigator, just follow these steps:

1. In Page view, click to place the insertion point at the spot on your page where you want the image.

2. From the menu bar, select Insert ➤ Picture ➤ From File. The Image dialog box appears.

 3. Click the blue globe icon. In a moment, your default Web browser opens, where you'll see a message that says "Browse to the page or file you want to use, then return to Microsoft FrontPage to continue..."

4. Locate the image you want on the Internet by any method you like (open a Web site, use a bookmark, find it with a search engine, or what have you).

5. When you've opened the page bearing the image you want, view the image in its own window by right-clicking the image. From the pop-up menu that appears, select View Image.

6. When the page bearing the image (or the image itself) is visible in the browser window, return to Page view by using the Windows taskbar. The Image dialog box is still open, where you'll see the URL of the image in the URL text box.

7. Click OK, and the Image dialog box closes, returning you to the Page view window.

There's your image, plain as day. Of course, be certain that you do not violate any copyright laws by using images belonging to others.

You can change image settings as often as you like until you're satisfied with the size, alignment, and spacing of your images. Now that you know how to place and adjust images, let's look at the various kinds of paragraph styles you can use to organize the information on your pages.

Using Ruled Lines

Horizontal rules are pretty much what they sound like: horizontal lines drawn across a page that visually separate parts of a document. You can insert ruled lines beneath document heads, between parts of a memo or article, or anywhere else you please. There are basically two kinds of ruled lines: horizontal rules created through the <HR> tag in HTML, and graphics that look like lines (and act to divide space) but don't share their HTML properties. Many of the decorated ruled lines that you have seen on the Web are probably graphics. Figure 4.14 shows several different ruled lines; the two at the bottom are graphic images.

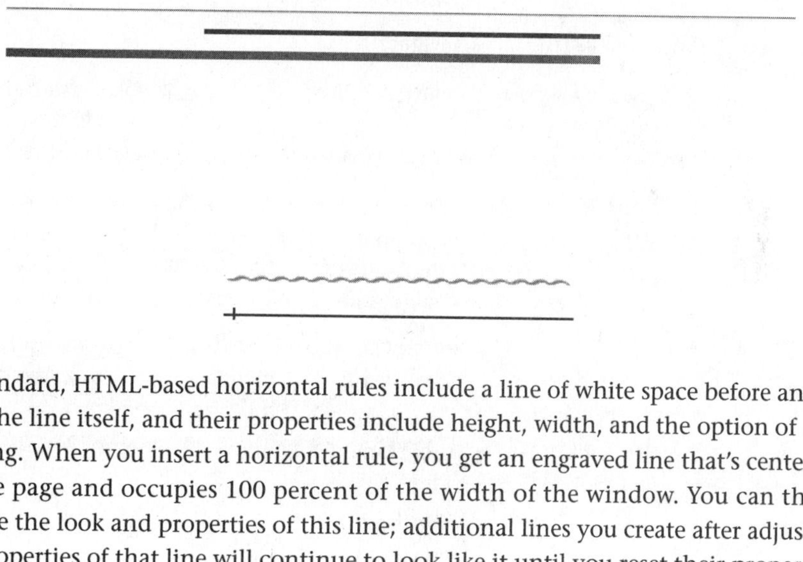

FIGURE 4.14

The two objects at the bottom of this picture are actually images, while the rest are ruled lines.

Standard, HTML-based horizontal rules include a line of white space before and after the line itself, and their properties include height, width, and the option of 3-D shading. When you insert a horizontal rule, you get an engraved line that's centered on the page and occupies 100 percent of the width of the window. You can then change the look and properties of this line; additional lines you create after adjusting the properties of that line will continue to look like it until you reset their properties.

Inserting a Ruled Line

Drawing a ruled line in Page view is even easier than it would be if you were using a ruler and paper. In this section, we're going to draw a line. In the next section, "Changing the Look of a Ruled Line," we're going to adjust the properties of a line drawn with Front-Page; and in the section called "Using Graphical Ruled Lines," we'll tell you how to use a graphic image that acts as a ruled line.

To drop a ruled line onto your page, just follow these quick steps:

1. In the Page view window, open a page. Click the page to place the cursor's insertion point where you want the line to appear.

2. From the menu bar, select Insert ➤ Horizontal Line. A 3-D line appears across the page.

Now let's find out how you can change the look—the size, color, and shading—of lines like these.

About Pixels

When you're choosing the size for a Web page element, you're often given two choices for the unit of measure: *percentage* or *pixels*. Percentage means that the measurement is drawn to occupy a certain portion of the available screen size—usually the screen's width.

Pixels are actually (and generally) a unit of projected light. There's no precise size for pixels; a pixel is just a dot of light on a screen. Televisions and computer screens both use pixels as their basic unit of measure, although the pixels on TV are generally much bigger than those on computer screens. The higher the resolution of the medium, the smaller the pixels are.

When you're using pixels as your unit of measure, you should realize two things: One pixel is pretty small, but it's not invisible; and pixels are different sizes when viewed on screens of different sizes or resolutions. The lowest resolution screens these days are 640 pixels by 480 pixels. In recent years, screens with a resolution of 800 pixels by 600 pixels and even 1024 pixels by 768 pixels are also becoming common. Some high-end computers come with screens of much higher resolution; they'll have lots more pixels.

In designing Web pages, you ought to consider the size of screen you'll generally design for (this goes back to what sorts of machines you expect your audience to have). You'll also want to consider this in choosing a pixel size for elements that appear on your pages.

Changing the Look of a Ruled Line

You will rarely want to use the default ruled line that's plain, engraved, and occupies 100 percent of the browser window. Leaving a ruled line at this default breaks up a page too dramatically. You can soften the effect and improve readability by making the line shorter, varying thickness, or applying color. Adjusting the properties of a line gives you a great deal of design flexibility; you can adjust the height (thickness), width (length), and appearance of lines with the greatest of ease. Just follow these steps:

1. Place a horizontal line on your page as described earlier in "Inserting a Ruled Line."

2. Right-click the line you just placed and, from the pop-up menu that appears, select Horizontal Line Properties. The Horizontal Line Properties dialog box appears, as shown in Figure 4.15.

FIGURE 4.15

You can use the Horizontal Line Properties dialog box to change the look of horizontal lines on your pages.

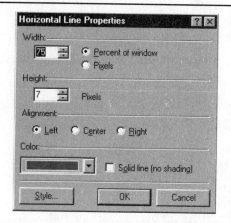

3. To make the line longer or shorter, you can adjust the line's width (make it span more or less of the page). In the Width area of the Horizontal Line Properties dialog box, select a unit of measurement:

   - If you want your line to occupy a certain percentage of open window space, click Percent Of Window.

   - If you want your line to occupy a certain number of pixels, click Pixels.

   Type a number in the Width text box (or click the arrows to increase or decrease the number) to indicate the percentage or number of pixels you want.

4. To change the thickness of the line, in the Height area of the Horizontal Line Properties dialog box, choose the number of pixels high you want your line to

be. The default is 1; you could make your line 800 pixels high if you felt like it, but it would look pretty silly (and it would sort of cease to be a line at that point).

5. By default, ruled lines appear in the center of the page. But you may want some lines, particularly short ones, to be aligned to the left or right of the window rather than smack dab in the center. Click Left, Center, or Right to choose an alignment.

6. Generally, a line takes on the appearance of the background—its color, for example—but if you'd like it to stand out more, you can adjust the line's color by opening the Color drop-down box and selecting a color you prefer.

7. If you'd like to remove the beveling (the 3-D shading) from your line, place a check mark in the Solid Line (No Shading) checkbox.

8. For advanced users who are using style sheets to add design to pages (see Chapter 13), you can modify the rule with style information. Click the Style button, and the Modify Style dialog box appears. Use this box to change the rule.

9. Click OK to close the Horizontal Line Properties dialog box. The Page view window reappears, and you'll see your new and improved ruled line on the page.

You can get really fancy if you'd like and create ruled lines that are actually graphics. Read on.

Too Many Lines Spoil the Web Page

You might be tempted to put fancy, flashy, engraved, colorful, beveled dividing lines all over your page. Don't do it, we beg you! It's way too easy to drop ruled lines onto a page, in different sizes and widths, in lieu of spending actual time thinking out an effective design that helps people read and comprehend your message. Instead of using ruled lines, try a few other tricks. Generally, white space works well as a division between paragraphs, or between paragraphs and headers, or between paragraphs and images. When working with blocks of text, you might also try using different alignments (left, right, and center) in combination. Consider using different text colors to make one paragraph stand out (see Chapters 5 and 6, where we examine text and type in detail). Use indents or tables (see Chapter 11, *Using Tables for Advanced Layout*) to lay out the page so that it has different options for areas of white space and overall layout. Return to Chapter 1 for a quick tour of well-designed sites. Ruled lines are okay in their place, but they're easy to overuse.

Using Graphical Ruled Lines

As you know, when you create Web pages using a WYSIWYG authoring tool like Front-Page, you are actually creating HTML; you just don't see it that way while you're doing the deed. Instead of typing in the code—the HTML instructions for how a page should look—you create the text, images, and other objects, making them look as you want them to appear to users. All the while, little HTML elves work behind the scenes to write the code that allows those instructions to be carried out by the user's browser software. A simple ruled line is just that—simple. It does not show up as a string of teddy bears holding hands, a multi-colored zigzag line, or anything very fancy at all. You might wonder how to create such nifty effects. The answer is simple: These are not really ruled lines; they are graphics masquerading as ruled lines.

Using graphics for ruled lines involves different HTML. Horizontal rules in HTML are represented by the <HR> tag, which can include other attributes (such as height and color—we described creating and modifying a ruled line like this in the previous sections.)

You can insert an image that *acts* and *looks* like a ruled line quite easily. In fact, FrontPage's Clip Art Gallery comes with an assortment of images intended for this purpose. It's best to start with an image that's pretty long and narrow, but even that's not a prerequisite. You can use an image of your own or a line from the FrontPage Clip Art Gallery.

Using a Clip Art Line

Let's add a line from the FrontPage Clip Art Gallery first. Just follow these steps:

1. With the Page view window open and a Web page in view, from the menu bar, select Insert ➤ Picture ➤ Clipart. The Clip Art Gallery dialog box appears.

2. In the Pictures area, you'll see a nice selection of categories. Select one that appeals to you. For rules, try either Dividers and Decorations or Web Dividers. These categories have plenty of graphic rules that can add panache to your page. Click your choice, and a selection of clip art appears.

3. Look around for a rule that suits your fancy. Right-click your choice, and a caption menu appears. The first selection in this menu is Insert Clip. Click that and your image appears on your page.

4. Close the dialog box and the Page view window reappears. Your page is in view, and it now includes the line you just inserted.

In Figure 4.16, you can see some of the graphical lines available from the Clip Art Gallery's Web Dividers category.

FIGURE 4.16

*The Clip Art Gallery
includes lines and
icons such as these.*

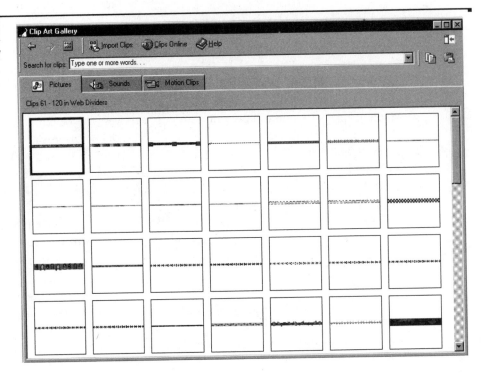

Now let's find out how to use a graphical line you created or found. And in the upcoming section, "Making Changes to Your Graphical Line," we'll find out how you can adjust your line's size, shape, and alignment.

Adding a Graphical Line of Your Own

You can create your own images to use as graphical lines, or you can find them in clip art collections on the Web. In either case, you'll want to save the image file locally to store it. Once you have the image saved on your hard drive or on your FrontPage web server, just follow these steps to place it onto your page:

1. With a page open in Page view, from the menu bar, select Insert ➤ Picture ➤ From File. The Image dialog box appears.

2. The Image dialog box displays the folders in your current FrontPage web. Click the folder that contains the image (probably the Images folder) to display the contents of that folder, and then click the name of the image. The image's location appears in the URL area of the dialog box.

TIP It's best to import images into your FrontPage web before you insert them into your page. See the section titled "Importing Images into Your FrontPage Web," earlier in this chapter, for more information.

3. Now that you've specified the location of the image you want to add, click OK to close the Image dialog box. The Page view window reappears, and you'll see the image placed right on your page.

Now let's find out how to adjust your image properties to make the image act as much like a line as you want it to.

Making Changes to Your Graphical Line

Once you've got an image you want to use as a graphical line, you may want to fiddle with it a bit to make it do and be just what you envision. Here's how:

1. With a page containing an image open in Page view, to change the alignment of your graphical line, select it with your mouse, and click one of the alignment buttons (left, right, or center) on the Formatting toolbar.

2. If you'd like to change the length of your graphical line, right-click it and, from the pop-up menu that appears, select Image Properties. The Image Properties dialog box appears.

3. Click the Appearance tab. The contents of the dialog box change to reflect your choice.

4. In the Size area of the dialog box, click the Specify Size checkbox.

5. In the Height and Width text boxes, specify either a percentage width or a pixel width for each value. For example, if you'd like your graphical line to take up 90 percent of the width of the window, click the Percent Of Window button (under Width), and then type 90 in the Width text box. If you'd like the line to be a certain number of pixels wide, click the Pixels button, and then type that number in the Width text box. You can adjust the height of your image in the same way, if you like.

 TIP You can also click the image and drag the borders of the image to resize it.

6. Click OK to close the Image dialog box. The Page view window reappears, and you can see the changes you made to your graphical line.

If your image looks a little funny or is not what you had in mind, keep playing with it by repeating the steps above until you get it right.

Another great use of images is to create a background. This kind of background is often referred to as *wallpaper* and can be a great decorative or design element. Read on to take an up-close look.

Using Special Backgrounds

While Web browsers in the olden days (a couple of years ago) displayed all backgrounds as a uniform drab gray, most popular browsers today can display full-color backgrounds, as well as backgrounds comprised of images—in fact, any image that can be displayed on a Web page can be used as a background. This is great, and it's also a potential design pitfall. Take care when designing your pages that you choose simple, harmonious color schemes—not many people will stop to read a page with orange text superimposed over a bright green golf course.

NOTE Older browsers, which some people still use, don't display background colors or images. Make sure that your page doesn't depend on such elements in order to be grasped, especially if your audience is very broad or may not be up on the latest hardware and software. See Chapter 16, *Cross-Browser Design.*

Setting a Background Color

Setting a background color for your page is easy. Just follow these steps:

1. With the page whose background you want to adjust open in the Page view, from the menu bar, select Format ➤ Background. The Page Properties dialog box appears, with the Background tab at front (see Figure 4.17).

2. Click the Background drop-down box and choose a color from the available selection. To choose a color other than the default colors available, select Custom. The Color dialog box appears.

FIGURE 4.17

*Use the Background
tab of the Properties
dialog box to change
the color of your
pages.*

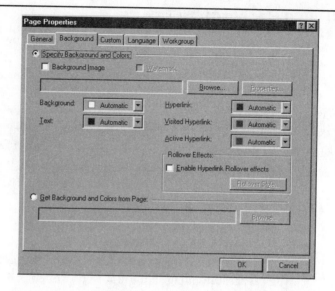

 WARNING   Selecting a color from outside the default range can be problematic for older browsers. The default color palette in FrontPage is made up of a series of colors referred to as "browser-safe" or "Web-safe" colors. These colors are best suited to be managed across different browsers, computer platforms, and hardware types. It's always best to stick with the browser-safe color selection.

3. Click in the Hue area of the Color dialog box to choose a color, and then click in the shade area (the narrower panel to the right of the rainbow array of hues) to adjust the brightness and darkness of the color. The color you chose appears in the Color/Solid area of the Color dialog box.

4. Click Add To Custom Colors, and the color you chose appears in the Custom Colors area of the Color dialog box.

5. Click OK to close the Color dialog box. The Page Properties dialog box reappears. The color you chose is there, along with the word Custom, in the Background drop-down box.

6. Click OK to apply the background color you just chose to your page. The Page Properties dialog box closes, and the Page view window reappears. You'll see the new color of your page in use.

You can repeat these steps as often as you like until you find a color that suits your needs.

Setting a Background Image

Choosing a background image is quite similar to specifying a background color. The image you choose should be subtle and serve the purpose its name suggests—a background for the text on the page. Web browsers that can display background images will *tile* the image—that is, repeat it over and over—until it fills the browser window completely (no matter what size the user's browser window is). If you've ever changed your Windows Desktop wallpaper, you're probably familiar with the concept.

Setting a background image for your page is easy. Just follow these steps:

1. With the page whose background you want to adjust open in the Page view, from the menu bar, select Format ➤ Background. The Page Properties dialog box appears, with the Background tab at front.

2. Place a check mark in the Background Image checkbox. The Browse pushbutton becomes active (not grayed out).

3. In the Background Image text box, type the full path name of the location for the background image you want to use, or click Browse to specify a location within a FrontPage web or on your computer.

4. If you're using a large image for your background (an image that takes up a screenful or so of page real estate), you can place a check mark in the Watermark checkbox.

 NOTE Watermarks don't scroll along with any text or other page elements in the latest browsers; instead, they remain anchored on the page while everything else scrolls by.

5. When you're ready, click OK to close the Page Properties dialog box. The Page view window reappears.

Double-check that the image looks like you thought it would, now that it's tiled across the screen—this is pretty much how it will look when people see it on the Web. If you like what you see, you're all set. If not, go back and change it.

At this point, you'll have great looking pages. But, you still have to add one of the most critical pieces of the Web page puzzle: links!

Adding Hyperlinks

Hyperlinks, or just plain *links*, are the big difference between the Web and other media—no matter how hard you try, you can't click on a map on TV, an author's name in a magazine, or a song title in a book. (At least not yet!)

As you're undoubtedly aware if you've been on the Web for even 15 minutes, a link can point to any address on the Internet—which may in turn represent the path to an item such as another file; an FTP server; a downloadable file or application; a sound, video, or multimedia clip; an e-mail address; or a newsgroup. Any public location on the Internet can be accessed through the Web using links.

There are many kinds of URLs, but when discussing links, there are only two kinds of addresses: *relative* and *absolute*. Relative addresses contain only a filename, its extension, and possibly its location within the file directory. The URL of a relative address points to a file that resides on the same Web server. For example, when you're linking from one page to another within the same folder on your FrontPage web, you can simply point to its filename: `figs.html`. If you're in your main directory but have an image in the `images` directory, you can point to that with a relative address, too. That would look like this: `images/figs.gif`. Using relative addresses is a good practice when you're linking items together within a single site, because they make it much easier for you to maintain your site. If you've used relative addresses, you can move files from one directory on a Web server to another without having to make major changes to your HTML.

On the other hand, if you were to spell out the entire URL, such as `http://www.mysite.com/figs.html`, you'd be using an absolute address instead. Absolute addresses start with `http://`, `ftp://`, or another *protocol* type. (A protocol, of course, is simply an agreed-upon way of doing things. HTTP is the name of the protocol for Web pages, for example.) The protocol is then followed by the rest of a full URL. The term *absolute* indicates that not only the name of the document on a server is given, but the full, exact, honest-to-john location of the entire server itself is also spelled out.

Generally, links that point to *local* resources—items on the same server—use relative links, while links that point out into cyberspace use absolute links. If you still don't get this stuff, FrontPage will make it all absolutely, relatively clear. Read on.

Linking to a Page in Your FrontPage Web

Linking two pages within your FrontPage web is a perfect example of relative linking—called *internal linking* in FrontPage parlance. Internal linking is linking that points to documents within the same FrontPage web. You may also hear this term used to describe links to different parts within a given Web page.

Suppose there are two pages in your FrontPage web: `default.html` and `new.html`. You'll probably want the two to be linked together. Let's say you have `default.html` open in the Page view, and you want to create a link to `new.html`, which is in the same directory as `home.html` on your FrontPage web. Just follow these steps:

1. With FrontPage open and your document visible in the window, type the word you'd like to use as a link, and then highlight it. In our example, you might type **What's New** on the page `default.html`.

2. From the Page view menu bar, select Insert ➤ Hyperlink (or click the Hyperlink button on the Standard toolbar, or use the key combo Ctrl+K). The Create Hyperlink dialog box appears, as shown in Figure 4.18.

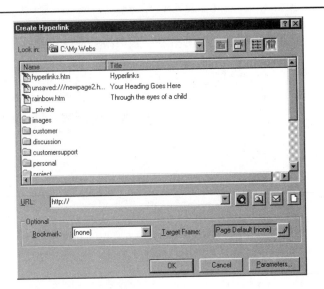

FIGURE 4.18

You'll use the Create Hyperlink dialog box to specify the URL for your link.

3. In the Create Hyperlink dialog box, you'll see the filenames and page titles of the current FrontPage web's pages. Select the file you want to link to by clicking it, and its URL appears in the URL text box.

4. Click OK to close the dialog box; the Page view window reappears.

Now you'll see the word you used as a link (What's New, in our example) underlined and in a different color. Pass your mouse over the link (called a *mouseover*), and you'll see the address of the page displayed in the status bar of the Page view window.

You could follow the same steps to put a link that leads back to your home page on your resume page.

Linking to a Page on the World Wide Web

Creating links to the outside world is generally done through absolute addressing, in which you specify the entire path name of the file—also known as its Internet address or URL. Although you're most likely to link to Web files, there are many other types of Internet addresses you can link to using the methods described in this section, for example:

- FTP
- HTTP
- HTTPS (Secure HTTP)
- Mailto (for e-mail addresses)
- News (for newsgroup names)
- Telnet (to launch a Telnet session)

 TIP You can also link to File, Gopher, or WAIS files; however, these types are no longer in general use. A File link goes to a file on the local machine (rather than a Web server), while Gopher and WAIS links go to two special sorts of Internet servers that have faded in prominence since the advent of the Web.

Let's say you want to create a link to www.microsoft.com/, which is the address of Microsoft on the Web. The simplest way to do this in FrontPage 2000 is simply to type the URL into Page view. It will automatically be linked.

However, if you want to link a word or series of words that are not full addresses, just follow these steps:

1. With FrontPage open and your document visible in the window, type the word you'd like to use as a link, and then highlight it. (In our example, you might type **Microsoft**, then highlight that word.)

 TIP If you prefer to use an image for a link, simply highlight that image.

2. From the Page view menu bar, select Insert ➤ Hyperlink. The Create Hyperlink dialog box appears.

3. If you already know the address of the page you want to link to, in the URL text box, type (or paste) the Internet address of that page. In our example, this would be www.microsoft.com. (Alternatively, to use your Web browser to locate the page you want to link to, click the Web Browser button in the Create Hyperlink dialog box.) FrontPage launches your Web browser (if it's not already open). Use your browser to locate the page you want to link to (by using a bookmark, clicking a link, using a search engine, or whatever you like). Once it's in the browser window, return to FrontPage, where you'll see the page's address in the Create Hyperlink dialog box's URL text box.

 WARNING FrontPage assumes that you're going to be linking to a page on the Web, so it includes the first part of the address (http://) in the URL text box. If you're pasting in a URL you copied from another document or program, make sure that you delete the http:// from the URL text box first; you need to include that information only once. Pay close attention to how the address appears in the URL text box, especially if your address is an FTP, Telnet, or other kind of address.

4. Once you have the address in place, click OK to close the dialog box; the Page view window reappears.

Now you'll see the word you specified as a link (Microsoft in our example) underlined and in the link color. Mouseover it, and you'll see the address of the page it links to displayed in the status bar of the Page view window.

Creating a New Page and Linking to It

Let's say you started to link to your What's New page and then realized you hadn't created it yet; you may wonder whether you can make the link anyway. The answer is *yes*—not only can you create the new link, you can create the new page, too! Just follow these steps:

1. With FrontPage open and your document visible in the window, type the word you'd like to use as a link, and then highlight it. (In our example, you might type the words **What's New**.)

2. From the Page view menu bar, select Insert ➢ Hyperlink. The Create Hyperlink dialog box appears.

3. Click the New Page button. The New dialog box appears.

4. If you'd like to use a template for your new page, select one from the list by clicking it; otherwise, click Normal Page.

5. Click OK. The New dialog box closes, and so does the Create Hyperlink dialog box. You'll be returned to Page view, where you'll see your new blank page in the window.

6. From the menu bar, select File ➢ Save As to save your new page. The Save As dialog box appears.

7. In the Title text box, type a title for your new page, and then, if you like, edit the filename in the URL text box.

8. Click OK to close the Save As dialog box and return to the Page view window.

When you return to the page you were working on previously, you'll see that the word you highlighted in step 1 is now linked to the page you just created.

NOTE When you use this method, be sure to save the new page before you return to the one already in progress. Otherwise, you'll see that your link points to new_page_1.htm or something like that, which can be horribly confusing if you are trying to create a link to new.htm.

Creating Links within Single Documents

Links within a single document (also known as *intra-page links*) allow visitors to your page to click and then quickly jump to another part of that document. For example, you can create a table of contents at the top of your document, and users can click an item there to jump down the page and see the section of the document that item points to. However, if your document is quite long, it might make sense instead to break it up into more than one document. A single, gigantic page takes longer to load than several smaller pages. Only you can say which navigational method makes better sense for your content and your users. Both are quite viable options.

Linking to a Section in the Current Page

Creating an internal link to part of the page you're on is a simple, two-part process. First you need to create a bookmark, which means that you name a part of your document—the part you want people to be able to jump to. Then you need to create a link to that bookmark.

Creating a Bookmark

Creating a bookmark for linking involves these steps:

1. With a page open in Page view, click the cursor at the place in the text where you want your bookmark. For example, you may want to place bookmarks at subheads in your document, at the beginning of each new article (or recipe, or what have you) on your page, or somewhere else that's logical.

2. From the menu bar, select Insert ➤ Bookmark. The Bookmark dialog box appears.

3. In the Bookmark Name text box, type a name for the bookmark.

4. Click OK. The dialog box closes and you return to the Page view window.

A small flag appears next to the text you selected in step 1, indicating that this text has been bookmarked.

 TIP To delete a bookmark, select Edit ➤ Bookmark. The Bookmark dialog box appears. In its list of bookmarks, select the one you want to delete. Click the Go To button, then Clear. The bookmark will be gone.

Linking to a Bookmark

Now we're going to create a link to this bookmark. This process is quite similar to creating an ordinary link:

1. In Page view, select the text you plan to turn into a link. From the menu bar, select Insert ➤ Hyperlink. The Create Hyperlink dialog box appears.

2. In the dialog box's Bookmark drop-down list, select the bookmark you previously created.

3. Click OK. The dialog box closes and you are returned to the Page view window. The link you just created is indicated by the appearance of a solid line underneath the text you selected.

Now, when you save this page and load it into a browser window, you'll be able to click the link you just created in order to jump to the bookmark we created earlier, in the section called "Creating a Bookmark."

Linking to a Bookmark in Another Page

To link to a bookmark on another page, you need to make a bookmark on one page, just like you did in the section called "Creating a Bookmark." On the other page, you then need to create a link. Follow the steps in the section called "Links to a Page in Your FrontPage Web." In step 3, after you select the file you want to link to, type the bookmark into the Bookmark text box.

Creating Links to E-Mail Addresses

After Web addresses, the most common type of address you'll want to provide a link to is your e-mail address. You want people to be able to reach you, so they can provide valuable feedback about what they enjoy about your pages, as well as notify you of any buggy or problematic stuff kicking around your site.

> **NOTE**   As with any other absolute URL, if you type the literal e-mail address, such as `molly@molly.com`, directly into your editor, it will automatically be hyperlinked.

Also known as a *mailto*, linking a word or phrase to an e-mail address is easy to do:

1. With FrontPage open and a page visible in the window, type something to indicate that the link will lead to you—this could be your name, the words **Webmaster**, **mail me**, **feedback**, or whatever you like. Type it wherever you want it to appear on the page, and then highlight it.

2. From the Page view menu bar, select Insert ≻ Hyperlink. The Create Hyperlink dialog box appears.

3. Click the e-mail button shown here (it looks like a little envelope). The Create E-Mail Hyperlink dialog box appears.

4. In the text box labeled Type An E-Mail Address, type your full e-mail address, which should look like this: **user@site.com**.

5. Click OK. The Create E-Mail Hyperlink dialog box closes, and the Create Hyperlink dialog box reappears.

6. You'll see your e-mail address printed in the URL text box, preceded by `mailto:`. This is exactly what's supposed to happen. Click OK to close the Create Hyperlink dialog box and return to the Page view window.

Now, when your page is loaded onto the Web and someone clicks on the link to your e-mail address, they'll be able to send you a message and tell you how cool you are. Now that you know how to make your pages go, you can learn more about making them look good.

Themes and Variations

FrontPage 2000 has a feature called *themes*, which may have a familiar ring to it—the Windows 95 and 98 Plus Packs also feature themes, which in that case means collections of screen savers, desktop patterns, and mouse pointer animations, each of which was designed around a designated *theme*.

In the case of FrontPage, a theme is a collection of page design elements that have a given look and feel, which you can use to get your pages off to a good start. Themed pages start off with a banner image and a navigation bar at the top of the page, and a nice background image that goes with them. You'll also find that there's some explanatory text to get you started. You can choose from among the many themes offered, and base the design of your site on whichever seems appropriate. This makes Web "design" easy for the non-designer; however, it also denotes that your page has used FrontPage to create the design. If you're going for practical, that's fine, but if you want to stand out as unique, you'll need to use or refine your design skills, or get a professional to help with the look and feel of your site.

You don't *have* to use themes. You can change horses in the middle of the theme, or you can start with a theme or two or more and then do away with themes on your pages altogether. Further, you can select a theme for an entire FrontPage web, or for just a single page within a FrontPage web.

Selecting a Theme for an Entire Web

One way to go in designing your site is simply to choose a single appropriate theme and apply it to the entire FrontPage web. This is certainly quick and easy. Just follow these steps:

1. With a web open, from the menu bar, select Format ➢ Theme. The Themes dialog appears (Figure 4.19).

2. Browse the list of themes that appears along the left side of the window, and select one you like. A preview of that theme appears in the window's right side so you can see what you're in for.

3. Make sure the All Pages button is checked.

FIGURE 4.19

The Themes dialog box
allows you to select
and modify themes.

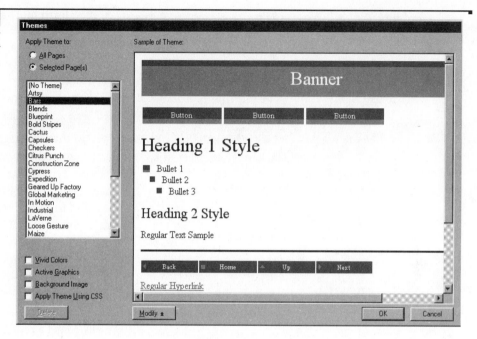

 TIP You can modify the look of any given theme to include a background color instead of a background image, to include colors that are more vivid or less vivid, or to use animated ("active") buttons and images. To adjust these properties, select (or deselect) the checkboxes marked Vivid Colors, Active Graphics, or Background Image. Advanced users interested in adding style sheet information to control the appearance of the page can check the Apply Theme Using CSS checkbox, too.

4. When you find the theme you want applied to your web, click OK. The theme is applied to your entire FrontPage web.

 NOTE If you've applied a theme to your web and then changed your mind about it, follow the same procedure for applying the theme, but in step 2, instead of choosing a theme, select No Theme.

Selecting a Theme for a Single Page

As mentioned, you can apply a theme to your entire web, or to any given page within it. If you're practicing, feel free to mix and match themes 'til the cows come home. However, it's a fair caution to say that when you're ready to publish your site, a consistent look is going to be more professional and appealing to site visitors.

To apply a theme to an individual page, just follow these steps:

1. Open a theme-ingly attractive page in Page view.

2. From the Page view menu bar, select Format ➤ Theme. The Themes dialog box appears.

3. Browse the themes, clicking the name of the theme that most interests you. A preview of the theme appears in the Theme Preview area of the dialog box.

4. In this case, make sure that the Apply Theme To option is set to Selected Page(s).

 WARNING If you don't click the Selected Page(s) button, the theme will be applied to the entire web.

5. When you're satisfied, click OK to close the Themes dialog box. The Page view window reappears, and you see your changes in effect.

That's all there is to that.

 NOTE If you've applied a theme to one page or another and then had second thoughts, you can easily remove the theme. Follow the same procedure for applying the theme, but in step 3, instead of choosing a theme, select No Theme. If you want to wipe out themes in the whole web, see "Selecting a Theme for an Entire Web," previously in this chapter.

If you'd like to remove the banners and buttons and such that are on your page and start with more or less a clean slate, just select the bits you want to remove with your mouse and then press the Delete key.

Again, using themes is a very handy shortcut, but as such it holds the danger of many Web pages on many sites looking alike. Be sure it doesn't matter to you that your site looks generic before you rely heavily on themes. As an alternative, you might consider cruising through Chapters 1, 6, and 9 of this book to find out more about how to add visual diversity to your sites.

Up Next

If you're a bit tired at this point, take heart. You've learned a *lot* in this chapter—how to work with text, images, and links, and how to use the specialty FrontPage feature, themes.

The next chapter, *All About Text*, will take you from the basics learned here to more sophisticated techniques you can use to layout text. This is an important part of design. After all, your text is critical—it's a primary aspect of the message you're sending to your site visitors. Proper formatting of text will help you refine your pages, adding impact as well as maximizing the visitor's ability (and desire) to read your carefully prepared content.

CHAPTER 5

All About Text

Sure, you can type text onto a Web page, but you want your pages to look *good*. Many people actually hire professional editors to ensure that their written work is presented well. While you don't have to go to that trouble to make your pages worth reading, you can use the tools FrontPage gives you to spruce up your text.

In this chapter, we'll learn how to use text styles and paragraph styles, how to use headers effectively to label your document, and how to create lists to organize your ideas. While we discuss how to manipulate each text attribute individually, remember that a well-designed page integrates these elements into a unified design.

NOTE Chapter 6, *Fantastic Fonts*, and Chapter 13, *Getting in Style with Cascading Style Sheets*, cover the more design-oriented aspects of text. This chapter, however, will teach you all about the basic attributes of text on Web pages.

Even if your site's content *is* largely comprised of images, it certainly will include some textual elements, and the construction of these is as important as any image. For instance, the Museum of Modern Art, New York, has exhibits filled with images, but also uses text to create a powerful design (see Figure 5.1).

While your project may not be as ambitious (or as image-driven) as an overview of art history, you should hold your work to high standards. After all, you're going to be putting it on the Web, where countless millions of people have potential access to it.

MASTERING WHAT'S ONLINE

Visit the Museum of Modern Art (MOMA), New York , at www.moma.org/.

FIGURE 5.1

*Even if images are
your site's focus, you
still need to work
well with text.*

Communicating with Text

While making a page look terrific is all well and good, it's not going to get you anywhere if that page isn't *readable*. All too often, people forget that they're supposed to
be presenting *content*—that's the point of having a Web page in the first place. Put too
much gigantic, blinking, scrolling, orange text overtop of a neon purple background,
and most Web surfers will simply flee in horror. They'll miss your message—and
what, then, was the point of all your hard work?

In general, the same rules that apply to using text on paper apply to using text on the Web. There are some special issues, though, and you'll want to keep them in mind. These tips, while not steadfast rules, are a good set of guidelines to work from:

- Readability is key.

- On Web pages, reserve underlining for links. Italics is the proper format for book titles, and works well for emphasis in general.

- When you're emphasizing a word, choose either bold or italic type. Using too many different type styles at once makes text look **_weird_**.

- Reserve large, bold type for headlines, which should properly stand out from the rest of the page.

- Limit your use of italic type; in particular, ask yourself if entire paragraphs really need to appear in italics. It can be difficult to read, particularly on a computer screen.

Now let's find out how to put text to work.

Understanding the Purpose of Text

It's been said that "Content is King." Just what is *content*, though? Is it images and media? Written copy?

The easy answer is "yes." If your text information is weak in both written and visual form, it will dramatically reduce your Web site's efficacy.

We'd like to make one thing clear in this chapter: It's not simply the way your text looks that's important to a good Web page; what it does while it's looking good is just as critical. Contrary to what some erstwhile Webmasters seem to believe, text is not just that stuff that fills in the space between flashing animated GIFs and blinking Java applets. As discussed in Chapter 1, it doesn't matter what kind of gadgets you have, or how flashy your design is, if your site doesn't have good content.

 MASTERING THE OPPORTUNITIES

Five Steps to Better Content

Here's a checklist of questions and concepts to help you make your text terrific:

Audience Do you know your audience? Have you defined them well enough so you can write to them and make the content not only understandable, but also

 Continued

MASTERING THE OPPORTUNITIES CONTINUED

appropriate? For example, if you're writing for children, your words are going to be decidedly different than if you're writing for adults. A Web page written for sports enthusiasts is remarkably different from one written for classical music lovers. Get to know your audience, and they'll stick around your Web page longer and get to know you!

Intent What is the *intent* of your message? In other words, do you want to sell, to entertain, or to inform? The intent of a message significantly influences the manner in which you prepare your content.

Clarity Once you do have an idea of who you're writing for (audience) and what you're writing about (intent), it's important that your content is clear. Are there words you don't need, or areas where you need to be more descriptive? Your Web site visitors will need to know your intent on each page within your site. Are you using words that make this clear?

Voice Voice is an important part of writing that has to do with the tone and general feel of the words. Consider the way you speak to others. When you speak to authority figures, you have one means of talking. When you speak with children, you use a different voice. The same thing is true of written text; the voice you use should be appropriate to the people reading your text. Proper voice is impossible to achieve without knowing your audience. Once you do, write to them using a method that captures the message you want to express. Are you being casual, using lots of jargon? Or do you need to be more formal, as in a corporate setting?

Web Style Writing for the Web is a precise art. It's important to understand that people don't hang around terribly long on a Web site, unless the content is interesting enough for them to do so. Using short, concise sentences while maintaining an appropriate voice is part of writing for the Web with style. Think in "capsules," or short bursts of text. This makes a page interesting and easy to read.

Just as you pay less attention to speakers who mumble or ramble on and on, people pay less attention to text that isn't letter-perfect. Remember that people are actually going to be reading the words you put on your pages, and that a lot of people really *do* care about things like spelling, punctuation, and grammar. Not paying attention to these important concerns will cause your site to look amateurish and unprofessional.

TIP Want to check your spelling? With your page open in Page view, from the menu bar, select Tools ➤ Spelling (or press F7). The FrontPage spelling checker (shown in Figure 5.2) will start, and it'll check all the words on your page while skipping the links and other HTML.

Just as you check your pages to make sure there are no broken links or missing images, you should check your text to make sure that it's grammatically correct and free from typos and spelling errors. Enlist a friend to help you; we certainly know what it's like to work on a page for so long that the words all look the same.

 TIP Don't forget to check your page titles, headings, and captions for spelling errors and incorrect capitalization.

FIGURE 5.2

FrontPage's spell checker will help you mind your p's and q's.

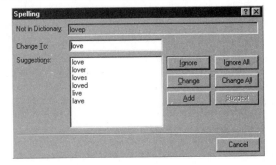

 MASTERING WHAT'S ONLINE

To learn more about English usage, enlist the help of a good copyeditor—or learn how to become one—at The Slot (www.theslot.com). Or you could try the classic editor's guidebook, Strunk and White's *The Elements of Style*, at www.columbia.edu/acis/bartleby/strunk. The editors of Wired magazine have published a very useful guide, *Wired Style: Principles of English Usage in the Digital Age*, edited by Constance Hale (Hardwired, 1997). Of course, you could always go buy the book, so to speak, and get yourself a copy of *The Chicago Manual of Style* or *The AP Style Handbook*. The Indispensable Writing Resource (www.stetson.edu/~rhansen/writing.html) lists dozens of other books and Web sites that you might find helpful.

Working with Browser Defaults

When you're getting ready to work with text in your page design, you should to be aware of how your efforts are going to show up on the other end: the Web browsers your readers are surfing with. While there are as many different kinds of browsers as there are kinds of cheese, a few basic rules will help you get your ducks in a row.

Your basic Web surfer is probably using some version of either Netscape Navigator or Microsoft Internet Explorer; only about 10 percent of the Web population use any other browser. Both of these browsers, as well as many of the others, use two kinds of fonts to present text: proportional and fixed width.

Each character in any font consists of a letter, number, or symbol together with a certain amount of surrounding white space. Proportional and fixed width fonts differ in the amount of space taken up by each character. The *proportional* font is called that because, like the text on this page, each character is a different width, and therefore takes up an amount of space proportional to its size. The amount of space a word occupies on a line is dependent on *which* letters it contains, not on *how many* letters it contains. As you can see here, the letter *i* takes up much less space than its friend *w*:

> Times New Roman is a proportional font.
> Note that these five letters:
> iiiii
> take up less space than these five letters:
> wwwww

The factory default for most browsers' proportional font is Times New Roman, 10- or 12-point. Proportional fonts are generally used for most body text and headlines, because they are usually much easier to read.

NOTE *Point size* is a measurement of how big the letters in a word appear on the page. In old-fashioned, hand-set type, one point is equal to 1/72 of an inch (meaning that 72-point type is one inch high). In digital type, point size is more relative. Some fonts (such as Courier or Bookman Old Style) appear bigger than other fonts (like Times or Garamond), even when they're set to the same point size. This is generally due to how wide the characters are or how the type is spaced.

Fixed width fonts, on the other hand, employ letters that all occupy an equal amount of space. Imagine that each character occupies a little square of space. In a fixed width font, that square is the same size for all characters, yet there might be more white space in the square for the *l* than there is for the *m*. When we look at *i*'s and *w*'s in a fixed width font, they take up the same amount of space:

```
Courier is a fixd-width font.
Note that these five letters:
iiiii
Take up the same space as these
five letters:
wwwww
```

Courier or Courier New, which looks suspiciously like old typewriter or telegram text, is the default font for most people's fixed width fonts.

Fixed width fonts are used to emulate computer code, quoted e-mail messages, mathematical and scientific equations, and so on. Because it is a fixed width font, Courier New is also a popular choice for e-mail and Telnet programs.

Now, having said all this, there's still the chance that the folks at home have completely reconfigured their default font faces and sizes. Most Web browser software programs, in particular Netscape Navigator and Microsoft Internet Explorer, afford the user a lot of opportunity to customize the way their interface to the Web looks and acts. Users can, for instance, customize the default font faces and sizes used to display text on the Web. Nearsighted folks can set their default text size to 14- or 16-point for easier reading; others may choose to use a smaller font size to fit more text per square inch on the screen. And anyone at all can decide to up and change their default font faces, which can give a totally different look to pages that maximize on the distinction between proportional and fixed width fonts.

Some browsers even allow users the option of using Times New Roman, a decidedly proportional font, for their fixed width font, simply because they like the way it looks. One of the things we'll explore in this chapter is how to maximize your control over which font faces and sizes your users see, so that your pages will appear the same on every screen—or as close as you can get. This is why you should learn as much as you can about typography: to ensure that your audience sees the page *you* designed.

Using Text and Paragraph Styles

In computing parlance, *text style* is a generic term for specially formatted text. Bold is one example of a text style; underlined is another. Manipulating the weight of text, as in bold type, and the orientation, as in italic type, serves to emphasize words. Watch out for overemphasis, however, as described in the sidebar "Blinking Red Eyes."

NOTE   *Text style* is a standard term used by most word-processing and page layout software to mean the way formatting (bold, italic, etc.) is applied to text; in FrontPage, text styles are also referred to as *font styles*. *Paragraph style* describes how HTML formatting affects the way a paragraph is treated by a Web browser—note the Paragraph Style drop-down menu on the Formatting toolbar. *Style sheets*, described in Chapter 13, are a relatively recent invention and should not be confused with text or paragraph styles.

Blinking Red Eyes

Did you ever wonder why it is that newspaper headlines are so easy to read? Well, they're bigger than the stories they describe, and they're bold.

Unfortunately, some folks with Web pages have taken this little fact of life to mean that all the text on their pages should be pretty big, and bold—and italic, and red, and flashing (courtesy of the <BLINK> tag).

Have you ever gotten an e-mail message written ALMOST ENTIRELY IN CAPITAL LETTERS? Did you actually read the whole thing? Didn't it feel like someone was shouting at you?

The thing about emphasis is that, in order for it to do its job—that is, make part of the text stand out from the whole—it needs to *stand out* from the whole. If all the text on a page is bold, italic, and large, then you'd need to make your point in really tiny letters in order for it to garner notice.

Your eye has to do some work in order to read at all. A nice serif font in 12-point type is not only perfectly readable, but very easy on the eye (see "Choosing Font Faces" in Chapter 6). However, the more doo-dads you add to that type, the more difficult it is to read.

In other words, if all the text on your page is bold, then nothing stands out; the non-bold text on such a page almost recedes away from the eye, which has to work much harder to read a page composed entirely of bold and italic letters.

When you're designing a page, make sure that the text stands out from the background, rather than clashing with it; make sure the words that need to be *emphasized* have a chance at **standing out** from the rest of the text; and make sure that people can tell the headlines from the text.

Formatting Text for Emphasis

If you want to add emphasis to your pages with bold, italic, or underlined text styles, FrontPage will be happy to oblige you. Just follow these steps:

1. With your page open in Page view, highlight the text you wish to format for emphasis.

2. Click the appropriate button on the Formatting toolbar:

B for bold, *I* for italic, or <u>U</u> for underlined. Your text is emphatically changed.

To remove this formatting, just repeat the steps above, and the text style reverts to normal. Remember to use caution when choosing to underline text. As we mentioned, it confuses people to see underlined words that are not links on a Web page.

 NOTE Something a bit odd happens when you use the Bold or Italic buttons to bold or italicize text. Take a look at the HTML source code, and you'll see that instead of the tags for bold or italics, the tags for emphasized or strong text have been used. The visual result in most (but not all) browsers will look like bold or italics as you intended—but the actual HTML tags may not be the ones you expected to generate by using the Bold or Italic buttons. Read on for details.

Using Other Physical Text Styles

There are other text styles that you can use to modify your type. Physical text styles allow you to manipulate text in a very precise way in order to draw attention to that type for the following purposes:

Physical Text Style	What It Does	How to Achieve It
Strikethrough	~~Draws a horizontal line through~~ selected words. May be useful if you want to show corrections.	Select Format ➤ Font; then in the Font dialog box's Effects area, click Strikethrough.

Physical Text Style	What It Does	How to Achieve It
Superscript	Shrinks selected letters or words and raises them slightly above the line surrounding text sits on. Used for text such as footnotes and equations, as in $E=MC^2$.	Select Format ➤ Font; then in the Font dialog box's Effects area, click Superscript.
Subscript	Shrinks selected letters or words and lowers them slightly below the line surrounding text sits on. Used most often in chemistry and mathematics, as in H_2O.	Select Format ➤ Font; then in the Font dialog box's Effects area, click Subscript.
Keyboard	Makes text appear in a font that `looks like typewriter text`. Although this is technically a physical style, the way it will appear on screen depends on the fonts that users have installed and specified as defaults.	Select Format ➤ Font; then in the Font dialog box, click the Keyboard checkbox.
Blink	Makes words flash on and off on the screen, which can be very annoying. Luckily, we can't reproduce this effect in print.	Select Format ➤ Font; in the Font dialog box's Effects area, click the Blink checkbox.

Use these styles with caution. A lot of strikethrough text, for example, might seem clever at the time you're using it, ~~but have you ever tried to actually read several lines of text that were struck through~~? This warning goes double for blink. It's true that flashing text is a uniquely digital phenomenon, but once you've seen the word NEW!!! blinking on and off a hundred times, you've seen it a million times.

Using Logical Text Styles

Logical text styles, in the wild, wild web of yesteryear, told a browser that a piece of text was somehow *different* from regular old text, but the interpretation of this difference was left up to the browser software. For example, two logical text styles that FrontPage doesn't directly support are emphasis <EM> and strong emphasis <STRONG>, although those tags are what the Italic and Bold buttons produce, respectively. Most browsers interpret these tags as italic and bold, but other browsers do different things with these tags.

 NOTE In addition to the browsers we've mentioned, there are other types of browsers such as Braille browsers, text-to-speech browsers, and telephone-based browsers—all of which use the <EM> and <STRONG> tags to emphasize passages with volume, stridency, pauses, and the like. The visual design focus that many Web designers lean toward often doesn't consider browsers that work for the disabled.

When decisions were being made about basic HTML code, there were a lot of people at bat for all kinds of logical text styles, from <strong> to <person> (which, believe it or not, was supposed to indicate a proper name).

 NOTE There actually was a logic in developing HTML tags this way—the logic of logical styles had to do with the underlying cross-platform logic of the Web; it was thought that allowing the browser software to have some say in how to interpret a tag helped to make the original Web cross-platform. Also, the Web was not originally intended as a true publishing medium, but as a means for scientists and researchers—who did not care about fancy layout—to share information about research, academics, and hobbies. Cool fonts, fancy layout options, and the like were considered frivolous and irrelevant—and to some old-school types, they still are.

Little did the code standard-makers realize how infrequently their painstaking inventions would be used. Let's take a quick look at these logical styles—while you may never find a use for them, someone may ask you to, or you may find yourself updating an old relic of a page that does use them.

You can apply any of these text styles by following these steps:

1. With your document open in Page view, select the text you want to change.

2. From the menu bar, select Format ➤ Font. The Font dialog box appears.

3. Click any of the Effects checkboxes in the Font dialog box, and the Preview text at the bottom of the dialog box changes to reflect your choices (see Figure 5.3).

4. When you're finished, click OK, and the Font dialog box closes. The text you selected has changed its spots.

FIGURE 5.3

The Effects checkboxes in the Font dialog box let you choose from a number of logical text styles.

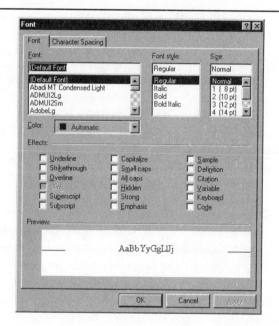

Now let's take a quick look at what these styles actually do. Because these are logical styles, different browsers interpret these tags in different ways. In the following table, the "What It Looks Like" column indicates how the listed styles are interpreted by popular browsers such as Microsoft Internet Explorer and Netscape Navigator.

Logical Text Style	What It's Usually Used For	What It Looks Like
Citation `<cite>`	Quotations in papers and essays	*Italic text*
Sample `<samp>`	Samples of non-formatted text in documents about formatting text	`Fixed width font, slightly smaller than regular text`
Definition `<dfn>`	Definitions of words in online glossaries	*Italic text* in Explorer; normal text in Navigator
Code `<code>`	Examples of computer code	`Fixed width font`
Keyboard `<kbd>`	Emulating keyboard or typewriter text; a fixed width or monospace font	`Fixed width font, slightly smaller than regular text`

Although many of these tags look similar, you may find them useful for their original purpose, in particular if you're working with example code on your Web pages. Generally speaking, however, you won't be using logical text styles too often.

Using Paragraph Styles

What's the difference between *text* style and *paragraph* style? Simply put, text style can be applied to a few words, a single word, or even a single letter anywhere on a page, while paragraph style affects an entire paragraph. As you'll recall from Chapter 4, a paragraph in HTML is a unit of text followed by a line break or a paragraph break; it is not the three-sentence model of perfect composition you may have learned in school. HTML paragraphs can be single lines of text or even single words. (But don't tell that to a third-grade teacher!)

Technically, headings, lists, block quotes, and other formatting styles are paragraph styles, but for our purposes, there are three kinds of paragraph styles: Normal, Preformatted, and Address. (We'll cover headings and lists in upcoming sections.)

Normal style is what it sounds like: regular words on a page. You can apply any kind of text style such as bold, code, or subscript—to normal text. Any time you want to remove text styles and make text normal, just do this:

1. In Page view, select the text you want to change back to normal.

2. On the Formatting toolbar, click the Paragraph Style (also called Change Style) drop-down menu, and select Normal (it's the default, so it may already be selected).

Ta-da! Your text is normal—at least style-wise. Normal is the default paragraph style FrontPage uses for text as you type. You don't actually have to change most text into Normal style, unless you want to change it *back* to Normal from some other paragraph style.

 NOTE Normal style, as a paragraph style, can contain any number of text styles, such as bold, italic, typewriter, and the like. If you want to remove text formatting from your paragraphs, select the text you'd like to make plain and, from the menu bar, select Format ➤ Remove Formatting. All text styles are removed from your selection.

Preformatted style paragraphs look like typewriter text but the HTML code behind them is not the same as the logical styles we discussed earlier in this chapter. In normal HTML, formatting done with multiple spaces or multiple line breaks is pretty much ignored. In preformatted paragraphs, the formatting of the text is preserved.

To choose the preformatted paragraph style, just follow these steps:

1. In Page view, highlight the paragraphs you want to change.

2. Select Formatted from the Formatting toolbar's Paragraph Style drop-down menu.

Your text appears like typewriter text, with all the spacing preserved. This is especially nice for things like ASCII art, text-based tables, poems, and other blocks of text designed in a text editor with spaces used for formatting.

 NOTE You may want to specify that text is preformatted before you paste in a big chunk of preformatted text from an e-mail message or text editor window. Just select the Formatted text option *before* you paste in the text to guarantee that your plain text formatting will be preserved.

Address style was initially intended to indicate the name and contact e-mail address of the Webmaster or administrator of the page. In most Web browsers, address style text is displayed in italic font. Once upon a time, the Address style may have been considered valuable because of the possibility of standardization of Web pages. If all pages on the Web used the <ADDRESS> tag to indicate the page's owner, it would have been trivial to employ search engines to locate and file away that information. These days, the address style is rarely used for its intended purpose, although with the increasing popularity of style sheets, some of the old logical styles may see a resurgence in popularity. To format a paragraph as address style, just follow these steps:

1. With a page open in Page view, highlight the paragraph(s) you want to change to address style.

2. Select Address from the Formatting toolbar's Paragraph Style drop-down menu.

Your text appears italicized; it is also recognized as address style text by any Web browsers or indexing programs that care to note it.

TIP You can also format paragraphs by using the menu bar. Select the paragraph(s) you want to format, then select Format ➢ Paragraph. The Paragraph Properties dialog box appears, where you can select Normal, Formatted, Address, or any of the six levels of headings described in the section "Including Headings."

Margin of Defeat

You can arrange elements and white space on a page in many ways; just keep in mind that white space *is* one of the elements on your page. The more things you cram together, the less likely someone is to stop and read the pages; pages that look cramped and dirty are apt to get overlooked.

When you're laying out type in FrontPage, wouldn't it be convenient if you could somehow change the margins? There are several ways to get your content to spread out into the gutter of the page, even though there's no simple "Change Margins" command in FrontPage.

- Use paragraph indents and vary the alignment of chunks of text to create a look that's different from the regular old block of text on a page (see Chapter 4, *Creating Basic Pages*).
- Use tables without borders to divide up the space on the page—try using empty table cells to create extra room to maneuver in (see Chapter 11, *Using Tables for Advanced Layout*).
- Use the HTML tag <blockquote> around the text that requires margins. Or, set the margin information in the <body> tag, using margin attributes. To learn how to do this manually, visit www.microsoft.com/workshop/author/dhtml/reference/objects/BODY.htm.
- Delve into the world of Cascading Style Sheets (see Chapter 13).

Using Lists

You're undoubtedly familiar with the use of lists to display related tidbits of information. You can use three different kinds of lists on Web pages: bulleted lists, numbered lists, and definition lists. You can use any kind of list on your page, in combination with practically every kind of paragraph formatting other than headings.

Lists are particularly good for Web pages because they break up space, which makes reading easier, and they highlight specific points of interest with short, simple language—the best kind for the Web.

Using Bulleted Lists

Bulleted lists are good for lists in which each item should stand out, but the order the items are listed in does not matter. Bulleted lists look like this:

- Printer
- Telephone
- Modem

Creating a Bulleted List

To create a bulleted list, follow these steps:

1. With a page open in Page view, type (or paste) your plain text list on the page.
2. Highlight the items in the list, and then, on the Formatting toolbar, click the Bulleted List button.

Your list is now riddled with bullets.

Changing the Style of Bullets

Not all browsers are up to this challenge, but many can display different kinds of bullets, such as solid circles, open circles, or solid squares. To change the way your bullets look, try this:

1. Create a bulleted list (as described in the preceding section) or display a page containing a bulleted list.
2. Highlight the list items whose bullets you want to change. Right-click on the highlighted text and, from the pop-up menu that appears, select List Properties. The List Properties dialog box appears, looking like it does in Figure 5.4, with the Plain Bullets tab selected.

TIP You can select a single item in a list and choose List Item Properties (instead of List Properties) from the pop-up menu to change just one bullet in your list.

3. Click the kind of bullet you want to use for the selected list item(s), and then click OK to close the List Properties dialog box. Page view reappears, and you'll see your new-fangled bullets displayed there.

 NOTE The use of themes to control the look of your pages, as described in the section titled "Themes and Variations" in Chapter 4, can also affect how bulleted lists look.

FIGURE 5.4

The Plain Bullets tab of the List Properties dialog box lets you choose a new look for your bullets.

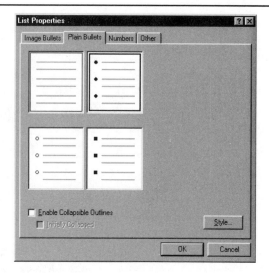

Now let's make a different kind of list: one with numbers.

Using Numbered Lists

Numbered lists are good to use when the order of your list items is important; for example, the procedures we take you through in this book might not be as easy to follow if the steps weren't numbered list items.

Numbered lists look like this:

1. Lather
2. Rinse
3. Repeat

Read on to count your blessings.

Creating a Numbered List

Making a numbered list is easier than counting to three. Just do this:

1. With the page you're working on visible in Page view, type (or paste) your list onto the page. Omit any numbers that might appear in the original list; the numbers are added automatically when you make the list using FrontPage.
2. Highlight the items in the list, and then, on the Formatting toolbar, click the Numbered List button. (Easier than counting on your fingers!)

You'll see your list displayed with the numbers inserted. The cool thing about numbered lists in FrontPage is that if you decide to add a list item anywhere in the list, the list items are automatically renumbered for you.

Renumbering Lists

FrontPage automatically renumbers your lists for you, even if you don't want it to. Suppose that within a numbered list of directions, you want to insert a small map. If you press Enter within the list, you'll insert a paragraph break, and with it, extra numbered lines. Trying to get your list items to maintain their proper numbers around elements inserted in the middle of the list can be an incredible pain. You can end up with a list that has every item numbered 1, because FrontPage assumes that it's supposed to start a new list after every inserted image.

The solution? Insert *line breaks*, rather than paragraph breaks, before and after images if you want to put them in the middle of your list.

If you do need to renumber a list, though, just delete any extraneous lines, select the entire list, and select Numbered List from the Formatting toolbar's Paragraph Style drop-down menu. Your list is renumbered.

Changing the Style of Numbering

You may want to get fancy and use letters (A, B, C, or a, b, c) or Roman numerals (I, II, III or i, ii, iii) to number your list instead of standard Arabic numerals. To change the way your numbers look, try this:

1. Create a numbered list (as described in the preceding section, "Creating a Numbered List") or display a page containing a numbered list.

2. Highlight the list, right-click it, and from the menu that appears, select List Properties. The List Properties dialog box appears, with the Numbers tab selected. You can see it in Figure 5.5.

3. Click the kind of number you want to use, and then click OK to close the List Properties dialog box and return to Page view. Your choice of number style now appears in your numbered list.

FIGURE 5.5

The Numbers tab of the List Properties dialog box lets you play the numbers.

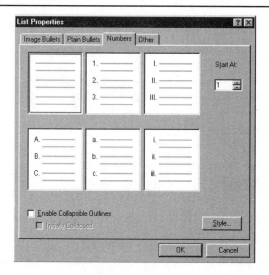

Using Definition Lists

Definition lists offer you the option to show each list item with associated text indented on the line beneath it. The most common use of a definition list is to show terms with their definitions:

Apple

A round fruit

Carrot

A long, root vegetable

Potato

A root that is (nutritionally) neither a fruit nor a vegetable, but a starch

Creating a Definition List

To create a definition list, follow these steps:

1. With the page you're working on displayed in Page view, type the first word you want to define at the place where you want it to appear. Press Enter, and type in the definition.

2. Highlight the word you are defining. From the drop-down list on the far-left side of the Formatting toolbar, select Defined Term.

3. Now, highlight the definition of the term. From the same drop-down list, select Definition. FrontPage will now indent and arrange both the definition and the term according to the definition style.

4. Repeat steps 1 through 3 for each additional term you want to add to the definition list.

Keep in mind that any time you want a paragraph to be indented beneath other text, a definition list may be your best option.

Now let's make today's headlines.

Including Headings

Just like headlines in newspapers and magazines, *headings* (also called headers, headlines, or heads) in Web pages often denote a title for a page or story. They also break text into smaller, more readable sections, allowing people to find what they seek more easily (just as we've done in this book.)

The principle for using headings in Web pages is exactly the same as in traditional print: Headings are larger than regular text, they often appear in bold type, and they're usually offset from the preceding and following text by a blank line of space.

 TIP Often, in print, the amount of blank space that follows a heading is less than that above it; this helps the reader's eye create more of a connection between the heading and the text it is introducing. HTML and FrontPage both place the same amount of blank space before and after a heading. However, you can change this by using a method such as style sheets, which are covered in Chapter 13.

You can use a heading to announce the title of your page, or you can use headings of different sizes for different levels of emphasis. For example, again in this book, the headings for chapter titles are in the largest type size, while each section of the chapter gets a smaller head, and the headings for subsections get increasingly smaller as the subsections become sub-sub sections.

In HTML, there are six sizes of headings. Not all of these would make really effective headlines; the sixth, or smallest, heading size is tiny and is smaller than the body text. Headings 1 through 6 are shown in Figure 5.6.

To create a heading using FrontPage, just follow these steps:

1. With your page-in-progress open in Page view, highlight the text you want to turn into a heading.

2. From the Formatting toolbar's Paragraph Style drop-down menu, select a heading size (Heading 1 to Heading 6). You'll see the effect immediately.

FIGURE 5.6

Heading sizes

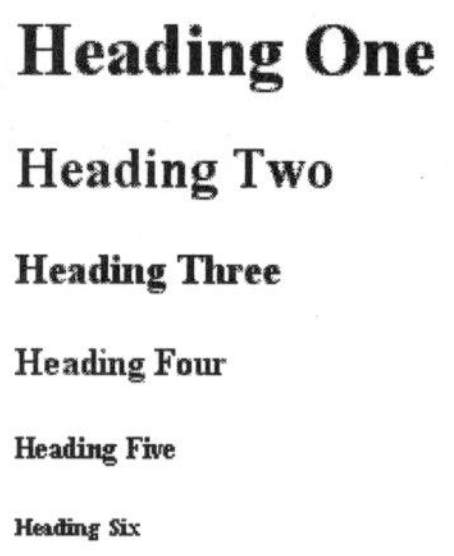

Heading One

Heading Two

Heading Three

Heading Four

Heading Five

Heading Six

 NOTE Because headings are considered to be a type of paragraph style in HTML, applying the heading formatting to even a single word selected from the middle of a paragraph turns that entire paragraph into a heading. If you want a word in the middle of a paragraph to be big and bold, you need to apply that formatting as a separate text style, rather than trying to make a heading appear in the middle of your text.

 TIP You can convert a heading back into normal body text by selecting it and then choosing Normal from the Paragraph Style drop-down menu on the Formatting toolbar.

Up Next

Now that you know how to work with basic text, it's time to add power and impact to that text. This is done through the use of *typography*. As you'll see in Chapter 6, *Fantastic Fonts*, using proper type, or *font* styles, your pages can begin to approach a sophisticated, professional level of design.

CHAPTER <u>6</u>

Fantastic Fonts

Early in HTML's life, there wasn't really much you could do with it to *design* your Web pages—you simply had to work within the constraints of the language. HTML, after all, was never intended to be a page design or layout language.

However, the demands of designers and audiences, as well as the competitive nature of browser developers, have each lent influence. HTML has changed from a simple document-formatting language to the skeletal system of Web page design and layout, giving more flexibility and options to the designer.

One area in which the changes in HTML have influenced design is in using *typography*—type, also referred to as *fonts* in the computer world—to enhance the textual message. While still filled with challenges, there are now many more typographic options based in HTML than ever before. There are two main areas where this is most obvious—with the use of the font tag and with Cascading Style Sheets, covered in Chapter 13. In this chapter, we'll focus on type that you can create with HTML, or "HTML-based" type.

 NOTE Of course, you can always opt for placing your type in a graphic—and this is often a good choice for headers or logos. However, the more type options you include in the HTML, the faster your pages are going to load. This is one of the reasons the growth of type technology in HTML is so important.

Entire volumes—including many good ones—have been written about the power of typography and the manipulation of text on the page. The use of typefaces on the Web might be a relatively new concern, but it's an extremely important one. Typefaces can not only serve as decorative elements, but they can help send a powerful message about who you are and what you do.

In this chapter, you will get a short course in basic typography for the Web. We'll demonstrate different kinds of type and explain when it's best to use which kinds. Then, we'll look at how to use FrontPage and HTML tricks to add different kinds of type to your pages. We'll also look at how to add color to text and links. A list of typographic do's and don'ts is included, helping you to make sure your pages get the added benefit of type design, without ever sacrificing the style and impact that type can bring.

Looking at Types of Type

There are so many different kinds of type that they've been grouped into sensible containers in order for designers to be able to keep track of them. The Web isn't as sophisticated as print, however, so we can focus in on which kinds of type can be used, and why you'd want to use one kind over another.

Ultimately, our concern will be with typefaces, referred to in the Web world as *fonts*. A font is a distinctive and specific kind of type that is part of a larger category of type. We'll take a closer look at specific fonts in just a bit. First, let's get comfortable with type categories.

 NOTE   The word *font* is actually a carry-over from the days of the printing press. It is used interchangeably these days with *typeface*.

There are five categories of type that are important to the Web:

Serif This is a standard, familiar group of fonts that are identified by *serifs*, which are tiny horizontal strokes, or "feet," on the individual letters. Serif fonts are said to be the easiest to read in print, but this may not be true for the screen. While the verdict is still out, it can confidently be said that serif fonts are often the default fonts used in software programs. In general, serif fonts are excellent for body text (longer sections of text).

Sans serif A very common group to Web design is the *sans* (meaning without) *serif* category. These font families have no tiny horizontal strokes, or "feet." Fonts in this category are felt to be highly readable on the screen. Sans serif fonts are very popular for body text on the Web.

Monospaced In this font group, each character and the white space around it takes up the same space, similar to the fixed width text described in Chapter 5. Like fixed width text, monospaced fonts are often referred to as *typewriter* fonts, because they resemble the monospaced type used by those old-fashioned typewriters. In Web design, monospaced type is used mostly as a decorative element.

Script This category includes all families that resemble handwriting. Most script fonts are very difficult to read in longer sections, and therefore should not be used for body text. Script can be used most effectively for short headers or decorative elements.

Decorative This group is identified as having special decorative features such as dots, scrolls, and other designs. As the name indicates, you'll want to use decorative type only for headers or decoration.

The following table lists the five categories of Web type and some of the fonts in each category.

Category	Faces
Serif	Times, Century Schoolbook, Garamond
Sans serif	Helvetica, Arial, Verdana
Monospaced	Courier, Courier New
Script	Nuptial Script, Boulevard, Signature
Decorative	Whimsy, Arriba!, Bergell

In Figure 6.1, you can see the table with an example of each type of type.

Category	Faces
Serif	Times, Century Schoolbook, Garamond
Sans-Serif	Helvetica, Arial, Verdana
Monospaced	Courier, Courier New
Script	Nuptial Script, Boulevard, Signature
Decorative	Whimsy, Arriba!, Bergell

 TIP Many designers spend their entire lives learning how to design with and create type. This is a good indication of how powerful a design element it is! Choose the right type, and your work will have the impact you're after. Choose a clashing or inappropriate typeface, and your work will be unattractive—or worse, boring!

Adding Fonts to a Page

When you don't specify a font face, most Web browsers use Times, a serif font, for "normal" text and Courier, a monospaced font, for preformatted and other code-like text. Using FrontPage, you can use any font you have installed on your machine in your Web page, but be forewarned: If the person looking at your site doesn't have that font installed on his or her machine, the text will instead be displayed in whatever he or she has chosen as a default font face.

Nonetheless, it's very likely that you'll want to specify fonts. This is a big part of Web design, and in fact, anyone who does choose to override your specified font choices may be missing out on your terrific design! As a Web designer, you can tremendously control a user's experience of text through the magic of typography—and that means specifying fonts.

To choose a font, just follow these steps:

1. With your document open in Page view, select the text whose font you want to change.

2. Click the Formatting toolbar's Font drop-down menu (see Figure 6.2), and select a font from the list that appears. Just click the name of the font, and the selected text changes to the font you selected.

FIGURE 6.2

*The drop-down
Font menu*

When you change fonts, FrontPage uses the HTML code `<FONT FACE="fontname">`. This code tells the browser that loads the page to check and see if that font is on the user's computer; if it isn't, the browser just uses the default font instead.

 TIP Alternatively, you can use the menu bar to select Format ➤ Font, and use the Font dialog box to choose a font. This will allow you to see a preview of the font before you apply the changes to your page.

You can repeat these steps as often as you like until you find a font that appeals to you.

 MASTERING WHAT'S ONLINE

Font FAQ

An extensive resource about fonts—their origins, their limitations, whether or not they have serifs, even the pronunciation of their names—can be found in the Font FAQ at www.rz.go.dlr.de:8081/info/faqs/fonts/.

Managing Web Fonts

At this point, you might be thinking to yourself, "Cool! Lots of categories, lots of fonts to choose from, and it's real easy to do!" Unfortunately, this isn't really the case.

As we warned, the problem is that in order for an HTML-based font to be seen, the specified font *must reside on the site visitor's computer*. This means if Jane Doughie doesn't have the font you want, she's going to see a default font. So if you just walked through the exercise in the previous section and added a fancy, decorative font such as Whimsy to your pages, chances are that very few people are ever going to see the font, since most people don't have Whimsy installed or active on their computers. They're just going to see their browser's default font, and whoosh! Your nice design is gone.

There are some workarounds for this problem, including using fonts that show up on almost everyone's machines. Unfortunately, this is limited to two fonts: Times and Courier. You can use a technique called *stacking* fonts (something that FrontPage doesn't do automatically, but you can add yourself), or a very new technology known as *font embedding*. Or you could request that your visitors download a specialty set of fonts from Microsoft known as *core* fonts. The following sections describe these methods.

Cross-Platform Typography

Remember, the caveat to remember in typography is that if you use a font that isn't resident on your visitor's machine, he or she isn't going to see the font that you're coding, unless you are using Times or Courier, or make some special arrangements.

Arial is a font native to Windows machines, but rarely, if ever, is it found on a Macintosh. Without that font being resident on a Mac, the Mac's browser will simply display the default font, which is normally set to Times. It's easy to see how quickly this substitution can disrupt your design!

Fortunately, HTML allows you to *stack* font faces (provide a list of acceptable fonts to use). You can use any font face that you want, but you need to keep in mind that the Mac typically uses a different series of fonts than Windows does. In order to use this technique effectively, you really need to understand the categories of type, and some popular fonts that fit into each category. The browser looks for the first font you name, and if it doesn't find it, it moves on to the next named font, and so forth. To do this, you're going to have to get into the HTML itself, since FrontPage cannot do it for you.

Despite the fact that you have to do a little hand-coding work here, there's a big advantage to using this technique. It gives you better control than just letting the browser do the thinking for you. You can put as many font names as are appropriate and reasonable into the stack. This way, the browser looks for your preferred font first, and if it doesn't find it, then it looks for a similar font that you have specified. In the case of the Macintosh, Helvetica is a sans serif font that is commonly found on Macs and is very similar to Arial. So you could include Helvetica in your font stack in case a Mac browser is used to view your page.

First, let's take a look at the way the HTML works. Then, we'll go in and add this technique step-by-step using FrontPage.

Stacking Fonts in HTML

Here's how you make a bit of text appear in the Arial font using FrontPage's HTML:

```
<FONT face="arial">
Through the eyes of a child<br>
    love paints a rainbow<br>
    With each passing day<br>
    the colors unfold<br>
    A story of enchantment<br>
    that touches my heart.<br>
</FONT>
```

This poem appears in Arial—provided that the person looking at the HTML code through his or her browser *has* the Arial font.

Since Macs don't usually have this font, you can go ahead and stack a sans serif font that is common on Macs, such as Helvetica.

 TIP   While there is conceivably no limit on the way you stack fonts, there are two simple and stable options for body text. If you want a serif font, you can set the font stack to include the serif of your choice, such as Garamond, followed by Times (which is available on Mac and PC). The opening tag and attributes will look like this: `<FONT face="Gara-mond, Times">`.

For a sans serif body, set the serif of your choice, such as Verdana. Follow it up with Arial, which will be available to your Windows users, and then with Helvetica, which will be available to your Mac users: `<FONT face="Verdana,Arial,Helvetica>`.

In order to accommodate both machines, you can create HTML code that looks like this:

```
<FONT face="arial, helvetica">
Through the eyes of a child<br>
    love paints a rainbow<br>
    With each passing day<br>
```

```
    the colors unfold<br>
    A story of enchantment<br>
    that touches my heart.<br>
</FONT>
```

With this coding, the browser looks for Helvetica if it cannot find Arial.

There's another option that you can add to stacking as well. It's supported only by later browser versions. This technique allows you to put a category name into the string, as follows:

```
<FONT face="arial, helvetica, sans serif">
Through the eyes of a child<br>
    love paints a rainbow<br>
    With each passing day<br>
    the colors unfold<br>
    A story of enchantment<br>
    that touches my heart.<br>
</FONT>
```

Now if the browser cannot find Arial or Helvetica, it seeks out the first sans serif font it can find on the resident machine and uses that.

How do you know what fonts are resident on what Macs and PCs? If you've already been wondering about this—good for you! The following table shows the fonts that are always native to Windows and Macintosh. This means that they come shipped with the operating system. Of course, the owner of the machine may have added many fonts, but you can be sure that at least these fonts are going to be available. Please keep in mind that these fonts do not correlate to one another in terms of their category; these are merely lists of resident fonts for these operating systems. For a good rule of thumb on how to manage fonts for cross-platform consistency, read the information in the "Cross-Platform Typography" section earlier in this chapter.

Windows		Macintosh
Arial	Courier New	Chicago
Arial Black	Garamond	Courier
Arial Narrow	MS Dialog	Helvetica
Arial Rounded MT Bold	MS Dialog Light	Monaco
Book Antiqua	MS LineDraw	New York
Bookman Old Style	MS LineDraw	Palatino
Century Gothic	MS SystemX	Times
Century Schoolbook	Times New Roman	
Courier	Verdana	

You can see from this table that the *only two fonts* that are always native to both Windows and Macintosh are Times and Courier! This is unnerving, to say the least.

However, if you combine typographic knowledge with an understanding of the cross-platform limitations of fonts, you can gain some control over standard HTML documents.

Even if you want to use a fancy, decorative font that isn't available on an end user's machine, you can stack alternatives so that the user still gets a stylish page:

```
<FONT face="whimsy ICG, garamond, times, serif">
Through the eyes of a child<br>
    love paints a rainbow<br>
    With each passing day<br>
    the colors unfold<br>
    A story of enchantment<br>
    that touches my heart.<br>
</FONT>
```

This way, if the person doesn't have Whimsy, there's a chance he or she might have Garamond. If not, the browser will look for Times, which the site visitor is very likely to have.

Stacking Fonts in FrontPage

Now that you know how the stacking technique works, let's go ahead and give it a try using FrontPage.

1. With your document open in Page view, select the text you want to modify.

2. Click the Formatting toolbar's Font drop-down menu and select the font you want to use. Just click the name of the specialty font you want to use (we've selected Gill Sans MT, and the selected text will change faces.) Behind the scenes, this action adds the necessary HTML for controlling fonts.

3. To begin stacking the font faces, you'll need to switch to the HTML editing view. Simply click the HTML tab, and you'll be taken right to the HTML you want to modify (see Figure 6.3). Since we know that Gill Sans is only going to be on some computers, we're going to make sure that our visitors who don't have the font get to see something close to what we want them to. Gill Sans is a sans serif font. We're going to add Arial as the next choice.

4. Place your cursor after the first instance of the Gill Sans face code.

5. Add a comma, one space, and then type in **Arial**. Your code should now look like this:

```
<font face="Gill Sans MT, Arial">
```

From the list we provided earlier, you can see that Arial shows up with any certainty only on Windows machines. So, since we want to include our Mac site visitors, we're going to add Helvetica to our code.

FIGURE 6.3

HTML code for fonts as created by FrontPage

```
<html>

<head>
<meta name="GENERATOR" content="Microsoft FrontPage 4.0">
<meta name="ProgId" content="FrontPage.Editor.Document">
<title>Through the eyes of a child</title>
</head>

<body>

<p><font face="Arial">Through the eyes of a child<br>
love paints a rainbow<br>
With each passing day<br>
the colors unfold<br>
A story of enchantment<br>
that touches my heart. </font></p>
<p> </p>

</body>

</html>
```

6. After Arial, type in Helvetica, following the instructions in step 5. Your code should now look like this:

```
<font face="Gill Sans MT, Arial, Helvetica">
```

7. For extra safety, you can add the sans serif value:

```
<font face="Gill Sans MT, Arial, Helvetica, sans serif">
```

Your final work will appear in the HTML as follows:

```
<p><font face="Gill Sans MT, Arial">Through the eyes of a child<br>
love paints a rainbow<br>
With each passing day<br>
the colors unfold<br>
A story of enchantment<br>
that touches my heart. </font></p>
```

Now save your file, and the changes will be incorporated. Since we have Gill Sans, our sample shows that font, as you can see in Figure 6.4.

You now have a cross-browser solution for font viewing. Your visitors may not see your first choice, but they'll at least see a font style that you've created for your site.

FIGURE 6.4

The font face results in our browser

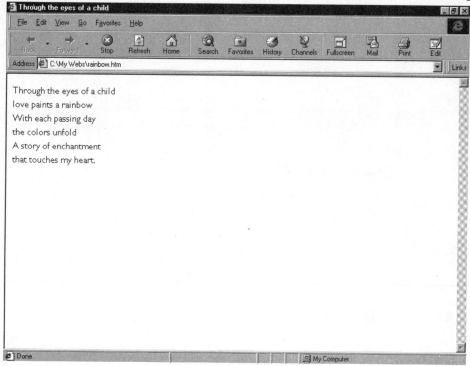

Through the eyes of a child
love paints a rainbow
With each passing day
the colors unfold
A story of enchantment
that touches my heart.

Embedding Fonts

Another method to guarantee the look of a page is to embed fonts directly within the Web page itself.

Embedded fonts are an interesting concept that allows you to embed a font within a page so that it is downloaded to end-users while they load the page. The user will then have the information to properly display the page as you've set it up to be!

Both Internet Explorer and Netscape have methods by which to offer embedded fonts. In IE, font embedding is delivered using a font format known as OpenType. In Netscape, font embedding is dealt with using a technology developed by Bitstream known as TrueDoc. It's interesting to note that OpenType is also backed by Adobe, which gives the format a lot of respectability and punch for future font issues on the Web.

While there is a lot of general interest in the idea of font embedding, it's currently being used only in test cases or experimental design sites. Embedding itself is not a new concept, however. You can already embed TrueType fonts within documents that have embraced the TrueType standard, notably Microsoft Office applications and many programs for the Macintosh.

In those cases, you simply use the font you want, give the document to someone via e-mail or disk, and they can see the font—and print it. It seems like a logical step to extend the TrueType specification to the Web, but this is not yet a standard.

MASTERING WHAT'S ONLINE

Embedded Fonts

For Bitstream's TrueDoc, check out www.bitstream.com/.

Microsoft covers the OpenType format at www.microsoft.com/truetype/.

Microsoft Core Fonts

Microsoft is more than willing to give away free fonts so that Windows and Macs can share the same font family. You can add these core fonts to your own collection, and if you're a font-maniac showing off a home page, you can ask your visitors to download this package, too.

WARNING If you're designing a commercial site, it's never wise to tell visitors what they need to properly see the site. You should design commercial Web sites that will receive a lot of visitors by following cross-browser design techniques, found in Chapter 16, *Cross-Browser Design*. You can include some recommendations on a Help page, but don't rely on this for your commercial visitors.

MASTERING WHAT'S ONLINE

The Microsoft Core Fonts collection includes several serif, sans serif, monotype, and decorative fonts. To download these fonts, visit www.microsoft.com/typography/fontpack/.

Using Font Tips and Tricks

If you want more fonts, there are plenty on the Web that you can download and install for free—but the more fonts you have, the more choices you have! Not to mention the fact that having many fonts installed can impact your computer's performance. It's difficult to remember which font looks like what, and choosing between dozens or hundreds of fonts can leave people stymied.

One thing you might do is use your favorite word processing program to create a font list that you can print out for easy reference while you're choosing a font. You can group your fonts alphabetically or by category, with all of the script fonts in one section, the handwriting fonts in another, and the heavy, decorative fonts in still another.

Now, just because you have a font doesn't mean you should use it—and just because you have 57 fonts doesn't mean you should use all of those, either! Using a light hand with fonts is *always* the best trick of all.

Here are some other helpful guidelines:

- Using more than two or three fonts on a page makes it look cluttered and confusing. Figure 6.5 shows an example of mixed fonts that works, and Figure 6.6 shows one that doesn't. Note that both examples use not only more than one font face, they also mix alignments, sizes, colors, and styles (bold and italic).

FIGURE 6.5

Mixing fonts well
means using a
light hand.

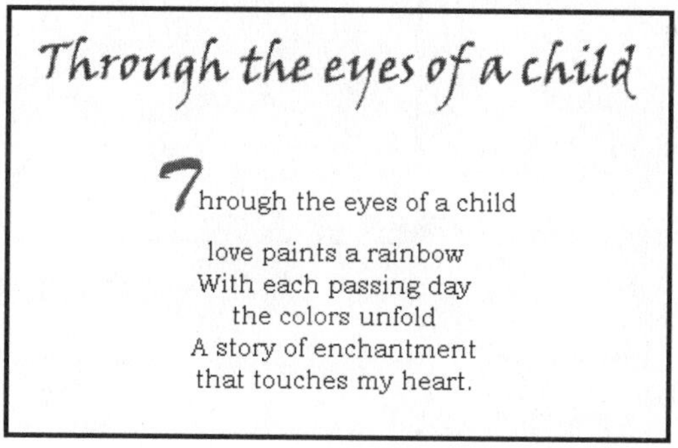

Through the eyes of a child

*T*hrough the eyes of a child

love paints a rainbow
With each passing day
the colors unfold
A story of enchantment
that touches my heart.

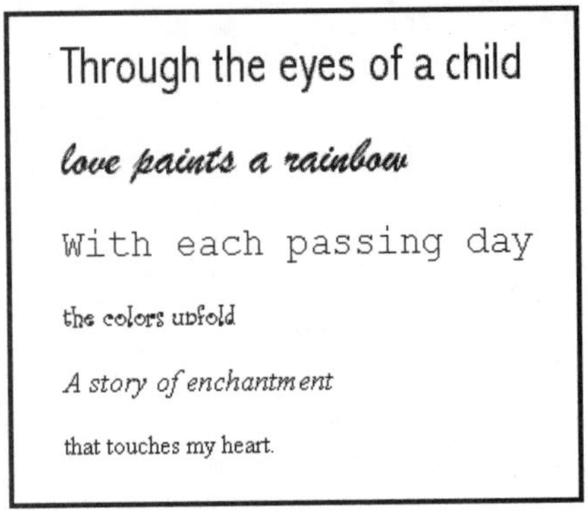

FIGURE 6.6

Too many fonts can spoil the soup.

Through the eyes of a child

love paints a rainbow

With each passing day

the colors unfold

A story of enchantment

that touches my heart.

- When choosing a font, contrast can make a page look very professional. This means choosing headers that differ from body text. For example, you can choose a sans serif font for your headers, and a serif font for your body text (see Figure 6.7), or vice-versa (see Figure 6.8). Either way can work well, but be consistent!

FIGURE 6.7

A sans serif font for headers and a serif font for body text is a professional mix.

Through the Eyes of a Child

Through the eyes of a child
love paints a rainbow
With each passing day
the colors unfold
A story of enchantment
that touches my heart.

FIGURE 6.8

A serif font for headers and a sans serif font for body text looks good too, but be consistent!

Through the Eyes of a Child

Through the eyes of a child
love paints a rainbow
With each passing day
the colors unfold
A story of enchantment
that touches my heart.

- Limit your font color palette, and make sure that text stands out from the background without clashing with it. More on colors in just a bit.

MASTERING WHAT'S ONLINE

Font Resources

You can get a lot of information about fonts, including downloads of specialty fonts, by visiting these sites:

Web Wonk—www.dsiegel.com/tips/

The Dezine Café at Design Online—www.dol.com/Root/

The comp.fonts page—www.ora.com/homepages/comp.fonts/

Web Page Design for Designers—ds.dial.pipex.com/pixelp/wpdesign/wpdin-tro.shtml

Changing Font Size

Just as different fonts can add variety and interest to a page, so can font sizing. You've already learned that headings come in different sizes. As you will recall, headings come in sizes from 1 to 6, where size 1 is very large and size 6 is very small.

Similarly, text sizes in HTML range from size 1 to size 7, although the scale goes the other way: size 1 text is rather small, while size 7 is large. "Regular size" type, or the default setting, is size 3, which generally corresponds to 12-point type. Size 4 is generally size 14, on up to size 7, which translates to 36 points. At the other end of the scale, tiny size 1 type is generally displayed at 8 points—small print indeed. This numeric method is referred to as *absolute*. However, because different browsers interpret information in their own unique ways, and because there are many variables—such as customizing default fonts or changing the resolution on one's monitor—font sizing in HTML is not very specific or accurate.

You can see the different font sizes illustrated in Figure 6.9, where the base font is size 3.

FIGURE 6.9

HTML uses seven different font sizes.

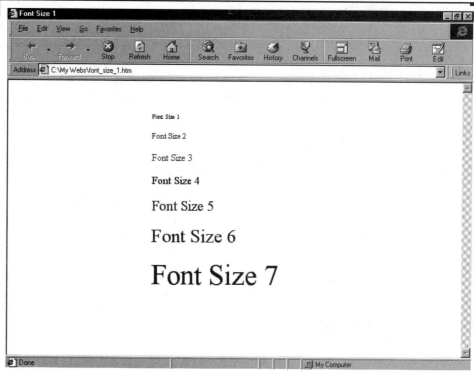

Of course, font sizes are also *relative* to the default font size settings in your visitors' browser software. Nearsighted folks, or people with Really Big Monitors, may have their default font size set to 14 or bigger, and some exceptionally keen-eyed people may decide to set their default font size to 10, to fit more text on the screen. What this means is that the font size you set will not be based on 12 points, but on the user's own private standard.

Because users can change their browser's font size settings, all HTML font sizes are really relative, but some are more relative than others. FrontPage uses two different scales: the absolute type scale, which specifies font sizes as ranging from 1 to 7, and the relative scale. The relative scale uses a numeric scale based on plus and minus values. This method tells the browser to knock the point size up or down a notch.

In the absolute scale of 1 to 7, size 3 is the default font size; it's also known as the *base font* size. The other font sizes on the relative scale then use 3 as the "zero" setting. These seven settings act the same as the 1 to 7 point scale used by FrontPage.

The +1 size, for instance, is the same as font size 4. The code for these fonts looks rather similar:

Relative type scale   `<FONT SIZE=+1>14 point</FONT>`

Absolute type scale   `<FONT SIZE=4>14 point</FONT>`

Each of these pieces of code would produce a piece of text the same size; to use relative sizes instead of absolute sizes, you'd simply open the HTML view in Page view and make the changes there.

The one relative size that's the most important is the base font size. If you set the base font size (usually equivalent to size 3) to size 5, for instance, all the + and – settings would be based on size 5 rather than size 3.

 NOTE Absolute or relative: Which is better? This depends upon your preference—and your audience. In most cases, it's going to be best to stick to the absolute method. However, if you know that your audience tends to modify their browser defaults (such as an audience with known vision difficulties), you may opt for the relative method.

Setting Font Sizes

To set an absolute font size:

1. Select the text you want to size.

2. From the drop-down sizing menu on the formatting toolbar, select the numeric size you want.

or

1. Select the text you want to size.

2. Select Format ➢ Font. The Font dialog box will appear (see Figure 6.10).

FIGURE 6.10

The Font dialog box offers a variety of font modification options, including sizing.

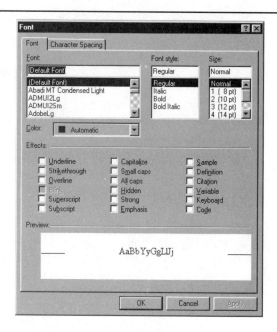

3. Choose the size you want the font to be.

The size of your text will now change accordingly.

To set a relative font size, you can go right into the HTML and add your changes.

1. With your document open in Page view, select the text you want to modify.

2. Click the Formatting toolbar's Font size drop-down menu, and select the font size you want to use. Behind the scenes, this action has added the necessary HTML for a standard font size.

3. To change to a relative size, you'll need to switch to the HTML editing view. Simply click the HTML tab, and you'll be taken right to the HTML you want to change.

4. Place your cursor in front of the numeric value described. Now type in a plus or minus sign, and the relative numeric value you want the font size to be.

5. Save your file, and you're all set!

MASTERING THE OPPORTUNITIES

Nifty Font Size Effects

So you can make some pieces of text bigger than others—what's the big deal? You can achieve a polished look by mixing the font sizes on a page, or you can make your page look weird and haphazard (we don't recommend the latter). Here are some ways you can use different font sizes to great effect:

- Initial caps, as in **O**nce upon a time. Just increase the size of the first letter in a paragraph.
- Small caps, as in **I**N THE **B**EGINNING. Type your text in all capital letters, and then make the initial letters in the word a size or two bigger than the rest.
- Varied font size, as in sup**e**rman. This effect usually serves no real purpose, but you can achieve it by changing the size of each letter in a word. If you're careful, you can use this for a nice graphic effect, although most people just do it to show off.
- Try making your address information (usually found at the bottom of the page) a bit smaller than body text. You can also make captions and sidebars appear in a smaller font size.

Changing Colors

Using colors for text can add visual contrast and interest to pages. As we've discussed, links have usually appeared underlined and in a distinct color, but you couldn't always determine what that color would be. Similarly, link colors were often the only spot of color to be found in the text. Now you can set both the link color and the text color, and you can also highlight areas of your text by using additional font colors within the body text.

Most of the time you're going to want to use a text color that contrasts strongly with the background; black text on a white page and white text on a black page are two obvious examples. In either case, you'll want to choose a link color that goes well with the background as well as the other text on the page, but still makes the link stand out in some way.

Sometimes, too, you're going to want to highlight portions of your pages by using an additional font color different from that used for text and links. Some pages look elegant with headings set in their own color, for instance. But you want to be sure not to confuse your users with too many additional colors. As with face and sizing, a light hand is often the most effective.

When choosing your color scheme, remember your audience. If you're creating a lively page about gardening, you might opt for pale yellow text on a dark green background, with light green or gold link colors for the entire site. On the other hand, if your site is a post-industrial wasteland of punk bands, skateboards, and splatterpunk fiction, you might use a more grisly look with a black background, silver text, and blood red links.

 TIP No matter the palette you choose, you should keep colors consistent throughout a site. For example, you should use the same text and link colors on the main page as you do on any of the internal pages.

 MASTERING WHAT'S ONLINE

Two sites that choose their color schemes to suit their audience are HotWired and Salon. HotWired, at www.hotwired.com/, uses a neon array of bright, mind-bending colors to challenge the paradigms of the technocracy (and the patience of the people who actually try to read the stuff).

Salon, an online features magazine for highbrows, uses a traditional print color scheme of black body text on white pages. They highlight not only links with color, but also headlines, initial caps, and introductions, usually by using dark red, blue, brown, or some other stately color to attract attention to part of a page. Their high-design pages are worth looking at—and reading—at www.salonmagazine.com/.

Setting the Color of Links and Body Text

You probably know that links are traditionally a brighter color than the rest of the page, but you may not be aware that links actually have *three* color attributes.

Link color is the color of a new link—one that your guest has never before clicked. *Visited links* may prompt déjà vu: You know you've seen that link before, and its color has changed to assure you that that is the case. Finally, when you're in the act of clicking a link, it may change color while you're clicking and holding the mouse button down, if the Webmaster has set an *active link* color.

You can set all three of these colors using FrontPage. Just follow these steps:

1. With a page open in Page view, from the menu bar, select Format ➤ Background. The Page Properties dialog box appears, with the Background tab selected (see Figure 6.11). (If you need to, just click the Background tab of the Page Properties dialog box, which changes to reflect your choice.)

FIGURE 6.11

In the Page Properties dialog box you can change text and link colors, among other things.

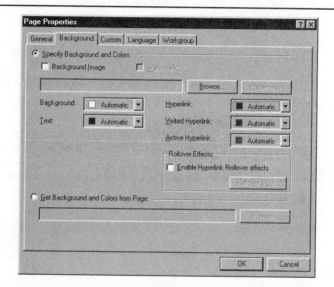

2. Decide on a text attribute whose color you want to change—Text, Hyperlink, Visited Hyperlink, or Active Hyperlink—and click the drop-down list for that color. From the list of colors that appears, choose a color that appeals to you. If you select Default, no color is chosen, and the colors that appear on the user's screen when he or she views your page will be determined by the default browser settings that the individual user has set. Move on to step 7.

or

If you'd like to choose a custom color that doesn't appear in the drop-down menu, click Custom. The Color dialog box appears (see Figure 6.12).

Choose a color from the box, and then you can color with it.

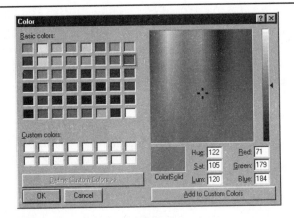

 NOTE The basic color choices offered to you as menu options may not be very exciting, but they do offer a distinct advantage over colors you create yourself: They're *standard*. That means that no matter which platform or what kind of awful, low-resolution color monitor your guests use to surf the Web, they'll see pretty much the color you choose, if you stick to basic colors.

 NOTE Brief color theory lesson: The *hue* of a color is its main characteristic. Orange, green, and red are all distinct hues on the color wheel. Lighter colors (hue plus white) are called *tints*, and darker colors (hue plus black) are called *shades*. When you're talking about relative lightness and darkness of a color, it's common to refer to its *shade*—for instance, pink, scarlet, and crimson are all different shades of red.

3. In the Color dialog box, select a hue by clicking in the color box in the center. (It looks like a rainbow of colors!) Then, you can use the slide on the far right to select a lighter or darker tone. The combined result of your clicks will be displayed in the Color|Solid color box.

4. When you've settled on a color you like, click Add To Custom Colors, and that color will appear in one of the Custom Colors color boxes, at the lower left of the Color dialog box.

5. Click the Custom Color box that contains the color you just chose, and then click OK to specify that color. The Color dialog box closes and the Page Properties dialog box reappears. The color you specified is displayed as the Custom color in the drop-down menu. For example, if you clicked the Text drop-down menu in step 2, and chose a Custom color in steps 3 through 6, that custom color is now displayed in the Text drop-down list.

6. You can repeat step 2, or steps 2 through 6, for each of the four color options: text color, link color, visited link color, and active link color.

7. When you're done, click OK to close the Page Properties dialog box. The Page view window reappears, where you'll see your new color choices (if you've already got text and links on your page, of course).

 TIP You can control only the background properties of pages that do not use themes. If your page does use a theme, you'll have to turn it off before you can make changes to the background properties. See Chapter 4 for more about themes.

 NOTE You won't see visited and active link colors in action until you've loaded your page into a Web browser and tested your links.

Now that you know how to set the text color for the main body text and for the links (and their various attributes), let's take a look at how you can set different colors for parts of the text on a page.

Changing Font Colors

While the main body of your text will generally be all one color, you may want to change the colors of headings, captions, addresses, particular words, or whatever else you feel like sprucing up. One good use of this is on a page that has tables (see Chapter 11, *Using Tables for Advanced Layout,* for instructions on working with tables).

Another effective way to use color on your pages is to assign an entire paragraph a slightly different color from the rest of the text to make the reader's eye jump to it. Salon Magazine, which we referred to earlier, uses black text for most of its pages, but you'll see an occasional dark red paragraph that just ever so slightly stands out—just enough to bear notice.

 NOTE Manipulating text colors on your pages can create lovely effects, especially in combination with tables, background colors, and a mix of paragraph alignments or indents. Beware of overuse, however. Too many colors of text on a page can make it look busy—and worse, difficult to read.

To change the color of a specific piece of text, follow these steps:

1. With a page open in Page view, highlight the text whose color you want to change.

2. Click the Formatting toolbar's Text Color button. The Color dialog box appears.

3. Click one of the color boxes in the Basic Colors area of the dialog box to select that color. Or, click Define Custom Colors. The Color dialog box expands to display the hue (large) and shade (narrow) areas. Select a hue by clicking it in the center "rainbow" box, and then choose a shade by sliding to a lighter or darker tone in the narrow panel to the right of the color selection box. The combined result of your clicks is displayed in the Color|Solid color box. To use this color, click Add To Custom Colors, and the color appears in one of the Custom Colors boxes at the left of the dialog box. (You might want to click it, to make sure it's selected, but it's selected automatically when you add it to your Custom Colors palette.)

4. When you're done selecting colors, click OK to close the Color dialog box. The page reappears, and there you see your colors shining through.

That's all there is to that.

Now we've learned how to change the look of text, including its color, font, size, and style. Combined with what you learned about paragraphs, text alignment, and indents in Chapter 5, *All About Text*, you're ready to tackle text in any form.

Other Typographical Issues

Entire books have been written on typography—indeed, entire courses of study are devoted to learning how to present text on a page. We've looked at what you can do with type on the Web using FrontPage 2000, but let's touch on some other typographical issues you may hear mentioned in your travels with type:

Anti-aliasing When you're using words as part (or all) of an image, as you might do with logos, headlines, button bars, or pull quotes, you're fixing text into the image, which means that it loses its font qualities and becomes just pixels in the image. When you use an image program to place text, be sure to anti-alias the text (in Microsoft Image Composer, this is called *smoothing*). (Chapter 9, *Designing Graphics for the Web*, covers some other image issues, such as transparency and reducing the number of colors per image.)

Continued

CONTINUED

Kerning and Tracking Most computer fonts employ *proportional spacing*; that is, the space between each letter in a word is adjusted depending on the size and shape of each unique letterform. Typographers often want to adjust the way lines of type are spaced. *Kerning* refers to adjusting the space between pairs of letters, while *tracking* refers to adjusting the spacing of an overall line. Page design and imaging programs such as Adobe Photoshop 5, Adobe Illustrator, Adobe Page-Maker, and Quark Express include tools for kerning and tracking; if you design a block of text using one of these programs, you could create an image based on this picture-perfect type.

Margins Part of what makes a page look either lovely or cluttered is the space between text or images and the edge of the page, or the space between columns (which you can create through the use of tables, as discussed in Chapter 11).

Vertical Spacing Balancing the white space between paragraphs, between images and their captions, and between headlines and stories can help unify the overall look of a page. Chapter 9 describes how to adjust the space between text and images, and Chapter 4 discusses the use of horizontal rules to divide space. However, be aware that simple white space is rarely overused.

Up Next

Believe it or not, you now have enough skills to create a fine-looking page! In order to help bring you to the next level, we're going to focus first on how to manage your things-to-do list, helping you organize the various pieces of the basic webs you can now create.

Chapter 7, *Managing Tasks*, will not only help get your work organized, but also get you in position to move toward publishing your pages.

CHAPTER 7

Managing Tasks

C reating a great Web site is a lot of work, even with all of FrontPage's wizards and shortcuts giving you a hand. If your FrontPage web has lots of pages, you'll find it challenging to keep track of everything you must do to finish the job. To help you manage your web creation and maintenance duties, FrontPage includes a task manager called the *Tasks view*.

You can think of the Tasks view as an organizer that's integrated with your Web site. For example, suppose you're too busy to spell check your web at the moment, but you want to remind yourself to do it later. Instead of writing "Spell Check!" on a Post-It note and attaching it to your monitor, you can enter a new task into the Tasks view. Later, FrontPage can help you complete the task by showing the pages that need spell checking and even tracking when the spell check has been completed for each page.

A *task* is an item associated with a particular FrontPage web that represents an action you need to perform. Some tasks are automatically created for you by FrontPage's wizards (such as the Corporate Presence Wizard, which creates tasks to remind you which pages to customize). You can also add your own tasks to the Tasks view whenever you want. All tasks are always listed in the Task list, which is routinely displayed by FrontPage's Tasks view. In this chapter, you'll learn how to work both with tasks created by FrontPage wizards and those created by you or team members from scratch.

 NOTE Remember, the Tasks view is available on the Views toolbar, which opens automatically with FrontPage. You can find it to the left, with the Tasks view button the bottom button on the toolbar.

If you're working on a big Web site, you might need to coordinate changes and tasks among members of a team or workgroup. FrontPage's Tasks view keeps track of who created each task, who's supposed to complete the task, and when the task was last modified (so you can congratulate team members who complete their tasks on time, or send nasty notes to shirkers). We'll show you in this chapter how a team of Web authors can use the Tasks view to coordinate their efforts. But first let's look at simpler situations.

When FrontPage Wizards Create Tasks

When you use FrontPage to create a web using a wizard, tasks may be added to the Tasks view automatically. The Tasks view simply lists actions that are not yet completed, and keeps track of who is working on each of those tasks.

One wizard that creates several tasks is the Corporate Presence Wizard, which helps you create a Web site for a business. When you create a Corporate Presence web, Front-Page adds and tracks tasks to remind you which pages need to be completed. Let's take a look at working with wizard-generated Task lists. To start the Corporate Presence Wizard and create a new Corporate Presence web, follow these steps:

1. From the FrontPage menu bar, select File ➤ New ➤ Web. The New Web Sites dialog box appears (as shown in Figure 7.1).

2. Highlight the icon for Corporate Presence Wizard.

3. In the drop-down menu labeled Specify The Location Of The New Web, choose a pre-existing location from the drop-down list, or add a new location by typing it into the text box.

FIGURE 7.1

The New dialog box offers several wizards and templates for creating a new FrontPage web.

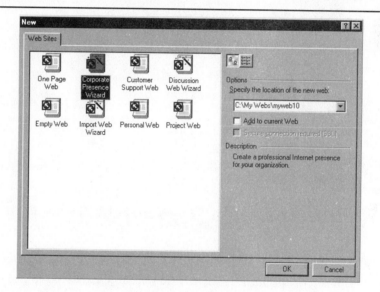

4. Click OK. The Create New FrontPage Web dialog box appears and remains on screen while the web is being created. Then the dialog box closes automatically, and the first Corporate Presence Web Wizard dialog box appears.

5. The first Corporate Presence Web Wizard dialog box includes some information about the wizard—read it. You can customize the Web pages about to be generated, but for the moment, our goal is to investigate how the Corporate Presence Web Wizard works with the Tasks view. (See Chapter 2, *Exploring FrontPage 2000*, for more information about using wizards and templates to create Web sites.) For

now, simply click the Finish button. The Corporate Presence Web Wizard dialog box closes after a few moments and the FrontPage window reappears, with the Web site you just created displayed in the Tasks view, as shown in Figure 7.2.

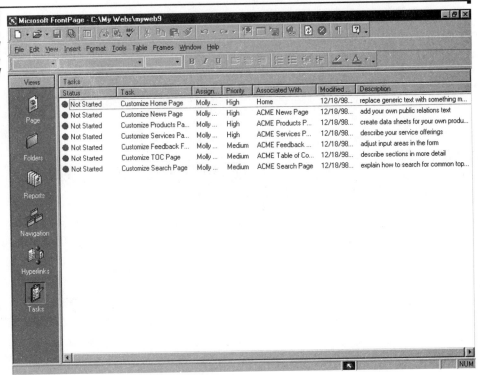

Each task you see in the Tasks view points out something that needs to be done to finish a page in the newly created web. You don't have to complete the tasks now; the purpose of the Task list is to remind you of what needs to be done so you can go about doing other things and return to these tasks when you're ready. Feel free to explore the new corporate web first. Go ahead and check out your new corporate web with the other views, consider your overall plan of action, then return to the Tasks view later.

NOTE   When you are ready to work with existing tasks, you can switch to the Tasks view by selecting the Tasks icon from the Views toolbar, or select View ➤ Task from the main menu.

Working with the Tasks View

When you open the Tasks view for a given web, a Task list appears showing which tasks need to be completed. For example, Figure 7.2 showed tasks that were created by the Corporate Presence Wizard. (The number of tasks on your screen will vary depending on several factors, including how many pages were created by the wizard, if you used one.) In general, tasks are displayed in rows with information about the tasks shown in columns:

- The *Status* of the task designates the task as Not Started, In Progress, or Completed. Initially, all tasks are assigned a status of Not Started.

- The *Task* column lists the name of each task. (Every task has to have a name.)

- The *Assigned To* column lists the name of the person assigned to complete the task. (By default, the user who created the task is responsible, but you can assign the task to someone else if you want; see "Assigning a Task to a User.")

- The *Priority* column indicates whether the task is given High, Medium, or Low priority.

- The *Associated With* column shows which Web page is associated with each task. (Not every task has to have an associated Web page, but most tasks are specific to a particular page.)

- The *Modified Date* column indicates when the task was last modified; initially, this is when the task was created, but later it's presumably when the task was last addressed.

- The *Description* column shows detailed information about each task (whether that information was entered by a wizard or by an individual).

Depending on your screen's resolution, you might not be able to see all of the columns in the Task list at once. (If this is so, you can scroll horizontally to see additional columns.) To learn to modify the layout of columns in the Task list, see the sidebar "Customizing the Task Column Layout and Sorting Tasks by Column." To delve into working with tasks, read on.

Starting a Task

When you're ready to start working on a task, you must first indicate which task you want to tackle, so the appropriate page will appear and your progress on the task can be tracked. Just follow these steps:

1. With a web open in FrontPage, select View ➢ Tasks (or click the Tasks button). A Task list appears, showing the outstanding tasks for this web.

NOTE To find out more about a task, just double-click it. A Task Details dialog box appears, as shown (for the first task in our list) in Figure 7.3. To complete the task, click the Start Task button and go to step 4.

FIGURE 7.3

In the Task Details dialog box, you can see all of the information about a task in more detail.

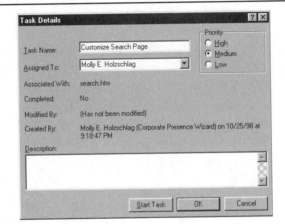

2. In the Task list, highlight the task you want to work on.

3. From the menu bar, select Edit ➢ Task ➢ Start. The Web page associated with that task opens in the FrontPage Editor window.

 TIP As a shortcut, you can simply right-click a task, and from the pop-up menu that appears, select Start Task.

4. Now you can use the techniques described in the rest of this book to make changes to the page in Page view. When you're finished, save your work by selecting (from the menu bar) File ➢ Save.

If you have indeed completed the task at hand, you can mark it as complete (see "Completing a Task" to learn how to do this).

MASTERING THE OPPORTUNITIES

Customizing the Task Column Layout and Sorting Tasks by Column

If you can't see all of the columns when you open up the Tasks view, you can change the width of each column. Just follow these steps:

1. With a web open, click the Tasks icon. The Task list appears.

2. Move your mouse pointer to the vertical bar at the right edge of the heading for the column you want to resize. The mouse pointer changes into a two-headed arrow.

3. Click and drag the mouse to the left to shrink the column, or to the right to widen the column. (You can always adjust a column's width again later if you change your mind.)

Alternatively, if you want to make a column exactly as wide as needed to display the information for each task, you can simply double-click the vertical bar, and the column's width adjusts accordingly.

By default, tasks appear listed in the order they were created. You can sort tasks by clicking the column heading you want to use as sort criteria—for example, to sort tasks by priority, click the Priority heading. The Task list rearranges itself and sorts all the tasks in the list (in ascending order) as you specified. Click a second time to reverse the order to descending. To restore the default order, click once on the Modified Date column heading, and the Task list displays the tasks in the original order.

Completing a Task

You can mark tasks as completed whenever you want, but there's no going back. Once a task is marked completed, you can't change its status. Therefore, you should mark a task as completed only when *everything* needed to finish it has been done. For example, if several team members are responsible for completing a given task, the task should not be marked as completed until all team members have finished their contributions. Similarly, if this team has finished its work on the page, but it needs to be reviewed and approved by a higher authority, do not mark it as completed until it's been reviewed, any last-minute corrections have been made, and the page is approved for posting.

To indicate that a task has been really, truly completed, follow these steps:

1. With a web open in FrontPage, from the menu bar, select View ➤ Tasks. The Task list appears.

2. In the Task list, highlight the task that's been finished.

 WARNING Remember: Once you have marked a task completed, it's done. Be sure you've finished a task before marking it as complete. If you do mark a task completed prematurely, you'll have to delete it and create a new task from scratch to replace it. See "Creating a Task from Scratch" for more information.

3. Now, from the menu bar, select Edit ➤ Task ➤ Mark As Completed. In the Task list's Status column, the task is marked completed.

 TIP Alternately, you can right-click a task in the list and, from the pop-up menu that appears, choose Mark As Completed.

From here, you can switch to a different view to continue working on your Front-Page web, or you can add new tasks using the techniques we'll show you later in this chapter.

Creating a Task from Scratch

Most wizards don't add tasks automatically. Furthermore, you won't always be using a wizard. If you're creating a web using a template or from the ground up, you will have to add tasks to the Task list manually.

You can create two types of tasks: *linked tasks*, which are associated with a particular page or file, and *unlinked tasks* (also known as general tasks), which are associated with the current web (but not with any particular page or file in that web). As examples, you might use a linked task to write a single paragraph of text for a specific page, and use an unlinked task to add a copyright notice or a text-link navigation bar to every page on the site.

NOTE Some FrontPage 2000 features give you an opportunity to add tasks automatically (see "Adding Tasks Using Other FrontPage Features" later in this chapter). For example, you can create a link to a new page without actually creating that page; instead, you just add a task to remind you to create the page later. You can also create tasks in the course of doing routine things to a large site—for example, as you run a spell check, you might want to create tasks as reminders to correct misspelled words, or when you verify hyperlinks you might want to create tasks as reminders to fix the broken ones.

Adding a Task Linked to a Web Page

A linked task, as we've mentioned, is one that's associated with a particular page or file. To create a task that's linked to a particular Web page, follow these steps:

1. With a web open in FrontPage, and with any view that lists the file you want to link as active, highlight the file (see Chapter 2 for more on changing views).

2. From the menu bar, select File ➢ New ➢ Task. Or, right-click the filename, and from the menu that appears, select Add Task. The New Task dialog box appears. (Figure 7.4 shows the dialog box after it's been filled in.)

FIGURE 7.4

*This new task
will remind us to
do a spell check.*

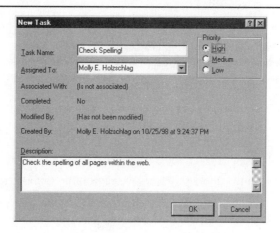

3. In the Task Name text box, type a brief phrase to identify or describe the task. You can include spaces, but try to keep the task name to three words or less because of space limitations in the Task list. You can add a longer description later, as you'll see in step 6.

4. In the Priority area, set an appropriate priority for the task by clicking one of the radio buttons labeled High, Medium, or Low.

5. To assign the task to someone else, type that person's name in the Assign To text box. (We cover this option in more detail later, in the section called "Using the Tasks View in a Team Setting.")

6. If you'd like to add more details about the task, simply type those details into the Description text box.

7. Click OK. The dialog box closes and the view you were in reappears.

You won't see the task listed immediately upon your return to FrontPage, but it will appear next time you change to the Tasks view. To do so, from the menu bar, select View ➢ Tasks.

Adding an Unlinked Task

As mentioned, an unlinked (or general) task is one associated with the current web rather than a single page. It's easy to create unlinked tasks; simply follow these steps:

1. With a web open in FrontPage, from the menu bar, select File ➢ New ➢ Task. The New Task dialog box appears. (Figure 7.4 shows the dialog box after it's been filled in.)

 TIP As a shortcut, you can right-click a blank area of the Task list and, from the pop-up menu that appears, select New Task. Again, the New Task dialog box appears.

2. In the Task Name text box, type a brief phrase to identify or describe the task. You can include spaces, but try to keep the task name to three words or less because of space limitations in the Task list. You can add a longer description later, as you'll see in step 5.

3. In the Priority area, set an appropriate priority for the task by clicking one of the buttons labeled High, Medium, or Low.

4. To assign the task to someone else, type that person's name in the Assign To text box. (We cover this option in more detail in "Using the Tasks View in a Team Setting.")

5. Optionally, you can type in the Description text box an exhaustive description of the task with as much detail as you'd like. This might be helpful, for example, if you are assigning the task to another team member.

6. Click OK. The dialog box closes, the task is saved automatically, and the task you've created appears at the bottom of the Task list.

To confirm the task you just created, double-click its name in the Task list. The Task Details dialog box appears, bearing the information you just entered. Review the information as you like, then click OK to return to the Task list.

 WARNING Because unlinked tasks aren't associated with a particular page, your headway on them cannot be monitored automatically. Thus, if you double-click an unlinked task and the Task Details dialog box appears, it will have no Start Task button in it. You must manually mark the task complete when the time comes. To do so, right-click the task in the Task list and from the pop-up menu that appears, select Mark As Completed.

Adding a Task from Page View

You may find yourself wanting to add a new task to a page you are currently working on in Page view. For example, if you place dummy text on your page as a placeholder, then you'll need to remember to replace that text with the real thing. You can simply add the task from Page view; when you do, the task will be added to the Task list as usual. Follow these steps:

1. With a page open in Page view, from the menu bar, select Edit ➢ Task ➢ Add Task. The New Task dialog box appears.

2. In the Task Name text box, type a brief phrase to identify or describe the task. You can include spaces, but try to keep the task name to three words or less because of space limitations in the Task list. You can add a longer description later, as you'll see in step 5.

3. In the Priority area, set an appropriate priority for the task by clicking one of the buttons labeled High, Medium, or Low.

4. To assign the task to someone else, type that person's name in the Assign To text box. (We cover this option in more detail in "Using the Tasks View in a Team Setting.")

5. Optionally, you can type in the Description text box a long, detailed description of the task. This will help you or other team members to fully understand the task.

NOTE You'll notice that the Created By, Modified By, Completed, and Associated With fields also appear. These fields are already filled in based on the current page, and you cannot modify them.

6. Click OK. The dialog box closes, the task is saved automatically.

You won't see the results of your efforts immediately, because tasks are visible only in FrontPage's Tasks view, and you are now in Page view. You'll need to switch to Tasks view in order to see your new task. Note, too, that you can modify the newly created task or complete it as usual (see the sections "Completing a Task" and "Modifying a Task" for more information).

Adding Tasks Using Other FrontPage Features

Suppose you're checking spelling on your web. In the course of that, a list of the web's pages appears, along with a summary of how many spelling errors were found on each page. If you aren't ready to deal with this tedium right now, you can check the Add A Task For Each Page With Misspellings checkbox in the Spelling dialog box, and new tasks will be created for you automatically—one task for each page that includes spelling errors.

This is a classic example of how you can use the Tasks view in conjunction with other FrontPage features. You can also use the Tasks view in the course of creating new pages and verifying hyperlinks. Let's take a brief look at each of these options.

Using Tasks to Help You Complete a Spell Check

Typos happen. But you don't want to present your finished site to the public with typos lying about, any more than you'd wear an Armani suit with loose threads and tailor's marks showing. To make sure your site looks professional, give it a thorough proofreading, then make corrections. In Chapter 8, *Publishing Your Pages*, we cover checking spelling on your site before you go public. Here we'll give you a brief taste of the process, focusing on using the Tasks view to facilitate it.

If you've spent any time with a word processor, you know how spell checks work in general. Because FrontPage is part of the Microsoft Office family, FrontPage's spell-checking process is very similar to spell checking in Microsoft Word. The difference is that FrontPage can check spelling in all of your web files at once, compiling a report of all pages with spelling errors.

If yours is a large web and you didn't win any spelling bees at school, fixing the spelling mistakes in each file can be a long and drawn-out matter. Rather than completing this in one tedious session, you can have a task created for each page that contains spelling errors. You can then share the chore of making corrections among several members of your team or over a manageable period of time.

To create tasks from a spell check, follow these steps:

1. With a web open in FrontPage, if you want to check only the spelling in a single file, highlight that single file; if you want to check the spelling in your entire web, just move on to step 2.

2. From the menu bar, select Tools ➤ Spelling, and the Spelling dialog box appears.

3. If you want to check spelling on the single page you selected in step 1, click the Selected Page(s) button. To check spelling on all pages in the web, click the Entire Web button.

4. Click the checkbox labeled Add A Task For Each Page With Misspellings.

5. Click the Start button. The spell check begins, and its progress is shown in a dialog box. When it's done, the Spelling dialog box appears, detailing the number of tasks that have been added to the Task list. You won't see this just yet—the only evidence is the Spelling dialog box's notification. One task is added for each page that had misspellings.

6. Close the dialog box.

When you're ready to fix the errors found during the spell check process, follow these steps:

1. With the spell-checked web open in FrontPage, switch to the Tasks view by selecting View ➤ Tasks. A list of outstanding tasks appears.

2. The entries for misspelled words say Fix Misspelled Words. Double-click one of these entries. The Task Details dialog box appears.

3. The dialog box's Description text area will include a list of misspelled words that appear on the page associated with the task. Click the Start Task button and the page itself opens in Page view.

4. The spell checker goes to work, telling you what is misspelled and offering suggestions and options. Fix the spelling, then save the file by selecting (from the menu bar) File ➤ Save.

5. An alert box appears, asking you if you want to mark the task as completed. If you do, click Yes. If you want to come back to the task again, click No, and the file is saved In Progress.

MASTERING WHAT'S ONLINE

Spell checkers don't define words for you. If you want to look up a word to find out what it means, you can't go wrong with the Web's online dictionaries:

One of the most useful is Merriam-Webster's WWWebster Dictionary (www.m-w.com/netdict.htm).

OneLook (www.onelook.com/) offers a one-stop search of over 150 dictionaries; type in your word and you'll get back a wide range of definitions.

For computing terms, check out the PCWebopaedia (www.pcwebopaedia.com/).

The Free Online Dictionary of Computing (FOLDOC) is a straightforward search engine of computing terms, wombat.doc.ic.ac.uk/.

Using Tasks to Help You Create New Pages

Using tasks can help you to manage the creation of new pages, when you know that you need to create a page or even a link but you're tied up with other business. If for some reason you don't want to create a page right away (and don't want to risk forgetting about it later), you can create a new task reminding you to handle the matter. This type of task is called a *Finish* task (because you'll have to *finish* the page later). Follow these steps to create a Finish task:

1. From the FrontPage menu bar, select File ➢ New. The New dialog box appears (see Figure 7.5).

TIP When you are creating a link, instead of targeting an existing page, you can target a page that does not yet exist and add a task reminding you to create the page in the future. To do this, from the menu bar, select Insert ➢ Hyperlink. The Create Hyperlink dialog box appears; in it, click the New Page button. The New dialog box appears, and you can continue on with step 2.

2. From the dialog box's list of templates and wizards, select the type of page you want to create. Along the right side of the dialog box is a description of the selected page and a preview of how it will appear.

FIGURE 7.5

*You don't have to
create a new page
immediately; you
can defer that chore
until a later time.*

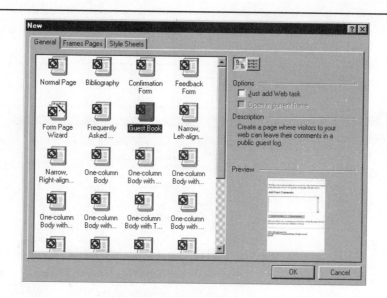

3. Select the Just Add Web Task checkbox.

4. Now click OK and the Save As dialog box appears.

5. In the dialog box's text boxes, type a filename and title for the page.

6. Click OK. The dialog box closes with the page you were originally editing in view again.

You can now continue editing the original page. When you switch back to Front-Page and view your site in the Tasks view (see the section titled "Switching to the Tasks View," earlier in this chapter), you'll see a new task—named *Finish*—added to the Task list.

When you want to complete the task by adding the new page, simply do the following:

1. From FrontPage's menu bar, select View ➢ Tasks. The Tasks view appears.

2. In the Task list, you'll see the new Finish entry for the page you just added. Double-click it. The Task Details dialog box appears (see Figure 7.6).

3. In the dialog box's Description text box, if you plan to work on the task further in the future, type a description of your progress and what still needs to be done to remind yourself or any team members who may also work on the page.

TIP You can also take this opportunity to modify other details of the task. See the section titled "Modifying a Task" for more information.

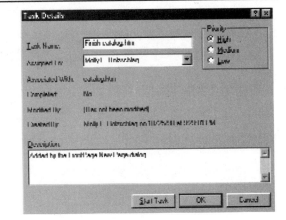

5. To start working on the page, click the dialog box's Start Task button. The new page appears.

6. You can now use all of the tools and methods we describe in the rest of this book to create or change the page. When you're ready to save the page, from the menu bar, select File ➤ Save.

The advantage of this technique is that the Finish task will remind you to create the page later, and you don't have to worry about forgetting your intentions when you do so. You can "sketch" out whole sections of your web and fill in the details at an appropriate time later.

 NOTE Using techniques very similar to those described in the preceding two sections, you can take advantage of the Tasks view's features to assist you or team members in verifying links. We cover verifying links in Chapter 24, *Site Maintenance and Promotion*; turn there for more information.

Modifying a Task

Sometimes you'll want to modify some details about a task. For example, you might want to change its priority, assign the task to someone else, or update its description. Follow these steps:

1. With a web open in FrontPage, from the menu bar, select View ➤ Tasks. The Tasks view appears.

2. Double-click the task you want to modify. The Task Details dialog box appears.

NOTE   With most tasks, there are four fields that you can change: the Task Name text box, the Assigned To text box (which displays the name of the user to whom the task is assigned), the Priority area, and the Description text box. (Any tasks that were added by a wizard will have a fixed task name that you can't change. And with completed tasks, you'll be able to change only the description.) The other fields can't be changed directly, but to get around this you can always just create a new task.

3. Change any of the fields by typing in the appropriate text boxes.

4. Click OK to close the Task Details dialog box. FrontPage's Tasks view reappears. Any changes you made to tasks are visible in the Task list.

You can continue working with the Tasks view of your web by following the directions in the other parts of this chapter, or start working with other views of your site (see Chapter 2 for more information about changing views).

Deleting a Task

While completed tasks are normally hidden, as we mentioned earlier in the section "Completing a Task," they do take up space on the Web server's hard drive. You might want to delete your completed tasks, along with any other tasks that you have no intention of completing.

WARNING   There's no way to undelete a task. Even the Undo command won't work. Be very sure that you really want to delete the task, because there are no second chances.

To delete a task, follow these steps:

1. With a web open in FrontPage, from the menu bar, select View ➤ Tasks. The Tasks view appears.

2. All of the completed tasks appear in the Task list with a green circle (as opposed to a red one) next to them. To delete other sorts of tasks, move on to step 3.

3. Now you can:

   - Click the task you want to delete and press the Delete key.

   - Right-click the task you want to delete and from the menu that appears, select Delete.

   The Confirm Delete dialog box appears.

4. In the dialog box, click Yes. The dialog box closes and the Tasks view of the Front-Page window reappears. The targeted task no longer appears in the Task list.

That's it! The task is gone, never to return. You can now switch to another view in FrontPage or continue to work on other tasks.

Using the Tasks View in a Team Setting

As you've seen throughout this chapter, FrontPage keeps track of who created each task and who is assigned to complete each task. You can also see who last modified a page linked to a task (and the time of the modification as well). These tracking features make using FrontPage 2000 in a workgroup or web team setting a project manager's dream.

 TIP FrontPage doesn't keep a detailed log of changes to a task. Only the most recent change is listed in the Task list's Modified By field. However, you can use FrontPage in conjunction with Microsoft Visual Source Safe (mentioned in Chapter 2), a revision control system that is available as a separate product, to track changes more closely. Visual Source Safe keeps an audit trail of revisions; it allows you or team members to return to any version of the file at any time, so if you decide you preferred an iteration that occurred two weeks ago, you'll still have access to it. This can be very handy indeed.

To work properly as a team, you'll need to make sure each person logs into the network correctly (with his or her own unique username) and that the web is set up correctly, with the proper permissions in place for each member of the team. (Chapter 24 covers making assignments and setting permissions for webs.) In organizing a team or workgroup to work on a Web site, the most fundamental consideration is whether the team will have assigned areas of the site (a decentralized approach) or assigned tasks that will occur all over the site (a centralized approach).

There are pros and cons either way: In a decentralized approach, individuals (or smaller teams) "own" that area or web, providing for an increased sense of pride and responsibility (as well as increased accountability).

In a centralized approach, one key player can have greater control over the big picture, with team members carrying out various functions in a more assembly line–like manner that can be very efficient. As team leader or manager, you need to decide which approach you will take and make assignments and set permissions accordingly. You may want to assign and set permissions for a whole area of the site or a specific web to a given person, or you may want to assign and set permissions on a task by task basis. Again, Chapter 24 covers setting permissions; you must set appropriate permissions before you can assign tasks to individuals.

 TIP Remember to set permissions for team members who are to check other people's work. For example, if you have a review team or quality assurance person who has to check the work of others, permissions must be set accordingly.

Assigning a Task to a User

By default, FrontPage assigns a task to the person who created it. You may want to assign things differently, however. You can assign any user to a task. Follow these steps:

1. With a web open in FrontPage, from the menu bar, select View ➢ Tasks. The Tasks view appears.

2. In the Task list, double-click the task you want to reassign. The Task Details dialog box appears.

3. In the Assigned To text box, type the name of the user who should do the task, or select a name from the drop-down list. (See the sidebar "On Usernames and FrontPage" for tips and cautions.) You can use a group name here, or you can type whatever name you want in this space, as shown below.

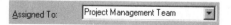

4. Click OK. The Task Details dialog box closes and the Tasks view of the FrontPage window reappears. The entry for the task you selected in step 1 now includes the new name.

 TIP Whenever you create a new task (regardless of how you go about creating it), you can quickly assign it to a user other than yourself by entering that person's name in the New Task dialog box's Assigned To text box. See "Creating a Task from Scratch."

 MASTERING TROUBLESHOOTING

On Usernames and FrontPage

When you first switch on your computer, Windows displays a login dialog box, with text boxes for your username and password. It's best and simplest all the way around if you use that same username here. Usernames are usually only one word long.

Note that you will not be forced to use a username from the list of users and groups assigned to the web as a whole. This means that you have to make certain the correct username is listed for each task. It's helpful to make a list of usernames for your team members and distribute it to ensure that everyone is using this list consistently.

 NOTE Anyone who has the correct permissions can complete a task, whether or not it was originally assigned to that person.

Tracking Modifications

Knowing who completes or modifies a task is of great concern to you, the team leader. FrontPage keeps track of the last person who worked on a task along with the last time they saved the file. This information is recorded in the Task list's Modified By field, in FrontPage's Tasks view.

If you want to know who last worked on a task and when, follow these steps:

1. With a web open in FrontPage, from the menu bar, select View ➤ Tasks. The Tasks view appears.

NOTE Make sure that everyone working on a task has used the correct username and has logged in properly.

2. Double-click the desired task. The Task Details dialog box appears. Note especially the information listed in the Created By and Modified By fields. (If the task is already completed, the Modified By field will have been replaced with a Completed By field. If the task is an unlinked task, the Modified By field will always say Has not been modified.)

3. Click OK. The dialog box closes and the FrontPage window reappears.

MASTERING WHAT'S ONLINE

In some ways, FrontPage's Tasks view acts like scaled-down project management software.

Microsoft Project is a full-featured project manager program you can use in addition to FrontPage; read more about this popular application at the Microsoft Project home page (www.microsoft.com/project).

Plenty of other companies also sell project management software; Yahoo!'s list (www .yahoo.com/Business_and_Economy/Companies/Computers/Software/Business/ Project_Management) will keep you busy if you want to comparison shop.

Up Next

Now that you've learned not only how to create and modify pages in FrontPage, but also basic web management skills, it's time to try out the next logical step: making your site live on the Internet!

Don't worry if you feel as though your site isn't ready for prime time. We're going to work on advanced design concepts in upcoming sections of the book. However, it is time to get your feet wet with the aspects of FrontPage that you'll need to use when you do feel confident about your site. So, let's move on to Chapter 8, *Publishing Your Pages*.

CHAPTER **8**

Publishing Your Pages

You've been having fun designing your Web pages, but those pages won't do you any good if they sit on your computer, unread and unloved. What you want to do is share them with the world! So far in this book, you've seen how to use FrontPage and design Web pages—now we'll show you how to take your labor of love and *publish* it on the Web so that it can be admired by Web surfers around the world, everywhere from Australia to Zimbabwe.

To be a part of the World Wide Web, your FrontPage web must be *published* (or uploaded) to a Web server. You'll need an account with an *Internet service provider (ISP)* or access to your company's Web server. If you need help choosing an ISP, see the section titled "Choosing an Internet Service Provider or Internet Presence Provider" later in this chapter.

 NOTE To publish online, your computer must be connected to the Internet; you can then use a Web server that belongs to you (or your organization), or rely on your ISP's Web server. In this chapter, we'll talk about those options.

Publishing, in this context, is simply the process of copying all the files that make up a page or a site to the proper computer. Without FrontPage, this can be a complex task requiring knowledge of *FTP (File Transfer Protocol)*, file permissions, and other technology skills. One of FrontPage's many qualities is that it takes care of these details and makes them easy for you to manage.

Once you've specified the name of the Web server to publish to, the URL (Uniform Resource Locator, the address assigned to you by your ISP), and some other basic information, you can forever after publish changes and new pages with the click of a button.

MASTERING THE OPPORTUNITIES

Types of Sites

There are three important types of Web sites you should know about, as they immediately relate to the publishing process. They are:

Internet An Internet Web site is a typical, public site that all people with Internet access can visit.

Continued

MASTERING THE OPPORTUNITIES CONTINUED

Intranet An intranet site is a site that's restricted to a company's in-house networking needs. The company's internal network is built using the same technologies used to build an Internet, but the material is private and accessible only by those with access privileges.

Extranet Many times, companies want to exchange specific internal, intranet-based information with sub-contractors, vendors, and related companies without allowing access to certain other internal data. An extranet is a proprietary and private Web site that allows access to specified external entities.

Alternatively, you can create a FrontPage web and set it up as an intranet so that everyone on your company's in-house network can browse it. Or, you can restrict access to just those people to whom you give permission to visit the site. In that case, no one outside your organization's intranet will have access to it, and you can create and publish on it private company Web pages about your department or your projects. In this chapter, in addition to showing you how to publish a public Web site, we'll show you how to publish your FrontPage web to an intranet. Finally, we'll make sure you are familiar with making changes so you can regularly update your Web pages with ease.

The Stages of Publishing

When software manufacturers are in the process of creating a product, they go through two distinct stages: *alpha* testing, which is internal testing that occurs while the software is being developed, then *beta* testing, which is broader-based testing by a larger group of interested parties, sometimes including outsiders. When beta testing is finished, the product is ready to be shipped to the manufacturer or otherwise presented for public consumption.

Your Web site will go through both of these stages before it is launched. During page or site development, think of yourself (and the site) as being in the alpha stage. Because you have FrontPage, you'll be using your local computer as a Web server, but the only person who will use that Web server is you (and your team, if more than one person is building your site). As you work on your Web site, you should constantly test your page using various browsers, and refine your design and content as necessary. (See Chapter 16, *Cross-Browser Design*, for information about which browsers are in use and how you can design your pages to accommodate their capabilities.)

TIP Use the techniques we showed you in Chapter 1 for creating a storyboard and structure, working out navigational elements, and building a prototype. Show your work to a small group of colleagues if you like—it doesn't hurt to get feedback along the way.

When you've gotten your site more or less together, prepare to enter *beta* testing. Round up some good people who can test your Web site and give you detailed feedback. It's a good idea to set up or borrow space on a temporary Web server called a *staging server*. (You can simply use a secret directory on your normal Web server if you like.)

Later in this chapter, in the section titled, "Publishing Your FrontPage Web to a Web Server," we'll describe how to publish your FrontPage web to this staging server, by setting up a temporary URL. Distribute this temporary URL only to your beta testers and ask them to let you know what they think. Keep your FrontPage web on the staging server during its testing and refining. You may go through several major revisions, publishing different versions of your site and going through a new cycle of soliciting more feedback (recruiting new beta testers if necessary). When you've resolved the beta testers' issues to your satisfaction, beta testing is finished—and you're ready to publish your Web site to its final location.

 TIP You can assign beta testing to a select group of co-workers if yours is a company site, or you can hire freelance editors and reviewers to look at it. Or, whether you have a company site or personal site, you may be able to get volunteers by posting a request to a Usenet newsgroup such as comp.infosystems.www.authoring.html, or a newsgroup related to your Web site's topic. Be sure to keep your postings short, relevant, and specific. Don't post to more than two or three newsgroups; be familiar with the newsgroup and what is normally posted there; read the newsgroup diligently after you post to follow up on any questions or comments; and don't post your announcement more than once. Any other approach is a violation of Usenet etiquette and will earn you a bad reputation and no beta testers.

Web Publishing Options

Now that you know about the publishing process, let's look at how to get your Front-Page webs onto a remote Web server. As mentioned, to publish on the Web, you need an Internet connection. You also need access to a Web server, which can be had either through your company (if it runs its own servers) or through your ISP, which will usu-ally offer you space on their Web server as part of a package deal.

MASTERING WHAT'S ONLINE

Within limits, you can publish on the Web for free. Geocities (www.geocities.com/) offers free Web home pages and e-mail on the Web. Many other free Web services are available; to find a long list, go to Yahoo! (www.yahoo.com/) and search for *Free Web Pages*. Note, however, that some free Web page services focus less on customer service or will offer you only a tiny amount of space. Others operate on a shoestring. Almost all place advertisements somewhere on your page. For a truly professional site, you're going to have to purchase service.

Choosing an Internet Service Provider or Internet Presence Provider

The world of Web-hosting services is divided into two categories. ISPs provide hosting but no assistance with content, presentation, or other issues one might want a consultant for. *IPPs* (*Internet presence providers*) offer a range of services that might include devel-oping concept, design, implementation, hosting, and consulting on a range of topics such as site promotion, managing online transaction systems, and so on. Which is best for you is usually a matter of your budget and what resources you have on hand to handle strategy, design, and implementation. (Obviously, you'll pay more for a wider range of services.) Most people opt for the ISP route; let's look at that one.

Assuming you have an e-mail account and a Web browser, you might first investi-gate what the provider of your Internet service offers; if yours is a small site, this may be the simplest and best way to go. If yours is a larger site, you'll need more server space and perhaps more attention from the folks running the ISP that hosts your site, and the expense will go up accordingly. In that case, you'll want to shop around. Your best bet is to ask around, to look in print publications including the local phone book, or to search the Web for a local or national provider, and compare and contrast prices and services.

MASTERING WHAT'S ONLINE

Microsoft lists registered companies that will host your FrontPage webs, and each of these has the FrontPage Server Extensions installed, which is a plus. For more information, check out `microsoft.saltmine.com/frontpage/wpp/list/`.

Other hosting companies include budgetweb (`www.budgetweb.com/`) and The Blade (`www.theblade.org/`), and a big, famous list is at The List (`www.thelist.com/`). Yahoo!'s general listing is at `www.yahoo.com/Business_and_Economy/Companies/ Internet_Services/Internet_Access_Providers`.

Most ISPs offer information about themselves—once you have some likely candidates, go to their home pages and have a look (for example, the home page for DNAI, a good local ISP in the San Francisco area, is `www.dnai.com`). Many ISPs even let you sign up online.

What to look for? Well, local ISPs typically offer more personal service and lower overall fees than national ISPs. They are also often familiar with local businesses and computer groups. National ISPs, on the other hand, can sometimes provide more consistent service than local ISPs because they have the resources to continue on during such temporary emergencies as poor weather conditions, power outages, or equipment failure.

Phone each ISP and ask questions. What's most important to you will vary depending on the purpose, content, and audience of your site. Here are some things to focus on:

Reliability Does the ISP have onsite technicians? Are they there 24/7? How often are backups performed? How will they handle power outages, earthquakes, bad weather conditions, and other potential disruptions to service?

Disk space How much disk space is allocated? Usually 5 to 20MB will be included in the basic monthly fee; find out what they charge for more if you need it. Remember that sites get bigger as they grow older and include more content. Remember, too, that one AVI file can take as much disk space as 1,000 HTML files, so how much disk space you need depends heavily on what sort of content you'll publish.

The FrontPage Server Extensions Do they have them installed? If not, will they install them? (Some of the advanced features of FrontPage just won't work without them.)

Scripting Can they handle any scripts your site might use?

Live content Are they set up to handle any sort of live content you plan?

Traffic levels What if your site goes through the roof? How much traffic can they manage successfully? Also, will they charge extra for heavy traffic should you be lucky enough to experience it?

Databases Do they support databases? If so, can they help you get your database into the format they support? And can they deal with Active Server Pages (ASPs)?

Transactions Do they offer a secure server for online transactions? Do they charge extra for using it? What sort of technical and customer service support is provided for this, if any?

Domain name Will they allow you to have your own domain name? (Most do, but you should check, just in case.)

Consulting vs. hosting How much consulting or general assistance will they provide? Are they actually an ISP or an IPP? Are there stepped-up package deals—for example, design plus hosting at one price, design plus hosting plus concept development at another?

Customer service How is customer service? Ask them about this, for sure, but also pay attention to your experience with them—are they helpful and polite? Do they answer questions quickly and accurately? Do they answer the phone and respond to messages in a timely way? Actions speak louder than words; how does their actual treatment of you compare to what they say their customer service policy is?

Cost What's all this going to set you back? Be sure to ask about any extra expenses hidden in the potential use of databases, extra disk space, high traffic, and so on.

Any additional offerings What sets this service apart? Ask them this outright, but again, make your own assessment not only by comparing Company A's answers to Company B's answers, but also by comparing what each company says to what you experience from them in the course of your investigations. Do they fulfill the stated or implied promises of their marketing hype? Do they seem, after all your questioning, to be a good, reliable company? What makes them stand out in a way that's useful to you?

Registering a Domain Name

A business Web site, to look professional, must have its own domain name. Using a virtual domain name (one that is actually the domain name of your ISP, with a little identifier tacked on, like `www.ispco.com/~joe`, is like having a P.O. box as your company address—it just points out that you are small-time stuff. A custom domain name is usually also easier to type and remember. For example, Rupert's URL for his site hosted at Best would be `www.best.com/~rupert/`. But if Rupert gets a custom domain name, then his URL becomes `www.rupert.com/`. Rupert's customers won't know if Rupert has his own Web server or if he uses an ISP; what they will sense, however, is that Rupert's business is more professional and credible, and they'll remember where it is (at `rupert.com`). Perhaps most beneficial of all, domain names can be transferred from one ISP or IPP to another, if you decide to switch to a different provider.

Getting a domain name is inexpensive and relatively easy. (The hard part is finding one that isn't already taken.) All domain names that end in `.com` or `.org` must be registered through InterNIC (`www.internic.net/`). Geographical domains like `.uk`, `.jp`, and `.us` are handled by individual country registries. Your domain name for a U.S. business should end in `.com`; but if you're nonprofit, your domain name should end in `.org`. InterNIC requires a contact person and their name, phone number, and address for each domain.

To find out if your desired domain name is available, visit InterNIC's "whois" service at `www.internic.net`. By following the instructions on the page, you can check for your desired domain name's availability. Another quick trick is to use your browser to try to access a site with your potential domain name; just type it in as part of a basic URL and see if you turn up anything.

In researching potential domain names via InterNIC, don't type in a URL or machine name—just type the domain name (for example, `rupert.com`). Don't be surprised if your first choice is already taken. There are only so many words in the language. Remember, domains can contain only letters, numbers, and a hyphen; other punctuation (including spaces) is not allowed. In addition, domain names can be only 26 letters—and after the period and three letters for `.com` or `.org`, that leaves you only 22 letters. You'll have to be creative about this. For example, if your site promotes fresh produce, you are quite likely to find that `freshproduce.com` and `vegetables.com` are taken; but `rutabagas.com` or `vegco.com` *might* not be.

Continued

MASTERING THE OPPORTUNITIES CONTINUED

Once you find an available domain name you like, you'll have several forms to fill out. Rather than do this yourself, the easiest way to register a domain name with InterNIC is through your ISP or IPP. The typical setup fee can range from $20 to $200. In addition, InterNIC charges $70 for the first two years, and then $35 per year after that; these fees are not negotiable. Your ISP or IPP may charge a monthly fee or yearly fee on top of the setup fee and in addition to the InterNIC charges. As usual, our advice is to shop around; many ISPs and IPPs will register a domain name for a small setup fee when you sign up, as an incentive, and won't charge any fees after that.

Publishing Your FrontPage Web

Now let's look at how to actually publish your FrontPage web to a Web server. In this discussion, there are two types of Web servers: those with the FrontPage Server Extensions, and those without. The procedures for publishing to each vary a bit. It will help somewhat if you know in advance whether the machine to which you'll be publishing has the FrontPage Server Extensions. But if you don't know, you'll be notified along the way and adjustments will be made automatically, so you can in fact start out assuming that the FrontPage Server Extensions are there.

 TIP If you're still in the alpha or beta stages of designing your Web site, you can use these publishing techniques to put your Web site on a staging server. Then finish your site and be sure that testing is complete. Be sure that every link works (use the Verify Hyperlinks command discussed in Chapter 24, *Site Maintenance and Promotion*), and that you've tested your site using as many browsers as possible. Are all of your tasks completed? (See Chapter 7, *Managing Tasks.*) In Chapter 3, *Working in Page View*, we showed you how to spell check your pages, and in Chapter 7, how to spell check an entire web using FrontPage's Task feature. Once you've actually published your Web site, you can begin maintaining and promoting the site (see Chapter 24).

Table 8.1 lists which features depend on the FrontPage Server Extensions and which ones work without them. If you find that you don't have the Server Extensions installed at all, you can simply install them, as described in Appendix C.

A common problem that may exist with installed Server Extensions is that the FrontPage 97 or 98 Server Extensions are installed instead of the 2000 version. FrontPage 2000 includes some features that earlier versions do not support. Of course it's best to simply upgrade your Server Extensions to the 2000 version, but if that's not possible, keep in mind these issues:

- Text on images and navigation bars or page banners in the body of the page can simply vanish.

- Pages that connect to a database (see Chapter 23, *Adding Databases for Maximum Impact*) might not work correctly.

- Certain themes, image bullets, and page banners will not be supported. Because these features are only decorative, this may not be a terrible loss.

Shared borders and the automatic FrontPage navigation structure are also unsupported, which is a much bigger problem. When you publish your web, FrontPage 2000 will detect that earlier FrontPage Server Extensions are installed, and will give you a choice. You can publish your web without these features, so that people browsing the site won't see them but you'll still be able to author your site on the remote server. Or, you can publish your web with those features, so that people browsing the site will see them but you won't be able to author the site on the remote server. In that last case, you'll instead have to keep your web on your local computer, make changes locally, and republish the web whenever you've made a change.

TABLE 8.1: FEATURES THAT REQUIRE FRONTPAGE SERVER EXTENSIONS	
Require Server Extensions	**Do Not Require Server Extensions**
Easy publishing (without the Web Publishing Wizard)	FTP publishing (with the Web Publishing Wizard)
FrontPage form handlers (see Chapter 14)	CGI form handlers that you install yourself, or mailto form handlers (see Chapter 14)
Many FrontPage components (Confirmation Field, Hit Counter, Search Form, Scheduled Image, and Scheduled Included Page; see Chapter 15)	HTML tags and attributes (including links, frames, tables, images, and multimedia) and basic formatting

TABLE 8.1 (CONTINUED): FEATURES THAT REQUIRE FRONTPAGE SERVER EXTENSIONS	
Require Server Extensions	**Do Not Require Server Extensions**
Server-side image maps (see Chapter 9)	Client-side image maps (see Chapter 9)
Some active elements (including the Banner Ad Manager)	Advanced features that do not require special server support (Java applets, plug-ins, ActiveX controls, scripts; see Chapters 21 and 22)
Active themes (any of the advanced themes that incorporate the above features)	Basic themes
Any page templates that depend on the above features, including Confirmation Form, Feedback Form, the Form Page Wizard, Guest Book, Search Page, and User Registration	Any page templates that build static pages or pages that can be generated by FrontPage ahead of time (including a table of contents, navigation bars, and shared borders)
Any FrontPage web templates that include pages that depend on these features, including the Discussion Web Wizard	Normal FrontPage web templates that don't include pages that are not supported

 NOTE Because in an intranet setting you usually have physical access to the computers involved (as well as the appropriate permissions), you can install the FrontPage Server Extensions to the server manually if they're not available. But if your ISP's remote Web server doesn't have the Extensions, you'll have to contact your ISP and persuade them to install those Server Extensions designed for their operating system and Web server. Direct them to Microsoft's FrontPage Server Extensions Web site, at www.microsoft.com/front-page/IPP/.

Publishing to a Web Server

Because FrontPage 2000 can automatically detect whether the FrontPage Server Extensions are installed (and compensate if they're not), it's quite safe to assume that they are and proceed as if they are.

Publishing to the Internet

Before you get too revved up, make sure your computer is connected to the Internet and that you know the full URL for the machine to which you'll be publishing your web—the target server. Once you've got that info, follow these steps:

1. With the web you want to publish open in FrontPage, from the menu bar, select File ➤ Publish Web. The Publish FrontPage Web dialog box appears (Figure 8.1).

FIGURE 8.1

The Publish FrontPage Web dialog box

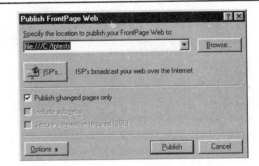

2. Near the top of the Publish FrontPage Web dialog box, you'll see a text box labeled "Specify the location to publish your FrontPage Web to." Type a location in the text box, or click the arrow to see a drop-down list of all the places you've published webs before. If you see the location for today's target server there, select it.

 NOTE If yours is a custom domain name, you may have to use your ISP's or IPP's machine name instead of your custom domain name while publishing your web. The technical support people at your ISP or IPP can help you determine the proper name to use.

3. In the Publish FrontPage Web dialog box, by default, a check mark will appear next to the Publish Changed Pages Only checkbox. Because this is the first time you're publishing this web, deselect this option.

 WARNING When you publish to a location you've published to before, the old files are erased from that server and replaced with the new files. Before you do this, make certain that this is your intention. The last thing you want to do is accidentally erase your important documents.

4. Click OK. The dialog box closes and the publishing process begins in FrontPage. If the Server Extensions are installed, the installation process proceeds and uploading starts. The upload's progress is indicated by the Microsoft FrontPage Web status box.

A large web can take five minutes or more to publish. Go get coffee or something, because even after the progress counter in the status bar reaches 100%, you'll have to wait while FrontPage updates the target Web server at the remote location. When your upload is finished, you'll see a dialog box telling you that your new web has been successfully published.

At this point you will want to test your web on the remote Web server. Launch your Web browser and type in the URL for the remote Web server (including any folder name at the end, if you used one). The Web pages that make up that web should appear; be sure to test all of their features.

Notes on Publishing on an Intranet

To publish your web to an intranet machine, you'll need to know the name of the computer ahead of time. Then you can follow exactly the same procedure outlined in the section before this one. The only difference is that things should go a lot faster—since you're managing the site via a network rather than a mode. Also, the name of the Web server you select in step 2 will be the designated computer's name on your intranet, such as fargo or server or bob.

Using the Web Publishing Wizard

In the previous section, "Publishing to the Internet," if you got to step 4 and learned that you did not have the Server Extensions installed, the Web Publishing Wizard appeared (see Figure 8.2). Proceed by following these steps:

1. In the Web Server Name text box, type the name of the Web server to which you are uploading your web.

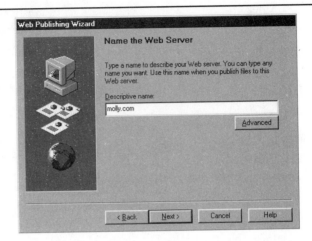

2. In the Directory Path text box, type the name of the directory into which the files should be uploaded. (Your ISP or IPP can provide this information.)

3. Click Next to continue. The second wizard panel appears.

4. In the User Name text box, type your username.

5. In the Password text box, type your password.

6. Click Finish and the upload begins. If any of the pages you are publishing require the FrontPage Server Extensions, a warning dialog box appears; you can click Cancel to return to the Editor and change the problematic page so that it does not require the Server Extensions (see Table 8.1), or you can click Continue to continue publishing the web (including the page that does not function correctly). The Transferring Files dialog box appears.

7. When the whole process is over, the dialog box closes and the words "Published to," followed by the remote server's URL, appear at the bottom of the window.

Publishing is a success! You'll want to test your Web site in several browsers and make sure that you remember to fix pages that aren't working.

Publishing What's Changed on Your Web

There are two common approaches to making changes to your Web site: live updating and local authoring. *Live updating* is the process of editing the Web site at its actual remote location, so that any changes are reflected as soon as you save the file. *Local authoring* is a process by which you make changes on your local computer, and go through the publishing procedure to copy these changes to your site.

WARNING Use one method or the other. And make sure your whole Web team uses the same method, too. If some people are making changes on the remote site while you make changes to the local site, you'll have no way to synchronize the differences. You'll either have to overwrite the changes made remotely when you publish your changes, or import the remote file to get the remote changes, which will cause you to lose the changes you've made locally.

Making Changes Directly on the Remote Web Server

To use the live updating approach, you'll either have to edit the files on the Web server directly (not recommended because it leaves you without a backup copy of the work you are currently doing), or open the web by using FrontPage's remote authoring capability. To use remote authoring, follow these steps:

1. From FrontPage's menu bar, select File ➤ Open FrontPage Web. The Getting Started dialog box appears.

2. Click the More Webs button. The Open FrontPage Web dialog box appears.

3. In the "Select a Web server or disk location" text box, type the name of the remote computer (such as `fargo` or `www.happyfunco.com`). Then click the List Webs button. After a few seconds, the FrontPage webs stored at the remote location appear. (If they don't, either you've mistyped the remote computer's name or remote authoring has been disabled. This could be because the remote computer requires special permissions, is protected by a firewall, or doesn't have the FrontPage Server Extensions installed.)

4. Click the name of the FrontPage web you want to work with, then click OK. The selected web appears in Page view.

Now you can use the methods and techniques described throughout this book to make changes, and when you save the file, it will be saved and automatically published to the remote Web site, so that any changes are immediately available on the Internet or your intranet.

Publishing Local Changes to a Remote Web Server

Things change—especially on the Web. After you've published your web to a Web server, you'll probably find yourself wanting to change or add a few pages. When you're ready to upload fresh pages to the Web server, you don't have to wait and upload the entire web. You can elect to upload only those files that have changed since the last time you uploaded. This can save a great deal of time, especially if you're dealing with a large Web site. Follow these steps:

1. With the web page you want to upload open in FrontPage, select File ➢ Publish Web. The Publish dialog box appears.

2. In this dialog box, verify that the "Publish changed pages only" checkbox is selected.

3. In the list of sites to which you've recently published, select the target server—the one to which you plan to publish.

4. Click OK, and files are copied to that Web server. The Publish dialog box closes, and the status bar shows that publishing is a success.

In the following section, we'll cover how to delete a web you've uploaded in the past and no longer want on the server.

Deleting Remote Webs That You've Published

Okay, the day might come when you need to delete a FrontPage web. Perhaps it was just a test web. Perhaps the company has folded. Perhaps it's a remote copy that's outdated and you're about to replace it. Bottom line: you need to kill the pages. How? Simply delete the FrontPage web on the remote Web server.

 WARNING A deleted web cannot be resurrected. The Undo command won't work, and there's no recycle bin or trash can from which to recover the files. Make sure you mean it when you kill a web—deleted webs are really, truly, absolutely gone.

 TIP If you've kept a copy of the web locally, however, you can republish it in place of the web you've deleted.

To delete a web on a remote server, follow these steps:

1. From the FrontPage menu bar, select File ➤ Open FrontPage Web. The Getting Started dialog box appears.

2. If the doomed web's URL appears in the list of recently accessed webs near the top of the dialog box, select it.

 TIP   If the doomed web does not appear in the list, select the More Webs button to display the Open FrontPage Web dialog box. In the Select A Web Server Or Disk Location text box, type the name of the Web server on which the doomed web resides. Now click OK, and a complete list of the webs on that server appears. Highlight the one you plan to kill off and click OK to proceed to step 3.

3. In the Getting Started dialog box, click OK. The web of interest appears in Page view.

4. From the menu bar, select File ➤ Delete FrontPage Web. The Confirm dialog box appears.

5. Click Yes. The Confirm dialog box closes and the web is deleted. The Getting Started dialog box reappears.

 NOTE   To delete a web this way, the server that holds the web must have the FrontPage Server Extensions installed. If it doesn't, you'll have to delete the files manually on the remote Web server—a procedure that varies depending on the computer's operating system.

Up Next

Now that you know how to publish your FrontPage webs to an intranet and onto the Web, you've learned all of the basics and finished Part I! Give yourself a pat on the back. But don't relax for too long: Your competitors are jazzing up their sites with advanced features like multimedia, tables, and frames. To find out about these features, Part II will tell you everything you need to know—starting with a lot of information about graphics, animation, and image maps.

Creating Sophisticated Designs

LEARN TO:

- Design great Web graphics

- Add multimedia to your sites

- Create framed pages

- Use style sheets

- Make feedback forms

- Add special effects

- Design across browsers and platforms

CHAPTER <u>9</u>

Designing Graphics for the Web

Once upon a few short years ago, a Web site was mainly very plain text on a very dull gray background, with few images in sight. Well, the times they sure have a-changed, and these days Web sites are rich, lively, highly visual presentations. From drawings to photographs, artistic treatments of text, and even animations, the Web is alive with color, texture, and motion.

In this chapter, you'll learn to create and modify visual elements for your Web page, allowing you to add features that will bring your site from the simple to the lively and colorful ranks of the sophisticated.

Imaging Programs and File Formats

On the Web, art is rarely art for art's sake; plenty of art exists as something to aid navigation or entertain, inform, or attract users. In this chapter, you'll get a good look at how to create standard graphics, how to produce *image maps* (images with clickable hotspots), and even how to include lively animations in your pages.

To create images, you'll need an imaging program. There are many available, and two of importance are from Microsoft: PhotoDraw and Image Composer. The examples in this chapter use both of these programs. PhotoDraw is featured due to its membership, like FrontPage, in the Office family. (The evaluation version of PhotoDraw is included on the CD-ROM accompanying this book.) Image Composer is looked at in detail because of its wide popularity among users of earlier versions of FrontPage, as well as the general public.

However, before we show you how to make Web graphics with these two programs, there are a variety of other imaging programs, also referred to simply as *graphics software*, that demand attention. Different graphics software packages work for different folks; which one works for you will depend on your work habits and what sorts of imaging tasks you do most often. While both PhotoDraw and Image Composer are sturdy choices and may be just right for you; you also might want to consider other options. (For more about graphic imaging programs, see Chapter 18, *Working with Professional Graphics Programs*.)

If you are a graphic designer, or aspire to a profession in graphics, Adobe Photoshop and Adobe Illustrator are considered industry standards. Less costly alternatives from the Adobe family include Adobe ImageStyler and Adobe ImageReady. Fans of Macromedia products will enjoy Macromedia Fireworks, a graphics software package built just for the Web. Corel Draw! is a popular product, and even more popular among personal Web page enthusiasts is Jasc's Paint Shop Pro, a low-cost shareware solution that packs a powerful punch and offers many of the same features as the more expensive alternatives. Another suite of popular Web graphics tools is available from Ulead. Be sure to visit the sidebar in this section for a list of Web sites where you can download demos of these programs. Macromedia Fireworks, Jasc's Paint Shop Pro, and several

Ulead products can be found on this book's CD-ROM. (Learn to think like a designer with a visit to Chapter 16, *Understanding Advanced Web Design*.)

Choose the package you find most suitable for your budget and needs, and you'll be well equipped to create your own images especially for the Web. And, once you have the program in hand, the real work begins!

MASTERING WHAT'S ONLINE

To take a look at Adobe's offerings, visit www.adobe.com. Macromedia's Fireworks can be found at www.macromedia.com. Corel Draw! and related software is a short jump away, at www.corel.com, as is Jasc's PaintShop Pro, at www.jasc.com. Finally, visit www.ulead.com for a look at these lower cost but punch-packing packages.

PART

II

Creating
Sophisticated
Designs

GIFs and JPEGs

It's important to know that almost all graphics on the Web exist in one of two file formats: *GIF* or *JPEG*. These two file types are universally supported by most browsers, which accounts for their popularity. While many other graphics formats exist, support for GIF and JPEG is the most comprehensive, and therefore the most desirable.

On the Web, small files are good files, and both GIF and JPEG can make small files, although they do this in different ways. Much of how small, yet clear, your Web graphics will be depends upon choosing the appropriate file format for each individual graphic placed on your page.

GIF stands for *Graphic Interchange Format*; this friendly format was originally designed for CompuServe specifically for the online display of graphics. It is an 8-bit file format, meaning it can contain a maximum of 256 unique colors within an image. When an image is saved to a GIF file, any color that is not one of those 256 is forced into becoming one of the 256. That keeps the file size down but it can also result in a loss of image quality—therefore, GIF is not a great option for storing photographic images, which often want subtle gradations that require more than 256 colors. But it is terrific for simpler images without lots of subtleties—images with big blocks of solid color, geometric shapes, or text that is being handled as an image (see Figure 9.1). In fact, you can reduce GIFs below the maximum of 256 colors, so if you have very few colors, your graphic files will be greatly reduced in terms of their weight.

FIGURE 9.1

Use the GIF format for simple shapes of solid colors.

The JPEG file format was named after the folks who invented it, the *Joint Photographic Experts Group*. JPEG files start by allowing an image to include over 16 million colors, which is actually more than the human eye can see. JPEG does not reduce file size by reducing color range as GIF does. Instead, this file type uses a built-in file reduction technique called *lossy compression*.

When you save a file in JPEG format, you can actually control how much the file is compressed, which is important in Web work, because as you know, small files are good files. However, the more a file is compressed, the worse its quality gets. Figure 9.2 shows a JPEG photograph saved at a "maximum" compression. At this most bloated of compression ratios, the file is 17 kilobytes in size. Figure 9.3 shows the same photograph, saved as a JPEG with a low compression—it's only 9 kilobytes in size and, for use on the Web, is of nearly identical quality. Unlike GIF files, JPEGs are well suited for storing photographic images or other art that requires subtle gradations of color.

FIGURE 9.2

The original JPEG file

FIGURE 9.3

This file was saved at low compression, and then magnified to demonstrate the degradation in the image's integrity. Note all the blurry patches.

Getting Started with PhotoDraw

PhotoDraw has been specially designed to work with all Office products. This means that it offers you not only the flexibility of creating images on your own, but also the opportunity to use a variety of templates appropriate to your needs. PhotoDraw makes graphics for menus, envelopes, letterheads, business cards, and of course, Web pages.

The PhotoDraw interface contains a drawing area and standard toolbars (Figure 9.4). PhotoDraw also adds toolbars or effects boxes as you work through a specific task.

FIGURE 9.4

The PhotoDraw interface with a blank canvas ready for your creation

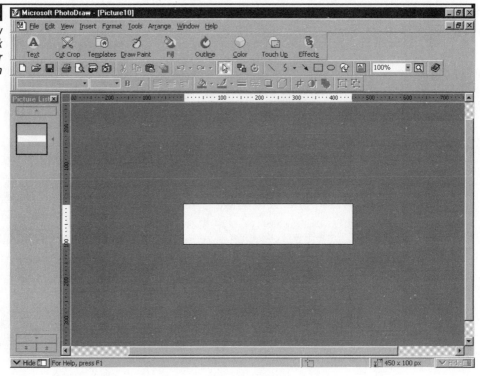

PhotoDraw is a very handy application that allows you to make changes to existing FrontPage graphics, to work from a template to create graphics for your pages, or to create specialty graphics from scratch.

Let's begin by starting PhotoDraw and opening an existing image.

Opening an Image in PhotoDraw

You can easily load existing image files for editing. PhotoDraw recognizes a very wide range of graphics file formats, including the Web-specific GIF and JPEG, as well as TIFF, BMP, and Photo CD files.

 NOTE PhotoDraw images use the .mix extension, unless they are saved in another format.

To open a local image in PhotoDraw:

1. Select File ➤ Open. The Open dialog box appears (see Figure 9.5).

2. Using the dialog box, navigate your local files until you find the desired file.

3. Highlight the file you want and click Open.

4. The file opens in the drawing area of the application (see Figure 9.6).

FIGURE 9.5

The Open dialog box in PhotoDraw

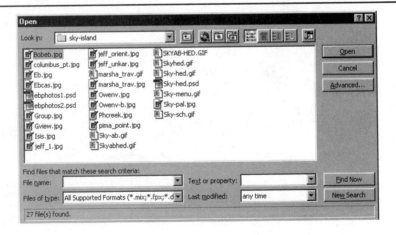

FIGURE 9.6

An existing figure open in the drawing area

MASTERING THE OPPORTUNITIES

Zoom a Zoom Zoom

As you work with images, you'll find the need to zoom in or out. You can do this one of two ways in PhotoDraw. From the main toolbar, you can type in a zoom percentage (100% being normal view) or select one from the drop-down zoom percentage menu. Or, you can click the Pan And Zoom button, which appears to the immediate right of the drop-down menu.

Continued

MASTERING WHAT'S ONLINE CONTINUED

This will display a small dialog box that allows you to zoom in or out, or pan to a specific area of your image.

Scanning an Image into PhotoDraw

Photographs and other artwork may be scanned directly into PhotoDraw with a standard, TWAIN-compliant scanner. TWAIN is a standard interface that exists between scanners and computers. Most scanners on the market today are TWAIN-compliant.

Scanning an image into PhotoDraw has been made especially simple:

1. Select File ➢ Scan Picture. The Scan workpane appears (see Figure 9.7).

2. Use the options in the workpane to adjust your settings.

3. Click Scan.

4. PhotoDraw scans your image and opens it in the drawing area of the application.

Now you can use the techniques described throughout the rest of this chapter to edit the image. Also see Chapter 4 for information about incorporating images into Web pages.

FIGURE 9.7

PhotoDraw's Scan workpane

Opening a Template Image

PhotoDraw has a variety of template images that you can modify for Web use. To access these images:

1. Select File ➢ New Template. The Templates workpane appears (see Figure 9.8).

2. Using the drop-down menu at the top of the workpane, select the category for your graphics. Web Graphics is most likely to be your choice in this case.

3. From the sample graphics displayed below the menu, click the style and image you'd like.

4. PhotoDraw opens that image into the drawing area.

5. You can modify your image by following the steps in the Templates workpane (click the Next button), or by using some of the methods described in upcoming sections.

Creating Sophisticated Designs

FIGURE 9.8

*PhotoDraw's
Templates
workpane*

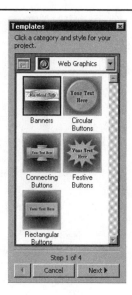

Preparing a New Image

Using PhotoDraw to create new images is perhaps the most creative use of the application. To prepare a custom graphic with PhotoDraw:

1. Select File ➢ Picture Setup. The Picture Setup dialog box appears (see Figure 9.9).

2. Be sure Default Picture is highlighted in the Picture size drop-down menu, then choose Pixels from the Units drop-down menu.

3. Enter the width and height in pixels that you want your image to be.

4. Click OK.

5. Select File ➢ New. The New Image dialog box opens.

6. Highlight the default image and click OK.

7. The new image canvas appears.

FIGURE 9.9

*PhotoDraw's Picture
Setup dialog box*

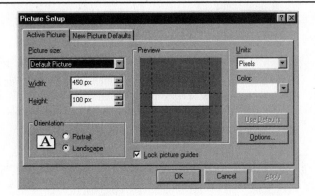

Working with PhotoDraw

Once you have opened an existing image or template, scanned in your artwork, or created a clean canvas upon which to create an image, you will want to be aware of several techniques to help you work with that image.

These include drawing and painting, working with text, moving and resizing your image, and applying special effects.

Drawing, Painting, and Creating Shapes

PhotoDraw offers an interesting array of methods to draw, paint, and create shapes. Drawing consists of the application of lines via points. You can select from a variety of line and brush types and colors. Painting works the same way—you can freely paint using a selection of lines and various brush types and colors. You can also create shapes with PhotoDraw, using the same selection of lines, brushes, effects, and color.

To work with the image of your choice:

1. Open an existing image, scan an image, create an image from a template, or begin with a clean canvas.

2. Make sure the Visual menu is visible by selecting View ➢ Visual Menu.

3. From the Visual menu, click Draw Paint. The drawing and painting options pallette slides open.

4. Move your mouse over the Draw option and click. PhotoDraw switches to its drawing view (see Figure 9.10). You'll see your canvas, the AutoShape toolbar, and the workpane (including line and color options) on your screen. When the image has fully loaded, click the canvas, and a bounding box appears around your drawn image.

 NOTE A *bounding box* is a box that contains the specific elements with which you are working. You use this box to move or modify the elements within the box itself.

FIGURE 9.10

PhotoDraw's drawing view

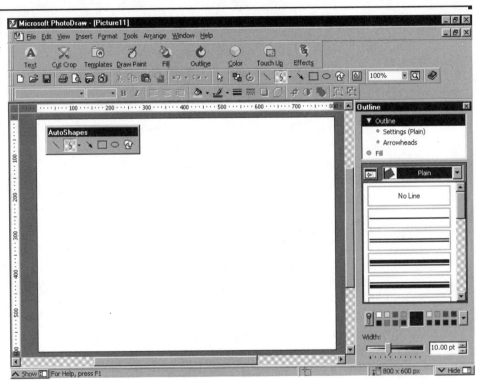

5. Now select your desired line style, width, and color from the workpane.

6. In the canvas area, click and move from point to point until you've drawn the desired image.

7. PhotoDraw automatically adds the specified line style, width, and color to your drawing (see Figure 9.11).

FIGURE 9.11

Drawing in PhotoDraw

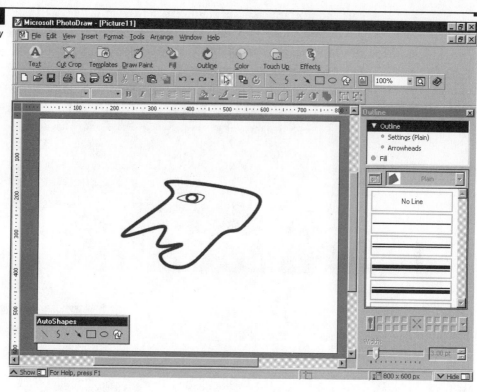

Painting with PhotoDraw is similar to drawing. Here's how to do it:

1. Open an existing image, scan an image, create an image from a template, or begin with a clean canvas.

2. Make sure the Visual menu is visible by selecting View ➤ Visual Menu.

3. From the Visual menu, click Draw Paint. The drawing and painting options palette slides open.

4. Move your mouse over the Paint option and click. PhotoDraw switches to its painting view. This view looks very much like the drawing view, shown in Figure 9.11, but the workpane is slightly different, with brushes rather than lines available to you.

5. Now select your desired brush style, width, and color from the workpane.

6. In the canvas area, click once at the spot where you want to begin painting, and move in a free form manner until you've painted your desired image. You can

start and stop as you wish, but unlike drawing, the lines won't be automatically connected.

7. PhotoDraw automatically adds the specified brush style, width, and color to your painting (see Figure 9.12).

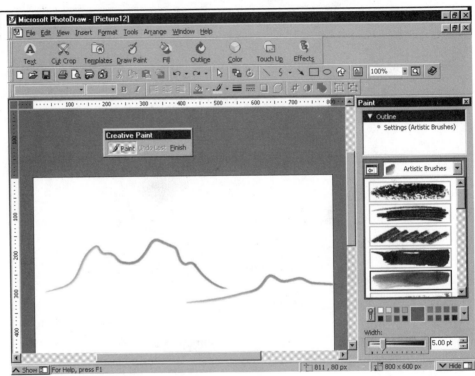

FIGURE 9.12

Painting in PhotoDraw

To create shapes in PhotoDraw:

1. Open an existing image, scan an image, create an image from a template, or begin with a clean canvas.

2. Make sure the Visual menu is visible by selecting View ➤ Visual Menu.

3. From the Visual menu, click Draw Paint. The drawing and painting options palette slides open.

4. Move your mouse over the Shapes option and click.

5. Now select your line brush style, width, and color from the workpane.

6. From the AutoShapes menu select a shape. You can use a square or circle, or you may select the AutoShapes button for more options.

7. In the canvas area, click once at the spot where you want to start drawing your shape, and move the cursor until you've created the desired shape. Click a second time to stop drawing.

8. PhotoDraw automatically adds the specified line brush style, width, and color to your shape (see Figure 9.13).

FIGURE 9.13

Creating shapes

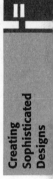

Once you are satisfied with your results, you can save the file in native PhotoDraw format for further editing, or read the sections below about how to modify and save your files for the Web.

Working with Text

Whether you use graphic text alone to add a specific style and color not easily achieved with FrontPage itself, or you use text along with an image to enhance that image, being able to create graphic-based text is extremely important.

PhotoDraw makes it quite simple to add text to any existing or new image:

1. Open an existing image, scan an image, create an image from a template, or begin with a clean canvas.

2. Make sure the Visual menu is visible by selecting View ➤ Visual Menu.

3. From the Visual menu, click Text. The text options palette slides open.

4. Move your mouse over the Insert Text option, and click. PhotoDraw switches to its text view, and a bounding box appears on your canvas (see Figure 9.14).

FIGURE 9.14

PhotoDraw's text view

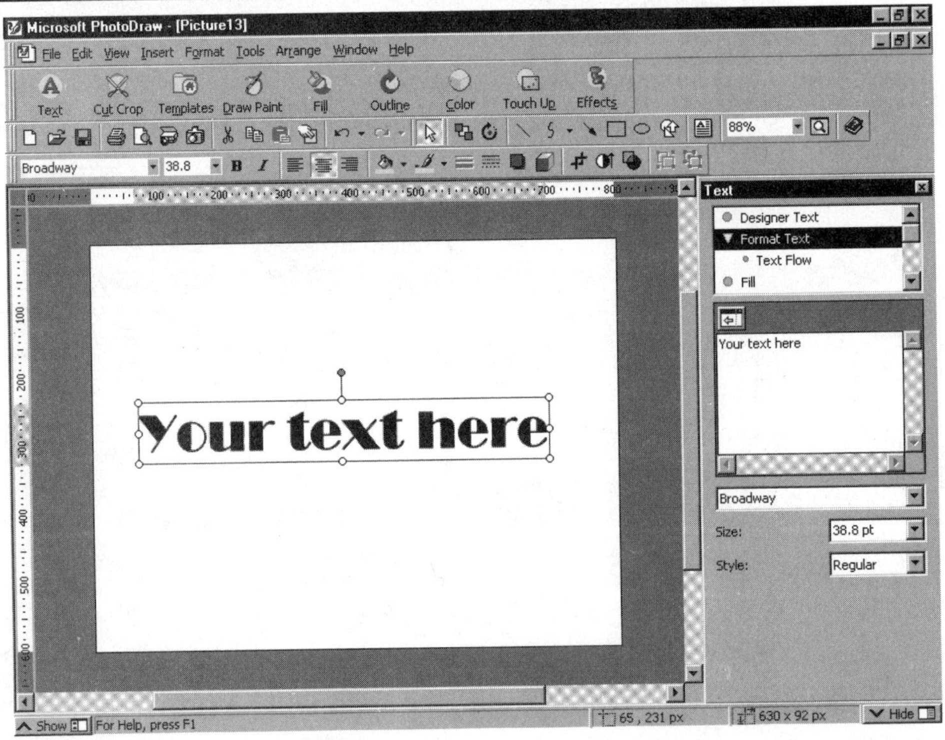

5. In the text workpane, make your font, style, and size selections. In the mini text box, type the text you wish to appear within the bounding box. The text simultaneously appears within the bounding box.

6. To change the color of the text, select Fill from the text workpane, and click the color of your choice. Your text fills with the selected color.

Using Text Effects

Before saving your file, you might want to consider adding effects to your text. Photo-Draw offers a wide range of text effects, including the ability to bend text, make it three-dimensional, or give it a specialty look and feel.

Each of these category options is available from the text button on the Visual menu. Simply click the Text button, and slide down to the desired effect category. In the workpane, the category loads, along with a variety of specific styles that you can use to modify your text. Simply click once on the effect you'd like to apply, and PhotoDraw does the rest (see Figure 9.15).

PART
II

Creating
Sophisticated
Designs

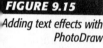

FIGURE 9.15

Adding text effects with PhotoDraw

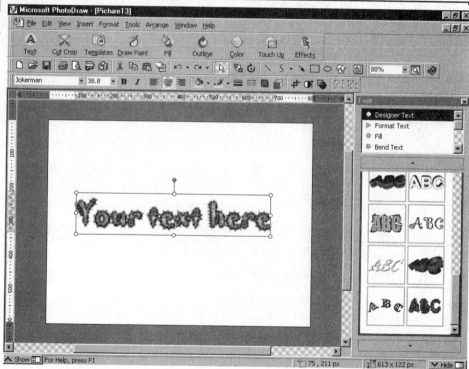

Moving and Resizing Your Image or Text

As you've seen, the bounding box contains all of the image or text elements that you are creating or modifying. Using this box, you can move or resize an image or text:

1. Pass your mouse over the bounding box until the Move symbol appears.
2. Click the mouse and hold down the button.
3. Move the mouse, and the bounding box, to the new area where you'd like it to be.
4. Release the mouse, and the image is now in its new home.

To rotate an image or text:

1. At the top of the bounding box, you'll see a small green circle. Pass your mouse over this circle until the Rotate symbol appears.
2. Click the mouse and hold down the button.
3. Rotate the image until its appearance is acceptable to you.
4. Release the mouse button.

You can resize an image either vertically or horizontally, or both. To resize an image vertically:

1. Pass your mouse over the white circle in the center of the bounding box's bottom line until an arrow appears.
2. Click the mouse and hold down the button.
3. Drag the line until vertically you're satisfied with the size of the image.
4. Release the mouse button.

To resize an image horizontally:

1. Pass your mouse over the white circle in the center of the bounding box's right or left vertical line until a horizontal arrow appears.
2. Click the mouse and hold down the button.
3. Drag the line horizontally until you're happy with the size of the image.
4. Release the mouse button.

To resize an image both vertically and horizontally while retaining its perspective:

1. Pass the mouse over one of the white circles in either corner of the bounding box until an arrow appears.
2. Click the mouse and hold down the button.

3. Drag the box in or out depending upon how you want to resize the image.

4. When you are satisfied with the size of the image, release the mouse button.

You can always return to the bounding box and resize or rotate your image again. Also, remember that you can undo any change by selecting Edit ➤ Undo or by pressing Ctrl+Z.

Using Special Effects

PhotoDraw offers a very appealing range of special effects that you can add to your images and text. To cover all of them would take much more room than we have here, but we'll show you how to use three popular effects to get you started.

Making a Drop Shadow

Drop shadows are used frequently in the graphic design world. They add dimension and visual interest to graphic images or type. This dimension is coveted on the Web, which tends to offer up flat designs. Adding a shadow can really spruce up a graphic and make your site look more professional and sophisticated.

PhotoDraw allows you to create a variety of drop shadows, instantly adding a shadow with direction and specific softness to your graphic. To add a shadow to your graphic using PhotoDraw:

1. Open the image you'd like to add the shadow to.

2. From the Visual menu, click the Effects button. The Effects palette slides open.

3. Click Shadow.

4. The Shadow workpane opens, displaying a variety of available shadow styles.

5. Choose a shadow style by clicking it once.

6. PhotoDraw inserts the shadow (see Figure 9.16).

7. You can modify the shadow's position, transparency, and softness using the tools found in the workpane.

When you're happy with the results, you can save the file in native PhotoDraw format, or read the "Saving Your Image" section later in this chapter to modify the image for the Web.

PART

II

Creating
Sophisticated
Designs

FIGURE 9.16

A drop shadow adds
dimension.

Softening Edges

Another way to give a graphic or text visual interest is to soften hard edges. As with a shadow, softening an edge also adds a professional touch to your work.

To soften the edges of a graphic image using PhotoDraw:

1. Open the image you'd like to add the soft edge to.

2. From the Visual menu, click the Outline button. The Outline options palette slides open.

3. Click Soft Edges.

4. The Soft Edges workpane opens and displays a slider bar that will allow you to adjust the edge softness.

5. Slide the bar until you're satisfied with the edge effect.

As you can see in Figure 9.17, the results are definitely more appealing to the eye than a flat edge!

FIGURE 9.17

Use a soft edge to add a sophisticated look to your graphic.

Adding an Artistic Look

If you have a photograph, image, or text that you'd like to stylize to look as though it had been drawn or painted, you can do this with PhotoDraw's Designer Effects.

To add an artistic look to an image using PhotoDraw:

1. Open the image you'd like to modify.

2. From the Visual menu, click the Effects button. The Effects palette slides open.

3. Click Designer Effects.

4. The Designer Effects workpane opens, and you'll see a broad selection of artistic styles to choose from.

5. Select a style that interests you and click it.

PhotoDraw now modifies the image (see Figure 9.18). At this point, you can save the image as is, or add an edge effect such as a drop shadow or soft edge.

PART

II

Creating
Sophisticated
Designs

FIGURE 9.18

*Designer Effects
add an artistic
look to your
graphics.*

Saving Your PhotoDraw Image

As mentioned earlier in this chapter, when you save a file in PhotoDraw's native format, it will have the extension `.mix`. This is a good way to save files for future editing, but these files cannot be used for the Web itself. In order to do that, you'll have to use PhotoDraw to save the image in a format that is acceptable for the Web.

There are two methods available for saving your image for the Web in PhotoDraw. One is by using the Save As option, and selecting your choice of image. This is good if you know a bit about when to use GIF and when to use JPEG.

The other method is to let PhotoDraw help you make decisions about the image using the Save For Use In Wizard. This wizard walks you through a process by which you can make parts of an image transparent or save the image at a specific size.

To save an image using the Save As feature:

1. Select File ➤ Save As. The Save As dialog box opens. Your file's name appears in the File Name text box. You can change the name if necessary by typing the new name into the text box.

2. From the drop-down Save as type menu, select the file type you want the image saved as.

3. PhotoDraw saves the image.

You can now either open the .mix file for further editing, or import your finished GIF or JPEG into FrontPage for use on your Web page.

To save an image using the Save For Use In Wizard:

1. Select File ➤ Save For Use In. The Save For Use In Wizard opens (see Figure 9.19).

2. Click the On The Web button.

3. Click Next. You'll now be asked to step through a number of customized settings such as transparency or color fill, and best time for modem speed. Fill in each section as the wizard suggests, clicking Next until you are happy with your choices.

4. Click Save, and the wizard processes the file for you.

You've now created an image that's ready for use on the Web. Be sure to visit Chapter 4, *Creating Basic Pages*, to add your images to your FrontPage webs.

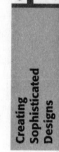

FIGURE 9.19

The Save For Use In Wizard dialog box

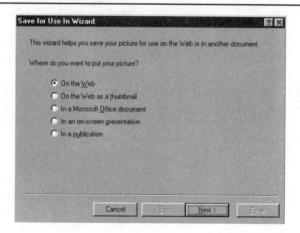

Creating and Editing Graphics with Image Composer

Image Composer is a very popular imaging program with many FrontPage users, as well as with the general public. While PhotoDraw is very useful because of its inclusion in the Office 2000 family, Image Composer is an excellent choice for people seeking options when working with their graphics. Image Composer works in a way that allows you to manipulate graphic objects with more precision than PhotoDraw.

The method by which Image Composer allows this precision is the fact that it works in layers. Each new Image Composer file is called a *composition*, and a composition is actually a collection of these layers, which are actually tiers of visual objects known as *sprites*. A sprite is a single visual object; it can be a simple graphic such as a solid blue circle, or some text, or a photograph. Each sprite is contained within a *bounding box*, a rectangular border that appears around the sprite when you select it. This allows you to see the boundaries of the sprite and resize and move it around.

Image Composer allows you to manipulate sprites as if they were square boxes, but that does not mean all sprites appear as square boxes on the final image, and certainly not on the final page. The background within the box that contains the sprite is transparent; basically, only the actual sprite shape has any color that shows (see Figure 9.20).

*Layered sprites in
Image Composer*

NOTE *Transparency* is actually the process of making one color "clear" so that whatever is behind it shows through. The "clear" color doesn't have to be the background color in a sprite, but that's the most commonly used approach.

 TIP Image Composer comes with a handy supply of free sample sprites you can use for experimentation or for real. Find them via the online help system by selecting, from the menu bar, Help ➤ Sample Sprite Catalog. Note that the sample sprites are not installed by default when you Install Image Composer. You have to select them specifically. See Appendix A for information about installing Image Composer and all of its components.

Starting Image Composer

If you have Image Composer installed on your hard drive, you can begin by opening the program. From the Windows Start menu, select Programs ➤ Microsoft Image Composer ➤ Microsoft Image Composer. Otherwise, you'll need to visit www.microsoft.com/imagecomposer/ to download and install the program on your hard drive.

 TIP You can also open Image Composer and load an image in one step from within FrontPage. Just double-click an image you have placed in a Web page and the Image Composer window appears.

Image Composer now opens, providing a blank workspace for you to begin your project (see Figure 9.21).

PART

II

Creating
Sophisticated
Designs

FIGURE 9.21

*Image Composer
as seen immediately
after launch*

Tool	What It's Called	What You Can Do with It
	Selection	Select an item
	Arrange	Move a sprite within a stack of sprites
	Cutout	Remove portions of sprites to create a new sprite
	Text	Create text block sprites
	Shapes	Form sprites using geometric shapes

Tool	What It's Called	What You Can Do with It
	Paint	Access brushes, pens, and pencils for hand drawing
	Effects	Apply artistic looks, patterns, and warp enhancements to your sprites
	Texture Transfer	Copy the properties of one sprite onto another
	Zoom	Increase or decrease magnification of the current view
	Pan	Pan the window and move to a different area of the image
	Color Tuning	Adjust color values and brightness
	Color Swatch	Select a color to use

Clicking some of these tools displays a dialog box, which contains the options available for that task. We'll go over those options as we actually create sprites in upcoming sections.

 TIP You can use the area outside the composition area as an organizing or staging area for sprites before they are arranged within your image. Simply drag them off the space as they are created or imported. Note, however, that sprites (or portions of sprites) that lie outside the composition area are *not* saved as part of the image if you save the image as a GIF or JPEG file. They will then be lost, never to be recovered.

Opening or Creating an Image

As mentioned in the preceding section, when you start Image Composer, a new blank document appears, as shown in Figure 9.21. In this blank document, you can add those nifty sprites to your empty composition and transform it into the image you want for your Web page. Or, you can load existing image files on disk or via scanning. Image Composer recognizes most major graphics file formats, including the ever-popular GIF and JPEG, as well as TIFF, BMP, and Photo CD files.

Photographs and other artwork may be scanned directly into Image Composer with a standard, TWAIN-compliant scanner. TWAIN is a standard interface that exists

PART

II

Creating Sophisticated Designs

between scanners and computers. Most scanners on the market today are TWAIN-compliant.

Opening an Existing Image

While editing images is not Image Composer's forte, it can certainly be done, and done to good effect. First, you must open an existing image, which you can then edit. To open an existing image, follow these steps:

1. Start Image Composer as described earlier. From the menu bar, select File ➤ Open. The Open File dialog box appears.

2. In the dialog box's list of filenames, find and select the image file of interest. Click Open. The dialog box closes. If the file you're opening is one that was created using Image Composer (in other words, if it has the extension .mic), the image appears in the composition area looking just as it did when it was last modified. If the file is some other type of image file, the composition area is resized to match the size of the image, and the image is placed in that area as a single sprite. (This makes it possible for you to work with the image as if it were a sprite, using Image Composer's various tools and abilities.)

Now you can use the techniques described throughout the rest of this chapter to edit the image. Also see Chapter 4 for information about incorporating images into Web pages.

Creating an Image

Creating an image is Image Composer's true purpose in life. Here's where this software really shines, offering a variety of easy-to-use tools and a simple process to follow. Creating an image with Composer involves:

- Choosing a color
- Placing sprites of the appropriate types and, if required by those types, the correct shapes
- Rearranging and manipulating the sprites
- Saving the file

This is true whether the image you're aiming for is a graphic image or text that you'll be treating as a graphic. Read on.

Choosing Colors

On the Web, color is critical. Okay, well, it's also critical in design for reproduction on paper, but that medium is a lot easier to control and more is known about it.

The colors you choose for your Web-displayed graphics and text will look different on the various machines users use to view your pages—this is just a fact.

On the Web, depending on his or her system, Joe or Joanna User may be viewing your work in 16 colors or 16.7 million colors. Some users may not see color at all, as they may have a gray-scale monitor that doesn't display color. They may see your graphics on a tiny laptop screen, or on a 21-inch professional graphic artist's monitor. How can you get as much control of all this as possible, so your graphics will look their best? By learning to live with and make the most of the colors most computers and most Web browsers recognize.

Most computers recognize a standard palette of just 256 colors (although many Windows 3.1-era machines recognize only 16 colors). Internet Explorer and Netscape Navigator both recognize a basic color palette taken from that "system" palette—both browsers recognize the same 216 colors that are recognized by the Windows and Macintosh operating systems. (At least everyone can agree on *something*.) The other 40 colors available to Windows and Macintosh machines are recognized by Internet Explorer and Netscape Navigator, but appear different in each browser—in fact, they appear different depending on which platform each browser is running on.

Image Composer also lets you specify "true color" colors. These are colors that are not taken from any palette—they can theoretically take on any possible color! When a user with a 256-color display loads a page that includes a true color image, what they see can look pretty bad. This is because the user's computer can display nowhere near as many colors as you can specify using true color, so the browser dithers the image.

Dithering is the process of putting pixels of different colors next to each other to create a third color. While this works well for TV (your TV actually displays all colors by combining red, green, and blue dots), it does not produce good results on computer screens, where dithered images usually look grainy and lose their sharpness. In general, avoid using true color images in your Web images, because they just don't work.

When you select colors for use on the Web, stick to the 216 everyone can see correctly. Image Composer calls these "Web (Solid)" colors. Take our advice and don't try to exercise additional options; if you do, not all your users will see the colors you selected, and some of them will see only a mishmash of color instead.

Image Composer provides you with the ability to form complex images combining many sprites in a single composition. Each time you create a sprite, you'll first choose a color for that sprite. (In the end, you can have many sprites of many colors, you just have to start each one by specifying its color.) Here's how to choose a color for a sprite:

1. With Image Composer open and either a new, blank composition area open or the existing composition of interest in view, from the toolbox, select the Color Swatch tool (see Figure 9.22). The Color Picker dialog box appears (see Figure 9.23).

PART

II

Creating
Sophisticated
Designs

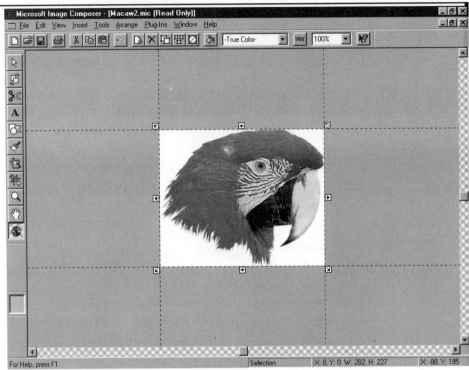

2. The Color Picker dialog box opens with either the True Color tab or the Custom Palette tab selected.

- With the True Color tab selected, you can select any color, regardless of palette concerns. The drawback is that you can select colors that will not properly display on the Web. (See the sidebar "Color Palettes and the Web" for background information about Web-safe colors.)

- With the Custom Palette tab selected, you can choose a palette from the Color Palette drop-down list. This tab leads you on the true path toward Web-safe colors.

3. Because you are creating graphics for the Web and want them to be successful, select the Custom Palette tab. The contents of the dialog box change to reflect your choice.

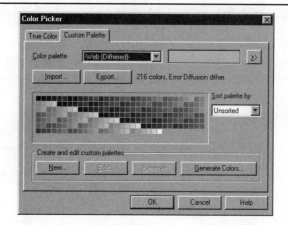

FIGURE 9.23

Select a color from the Color Picker dialog box.

4. In the Color Palette drop-down list, select Web (Solid) if you are creating a color image, or Gray Scale if you are creating colorless images. The contents of the dialog box again change to reflect your choice.

5. In the rainbow grid of colors in the middle of the dialog box, select the color you like. A sample of the selected color appears in the upper-right corner of the dialog box.

6. Click OK. The Color Picker dialog box closes, and you are returned to the Image Composer window with the selected color displayed in the toolbox's Color Swatch tool.

MASTERING WHAT'S ONLINE

Some designers have kindly provided the 216-color palette online for the reference of others. Victor Engel's No Dither Netscape Color Palette is at www.onr.com/user/lights/netcol.html, and Lynda Weinman's excellent discussion of the Browser Safe Color Palette, complete with examples to download, is at www.lynda.com/hex.html.

Creating Sophisticated Designs

Adding Shape Sprites: Rectangles, Ovals, Circles, and Curves

There are two types of sprites: shapes and text. Shape sprites start as actual shapes—these rectangles, ovals, circles, and curves are the basic building blocks you'll use to create images with Image Composer. Which shape you'll use for what image depends on what you're trying to do; experimentation is the key to success here. Remember that you'll be layering these shapes on top of each other to produce images later.

To create or edit shapes, you'll use the toolbox's Shapes tool. Follow these steps:

1. With a composition open in Image Composer, from the toolbox, select the Shapes tool. The Shapes dialog box appears.

2. If you are creating a Curve or Polygon, you can choose to create either a *closed* or *open* shape. A closed shape is one in which the last point in the shape is connected back to the first point—an example of a closed polygon is a square, while a closed curve might be a circle. An open shape is one in which the last point and the first point are not connected, as in a curved line. To create a closed shape, click the Close checkbox.

3. If you chose to create a closed shape, you can also either fill it or not fill it with a solid color. To fill the shape with a solid color, click the Fill checkbox.

4. Along the left side of the dialog box, you'll see four radio buttons that represent the four sprite shapes you can create:

   - Rectangle (which includes the option of creating a square)
   - Oval (which includes the option of creating a circle)
   - Curve (a set of points connected via a curved line)
   - Polygon (a shape with straight edges and any number of sides)

 TIP A commonly cited example of a five-sided polygon is the Pentagon building. Stop signs are eight-sided polygons. But in these examples of polygons, none of the lines cross. A sprite shaped as a polygon can bend and twist in any direction using straight lines, even crossing back over itself one or more times.

Select the button for the sprite you want to add to the composition.

5. To place the sprite on your composition, use one of two methods, depending on the shape you're dealing with:

- If you are placing a rectangle or oval sprite in the composition, click and drag over the area where you want the sprite to appear. When you release the mouse button, you'll see an outline of the shape.

 TIP Holding down the Shift key as you drag the mouse to define the sprite's outline causes the outline to be a "perfect" shape. If you do this with the Rectangle tool selected, you'll create a perfect square. Likewise, if you do this with the Oval tool, you'll create a perfect circle.

- If you are placing a curve or polygon in the composition, click at spot where you want to place the first point of the shape. Now click into place each additional point in turn until you have clicked into place all the points that will define the shape. As you click, you'll see the shape itself appear. You don't have to close up the end points of the shape. This happens automatically.

6. In the Opacity For New Shape area of the dialog box, use the slider to set the opacity for the sprite you are adding. (See the sidebar "Opacity and Edges: Controlling the Look of Sprites" for more information.) Your options range from 0 (completely invisible) to 100 (completely solid).

7. In the Edge area, use the slider to specify the sharpness of the sprite's edges. (Again, see the sidebar "Opacity and Edges: Controlling the Look of Sprites" for more information.) Your options range from Hard to Soft.

8. Click the Create button. The sprite as you've defined it appears on the composition area. Here is a polygon we had a good time playing with:

PART

II

Creating
Sophisticated
Designs

MASTERING THE OPPORTUNITIES

Opacity and Edges: Controlling the Look of Sprites

The sprites that make up your composition can overlap each other. That is, one sprite can be placed right on top of another sprite. So what would happen if you placed a blue circle on top of a red square? The answer depends on the *opacity* of the sprites involved. When something is *opaque*, you can't see through it. A fully opaque sprite (one you can't see through at all) has an opacity value of 100, which is the default setting for the opacity option in Image Composer. The lesser the value, the more *transparent* the image becomes.

Lower opacity numbers indicate more *translucency* or *transparency*. When a sprite has a lower opacity level and it is placed on top of something else (say, another sprite), whatever is behind it can be seen through it.

Sprites also have a quality called *edge*. This refers quite simply to how hard (sharp) or soft (blurry) the edge of the shape looks.

You can continue creating more shapes for your composition, or you can save the individual sprites as described in the procedure at the beginning of the section "Save Your Image Composer Image," later in this chapter.

Working with Text Sprites

Often you'll create graphics for your Web pages that actually consist primarily (if not totally) of text. Perhaps you want a label or button to appear in a particular font and size that aren't available in HTML. ("New!" in a starburst, for example, just isn't an HTML option. It has to be done as a graphic.) Or you may want to twist and bend the text into some expressive shape that better conveys its message. Perhaps you want your company name to look just as you designed it, without any differences based on individual users' Web browsers. Create a text image in the font and point size you like, with special effects as needed, and you are guaranteed that it will look the way you like, no matter what browser tunes into it.

TIP Don't go overboard by replacing too much text on your page with text graphics. Every graphic you add to a page increases the page's combined file size, and that slows the process of loading the page when a user views it—not good. Users like pages to load quickly, but when they arrive, the pages should look good, too. Balance the look of your page against download time, and make sure that any graphic element you add furthers the overall purpose of your page.

WARNING Because Web graphics that include text are designed to appear on screen, they often print poorly—computer monitors and printers operate at different resolutions.

A basic text sprite is a breeze to create. Much of what you'll do here is just like typing in a word processor, but the results can be pretty dazzling. Follow these steps:

1. With a composition open in Image Composer, switch to 100-percent zoom by clicking the 100% button on the toolbar along the top of the Image Composer window. Unlike other Image Composer tools, the Text tool works only when you are viewing your composition in 100-percent zoom. (See the section titled "Zooming In or Out.") The view of the image changes (unless it was already at 100 percent).

2. From Image Composer's toolbox, select the Text tool. The Text dialog box appears, as shown in Figure 9.24.

FIGURE 9.24

Create cool effects with the Text dialog box.

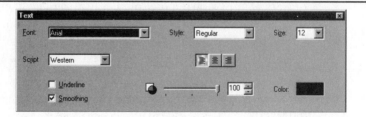

3. From the dialog box's Font drop-down list, select the font you prefer. (See Chapter 6, *Fantastic Fonts*, for information about choosing the optimal font for your purpose.)

4. From the Style drop-down list, select a style for the text. Your options vary depending on which font you selected in step 3, but generally they are:

- Regular for regular, nothing-special type
- **Bold** for darker, heavier type
- *Italic* for slanted type
- ***Bold Italic*** for darker, heavier, slanted type

Choose one of the available options. If you're unsure, choose Regular. (You can always change it later.)

5. From the Size drop-down list, select a size for the text to be created. The numbers you see here represent *points*; this is just like what you do when you select a size for text in word-processing software. If the size you prefer is not apparent in the drop-down list, you can type it directly into the text box.

TIP When you specify font sizes from within FrontPage, as described in Chapter 6, you are specifying *relative* font sizes; they are relative to some font size set by the user who finally views the page. But here you are actually choosing the real, true font size. If you try to match the font size you selected for HTML pages, be aware that to many users, the two seemingly same-sized fonts will not look the same.

6. In the bottom-left area of the Text dialog box are two checkboxes:

- *Underline* is self explanatory; if you want your text underlined, click this checkbox.
- *Smoothing* (known more commonly as *anti-aliasing)* is the process of blending an object's edge in relation to the color behind it, so the edge looks *smooth*. Without smoothing, edges of characters may look jagged. Generally, it's a good idea to smooth all the text you add to a composition.

WARNING If you are going to use smoothing on the text you add to a composition, the text should be the last sprite you add. For example, if you smooth the text while the sprite is over a white background, then move the sprite so some other color is behind it, you'll lose the benefits of smoothing and actually make the text look worse.

7. In the Text dialog box, click the Color box. The Color Picker dialog box appears. For detailed information about using the Color Picker dialog box, see the section titled "Choosing Colors" earlier in this chapter. For now, in the rainbow grid of colors in the middle of the dialog box, select a color you like.

8. Click OK. The Color Picker dialog box closes and the Text dialog box reappears, with the Color box containing the color you selected.

9. Use the slider bar at the bottom of the dialog box to specify the opacity of the sprite you are adding. (See the sidebar "Opacity and Edges: Controlling the Look of Sprites" for more information.) Your options range from 0 percent (completely translucent) to 100 percent (completely solid). As you drag the slider bar left or right, the percentage changes.

10. Just above the opacity slider bar are three buttons that control the alignment of the text within the sprite. You can align the text using alignment options much like those the editor offers for HTML—left aligned, center aligned, or right aligned. Click the button that corresponds to your preferred alignment.

 TIP This refers to the centering of the text *within* the sprite's bounding box, not the centering of the sprite on the composition.

11. Now you're ready to add text. Click your mouse anyplace within the composition. An empty text editing box appears with a cursor in it, as shown here.

12. If you need more space for your text than the text editing box provides, click and drag the edges of the box in any direction. Don't worry if you make the box too large; when you finish typing, Image Composer will shrink the sprite's bounding box down to fit the text.

13. Type the text of your dreams within the box. Then click the mouse anyplace on the composition area but *outside of the text box*. The text editing box closes and your finished text sprite remains on the composition as shown here. (We simply added text to the shape we created earlier in this chapter.)

Are you ready to get really creative? You've now got basic Image Composer skills under your belt; in the next section we'll show you how to apply dazzling effects to your shapes and text. (You can even do this with images you've created or obtained elsewhere.)

Moving, Arranging, and Rotating Sprites

You can shuffle around, rearrange, rotate, and manipulate sprites all you like. Here's how to move a sprite:

1. Click the sprite and hold down the mouse button. A bounding box appears around the sprite.

2. Drag the sprite to a new location in the composition area. An outline of the sprite moves as you drag the mouse. When you reach your target destination, release the mouse button. The sprite appears there.

To rotate a sprite, do this:

1. Click the sprite and hold down the mouse button. A bounding box appears around the sprite.

2. In the upper-right corner of the bounding box, find the rotate symbol. Click it and drag the sprite around in circles as you like. An outline of the sprite moves as you drag the mouse. When you stop and release the mouse button, the sprite appears there, with a new bounding box around it and the rotate symbol again in the upper-right corner. Click within the bounding box to resume editing. The box disappears and you can continue working.

Now, with at least two sprites that overlap in view, to change their layering, do this:

1. Click the sprite. A bounding box appears around it.

2. You have four choices for layering your sprites:

- To move the selected sprite to the top, from the menu bar, select Arrange ➤ Bring To Front.

- To move the selected sprite to the bottom, from the menu bar, select Arrange ➤ Send To Back.

- To move the selected sprite up one level, from the menu bar, select Arrange ➤ Bring Forward.

- To move the selected sprite down one level, from the menu bar, select Arrange ➤ Send Backward.

The change occurs immediately. The extent of change depends on the opacity and other settings of the sprites involved.

Zooming In or Out

For the most part, you'll be creating small images for your Web pages. Smaller images make smaller files, and small files—as we keep saying—are good. But that does not mean that you have to plaster your head to your monitor to see the things. You can zoom in (or reverse the process and zoom out) of a composition to make it appear much larger (or smaller) as necessary, and thereby make it easier to work with.

To change the zoom of a composition:

1. With the composition open in Image Composer, from the toolbox, select the Zoom tool. The mouse pointer changes to a magnifying glass.

2. Click anywhere inside the composition. Each time you click, you zoom in on the composition (with the center of your field of view being the spot where you clicked) and all of the sprites appear larger. If you hold down the Ctrl key while clicking, you zoom out each time you click and all of the sprites appear smaller.

3. To return to the normal zoom, select the 100% button from the toolbar. The composition pops back to normal size.

 TIP You can also jump to any zoom you like—from 10 percent to 1000 percent — by selecting a percentage from the toolbar's Zoom drop-down list.

Applying Effects in Image Composer

Until now in this chapter, we've dealt with the basics: creating shape sprites and text sprites, then moving them around. You can tweak the way those individual sprites look—you can change their color or opacity, for example. But there's much more—you can apply an array of special effects to any sprite in your composition. You can blur, smudge, or add a drop shadow to a sprite; you can also apply a cool radiating spoke-like effect. The sky is (kind of) the limit.

To apply an effect to a sprite in your composition:

1. With the composition open in Image Composer and with a sprite already added (see the section "Adding Shape Sprites: Rectangles, Ovals, Circles and Curves" or "Working with Text Sprites" for details), select the sprite to which you want to apply an effect.

2. From the Image Composer toolbox, click the Effects tool. The Effects dialog box appears, as shown in Figure 9.25.

FIGURE 9.25

The Effects dialog box offers previews of how each effect will affect the selected sprite.

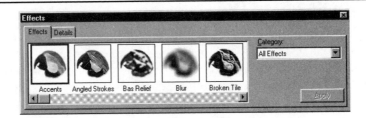

3. If the Effects tab along the top of the dialog box is not already selected, select it. The contents of the dialog box change to reflect your choice.

4. Effects are grouped into categories here. From the Category drop-down list, select the category you want to see. All the effects in that category then appear in the dialog box. (Select the All Effects category to have all of the effects appear.)

5. Select an effect by clicking it. (You may have to use the horizontal scroll bar below the list of effects to see them all.) A highlight appears around the selected effect.

6. Each effect has its own options you can set—angle for the Radial Sweep effect, foreground and background levels for the Conté Crayon effect, and so on. To set options for the effect you selected in step 5, select the dialog box's Details tab. The contents of the dialog box change to reflect your choice. Set the options you like.

7. In the dialog box, click the Apply button to apply the effect to your sprite. Your sprite appears with the effect you chose. The result of applying the Drop Shadow effect to the shape sprite in our sample composition is shown here.

TIP If you are not satisfied with the results of applying the effect to your sprite, *before you save it or do anything else,* select Edit ➤ Undo from the menu bar.

8. You can combine effects as you like. Choose one effect to apply on top of another, click the Apply button again, and there you go. Your sprite appears with the additional effect. Here you can see the Spoke Inversion effect applied on top of the Drop Shadow to the shape sprite in our sample composition.

Play around with this—it's really fun! Getting familiar with what can be done will take some time, but in the end you'll find that you can combine effects with panache. You might want to save various versions of your work as you go, however, so you can go back to some version you liked after heading off on a track you don't find quite so satisfying. The key here, as in all creative endeavors, is experimentation.

Transferring Textures between Sprites

As you overlap sprites (see "Moving, Arranging, and Rotating Sprites" earlier in this chapter), you may want the overlapping area of the topmost sprite to take on some of the effects you've applied to the sprite behind it (or vice versa). You can do this using the Texture Transfer tool. Follow these steps:

1. With a composition open in Image Composer, select *both* of the sprites you want to work with.

NOTE Image Composer supports the standard Windows ways of selecting multiple objects. You can either press and hold down the mouse button as you drag the pointer around all the objects you want to select, or you can hold down the Shift key as you click in turn on each object you want to select. Either way, handles appear on each object to indicate that it is selected.

2. In the toolbox, select the Texture Transfer tool. The Texture Transfer dialog box appears, as shown in Figure 9.26.

PART

II

Creating
Sophisticated
Designs

FIGURE 9.26

*The Texture Transfer
dialog box*

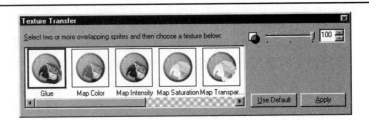

3. You can choose among many different types of transfers. The best way to get to know what each one does is to try them out, one after the other. Choose any of the texture transfers by clicking its button. Options that are available for that texture transfer appear along the right side of the dialog box.

4. Set the options available for the texture transfer you selected in step 3 as you like, or leave the defaults in place.

5. Click the Apply button. The texture transfer is applied to the selected sprite. You'll see the results immediately.

TIP If you are not satisfied with the results of applying a texture transfer, before you do anything else at all, select Edit ➢ Undo from the menu bar.

Adding Buttons

Buttons are almost as common as links on the Web. In fact, buttons are often used to link pages or to signal some other sort of interactivity. Image Composer comes with a Button Wizard that lets you create stylized buttons for your Web site in the blink of an eye. It all starts with a sprite. To create a button sprite, follow these steps:

1. With the composition of interest open in Image Composer, select Insert ➢ Button. The first panel of the Button Wizard appears, as shown in Figure 9.27.

2. In the Button Style list box, select a likely style. Play around to preview the choices—as you select different styles, a preview of each appears in the right portion of the panel. When you find one you're happy with, leave it in place and click Next. The next panel appears.

FIGURE 9.27

The Button Wizard creates stylized buttons for you.

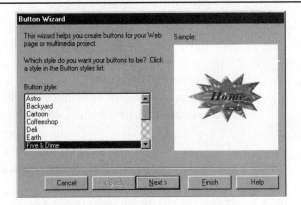

3. In the How Many Buttons Would You Like To Create? text box, type the number of buttons you plan to create. Each button will share the same style (the one you specified in step 2) and will be placed on the composition as a separate sprite. Click Next. The next Button Wizard panel appears.

4. In the Enter The Text Label For The Button text box, type the text you want to appear on the first button. Generally, when it comes to text on buttons, the shorter the text, the better.

TIP You can specify an image file to include on the button. To do so, click the Image checkbox and click the Browse button. The Insert An Image File dialog box appears. In the dialog box, select the image file you want to use and click OK. The Button Wizard panel reappears, this time with a preview of the image you selected. Go on to step 5.

5. Click Next. If you created multiple buttons in step 3, then the panel you saw in step 4 reappears, this time asking for the text for the next button, so take care of that. When you've specified text (or images) for all the buttons you are creating, the next Button Wizard panel appears.

6. In this panel, you can control how the buttons will look. For example, you can make the buttons different sizes (each button sized based on the text that appears on it) by clicking Exact Fit For Each Button.

or

You can make all buttons the same size by clicking the Same Size For All Buttons button. If you select this option, you can either accept the default (which is

PART

II

Creating Sophisticated Designs

designed so that the longest text specified for any one button will fit in *all* of the buttons), or you can specify a preferred width and height for all of the buttons in the appropriate text boxes. You can preview what the buttons will look like by clicking the Size Preview button.

7. Click Next. One last panel appears; this one includes general information about modifying the buttons. Read it and click the Finish button. The Wizard closes and you are returned to the Image Composer window, where those charming buttons you just created are visible in the composition area.

TIP After you have created a button, you can make changes to it by double clicking it. The Button Editor dialog box will appear, providing you with the ability to change just about every aspect of the button.

If it's just a single button image you need, follow the directions in the section titled "Saving Your Image Composer Image" to save the button sprite as an image file, Then, to make it live, turn to the section in Chapter 4 titled "Adding Hyperlinks," and follow those steps. If the buttons are instead going to become part of a larger, more involved image, see the section titled "Moving, Arranging, and Rotating Sprites" earlier in this chapter for information on how to move them to their final resting spot on the overall composition.

Using the Image Composer Paint Tool

Getting or creating graphic images and simply placing them on a Web page does not an artist or designer make. You may want much more detailed control of your images—you might even want to manipulate them at the *pixel* level. Image Composer offers the Paint tool for your nitty gritty design-crunching use.

Using the Paint tool, you can "paint"—that is, draw freehand—on top of any sprite in your composition. Circles, squares, text sprites, what have you—you can mess with all of their pixels.

To use the Paint tool:

1. With a composition open in Image Composer, select the Paint tool. The Paint dialog box appears.

2. Select the sprite you want to play with.

TIP If you just want to make a big freehand drawing, make one big white square sprite and paint on top of it. (Unfortunately, there is no way to use the Paint tool without having a sprite to paint on.)

3. Select any one of the paint effects available to you in the Paint dialog box:

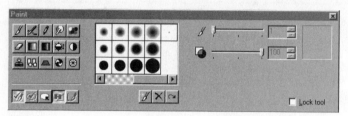

The mouse pointer changes to indicate which tool you chose.

4. In the middle of the dialog box is a box with examples of different brush thicknesses. Select a thickness by clicking the corresponding button. Use the scroll bar at the bottom to see all the thicknesses available.

 TIP To manipulate images at the pixel level, select the smallest brush, then zoom the image up until you can see each pixel clear as day, and start painting them.

5. You're now ready to paint away. Click the spot where you want to start painting on the sprite, and hold down the mouse button as you move the pointer. You'll see the results of your handiwork as soon as you move the pointer. Exactly what you see depends on which of the Paint effects you selected in step 3.

The Paint tool can be very useful and just plain fun. Don't be afraid to experiment with it—you'll learn a great deal that way.

Saving Your Image Composer Image

Once you have all those dandy-looking sprites arranged as you prefer, remember to save them. You must save them before you can actually incorporate them into your Web pages, but you'll also want to save compositions so that you can go back and

PART

II

Creating
Sophisticated
Designs

make changes to them later. As mentioned earlier in this chapter, when you save a file using Image Composer, it will have the extension `.mic`. That's fine for picking up that file and working with it again in Image Composer, but to actually use the image file on the Web, it has to be in a file format that the Web and Web browsers can deal with. Read on.

 TIP You should save your compositions in Image Composer format as you work on them, and wait until you are ready to put them in a Web page before saving them in GIF or JPEG format. This will allow you to make changes to them more conveniently than if you save the images in GIF or JPEG format while they are still under construction.

Saving for the Web

Image Composer comes with a Wizard that can guide you through the process of preparing and saving sprites and compositions for use on the Web.

To use the Save For The Web Wizard to save your sprites or composition in one of the correct file formats for the Web, follow these steps:

1. With a composition open in Image Composer, select the sprites you want to save by clicking them. A border appears around them to indicate that they are selected. (To select more than one object, you can either press and hold down the mouse button as you drag the pointer around all the objects you want to select, or you can hold down the Shift key as you click in turn on each object you want to select.) Alternatively, if you want to save the entire composition, select nothing—by default, everything in the composition is selected.

2. From the menu bar, select File ➢ Save For The Web. The Save For The Web Wizard dialog box appears.

3. If you want to save the entire composition, click the All Sprites Inside The Composition Area button. If you want to save only the specific sprites you selected in step 1, click the The Selected Sprite Or Group button. Click Next. The next wizard panel appears.

4. In this panel, you determine whether or not the background of the Web page will appear through the image. If you want the image to appear on the Web page as transparent (so the Web page's background *can* be seen), click the Let The Web Page Background Show Through button. If you want the image to appear on the Web page as not transparent (so the Web page's background *cannot* be seen),

click the button labeled Fill Them With The Background Color. Click the Next button. The next wizard panel appears.

5. Which panel appears now depends on whether or not you chose to save the image as transparent:

- If you chose to save the image as transparent, you must specify whether a titled image or a solid color will appear behind it (as a background) on the final Web page. If the page uses a titled background, click the button labeled My Web Page's Background Is A Titled Image. If the page uses a solid color, click the button labeled My Web Page's Background Is The Following Solid Color and click the Color button. The Color Picker dialog box appears. In the dialog box, select the color to be used as background for the page, then click OK.

- If you chose to save the image as non-transparent, you must specify the background color you wish to use for the image. In the panel that appears, click the Color button. The Color Picker dialog box appears. In the dialog box, select the color to be used as background for the page where the image will appear, and click OK.

The dialog box closes and you are returned to the Save For The Web Wizard panel, with the color that you just selected now shown.

6. Regardless of whether or not the image is transparent, click the Next button to continue. The next wizard panel appears.

7. If in step 5 you chose to save a non-transparent version, you must select a file format and compression method to be used for the image. In the current panel (see Figure 9.28), you'll see your original image on the left (note that transparent images can be saved only in GIF format, so if you choose to create a transparent GIF in step 5, you will not be offered a choice of file formats). On the right you'll see renditions of the image using different file formats and compression rates. Select the image that corresponds to the method you want to use to save the image. We recommend that you choose either GIF or JPG. (See the section titled "GIFs and JPEGs" earlier in this chapter.) Click the Next button. The next wizard panel appears.

or

If in step 5 you chose to save a transparent version, simply go on to step 8.

PART

II

Creating
Sophisticated
Designs

TIP To determine how long it will take a typical Web user to download the image in each of the possible file formats and compression rates, select a modem speed from the Connection Speed drop-down box. The download time for each of the possible file formats and compression methods then appears above each preview.

FIGURE 9.28

You can choose among formats to save your image, and you can see how long it will take a typical user to download the image in each of those formats.

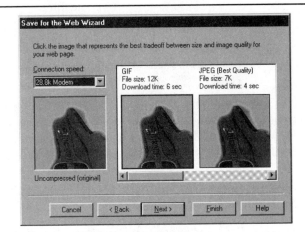

8. Review the summary of the options you have selected. If they look okay, click Save. (If you want to make any changes, click the Back button to return to previous panels, make adjustments, then click Save.) The Save The Current Selection dialog box appears.

9. In the dialog box's list of files and directories, select the directory into which you want to save the file. Also, type a name for the file into the File Name text box. (As always, keep it short but descriptive.) Be sure to use only letters and numbers in the filename. Do not use punctuation or spaces. Also, keep the proper file extension: `.gif` for GIF files or `.jpg` for JPEG files. Click Save. The dialog box closes and the Image Composer window reappears.

That's it—success! You've created an image that's Web-ready. Use the methods outlined in Chapter 4 to incorporate your new image into a Web page.

Saving Compositions

If you save your Image Composer images only as Web-ready files and not as MIC (Image Composer) files, your options for opening and modifying the images will be limited. The entire image will then open in Image Composer as a single sprite—regardless of the number of sprites originally created to make that image. And, instead of being able to isolate and modify a single sprite in the image (say, to change the text in a text sprite), you'll have to struggle with editing the whole thing—and trust us, this (even when it is possible) is a big, big pain. For this important reason, we suggest that you save every Image Composer file as an MIC file. To do so, follow these steps:

1. With a composition open in Image Composer, select File ➢ Save As. The Save As dialog box appears.

2. In the dialog box's list of directories, select the directory into which you want to save the file.

3. Type a short, descriptive filename into the File Name text box.

4. Click Save. The dialog box closes, your composition is saved, and the Image Composer window reappears.

Done deal. You can now open this file in Image Composer any time you like using File ➢ Open.

Closing Image Composer

At the end of your image creation and editing session, it will be time to close down the program. To do so:

1. From the Image Composer menu bar, select File ➢ Exit.

   or

   Press the keyboard combination Alt+F4.

   or

   In the upper-right corner of the Image Composer title bar, click the close program button (the one with the X in it).

2. If at any time during your work you've cut or clipped sprites or images, the program will alert you that the contents of the Clipboard will be unavailable should you continue with the shutdown operation. To accept that, click Yes within the alert box.

   or

   If you've forgotten about something on the Clipboard, and wish to retrieve and save it by pasting it, click No within the alert box. Paste the item into a composition and then repeat step 1 to close the program.

PART

II

Creating
Sophisticated
Designs

3. Image Composer closes, leaving you with the desktop in view.

 NOTE See the section titled "Working with Images" in Chapter 4 for information about incorporating images into Web pages.

How Animation Happens on the Web

Remember the cartoon images that populated the upper right-hand corner of some children's paperback books? When you flipped through the pages of the book quickly, the characters danced and moved about? That same concept of animation—*flipbooks*—can be included in your graphics, in the form of *animated GIFs*. An animated GIF (often called either a GIF89a or just a GIF89) contains multiple images in one single GIF file, with each image resembling the previous one but showing a slight change in position. When these files are displayed one after another in a quick sequence, a miniature animation occurs; it can then be repeated as it reaches the end of each cycle. Each image, or *frame*, of an animated GIF can be edited individually before being combined into the final animation. So the smaller each individual frame is, the smaller the final animated GIF will be.

 TIP Not all browsers support animated GIFs. Internet Explorer has, since version 3, and Netscape Navigator has, since version 2, but some others don't. Those that don't will generally display only the first frame of your animation, as a still image.

 MASTERING WHAT'S ONLINE

The Animation Zone is filled with classic and clever animated GIFs you can use; have a gander at www.anizone.com/.

Creating Animated GIFs with Image Composer

When you installed Image Composer, you also installed a program called Microsoft GIF Animator. This little program allows you to bundle images you've created in Image Composer or gotten elsewhere into an animated GIF. Here's how:

1. Using Image Composer, as described earlier in this chapter, create a sprite for each of the frames to be included in your animated GIF. Each frame should be a separate sprite, although they can all appear (separately) within the same composition area.

2. From Image Composer's menu bar, select Tools ➤ Microsoft GIF Animator. The Microsoft GIF Animator window appears (see Figure 9.29).

FIGURE 9.29

Microsoft GIF Animator

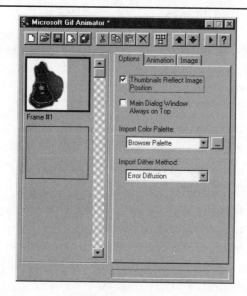

PART

II

Creating
Sophisticated
Designs

3. Resize the Image Composer and Microsoft GIF Animator windows so you can see both at the same time (you'll be dragging sprites between the two windows).

4. From the Image Composer window, click and drag the first sprite over and drop it on the left side of the Microsoft GIF Animator window.

5. Continue to drag and drop sprites from Image Composer into GIF Animator in the order you want them to appear in the final animation.

6. Once you have dragged over all the sprites you want to include in the final animation, in the Microsoft GIF Animator dialog box, click the Animation tab. The contents of the dialog box change to reflect your choice.

7. If you want the animation to repeat one time or more (or even infinitely), click the Looping checkbox. Type the number of times you want the animation to repeat in the Repeat Count text box, or click the Repeat Forever checkbox if you want to create an endless animation.

8. In the Microsoft GIF Animator window, click the Image tab. The contents of the dialog box change to reflect your choice.

9. In the dialog box's Duration text box, type the delay time you'd like to see between images (in hundredths of seconds). The smaller the number, the faster the animation will go. You'll need to experiment here to find a rate that's pleasing to the eye.

TIP You can preview your animated GIF; on Microsoft GIF Animator's toolbar, click the Preview button (it looks like a VCR play button).

10. To save your animation file, on the GIF Animator toolbar, click the Save button (the single floppy disk icon). The Save As dialog box appears.

11. In the dialog box's list of directories, select the directory into which you want to save the file.

12. Type the filename into the File Name text box.

13. Click Save. The dialog box closes, your composition is saved, and the GIF Animator window reappears.

14. Exit GIF Animator by clicking the close box (the X) in the window's upper-right corner. The window closes.

Your animated GIF is now complete and you can incorporate it into your Web pages using the methods outlined in Chapter 4.

TIP FrontPage comes with some pre-made animations, referred to as "motion clips." You can add these by selecting Insert ➢ Picture ➢ Video. In the Video dialog box, click the Clip Art button. The Clip Art Gallery opens, and you can choose available motion clips to add to your page.

Making Better Image Maps

Just what is an *image map*, anyway? Put very simply, an image map is an image that contains hyperlinks. How is that different from an image that *is* a hyperlink? Generally, an image map contains at least two hyperlinked *hotspots* within its borders. A hotspot is a distinct area of the image that is defined as a hyperlink. For example, a national retail shop may want to provide its Web site users with information about the locations of its locations. To do so, the site's designers create a map of the United States with icons that identify each national location of the store (see Figure 9.30). Each of these icons is then defined as a hotspot and is hyperlinked to information about that airport.

FIGURE 9.30

An image map with hotspots

Buffalo Exchange Franchise Stores:
Boulder, Denver, Flagstaff, Bozeman and Buffalo Kids in Tucson
are independtly owned and operated.

More than any other graphic you may use on your site, an image map that aids navigation has to be viewable by all. You really must consider color depth and file size carefully. Your map may be the most beautiful image on your site, making use of tens of thousands of colors, but will that work? If those colors don't view well on a 256-color system, or if they blend together when viewed in gray scale, your visitors may lose the visual clues you've so carefully provided them to aid in navigation on your site. If they can't navigate easily, they won't stay long. Read the early sections of this chapter for more information about what to consider when creating images for the Web.

TIP To accommodate users with text-based browsers, or older browsers that may not support image maps, provide a text alternative for navigation. This is usually accomplished with a row of small text-only links at the bottom of a page that are linked to the same areas as your image map.

Creating an Image Map

In days gone by, there were several types of image maps, and designers had to determine whether the format of the image map matched the format required by the server it sat on. No more; these days, this determination doesn't matter at all. Also, unlike many other image-editing programs, FrontPage includes all the tools you need to create image maps—there is no need to use another piece of software for any part of the process. To create an image map, you essentially create the image, then place it on a Web page, and then place the hotspots—the links—in it.

To create and place an image map on your Web page, follow these steps:

1. Using the methods discussed in this chapter, create an image to use as the image map using PhotoDraw or Image Composer. Be sure to save the image in proper GIF or JPEG format.

2. With the page where you want the image map to appear open in Page view, click where you want to place the image map.

3. From the menu bar, select Insert ➤ Picture ➤ From File. The Image dialog box appears.

4. In the Image dialog box, click the file icon in the lower right-hand corner.

5. In the Select File dialog box, locate the image you created in Image Composer and select it. Then click the OK button. The Select File dialog box closes and you are returned to the Image dialog box, where the filename you just selected appears in the URL text box.

6. In the Image dialog box, click OK. The dialog box closes and Page view reappears, with the image visible.

7. Click the image. A toolbar appears along the bottom of the window.

8. You need to outline each hotspot for the image map. Each hotspot will have a certain shape. To select a shape for a given hotspot, from the toolbar, select the tool for that shape and click and drag over the area that should become the hotspot. (Note that the tools behave much as the tools of similar names do in Image Composer.) When you release the mouse button, the Create Hyperlink dialog box appears, as shown in Figure 9.31.

FIGURE 9.31

The Create Hyperlink dialog box allows you to specify where each hotspot will link to.

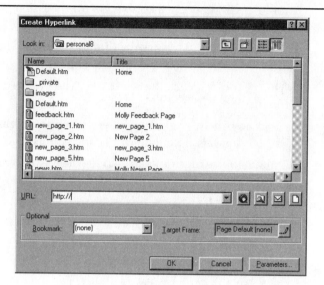

 TIP When novices design image maps, they often try to define small hotspot areas; however, most users don't search diligently for those itty-bitty hotspots. It's a far better strategy to create larger, easier to find hotspots in your image map.

9. In the Create Hyperlink dialog box, specify the target for the hotspot you just defined. (You have all the same options you do when you create regular hyperlinks; see Chapter 4 for more information.) In the list of files and directories that are in your web, select the file to which you want to link, or type the target URL into the URL text box.

10. Click OK. The dialog box closes and the editor window reappears, with an outline around the hotspot you just defined apparent in the image. Repeat steps 6 through 8 for each additional hotspot you want to add.

Adjusting Hotspots

One problem with image maps has always been that when links change on the site—or indeed when whole sections of the site go defunct or launch anew, you have to go into the image map and fix up its links. But this becomes a far easier task with a FrontPage-created image map. To add a new hotspot, simply open the image map in Page view and follow the steps outlined in "Creating an Image Map."

To move, resize, or delete a hotspot, follow these steps:

1. With the Web page that includes the image map open, select the image map by clicking it. Outlines appear within the image to show you where the hotspots are. The Image toolbar also appears along the bottom of the window.

2. On the toolbar, click the Select tool. The mouse pointer changes to an arrow pointer.

3. Click anywhere within the hotspot you want to change. The hotspot's bounding box appears around it, with handles on its edges.

4. Now, to move the hotspot, click anywhere within the bounding box (except on a handle) and drag the hotspot to the new location you prefer.

   or

   To resize the hotspot, click and drag one of the handles on the border of the bounding box until it is the size you prefer.

   or

   To delete the hotspot, press the Delete key.

5. To deselect a hotspot, click anywhere else in the image or press the Esc key.

MASTERING THE OPPORTUNITIES

Creating Image Maps with Professional Savvy

When producing image maps, keep in mind the following tips for best results:

- Because image maps tend to be larger than other graphics, be sure to keep the file size as small as possible without losing quality.

- Put some space between hotspots. At the same time, make hotspots large enough to accommodate a click in the general area rather than requiring users to hunt them down carefully.

- If you use bullets or other small accent graphics near each item in the image map, be sure those visual accents are located within the hotspot—they provide a target for clicking.

- As a courteous, helpful nod toward those with minimal screen capabilities or those browsing the Web with images turned off, always offer a text alternative to the image map. This can be a small navigation bar of text links placed immediately below your image map, or one placed neatly at the bottom of the page.

Making Image Maps Work for Multiple Browsers

Image maps are yet another of the many things on the Web for which no single standard exists. Instead, several types of image maps are used. To understand this, you first need to know how image maps work, which is that they map areas of an image to URLs. Although the creator of an image map decides what areas of the image will map to which URLs, either the user's browser or a special program on the server side translates the image map into something the user can use.

By default, FrontPage uses client-side image maps. Client-side image maps are actually sent to the Web browser by the server along with the Web page they live on; it is the browser that then sorts things out so that the image map works. Client-side image maps are the most common type and they are supported by all modern Web browsers (though not by old versions of Netscape, Mosaic, and the like). Because of this, using client-side image maps is a fine route.

This leaves a bit of a problem, though, regarding what will happen when a user encounters your site using a browser that doesn't support client-side image maps. To address this, you can use server-side image maps along with the client-side image maps you may know and love. Server-side image maps rely on a special program that runs on the Web server, but you don't have to deal with that to make this option work in FrontPage. You do have to choose among the three formats the various servers recognize, but again, that's no big deal. In the end, all you have to do is specify the type of server your site will be hosted on.

To do so, follow these steps:

1. With a web open in FrontPage, select Tools ➢ Web Settings. The FrontPage Web Settings dialog box appears.

2. Click the Advanced tab. The contents of the dialog box change to reflect your choice.

3. In the Image Maps area, from the Style drop-down list, select the type of format your server recognizes. You can find out by consulting your server's documentation or asking your network administrator. Your choices are:

    - FrontPage
    - NCSA
    - CERN
    - Netscape

4. Verify that the Generate Client-Side Image Maps checkbox is checked.

5. Click OK. The dialog box closes and you are returned to the Explorer window.

PART

II

Creating Sophisticated Designs

Although the changes you just made to your page take effect immediately, you won't see any visible changes. To verify your success, preview the image map in both a modern browser like Internet Explorer 4 and above, and an older browser, like Mosaic 1.

Up Next

In this chapter, you learned how to use two popular programs, PhotoDraw and Image Composer, to make graphics for your Web page. Now you're ready to learn about another aspect of sophisticated design: adding multimedia.

Multimedia—especially audio and video—are becoming quite popular on the Web. Chapter 10, *Adding Multimedia*, will introduce you to audio and video on the Web and teach you how to add such media to your own pages.

CHAPTER **10**

Adding Multimedia

Strike up the band and listen here: You don't have to stick to text and images on your Web site; you can add video, sound, and music! In days gone by, experiencing video and audio on the Web was a pretty limited affair—users had to actually download the files and use special viewers and players to see and hear the stuff. But nowadays a wide variety of options are available. The tried-and-true downloadable files are still a great way to go—newer browsers can play them automatically without additional viewers and players, while older browsers still allow users to do the download two-step. But other, newer options allow video and sound to "stream" to a user's machine, appearing and playing seamlessly with no apparent wait for downloading.

Adding video and sound to your site can jazz things up quite a bit. But keep in mind that video for video's sake is no better than gratuitous blinking text. As always, keep in mind your audience's real needs, what equipment they might have, and how you'll most effectively get your message across.

One choice you'll make is which file type to use, both in video and sound. There are pros and cons all around. The most common file types for video are AVI and QuickTime; for sound, they're WAV, AU, and MIDI. In this chapter we'll tell you about the various formats and technologies available for digitizing video and sound for delivery via the Web. We'll also step you through your options for incorporating video and sound into your Web pages using FrontPage.

NOTE   Rule number one in delivering video and sound via the Web is that you must tell users the size of the file. Video and sound files can be very BIG, and the size of these files can overload some users' systems and bring them crashing down. Not only would that be no fun for them, it can kill their interest in your site in a frustrating instant. Do yourself and your users a favor and let them know just what they're getting into when they play video or sound files you've offered.

MASTERING WHAT'S ONLINE

Thousands of sound and video files are available for you to peruse (and sometimes use) at many Web sites. One good site with a large collection of great files is at www.yahoo.com/Computers_and_Internet/Multimedia/Video/Collections/. Apple maintains collections of QuickTime videos at quicktime.apple.com/sam/. Finally, a vast collection of MIDI files is available from www.midi-jukebox.com/.

Using Video with Your FrontPage Webs

In many ways, video is just another file format. Like other file formats, you can store it on a Web server and serve it to a Web browser—nothing special about that. But depending on the format you use to store the video and the software the user uses to view it, the user may or may not be able to see that video you so carefully prepared and offered up. Your challenge is to choose the video format best suited to your audience and your presentation needs. In the upcoming sections, we'll describe the formats that are currently popular for video on the Web. Then we'll dig into how you can embed video in your Web pages.

 TIP In some cases, video is not the way to go. You can have motion on your site without a video-sized investment through the use of *animated GIF* files. These are simply a fancy application of the ubiquitous GIF image files—basically, an animated GIF is like those simple paper "flip-books" that so amuse kids and adults alike. See Chapter 9, *Designing Graphics for the Web,* for information about using Image Composer to create animated GIFs.

About Video Formats

If a picture is worth a thousand words, video can be (and often is) worth a thousand or more pictures. A quick video clip can often grab attention and relay your message instantly. Tune into CNN Interactive, for example, and you'll see that video clips complement many stories, from celebrity deaths to the latest doings of a robot roving around Mars. Keep in mind, though, that a video file can grow to gargantuan proportions; you must take care to keep the file size down and let folks know how big it is before they start to download or play the thing.

 MASTERING WHAT'S ONLINE

News sites are known to incorporate lots of video onto their pages; take a look at MSNBC (www.msnbc.com) and CNN Interactive (www.cnn.com). Many movie studios, such as Fox (www.fox.com) and Paramount (www.paramount.com), also take advantage of video to offer previews of new releases.

PART

II

Creating
Sophisticated
Designs

TIP Bloated video files embedded into your pages without any warning of their size are a quick, sure route to alienating users. One way to address the download problem (although not the only way) is to use a *streaming protocol*. For more on that option, see the section titled "Streaming Video and Sound" later in this chapter.

Plenty of video formats are floating around. A lot of them are perfectly viable, but the problem in using them for your Web site is that not every user can play every file format. For that compelling reason, the best idea by far is to stick to the more popular, commonly used file formats. There are two:

- Microsoft Video for Windows files (which have the extension `.avi` and are commonly called AVI files) can be played on all Windows computers (and that's a heck of a lot of computers). Mac users can also download and use freely available software to play these files, so no one is left out.

- QuickTime is Apple's own video software, but freely available players are in common use on Windows machines, too; the files involved have the extension `.mov` or `.qt`.

Which of these formats you should use is mostly a matter of which format has been used to create the files you plan to offer. Each is strong and has a good following; if your company has a bunch of files of one type or the other in stock, then that format is the one to use. If you are jobbing out creation of the files to a service, they may have systems for one or the other, so that will be your choice. Do try to stick to one of them for your entire Web site, if you can—requiring users to have two players is a bit inconsiderate.

 MASTERING WHAT'S ONLINE

You can find out all about QuickTime at Apple's QuickTime site at `quicktime.apple.com/`.

Placing Video on a Page

When it comes to incorporating video into your Web pages, you have two basic choices. You can:

Embed the video such that it appears in a page much as an image does; how the user experiences the video depends on what sort of browser is used.

Create a link to a video file such that the user downloads the file and then a program on the user's computer plays it.

Let's see how these tasks are accomplished.

Embedding Video for Playback via Both Internet Explorer and Netscape Navigator

Embedding video directly on the Web page allows users to click an image that represents the video and play the video quite seamlessly. No need to download the video file and no need to use any external player software. Because we believe developers of most sites will want as many users as possible to view their content, we suggest you use a method for doing this that enables both Internet Explorer and Netscape Navigator to view the video you present. (There is another, simpler method, which we'll get to in the next section, but only users of Internet Explorer are able to play the files created using that method.)

 NOTE While most users have either Internet Explorer or Netscape Navigator, not all do. Some browsers, such as Mosaic and Lynx, simply won't recognize plug-ins or video files, and that's that.

In using this method to embed a video, you'll actually be setting things up so that the user's browser will employ a *plug-in* to play the file. A plug-in is a helper program that enables a browser to play files it would not otherwise recognize. Both Internet Explorer and Netscape Navigator come with the necessary plug-in for this to work with AVI files. Many users have the plug-in for QuickTime files; those who don't can get it easily. A video file embedded using this technique will appear on the Web page as an image; when the user plays the video file, it will simply *play*—the use of the plug-in will be essentially invisible to the user.

Here's how to get this job done:

1. With a page open in Page view and the cursor placed where you want the image to appear, from the menu bar, select Insert ➢ Advanced ➢ Plug-In. The Plug-In Properties dialog box appears, as shown in Figure 10.1.

2. In the Data Source text box, type the URL for the video you want to include. Be sure to include the proper file extension (.avi for a Video for Windows video or .qt or .mov for a QuickTime video).

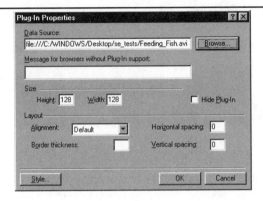

3. In the Message For Browsers Without Plug-In Support text box, type the message you want to appear when users of browsers that don't support plug-ins visit the page. (A good choice might be: "Sorry, but your browser does not seem to support either video or the use of plug-ins needed to play this video.")

4. You can now set any of the following options that affect the way the video will appear on screen:

- Alignment allows you to choose how you want the video to be aligned on the page. (Your choices are the same as they are for images; see the section titled "Adjusting Image Properties" in Chapter 4 for details.)

- Border Thickness allows you to specify the width of a border if you want one to appear around the video image on the page; leave the text box blank to suppress a border.

- Horizontal Spacing and Vertical Spacing allow you to specify (in pixels) the amount of white space you want to appear between the video and any surrounding elements.

- The Size area allows you to specify the height and width of the image that appears on the page representing the video, and therefore, the size of the video.

TIP The default size, 128 by 128, works just fine for most videos, but as always, you ought to test your page by viewing it with a number of browsers and adjust the size as needed so it looks as good as it can in as many browsers as possible. (See Chapter 16, *Cross-Browser Design,* for more on designing for multiple browsers.)

5. Click OK. The dialog box closes. An icon is there on the screen to indicate where you just embedded the video.

The video you just placed in your Web page will not be visible in Page view, but if you view the page using either Internet Explorer or Netscape Navigator, you'll see the video incorporated nicely into the page. Again, when a user clicks on the image representing the video (assuming the user has a browser that recognizes video and can use plug-ins, which means most users of Internet Explorer or Netscape Navigator), the browser seamlessly and invisibly launches the necessary plug-in and the video plays.

Embedding Video for Playback via Internet Explorer Only

One method for embedding video into your Web page via FrontPage has a pretty severe limitation: The files you embed in this manner will be viewable only to users of Internet Explorer. This method may be of interest to those developing an intranet for use within a company that relies exclusively on Internet Explorer as the Web browser of choice, but on the whole it's no easier than the previously described method and carries the handicap of limiting your audience.

As is true of other embedding methods, this one will plop the video right onto your Web page. When a user loads the page, the first frame on the video appears on screen looking much as any other image does. When the user plays the video, that happens right on the Web page. Nice. Too bad it works only for Internet Explorer.

To use this method to place a video on one of your Web pages, follow these steps:

1. With a page open in Page view and the cursor placed where you want the video to appear, from the menu, select Insert ➤ Picture ➤ Video. The Video dialog box appears.

2. In the dialog box's list of files, select the video file you want to incorporate into your Web page.

or

In the URL text box, type the URL of the video file you want to incorporate onto your page.

3. Click OK. The dialog box closes. You'll see the first frame of the video you just inserted there, masquerading as a simple image.

 TIP When you insert a video using this method, FrontPage uses the same tag that's used to insert actual images. You can format the image (setting such nifty options as its alignment) using the same basic techniques you learned in Chapter 4, *Creating Basic Pages,* for images. You can also control the position of a video on a page using tables (see Chapter 11, *Using Tables for Advanced Layout*).

The only way you can tell that this is actually a video and not an image is to right-click it and, from the menu that appears, select Image Properties. The Image Properties dialog box appears. If the item you selected is a video (as opposed to an image), the dialog box's Video tab is selected. From a user's perspective, when the page is viewed in Internet Explorer, clicking the image causes the video to play.

Linking to a Video

An old, tried-and-true, easy-as-pie method for including a video on your site is to place a regular link on the Web page, with that link leading to a video file. (This is the way it was done before plug-ins and streaming video.) When a user clicks such a link, the linked file is downloaded to the user's computer. Then the user can play the video using the appropriate application. If the file is an .avi file, it can be played using Windows; if it is an .mov or .qt file, the user will need the QuickTime player.

 TIP To link a file, see the section titled "Adding Hyperlinks" in Chapter 4. And remember that because video files can be very large, it is customary and common courtesy to indicate the size of the file right there next to the link.

Using Sound and Music with Your FrontPage Webs

In the right place at the right moment, sound and music can make all the difference. For sites like IUMA or CDNOW, both of which present or sell music over the Web, sound clips are downright necessary—they "show" users the company wares. In addition, sound can provide an audio recollection of your company or product—think of all those commercial jingles you end up humming all day! Sound files can also set the stage with mood and tempo for additional multimedia elements.

And, to nab the attention of users in a heartbeat, an appropriate sound file that arrives and plays with the site's splash screen can be a real kick. A sound file like this should be quick, and relevant to the site. A clever example might be a doorbell when you get to the entrance of an online shop. Sound is a relatively low-bandwidth method of adding multimedia features to your Web site.

However, you can quickly alienate users by embedding big, downloadable sound files into your pages without warning users of their size. You might consider using a *streaming protocol* to deliver sound. For more on that option, see the section titled "Streaming Video and Sound" later in this chapter.

About Sound Formats

While there are only two really common video file types in use on the Web, sound file types proliferate. Computers have been capable of producing and playing sound far longer than they've been able to play back video. So, way back when, everyone making computer systems developed their own file type and lots of 'em are still around. Not to worry—even if a sound format was originally developed for use on a system unlike your own, software has almost certainly been created to allow most other types of computers to play that file type.

In general, your decision regarding which file type to use for your own site will rest on what format your sound files are already in, or on what platform you will be using to develop them. Music poses some special considerations, but we'll get to those in a moment. Here are the most commonly used sound file formats for the Web today:

Microsoft WAV files use the extension .wav. This widely used standard format was developed (big surprise!) by Microsoft, so all Windows computers can play WAV files.

Macintosh Sound files, which use the extensions .snd or .mac, are standard for Macs. All Macs, as well as most other types of computers, can play sounds stored in this format.

Sun Audio files, which have the extension `.au`, are standard for Sun computers, so almost all Unix-based computers, as well as most other computers, can play sounds stored in this format.

MIDI files, which use the extension `.mid` or `.midi`, were originally developed to send digital information between musical instruments, but later their use was expanded to include the storing of musical notes in a computer file. MIDI can store an equivalent amount of music in a much smaller space than the other formats discussed here. Because MIDI files actually are not digitized sound, they are not suitable for use in storing nonmusical sounds, such as conversations. MIDI files can be used universally on all computer platforms.

 NOTE The most recent versions of both Internet Explorer and Netscape Navigator are quite capable of playing all the formats listed without requiring the user to install any special software.

In choosing which format to use, again, your convenience is generally the deciding factor—if you have scads of WAV files around, make that your standard format. The only exception to this is if you are including only music on your page, and if the quality of that music is of urgent concern, then by far your best choice is MIDI. Using MIDI for music will produce much smaller files than any other format discussed here. The drawback to using MIDI, however, is that it doesn't store digitized sound, but rather a sequence of notes used to create the music. That's why it is only useful for music—conversation and other sounds don't occur in "notes" and can't be stored in MIDI files. In fact, MIDI files are usually created by someone sitting at a keyboard playing the music to be stored in the file.

This makes it impossible to convert files in other formats to MIDI. Either a file is in MIDI format or it isn't. If you can't use MIDI as the file format because the material is not music (the spoken voice, for example) or you already have it in another format, we recommend using either WAV or SND.

Using Sound on a Page

You have three basic methods for including sound in your Web pages. You can:

- Embed VCR-type controls that allow the user to play the sound at will
- Set a background sound to play automatically when the page is loaded

- Create a link to a sound file so that the user downloads the file and then a program on the user's computer plays it

Let's see how these tasks are accomplished.

Embedding Sound for Playback via Both Internet Explorer and Netscape Navigator

Embedding sound or music directly into a Web page allows users to click a set of VCR-type controls (see Figure 10.2) that represent the sound and allow the user to start and stop it. The sound or music will play fairly seamlessly, without need for downloading the file or using any external player software.

FIGURE 10.2

On the right are Internet Explorer's VCR-type sound controls; on the left are Netscape Navigator's.

NOTE While most users have either Internet Explorer or Netscape Navigator, not all do. Some browsers, such as Lynx, simply won't recognize plug-ins or sound files, and that's that.

Here's how to get this job done:

1. With a page open in Page view and the cursor placed where you want the VCR-type sound controls to appear, from the menu bar, select Insert ➢ Advanced ➢ Plug-In. The Plug-In Properties dialog box appears, as shown previously in Figure 10.1.

2. In the Data Source text box, type the URL for the sound you want to include.

3. In the Message for browsers without Plug-In support text box, type any message you want to appear when a visitor using a browser that does not support plug-ins happens on the page. (One option is: "Sorry, but our site offers sounds that require the use of a plug-in that your browser does not seem to support.")

4. You can now set a number of options that will affect the way the VCR controls for the sound will appear on screen:

   - Alignment allows you to choose how you want the VCR-type sound controls to be aligned on the page. (Your choices are the same as they are for

PART

II

Creating
Sophisticated
Designs

images; see the section titled "Adjusting Image Properties" in Chapter 4 for details.)

- Border Thickness allows you to specify the width of a border if you want one to appear around the sound controls on the page; leave the text box blank if you want to suppress a border.

- Horizontal Spacing and Vertical Spacing allow you to specify (in pixels) the amount of white space you want to appear between the sound controls and any surrounding elements.

5. Click OK. The dialog box closes and you'll see the media icon on screen to indicate where you've embedded the sound.

The VCR-type sound controls you just placed on your Web page will not be visible from the Editor, but if you view the page using either Internet Explorer or Netscape Navigator, you'll see them there. More importantly, when a user clicks the play button on the sound controls, the sound will play—if the user has a browser that recognizes sound and can use plug-ins (which means most users of Internet Explorer or Netscape Navigator).

 WARNING For some reason, pages that rely on the use of plug-ins do not always preview correctly when you select File ➢ Preview In Browser from the menu bar. If this happens, simply use a Web browser to view the stuff and everything will be fine.

Setting a Background Sound for Users of Both Internet Explorer and Netscape Navigator

Background sound can set a tone for a site or identify a product quickly (as in the case of a familiar jingle). Developers of most sites will probably want lots of users to hear any background sound they set, so we recommend that you use a method for doing this that enables both Internet Explorer and Netscape Navigator to play the background sound you offer.

 NOTE There is another method of including background sound that's somewhat easier, but only users of Internet Explorer will be able to play the files created using that method. We'll describe it in the next section, in case you want to use it.

This method actually involves the use of a plug-in to play the sound (much like the technique described in the preceding section). To set a background sound to play automatically when a user loads your page in later versions of Internet Explorer or Netscape Navigator, follow these steps:

1. Add the sound to the page in the standard way described in the section titled "Embedding Sound for Playback via Both Internet Explorer and Netscape Navigator."

2. Double-click the big icon that represents the sound (it made its appearance in step 5). The Plug-In Properties dialog box appears (you saw it in Figure 10.1), but this time, it's all filled in based on whatever you specified for the sound you inserted into your page.

3. In the dialog box's Size area, set the size to 1 pixel by 1 pixel.

4. Erase anything that appears in the Message For Browsers Without Plug-In Support text box.

5. Click the Hide Plug-In checkbox.

6. Click OK. The dialog box closes. The big funky icon is now a small one.

7. Now you're going to edit the HTML directly. This is necessary because the Front-Page Plug-In Properties dialog box doesn't directly support all of the features we are using for this procedure. To begin, click the window's HTML tab. The contents of the window change to reflect your choice—you'll see the HTML source code.

8. Locate the EMBED tag (that's the HTML tag that was inserted when you added the plug-in). It will look something like:

   ```
   <embed width="1" height="1" src="welcome.wav" hidden>
   ```

9. Type **autostart="true"** just before the word "hidden." Include the quotation marks as shown, and make sure you have one blank space before autostart and after "true".

10. Along the bottom of the window, select the Normal tab.

That's it, you're set. Now, regardless of whether a user has a later version of Internet Explorer or Netscape Navigator, when he or she loads your page, the background sound will play. (You can test this yourself by opening the page with one of those browsers.) If someone loads the page using a browser that does not support plug-ins, the background sound will not play, but the page will function fine silently, and they will never be the wiser.

PART

II

Creating
Sophisticated

Setting a Background Sound for Internet Explorer Users Only

The only reasons we can think of why you'd want to specify a background sound to play automatically only when a page loads in Internet Explorer are (a) if you are working in an intranet setting in which all users are known to use Internet Explorer, or (b) if you are creating a sound specifically intended to alert Internet Explorer users to something in particular that you don't want users of other browsers to hear—say, the Microsoft jingle, or an exhortation to switch to Netscape Navigator or something. (Just joshing about that last one.) The method we describe here is a bit easier than what we described in the preceding section, but it leaves out Netscape Navigator users, so think twice about using this method if you want all of your users to hear the fruits of your labor.

Follow these steps to get the job done:

1. With a page open, from the menu bar, select File ➢ Properties. The Page Properties dialog box appears.

2. In the Background Sound area's Location text box, type the URL for the sound you wish to play automatically when the page is loaded.

   or

   Click the Browse button. The Open dialog box appears; in it, select the sound file you want to play and click OK. The Properties dialog box reappears, with the URL text box filled in.

3. You can choose to have the sound file loop forever (that is, whenever the file is done playing it will start again...and again...and again...) or you can choose to play the sound a certain number of times and then stop.

   • To have the file loop forever, select the Forever checkbox. (Please don't use this, really. It's considered very rude, unless the sound file is extremely long.)

   • To have the file loop a specified number of times, deselect the Forever checkbox, and in the Loop text box, type the number of times you want the sound to play before stopping.

4. Click OK. The dialog box closes.

Because a background sound doesn't have any visual impact on your page, you won't see any indication of what you just accomplished. Preview the page in Internet Explorer (see "Previewing a Page" in Chapter 2, *Exploring FrontPage 2000*), and you should hear the sound play as the page loads.

Links to a Sound

That old familiar technique, placing a link on a Web page with that link leading to a sound file, is a perfectly good (if primitive) method for including a sound on your site. (It was done this way long before plug-ins and streaming audio arrived.) When a user clicks such a link, the linked file is downloaded to that user's computer. Then the user can play the sound using an appropriate application—if the file is a WAV file, it can be played using the Windows Media Player; if it is some other sound file type, the user will need the player appropriate to that file type. This is an especially good option if the sound file involved is big—that way, you don't force users to accept a file that might be overwhelming to their systems—or if your audience includes lots of folks with older browsers or text-only browsers.

To link a file, see the section titled "Adding Hyperlinks" in Chapter 4. As always, because sound files can be quite large, it is usual, customary, and courteous to indicate the size of the file next to its link.

Streaming Video and Sound

The traditional way to incorporate video or sound in your Web page is to treat them much like a graphic, as described throughout earlier portions of this chapter. In that case, the stuff is embedded on the page and generally appears as an image (a video still) or a set of sound controls representing the video or sound. (An exception is in the use of background sound, in which case there is no visual representation of the sound on the page.)

When you do incorporate video or sound into a Web page using these methods, the entire video or sound file must be downloaded to the user's computer before it is usable. This process doesn't always require the user to do something, but it does take a bit of time. This can be a problem if the files are multi-megabyte files for longer videos or complex sounds, because they can then take quite literally hours to download. Users simply haven't that much patience, and you'll lose them in the interim. The answer lies in *streaming video and audio*. This method "streams" audio or video files to a user's computer in small, bite-size chunks rather than as one big file.

Think of it like this: When you turn on your television and tune it to MTV (which is somewhat like tuning into a Web site), you don't have to wait until the entire episode of Real World has been sent to your TV before you can watch it. MTV is constantly broadcasting the *data stream* that makes up the television program, and your television tuner grabs it frame by frame and displays it on the television. Streaming technology for the Web works using a similar principle. Once a user starts to view a video or listen to a sound that is being delivered using a streaming protocol, the server starts sending a data stream—the digitized video or audio—to the player, which then grabs the data stream and plays each frame (or some quantum of audio) as it arrives. If the available bandwidth between your computer and the server becomes too low to support this real-time playing, either frames will be dropped out along the way or the video or audio will pause until the data stream catches up. Because streaming video and audio don't require the user to wait for an entire video or sound file to download before he or she can experience it, the likelihood is far greater that the user will play the video or sound just to find out what it is.

Performing all this magic requires that special software be running on your Web server. Also, the user's browser needs the help of a special plug-in designed to work with the particular streaming protocol you're offering. As a result, including some types of streaming audio and video may be more complicated than simply embedding a WAV or AVI file in your Web page.

At the very least, you'll need to check with your server administrator to make sure streaming audio or video support is available. At most, you'll have to buy and install a special server and the authoring tools required to create or convert files to the proper format for streaming. Software is available for the streaming of video only, audio only, or for a fully combined multimedia experience.

Programs such as Progressive Network's RealPlayer and VDOnet Corporation's VDOLive Player are popular options; Microsoft's Netshow uses *unicast* technology to send an individual stream that includes VCR-like controls for start, stop, rewind, and fast forward. Users can play the segment at will, just as they could with a videotape or cassette. Typically, the streaming video or audio software a user needs to experience the stuff is free, and can be easily downloaded; however you'll have to purchase the authoring software and the server software.

MASTERING WHAT'S ONLINE

You can learn more about Progressive Networks' RealPlayer at www.real.com. VDOnet Corporation is at www.vdo.net. A section of the Microsoft Web site dedicated to NetShow can be found at www.microsoft.com/netshow. VXTreme, a recent acquisition of Microsoft, is a leader in the area of streaming video delivery with its Web Theater product. That particular technology has been featured in high profile sites like CNN's, at www.cnn.com. Information about VXTreme's Web Theater and a download of the Web Theater plug-in can be located at www.vxtreme.com.

To use streaming video and/or audio with FrontPage, you must first make sure your ISP or in-house Web server can handle that technology. Ask the ISP tech folks or your network administrator. Having done that, your next step will be to set up the streaming media software on your server; how to do that varies widely depending on which software you use, so find out what you need to do from the company that provides the software. This process is not terribly simple, but it's necessary and the streaming server software company should provide plenty of support.

 NOTE You'll have to use the authoring software provided by the streaming software company you're working with to get your content into the correct streaming file format. This stuff does not convert from format to format.

Then, to make streaming stuff available to your users via FrontPage, you can simply follow the steps provided for embedding video in the section of this chapter titled "Embedding Video for Playback via Both Internet Explorer and Netscape Navigator." When you get to step 2, select the file in the streaming format for the software you're using, then proceed through the remaining steps as outlined.

Up Next

Now that you are familiar with how to add text and images as well as video and sound to your pages, it's time to take a look at better methods of controlling the way all of these elements are laid out.

One of the most powerful ways to manage layouts used on the Web today is with HTML tables. Chapter 11, *Using Tables for Advanced Layout*, will get you started thinking about and using tables as a way to make your page design more sophisticated.

PART

II

Creating Sophisticated Designs

CHAPTER <u>11</u>

Using Tables for Advanced Layout

Tables have traditionally been used, in print, for laying out data in easy-to-read columns and rows, and were originally adopted for that purpose in the early days of the Web. It turns out, however, that they also offer Web designers one of the most flexible ways to lay out very professional-looking pages. Chances are that most of the really beautiful pages you've seen on the Web were designed using tables, because they allow you to combine text, images, and white space in ways you can't accomplish otherwise.

In this chapter, we'll look at how to set up a basic table, and then we'll delve into some serious table work—how to control margins and how to combine spacing, colors, and everything else into a refined design using tables.

What Are Tables?

Tables in HTML are just like the tables you've seen in books, spreadsheets, and other documents. A table is a way of organizing and presenting information visually by using rows and columns to group related elements. Tide tables, temperature indices, train arrival and departure schedules, and Billboard's Top 100 music charts are all common examples of tables.

Scientists who need to present results with more than a couple of variables lay out their data into an easy-to-read grid so they can refer to it later, and so their colleagues can easily compare different parts of the results. That's exactly why tables were designed for use on the Web: so that the scientific community could share data without having to scan it into unwieldy images that take forever to download.

Once HTML table capabilities hit the Web, however (with Netscape Navigator 1.1), innovative Web designers exploited the page layout possibilities. Tables are now the cornerstone of Web page layout, and most layouts, such as CNET's (see Figure 11.1), wouldn't be possible without tables.

MASTERING WHAT'S ONLINE

CNET has used table-based layouts for longer than many sites have. Visit CNET's site at www.cnet.com/; then drop by www.builder.com/ for advice about working with all aspects of Web design.

PART

II

Creating
Sophisticated
Designs

FIGURE 11.1

CNET uses tables to create its advanced layout.

Each work area in a table is called a *cell*. In Figure 11.2, you can see a traditional data table with two columns and nine rows. The top rows of the table, together called the *table header*, explain the purpose of the table. Each of the subsequent rows provides a link to a different HTML tool, and you can find out more about a tool if you read across. As you can see, tables present information in a way that lets you easily look up just the bits you want.

FIGURE 11.2

This table demonstrates HTML reference tools.

A few cool HTML reference tools	
Tools	
Netscape Color Reference	An interactive Color Chart for Netscape
HTML Forms Tutor	How to write Forms for Web Pages
Table Tutor	How to make HTML tables.
Frame Tutor	Constructing Framed Sets of Web Pages
GIF Wizard from Raspberry Hill Publishing Inc.	A gif file size optimizing service. Bandwidth Karma builder

In HTML, tables are also used to present information visually in ways that simple heading-paragraph-break layouts can't do. For instance, you can use tables to create columns of text, to integrate text and images, to create wide margins or sidebars, and to create other sophisticated page layouts. Figure 11.3 shows another page that uses tables to lay out text and images on the page. (Some of the images are words.) You can, of course, use tables for their intended purpose, but the focus of this chapter is to show you how tables are used in layout design.

FIGURE 11.3

This page uses tables to create a sophisticated page design.

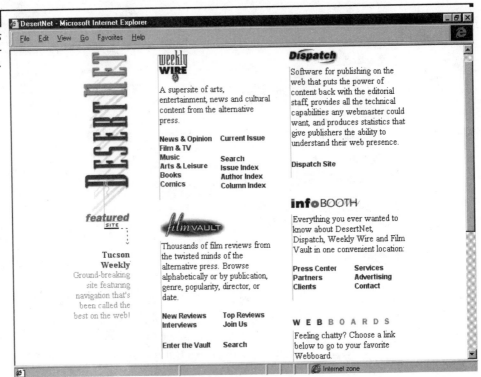

Creating Tables from a Template

You can begin exploring FrontPage's page design options by opening a template with a layout that uses tables to create columns and sidebars. FrontPage offers about a dozen page templates that use designs similar to those you see in well-designed newspapers and magazines—designs that wouldn't be possible on the Web without tables.

In Figure 11.4, you can see one of the templates for creating pages that use tables. Figure 11.5 shows the same page with the table borders turned on, so you can see how the page was set up. Most of the templates offered for creating new pages use tables, and you can view previews of them before you create the page.

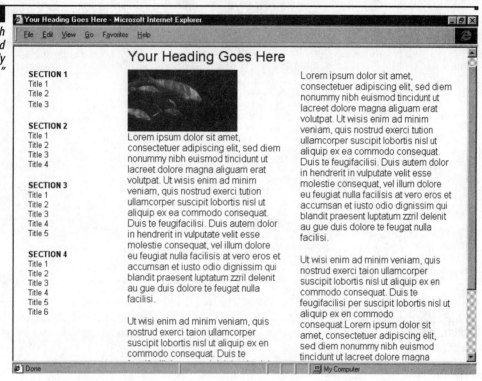

To create a Web page that uses tables from a template, follow these steps:

1. From the menu bar, select File ➤ New ➤ Page. The New dialog box appears, as shown in Figure 11.6.

FIGURE 11.5

This is the same template page as the one in Figure 11.4, but the borders are turned on so you can see where the table cells are.

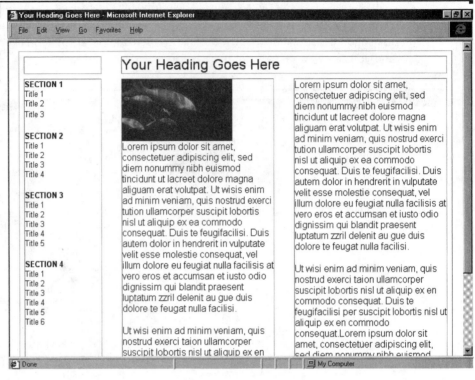

FIGURE 11.6

The New dialog box lets you choose from 14 different templates that use tables.

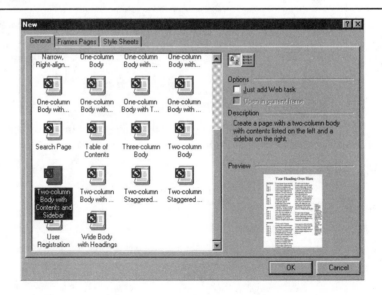

2. The Page tab is selected when the dialog box opens; in its list box, click any of the templates that use tables:

- Narrow, Left-aligned Body
- Narrow, Right-aligned Body
- One-column Body with Contents and Sidebar
- One-column Body with Contents on Left
- One-column Body with Contents on Right
- One-column Body with Staggered Sidebar
- One-column Body with Two Sidebars
- One-column Body with Two-column Sidebar
- Three-column Body
- Two-column Body
- Two-column Body with Contents on Left
- Two-column Body with Two Sidebars
- Two-column Staggered Body
- Two-column Staggered Body with Contents and Sidebar

When you click one of the templates, a preview of the template you've highlighted appears in the Preview area of the dialog box. Keep looking until you find one you like.

3. When you find a page design that appeals to you, highlight it and click OK. The New dialog box closes, and the FrontPage window reappears, displaying the template you just selected.

Now that you've got this template open in Page view, you can replace the text, headings, and images with your own material. Feel free to use what you've learned in this book to change font faces and sizes, text alignment, image sizes, and anything else you like to make the page truly your own. Throughout the rest of this chapter, you'll learn how to make changes to the table itself.

NOTE   You might notice that the text on these template pages is a little funny. "Lorem ipsum dolor sit" isn't written in any specific language; it's the standard dummy text (called *greeking*) used by page designers when mocking up magazine layouts, advertising text, and the like.

Creating a Basic Table

Inserting a table onto a Web page is as easy as setting a table for dinner—just make sure you know how many people you're expecting. You can create a table that takes up the entire page or just part of it—and you can change the table later if you change your mind about how big it should be. Until you put content into the cells, they will all be of equal size and may look rather small on the page.

One Way to Create a Table

The simplest way to create a table is to use the Insert Table button on the FrontPage Standard toolbar. Click it, and it drops a table right onto your page. You can create a 1-cell table this way, or a 4-by-5-cell table (20 cells big, right?). To do this, just follow these steps:

1. With a page open in Page view, click the Insert Table button on the Standard toolbar. A little table menu pops up onto your screen:

2. Click one of the cells on this menu to indicate the size of the table you want to create. For instance, if you want a table 3 cells wide by 3 rows long, you'd click the cell that's three cells over from the left and three cells down on the table menu. When you click one, the table menu closes, and a blank table appears on your page.

All the default settings for tables are in effect for the table you just created. For instance, your table probably occupies 100 percent of the screen width and has a 1-pixel border—but if you've changed these options, the last settings you defined will be the default settings. As we go through this chapter, you'll find out how to change settings to make the table look just the way you want it to.

Another Way to Create a Table

Now we're going to use the Insert Table dialog box to create a simple table that has two columns and four rows, making eight cells in all. Just follow these steps:

1. Open FrontPage and create a new page as you normally would (or open an existing Web page to which you'd like to add a table).

2. Click to place the insertion point at the place on the page where you want the table to appear, and from the menu bar, select Table ➢ Insert Table. The Insert Table dialog box appears, as shown in Figure 11.7.

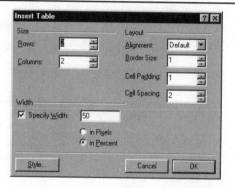

FIGURE 11.7

The Insert Table dialog box allows you to choose initial settings for your new table.

Creating Sophisticated Designs

3. In the Size area of the dialog box, you can see that the default setting for the number of rows is 2, as is the number of columns. These are the settings you adjust to create a different number of rows (across the page) or columns (down the page). To create a table with four rows, type **4** in the Rows text box.

4. In the Layout section of the Insert Table dialog box, you can choose to align your table to the left, center, or right of the page. If you choose to leave the Alignment as "Default," then your table will be aligned wherever the insertion point on the page was before you placed the table. To center your table on the page, select Center from the Alignment list box.

5. Tables are often easier to work with initially if they have a visible border. You can come back and remove the border later, but for now, set a 1-pixel border around all the cells in the table by typing in the Border Size text box.

6. We'll talk about Cell Padding and Cell Spacing later in this chapter; leave those settings alone for now.

7. The last area of the dialog box contains options for the screen width of your table. If you don't specify width, the table adjusts its size based on the biggest objects you place in the table's cells. To specify a width for your table, click the Specify Width checkbox to make the width options visible.

8. To make your table occupy a certain percentage of the window, click the In Percent button to make it active. To specify the number of pixels your table should occupy, click the In Pixels button. Either way, type a number in the Specify Width text box. For example, to make your table occupy 50 percent of the window, click the In Percent button and then type **50** in the Specify Width text box.

9. Now you're ready to place your table on the page. Click OK to close the Insert Table dialog box. Your table appears on the page, as shown in Figure 11.8.

Now you have your very own table, and you're ready to lay out your work.

FIGURE 11.8

Here's the new table you just made.

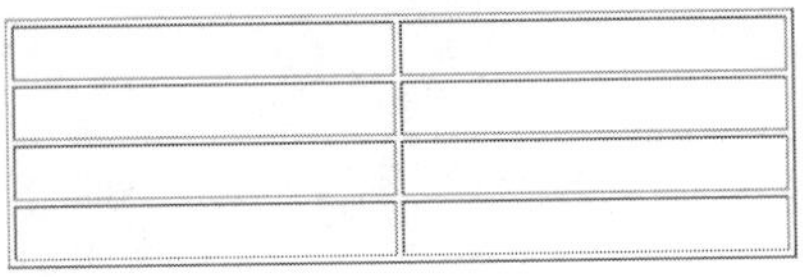

Drawing a Table and Using the Tables Toolbar

You also have the option of *drawing* a table right onto your Web-page-in-progress. The new Tables toolbar includes several different tools for manipulating a table; these tools and their buttons are listed in Table 11.1.

	TABLE 11.1: THE TABLES TOOLBAR	
Button	**What It's Called**	**What You Can Do with It**
	Draw Table	Draw a table or a cell wall
	Eraser	Erase the borders between cells
	Insert Rows	Add a row above the selected row
	Insert Columns	Add a column to the left of the selected column
	Delete Cells	Delete the selected cells
	Merge Cells	Combine the selected cells into a single cell
	Split Cells	Divide the selected cell in half
	Align Top	Align text with the top of the selected cell
	Center Vertically	Center text vertically in the selected cell
	Align Bottom	Align text with the bottom of the selected cell
	Distribute Rows Evenly	Even out the available space between rows
	Distribute Columns Evenly	Even out the available space between columns
	Background Color	Open the Color dialog box, which you can use to set the background color for your table
	Auto Fit	Automatically fit tables and rows in relation to one another after you're done drawing them

As we go along, we'll cover in more detail what all these buttons do.

Displaying the Tables Toolbar

Before you can use any of the options described in the previous section, you need to display the Tables toolbar. This is easy, just select View ➢ Toolbars ➢ Table from the menu bar. The Tables toolbar appears.

Once it's on screen, you can drag the Tables toolbar wherever you'd like, even onto the rows of toolbars at the top of the window. Just drag it up there and drop it, and it'll stay put.

 TIP You can click in any blank space on any toolbar and then drag it into the window to make it "float."

The Draw Table Button

Once the Tables toolbar is in view, you can use it to make tables. To use the Draw Table button to add a table onto your page, follow these steps:

1. With your page open in Page view, display the Tables toolbar, as discussed in the previous section (if it's not already in view).

2. Click the Draw Table button (see Table 11.1) to select that option. The cursor turns into a little pencil tool.

3. Position the pencil tool on the part of the screen where you want a table to appear. Your table must begin at either the left margin, the center of the page, or the right margin. For example, if you start drawing near the center of the page, you can draw toward either the right or left of the page, as well as up and down.

4. When you're ready to draw, click the mouse button and hold it down. A drawing box appears at the cursor beside the pencil to indicate that it's ready to draw a table:

5. Hold down the mouse button and drag it into the window; release the mouse button when the table is the right size. The table appears on the page.

You will see an outline that indicates the size of your table. All the tables that you draw with the Draw Table tool start off as single-celled organisms. As we go through this chapter, we'll learn how to add cells, rows, and columns, as well as how to split and merge cells—all of which will add space to your table. Many of the features of a table can be adjusted with both the Tables toolbar or with menu commands.

 TIP Tables are easy to resize, if you just want to adjust them a little. Just move your mouse over the right or bottom edge of the table. When the cursor turns into a double-sided arrow, click and drag the wall of the table to resize it, and release the mouse button when the table is the size you want it to be. You can resize individual table cells in the same way.

Placing Text and Images in a Table

Now that you have an empty table, you need to put some things in it. You can type or paste text into a table just like you do onto any other part of a Web page. Just click the insertion point where you want to type, and start typing. After you have some text in your table, you can manipulate it just like any text on a Web page, using FrontPage tools to create different text styles, fonts, colors, and headings, or whatever you'd like. While manipulating text and images in a table isn't much different from doing it else-where on a page, we'll cover a few specific elements you may want to use to enhance your tables.

 TIP You can use the Tab key to move from cell to cell in a table, and pressing Shift+Tab moves the insertion point back one cell.

Placing images in a table is also no different from placing them on a page without tables. Be advised, however, that when you insert an image into a table cell, the cell's dimensions expand to fit the image. This can work both for you and against you; of course it's easier to place an image and have the cell expand than it is to try to create a cell that's the exact size of your image. On the other hand, if you're wedded to a certain height and width for your table, you may have to rethink your plans in order to work with the images you have.

PART

II

Creating
Sophisticated
Designs

Aligning Text and Images in a Table Cell

Just as you can change the alignment of text on a page, you can change the alignment of text (and images) in a table. On a standard Web page, you can align text and paragraphs toward the left margin, the right margin, or the middle of the page. In the context of a table cell, you have these options, as well as the option of having text aligned with the top, bottom, baseline, or middle of a cell. Figure 11.9 shows a table that displays the various text alignment options in combination.

NOTE The *baseline* of text is the imaginary line that the letters sit on. *Descenders* of letters, such as the vertical lines in the letters *p* and *q*, dip below the baseline. (Their counterparts that reach upward are called *ascenders*, as in *d* and *h*.) If you adjust the vertical alignment of the cells in a row so that the text in each cell is aligned with the baseline, then the text will sit on the same imaginary line, regardless of whether or not the font sizes are the same. You can see this effect illustrated in Figure 11.9.

FIGURE 11.9

Vertical and horizontal alignments can be combined in many different ways.

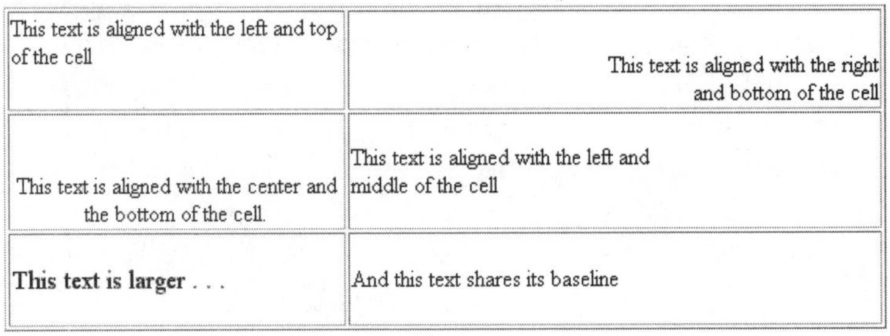

This text is aligned with the left and top of the cell	This text is aligned with the right and bottom of the cell
This text is aligned with the center and the bottom of the cell.	This text is aligned with the left and middle of the cell
This text is larger . . .	And this text shares its baseline

To change the alignment of text in a cell, just follow these steps:

1. With a page and its table in view, right-click in the cell whose alignment you want to adjust. From the pop-up menu that appears, select Cell Properties. The Cell Properties dialog box appears (see Figure 11.10).

PART

II

Creating
Sophisticated
Designs

FIGURE 11.10

The Cell Properties dialog box allows you to adjust text alignment in a cell, among other things.

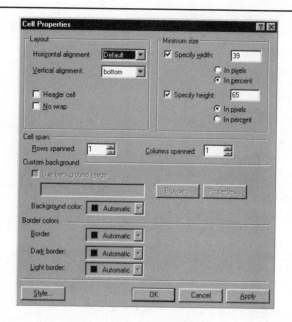

2. In the Layout area of the dialog box, click the Horizontal Alignment list box and choose an alignment (Left, Right, or Center). The Default setting allows the browser to interpret the alignment, generally as left.

3. Also in the Layout area, click the Vertical Alignment list box to choose a vertical alignment (Top, Middle, Baseline, or Bottom). The Default setting allows the browser to interpret the alignment, generally as middle.

4. Click OK to close the Cell Properties dialog box.

Any text or images in that cell are realigned according to your specifications. If the cell does not yet contain any text or images, they'll be aligned according to your instructions whenever you do place them.

 TIP If you already have text in a cell and you want to align it, you can use the Tables toolbar to adjust the vertical alignment. Just click in the cell containing the text you want to align, and then click one of the three alignment buttons: Align Top, Center Vertically, or Align Bottom (see Table 11.1). Remember that you can use the alignment buttons on the Formatting toolbar to align the text with the left, center, or right side of the cell.

MASTERING TROUBLESHOOTING

The No Wrap Option

When a user resizes the browser window, the table may look slightly different from the way it looked when you designed it. For example, text that looks perfectly shaped in a table cell you design may stretch out differently when it's in a bigger browser window. To keep this from happening, you can select the No Wrap option. Cells with this option checked will retain their original dimensions when browser windows are resized.

To turn on the No Wrap option, follow these steps:

1. With your page containing the table open, right-click in the cell where you want to add the No Wrap option. From the pop-up menu that appears, select Cell Properties. The Cell Properties dialog box appears (see Figure 11.10).

2. In the Layout area of the dialog box, click the No Wrap checkbox to make that option active.

3. Click OK to close the dialog box.

This option won't have any immediate visible result; if you want to see it in action, you can play around with turning it off and on and previewing the results of each in your browser window. Once your page is in the browser, resize the window several times and watch what happens to the text in your table.

Creating Table Headings

You can designate one cell as a *table heading*, if you'd like. Table headings, found at the tops of tables, generally announce the title of a table. Text typed into table headings is boldfaced, but isn't much different otherwise. Different browsers may give slightly different treatment to table headings, but the idea is generally the same.

To create a table heading, follow these steps:

1. With your page (and its table) in view, decide on the table cell you'd like to make into a table heading. It might make sense to choose a cell that's at the top of the table; you can also scatter headings throughout a table where appropriate.

2. Right-click the cell you just chose, and from the pop-up menu that appears, choose Cell Properties. The Cell Properties dialog box appears, looking as it does in Figure 11.10.

3. In the Layout area of the dialog box, click the Header Cell checkbox to make that option active.

4. Click OK to close the Cell Properties dialog box.

Any text already in that cell appears centered and bold when you close the dialog box. Any text you type in that cell later will also be centered and bold.

Creating Table Captions

A table caption is a special, borderless cell that extends the entire width of the table. It can be used for a table heading or as a note at the bottom of the table that defines or explains the table's contents. Although a table caption does not have borders, even if your table does, it shares any background color you apply to your table. Figure 11.11 shows a table that has a caption at the bottom.

PART

II

Creating
Sophisticated
Designs

FIGURE 11.11

This table's caption tells what the table is all about. Notice how the caption doesn't have any borders.

Mixing Colors

red	yellow	blue
+ yellow	+ blue	+ red
= orange	= green	= purple

To create a table caption, just follow these steps:

1. Click anywhere in the table to which you want to add a caption. You can use a cell that already contains text, or you can add the text when you're finished.

2. From the menu bar, select Table ➢ Insert Caption. The table caption cell appears. By default, the caption cell appears at the top of the table.

3. If you'd like to change the location of the caption, click in the caption and, from the menu bar, select Table ➢ Properties ➢ Caption. The Caption Properties dialog box appears, as shown in Figure 11.12.

FIGURE 11.12

The Caption Properties dialog box lets you place your caption at the top or bottom of the table.

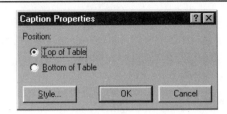

4. Click either Top Of Table or Bottom Of Table, whichever you prefer.

5. Click OK to close the Caption Properties dialog box.

You can add text to your table caption, if you haven't already done so. You can edit a caption with any of the FrontPage text tools to change the font, size, text style, or whatever you'd like.

Editing an Existing Table

So you put a table on your page, and all of a sudden you realize you need four columns, not three, or you have a few rows to add. Perhaps you want the table to occupy more (or less) of the screen, or you want to turn off the border you initially put in (or change the thickness of an existing border). There are several methods for changing a table you've already created. Let's take a look.

Changing the Size of a Table

Although cells expand according to what you put in them, you may want to define the size of your table, especially if you want it to occupy a particular percentage of the screen. Changing the size (both height and width) of a table you've already created is quite simple.

 WARNING If a table cell has text in it, then absolutely do *not* add a height to the table's size. You can't guarantee the amount of space text will need to take up, since that table dynamically moves to fit the text. If there is only an image in a cell, you can use the height attribute, but the height you specify must exactly match the height of the image. This approach is rarely used by professional HTML coders.

Here's how to change the size of a table:

1. With your page in view, right-click the table you want to edit. From the menu that appears, select Table Properties. The Table Properties dialog box appears, looking like it does in Figure 11.13.

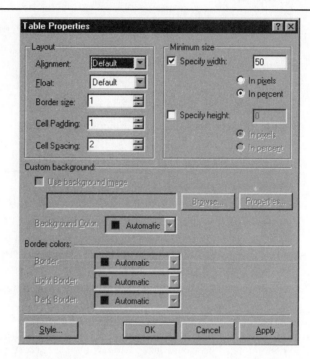

FIGURE 11.13

The Table Properties dialog box allows you to edit many of the table's settings.

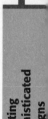

2. In the Minimum Size area of the dialog box, click the Specify Width checkbox, if that's what you want to do. Those options become active (not grayed out).

   or

   If you'd rather have the table size itself automatically, depending on its content, deselect this option by unchecking the Specify Width checkbox.

3. Decide whether you want to specify a width in Percent (of the browser window) or in Pixels, and click that option's button to select it.

4. Type a number (either a percentage or a number of pixels) in the Specify Width text box.

5. You can specify a table height in much the same way. In the Minimum Size area of the dialog box, click the Specify Height checkbox, if that's what you want to do. Those options become available (not grayed out).

6. Decide whether you want to specify a height in Percent (of the browser window) or in Pixels, and click that option's button to select it. Then, just type a number (either a percentage or a number of pixels) in the Specify Height text box.

7. If you need to change page alignment, in the Layout area of the Table Properties dialog box, select an alignment (Left, Center, or Right) from the Alignment list box.

8. Click OK to close the Table Properties dialog box.

NOTE Remember that `<table align="right">` does not cause the elements within the table to align right. Instead, it tells the whole table to align to the right, much like `<img align="right">` does. In fact, image alignment is quite similar to table alignment.

Your table is resized based on the width and/or height you specified. You can repeat this process until you are satisfied with the table's looks.

TIP You can change the border of your table in much the same way as you changed the size. Follow step 1, above, to open the Table Properties dialog box. In the Layout area, type a number between 1 and 100 in the Border Size text box. Click OK to close the dialog box and see your fancy new border. You may want to experiment with borders; some designers prefer not to use them at all, while others find them useful, particularly for large data tables. In general, borders are not used when the table is creating the underlying layout grid.

Changing the Alignment of a Table

If your table is anything other than 100-percent wide, you can align it on the page so that it's in line with the left or right margin, or so that it's in the middle of the page.

1. With your page in view, right-click the table you want to edit. From the menu that appears, select Table Properties. The Table Properties dialog box appears (see Figure 11.13).

2. If you need to change page alignment, in the Layout area of the Table Properties dialog box, select an alignment (Left, Center, or Right) from the Alignment list box.

3. Click OK to close the Table Properties dialog box. You see your table realigned on the page.

Most of the time you'll probably want your table to stay on the left side of the screen, but it's always good to know that you have options.

Adding Rows and Columns

If you want to increase the number of rows or columns in a table, FrontPage makes it easy. Just follow these steps:

1. With the page containing the table to which you want to add rows or columns in view, click the table, placing the insertion point near where you want to add the new elements.

2. From the menu bar, select Table ➤ Insert Rows Or Columns. The Insert Rows Or Columns dialog box appears, looking just as it does in Figure 11.14.

3. Click either the Rows Or Columns button. Notice that the options in the dialog box change depending on which button you select.

4. In the Number Of Rows (or Columns) text box, type the number of rows or columns you want to add.

5. If you're adding rows, click Above Selection to place the rows above where you clicked in step 1, or click Below Selection to place the rows below that spot.

   or

   If you're adding columns, click Left Of Selection to add the rows to the left of where you clicked in step 1, or click Right Of Selection to add the columns to the right of the insertion point.

6. When you're finished, click OK to close the Insert Rows Or Columns dialog box. The page reappears with the new elements added to your table.

FIGURE 11.14

The Insert Rows Or Columns dialog box lets you add elements to your table.

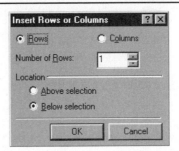

PART

II

Creating
Sophisticated
Designs

You can repeat these steps as often as you need to keep enlarging your table as you see fit.

 TIP You can also use the Insert Columns button and the Insert Rows button on the new Tables toolbar to accomplish the same thing (see Table 11.1). Just click your mouse where you want the new elements to go, and then click one of these buttons.

Adding Single Cells

Sometimes you just want to add a single cell to your table; most often this is done to tables that are being used for visual effect rather than the presentation of tabular data. Figure 11.15 shows a table to which a single cell has been added. Notice that above the added cell, there's some funny-looking blank space that's neither a cell nor available space. This sort of placeholder space shows up because tables are only really comfortable when they're rectangular, and if there's an awkward number of cells, the rest of the space is filled in with border stuff.

FIGURE 11.15

Adding a single cell instead of a row or column lets you make funny-shaped (and funny-looking) tables.

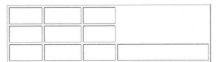

By default, cells are added to the right of a table (or to the left, if the table is right-aligned). To add a cell, follow these steps:

1. With the page your table is on visible, click anywhere in the table.

2. From the menu bar, select Table ➤ Insert Cell. Voilà! You have yourself a new cell.

Of course, you can add a bunch of new cells this way, one at a time, but if you want to add whole new rows or columns, you're better off following the instructions in the previous section, "Adding Rows and Columns."

Splitting Cells

If you'd like, you can create some interesting effects by splitting one or more of the cells in your table. Splitting effectively cuts a cell into pieces so that it forms its own set of mini-columns or rows. Figure 11.16 shows a table whose upper-left cell has been split into two rows, while the lower-right cell is split into two columns.

The upper-left cell of this table was split into two rows, while the lower-right cell was split into two columns. Note how the size of the upper row increased when the left-hand cell in that row was split in two.

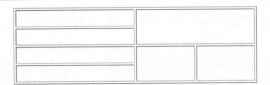

To split a cell, follow these steps:

1. With your tabled page in view, click within the cell you want to split.

2. From the menu bar, select Table ➢ Split Cells. The Split Cells dialog box appears, as shown in Figure 11.17.

3. In the dialog box, click either the Split Into Columns button or the Split Into Rows button, depending on the effect you want to achieve.

4. By default, a cell divides in two when you split it, but if you'd like to choose another number, type it in the Number Of Columns (or Rows) text box.

5. Click OK to close the Split Cells dialog box. The page reappears, and you'll see that your cell has gone through mitosis in the blink of an eye.

The Split Cells dialog box

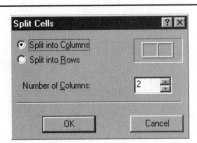

Once you split cells, you can do whatever you like with them, including making them different colors (see "Adding Color to Tables," later in this chapter).

PART

II

Creating
Sophisticated
Designs

MASTERING THE OPPORTUNITIES

Tables within Tables (within Tables...)

You can place nearly any HTML element within a table, and that includes other tables. This is referred to as *nesting*. Just click in a cell and add a table there, and you've got a table within a table. You'll get an effect similar to what you'd see if you'd split a cell into pieces, only when you add a table to your table, you have even more freedom to change the background, the borders, the width—just about anything. You could theoretically keep repeating this process until your page became like a hall of mirrors.

In general, if you can't achieve what you need by nesting two to three levels deep, you are probably not evaluating your needs accurately. You should be able to achieve virtually anything within three levels of tables. Avoid unnecessary code and overly complex tables, because they take longer for browsers to render, resulting in visitors that will click away to a faster-loading site.

This graphic shows a table within a table, and another table inside that one:

Generally, this technique is useful when *all* the content on your page takes place within the framework of a table, and you need to use other tables to place content effectively on the page. This is one of the things that FrontPage is great for—coding tables by hand isn't fun by any standards, but trying to code a table inside a table (by hand) can best be described as migraine material.

Merging Cells

Splitting cells allows you to divide available space into smaller components. You can also merge cells to create larger available spaces in which to put graphics or other elements. For example, you might want to merge two or more cells in one column to create a tall cell, while leaving the cells in another column divided into smaller chunks. Figure 11.18 shows a table in which the first four cells in the left column have been merged.

The first four cells in this table's left column have been merged.

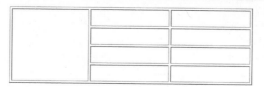

To merge two or more table cells, just follow these steps:

1. With your page and its table in view, click in the table. From the menu bar, select Table ➤ Select ➤ (Column or Row). The column or row appears highlighted.

   or

   To select more than one cell, but not an entire column or row, click in one of the cells you want to merge, and from the menu bar, select Table ➤ Select Cell. That cell is highlighted; with the cell still selected, hold down the Shift key and click the mouse button in the other cell(s) you'd like to select.

2. With the cells to be merged selected, from the menu bar, select Table ➤ Merge Cells. You'll see the lines between the cells disappear.

That's all there is to it.

Removing Rows, Columns, and Cells

Just as you might end up with more data than you have available space, you may end up with some extra spaces and nothing to fill them. You can remove rows, columns, or cells quite easily. *Remember, however, that any content in the row, column, or cell you delete will also be deleted.* Removing table elements is a two-step process:

1. With your page and its table visible, click the cell that you want to remove, or a cell that's part of the row or column you want to remove. From the menu bar,

PART

II

Creating
Sophisticated
Designs

select Table ➢ Select Cell (or Row, or Column). The element you selected is highlighted.

2. Now just wield your Delete key, and your unwanted cells will be gone.

 TIP You can also use the Remove Cell button on the Tables toolbar (see Table 11.1). Just click in the cell you want to remove and then click the Remove Cell button.

 TIP You can remove an entire table the same way, if you'd like. Just follow the steps above, choosing Select Table instead of Select Cell in step 1.

 MASTERING THE OPPORTUNITIES

Evening Up Your Table

Once you've got a table drawn and all the stuff in it, you might be looking at it and wondering if you can make the dimensions of the columns a little more uniform without having to specify pixel or percentage widths for each and every cell. Luckily, the answer is yes. Just follow these steps:

1. With your table in view, select the rows or columns you want to even up. You can use the Table ➢ Select Column/Row menu command, or you can select the elements with your mouse.

2. From the menu bar, select Table ➢ Distribute Columns Evenly or Table ➢ Distribute Rows Evenly.

or

Click either the Distribute Columns Evenly or the Distribute Rows Evenly button on the Tables toolbar (see Table 11.1).

Either way, your table is resized so that the dimensions of the cells in the column or row you selected are the same size as the largest cell in that column or row. You can even select an entire table and then follow these steps, if you'd like.

Some Fancy Table Options

Okay, now that you know how to put a table on your page, change its width, alignment, and borders, and add and remove cells, rows, and columns, you're ready to get busy making those fancy tables you've always dreamed of having for your very own. We're going to learn about spacing the items in your table with cell padding and cell spacing, adding color to your table, and even adding background images to your table and its cells.

MASTERING THE OPPORTUNITIES

Editing One Cell at a Time

You can make changes that affect only certain cells in your table, although some of the options available are slightly misleading. For instance, using the Cell Properties dialog box, you can specify a pixel or percentage width for your cell. Tables are reticently rectangular, however, so if you make one cell wider, the entire column it's in also increases in width. Let's quickly go through the options you have in the Cell Properties dialog box:

- Text alignment options (in the Layout area of the dialog box) allow you to place text at the left, center, or right of a cell, on both the horizontal and vertical scales.

- Width options allow you to change the width of a cell, although these specifications affect the entire column that contains the cell.

- Custom Background options, described in the section "Using Table Background Images," allow you to specify a background color or image for a single table cell.

- Custom Color options, described in the section "Adding Color to Tables," allow you to specify colors for the border of an individual cell.

- Cell Span options let you define how tall or wide a single cell should be. For example, you could set the number of rows spanned to 2 and the number of columns spanned to 3, and the cell would effectively occupy six cells' worth of space.

You can experiment with these options to exert even more control over the look and dimensions of your tables. To open the Cell Properties dialog box, which we looked at in Figure 11.10, just right-click a cell and, from the menu that appears, select Cell Properties.

PART

II

Creating Sophisticated Designs

Cell Padding, Cell Spacing, and Border Width

Cell spacing and cell padding both involve adjusting the amount of white space in a table. *Cell spacing* is the amount of space between a cell's walls and its content, and *cell padding* is the amount of space between cells. While different-sized border widths also affect the amount of space between cells, cell padding allows you to fine-tune the layout of the table even when your border width is zero.

Default cell padding is 1 pixel, and default cell spacing is 2 pixels. These measures are shown here in a four-cell table 100 pixels wide, with a border width of 1 pixel and FrontPage default settings for both cell padding and cell spacing:

pennies	nickles
dimes	quarters

Here's the same table with a cell padding of 10:

pennies	nickles
dimes	quarters

And in this table, the cell spacing is 10, while the cell padding is back to 1 pixel:

pennies	nickles
dimes	quarters

Here, the table's cell padding and spacing are back to default levels (1 and 2 pixels, respectively), while the table's border width is 10:

pennies	nickles
dimes	quarters

In this table, both the cell padding and cell spacing are set to 10 pixels, while the border width is set to 1 pixel:

pennies	nickles
dimes	quarters

Finally, here's the same table with the borders turned off (border width is set to zero):

pennies   nickles

dimes   quarters

As you can see, the options are almost limitless. You can experiment with different settings for all three options until you find a look that's right for the information you want to present. A lot of cell padding, particularly with borders turned off, might be a good way to present images and text together. Figure 11.19 shows just such a table.

 **a mighty lion**

another mighty lion

To adjust the amount of cell padding, cell spacing, and the border width of a table, just follow these steps:

1. With your table and its page in view, right-click the table. From the menu that appears, select Table Properties. The Table Properties dialog box appears (we looked at it in Figure 11.13).

2. To adjust the border size, in the Layout area of the dialog box, type a number (in pixels) in the Border Size text box (or use the arrows to increase or decrease the number).

3. To adjust the cell spacing, in the Layout area of the dialog box, type a number (in pixels) in the Cell Spacing text box.

4. To adjust the cell padding, in the Layout area of the dialog box, type a number (in pixels) in the Cell Padding text box.

5. Click OK to close the Table Properties dialog box. The page reappears, and you'll see the changes you made to your table.

You may have to adjust these properties several times before the table looks exactly like you want it to, but you can wield great control over your page layout with a little bit of experimentation.

WARNING If you're using tables to fit a page to the exact dimensions of a graphic or a specific screen resolution, cell padding and cell spacing can cause trouble by adding space that you do not need. In this case, you'll want to make sure your cell padding and spacing values are set to "0."

Adding Color to Tables

You learned to add background color to your pages in Chapter 4, and you can do the same thing for tables. Not only can you specify a different background color in your table than the color you used for the main body of the page, you can use a different background color for every single cell, if you like—although that would probably look a mite silly.

To change the background color of your table, follow these steps:

1. With your page open, right-click the table whose background color you want to change and, from the menu that appears, select Table Properties. The Table Properties dialog box appears.

TIP To access the Color dialog box quickly and adjust the table's background color, click in the table and then click the Background Color button on the Tables toolbar (see Table 11.1).

2. In the Custom Background area of the dialog box, click the Background Color list box and choose a color to use for your table's background. (Proceed to step 5.)

or

To choose a custom color not shown in the dialog box, click Custom. The Color dialog box appears (see Figure 11.20).

FIGURE 11.20

The Color dialog box lets you pick a color by clicking.

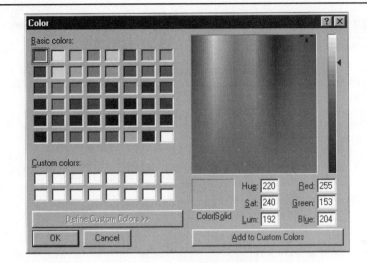

3. In the Color dialog box, select a hue by clicking in the large color box, and choose a shade (lighter or darker) by clicking in the slider box to the right of the color box. The resulting color appears in the Color|Solid box.

4. You can keep clicking, or you can choose this color by clicking the Add To Custom Colors button. Your color appears in the Custom Colors area of the Color dialog box.

5. To choose this color, click OK to close the Color dialog box and return to the Table Properties dialog box, where your new color is displayed as the Custom color in the Background Color list box in the Custom Background area of the dialog box.

6. When you're all set, click OK to close the Table Properties dialog box.

Now your table is bright and colorful.

TIP You can also color table cells by selecting the paint bucket icon on the Tables menu. Select your color and drop it into the cell you want to colorize.

PART

II

Creating
Sophisticated
Designs

NOTE Remember that not all browsers display background colors—this goes double for table backgrounds, as that's an even newer innovation. Make sure to choose a text color that goes well with your background—you can use the <FONT COLOR=n> tag to specify a different text color in your table than you do on the rest of the page.

Coloring Single Cells

You can also color one cell at a time, if you'd like. Follow the steps in the last procedure, selecting Cell Properties instead of Table Properties in step 1.

Coloring Borders

You can make colorful borders for your table, provided you set a border width of 1 pixel or larger. Follow step 1, above, and in the Custom Colors area of the dialog box, choose a color for Border, Light Border, or Dark Border. You can achieve different optical effects depending on the border width and the colors you choose, but generally, all three colors don't show up at the same time. As mentioned earlier, borders are not typically used when creating tables for layout design.

Using Table Background Images

Instead of adding a background color to your table, you can add a background image that's distinct from the background (color or image) of your page. Again, you can also use different background images in different table cells, if you like—but watch that your table doesn't get too cluttered. Just follow these steps:

1. With the page and tables you're working with in view, right-click the table (or cell) that you want to put a background image into. From the pop-up menu that appears, select Table (or Cell) Properties. The Table (or Cell) Properties dialog box appears.

2. In the Custom Background area of the dialog box, click the Use Background Image checkbox to select that option.

3. Click Browse to locate the image you want to use for a background, and use the Select Background Image dialog box that appears to find the image in a current FrontPage web, your local computer, the World Wide Web, or the FrontPage Clip Art Gallery. If you need more help selecting an image, see the section titled "Working with Images" in Chapter 4.

4. When you're done, click OK to close the Table (or Cell) Properties dialog box.

Your background image should be visible where you asked for it (see Figure 11.21).

FIGURE 11.21

We put the back-ground image in the first table cell. Because the lion image is trans-parent, it blends evenly into the background.

Up Next

One of the best advantages of knowing how to lay out pages using tables is that you can really stretch your creativity. No longer are you limited to standard HTML lay-outs, which, while effective, tend to restrict the many variations that tables afford.

With a knowledge of table structure, including cells and rows, as well as the tools available within FrontPage to modify that structure, you're going to be able to set a table everyone will be impressed with. Now it's time to move on to another method of layout control: frames.

CHAPTER 12

Fantastic Frames

Frames can make an entire Web site accessible from a single screen. Frames divide the browser window into individual windows, each of which can hold an individual page. A page that appears within a frame can include any element you can include on a standard Web page. The navigational power of frames can be amazing, and FrontPage is just about the easiest way in the world to get a frames-based page up and running.

In this chapter, we'll start with a frames template, then modify the layout, content, and navigational scheme. Because frames work only with certain browsers—Netscape Navigator version 2 or later, and Microsoft Internet Explorer version 3 or later—we'll also look at what you can do for your technically-challenged visitors.

How Frames Work

When designed properly, frames look great. They act even better than they look, unlike most children. Children are a pretty good metaphor for frames-based pages, because there is a parent page, called a *frames page* in FrontPage parlance, which sets the guidelines for how its children, called *content pages*, act. The whole batch of pages—the frames page and its attached content pages—is called a *frameset*.

Each frame in a frames page is a separate HTML file. You can create any number of documents to go within a frames-based site. The good news is that FrontPage makes it very easy to assign pages to frames. The bad news is that it doesn't create the pages for you. The best way to create a frames-based page is to create some of the content pages before you even start the frameset. Once you place the default pages in the frameset, you can tweak them right there to make sure they look okay once they've been framed.

The frameset page includes guidelines for how many frames will appear in the window, how big those frames will be, and how they will act. Each frame has an initial page setting, and can have any number of subpages connected to the frameset by links. Figure 12.1 shows an example of a frames-based page divided into three columns. Each of the two side frames has scroll bars, while the central frame does not. In this case, if you click a link in either the left or right frame, the middle frame changes. If you click a link in the middle frame, the page that results from that link appears in a new window.

The determination of which link goes to which frame is called *targeting*. The default target for each frame is itself; in other words, if you don't set any targets for a frame, any links the user clicks in that frame will open up the linked document in the same frame. You can set targets to open up a page in a frame, to open up a new page in the same browser window (but not in a frame), or to open up a new page in an altogether new window.

FIGURE 12.1

A three-column frames-based page

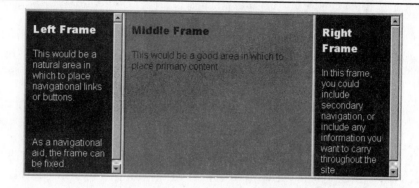

Using FrontPage, it's easy to create pages like this one, and with just as many different design options. Because each frame contains a different page, each page can have its own background color, text color, and link colors, although it's certainly best if the whole thing is designed with some idea of unity in mind. In the frameset shown in Figure 12.1, all the pages were given the same font, and the colors were chosen to complement one another rather than clash. The basic rule to remember is that while different pages are appearing, they combine to make a unified site, and as such they should not clash or conflict with each other.

Table or Frame: The Big Difference

Netscape introduced two of the biggest-ever layout and design innovations in Web pages: tables and frames. (The third, style sheets, was designed by the World Wide Web Consortium, the group that approves HTML standards.) Tables (discussed in Chapter 11) were designed to make it easier for scientists to present their data tables in the traditional columns-and-rows layout. Page designers quickly took advantage of this capability and made it their own, to create classy page designs that make positioning objects on a page more science than guesswork.

Most browsers of the "second generation" variety, such as Netscape 1.1, Internet Explorer 2, AOL 3, Mosaic 2, and newer versions of Lynx (version 2.5 and later), support the use of tables. As discussed in Chapter 16, each of these browsers treats tables slightly differently, but the basic design across and down the page remains the same.

Frames came along later. Navigator 2 or later and Internet Explorer 3 or later support frames, but few other browsers do, or if they do, they don't support frames too well. Because each frame in a frames page is a separate HTML document, you need a powerful browser and a 28.8 or higher connection to load frames in any manner even resembling speedy. The browser first requests the frameset page, which then draws the borders of the frames page and tells the browser to go get the content pages to fill in

PART

II

Creating
Sophisticated
Designs

the blanks—plus any images, Java applets, or other multimedia components contained in any of the content pages.

When you see a page designed with tables, you may not ever be aware of their existence—but you may not need to be. Pages designed with frames, on the other hand, usually command one's attention. Even pages designed using frames with the borders turned off (so you don't see an outline of the frames on screen or a scroll bar within the frame) are pretty recognizable—when you click a link, part of the page changes, while the rest of the page sits pretty without so much as a reload.

Frames pages can use tables as part of their design—each frame can contain any elements a standalone Web page can contain. Generally, frames pages should be used for unique or useful navigational schemes; form should follow function. You can pretty much use tables as you like, because you're much less likely to alienate a portion of the population by using them. Frames, on the other hand, are not available at all to some sectors of the browsing population, and some of the people who can see frames don't like them much. See the sidebar "Why Some Folks Hate Frames (and How You Can Ease Their Pain)" to find out why.

 NOTE Interestingly, designers often use tables to replicate the kind of design used in print publications such as magazines and newspapers. Frames, on the other hand, are a decidedly electronic way of presenting information, and, if used well, can really convey a sense of media mastery.

 MASTERING TROUBLESHOOTING

Why Some Folks Hate Frames (and How You Can Ease Their Pain)

Some people just can't stand frames, no matter how well the frames page is designed or how ingeniously it functions. One reason for this is the aforementioned pull on system resources: It takes a lot more out of a computer to download four pages (and their images) concurrently than it does to download one page and follow its links.

Navigational issues are also a reason. When frames were introduced, the browser Back button didn't act as users expected it to. Instead of taking you back to the previous frame, the entire frameset was treated as one page, and a click of the Back button sent

Continued

MASTERING TROUBLESHOOTING CONTINUED

you back to where you came from—to the location you were viewing before hitting the frames site to begin with. A pop-up menu command, Back In Frame, allowed you to go back through the history list one frame at a time, but many people never discovered its existence. Although this problem has been fixed in more recent browser releases, some folks were permanently traumatized by the disorientation that navigating through frames caused them. Another reason to hate frames is the reason so many people love them: targeting. A link in a frames site, when clicked, can make a page appear in any frame in that frames page, or in the same window (replacing the frames page), or in a new window. Some frames sites inappropriately link to outside sites within the tiny space of a frame on their own page, while others pop up new windows randomly. Many people get annoyed with either or both targeting options, and it's true that designers often use targeting unwisely.

Some folks think frames are just plain ugly. Visually speaking, frames can make the small space available on a Web page seem even smaller. One trick to avoiding this is using borderless frames, and keeping the number of frames you use on a given site down to no more than *three*.

Others have never gotten the hang of printing or bookmarking a single frame, and there's no way to bookmark a particular frames configuration once you start clicking around. Still more don't have, or don't plan to use, a browser that supports frames, and many browsers for the visually impaired aren't frames-compatible, either.

In other words, it couldn't hurt to offer a non-frames alternative to your site. (The non-frames version clearly should include the same content as the frames version.) Another solution is to offer a help page that includes instructions for working with the frames.

It is quite possible for users to print out the frameset from most Web browsers, either as individual frames or as a whole set. In later versions of Navigator, selecting File ➢ Print Frame from the menu bar prints a single frame, or File ➢ Print Preview double-checks what's being printed. In later versions of Internet Explorer, from the menu bar, select File ➢ Print and from the Print dialog box that opens, you can select any of several frame-printing options.

Bookmarking a single frame is also deceptively easy. In either browser, just right-click some blank space in the frame you want to bookmark. From the pop-up menu that appears, select Add Bookmark (Navigator) or Add To Favorites (Internet Explorer). The page displayed in the current frame will be bookmarked. Of course, this bookmarks only the single page and not the frames configuration, but if that page has the content you want, it's better than nothing.

Frames are not the evil, difficult beasts many people think they are. They can, in fact, be extraordinarily useful as a navigation device, and with a bit of nudging, users can benefit from an encounter with a framed site.

PART

II

Creating
Sophisticated
Designs

Uses for Frames

So are frames good for anything? Yes, yes, indeed yes! Any time your page would benefit from displaying multiple documents in the same window, you'll find frames quite handy. Let's take a look at some common and creative uses of frames:

Search engines The query form appears in one frame, and the results in another, so that the two are side by side. In this case, you'd want to target the links of the query results to appear in a new window.

Tables of contents These often appear as a long, thin frame on the left side of the window. When you click a link in the table of contents, its target appears in a larger frame in the same window.

Button bars Similar to a table of contents, a button bar or navigation tool set is visible during the whole visit in a frame at the top, bottom, or side of the central navigation area.

Footnotes Scholarly research papers don't take advantage of the frames footnotes idea nearly often enough. Users click the noted word in the main body of the window, and the footnote appears simultaneously in a smaller frame at the bottom of the window.

Guestbooks Visitors type comments in a form in one frame and, when they click Send, their comments appear in another frame.

Art catalogs You place an image in one frame, and the text that corresponds to it in another, complete with scroll bars. While the general idea is of the exhibition catalog, frames work beautifully in any instance in which an image is visible on screen while its related text is being read.

Banner ads Many sites use a separate frame in which to present their banner advertisements. For some, this solves the problem of how to integrate ads into the design of an overall page.

Multimedia Use one frame as the container for a sound file, a Shockwave movie, a Java applet, or an inline video clip.

You're bound only by your imagination and the limits of good taste.

MASTERING THE OPPORTUNITIES

Make a Navigational Frame

One clever use for frames is including a navigational frame that stays the same throughout the user's visit. The user clicks links or buttons in that frame to visit a new part of your site or to return to a part they're not finished with yet. Those links, of course, are targeted to open up in another frame on that page—usually the largest frame.

A navigational frame can take many different forms. You could put a full or abridged table of contents in a column-frame spanning the left side of the window. You could create a button bar and put it in a frame at the top or bottom of the window. The main thing is that this frame has links, in the form of words, buttons, or icons, which the user can click to move through your site.

The contents of this navigational frame should also appear on the nonframes page. That way, you've already got all the links for your site on one handy page; put the contents of this page on the nonframes page, and people will be able to navigate your site by clicking the same links your frames visitors use. You can create a navigation bar in a snap using the Navigation Bar component described in Chapter 15.

PART

II

Creating
Sophisticated
Designs

Planning Your Frames Page

Because there are so many variables, it's quite important to plan your site before you start creating one that uses frames. Planning a frame site might involve steps like these:

1. Make a rough sketch, on paper, of what the frames page will look like, including the number of frames, how much screen space each will occupy, whether they'll have borders, and whether they'll have scroll bars.

2. Plan a background, text, and link color scheme for each frame, keeping in mind the site as a whole. For instance, are you going to use a black background and yellow text in every single frame, or just in one part?

3. Create the pages that will fill in the blanks. Ideally, you should at least have a basic page for each frame in your frameset, although creating the content pages before you start the project isn't essential. You can use pages you created

months ago for another project in a new frames page, or you can create the whole thing on the fly.

4. Open up FrontPage and get to work putting the thing together!

5. Target your links: Define what will happen when you click each and every link in your page. (You can set defaults for each frame, in which case you need only specify targets for single links that depart from your default settings.)

Once you've planned your frames site, it's time to get to work making it.

MASTERING WHAT'S ONLINE

Interested in the HTML code behind frames? Netscape, the company that pioneered frames, offers an excellent frames tutorial at `home.netscape.com/comprod/products/ navigator/version_2.0/frames/`. You can also learn about frames from HotWired's HTML reference site, Webmonkey. The frames tutorial starts at `www.hotwired.com/ webmonkey/html/96/31/index4a.html`.

Creating Frames Pages from a Template

FrontPage offers several template options and frames editing methods. You can create any frames design under the sun by starting with the templates provided by FrontPage.

NOTE Unlike other FrontPage templates, such as those for forms and tables, there is no easier way to create a frames page than by starting with a template. As you pick up the knack of creating frames pages, you can save your creations under different names and work with templates of your own design. Starting from scratch may seem like a noble goal for the erstwhile purist, but in this case it ain't worth it.

Table 12.1 shows FrontPage's frames layouts. Choose the layout that's closest to your sketch of how your page should look, and start with that one. You can add and delete frames to any template.

TABLE 12.1: FRAME PAGE LAYOUTS OFFERED BY FRONTPAGE TEMPLATES

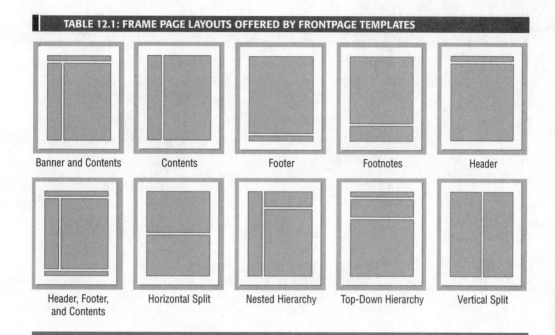

| Banner and Contents | Contents | Footer | Footnotes | Header |

| Header, Footer, and Contents | Horizontal Split | Nested Hierarchy | Top-Down Hierarchy | Vertical Split |

PART

II

Creating Sophisticated Designs

Let's make ourselves a frames page. Just follow these steps:

1. From the menu bar, select File ➤ New ➤ Page. The New dialog box appears.

2. Click the Frames Pages tab. The dialog box changes to reflect your choice, as shown in Figure 12.2.

3. You can choose from ten different frames layouts, as detailed in Table 12.1. Click the name of a layout, and a preview and description appears in the right side of the dialog box.

NOTE Remember that you can still add or remove frames after you choose a layout—you're going for a general similarity to your ideas here, rather than an exact match.

FIGURE 12.2

*Choose your layout
from the Frames tab of
the New dialog box.*

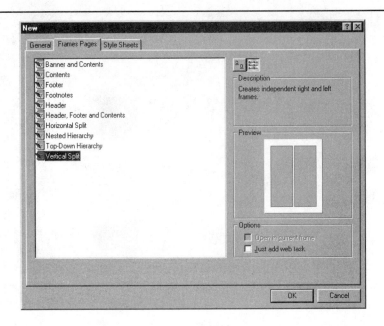

4. When you find a layout you like, click it, and then click OK. The New dialog box closes, and the layout of your frames page is displayed.

The gray fields that appear are mockups of your frame pages. They're what you'll use to assign individual HTML pages to each frame. Each pane in the frameset is represented by a blank, gray frame with its own set of buttons. Figure 12.3 shows an example of what you'll see in Page view when you create a frame using a template.

When you want to edit a particular frame, you select it by clicking it. Click around in the frames on your new template and watch how the selected frame becomes highlighted at its borders. Now that you have a frames template to work with, let's start doing just that.

FIGURE 12.3

This template creates two horizontal frames. Note that each has its own set of buttons.

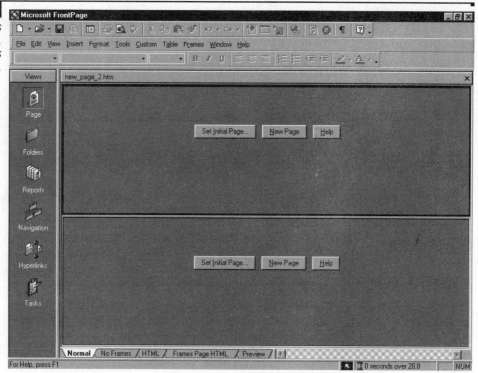

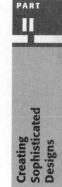

Editing Frames and Frame Pages

FrontPage's design for the frames editing tools is nothing short of brilliant. It's completely obvious when you use this tool that each frame contains a separate document—which is a concept that's tough to grasp for most Web users. Once you attach documents to the frames, they appear in Page view, where you can edit them. The few other frames editors in existence simply aren't this classy or easy to use.

You can start editing your frames page in any order you like. You can attach initial pages that are already finished to all the frames and just tweak them a bit to finish. Or you can attach some initial pages that are partially done one at a time, completing them as you go along. Or you can create the whole thing on the fly. Your working methods are up to you. We're going to go through each task you might consider doing one at a time.

MASTERING WHAT'S ONLINE

A classic in frames development is Cocktail, the HotWired site about the history and variations of the mixed drink. Point your browser at `www.hotwired.com/cocktail/`, and click around a bit. Note in particular the way that Cocktail's links are targeted to appear in different frames depending on the context.

Redesigning the Frames Page Layout

If the template's page layout is exactly what you want, you can skip this section. If you'd like to add frames to your template (or delete them), this is the place to be. You can redesign the layout of your frames page in three different ways: resizing frames, deleting frames, and splitting frames.

Just follow these steps to do any or all of the above:

1. With your frames template open in Page view, to resize a frame, just click the border between two frames and drag it right or left (for vertical borders); or up or down (for horizontal borders). (Obviously, you're going to resize both frames, and not just the one.) When it looks good, let go of the mouse button.

2. To split a frame, click in the frame you'd like to split. From the menu bar, select Frame ➢ Split Frame. The Split Frame dialog box appears:

3. If you'd like to split the frame lengthwise, click the Split Into Rows button. If you'd like to split the frame vertically, click the Split Into Columns button. A preview of your choice appears in the dialog box when you click either button.

4. Click OK to close the Split Frame dialog box. The FrontPage window appears, and you'll see your frame divided in half—each panel has its own set of buttons.

TIP After you split a frame, you can drag the border between the two halves to resize them, if you don't want them to be symmetrical.

5. To delete a frame, click in the frame you'd like to delete. From the menu bar, select Frames ➤ Delete Frame. The frame you selected disappears—or rather, because it's a portion of a larger page, its borders disappear—and its space is reabsorbed by an adjoining frame.

You can repeat any or all of these steps to add, resize, and remove frames until the page looks like you want it to. Starting with one of the FrontPage templates, you can achieve any layout you like by splitting, deleting, and resizing frames. Figures 12.4 through 12.7 demonstrate the redesign of a frames page following the steps we've described.

FIGURE 12.4

*This frames page
was created with the
Nested Hierarchy
template.*

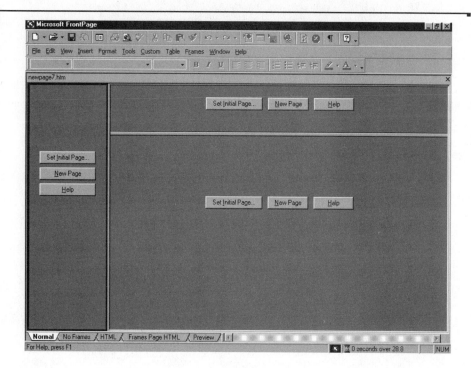

FIGURE 12.5

The two frames at the right have been resized by dragging the border between them.

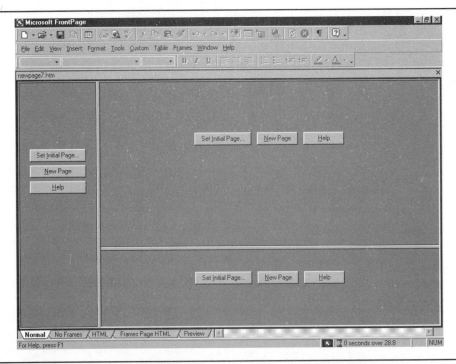

FIGURE 12.6

The bottom-right frame in Figure 12.5 was split into the two frames you see here.

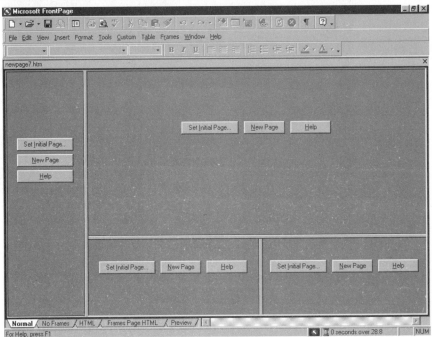

FIGURE 12.7

The left-side frame in Figure 12.6 was deleted, creating the layout you now see.

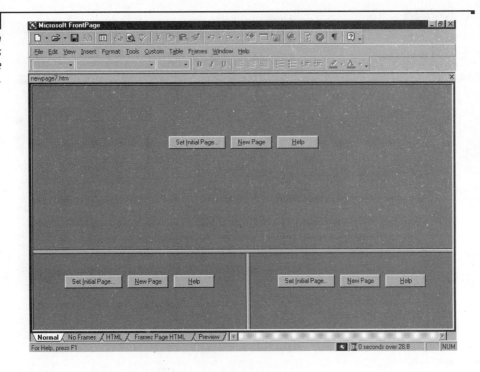

Attaching an Initial Page to a Frame

The *initial page*, also known as a *default page*, is the page that "belongs" to a frame. When the entire frames page is loaded into a browser window, each frame needs to be filled with something at the outset, and this something is the initial page. No matter what the frames get filled with over the course of clicking and backtracking and clicking again, the initial pages will always be the starting point for your frames-based site.

To attach an initial or default page to a frame, follow these steps:

1. With your frames template visible in Page view, click in the frame you'd like to work with to highlight it.

2. Click the frame's Set Initial Page button. The Create Hyperlink dialog box appears, as shown in Figure 12.8.

FIGURE 12.8

*Use the Create
Hyperlink dialog box
to attach an initial
page to your frame.*

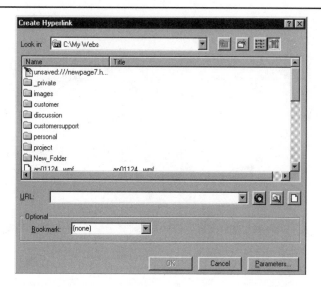

3. To attach a page that's open or available in your current FrontPage web, just click the name of the page in the file display area.

or

To attach a page that's on your hard drive, click the Attach Page button:

4. The Select File dialog box appears. Browse through the files and folders on your computer until you find the Web page you want. When you've selected your page, click OK to select your file. The Select File dialog box closes, returning you to the Create Hyperlink dialog box.

or

To attach a page that's already on the Web, type or paste its URL in the URL text box. To select a page using your Web browser, click the Use Web Browser button.

5. A browser window opens; you can use it to locate the page on the Web. When you're done, click the FrontPage button on the taskbar. The FrontPage window reappears with the URL of the page you selected in the URL text box.

6. When the address (either local or Internet) of the page is in the URL text box, click OK to close the Create Hyperlink dialog box. The window reappears, where you'll see the page you selected in step 3 displayed in its frame.

You can follow these steps for each and every frame in your page. You can also create a new page right in the frames template. See the following section, "Attaching a New Page to a Frame."

 TIP If you select an initial page for a frame and then change your mind, fixing it is easy. Click the frame whose initial page you want to replace and, from the menu bar, select Frame ➢ Set Initial Page. The Create Hyperlink dialog box appears, and from there you can follow steps 3 and 4, above.

 MASTERING THE OPPORTUNITIES

Dropping a Frames Page into a Frame

For a really interesting visual effect, you can embed a frames page into another frames page. In other words, you can set a frames page as one of your initial pages in a frameset, and the frames page will appear as the content of one of the frames.

This technique should be used sparingly, or it can look really cluttered and be overly demanding of system resources. It might be a nice approach for your initial splash screen page, however. You can set a frames page as an initial frame (see "Attaching an Initial Page to a Frame") and then set that frame's target as parent (see "Creating Target Settings"). Then, when someone clicks a link in that area of your site, the new destination page will replace the frames page as the content of your frame. Try it! You'll like it.

Attaching a New Page to a Frame

If you'd like, you can create a new page in your frame, a complete blank slate waiting to be filled with text, graphics, or other objects. For example, if one of your frames is simply going to include a title or a logo, there's no need to create it ahead of time. You can add a new page to your frameset and create it right in the frames template.

PART

II

Creating Sophisticated Designs

To add a new page to your frameset, follow these steps:

1. With your frames template visible in Page view, click in the frame you want to add a page to.

2. Click that frame's New Page button. A blank white page appears in the frame.

That's all there is to that. Now you can start working with the page as you would any other. In the section titled "Editing Pages within the Frames Page," we'll discuss some tips for working with pages in the frameset.

Saving a Frameset

A *frameset* is made up of several pages: the frames page, which is the behind-the-scenes page that holds the instructions for how the frameset should look and act; and the initial pages for every frame in the frameset. When you save a frameset, you must save all of these pages. If you've attached initial pages to your frameset that were previously saved within FrontPage, you have to save only the frames page to save the whole batch. If your frameset has any new or blank pages, including pages that initially came from the Web, you'll need to save those, too.

When you save a frameset, you need to specify the filename and the page title for the frames page and for each initial page in the frameset. FrontPage provides default suggestions, but specifying your own titles can be much more helpful than having tons of pages titled "New Page 1," "New Page 2," and so on.

The filename of the main frames page is used in the URL of the entire page: what you link to when you're pointing people there. The filename of each initial frame is stored as a URL in the frames page to let it know which initial pages to load.

 TIP If your whole web is frames-based, then your web's index file (`default.htm`, the home page file) should contain your web's frameset. This will cause the frames to appear automatically whenever anyone accesses your site.

The page title, which is displayed in your browser's title bar when viewing standalone pages, isn't absolutely necessary for each frame, but having a page title can be helpful while you're editing the frameset with FrontPage. When you click in a frame in FrontPage, the title bar displays both the title of the entire frameset and the title of the individual frame, so giving your frames a distinct name—even if it's something like *left* or *blue*—can help you distinguish what you're editing.

No matter what state of completion your frameset is in, just follow these steps to save the whole thing:

1. With your frames page visible in Page view, from the menu bar, select File ➤ Save. The Save As dialog box appears, as shown in Figure 12.9. Pay special attention to the preview area at the right of the Save As dialog box. The panel of the frame that's highlighted in this preview area indicates which frame you're saving.

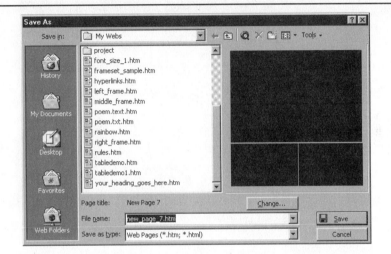

2. In the File Name text box, type the filename of the page you're saving. If you want to change the title, click the Change button, and the Set Page Title dialog box appears. Type in the name you want to use and Click OK.

3. Verify where you're saving the file. If you're saving it in your current FrontPage web, select the folder you want to save it in, if any, by clicking it in the file display area.

4. When you've verified the filename, page title, and location to your liking, click OK. The Save As dialog box closes and then reappears. Note that a different frame is highlighted in the preview area at the right of the dialog box.

5. Follow steps 2 through 4 for every frame in your frameset. A new Save As dialog box opens as soon as you finish saving each frame. When the dialog box looks like Figure 12.10, then you're saving the main frames page. The procedure is the same for this page, except that the filename and page title are slightly more important, because they will be the title and URL displayed to the world when they look at your frames page.

6. When you've finished saving the final frames page, click OK, and the last of the Save As dialog boxes closes.

Now you've saved everything. Click around in the frames displayed in the Editor window, and keep your eye on the title bar. Note how the title bar displays both the title for the main frames page and the title of each individual frame.

FIGURE 12.10

The heavy border around all the frames in the preview area indicates you're saving the frames page itself— it's mission control for your entire frameset.

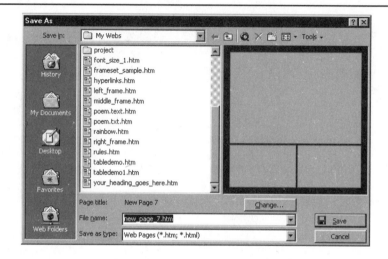

 TIP You can save changes to any individual frame at any time by clicking in it and then selecting File ➢ Save from the menu bar. You can also select File ➢ Save As if you'd like to save a different version of your frame, which you can connect to your frameset later by linking to it.

Editing Pages within the Frames Page

As we've said, you can put any kind of content into a frame that you'd put on a stand-alone Web page. Editing these pages is just like editing a new, blank page. You can set text and link colors, a background color or image, and a page title. You can add text in any form, including headings, lists, and formatted text. Forms and tables both feel right at home in a frame, as do images, plug-ins, and Java applets.

You're welcome to create a complete page and *then* attach it to a frameset. You can also attach a partially completed or completely blank page to a frameset and then edit it. The only difference is what you see on screen while you're editing. While it's helpful to see several pages all at once, editing pages within the frameset in FrontPage can be memory-intensive.

To find out more about editing pages in general, refer to Chapter 4, *Creating Basic Pages*. The principles are all the same, except that you can work with several pages all within the same window. Click in whichever frame you'd like to work with, and all the menu commands and toolbar buttons you use to edit standalone pages will apply to that frame.

TIP To view page properties for a frames page, click that frame to highlight it. Then, from the menu bar, select File ➢ Properties. The Page Properties dialog box appears, which you can use to adjust the page's title, background, and text and link colors, among other things. Refer to Chapter 4 for information about setting colors for your pages.

Adjusting Frame Properties

In addition to the properties that every Web page has, the frames in a frameset have properties of their own. These properties are saved in the main frames page, which stores information about the layout and functions of every frame in a frameset. When you're working with a frameset, however, you adjust the properties for each frame individually, rather than making the changes all at once.

Frame properties affect how the individual frame will look and act once it's up on the Web and viewable by Web browsers. These properties include whether a frame can be resized in the browser window, whether it will have scroll bars, what dimensions the frame will have, and what portion of the window it will occupy. You can also set margins for a frame, which will control the distance between the objects in a frame and its borders.

Let's take a look at the options available for each frame, and then we'll show you how to use the Frame Properties dialog box, shown in Figure 12.11, to achieve these effects.

The Frame Properties dialog box lets you adjust the size and margins of your frames, among other things.

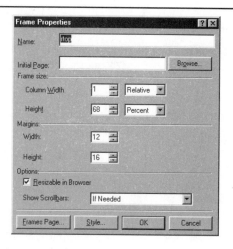

Resize Options

In the section titled "Redesigning the Frames Page Layout," we resized frames in the frames page by clicking their borders and then dragging them. If you set the frame properties so that frames can be resized, then visitors to your page will be able to do the same thing. You can turn off resizing for an individual frame if you don't want your page's layout changed, but it's generally more convenient for the user to be able to resize a given frame.

WARNING Remember, you should not assume that your page will be viewed by someone with the same screen size, resolution, or font sizes you use. What takes up a single line when you preview it may take up several lines on someone else's screen. Always design with a 640 × 480 screen resolution in mind, and in general, you should always enable resizing—or at least scroll bars—so crucial parts of your pages don't get axed on some other people's machines.

Scroll Bars

Each frame is perfectly capable of having its own scroll bars, either horizontal, vertical, or both. There are three scroll bar settings you can choose for each frame: If Needed, Always, and Never. In general, If Needed (also called Auto) is probably the best choice for most pages, and is also the default setting. The scroll bars show up if they're needed, and they stay out of the way if they aren't.

NOTE If you set the frame properties for scroll bars to If Needed, then a vertical scroll bar will be displayed in the window even if they're not needed to remind you that you've chosen this setting.

You can choose Never if you're dead certain that your frame will never include content that will scroll off screen. However, it's dreadfully annoying to see only half a word or two-thirds of a picture on your 15-inch monitor because some clever Webmaster with a 17-inch monitor has turned off scroll bars in his or her frames.

We can't think of a compelling reason to choose Always. You could select this setting if you predict that the frame will soon be filled with scroll-happy content resulting from some click or other, and you want your users to be prepared. Drawing the scroll bars in before they're needed might save the browser a few heartbeats.

Frame Size

Frame size is perhaps the most important property of each and every frame on your page. When you created your frames page using a template, FrontPage gave a cursory nod to frame size. If you resized your frames at all by dragging their borders, you may have unrhymed any reason the FrontPage size settings had.

In particular, sizing is important if you want two frames to be the same size, or any other important proportion. For example, you may want one frame to look twice as big as another, and there's no better guarantee than making the size settings stick.

 NOTE If you don't set the sizes of your frames in stone, your pages may look nothing like they do in Page view once you view them in a Web browser.

Framesets, like tables, are defined by columns (vertical divisions of space) and rows (horizontal divisions of space). In the Frame Properties dialog box, the setting for Height is also called Row Height, while the setting for Width is also called Column Width, depending on the dimensions of the frame. Additionally, the measurement for each column or row can be defined in pixels (we call this *absolute size*) or as a percentage of the screen. You can also set a frame's measurement as Relative, which means that its width and height will be based on the other frames on the page. The frameset shown in Figure 12.12 has two columns and two rows, although the rows are confined to the right half of the screen.

PART

II

Creating
Sophisticated
Designs

FIGURE 12.12

This frameset has two columns and two rows. The frame on the left spans 144 pixels, and the two right-side frames each occupy 50 percent of the window height.

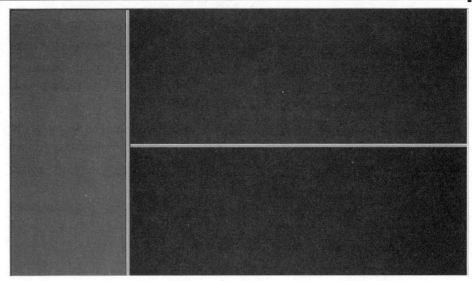

Because all the frames in a page are interdependent, you should set one frame's size first, and then base the other frames' sizes on that one. In the example shown in Figure 12.12, we decided to make the leftmost frame 144 pixels wide to exactly fit an image we're going to place there. Therefore, we made the column width setting for the remaining two frames Relative, so that they'll occupy the remaining screen width, regardless of the size of the browser window.

We also decided that the two frames on the right should be the same height. The Height setting for both of these frames is 50 percent. The Height setting for the frame on the left, which occupies 100 percent of the available height, is automatically set to Relative.

NOTE   When you set the dimensions of a frame to Relative, the Relative setting allows you to determine the proportion of the frames' sizes. For example, you can set one frame's width as 2 and Relative and another frame's width as 1 and Relative, and the available space will be assigned in a 2:1 ratio to these two frames. You can actually mix relative sizes with absolute sizes. The frames with relative sizes will divide up whatever is left of the window after the frames with absolute sizes are displayed.

Frame Margins

Unlike page margins, *frame margins* are not a property unique to Internet Explorer. Any browser that can view frames will respect the frame margins you set. Frame margins are particularly helpful for ensuring that content doesn't get lost in a window or frame resize. You set frame margins in pixels and measure them from the top-left corner of the frame. Therefore, the Width margin setting indicates the number of pixels of blank space between the left side of the frame and the content, and the Height margin setting indicates the number of pixels of blank space between the top border of the frame and the content.

Using the Frame Properties Dialog Box

Now that you know how the frame properties act, you can set them for your pages. Just follow these steps:

1. With the frameset visible in Page view, right-click the frame whose properties you want to adjust. If your frame is blank, a Frame Properties button appears. Click it, and the Frame Properties dialog box appears (see Figure 12.11).

   or

   If your frame has any content, a menu appears instead of a button. Select Frame Properties from the menu, and the Frame Properties dialog box appears (see Figure 12.11).

2. In the Options area of the dialog box, if you'd like the frame to be resizable in the browser window, leave the Resizable In Browser checkbox selected. If you don't want your users to resize your frames, deselect the Resizable In Browser checkbox.

3. Select one of the following options from the Show Scrollbars list box—If Needed, Always, or Never—as described earlier in the "Scroll Bars" section.

4. In the Frame Size area of the dialog box, set the height and column width of your frame by typing a number in the appropriate text box and choosing a measurement (Relative, Pixels, or Percent) from the corresponding list box. As described in the section Frame Size, you will probably want to specify exact height and width for some frames, while leaving the settings for others at Relative.

5. In the Margins area of the dialog box, you can specify margins for your frame, if you like. Type a number (in pixels) in the Width and Height text boxes.

6. When you're all set, click OK to close the Frame Properties dialog box.

Some of your settings, like size and scroll bar options, will be apparent immediately. Other settings, such as margins, will not show up until you preview the page in Page view or your Web browser (see Chapter 3, *Working in Page View*).

PART

II

Creating
Sophisticated
Designs

Adjusting Frames Page Properties

As we said earlier, the frames page basically acts as mission control for your frameset, storing information about which frame and which page goes where. In addition, the frames page will be visible in lieu of your frames to users with non-frames browsers who visit your site. We'll talk about this more in the section titled "Working with Non-Frames Users," later in this chapter.

For now, though, we're concerned with a couple of frames-specific settings you can specify that apply to all the frames on your page. *Frame spacing* is the amount of padding or blank space between the frames on your page; the default is generally 2 pixels. Be advised that frame spacing greater than 5 pixels can play weird tricks on most browsers.

Frame borders, when turned off, can disguise the fact that you've got frames to show at all. Figure 12.13 shows the same frames page we saw in Figure 12.12, but with the borders turned off.

FIGURE 12.13

Turning off the borders on a frames page makes the page look entirely different.

To adjust frame spacing or frame borders, follow these steps:

1. With your frameset visible in the FrontPage Editor window, from the menu bar, select Frames ➢ Frame Properties. The Frame Properties dialog box appears.

2. Click the Frames Page button. The Page Properties dialog box appears. Select the Frames tab.

3. In the Frame Spacing text box, type a number, in pixels, for the width and height of the padding between frames.

4. If you'd like to turn off frame borders, deselect the Show Borders checkbox; the frame spacing option automatically reverts to 0.

5. Click OK to close the Page Properties dialog box. The window reappears with the Frame Properties dialog box still open. Click OK, and you'll be back to your work in Page view.

Your changes may not be evident, or accurately displayed, in the FrontPage Editor window. We suggest that you preview your pages in both Internet Explorer and Navigator to make sure the changes display properly.

MASTERING THE OPPORTUNITIES

Placing Inline Frames Directly into a Page

Another type of frame you can include in your documents is called an *inline frame*. Inline frames (also known as floating frames) are supported by Internet Explorer versions 3 and later. They are also considered part of the HTML 4 standard, although implementation in browsers other than IE is still sketchy.

The advantage of using inline frames is that you can show a whole separate document in a specified area of the current Web page. An inline frame is just a rectangular region, sort of like an image, but instead of containing a picture, it contains another document.

FrontPage does not directly support inline frames, but you can insert the necessary tags manually using the HTML tab at the bottom of the FrontPage window.

Inline frames are defined using the HTML tag known as IFRAME. To learn more about HTML 4, turn to *The HTML Reference (Appendix E)* at the back of this book, or pick up a copy of *HTML 4.0: No Experience Required* by E. Stephen Mack and Janan Platt (Sybex, 1998). Once you've defined the inline frame, you can use it as if it were a standard frame. You can fill it with a particular page, or you can use it as a target for links.

You'll have to start the inline frame with an `<IFRAME>` tag and then include several attributes that define the inline frame's behavior. These are just variants on the attributes used for regular frames—after you create a frames page with FrontPage, you can click the Frames Page HTML tab at the bottom of the window to see the code.

In an inline frame, the `WIDTH` and `HEIGHT` attributes define the inline frame's size in pixels, the `ALIGN` attribute determines where the inline frame is horizontally aligned, and the `SRC` attribute indicates the filename of the page that should fill the frame (the source). The `NAME` attribute gives the inline frame a target name (which allows you to

Continued

PART

II

Creating Sophisticated Designs

MASTERING THE OPPORTUNITIES CONTINUED

target hyperlinks to the inline frame, using the same techniques discussed in the section titled *Setting Targets*). The `FRAMEBORDER="0"` attribute removes the inline frame's default border, and the `MARGINWIDTH` and `MARGINHEIGHT` attributes indicate the amount of pixels between the edge of the frame and the contents of the frame. After the `<IFRAME>` tag and its attributes, you must place some text that will appear in browsers that don't support the `<IFRAME>` tag. Then you must end the whole thing with an `</IFRAME>` end-tag.

Each inline frame defaults to automatic scrolling, just like regular frames. You can use the `SCROLLING` attribute to change this behavior (for example, use `SCROLLING="NO"` to remove scroll bars or `SCROLLING="YES"` to force them to appear).

To insert an inline frame, follow these steps:

1. With a page open in Page view, click the HTML tab. The contents of the window change to reflect your choice.

2. Place the cursor at the location you want the frame to appear and type:

```
<IFRAME WIDTH="300" HEIGHT="75" NAME="centerframe"
SRC="framepage.htm">

Sorry, you need a browser that supports Inline Frames.

</IFRAME>
```

3. Click the Normal tab to return to Page view. You'll see two question marks with a yellow background at the point you inserted the IFRAME tags. This is because FrontPage does not directly support the IFRAME tag.

When you preview the page, you'll see an inline frame that's 300 pixels wide, 75 pixels tall, and contains a file named `FRAMEPAGE.HTM`. The inline frame is named `centerframe`, and hyperlinks can change the contents of the inline frame by targeting it with that name. You can experiment with the look of inline frames by playing with these values.

Be sure to insert the code for an inline frame in between the `<BODY>` and `</BODY>` tags in your document. The best way to control the position of your inline frame is through the use of tables. (You can learn more about using tables to control the position of elements on the page in Chapter 11.)

To figure out where to place the inline frame code in a jumble of table code, type a recognizable word, like ZOOP, in one of your table cells. Then click the HTML tab and replace the word ZOOP with the code for your frame (or leave it there, if you actually like the word ZOOP).

Setting Targets

When you click a link in a frames-based page, what happens? That linked page could load into any of several different potential windows. *Targets* tell the destination link where to go. Setting targets is probably easiest once all of your pages are in place and you're reasonably satisfied that you won't be replacing all of your initial pages.

You'll follow as many as three steps when setting targets for links on your frames pages. The first is to name each frame. The second is to set a default setting for all the links in a particular frame. The third, which is optional, is to differentiate some links on your page so that they point to another location. Read on.

Naming Frames

Names for each frame, which are distinct from page titles and filenames, are stored in the frames page along with all the other information about the frameset. These names tell the frames page *where* to load each frame, both initially and when a link is targeted there. For instance, in Figure 12.14, the page in the frame on the left has the filename left.html, the page title Left Frame, and the frame itself is named left. When a link is targeted to load into the frame named left, the frames page, which works as mission control, loads it into the left-side frame.

FIGURE 12.14

This page has frames named left, nav, and body.

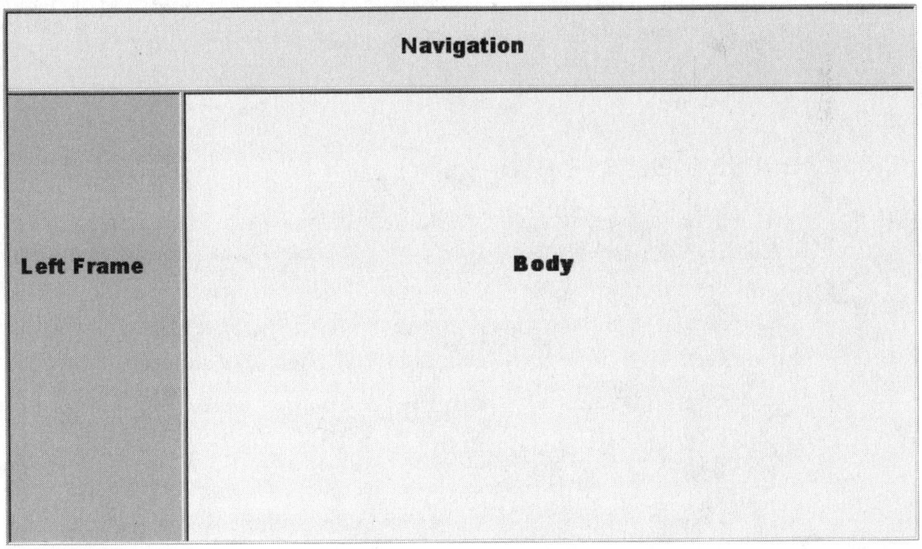

Navigation

Left Frame

Body

FrontPage designates names for each frame when you create the page from a template; it also suggests names for each frame you add after that. You can choose to use the frame names FrontPage gives you, or you can rename the frames to make them easier to remember.

To review or edit the names of your frames, follow these steps:

1. With your frameset visible in Page view, click the frame whose name you're confirming.

2. From the menu bar, select Frame ➤ Frame Properties. The Frame Properties dialog box appears (we saw it in Figure 12.11).

3. The name of the frame is displayed in the Name text box. To change this name, just type over it.

4. When you're satisfied with the name of the frame, click OK to close the Frame Properties dialog box.

5. Follow steps 1 through 4 for each frame on your page.

If you have a sketch of the design of your frameset, it might be helpful to write the name of each frame on the sketch so that you can refer to it when you're setting targets.

WARNING You should avoid certain words when naming frames: *top*, *self*, *parent*, and *blank*. We'll describe what these words mean in upcoming sections; for now, just trust us that it's a bad idea. It's also best to stick to lowercase letters and numbers when naming your frames, and to use underscores and dashes instead of spaces.

Creating Target Settings

The default target settings of a frame indicate where links, when clicked, will open the destination page. Unless you specify otherwise, links that appear in any given frame will open in that frame. You can target a link to open in any frame in a frameset, and you can set defaults for every frame. You can also specify some other, handy destination targets—all of which FrontPage simplifies. These special settings include:

• Same Frame (self) loads the destination page into the frame the link was in.

• Whole Page (top) loads the destination page into the browser window, replacing the entire frameset.

• New Window (blank) pops open a new browser window and loads the destination page into that window.

- Parent Frame (parent) loads the destination page into the browser window, replacing all of the current frames. If one of the frames contains a frameset, and from a frame in that frameset you refer to a parent, the document loads in the original frame instead of the browser window. (See the sidebar titled "Dropping a Frames Page into a Frame," earlier in this chapter.)

You can set the target for a link when you create or edit a link in that frame. If you're using the default settings for that frame, you don't need to set a target for your links, but you can follow the upcoming steps both to set a default target for your frame and to set a target other than the default for an individual link.

 TIP   You can set the default target for all the links that appear on the page by selecting from the menu bar File ➢ Properties. The Page Properties dialog box appears; in its Default Target Frame text box, select the default target for the links.

Just follow these steps:

1. With your frameset open in Page view, click in the frame to which you want to add a hyperlink.

2. Select the text or image that you want to make into a hyperlink and, from the menu bar, select Insert ➢ Hyperlink. The Create Hyperlink dialog box appears.

   or

   Right-click a link that's already in that frame and, from the pop-up menu that appears, select Hyperlink Properties. The Edit Hyperlink dialog box appears. (This dialog box is the same as the Create Hyperlink dialog box, for our purposes.)

3. Create or edit the link as you normally would. (See Chapter 4 if you have questions about how to use hyperlinks.)

4. In the Optional area of the Create Hyperlink dialog box, click the Change Target Frame button.

The Target Frame dialog box appears (see Figure 12.15).

The Target Frame dialog box lets you set default targets as well as targets for individual links.

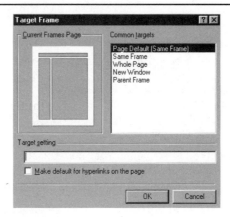

5. From this dialog box, you have several options for specifying a target frame. You can:

- Click the frame in the Current Frames Page preview area of the dialog box to use it as the default target

- Type the name of the target frame in the Target Setting text box

- Click one of the options in the Common Targets list box (these options are discussed at the beginning of this section)

In any case, the name of the target frame appears in the Target Setting text box.

6. To make this target setting the default for all the links in this frame, click the Make Default For Hyperlinks On The Page checkbox. Once you set the default target for a frame, all the links you add to that frame, or that exist on that frame already, will have the same target.

7. When you're done selecting a target for your link, click OK. The Target Frame dialog box closes, and the Create (or Edit) Hyperlink dialog box reappears, with the name of your target displayed in the Target Frame text box.

8. Click OK to close the Create Hyperlink dialog box.

To check that the targets for your links work properly, you must first preview your page in a Web browser and then click the link you want to verify.

WARNING It's important that you test all the links in a frames page to be sure that their target pages will open correctly. Otherwise, you could end up with frames piling up inside one another. If you link to a frames page, which in turn links to another frames page, and none of these pages have their links targeted outside the window, things can get browser-crashingly cluttered.

Adding Pages to a Framed Page

To add a page other than one of your initial pages to a frameset, simply link to that page from an initial page. The user who visits your framed site will click the link, and the new page will appear within the frame.

If you want additional pages to appear in the frameset, just create them with Front-Page. Using style sheets (see Chapter 13), themes, or templates (see Chapter 4), you can create pages with a consistent look to fit into the framework of your frames-based site.

MASTERING THE OPPORTUNITIES

Displaying Forms Results in a Frame

One great use for frames is to have a form in one frame, and have the form results displayed in another frame. This enhances the display of search engines and guest books, or any other forms in which the user would be interested in seeing the results of their input. (To get a head start on using forms, refer to Chapter 14.)

Getting form results to display in a particular frame is no more complex than setting a target for those results. (If you're unsure about the targeting process, refer to the section titled "Creating Target Settings.") Just follow these steps to set a target frame for your form results:

1. With your form page open in Page view (either in the frameset or on its own), right-click inside the form and, from the pop-up menu that appears, choose Form Properties. The Form Properties dialog box appears.

2. In the Form Properties dialog box, click the Target Frame button. The Target Frame dialog box appears.

3. Type the name of your target frame in the Target Settings text box. If you're working with this page while the rest of the frameset is in view, you can click the frame you want in the preview area of the dialog box to choose it.

4. Click OK to close the Target Frame dialog box and return to the Form Properties dialog box, where you'll see the name of your target frame displayed in the Target Frame text box (see "Creating Target Settings," earlier in this chapter, for more details).

5. Click OK to close the Form Properties dialog box.

As always, test, test, test those forms and targets.

PART II

Creating Sophisticated Designs

Working with Non-Frames Users

When a user with a browser like Netscape 2 or later or Internet Explorer 3 or later visits your frames page, they'll see the site you designed. When a user with an older or more ornery browser visits your page, something like this will appear:

This page uses frames, but your browser doesn't support them.

which basically tells that user to buzz off. You don't have to give those users the cold shoulder, however. You can create a page that contains the same basic information—at least a list of links to the same pages that would appear in the frames—so that they can get what they came for: your information.

When you create a frames page in FrontPage, a few additional tabs appear at the bottom of the window, in addition to the Normal and HTML tabs that are always there. The No Frames tab offers a view of what non-frames browsers will see when they visit your site, and the Frames Page HTML tab shows the HTML for this page, including both the frames page settings and the body of the page that you see in the No Frames window.

 TIP To see the HTML behind all the frames in a frameset, select the Frames Page HTML tab. To see the HTML for the frames laid out in the frames themselves, select the HTML tab (see Figure 12.16).

You can click the No Frames tab and create a page that will give your cutting-edge-challenged visitors something to do. You can edit this no frames page just like any other, using backgrounds, links, images, and what have you. Bear in mind, however, that it wouldn't make much sense to include things like Java, JavaScript, style sheets, or ActiveX in this page, because if they can't see frames, they can't see that other high-tech gadgetry, either.

It's best to include links in this page to all the files you can access from the frameset. If you offer thirty assorted fruitcake recipes, then provide links to them in the nonframes page, or create a link to a new page that includes links to them (you get the idea). People who visit your nonframes page should be just a few clicks away from any files they could see in the frames page.

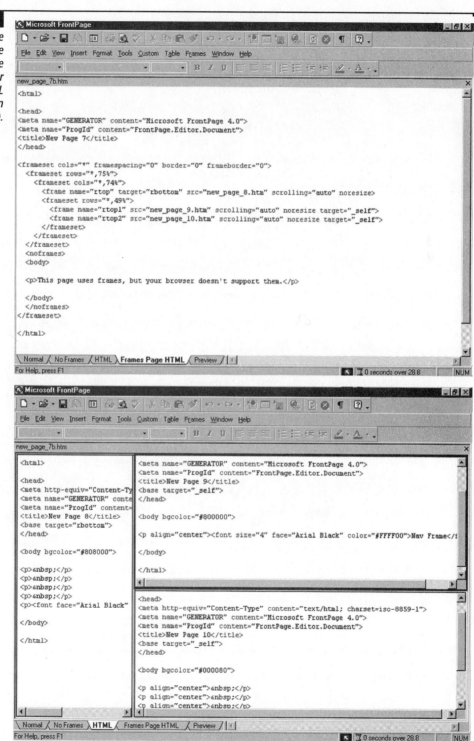

Creating
Sophisticated
Designs

FIGURE 12.16

Select the Frames Page HTML tab to see the HTML behind the frameset all together (top). Select the HTML tab to see it laid out in frames (bottom).

MASTERING THE OPPORTUNITIES

Creating a Frames/No Frames Button

Users like to be able to choose their experiences on the Web. It's great to create a non-frames page that users without frames-capable browsers can visit, but it's also a good idea to provide users who do have frames capability with the option of turning frames off. You can insert a link or a button in your frames page that will let your users do just that, and a similar button on that page to let the user turn frames back on.

Have your frameset open in Page view, then follow these steps:

1. On any frame in your page, insert some text or a button that says "Turn Frames Off" or "Unframe Me" or something similar.

2. Select that item and, from the menu bar, select Insert ➤ Hyperlink. The Insert Hyperlink Dialog box appears.

3. In the URL text box, type the URL or filename of a version of your page that does not use frames, or the URL or filename of one of the initial content pages in your frameset. (It would be futile to link to the frames page, because that would just reload the whole thing.)

4. Click the Target Frame button. The Target Frame dialog box appears.

5. In the Common Targets list box, click Whole Page. The word "top" appears in the Target Setting text box.

6. Click OK to close the Target Frame dialog box, and click OK again to close the Insert Hyperlink dialog box.

Now, if a visitor clicks the No Frames link, the new page or one of the pages in the frameset will open in the same window. You can use this same procedure in the non-frames version of the page to create a "Show Frames" or "Frame Me" link that will load the frames page. Just link to the frames page.

NOTE Chapter 16, *Cross-Browser Design*, offers tips for making your web work with as many flavors, shapes, and varieties of browsers as possible.

Up Next

Now that you're finished with the exercises in this chapter, you see that while working with frames is a bit more complex than some of the earlier exercises we've done, they're not that difficult! Furthermore, they offer a wide range of options for your site, including navigational and layout structure that would be impossible to achieve in any other way.

It's time to begin to add some style to our virtual soup. Up next is Chapter 13, *Getting in Style with Cascading Style Sheets*, where you'll learn how FrontPage manages a special form of HTML to cleverly enhance the layout and design of your pages.

PART

II

Creating
Sophisticated
Designs

CHAPTER 13

Getting in Style with Cascading Style Sheets

I n a desire to gain more control over the way a document is designed, developers have come up with *Cascading Style Sheets*, or *CSS*. While you've been adding color, type, and learning how to lay out pages using standard HTML elements, the reality is that HTML was never originally intended to be a design tool. Instead, it was meant to format documents simply: headers, plain text, and hyperlinks.

Of course, the Web has become an extremely visual environment since its inception, and HTML has had to accommodate the desire of audiences and developers for bigger, brighter, faster technologies. Clever developers used HTML to try to meet their needs for more interesting visual design. We saw a perfect example of this in Chapter 11, where tables—originally created to format technical information—became the underlying structure that almost all contemporary designs use for their infrastructure.

But the design elements found in HTML are imperfect. We've talked about the problems inherent with the FONT element in Chapter 6. We know that table and frame layouts, while effective, also have limitations.

In order to meet these limitations, CSS was proposed and eventually adopted as a part of the HTML standard. This means that CSS is the direction we're headed in to handle our page layout and design elements: color, type, and positioning.

Of course, in the fast-paced environment of Web development, there's a lot of instability. While CSS is a terrific concept, browser support is a concern. CSS is not backward compatible, meaning older browsers won't see it—a significant reason that it's taking time to be adopted full force. Furthermore, the support for it within individual browsers is inconsistent, creating even more challenges for developers.

 NOTE Internet Explorer 3 was the first commercial browser to have strong support for CSS. Internet Explorer 4 and above and Netscape Navigator 4 and above both support style sheets to varying degrees.

So why would you want to use CSS? Well, CSS is truly elegant and extremely efficient in the ways it can manage the design of a document. CSS separates the *content* of a page (stored in an HTML document) from its *presentation* (stored in a style sheet), and this has many advantages. You can change your document's appearance without changing its substance. Furthermore, using what's known as a *linked* style sheet, you can modify a single style sheet file and change the appearance of your entire site.

Many contemporary Web sites are employing style sheets, and if you're working on a personal page or a corporate intranet site, you can make the decision to use them based on your desired audience and favorite browser. And, because the technology itself is so powerful, it's a good idea to become familiar with style sheets in order to know how to manage them.

FrontPage 2000 has the most advanced CSS support of all the FrontPage versions. FrontPage 2000 lets you apply style sheet rules to individual elements on a page with terrific ease. Themes and other design-oriented features allow you to include style information, and there are a number of templates that you can use to set up a page based on style sheet concepts.

In this chapter, we'll start by teaching you the terminology, then show you how style works on individual elements and show you how to use FrontPage style sheet templates.

Remember, older browsers simply can't understand style sheet rules—so they ignore them. That means, for example, that a browser like Navigator 3 or Internet Explorer 2 won't display your fancy style borders at all. This is not necessarily a problem—because every browser will still be able to display your page's basic text and HTML appearance; only your document's style sheet appearance will be missing. This chapter will show you how style sheets work, in theory, and you'll become familiar with how to use style in FrontPage. Note, however, that style sheets are a very big topic involving complex syntax, and to cover every detail would take a complete book! So we'll give you the information you need to get going, and point out some online tutorials that will finish the job if you're interested in learning more.

Understanding Style Sheets

As you are already aware, when you create pages in FrontPage, it writes the necessary HTML for you. When you add formatting features such as a font color to your page, FrontPage inserts HTML to match your design.

But HTML is not really a layout language, page description language, or formatting language; instead, it's a markup language, intended to classify the different parts of a document by their functional roles. Specific HTML tags indicate a document's title, headings, paragraphs, images, and its author's address—but not how these elements will appear on a given computer screen. Using HTML, you indicate the role each part of your document will play, and the Web browser at the user's end takes care of the actual visual formatting. The Web is cross-platform and there are many different browsers (as well as many different versions of the same browser—for example, the hundreds of different versions of Netscape Navigator). For that reason, you can't guarantee that a WYSIWYG (What-You-See-Is-What-You-Get) editor like FrontPage will produce the same results for every browser.

HTML does include a few elements and attributes intended to allow site designers to make a document look attractive (for example, the font element and the various attributes of the horizontal rule element). However, these presentational features are not always recommended because they can cause problems in some browsers, including text-only browsers, text-to-speech browsers, and those used by the visually impaired. Instead, style sheets offer a chance for much better (and more complete) control over a document's appearance, in a way that doesn't interfere with the content of a document.

In theory, you can use any style sheet technology with HTML; in practice, the only style sheet technology that's well supported is CSS. This style sheet system was developed by the World Wide Web Consortium (W3C). The W3C is the organization now responsible for developing official standards for HTML and other Web technologies.

MASTERING WHAT'S ONLINE

To find out more about the W3C, visit its home page at www.w3.org/. To learn more about the W3C's work on style sheets in general, visit the style sheets page at www.w3.org/Style/. Find a list of CSS specifications, references, tools, tutorials, and recent work at www.w3.org/Style/CSS/. And for an especially well done CSS tutorial (from the Web Design Group), stop by www.htmlhelp.com/reference/css/. Finally, Microsoft's style sheet tutorial is at www.microsoft.com/workshop/author/css/css-ie4-f.htm.

Style Sheet Terms and Concepts

The most important thing to understand when working with style sheets is the difference between style rules, style sheets, and style.

- A *style rule* changes the appearance of HTML elements on your page in some way (such as by adding a border to all level-one headings, or by making every bold item appear in hot pink). To create a style rule, you must first create a style sheet.

- A *style sheet* is a list of style rules. A style sheet can be either embedded into a page (known as an *embedded style sheet*), or stored in a separate file (known as an *external* or *linked style sheet*) and then linked to one or more pages on your site. FrontPage lets you easily create an embedded style sheet in a document, or use one of the style sheet templates to create a linked style sheet.

- You can also apply style rules to an individual part of your page, such as making a particular paragraph have a border and some extra margins. Many FrontPage dialog boxes include a Style button. The Page Properties, Horizontal Line Properties,

Font, and Image Properties dialog boxes all have a Style button, as well as any other dialog box in FrontPage that allows you to control an HTML feature.

Technically speaking, the Style button is used to create an *inline style declaration*. Normally, style declarations are part of an embedded or external style sheet; they specify the visual appearance to be used. We'll see the difference between inline style declarations and style sheets later in this chapter, in the section titled "Working with Style Sheets in FrontPage."

FrontPage makes it easy to work with inline style declarations through the Style dialog box, and that's a fine way for FrontPage users to go. But if and when you want to employ the full power of style sheets, you'll have to learn how to create a style sheet of your own.

NOTE Currently, the most common type of style sheet technology is Cascading Style Sheets (CSS). The first official specification of CSS is called *level one*; we'll use the term *CSS1* in our discussion to mean "Cascading Style Sheets, level one." CSS2 is the current style specification under scrutiny by the World Wide Web Consortium.

MASTERING WHAT'S ONLINE

To read about the latest work being done on style sheets by the World Wide Web Consortium, visit www.w3c.org/style/.

Let's take a look at some style sheet specifics.

What Is a Style Sheet?

A style sheet is a collection of rules that affect the appearance of a document. Here's an example of a CSS1 style sheet with one rule.

```
H1 { text-align: center }
```

This example rule centers every level-one heading element in an HTML document by default. We'll learn how to create a style sheet like this one a little bit later in the sections titled "Embedding a Style Sheet in a Page" and "Structuring an External Style Sheet."

CSS style sheets consist of properties, values, declarations, selectors, and rules. A *property* is a browser behavior that can be affected by CSS. For example, font-family, background, border, and text-align are all examples of properties. The properties that can be changed are listed in the CSS specification; there are about 50 of them.

The *value* is whatever choice you can set for a property. For example, the font-family property's values can be specific font names such as Arial, Times, and Courier, or a generic name such as serif or sans serif.

A *declaration* is a property and its value (for example, `color: blue` is a declaration). While FrontPage usually creates the declarations for you, if you become an advanced style sheet user you'll want to create your declarations from scratch. To create a declaration, you'd start with a property name (be sure to specify it exactly, including any hyphens), followed by a colon, followed by the value for the property. (A semicolon at the end of a single declaration is optional.) For example, here are a couple of declarations:

```
text-indent: 5%
border: medium double
```

The first adds a 5-percent margin to the first line of a paragraph, and the second adds a double border of medium thickness.

A *selector* is the name of the HTML element to which you want to apply a declaration. For example, if you want to change the behavior of every block quote element, you would use BLOCKQUOTE as your selector. You can use *simple selectors* (the name of a single HTML element), or more complex *contextual selectors* (several HTML elements). To use selectors properly, you'll have to know HTML tags pretty well; Appendix E, *HTML Reference* can help you out with that. Selectors can also contain special attributes known as *classes*, which are discussed in greater detail in the upcoming section, "Class and Inheritance."

A *rule* is a selector plus a declaration. For example, `P { margin-left: 20% }` is a rule. The selector in this rule is the paragraph element (indicated by P), and the declaration is `margin-left: 20%`. The property being changed in this declaration is the margin-left property, which normally has a value of 0. In this rule, we're changing the left margin for every paragraph so that it takes up 20 percent of the window's default width.

NOTE Note the punctuation. In a rule, the selector is followed by the opening curly brace ({), then the declaration, and then a closing curly brace (}). (Curly braces are sometimes called *curly brackets* or *French braces*.) When you create an external style sheet, you'll need to know this punctuation. If you create an embedded style sheet, FrontPage usually handles this punctuation for you.

You can group declarations and selectors together when creating rules. For example, the code `H1, H2 { font-weight: normal }` groups two different selectors together to create two rules. Similarly, `H1 {background: black; color: white}` groups two different declarations together to create two rules. Grouped rules are called *rulesets*.

 WARNING When you're making a ruleset (for example, when you create an external style sheet), be absolutely sure to use semicolons to separate selectors with commas and multiple declarations. A single mistake (such as leaving out a comma) may cause the ruleset to have a completely different meaning or to just plain not work. FrontPage knows how to group declarations with semicolons, but it doesn't automatically group selectors properly.

By tradition, selectors are in uppercase and declarations are in lowercase. But this is only a tradition; CSS rules are not case-sensitive. When you create a style sheet, you'll have to type the selectors yourself. FrontPage lets you put selectors in uppercase or lowercase, but (as we'll see later) it uses lowercase for declarations created when you use the Style button.

PART

II

Creating
Sophisticated
Designs

Using CSS Units

CSS uses several different units of measurement. These units come in two categories: *absolute* units and *relative* units.

The common absolute units are:

- Inches, specified by "in" (for example, 0.5in means half an inch)
- Points, specified by "pt" (for example, 13pt means 13 points)

You can also use centimeters (cm), millimeters (mm), and picas (pc). Some of these are typographical terms: A pica is equal to 12 points, and 72 points is equal to an inch.

In electronic publishing, however, relative units are preferred because they scale better from one medium to another (and you don't have to make assumptions about a viewer's screen size or paper size). Here are the relative units:

- Pixels, specified by "px" (for example, 12px means 12 pixels)
- Ems, specified by "em" (where one em is equal to the element's font size, so 0.5em is half a line)

Continued

CONTINUED

- Ex-heights, specified by "ex" (where one ex is equal to the height of the lowercase letter x in the current font, so 2ex is twice the height of the letter x)
- Percentages, which are usually relative to the font size (so 200% usually means twice the current font size of the element)

Pixels might not seem to be a relative unit at first glance. But in actuality, pixels can vary tremendously. Take printers: A screen is often 72 pixels per inch, but a printer is typically 300, 600, or 1200 dots per inch. So browsers will scale pixel units appropriately when you print out a document, making pixel a relative term. Secondly and more importantly, the pixel size measurements for fonts are slightly different on Macintosh platforms than they are on Windows platforms. Still, pixels are the most common method of measuring type on the Web, and are the FrontPage default size for style-based type. If you want to be as safe as possible, try to use percentages and ems.

When specifying colors, FrontPage uses the RGB (red, green, blue) value of a color. For more details about color units and to see your options, check the CSS1 specification (www.w3.org/pub/WWW/TR/REC-CSS1#color-units).

Class and Inheritance

Sometimes you want style sheet rules to apply to only certain elements. To fill this need, you can use *class selectors*. A *class* is a name that you assign to one or more elements; you can create style sheet rules that apply only to members of that class.

To create a style sheet rule that selects by class, you simply use a selector name that's a little different. To create a class selector, just use the name you want for the class followed by a period.

You can create classes that only apply only to particular HTML elements by combining the element's name with a class selector, or you can create generic classes that can apply to every HTML element. For example, here's a style sheet that creates three classes (we've named our example classes *warning*, *note*, and *big*, but you can use any descriptive word you like):

```
<style>
<!-
P { font-family: Verdana, sans-serif }
P.warning { border: thick double rgb(0,0,0) }
P.note { background-image: url('clouds.gif') }
.big { font-size: 150% }
```

```
->
</style>
```

This style sheet has four rules. The first rule applies to every paragraph element (it changes the font face to Verdana, or a generic sans-serif typeface if Verdana isn't available). The second rule applies to only those paragraph elements in the warning class and gives them a thick black border made of two lines. The third rule applies to only those paragraph elements in the note class and adds an image background (assuming the image clouds.gif has already been added to the FrontPage web). The fourth rule makes the paragraph 50 percent larger than normal, and applies to any HTML element (paragraph, blockquote, table data cell, and so on) but only if that element is in the "big" class.

You'll be applying Class quite often with FrontPage, as you'll see in upcoming exercises and examples.

Inheritance is a concept that describes the flow of how style sheet information is processed. A CSS rule applies a declaration to a particular HTML element. That declaration also applies to any elements nested inside that element. For example, suppose you've made paragraphs green by inserting the following rule into a style sheet attached to your page:

```
P { color: green }
```

Consider an element nested inside another element, such as: <P>I am a <I>barrista</I></P>. The word *barrista* will appear both in italics and in green. This is an example of *inheritance*. The italics element here is said to "inherit" the green property from its *parent* element (which in this case is the paragraph element).

Other style properties will also be inherited, such as the font and font size. Some style properties are not inherited from the parent element by the child element. (Check with the CSS specification or a quick reference to see if a property inherits; FrontPage does not always show inheritance properly on screen.)

The best example of inheritance is applying declarations to the body element. For example, this style sheet

```
BODY { color: white; background: url(marble.gif) black; }
```

sets the text color to white and the background to an image named marble.gif, or black if the image isn't available. With this style sheet, every element in a document, including every heading and paragraph, will inherit the default text color.

Sometimes the value of a property is a percentage that refers to another property. For example:

```
P { font-size: 10pt; line-height: 150% }
```

In this example, the line height will work out to 15 points, because it is one-and-a-half times the paragraph's font size of 10 points. Elements nested inside a paragraph element will inherit the 15-point line height.

If you have more than one rule that applies to the same element, it doesn't matter where that rule comes from. The rule is this: The more direct and specific the source of the rule, the more weight it carries. If the rule comes from an inline style declaration, then that's very direct. If the rule comes from an embedded or linked style sheet, that's direct (but not as direct as an inline style declaration). If the rule is applied only through inheritance, then it's indirect and other rules will outweigh it.

When to Use Style Sheets

So, are style sheets really worth all of the potential problems and the hassle of learning and applying all that terminology? Well, there are three main advantages to using style sheets. First, you can create effects such as three-dimensional borders and paragraph indents that aren't possible with HTML tags. For example, Figure 13.1 shows a paragraph with a border style applied to it.

Second, style sheets can be an extremely efficient way of formatting a page that can actually speed up both the development and downloading time of your site in that style sheets can be reused and applied to every page on your site. You can define a style once, and apply it all over the place.

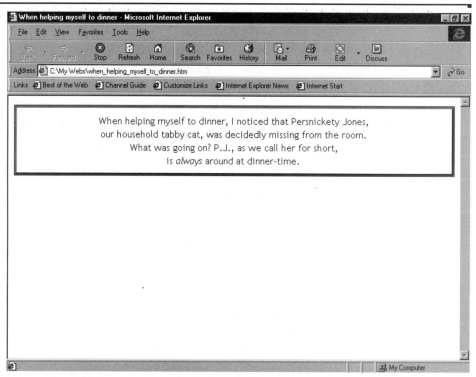

FIGURE 13.1

This border and the centered text were created with inline style.

NOTE This second advantage applies only when you create the external style sheets yourself, using the techniques in this chapter. If you create only inline style declarations, then that's actually *less* efficient because the code becomes more complicated and you can't reuse your style.

Third, style sheets are extremely unobtrusive; browsers that don't support style sheets simply ignore their presence.

There are two significant disadvantages to consider, however. First, style sheets are a somewhat complicated technology to learn, and using them is by no means a requirement of good site design. If you're pressed for time and don't want to learn something new right now, put style sheets on a back burner.

Second, browsers have flawed support of style sheets. Internet Explorer 3 was released before the specification for style sheets became finalized, so it has a large number of bugs. Navigator 4 copied a lot of Internet Explorer's bad decisions, and introduced a huge number of bugs of its own. (In contrast, Internet Explorer 2 and Navigator 3 just ignore the style sheets, which isn't a problem). IE 4 and 5 have better support, but there are still inconsistencies.

 NOTE For more about browser differences and how to create a page that works with all browsers, see Chapter 16, *Cross-Browser Design*.

Because many browsers don't yet support style sheets, you must weigh the advantages of style sheets (particularly the way in which a single style sheet can affect the appearance of your entire site) against how much of your audience is using Internet Explorer 3 and Navigator 4 and might see your styles incorrectly. Or if a big part of your audience is using even older browsers, they won't see your style sheet design at all. It's not worth the effort to put a lot of time into something that most of your audience won't be aware of.

 MASTERING WHAT'S ONLINE

For an absolutely essential list of which style sheet properties are safe with which browsers (as well as which properties are dangerous), check out the WebReview Style Sheet Reference Guide, edited by Eric Meyer (`style.webreview.com/`). There are also some helpful articles and tutorials here. For some demonstrations of the problems, with screen shots, hop over to Style Sheet Implementation Bugs (`www.emf.net/~estephen/htmlner/stylebugs.html`).

PART

II

Creating
Sophisticated
Designs

NOTE Style sheets promise important advantages to Web authors, particularly those working in corporate intranet environments, where control of software is pre-determined. Another strength is that style sheets integrate with other technologies to create special effects. In fact, you may have heard of a grouping of exactly such technologies referred to as *Dynamic HTML*, or *DHTML*. Style sheets play a large role in this group of applications, but the same limitations experienced with browsers interpreting current CSS code extend to DHTML, too. So for very broad distribution, the strengths of style sheets are still a questionable choice.

Certainly the current browsers' implementations of style sheets are imperfect and the differences between browsers pose problems, but the management, control, design, special effects, and future importance all make style sheets well worth learning. With a good knowledge of style sheets, there really is an infinite number of effects you can add to a page without using a single graphic image.

In the following sections, we'll show you the best and most efficient ways that you can use style sheets with your FrontPage webs.

MASTERING WHAT'S ONLINE

For information about the new absolute positioning CSS relationship to DHTML, see the W3C's draft in progress (www.w3.org/TR/WD-positioning). Another draft specification is Aural Cascading Style Sheets (www.w3.org/TR/WD-acss), which can add sound effects to a page and help control how your page is read by a text-to-speech browser (used by the visually impaired). CSS Printing Extensions allow you to specify page breaks at particular points when printing a document, among other things; see the draft (www.w3.org/TR/WD-print). The Web Fonts draft (www.w3.org/TR/WD-font) defines a way to use fonts more intelligently (including downloading fonts as needed). For some in-process suggestions that may become CSS level two, see a note on new style elements, including shadowed text, multiple columns, and cursors (www.w3.org/TR/NOTE-css-potential). Some of these drafts are already implemented by IE 4 and Navigator 4 (especially the positioning draft), but many have just recently been implemented within the 5 versions.

Working with Style Sheets in FrontPage

Three types of style sheets are available for use in FrontPage webs. To manage style using FrontPage, you can use a pre-existing template, or add style by hand. Either way, the style is controlled based on these three essential style foundations:

- To control the appearance of an individual page element, you can use *inline style declarations*. As we defined earlier, inline style declarations are CSS declarations that are attached to a part of a page, like a heading or a paragraph or the body of the page. While FrontPage 2000 is more interested in allowing you to use embedded and linked style, you can modify style using the inline method by following some simple directions, as we'll soon show you.

- To control the appearance of every element on a particular page, you can use *embedded style sheets*, which are stored in a special HTML tag at the beginning of a page. You'll use the menu bar's Format ➤ Style command to create or edit an embedded style sheet; we'll give you the skinny on this in the section titled "Embedding a Style Sheet in a Page." This is a terrific way of managing the style for a single page, and FrontPage enthusiastically supports using style in this fashion.

- To use a single file to control the appearance of your site, you'll use *external* (also known as *linked*) style sheets, which are style sheets stored in separate files. An external style sheet must be linked to some or all of the pages on your site, so that its effects are applied to the selected pages. External style sheets offer you the most bang for your buck in adding stylish effects to your Web site. An external style sheet lets you update your Web site by changing just one file. If you've ever gone through the time-consuming process of editing hundreds of pages to change their appearance, you'll appreciate being able to redesign an entire Web site by changing a single file. FrontPage 2000 lets you use linked sheets by helping you set them up via templates. You can also always write them yourself, and add an appropriate link to all the pages you want to influence with a particular style sheet.

Let's take a look at each of the available methods in FrontPage, and see how they can work to best suit your needs. We'll start with inline style declarations (also known as just plain style). Inline style declarations aren't as good as style sheets, because they don't let you reuse their effects and they mix content and presentation. However, it's important to learn what effects are available and how FrontPage lets you work with style using the Style button.

Applying Style

In this section, we'll show you how to create an inline style declaration, which is normally applied to an individual element on a page. Following the steps in this section will give you a little taste of what style can do. Although you won't be creating a style sheet (just an individual piece of style), the steps will show you inline style effects. You'll use a Style button on a FrontPage dialog box to dress up an element on a page. Follow these steps to use some style:

1. With a page open in Page view, select the element to which you want to add some style.

2. Right-click the element to which you'd like to add style. From the drop-down menu, choose the relevant Properties option. For example, if you want to modify the style of a paragraph of text, then select Paragraph Properties. When you select this command (see Figure 13.2), the appropriate Properties dialog box appears.

3. In the dialog box, you will see a variety of properties that you can modify. Some of these incorporate inline style. For example, in the Paragraph dialog box (see Figure 13.3), you'll notice options to change Alignment, Indentation, and Spacing. There's also a Preview area that gives you an idea of how the paragraph will look once you've made a change that you like. Go ahead and modify your element.

FIGURE 13.2

If you right-click a paragraph, a menu appears offering several Properties options.

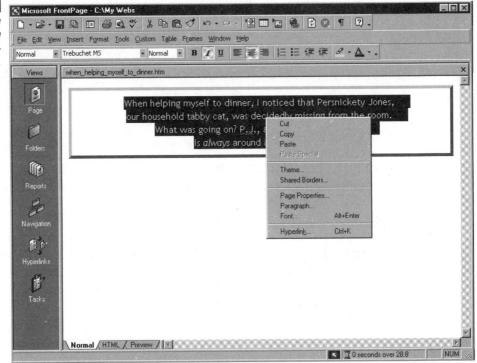

FIGURE 13.3

The Paragraph dialog box offers a variety of modification options that use inline style.

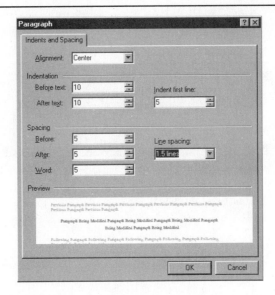

4. Click OK. The dialog box disappears. You can now see the changes you've made.

If you want to see the way the inline HTML code looks, simply click the HTML Tab from the editing window:

Style in Action: An Example

Here's an example of how to use the inline method to indent a paragraph differently than other paragraphs on the page. This technique can be employed to pull a quote or highlight an important concept.

1. With a page open in Page view, select the paragraph you wish to modify.

2. Right-click the highlighted selection, and choose Paragraph Properties. The Paragraph dialog box appears (shown previously in Figure 13.3).

3. Leave the Alignment as Default. In the Indentation area, set the Before Text and After Text measurements to 4em each. Leave the Indent First Line text box empty.

4. In the Spacing area, set the Before and After selections to 4em as well. Leave everything else as is.

5. Click OK. You'll see the changes you specified.

6. Select the Preview tab and look at how the modifications affect the look of the paragraph (see Figure 13.4). This is inline style in action!

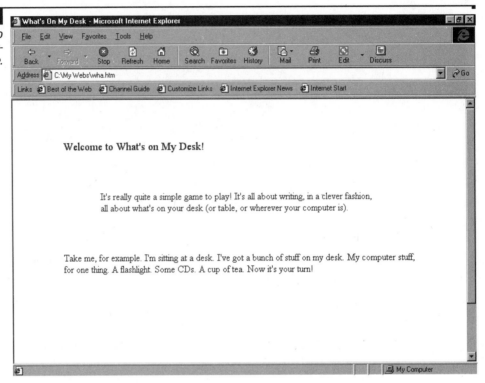

FIGURE 13.4

Inline style is used to format the first paragraph in this example.

Embedding a Style Sheet in a Page

In this section, we'll actually create a style sheet. When you use the menu bar's Format ➤ Style command, FrontPage opens a Style dialog box containing a variety of tags as well as a custom method of modifying by class. This is where you create a style sheet that will be embedded into the beginning of the current page.

 WARNING Again, it's important to understand the difference between a style sheet (with its style rules) and an inline style declaration. A style sheet applies to the entire page, but an inline style declaration applies to only one individual element.

To create an embedded style sheet, you must always start with the <STYLE> start tag and finish with a </STYLE> end tag. FrontPage automatically places these two tags for you, and puts them properly into your document when you're finished with the Style dialog box.

Be aware that older browsers might get confused by embedded style sheets and display the rules on screen. To prevent this from happening, FrontPage properly "comments out" the style sheet by using a comment tag. CSS1-enabled browsers will still obey the style sheet, but other browsers will safely ignore the content they don't understand. To comment out the style sheet, FrontPage puts the <!– characters before the style sheet, and the –> characters after the style sheet, as you can see in Figure 13.5.

FIGURE 13.5

To embed a style sheet, you must place your style sheet rules within comment tags.

```
<style>
<!--
h1          { font-family: Trebuchet MS; font-size: 18 pt; color: #800000 }
p           { text-align: Left; text-indent: 10; margin: 15 }
-->
</style>
```

PART

II

Creating
Sophisticated
Designs

To begin creating a style sheet rule, decide what HTML element you want to change; for example, you could change the behavior of paragraphs (P), level one headings (H1), indented quotes (BLOCKQUOTE), anchors (A), table cells (TD), the entire body of your page (BODY), or any other HTML element. That HTML element will be your selector.

 TIP At this point, you might want to review our earlier definitions of style sheet terminology in the section titled "Understanding Style Sheet Terminology." If you need to review the names of HTML elements, see Appendix E.

You can indicate any HTML element; you must use the name of the element's start tag, but without any angle brackets. If you want to change the style of bold items, you could use STRONG or B as the selector. Or if you wanted to change the appearance of first-level headings, you could use H1 as the selector.

NOTE When you click the Bold button on the Formatting toolbar, it actually inserts a <STRONG> tag, not a <B> tag. To insert a real bold tag, from the menu bar, select Format ➤ Font, and the Font dialog box appears. Click the Special Styles tab, and then click the *Bold* checkbox. If you have lots of legacy documents, they may already be using the <B> tag. If so, you should match this use. Or, if you don't have any documents with <B> tags, simply use STRONG as your selector.

Once you've chosen your selector, you will use the Modify button at the bottom of the Style dialog box to create the declaration.

Now that you know the theory, let's see it in practice. Follow these steps to create an embedded style sheet:

1. Have the page to be formatted open in Page view. From the menu bar, select Format ➤ Stylesheet. The Style dialog box appears.

2. Choose the selector you want to modify.

3. Click the Modify button in the Style dialog box. The Modify Style dialog box appears.

4. Click Format to display a drop-down menu with options including Font, Paragraph, Border, Numbering, and Position.

5. Select the option that you want to modify. For example, if you want to have all H1 tags to show up in dark blue Arial text, you'll choose Font. The appropriate dialog box appears.

6. Make your modifications and click OK. The Modify Style dialog box reappears.

7. Click OK, and the Style dialog box appears.

8. Click OK to save your changes, or start again from step 2 to modify any other tag element.

That's it! You've just created a style sheet that changes the behavior of an element in this document. Now every time you use that element, you'll see the rule in action.

Applying a Style Sheet to a Web or a Site

In the previous section, we learned how to create an embedded style sheet. This style sheet is attached to a particular page, and its style rules affect every element on that page. But let's say that you have a very large site that you'd like to have controlled by the same style sheets. You can avoid embedding style information into every single page in that site by simply creating one style sheet and linking to it. To connect a style sheet to your FrontPage web, link to an external style sheet using a special <LINK> tag.

You can create a style sheet on your own, or you can use a FrontPage 2000 template. There are several templates to choose from, and you can modify any of them, too!

Structuring an External Style Sheet and Including Comments

Your external style sheet will simply be a text file with your rules and rulesets and no HTML elements at all. Aside from style sheet rules, the only other element that can go in an external style sheet file is comments; we'll see how to create style sheet comments in this section.

 NOTE In particular, don't include <HTML> and <HEAD> tags, or any other HTML tags like <STYLE>. In the early days of CSS, some unclear examples of external style sheets encouraged this practice, but style sheets have become much more sophisticated since that time.

To create your own style sheet by hand, follow these steps:

1. Within FrontPage, select File ➤ New ➤ Page.

2. You can use a normal page to create your style sheet by typing in your rules or rulesets, one on each line. Alternately, you can paste in a style sheet if you have one somewhere.

 TIP Instead of typing your style sheet from scratch, you can create an embedded style sheet using the technique described previously in "Embedding a Style Sheet." Then view the HTML tab, select and cut (Ctrl+X) the style sheet, and paste (Ctrl+V) it into a new page. Don't forget to delete the <STYLE> and </STYLE> tags along with the <!- and -> comment characters.

3. Save the file with a `.css` extension. From the menu bar, select File ➤ Save As. Name the style sheet, such as `my_style.css`.

If you wish, you can include comments in your style sheet. Comments are simply reminders or notes to yourself or your team members that don't affect the style sheet. CSS has a format for comments that's different from HTML. CSS comments begin with /* and end with */. For example:

```
/* This is a CSS1 comment */
```

It's a good idea to begin your style sheet with a comment that explains its purpose. Also, any rules that might be complex should be explained with a comment. Here's an example of an external style sheet that uses comments:

```
/* CSS1 Style Sheet */
/* The ourdefaultfonts.css style sheet contains font settings */
BODY { background: black; color: white; margin-left: 10%; margin-left: 10% }
H1 { text-align: center }
TD { color: white; background: black }
/* Because Navigator 4 doesn't inherit properties to tables, you must
separately define the body rule for a table cell */
.warning { font-size: larger; font-weight: bolder; text-align: center;
color: red; background : yellow; border: thick groove gray; }
HR { text-align: center; margin-left: 25%; width: 50%; margin-right: 25%; }
```

Most of these rules should be fairly self-explanatory if you love HTML or computer languages. If these rules don't make any sense to you, you probably shouldn't be creating style sheets from scratch on your own. Instead, use one of the templates (described in the following section) or visit one of the recommended Web sites in this chapter that provide style sheet information and resources.

NOTE You have a fair amount of flexibility in how you arrange your style sheet rules; the order doesn't really matter much, and you can include extra spaces or carriage returns if you like (whatever makes it easier for you to understand).

Using a Style Template

FrontPage 2000 offers several style sheet templates. To use any one of the templates, follow these steps:

1. Select File ➤ New ➤ Page. The New dialog box appears.

2. Click the Style Sheets tab. You'll see a number of style sheet templates.

3. Choose the one you want. Click OK.

4. FrontPage opens the style sheet. You'll see rules and/or rulesets on the page.

5. Make any modifications to the style sheet that you like. Save the page with a name appropriate to your site. Be sure to save it within your web, or within an appropriate file directory, along with the pages for your site.

Now you've got an external style sheet! The next step is to link to the sheet from your pages.

Adding the External Style Sheet to Your FrontPage Web

Now that your CSS file is part of your FrontPage web, you can link it into each file quickly and easily using the Style Sheet Links selection, as follows.

1. Open the page or web you'd like to apply the style sheet to.

2. From the main menu, select Format ➤ Style Sheet Links. The Link Style Sheet dialog box opens (see Figure 13.6).

3. You'll see two buttons at the very top of the dialog box. If you want the sheet applied to all of the pages in your web, select All Pages. If you want only certain pages to be affected by the style sheet, choose Selected Page(s) and click the Add button to add those pages. Each page you select will appear in the Link Style Sheet dialog box.

4. Click OK. FrontPage now automatically links the style sheet to the pages you've chosen.

PART

II

Creating
Sophisticated
Designs

FIGURE 13.6

The Link Style Sheet dialog box allows you to link all, a handful, or only one of your pages to a single style sheet.

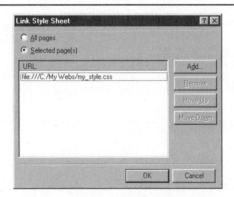

At this point, you'll want to review your web or page within a variety of browsers. Because style sheets are still quite bug-ridden, this review will help you to determine how different browsers are managing the style.

Previewing Style Results in a Browser

With the page affected by a style sheet or style visible in Page view, follow this single step to see how a browser would display your document:

1. Select File ➤ Preview In Browser.

2. The Preview In Browser dialog box appears. In it, you'll have a list of available browsers. Select the one you want to begin testing your pages in and click OK.

3. Review your pages, and repeat the process for any browser you have installed.

Up Next

If style sheets seem confusing and unstable, that's because they are! Why it's taking so long for browsers to fully embrace them is a mystery. Style sheets are a truly elegant and necessary part of Web design—which is one of the reasons we encourage you to learn them, even if you choose to not use them. However, we also hope that you won't get frustrated by the inconsistencies in the technology and give up on them altogether! They are powerful and useful, and if you're interested in professional design for Internet or intranet sites, you'll find opportunities to use them.

In the next chapter, we'll take a turn away from the appearance of a document and concentrate on how you can make your pages more interactive, by adding forms and form controls.

CHAPTER 14

Making Interactive Pages with Forms

O ne of the best ways to interact with users is through *forms*. If you've ever used a search engine, filled out an online survey, ordered products over the Web, registered to be a member of a site, or entered an online contest, then you've used a form.

Forms are designed to collect specific information, to let users interact with the site, and to let you find out more about your users. Forms are also the conduits for online catalogs, search pages, and anything else that requires the user's input. In this chapter, we'll show you how to construct a page that uses forms. We'll go through each element of a form page, and demonstrate how to collect data from submission forms.

What Are Forms?

In general, in the real world, forms are pieces of paper with blanks that are labeled so that everyone presents their information in the same way. They standardize and simplify the essential data.

Forms on the Web similarly standardize and simplify the way information is gathered and presented, but they can also be a simple and fun way to make your site interactive. In using a form, visitors will interact with either you or some scripts in a way that will make their visit interesting or helpful.

For example, suppose a Webmaster wants to know the favorite color of all her site's fans. She could post a note that says, "Hey, if you have a favorite color, drop me an e-mail at the address below." She might get a few responses, in essay form, in which users pontificate about the advantages of blue over orange. Or she could create a survey form in which users simply click a radio button to identify their favorite color, press a Submit button, and send the answer painlessly to the Webmaster, where a program on the other end counts the responses and auto-magically sorts the answers into percentages (6 percent burnt sienna, 40 percent cerulean, and 54 percent puce).

In Figure 14.1 you can see a Web form that's quite interactive. We made this form to include every single kind of box and button there is (for labeling purposes); you'll probably want to make your forms simpler than this one. Boxes and buttons on a form—in fact, any form element that requires input—are called *fields*. These fields are the part of the form with which users interact, either by clicking them or by typing information into them.

FIGURE 14.1

This form has all the fields covered.

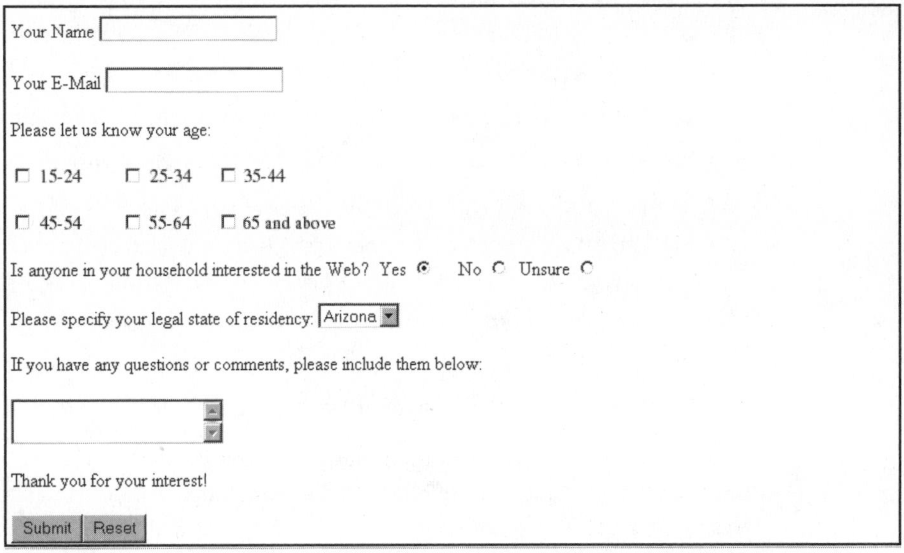

Your Name [   ]

Your E-Mail [   ]

Please let us know your age:

☐ 15-24   ☐ 25-34   ☐ 35-44

☐ 45-54   ☐ 55-64   ☐ 65 and above

Is anyone in your household interested in the Web? Yes ⦿   No ◯   Unsure ◯

Please specify your legal state of residency: [Arizona ▾]

If you have any questions or comments, please include them below:

[   ]

Thank you for your interest!

[Submit] [Reset]

MASTERING WHAT'S ONLINE

To learn about the HTML behind forms, visit the National Center for Supercomputing Applications (NCSA) forms overview, a part of their HTML for Beginners site: www.ncsa.uiuc.edu/SDG/Software/Mosaic/Docs/fill-out-forms/overview.html. Scroll down to the examples area; that's the best part.

What Can I Do with Forms?

You can put a form on any Web page, and you can apply any kind of HTML formatting to your form. You can also place any Web page element you like inside a form—except another form. For example, you can make labels on your fields into links, so visitors can click the links to find out more about their choices. Or you can use images or ruled lines in the design of your form to make it even more user friendly.

Forms can be used to gather just about any kind of input you want. For example, you can:

- Create a registration form to find out who your users are
- Ask users to fill out a longer survey to get even more information about them
- Supply a feedback form or guestbook to glean users' opinions
- Design a Web form as an interface to your company database
- Implement a search tool for searching your site (and remember, you can't use a search engine without a box to type search terms into!)
- Offer online registration for an event, conference, or contest
- Let the user choose variables (such as color or font) to personalize the site's look
- Create a username and password system to restrict access to your site

You're limited only by your imagination here—although some of these little tricks do involve scripts that work behind the scenes to make this stuff happen, so in some cases programming is required. (See Chapter 21, *JavaScript and Dynamic HTML*, for some scripting options that FrontPage supports.)

MASTERING WHAT'S ONLINE

Most really useful sites, from search engines to online dictionaries, use a forms interface to help you retrieve all that useful stuff they offer. Some incredibly useful forms pages include BigBook, an Internet Yellow Pages type of site, at www.bigbook.com/; and Amazon.com's catalog and search pages, at www.amazon.com/. You might also want to try the lookup services at the U.S. Post Office (www.usps.gov/), or the MegaConverter, at www.megaConverter.com/.

What Do Forms Do?

Forms, as we've explained, accept *input* from your users—input being whatever they type or click within the form itself. You can think of a Web form as being like a dialog box in a software program. When you open a dialog box in a program like FrontPage, you make choices. You might click buttons, check checkboxes, type text in text boxes, and select options from drop-down lists.

All this clicking and typing sends information that enables the software to obey your commands. The program either acts on your selections immediately, or stores the input as settings in the program to remember later. On Web forms, the same basic thing happens. After you fill out a form, you click a button like Send or Submit (the same as clicking OK in a dialog box), and the information is whisked away. You'll either see a change in the page you're viewing (a different page may load or an entry may be posted in a guestbook), or the information will be sent to the Web server to be used later. (This is what happens when you order something from an online catalog or register as a "member" of a site.)

When input is sent off, it is translated into *name-value pairs*. This is not a difficult concept. For example, the *name* of the field may be Phone_Number, and the *value* of the field (which, in this example, presumably will be different for each user) may be 301-555-6789. Thus, the name-value pair would be something like:

```
Phone_Number:301-555-6789
```

After users fill out a form, they generally click a button, which may then send the input to a *form validator*. This validator (a script, not a person) skims the information to make sure it fits the format specified for the fields on the form. If something isn't quite right, the validator tells the user to adjust his or her input—for example, the user may have to fill out a text box left blank, or type a phone number using numbers instead of letters. When everything's hunky-dory, the data gets relayed to a *form handler*, a little script that can do one of several things with the data:

- Store the input in a text file for later retrieval
- E-mail the input directly to the Webmaster
- Add the information from the forms into a database
- Post the data directly to a Web page on the site

While the data is being tucked safely away or sent on, most good little form handlers will also post a *confirmation page*, which tells the user the input was received and appreciated. The confirmation page also gives the user a link to follow—back to the home page, to the page that led to the survey, or to some other destination. If the form input was posted to another page, the confirmation page generally provides a link to that location.

 NOTE We've seen plenty of forms that don't include confirmation pages, which means that you click the button, then the little flying Web browser icon does its thing for a couple of seconds, and then all is quiet—too quiet. Did anything happen? Did my data go through? Should I send it again? We imagine that most Webmasters with sites like these find themselves with a hefty stack of duplicate responses from people who clicked the button again and again, waiting for something to happen. We'll tell you how to set up a confirmation page later in this chapter, in the section titled "Offering Confirmation."

PART

II

Creating
Sophisticated
Designs

As we go through this chapter, we'll describe how to create different types of forms, how to add different kinds of fields to your forms, and how to choose an event handler to process your forms. If you're using a Web server with FrontPage Server Extensions (see Appendix C), you can use the built-in handler that comes with FrontPage. If not, contact your Internet service provider's system administrator to find out how to use existing form scripts or to install scripts that will handle your forms.

Using the Form Wizard

One easy way to get started using forms is to use the Form Wizard, which will help you create a new Web page that contains a form with as many fields as you tell the wizard to put into it. Once you create this page using the wizard, you can edit it and add more content; you can cut and paste the form from the wizard page to an existing Web page; you can redesign the form altogether; or you can publish and start using it. We'll learn all about editing forms in the section titled (guess what?) "Editing Forms." For now, let's look at what the Form Wizard does.

NOTE   Instead of starting with the Form Wizard, you can get a head start on a form page by using a FrontPage template. The Feedback and Guestbook templates are both accessible from the New Page dialog box. From the menu bar, select File ➢ New ➢ Page, and the New Page dialog box appears. Select either Feedback Form or Guestbook from the list of possible templates, and then click OK to close the New Page dialog box and display the template in the Page view window.

Starting the wizard is quite easy. Of course, you may find yourself scratching your head trying to figure out what some of the options mean, but don't worry— we'll dutifully explain them all as we go along. For now, just start FrontPage and follow these steps:

1. From the menu bar, select File ➢ New ➢ Page. The New dialog box appears.

2. From the general list, click Form Page Wizard, then click OK to close the New Page dialog box. The Form Page Wizard appears.

3. This first panel describes forms; read it and click Next to proceed to the next panel of the wizard.

4. In this panel's Page Title text box, type your new page's title. In the Page URL text box, type its filename. The page URL, as always, should end in .html or

.htm. The title should describe what your form will be used for (something like "Company Survey" might be good), although "Form Page 1" may be okay for now. (You can change it later if you like.) When you're done, click Next to proceed to the next panel.

5. Now we get to the nitty gritty of the Form Page Wizard (see Figure 14.2). To start adding elements to your form, click Add, and the Form Page Wizard displays a list of options for form input.

PART

II

Creating
Sophisticated
Designs

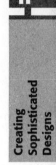

FIGURE 14.2

Use this panel to add elements to your form.

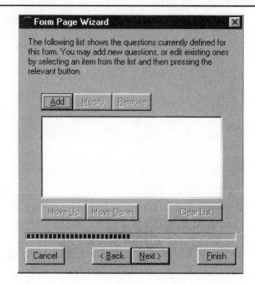

6. As shown in Figure 14.3, you have quite a few options to choose from when creating a form with the wizard. Some of the options we found are:

- Contact, Account, Product Information, Ordering, or Personal Information (each produces a series of text boxes and other fields)
- One of Several Options (produces radio buttons, a drop-down menu, or a list box)
- Any of Several Options (produces checkboxes)
- Boolean (produces yes/no or true/false buttons)
- Date or Time (produces fields whose inputs are limited to specified formats)
- Range (offers a range of buttons or menu options)

- Number (produces a text box that will accepts only numerical input)
- String (produces a text box)
- Paragraph (produces a scrolling text box)

Click any of the options, and you'll see a description of it in the Description area, while the text that will appear on the form is shown in the text box labeled Edit The Prompt For This Question.

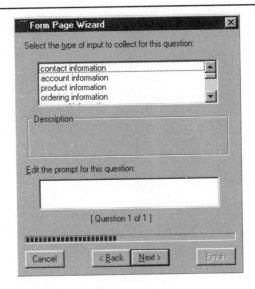

FIGURE 14.3

You can choose from any number of form field options, each of which places one or more form fields on your page.

7. When you find an option that meets your needs, click it, modify the question text if you like, and then click Next to display its options. Figure 14.4 shows a sample of what might appear on your screen (we chose Account Information).

8. In this panel, you'll find a series of buttons and boxes to fill out; these will differ depending on what option you selected in step 7. These buttons and boxes control how your form field looks and acts. You'll also find a text box labeled Enter The Base Name For This Group Of Variables. You must fill out this text box for any fields you include in your form—it's the name part of the name-value pair we mentioned earlier, in the section called "What Do Forms Do." When you're done selecting options for that question, click Next, and you'll return to the panel of the dialog box we saw in Figure 14.2. The question text you typed in step 7 is displayed in the list box.

FIGURE 14.4

Each kind of form in the Form Page Wizard has its own set of options; these are the options for the Account Information template.

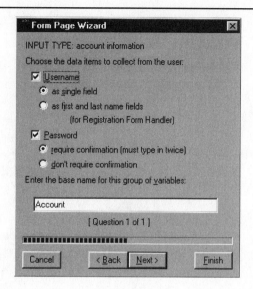

9. Repeat steps 5 through 8 to add other form fields to your page, if you like.

10. Once you have added one or more form fields to your page, you can delete or edit them, or change the order in which they appear. To delete a form field, in the list box of the panel shown in Figure 14.2 click its question text and then click Remove. To edit your choices for a form field, click its question text, and then click Modify. To change the order in which the questions will appear on the page, click the question to be moved and then click Move Up or Move Down until you're satisfied with the order.

TIP To remove all items from the list, click the Clear List button.

11. When you've finished adding questions and fields to your form, click Next to proceed to the Presentation Options panel of the wizard (see Figure 14.5). Here, you'll see options for formatting your form's questions. Click the appropriate button to lay out your table in normal paragraphs, as a numbered list, as a bulleted list, or as a definition list. If you'd like the wizard to add a clickable table of contents to the top of your form page, click the Yes button. If you'd like to give the wizard the option of using tables to align your form content, click the checkbox labeled Use Tables to align form fields.

PART

II

Creating
Sophisticated
Designs

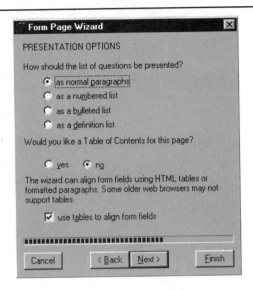

12. Click Next to move to the Output Options panel of the wizard. Use these options to determine how to process the data collected by the form. We discuss these options later in this chapter in the section titled "Setting Up a Form Handler," later in this chapter. For now, if you know whether you'll be saving your results as a Web page or a text file, or sending your results to a custom CGI script, click the appropriate button and type a name for your file in the text box labeled Enter A Name For Your File.

NOTE If you choose a custom CGI script to handle your form, the text box will become grayed out. Refer to "Setting Up a Form Handler," later in this chapter, for more information about setting up these options.

13. When you're done, click Finish. The Form Page Wizard closes, and the Page view window reappears with your new form displayed.

When your page appears, you'll notice a dashed line surrounding the parts of the page that make up the form itself. The Forms Toolbar is also displayed; we'll tell you all about it in the next section, "Editing Forms."

TIP Many of the forms generated by the Form Page Wizard include tables for formatting purposes. You can learn more about editing tables in Chapter 11.

In Figure 14.6, you can see a page created with the Form Page Wizard, before it's been edited. You can edit the text for any of the form field questions, or the text that says, "This is an explanation of the purpose of the form," just as you would any other text. Refer to Chapter 4, *Creating Basic Pages*, for instructions on basic text editing, or to Chapter 6, *Fantastic Fonts*, for details about fancy text options.

 NOTE Submit and Reset buttons will be added to your form page automatically; refer to "Adding Submit and Reset Buttons," later in this chapter, to find out how to make these work.

 NOTE You can see what your form will look like in the Web environment by previewing it in your browser (click the Preview button on the Standard toolbar, or use the menu bar to select File ➤ Preview In Browser). Your form won't *do* anything yet, because you haven't attached it to a form handler, but we'll get to that in the section called "Setting Up a Form Handler," later in this chapter.

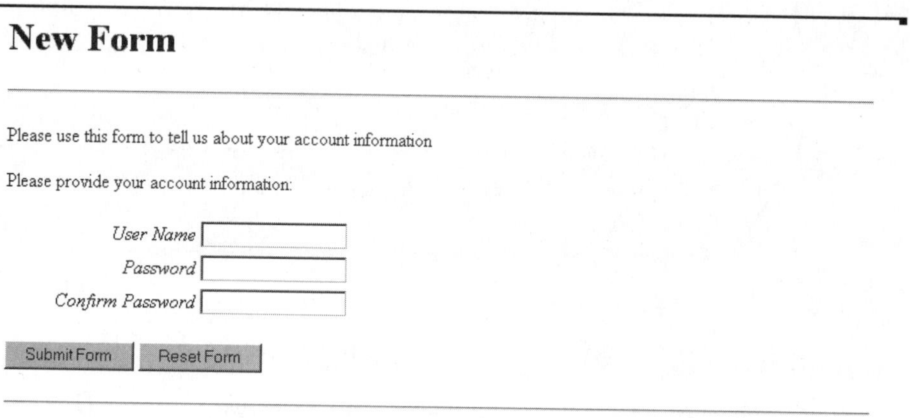

PART

II

Creating
Sophisticated
Designs

FIGURE 14.6

We made this page using the Form Page Wizard.

New Form

Please use this form to tell us about your account information

Please provide your account information:

User Name	
Password	
Confirm Password	

Submit Form   Reset Form

MASTERING WHAT'S ONLINE

Whimsical—nay, wacky—uses of forms abound on the Web. Try these on for size: The Dada Server, at www.smalltime.com/nowhere/dada/ is a tribute to the anti-art movement of the early 20th century. Similarly, most of the Surrealist Games at the Surrealism Server pharmdec.wustl.edu/juju/surr/games/games.html use forms to forward their maniacal end.

Mirsky's Drunk Browsing Test is a creative, if utterly useless, use of forms. Click away at www.turnpike.net/~mirsky/drunk/.

And the ever-popular Place of General Happiness uses forms to great ends for things like the Stalking Post BBS, the Punchline Server, and various other corners of the site. Point your browser at www.paranoia.com/~sorabji/.

Editing Forms

FrontPage makes it easy to edit and create forms on your Web pages without using the Form Page Wizard. You can also modify or add fields to a form created with the wizard. We'll even tell you how! Really, FrontPage makes it simple to put all the input fields on your pages. You use the Forms toolbar to create the boxes and buttons, each of which has its own Form Field Properties dialog box to let you change the details of the field. Read on.

TIP   The text on your page, whether in the form or outside it, can be edited and formatted just like any other text.

Copying, Cutting, and Pasting Forms and Form Fields

In Page view, you can cut (or copy) and paste just about any HTML element you can put on a page into another part of that page, or into a different page. This applies to forms, most certainly. As we've said, forms are indicated in Page view by a dashed, rectangular box that surrounds the form (see Figure 14.7).

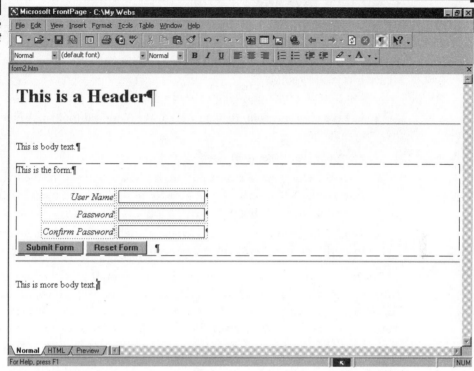

FIGURE 14.7

Here you can see the
form—it's the part
inside the dashed box.

You can select all or part of a form the same way you select text: by clicking and
dragging. When the part of the form you want to copy is highlighted, press Ctrl+C to
copy (or Ctrl+X to cut) the form, code and all, to the Clipboard. Then click your mouse
where you want that stuff to go, whether it's in the same document or another document, and press Ctrl+V to paste the form components. It's that easy!

Making a One-Line Text Box

If forms are like high school tests, then *one-line text boxes* are good for short answer
questions. (For example: "H_2O is the chemical symbol for what substance?") Other
text boxes work better for multiple choice or essay questions, but one-line text boxes
like the following one are perfect when all you want is a name, an address, or something else that requires just a few words.

Creating a Text Box

Creating and editing a one-line text box is a two-part process. The procedure for creating and editing all of these fields is pretty similar: First you use the Forms toolbar to place the element on your page, and then you right-click the element to pop up the dialog box used to edit it.

Let's start with a brand new blank page and put a one-line text box on it.

1. In Page view, click the New button on the Standard toolbar. A new blank document appears.

2. From the FrontPage menu bar, select Insert ➤ Form.

3. Click the One-Line Text Box button. A text box appears to the left of the insertion point. Notice that the area surrounding the text box is enclosed with a dashed line, indicating that there's a form in the making.

4. Type some text near your box (on either side, or above it, or below it) to indicate its purpose—whether it's for a name, an e-mail address, or what have you.

The text box behaves just like any other element on the page—you can click the insertion point before it and start typing, and it will move to the right to make way for the text. If you'd like people to use a particular format for the info in the text box, you can give them an example with your text. Instead of just typing **Name**, you could type **Name** (*e.g., Franklin D. Roosevelt*) or **Name** (*e.g., Roosevelt, Frank*).

 TIP Click your new text box, and little black squares called *handles* appear on the edges. You can click the handles and drag them to change the width and height of the text box.

Editing a Text Box

Now let's pop open the Text Box Properties dialog box and see what our options are. Follow these steps:

1. Right-click the text box, and from the menu that appears, select Form Field Properties (because the text box is, after all, a form field). The Text Box Properties dialog box appears, looking like it does in Figure 14.8.

2. Choosing a name for your form fields is generally helpful when you're sorting out the data later on. In the dialog box's Name text box, type a name for your own text box. Keep in mind that the names of form fields can contain only letters and numbers; although you can use underscores, you cannot use spaces.

FIGURE 14.8

The Text Box Properties
dialog box lets you edit
your text boxes.

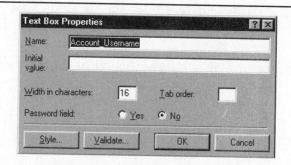

3. You can use the Initial Value text box if you'd like something to appear in your text box when it's loaded onto the page. For example, if your text box is for collecting country information, you might type **United States** in the Initial Value field to show people what you mean.

4. In the Width In Characters text box, type a width for your text box. The default is 20 characters, which isn't very long.

5. If you're going to be using your field to collect password data, in the Password field area, click Yes. Any characters typed in this field will be obscured by asterisks. (Or leave it with No selected if it's just a regular old text box.)

6. When a user is actually using a Web form in a Web browser, he or she can move from field to field by pressing the Tab key. (You can move between the fields in dialog boxes the same way.) The order this goes in for form fields on Web pages is generally top to bottom, but you may want to impose a different order, particularly if you're using tables to lay out your pages. In the Tab Order text box, you can type a number to set a tab rank for this field. (Tab order starts at 1 and increases from there.)

7. If you're all done with this form, click OK to close the Text Box Properties dialog box.

or

If you'd like to set limits for what your users can type in the box, hold tight and move on to the next section.

Creating Rules for Text Box Validation

Now that you have a text box that does what you want it to, you can make it practically autonomous and freethinking. Okay, maybe not quite—but you can have it weed out a lot of blank or improperly filled in fields for you by setting validation parameters. If people type unacceptable data into your text box and then submit it, a validation script will glance at the data and tell users that something's wrong with what they typed.

1. To restrict the input in this box to just letters or numbers, with the Text Box Properties dialog box still open, click Validate to open the Text Box Validation dialog box, which you can see in Figure 14.9.

   or

   To set these validation rules starting from a Page view window, just right-click the text box and, from the pop-up menu that appears, select Form Field Validation Properties. The Text Box Validation dialog box appears (see Figure 14.9).

FIGURE 14.9

You can limit acceptable input to either numbers or letters by using the Text Box Validation dialog box.

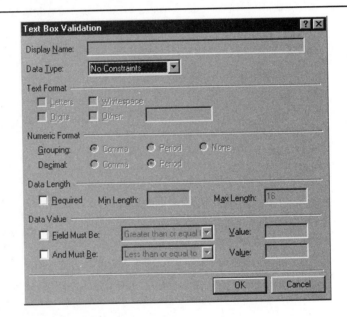

2. The Data Type drop-down menu offers four choices:

   - *No Constraints* lets you accept any kind of characters. This is the default.
   - *Text* allows you to limit the input yourself. (See step 4 to find out what your options are.)
   - *Integers* limits the input to whole numbers.
   - *Numbers* limits the input to whole numbers and decimals.

Click the Data Type list box, and then click one of the options. The Text Box Validation dialog box makes more options available.

3. If you chose Text, Integers, or Numbers, type a display name in the Display Name text box. If the user's input doesn't conform to your specifications, a dialog box will appear in his or her Web browser saying to change or enter data in the field. For example, if you want to require an e-mail address, type **E-mail address** in the Display Name text box.

4. If you chose Text, use the Text Format area of the dialog box to decide what sort of characters you want to accept. Select Letters or Digits to accept those; click Whitespace to accept spaces and the like. If you want to allow other characters, such as the @ sign, commas, or periods, click Other and type those characters in the box.

   or

   If you chose Integers or Numbers, in the Numeric Format option of the dialog box choose options for separating numbers typed in the box. You can choose commas or periods for separating decimals and for delineating discrete numbers—the option you choose probably depends on what the data will be used for (inputting it into a database, sorting it with a script, or casting magic spells to take over the world).

5. To make input into this field required, select the Required option. (If you're going to require that a field be filled in order to accept a form, make that fact explicit on the page.)

6. In the Min Length and Max Length text boxes, you can restrict your field to a minimum and/or maximum length. For example, if you're creating a hangman game and the correct answer is six characters long, you can make both the minimum and maximum number of characters 6. You might want to set minimums for things like names (who has a name one character long?) or maximums for questions like "What's your state's nickname?" (I doubt any state's nickname is over 80 characters.)

7. If you want to set parameters for what exact information can or cannot be entered in a field, you can use the Data Value area of the dialog box to set parameters for exact matches. For example, if you simply will not accept surveys from people named Santa Claus, you can select the checkbox labeled Field Must Be, and from the drop-down list, select Not Equal To, and then in the Value text box, type **Santa Claus**.

PART

II

Creating
Sophisticated
Designs

8. When you're all done setting parameters for validating this form, click OK to close the Text Box Validation dialog box. You'll return to either the Form Field Properties dialog box (which you can close by clicking OK) or Page view window.

You can use text box validation to run contests and games, to weed out practical jokers, and to make sure that people don't forget to type in their e-mail addresses, among other things.

MASTERING TROUBLESHOOTING

Preventing Form Failures

You already know that to see how your pages will look on the Web—with or without forms—you need to preview them in a Web browser. But form pages need to be tested, tested again, and then tested yet again to make sure they work. Before your site launch, make sure you install the pages on your Web site. Checking to make sure they look right is important, but checking to ensure that they *act* the way they're supposed to is imperative, particularly if you included any validation settings or if the form is supposed to do something snazzy. If the form is supposed to store the data sent to it, make sure it does that. If the form is supposed to display a validation screen or send the user somewhere specific, make sure it does that, too. Test the forms yourself, have co-workers test them, and then test them again.

Creating a Scrolling Text Box

If one-line text boxes are for short answer questions, *scrolling text boxes* are for essay questions. If you're creating forms to send e-mail, gather comments, or solicit posts to a guestbook, the scrolling text box is what you need. It does what it says: holds enough text to need its own scroll bars:

Creating a scrolling text box is simple. Just follow these steps:

1. On the page that's open, click the mouse where you'd like your scrolling text box to go. Click Insert ➤ Form ➤ Scrolling Text Box, and the scrolling text box appears on your page.

2. Right-click the scrolling text box, and from the pop-up menu that appears, choose Form Field Properties. The Scrolling Text Box Properties dialog box appears, as shown in Figure 14.10.

FIGURE 14.10

The Scrolling Text Box Properties dialog box lets you resize your brand new box.

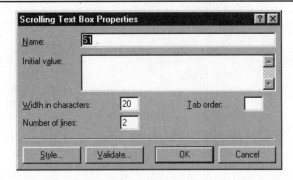

3. In the Name text box, type a name for this form field (such as "feedback").

4. If you'd like your scrolling text box to appear on your Web page with some text already in it, type this text in the Initial Value text box. For example, you might want to have your text box start out, "I think your page is great because..." if you're asking for feedback.

5. If you'd like to change the size of your scrolling text box, in the Width In Characters text box, type a number for the width (in characters) of your text box. In the Number Of Lines text box, type a number to set the height for the text box.

6. When you're using a Web form in a Web browser, you can move from field to field by pressing the Tab key. (You can move between the fields in dialog boxes the same way.) On Web page form fields, tabbing generally occurs top to bottom, but you may want to impose another order, particularly if you're using tables to lay out your pages. In the Tab Order text box, you can type a number to set a tab rank for this field (starting with the number 1).

7. When you're done, click OK to close the Scrolling Text Box Properties dialog box. You'll see your new scrolling, scrolling, rocking and rolling text box.

Be sure to type some introductory text for your scrolling text box, like "Please type your comments here."

PART

II

Creating
Sophisticated
Designs

TIP If you'd like to set validation restrictions for your text box, you can click the Validate button in the Scrolling Text Box Properties dialog box, or you can right-click the scrolling text box and choose Form Field Validation Properties from the pop-up menu that appears. This dialog box is exactly the same as the one we talked about in the previous section, "Creating Rules for Text Box Validation."

Creating Checkboxes

Checkboxes are for true or false questions. Each checkbox acts as its own entity, just waiting to be filled with a Yes! or No! You can also put a bunch of checkboxes together in a group, for those "Check all that apply" type of forms:

Dropping checkboxes on your page is easier than dropping a stack of plates. Just follow these steps:

1. With a page open in Page view, click where you'd like the checkbox to appear.

2. Select Insert ➤ Form ➤ Checkbox, and a checkbox appears.

3. Right-click the checkbox, and from the menu that appears, select Form Field Properties. The Check Box Properties dialog box appears, as seen in Figure 14.11.

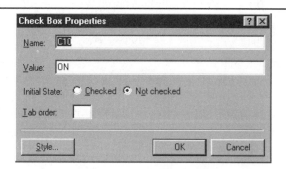

4. In this dialog box's Name field, type a name for your checkbox. Choosing a memorable name for your checkbox is especially important if you're going to have a bunch of them.

5. The Value text box is where you decide what Checked and Not Checked will mean. For example, if you want a check mark in the box to indicate "True," then you'd type **True**. If you want a checked box to mean, "Yes, please send my name to other companies," then you'd type something like **Sell**.

NOTE   If you're using a form with checkboxes to store data in a text file, you likely won't see evidence of those checkboxes that aren't checked. In other words, the names and values should be meaningful. A line that says *Stamp Collecting=Hobby* would be much more decipherable than one that said *SC=ON*.

6. The Initial State buttons determine whether your checkbox will appear on the page empty or already checked. If you want it to be checked automatically ("Yes, your page is a work of genius, please tell me more"), click Checked. If you'd like it to be blank initially ("Please check this box if you've declared bankruptcy in the last 10 years"), then click Not Checked.

7. When a user encounters a Web form in a Web browser, he or she can move from field to field by pressing the Tab key. (Moving between fields in dialog boxes works the same way.) On Web page form fields, the order is generally top to bottom, but you may want to impose a different order, particularly if you're using tables to lay out your pages. In the Tab order text box, you can type a number to set a tab rank for this field (starting with the number 1).

8. When you're done, click OK to close the Check Box Properties dialog box.

You can add checkboxes to your heart's content just by following these steps. Make sure you label each checkbox with some meaningful text.

Turning On Radio Buttons

Radio buttons were named for their similarity to rows of console buttons—when you push one of them to select it, it pops in and the others are deselected. Radio buttons are good for either true or false or multiple choice questions, particularly when there are only a few possible choices.

One radio button wouldn't do you any good, so let's create two of them:

1. With the page you want to add buttons to visible in Page view, select Insert ➤ Form ➤ Radio Button. A radio button appears.

2. Now repeat the process. Another radio button appears.

3. Double-click the first radio button to display the Radio Button Properties dialog box (see Figure 14.12).

4. In the Group Name text box, type a name for your entire group of radio buttons. You'll probably want to use a keyword from the question to which the radio buttons belong.

5. Now, in the Value field, type a name for this button. If it's a "Yes" button, type Yes. If it's a Choice 1 of 5 button—the first of five buttons, each of which represents to the user a different choice—you might type a word from that choice, such as **chocolate**.

6. If you'd like this button to be selected when the page opens (only one radio button can be selected in a group of named radio buttons), click the Selected radio button. Otherwise, click Not Selected.

7. When a user encounters a Web form in a Web browser, he or she can move from field to field by pressing the Tab key. (Moving between fields in dialog boxes works the same way.) On Web page form fields, the order is generally top to bottom, but you may want to impose a different order, particularly if you're using tables to lay out your pages. In the Tab Order text box, you can type a number to set a tab rank for this field (starting with the number 1).

8. Click OK to close the Radio Button Properties dialog box and return to your other radio button.

9. Follow steps 3 through 8 for the second button. Use the same Group Name, and a different Value name. Again, note that only one radio button can be selected initially.

You can follow step 1 to create as many radio buttons as you like, and then follow steps 3 through 8 for each of them. As long as you use the same Group Name for your buttons, they'll function as a set. As soon as you change the Group Name, you've got a whole new set of buttons on your hands. (Don't forget to add a text label for each of your buttons.)

 NOTE You can validate your radio buttons, if you like. Right-click any of the buttons, and choose Form Field Validation from the pop-up menu to open the Radio Button Validation dialog box. In the Display Name field, type a name for the set of buttons. This is the name that will show up in any error messages your users see if they don't click any of the buttons, so make it recognizable. To require that one of these buttons be selected to process the form, make sure the Data Required checkbox is selected.

Ordering from Drop-Down Menus

For multiple choice questions that have several possible responses, multiple checkboxes work well, especially if you want to let your users choose several (or all) of the possible selections. Another way to go is the drop-down menu. To let your users choose from dozens of options, all of which are indexed in one neat little box, drop-down menus are the perfect solution:

You can set up drop-down menus so that users can select more than one option at a time, too.

Creating a Drop-Down Menu

Creating a drop-down menu using the Forms toolbar is pretty easy:

1. Is the page you're working on still open in Page view? Good. To insert a drop-down menu on your page, select Insert ➤ Form ➤ Drop-Down Menu. A small drop-down menu appears on your page, along with the requisite Submit and Reset buttons:

2. Now, you may wonder how you'll be able to type anything in that little space. You don't—the Drop-Down Menu Properties dialog box is where you create all the content for your menu. To open it, double-click the drop-down menu, or right-click it and use the pop-up menu to select Form Field Properties. The Drop-Down Menu Properties dialog box appears:

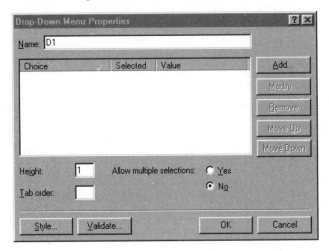

3. Before you forget, in the dialog box's Name field, type a name for your drop-down menu.

4. Now, to add your first item to the menu, click Add. The Add Choice dialog box appears.

5. In this dialog box's Choice text box, type the menu item exactly the way you want it to appear in the drop-down menu. If you would like the value of the item to be different from what appears in the menu, click the Specify Value checkbox and type the value in its text box.

6. If you'd like this menu item to be pre-selected when your Web page loads, in the Initial State area, click Selected; otherwise, leave the default at Not Selected.

7. Click OK to close the Add Choice dialog box and return to the Drop-Down Menu Properties dialog box, where you'll see the choice you just added displayed in the Choice list box.

8. Repeat steps 4 through 7 for as many items as you need to add to your drop-down menu.

9. Once you have added menu items to your drop-down list, you can modify or delete them, or change the order in which they appear.

- To modify an item, click it in the list, then click the Modify button. The Modify Choice dialog box appears; it is just like the Add Choice dialog box used previously in "Creating a Drop-Down Menu." Make any changes you like, and then click OK to return to the Drop-Down Menu Properties dialog box.

- To remove a menu item, click it in the list and then click Remove. The selected item disappears from the list.

- To change the order of items as they will appear in the menu, select the menu item you'd like to reorder, and click the Move Up or Move Down button to rearrange things. The order changes in the list as you click the buttons.

10. If you'd like your menu to display one item when your Web page loads, in the Height text box, type **1**. (Drop-down menu boxes that are one line high literally drop down to display the other choices when you click them.) If you'd like the menu box to display several choices at a time, and use scroll bars to display the rest, type a number greater than 1.

11. If you'd like your users to be able to choose more than one item for consideration, in the Allow Multiple Selections area, click the Yes button; otherwise, click No. Unpredictable things will happen if you set more than one choice item as selected and if Allow Multiple Selections is set to No, so be sure to double-check your options for selected items.

12. When a user encounters a Web form in a Web browser, he or she can move from field to field by pressing the Tab key. (Moving between fields in dialog boxes works the same way.) On Web page form fields, the order is generally top to bottom, but you may want to impose a different order, particularly if you're using tables to lay out your pages. In the Tab Order text box, type a number to set a tab rank for this field, starting with the number 1.

13. When you're through designing your drop-down menu, click OK to close the Drop-Down Menu Properties dialog box.

PART
II

Creating
Sophisticated
Designs

 TIP If you have a drop-down menu you need to use several times, such as a list of states or countries, you will be glad you remembered to copy and paste this menu on all the pages that need it. Also, you may want to borrow such a list from another page that already has one. Just open up the other page, and then copy it, paste it in your own document, and modify it for your use.

Using Validation with Drop-Down Menus

If you want to make sure your users choose *something* (not something in particular, just something) from your carefully constructed drop-down menu, you'll want to set validation parameters for it.

1. Right-click the drop-down menu you just created and, from the pop-up menu that appears, select Form Field Validation Properties. The Drop-Down Menu Validation dialog box appears.

2. To require that your users select something out of all the choices they have, click the Data Required checkbox. If you choose to require data, in the Display Name text box, type a display name for your drop-down menu (such as **Favorite Dog Breed**).

3. If you'd like to disallow the first (pre-selected) choice, click Disallow First Item. This is especially worthwhile if the first item says "Please select one."

4. All finished? Click OK to close the Drop-Down Menu Validation dialog box.

Those are all the boxes and buttons that you'll use to collect input from visitors to your page. In the next section, we'll cover *hidden fields*, which you can use to send data to yourself on the sly, as well as the push buttons that users will use to actually send the form to you. Read on.

Adding Hidden Fields

Hidden fields are data fields that don't show up on the Web page, but get sent in with the rest of the data nonetheless. Because the fields are hidden, they don't change depending on the input of the user, but rather serve as a tagline or reminder to you, embedded with the rest of the data. (The fields will appear to you later, along with the user's input, when he or she submits the form.) They are particularly useful if you will be processing data submitted from several different sources or pages. You might want to use hidden fields to identify the name of the form, the page that it came from, or an instruction for a custom CGI script.

Adding hidden fields is quite simple. Just follow these steps:

1. With your form page open, right-click any blank space inside the form. From the menu that appears, select Form Properties. The Form Properties dialog box appears.

2. In this dialog box, head straight to the bottom and click the Advanced button. The Advanced Form Properties dialog box appears, as shown in Figure 14.13.

FIGURE 14.13

This is where you create those hidden fields.

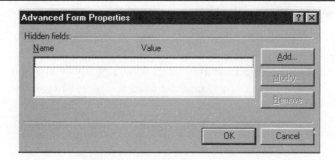

3. Click Add to open the Name/Value Pair dialog box:

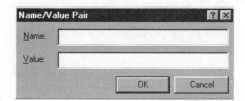

In the Name text box, type a name for the hidden field, and in the Value text box, type a value. Then click OK to close the Name/Value Pair dialog box and return to the Advanced Form Properties dialog box.

4. You'll see the name and value you just typed in the Hidden Fields list box. You can now add, remove, or modify additional fields by selecting the appropriate buttons.

5. When you're finished, click OK to close the Advanced Form Properties dialog box, and then click OK again to close the Form Properties dialog box.

You won't see the hidden fields because…they're hidden! Rest assured, however, that they'll be sent along with the rest of the input when people submit your forms. If you want to see them, just click the HTML tab at the bottom of the window.

 WARNING Although these fields are hidden from the casual user, they're visible to anyone who views the HTML source for your form page, so don't rely on them to hide confidential information.

Adding Submit and Reset Buttons

We still need to add buttons so that your users can send all this data to your home base—otherwise, your form will be like one of those Dapper Dan dolls that offer a lot of buttons to play with but that don't actually do anything. When your user clicks a Submit button, the data is validated and then whisked away to the form handler, which we'll get to later, in the section called "Setting Up a Form Handler." Many forms also offer a Reset (or Clear) button, which restores the form to its default settings, in case the user wants to start from scratch.

 NOTE FrontPage 2000 automatically adds a Submit and Reset button to your page when you create a form. You will still want to know how to add these buttons, though, in case you're working on a page started in another program, or in case you accidentally delete these buttons while you're working on the page.

Generally, you'll put these buttons at the end of your form (within the dashed outline), which may or may not also be the bottom of your page:

 TIP Most forms put the Submit button on the left and the Reset/Clear button on the right. A few forms do it the other way—we remember these forms distinctly as the ones we had to fill out four or five times in a row, because we kept pushing the left button instinctually. There's no requirement that you even include a Reset button if you don't want to. To delete it, just select it and wield your Delete key.

Making a Submit Button

Submit buttons, although you can call them whatever you like (Send, for example), are the buttons that get pushed to send the data to the form handler. FrontPage adds these buttons automatically, but if you need to add or replace one, it's easy enough. Just follow these steps:

1. Click in the area of your form where you want the button(s) to appear. Select Insert ➢ Form ➢ Push Button. A button labeled Button appears on your page.

2. Right-click Button and, from the pop-up menu that appears, select Form Field Properties. The Push Button Properties dialog box appears, as shown in Figure 14.14.

FIGURE 14.14

You can define buttons as Submit or Reset here.

3. Given that this is a Submit button we're making, in the Button Type area, click the Submit button.

4. In the dialog box's Name field, type a name for your button (such as Submit).

5. In the Value/Label area, type whatever it is you want the button to say. You can leave this button labeled Submit, or you can type something more specific, like **Enter Me in the Contest**, or something creative, like **Bring Home the Bacon**.

6. Click OK to close the Push Button Properties dialog box.

Now when your boss says that someone's pushing your buttons, you can assume he means the ones on your company's home page!

Making a Reset Button

Reset buttons, when clicked, clear the user's input and restore the form's default settings. FrontPage adds Reset buttons automatically, but if you need to add or replace one, it's easy enough. Just follow these steps:

1. Follow steps 1 and 2 in the previous section, "Making a Submit Button," to create a button and open the Push Button Properties dialog box. (The button will say Button when you create it initially.)

2. In this dialog box's Name field, type a name for your button.

3. In the Button Type area, click the Reset radio button, and the word Button in the Value/Label field changes to Reset.

4. You can change the wording in the Value/Label field to something like **Let Me Start Over**. When you're done, click OK to close the Push Button Properties dialog box.

Using Images as Buttons

Those standard gray boxy buttons that you see everywhere are so...standard. If you'd like, you can use images for Submit buttons instead (unfortunately, you can't use images for Reset buttons). It's probably worthwhile to create images that are obviously button-purposed. Having text outside the image that says "Click the carrier pigeon to send in your results" might help, but your images should be concise just the same.

Now, to make an image button, follow these steps:

1. With your form page open, click in your form where you want your image button to land. Then, from menu bar, select Insert ➤ Form ➤ Image. The Image dialog box appears.

2. You can choose any image on your FrontPage web, on your computer, or on the Internet, or you can use FrontPage clip art. Use the Image dialog box to select your image, then click OK to close the Image dialog box and return to the Page view window, where you'll see your image there, within the form.

 NOTE If you need help using the Image dialog box, see the section in Chapter 4 titled "Working with Images."

3. Right-click the image to open the Image Properties dialog box:

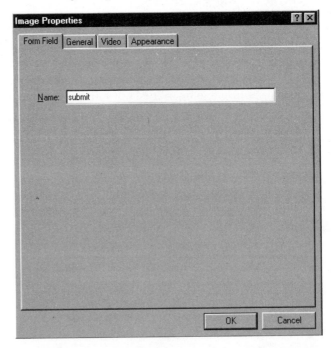

4. Click the Form Field tab, and in the Name text box, type a name for your image. If the image is going to act as a Submit button, for example, you might want to name it **Submit**.

5. Click OK to close the Image Form Field Properties dialog box.

When a user clicks the image, its coordinates are sent to the form handler, which understands it as a Submit button.

Now that you have everything in place, let's set up a form handler to tackle all the behind-the-scenes work.

 TIP To create attractive, graphical buttons, you can use PhotoDraw or Image Composer, as described in Chapter 9, *Designing Graphics for the Web*.

Setting Up a Form Handler

As mentioned, once the user clicks the Submit button on your Web page, that input is sent to the form handler, which then does something result-like with the results. You can choose from an array of FrontPage-based form handlers, or you can set up the form handler to work with custom scripts installed on your site. You have the following choices for form handlers:

- Save results to a file on the server.
- E-mail results to the Webmaster or some other person.
- Save results using a custom ISAPI, NSAPI, CGI, or ASP script.
- Use the results to register the user for a restricted web (for setting up username and password validation, see Chapter 15, *Special Effects*).

The Discussion and Registration webs are discussed in Chapter 15. To work with a custom ISAPI, NSAPI, CGI, or ASP script, contact your system administrator or your ISP's Webmaster or administrator.

 NOTE All the form handlers described in this section must be used with a server running the FrontPage Server Extensions, with the exception of custom scripts. ISAPI, NSAPI, CGI, and ASP scripts often run on servers other than FrontPage. The first three types run on various flavors of servers, while ASP scripts are most often associated with Microsoft servers.

Working with Custom Scripts

You can set up an ISAPI, NSAPI, or CGI script to do just about anything under the sun. If your Web server doesn't support FrontPage Server Extensions, or if you want more flexibility than FrontPage's scripting extensions can offer, a custom script may be the answer to your prayers.

 NOTE *CGI* stands for Common Gateway Interface. *ISAPI* means Internet Server Application Programming Interface, and *NSAPI* stands for Netscape Server Application Programming Interface. All three of these types of scripts are used to extend the functionality of Web servers. (Chapter 25, *Understanding CGI*, discusses CGI scripts in detail.)

However, custom scripts aren't a simple matter of clicking buttons and filling out dialog boxes. If you're not a programmer, you may need one—and a good script from a good programmer (for a good site) can be pricey. If you're dealing with an ISP (as opposed to working with your own or your company's Web server), you may be limited to scripts that they approve and install for you.

Don't panic, however. Most ISPs have a set of standard form-processing scripts, and they can tell you how to set up your forms so that they access these pre-existing scripts—a process that generally involves viewing the HTML and adding a few phrases here and there to the form code.

 WARNING Check with your system administrator or ISP to find out what your scripting options are before you get your sights set on a complicated form.

To set up your form to work with one of these scripts in the first place, follow these steps:

1. With your form open, right-click anywhere in the form and, from the menu that appears, select Form Properties. The Form Properties dialog box appears, as shown in Figure 14.15.

2. In the area labeled Where To Store Results, click the Send To Other button. Its drop-down menu will become visible.

3. From the drop-down menu, select a custom ISAPI, NSAPI, CGI, or ASP script.

4. Click the Options button. The Options For Custom Form Handler dialog box appears.

FIGURE 14.15

Choose your form handler.

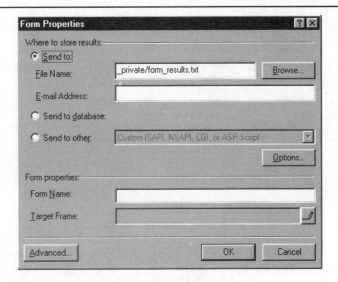

5. To fill out this dialog box, check with your system administrator (or, if you are the system administrator, fill it out). In the Method drop-down menu, select a method (POST or GET). The URL of your script goes in the Action text box, and the encoding method (if any) goes in the Encoding text box.

6. Once you're finished, click OK to close the Custom Form Handler dialog box. The Form Properties dialog box reappears. Click OK to close that dialog box.

Because these are instructions for the form's data rather than adjustments to the form itself, you won't *see* any visible result—be sure to test the heck out of your form to make sure it really does work with your script.

Saving Results to a File

The default setting for handling forms is to save them to a file. You can send results to a text file or an HTML file for later viewing, and you have several formatting options with either type. You can open up the text file that contains your users' input whenever you like. It'll look a little funny—raw data files often do—but if you gave memorable names and values to all your fields, you'll be able to make sense of it. You can crunch these numbers just as you do any others—although automating this process often involves the kind of custom script we talked about in the previous section. If you have a little bit of database or spreadsheet know-how, you can process these results in one of those programs, but that's a topic for a different book.

Setting up your form to save the results to a file, either an HTML file or a text file, is pretty simple. Follow these steps to do it:

1. With the form you're about to finish open in Page view, right-click inside the form and, from the menu that appears, select Form Properties. The Form Properties dialog box appears (we saw it in Figure 14.15).

2. In the area labeled Where To Store Results, click the Send To button, if it's not already selected.

3. Before you choose a filename for the results file, you must choose a file type. Click the Options button to open the Options For Saving Results Of Form dialog box, shown in Figure 14.16.

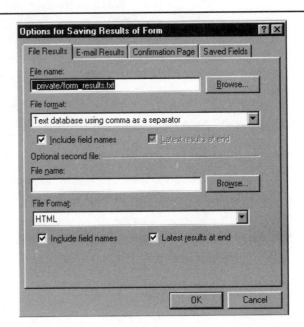

4. In the File Format area of the dialog box, click the drop-down menu. Several choices for both HTML and text files will be available: straight HTML; a definition or bulleted list; formatted text on an HTML page; a formatted text file; or text files with the fields delimited by commas, tabs, or spaces. (These last options are convenient if the file is going from FrontPage to a script, database, or spreadsheet.) Click the option you prefer.

5. Now, type a name for it in the File Name text box. Make sure the file ends in .htm or .html for HTML files, or .txt for text files.

 TIP You can include a directory in the name of the results file, if you'd like the file to be stored in a particular part of your Web site. If you're using a FrontPage server, you can make the filename something like private/formresults.txt to store the file in the private directory of your FrontPage web. To store the file in a particular directory of your Front-Page web, click Browse. The Current Web dialog box appears, and you can browse through the folders on your FrontPage web and select one in which to store your form results. Private is a good choice for storing form results, so that they won't be available to regular old folks browsing your site.

6. If there's some reason you don't want the field names sent to your file—for example, if you're going to post your form results as-is to the Web—deselect the Include Field Names checkbox. Otherwise, leave it alone. If you want the newest results from your form to appear at the bottom of your form results file, leave the Latest Results At End checkbox selected. To post the newest results at the top of the file instead of the bottom, deselect the Latest Results At End checkbox.

7. You can specify a second file in which your results are saved, if you'd like. For example, you may want to save your results as both HTML and comma-delimited text. To do this, follow steps 4 to 6, using the Optional Second File area of the dialog box for the second file. Specify the name and format of the second file in the same way you did for the first.

8. To specify which form fields are saved to these files, click the Saved Fields tab of the dialog box. The dialog box changes to reflect your choice (see Figure 14.17).

9. In this panel, you should see the names of all the form fields in your form. You can delete the names of any form fields that you don't want to save (for example, the name of the Submit button) by clicking them and pressing your Delete key.

 TIP If you delete form field names and realize you'd rather have kept them, don't worry. To restore all the form fields in your form, click Save All, and the deleted names will reappear.

PART

II

Creating
Sophisticated
Designs

FIGURE 14.17

*Decide what parts
of your form you
want to save here.*

10. In addition to saving the user's input from your form, you can save data that will tell you something about the user. In the Additional Information To Save area, select any of the checkboxes for the data you'd like added to the form results. FrontPage can add lines for the date and time the form was filled out, the name of the remote machine (alphanumeric or IP address), the username (if you're using FrontPage user registration for users to log into your Web page), and the browser type.

11. All finished? Click OK to close the Options For Saving Results Of Form dialog box, and then click OK to close the Form Properties dialog box.

Remember that URL (filename), because that's where you'll go to fetch your form results. When you're testing your form (as you will dutifully do before you launch your site) be certain to examine this file, as well, to make sure the results are satisfactory before you announce your form to the world.

E-Mailing Form Results

Another way to examine your form results is to have them e-mailed to you. That way, you don't need to remember to go and check up on your forms, because the results will come to your mailbox on a regular basis. The form results will be sent as the body of an e-mail message, rather than as attachments. You can then save the contents of e-mail messages as text files (and, by extension, as HTML files).

 TIP You can set up your form handler so that it both saves the files and e-mails them to you. Just follow the steps detailed in both this section and the preceding one, "Saving Results to a File."

To have your form results sent to you via e-mail, just follow these steps:

1. With the form you're about to finish open, right-click inside the form and, from the menu that appears, choose Form Properties. The Form Properties dialog box appears (we saw it in Figure 14.15).

2. In the area labeled Where To Store Results, click the Send To button, if it's not already selected.

3. In the E-Mail Address text box, type the e-mail address to which the results should be sent.

4. Click the Options button to open the Options For Saving Results Of Form dialog box, previously shown in Figure 14.16.

5. In this dialog box, click the E-Mail Results tab. The dialog box changes to reflect your choice (see Figure 14.18).

FIGURE 14.18

Use this tab to set up your e-mail message results.

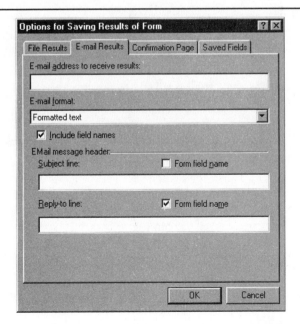

6. In the E-Mail Format area, click the drop-down list to choose a format for the data file. Several choices are available for both HTML and text files: straight HTML; a definition or bulleted list; formatted text on an HTML page; a formatted text file; or text files with the fields delimited by commas, tabs, or spaces. (These last options are convenient if the file is going from FrontPage to a script, database, or spreadsheet.) Click the option you prefer.

7. To include field names in your e-mail message, make sure the Include Field Names checkbox is selected.

8. Now you need to choose a subject line for the e-mail messages sent by the form handler. There are a couple ways you could go about this. If you want the subject line to reflect the simple fact that it contains results of your form, type something like **Results of Customer Survey** in the Subject Line text box.

   or

   If you'd like the subject line of the message to depend on how the form was filled out, you can make the subject line contain results of one of the form fields. For example, suppose one of your form fields is a drop-down menu that offers three choices: Compliments, Complaints, and Corrections. You may want to use these words in the subject line, because they probably have different priorities and may get handled by different members of your staff. So in the E-Mail Message Header area, check the Form Field Name checkbox, and, in the Subject Line text box, type the exact name of the form field whose results you want to display.

9. Another nifty feature of the e-mail form handler is the Reply-To option. If one of the fields in your form asks for the e-mail address of the respondent, your form handler can fill out each e-mail message's reply-to field with the respondent's e-mail address. To make this option active, in the E-Mail Message Header area, click the Form Field Name checkbox, and then, in the Reply-To Line text box, type the exact name of the form field that asks for the e-mail address.

 NOTE   In case you weren't aware of it already, e-mail messages include both a From field and a Reply-To field. The From field prints the exact e-mail address of the person who sent the message, while the Reply-To field prints the address that will show up in the To field when you click the Reply button. These can be two different addresses.

---

10. All finished? Click OK to close the Options For Saving Results Of Form dialog box, and then click OK to close the Form Properties dialog box.

Make sure you test this thing out a few times and ensure that the e-mail messages sent by the form handler actually make it to the proper e-mail box.

Offering Confirmation

When users click that Submit button, they want reassurance that *something* happened to all those boxes they filled out. It's a good idea to thank users for their time and to give them a link to click; beyond that, what your confirmation page does is up to you.

You can also include confirmation fields on your page; these fields verify the information the user sent, which is a great idea for things like conference registrations or password requests, because then users can save or print the results page for future reference.

 NOTE FrontPage 2000 doesn't come "out of the box" ready to support e-mailing form results. To make that option work, the Web server that hosts your web must be configured to send mail. If the server is with you, you'll do that; if your site is hosted on your ISP's server, your ISP must make the appropriate settings.

 NOTE Making a confirmation page is a two-step process. First you have to make the confirmation page itself (which can include confirmation fields), and then you have to set up your form page to request that the confirmation page be loaded when a user submits the form. Confirmation fields are available only to Web sites through the use of FrontPage Server Extensions (see Appendices A and C).

Setting Up a Confirmation Page

Now that you've made all these form fields, a confirmation page is exquisitely simple by comparison. FrontPage even supplies a template you can start with. Here's how to use it:

1. From the menu bar, select File ➤ New ➤ Page. The New Page dialog box appears.

2. In the General list box, select Confirmation Form, and click OK. The New Page dialog box closes and a new page, called Feedback Confirmation, appears in the window.

PART

II

Creating
Sophisticated
Designs

3. You can edit this page as you would any other, adding links and images, changing text and colors, and editing the title and headings.

4. The items in brackets, such as [UserName], are the confirmation fields supplied for this example page. Note that this template has no idea which fields are on your form pages, so be sure to double-check each and every one of them. To change a confirmation field, double-click it. The Confirmation Field Properties dialog box will appear:

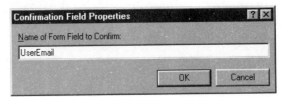

5. Type the name of the field you'd like to confirm in the Name Of Form Field To Confirm text box. The name must be exactly the same (including case sensitivity) as it appears in the code for the form. You can check the name of the form field by viewing your form page in Page view and double-clicking the form field it to display the Form Field Properties dialog box.

 TIP To have handy access to all these names and things as they appear on your page, you can view the HTML for your form page by clicking the HTML tab at the bottom of the window, and then print out the code. Or, you could just take notes as you go along.

6. Click OK to close the Confirmation Field Properties dialog box. You'll see the correct field name in the confirmation field you selected to change.

7. To add a confirmation field, click the page where you'd like it to appear, and from the menu bar, select Insert ➢ Component ➢ Confirmation Field. The Confirmation Field Properties dialog box appears.

8. In the dialog box, type the name of the form field you want to confirm.

9. Click OK to close the dialog box.

You're certainly welcome to create a confirmation page without using the template provided; just follow steps 7 through 10, above, to add fields you want to confirm.

Making Your Form Call Up the Confirmation Page

Your final task is to set up your original form to call up the confirmation page when a user submits your form.

1. With your form page open in Page view, right-click the form and, from the menu that appears, select Form Properties. The Form Properties dialog box appears (we saw it in Figure 14.15).

2. In the Form Properties dialog box, click the Options button. The Options For Saving Results Of Form dialog box appears (we saw it in Figure 14.16).

3. In this dialog box, click the Confirmation Page tab to bring it forward. The dialog box changes to reflect your choice (see Figure 14.19).

4. In this panel, type the target URL in the text box labeled URL Of The Confirmation Page (see the previous section, "Setting Up a Confirmation Page," for instructions on making a confirmation page). If your FrontPage web is open, you can click Browse to select the file from the available files.

5. You can specify a validation failure page in the same way, if you'd like to create a page (instead of a dialog box) that tells your users what they've done wrong. (Of course, this option is available to you only if you've used validation with one of your form fields. Otherwise, it'll appear grayed out.)

PART

II

FIGURE 14.19

Set up your confirmation page options here.

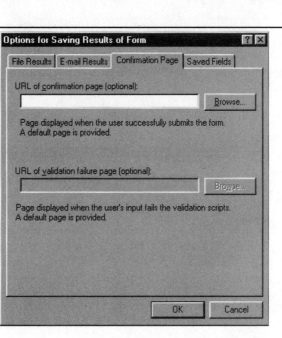

Creating Sophisticated Designs

6. When you're done, click OK to close the Options For Saving Results Of Form dialog box, then click OK to close the Form Properties dialog box.

Now your users will see your confirmation page when they click the form's Submit button (or the Show Me The Light button, or whatever you called it).

Up Next

If you've been feeling like the tasks in this book are getting more difficult, you're not alone! Working with forms—particularly setting them up to work on a server—can be frustrating for even an experienced Webmaster.

For those readers who come to FrontPage 2000 with little page-making experience, there is no doubt that the kind of work we're doing now is significantly more complex than the exercises earlier in the book. The good news is that you've learned how to do a lot of highly technical work without spending years learning how to operate Web servers or learn a language—FrontPage is doing most of the programming work for you.

This pep talk doesn't mean the experience of using FrontPage is going to get any less intricate, though! In Chapter 15, we're going to walk you through adding some pretty fun Web effects to your pages. While the technology in this book will continue to be sophisticated, you should be feeling confident that with FrontPage, you can easily accomplish these advanced techniques.

CHAPTER 15

Special Effects

Until recently, many of the strongest and most flexible features of Web site design actually required a more extensive knowledge of Web programming. Special programming skills were required in order to have different images display on a page at different times (say, over a holiday, when no one is actually in the office to change the image manually), or to add a hit counter to a Web page, or create a discussion group. All of these effects are supported by a variety of Web technologies that go beyond simple HTML.

But many of us are not programmers, nor do we have the time or desire to become programmers! Still, we want to implement these special but often site-enhancing features without spending extra money or time on programmers.

In this chapter, we'll focus on several approaches to adding programming-based techniques. One approach is known as *components*. Other approaches use various aspects of FrontPage and HTML technology to achieve effects that will spice up your pages nicely.

 TIP Be sure to drop by Chapter 21, *JavaScript and Dynamic HTML,* and Chapter 22, *Specialty Programming Techniques,* for a look at specific methods of programming effects within your pages.

Using Components

One way Microsoft FrontPage manages programming-based techniques is by taking many popular features that usually require programming and tying them up into neat little packages called *components*. Microsoft uses the term *components* as a catchall for a bunch of active elements that come with FrontPage. You can insert these handy items into your webs without any programming on your part. The components that come with FrontPage are actually implemented using a number of technologies, including server-side scripts, Java, and JavaScript (see Chapters 21 and 22 for more details).

 NOTE In Chapter 14, *Making Interactive Pages with Forms*, you were actually introduced to a component—the one that's used to save or e-mail the results of a form.

Components are prepackaged, preprogrammed elements you can easily add to your FrontPage webs. Those popular hit counters, for example (which count the number of times a page is visited), used to take two or three days of programming effort to create, and could be accomplished only by those who were familiar with a programming language such as Perl. The hit counter component, on the other hand, lets you install one on your page in only a few minutes!

If you know how to place an image on your page (as explained in Chapter 9, *Designing Graphics for the Web*), you are already well on your way to working with components.

Placing an Ad Banner on Pages

A commonly used component, the ad banner allows you to set up an advertisement with special effects on any page you choose.

To place an ad banner on a page, follow these steps:

1. With a page open in Page view, place the cursor at the point where you want to insert the banner (this will usually be the top).

2. From the menu bar, select Insert ➢ Component ➢ Banner Ad Manager. The Banner Ad Manager Properties dialog box appears (see Figure 15.1).

FIGURE 15.1

The Banner Ad Manager Properties dialog box

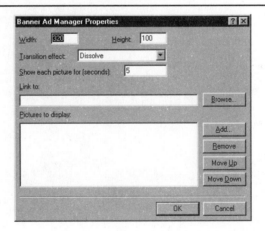

3. Set the height and width of the banner. These should be uniform if you're going to rotate banners.

4. Choose an effect. You can have the banner transition in a variety of styles, including a "blinds" effect, a dissolve, or a box. You can also leave this set to None if you do not want an effect.

5. In the Link To text box, add the page or URL you'd like the banner to go to. You can use the Browse button to find what you're looking for, or simply type in the location.

6. In Pictures To Display, you can select the banner graphics of your choice. Note that you can use more than one, but keeping the total number to three is probably most appropriate on smaller sites.

7. Click OK.

You now have a rotating banner, with special effects!

Adding a Hit Counter

Many people like to track the number of visitors to their site and broadcast this information for all to see. FrontPage makes this a breeze with the Hit Counter component, which counts every visit to your page and then proudly posts the tally. Several stylish display options are available (see Figure 15.2).

In the Hit Counter Properties dialog box, you can select a variety of fonts for numbers.

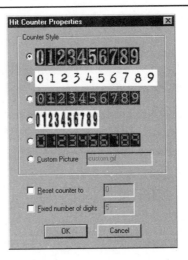

To use the Hit Counter component, follow these steps:

1. With a page open in Page view, position the cursor at the point where you want to insert the hit counter.

2. From the menu bar, select Insert ➢ Component ➢ Hit Counter (or click the Insert Component button on the toolbar). The Hit Counter Properties dialog box appears.

3. A variety of counter styles are presented for your consideration; select the one that appeals to you by clicking its button. (The numbers in your hit counter will appear in this font later.) Or, select the Custom Image button, if you have designed your own font or obtained one from elsewhere.

MASTERING WHAT'S ONLINE

You can find and use downloadable fonts from various online sources, including Digit Mania (www.digitmania.holowww.com).

4. By default, the hit counter will start its tally at 0, but you can make it start at whatever number you like. To set the number you prefer, click the checkbox labeled Reset Counter To and type a number in the text box.

5. Again, by default, the hit counter will count on forever—adding digits as necessary to count your ever-increasing number of visitors. If you like, you can change this so the hit counter will stick to a fixed number of digits. You might consider this so you can better control the layout of the page—lots of digits might cause the tallied number of visitors to wrap to the next line or even push text and images onto another line. Note that the hit counter defaults to five digits, allowing you to track up to 99,999 visits to the page. Because only five digits are displayed by default, and these are always the right-most five digits, visitor number 100,000 would actually see *00000*. To increase or decrease the number of digits displayed, select the checkbox labeled Fixed Number Of Digits and type the number of digits you prefer.

6. When you're finished making selections, click OK. The Hit Counter Properties dialog box closes and the Page view window reappears, with the text *[hit counter]* inserted into your page to mark the spot where the hit counter will show itself.

TIP A hit counter may seem like a cool gizmo to add to your pages, but in many circles it is considered the sign of a rank beginner. Take a look at any professional-looking site, and you'll see a complete lack of hit counters. Therefore, it's wise to use this component only if the subject matter of your page lends itself to a hit counter, or if you're creating a personal home page and want the counter more than you want a professional, clean look.

Creating Hover Buttons

Sometimes you'll visit a Web site and, as you move the mouse pointer over some image, that image changes. It might glow or change colors, for example. This is a pretty cool effect, and, with FrontPage's Hover Button component, you can add this oh-so-nifty *hover button* effect (also called a *mouseover*) to your own Web pages. Here's how:

1. With an unbuttoned page open, position the cursor where you want the button to appear.

2. From the menu bar, select Insert ➢ Component ➢ Hover Button. The Hover Button Properties dialog box appears, as shown in Figure 15.3.

FIGURE 15.3

Create special effects for buttons using the Hover Button Properties dialog box.

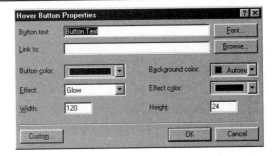

3. In the dialog box's Button Text text box, type the text you'd like to appear on the button. Change the font, if you like, by clicking the Font button and making your selection.

4. In the Link To text box, type the URL of the page you'd like to load when a visitor clicks on that button.

5. In the drop-down lists labeled Button Color, Background Color, and Effect Color, select the colors for the hover button. The color you choose for button color will be the basic color of the button, while the background color will appear behind the button (if you specify that some space should appear there). The effect color will be the color that's applied to the effect you select in step 6.

6. In the Effect pull-down menu, select the effect that should appear when the user points the mouse pointer at the button. You can choose only one—play around with all of them until you find one you like.

7. Click OK. The dialog box closes.

The button you just inserted will be visible; however, the special effects you chose are not visible (not even after you select the Preview tab). You'll have to preview the page in a Web browser that supports Java to see the full effects of the hover button.

Adding a Marquee

Marquees are scrolling text areas where you can deliver a specific message to your audience. To add a marquee:

1. With the unbuttoned page open, position the cursor where you want the marquee to appear.

2. From the menu bar, select Insert ➢ Component ➢ Marquee. The Marquee Properties box appears, as shown in Figure 15.4.

FIGURE 15.4

The Marquee Properties dialog box

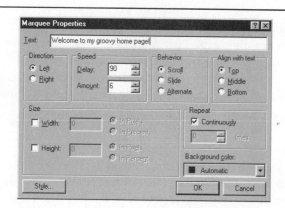

3. In the Text text box, type the text you'd like to have displayed on your marquee.

4. In the Direction area, you can choose to have the text scroll from either the left or the right simply by clicking the appropriate button.

5. In the Speed area, specify the delay (in seconds) before the marquee is to start scrolling, and how fast the marquee should move.

6. You can now select a behavior for the marquee. Options include a scroll, a slide, or having the marquee alternate styles.

7. Select a text alignment.

8. Set the size of the text box.

9. If you want the marquee to repeat, click the Continuously checkbox.

10. Select a background color.

You're set to scroll! You can simply click Preview to see how the marquee behaves. To make adjustments to any of the properties, you can right-click the marquee, select Marquee Properties, and make your changes in the Properties dialog box.

WARNING The Marquee, like many FrontPage components, is not a standard HTML tag. Therefore, the browser support for it is typically limited to Internet Explorer. See Chapter 16, *Cross-Browser Design*, for more details.

Including a Page within a Page

The Include Page component takes the content of one Web page and displays it within another Web page. While that might not seem very exciting, it can save you quite a bit of time maintaining your site. For example, many Webmasters like to have standard navigational controls on their Web pages. These can be buttons, icons, or simply text linked to major locations within the web itself. But typing the text, inserting the images, and creating the links for every page in your web can be time consuming. There's also a greater chance for error if you mistype something. Worse, should you decide to change anything, you'll have to load and edit every page that contains these navigational aids.

TIP This component is very similar to the Shared Borders component (covered in the section titled "Creating Effects across Multiple Pages" later in this chapter). Use Include Page when you want to place different content on each of a bunch of individual pages; use Shared Borders when you want to place a piece of content on the edge or edges of many pages.

Here's where the Include Page component comes to your rescue. You create one page that contains your navigational bar, then simply use the Include Page component to attach it to every page that needs the navigation bar. Changes are also a breeze—just change the original page, indicate that you've updated it, and all of the other pages will be updated automatically.

Include Page is also useful for those parts of pages that are frequently changed: headlines in a newsletter, entrees on a cafeteria menu, weekly activity schedules, and so forth. If you put these ever-changing items on a separate, relatively plain page, and then include that page within a more elaborately designed one, you have to change only the plain page (which is a lot easier to edit), protecting your elaborate design from inadvertent changes.

TIP You can also include other pages in a table cell that appears anywhere on your page. To do so, place a table on the page (see Chapter 11, *Using Tables for Advanced Layout*) and use the Include Page component to place your included page within a table cell.

Follow these steps to use the Include Page component:

1. With the page you wish to incorporate the second page into open, place the cursor where you want the inserted page to go.

2. From the menu bar, select Insert ➤ Component ➤ Include Page (or click the Component button on the toolbar). The Include Page Properties dialog box appears (see Figure 15.5).

3. In the Page To Include text box, type the URL of the page you want to include. Or, click the Browse button, and from the list that appears, highlight the page you want to include and then click OK. The URL of the page you want to include should appear in the Page To Include text box.

4. Click OK to close the dialog box.

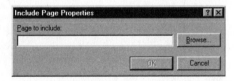

FIGURE 15.5

The Include Page Properties dialog box

The Page view window reappears, with the contents of the inserted page now displayed within the current page.

Scheduling the Inclusion of Pages

This interesting component allows you to set included pages to appear according to a defined start date, end date, or both. For example, you might want to replace a general navigation bar (see "Adding a Navigation Bar," later in this chapter) with a special-event one for a one-month promotion of a certain product. Or perhaps you want a different greeting to appear on your home page at different times of the day. These tasks are easily done with the Scheduled Include Page component, which combines the benefits of the Include Page component with those of the Scheduled Image component. Follow these steps to schedule an included page:

1. With the page that's going to include the component open, place the cursor where you want the Scheduled Include Page to appear.

2. From the menu bar, select Insert ➤ Component ➤ Scheduled Include Page (or click the Component button on the toolbar). The Scheduled Include Page Properties dialog appears (see Figure 15.6).

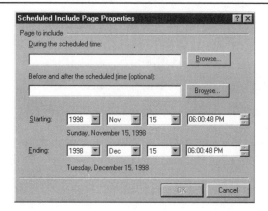

3. In the Page To Include text box, type the URL of the page you want to insert. Or, click the Browse button to display the Current Web dialog box. In the dialog box, you'll see a list of all of the files in the current web. Highlight the file of interest and click OK. The dialog box closes, and the Include Page Component Properties dialog box reappears. The URL for the file you just selected will be visible in the Page To Include text box.

4. In the area labeled Starting, set the date and time to begin displaying the page by selecting the appropriate information in the drop-down lists for year, month, day, and time.

5. Similarly, in the area labeled Ending, set the date and time you want to stop displaying the image by selecting the appropriate information in the drop-down lists for year, month, day, and time. (The default is one month after the date and time you selected in step 4.)

6. Finally (and optionally), you can choose an alternate page to be displayed before the start date and after the end date. (If you don't choose one, nothing will appear at that location.) In the text box labeled Before And After The Scheduled Time (Optional), type the filename of the page you want to display (or click the Browse button to select one from the dialog box that appears).

7. Click OK. The dialog box closes, and the Page view window reappears. If the current date falls within the schedule, you'll see the page you specified in step 3 incorporated into the currently open page. If it doesn't, the area where you inserted the Scheduled Include Page component will be empty.

Use the same procedure for any page you want included for a finite period of time. Good candidates for this are announcements that carry a date—such as the date of a meeting, a game, a contest, or special promotions that begin and end in a set time period. Set the ending date for the time of the event. No need to set an optional alternative page, the announcement will simply "go away" at the proper time.

Scheduling Picture Display

Web pages can be very dynamic, with new items and information added weekly or even daily. Many Webmasters like to "tag" these additions to identify the new elements with a small graphic such as this one:

NEW!

Of course, if you never remove that cute little tag, soon everything on your Web site will be identified as new. And it can't *all* be new, can it? Keeping track of when the tag was added, however, can be a very involved task. You could add an entry to the Tasks view (see Chapter 7, *Managing Tasks*) for each tag, or place the Comment component (described later in this chapter) with the tag. But why? The Scheduled Image component makes handling this matter a lot easier. When you insert the image, simply decide on which day and at what time (down to the second) the image should first be displayed, as well as the date and time it should be removed.

Additionally, you can specify a second image to be used before the start time or after the end time of your scheduled image. You might use this trick to show a "New" image followed by a "Featured Last Week" image, for example. Or you can use this option to display a special holiday logo only during the year-end holidays, while using a holiday-neutral one the rest of the year.

Here's how to use the Scheduled Picture component:

1. With a page open in Page view, place the cursor at the point where you want to insert the scheduled image.

2. From the menu bar, select Insert ➤ Component ➤ Scheduled Picture (or click the Component button on the toolbar). The Scheduled Picture Properties dialog box appears (see Figure 15.7).

PART

II

Creating Sophisticated Designs

The Scheduled Picture Properties dialog box

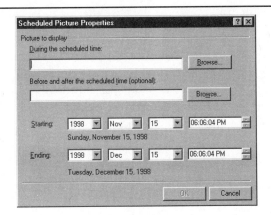

3. In the Picture To Display text box, type the URL of the image you want to incorporate into your page. Or, click the Browse button. The Image dialog box appears, and from the list box, select an image file—choose one from other images in your web, FrontPage's Clip Art Gallery, or elsewhere on your computer. Click OK to return to the dialog box. The appropriate URL will appear in the Picture To Display text box.

4. In the area labeled Starting, set the date and time to begin displaying the image by selecting the appropriate information in the drop-down lists for year, month, day, and time.

5. In the area labeled Ending, set the date and time to stop displaying the image, again by selecting the appropriate information in the drop-down lists for year, month, day, and time. (The default is one month after the date you selected in step 4.)

6. Finally (and optionally), you can choose an alternate image to display before the start date and after the end date. (If you don't choose an alternate image, no image at all will appear at that location.) In the text box labeled Before And After The Scheduled Time (Optional) text box, type the filename of the image file.

 TIP   You can also click the Browse button and, from the dialog box that appears, select a filename.

7. Now click OK. The dialog box closes and your page appears.

What you'll see depends on what you entered in the Scheduled Picture Properties dialog box. If the current date falls within the date range you set for the Scheduled Picture component, you'll see your selected image. If the current date falls outside of the scheduled dates, you'll see either the alternate image (if you've chosen one) or the text *[expired scheduled image]*. This text will not, however, appear in the browser displays of visitors to your site.

Including Specified Information throughout the Site

Earlier in this chapter, we discussed how the Include Page component lets you use the same text and images across many pages in your web while requiring you to create and maintain those elements on only one page. This is a whopping time-saver—it can make web maintenance a much easier chore.

Sometimes, though, only a word or phrase needs to be used multiple times, in different places—your name, a copyright notice, or similar "boilerplate" text. For this, FrontPage offers the Substitution component. Substitution uses *keywords* and *values*—whenever FrontPage encounters a specified keyword, it substitutes the value you assigned to it. For example, suppose you are creating a Web site for your company and plan to use a lot of copyrighted information, which you'll identify with the phrase *Copyright 1999 My Little Tiny Company*.

To save yourself lots of redundant typing time, you can use the Substitution component. You choose *co* as a keyword and give it the value *Copyright 1999 My Little Tiny Company*. Then every time you need to include the copyright, you simply access the Substitution component, select *co*, and presto! The entire phrase appears in its place. If, at some later time, you change the copyright notice, you need only make one change (resetting the keyword *co* to the new value, *Copyright 1997-99 My Little Tiny Company*), and everywhere you placed the substitution keyword, the new copyright statement will appear.

FrontPage comes with four defined keywords, but you can define as many as you'd like. The provided ones are:

- *Author*, which is replaced automatically with the name of the author who created the page.

- *Modified By*, which is replaced by the name of the author who most recently modified the page.

- *Description*, which is replaced by a description of the current page (by default, the title of the page is used as the description).

PART

II

Creating
Sophisticated
Designs

• *Page URL*, which is replaced by the page's location in the current FrontPage web.

You can create any other keywords you like. Just follow these steps:

1. With a web open in FrontPage, from the menu bar, select Tools ➤ Web Settings. The FrontPage Web Settings dialog box appears.

2. Click the Parameters tab. The contents of the dialog box change to reflect your choice (as shown in Figure 15.8).

3. Click the Add button. The Parameters dialog box appears.

4. In the Name text box, type a keyword (in our example, this would be **co**). In the Value text box, type in the word or phrase to be substituted for the keyword (**Copyright 1999 My Little Tiny Company**, in our case).

5. Click OK. The Parameters dialog box closes and the FrontPage Web Settings dialog box reappears, with the substitution you just added now listed.

6. Click OK again. The FrontPage Web Settings dialog box closes.

FIGURE 15.8

Here you can specify parameters and values.

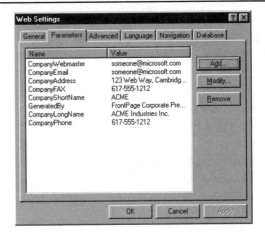

Now that you have associated a keyword with a value, you're ready to add the keyword to one of your pages. Here's how:

1. With a page open, place the cursor at the point you want to insert a keyword (and hence, its associated value).

2. From the menu bar, select Insert ➤ Component ➤ Substitution (or click the Component button on the toolbar).

3. In the Substitute With text box, type the keyword (the one you defined in the previous step list), or click the arrow next to the text box, and from the drop-down list of defined keywords select the one you want to use.

4. Click OK to close the Substitution Component Properties dialog box. The Page view window reappears with the value of the keyword you specified inserted into your page.

 TIP You may have to save, close, and then reopen the page for the substitution value to appear. You'll know this is necessary if the keyword itself (enclosed in square brackets, as in *[author]*) appears on the page.

When you've changed the value of a keyword (following the steps earlier in this section), open the page in Page view to see that the change has occurred on the page.

 TIP Variables are specific to each FrontPage web. This means that if you are building a big site that encompasses many different FrontPage webs, there is no way to share variables between the assorted webs. Instead, you will have to define a set of variables for each and every web.

Adding a Search Form to Your Web

You can grant users quick access to what they seek on your site by offering them a search feature. The user has only to type a word or phrase into a text box, then press a Search button, and—Poof!—up comes a list of items in your site that address that topic. Here's how you can use a handy component to provide just such a feature:

1. With a page open, place the cursor at the point you want to insert a search.

2. From the menu bar, select Insert ➤ Component ➤ Search Form (or click the Component button on the toolbar).

3. In the Search Form Properties dialog box (see Figure 15.9), select the Search Form Properties Tab (if it's not already selected).

FIGURE 15.9

*The Search Form
Properties dialog box*

4. You can change the defaults for the various labels and buttons by typing in different names in the text box fields. For example, to change the input label, simply type the preferred name of your label into the Label For Input text box field.

5. When you are happy with your selections, click the Search Results tab. You can now modify the search results and display. When you're satisfied that you've customized the search to your liking, click OK.

The dialog box disappears and you'll see the search form in edit mode. To preview the form, click the Preview tab and see your results (see Figure 15.10).

FIGURE 15.10

*Your search form,
ready for action*

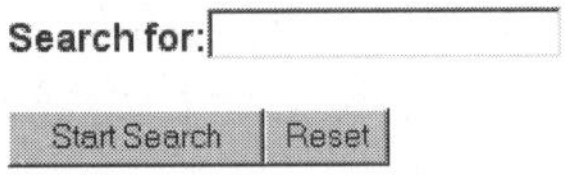

Search for: [   ]

[Start Search] [Reset]

You can also create a search form using the Search Page template. To do this:

1. With the page into which you want to add a search feature open, select File ➢ New ➢ Page. The New dialog box appears.

2. From the New dialog box's General list, select Search Page and click OK. The dialog box closes and a new page appears. This will be your search page—it includes a number of standard elements for search pages, like a text box and a Search button.

3. You can customize the search page as if it were any other page on your site. You cannot and must not change the area that includes functional items like a text box, the Start Search button, and the Clear button.

4. When you are happy with the search page, select File ➤ Save As and save it to your web. The window reappears with your search page in view.

 NOTE As with most FrontPage components, you will be required to publish your page on a Web server with FrontPage extensions in order for the component to function properly.

Building a Table of Contents

To help users locate what's on your site in a snap, offer them a table of contents like the one shown in Figure 15.11. A table of contents for a FrontPage web acts much like a table of contents for a book. The Table of Contents component creates a list of those pages that are linked from a web's home page.

FIGURE 15.11

Building a table of contents is easy when FrontPage does it for you.

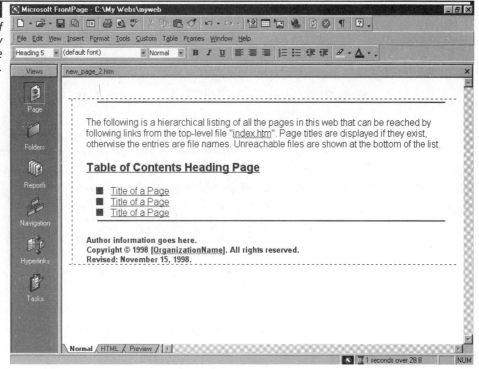

The following is a hierarchical listing of all the pages in this web that can be reached by following links from the top-level file "index.htm". Page titles are displayed if they exist, otherwise the entries are file names. Unreachable files are shown at the bottom of the list.

Table of Contents Heading Page

- Title of a Page
- Title of a Page
- Title of a Page

Author information goes here.
Copyright © 1998 [OrganizationName]. All rights reserved.
Revised: November 15, 1998.

To create a table of contents, follow these steps:

1. First, you'll want to work with an empty page. You can do this by opening a page in Page view. From the menu bar, select File ➤ New ➤ Page. The New dialog box appears.

2. Select Normal Page from the General area and click OK.

3. Now, from the menu bar, select Insert ➤ Component ➤ Table Of Contents (or click the Component button on the toolbar). The Table Of Contents Properties dialog appears (see Figure 15.12).

FIGURE 15.12

The Table Of Contents Properties dialog box

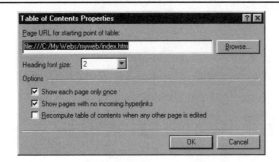

4. In the Page URL For Starting Point Of Table Text Field, add the name of the start page for your table of contents (this will usually be **index.htm** or **default.htm**).

5. Select a heading font size.

6. Customize your options. You can choose to show each page only once (a good idea—it's less confusing for your site visitors), show pages with no incoming hyperlinks, and have FrontPage re-compute the table of contents every time a page is added (this is quite a handy feature).

7. Click OK.

You'll see the table of contents laid out on the page for you. As with search pages, you can create a table of contents page using a template. To do so:

1. Open FrontPage, and from the menu bar, select File ➤ New ➤ Page. The New dialog box appears.

2. From the General list, select Table Of Contents and click OK. The New dialog box closes and you'll be returned to the window, with a new table of contents page visible.

3. You can now customize the table of contents using the methods discussed in Part I of this book. Be sure to change the page's title and remove any generic, descriptive text you don't want appearing on the table of contents final page.

4. Be sure to save your new page. From the menu bar, select File ➢ Save As. The Save As dialog box appears.

5. In the URL text box, type a name for the file (**TOC**—for Table Of Contents—is a good choice) and click OK. The dialog box closes.

It is customary to provide a link to the table of contents from the web's home page—that makes it easier for users to find and use the handy gadget you created. Use what you learned in Chapter 4, *Creating Basic Pages*, to add that link now.

Site Management Effects

In this section, we'll look at effects that can help you manage your sites—and your site visitors—more effectively. Each of these effects are handled using methods within FrontPage other than the component style you've just learned.

These effects include time stamping your pages, including comments within your code, and registering site visitors. As you'll soon see, these effects are very helpful in managing and adding impact to your site.

Adding Dynamic Date and Time

You may want to stamp your pages with the current time and/or date. This can lend your page a sense of currency or urgency. Many sites let users know when they were last updated; this component will do that job automatically. News sites can include this, for example, to suggest to visitors that the news presented is up to the minute—which it will be, if they update the page as news breaks, or at least daily. Usually, doing this requires attention to hard-coding HTML when changes are made to the page, or some fancy programming and server configuration. But, happily, FrontPage lets you add this effect easily, with no coding or programming necessary. Just follow these steps:

1. With the timeless page open, position the cursor where you want the timestamp to appear.

2. From the menu bar, select Insert ➢ Date And Time. The Date And Time Properties dialog box appears (see Figure 15.13).

3. You have two choices regarding which date will appear in the timestamp:

   • Date this page was last edited

   • Date this page was last automatically updated

Click one of the buttons.

FIGURE 15.13

The date and time of your site's most recent update can be stamped on pages using the Date And Time Properties dialog box.

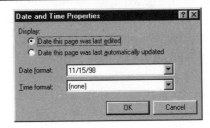

4. In the Date Format drop-down list, choose a format for the date's appearance.

5. In the Time Format drop-down list, choose a format for the time's appearance. If you do not want the time to appear along with the date, select "(none)".

6. Click OK. The dialog box closes.

You should now see the timestamp—formatted the way you specified in steps 4 and 5 above—on screen.

Including Comments

So you make your fine, upstanding Web page, and weeks, months, or even years after the thing was created, you or another team member goes back to it for some reason. Does that person know why you did what you did? Do *you* even remember? A good, standard programming practice can and should be applied to the creation of Web pages, and that is to insert *comments*—lines that aren't executed as part of a program—within the code. These comments explain exactly what a particular section of the code or program is meant to do.

 WARNING You can put anything you want into comments; none of that stuff will appear when a user views the page with a browser. However, anyone who views the *source* of your page (the code) will see the comments you have entered. You might want to watch what you say!

To insert a comment into a Web page, follow these steps:

1. With a page open in Page view, place the cursor where you want to insert your comment.

2. From the menu bar, select Insert ➤ Comment. The Comment dialog box appears.

3. In the Comment text box, type what you want to say.

4. Click OK. The dialog box closes. The comment you entered is placed on the page in a different color from the surrounding text. (The default color for comments is magenta.)

Again, when you preview the page in the Preview tab, or view the page in a Web browser, the comment will not appear. It is visible only when you are editing the page or viewing the source code via a Web browser.

Registering Users

You may want to track who has accessed what information on your site. You might want to know who's really who in a Discussion web (covered later in this chapter), for example, or you might want to have some sense of who's interested in a particular part of your site for marketing reasons. Using the User Registration component, you can require visitors to use a form to provide information about themselves before they are allowed access to your web.

 TIP Using the User Registration component is a bit more complex than using other components. In the course of setting things up, you'll have to place the registration form you'll create here into the root web—it cannot be located in any other web. (See Chapter 2 to find out about the root web.) Likewise, all links that go to the home page of the registration-required web must go to the registration page located in the root directory, not directly to a page in the web. Don't worry, we'll step you though this.

To add a registration form to an existing web, follow these steps:

1. With the root web open (the registration form for the web is not actually in the web itself, it is stored in the root web), select File ➤ New ➤ Page. The New dialog box appears.

2. From the General list, select User Registration and click OK. The New dialog box closes and you are returned to the Page view window, with a new registration page ready and waiting for you to modify it (as shown in Figure 15.14).

3. Locate the form area of the registration page (it starts with the label Form Submission) and right-click it. A menu appears.

FIGURE 15.14

As you customize this registration form, be sure not to change any of these text boxes or buttons.

Form Submission

Make up a username:

[   ] -- *you can use mixed case*

Make up a password:

[   ] -- *keep this private!*

Enter password again:

[   ] -- *for verification*

Enter e-mail address:

[   ] -- *if you have one*

[Register Me] [Clear Form]

4. From the menu, select Form Properties. The Form Properties dialog box appears.

5. Click the Options button. The Options For Registration Form Handler dialog box appears.

6. In the text box labeled FrontPage Web Name, type the name of the web you want users to have to register to use.

7. In the text box labeled URL Of Registration Failure Page (Optional), you can type the filename of a page to display when access to a web is denied (this usually happens when someone types the wrong password). This field is optional.

TIP Do not change the default entries in the rest of the dialog boxes. They are filled out correctly for the form created by the User Registration template. You need to modify them only if you want to use your own form—with different field names—to register users. That's a big job, and we suggest you skip it unless you're an advanced administrator.

8. Click OK. The Options for Registration Form Handler dialog box closes, and the Form Properties dialog box reappears.

9. In the Form Properties dialog box, click OK. The dialog box closes.

10. From the menu bar, select Edit ➤ Replace. The Replace dialog box appears.

11. In the Find What text box, type **[Other Web]**. This is placeholder text that will appear on the registration page in those locations where the name of the web you are requiring users to register for will later go.

12. In the Replace With text box, type the name of the web requiring registration.

13. Click the Replace All button. The web name you provided in step 14 will replace all the occurrences of [Other Web]. Once the replacement is done, a confirmation dialog box appears.

14. Click OK in that dialog box. The Replace dialog box reappears.

15. Click Cancel in the Replace dialog box. The dialog box closes and you are returned to the Page view window, with the user registration page in view. The substitutions you indicated will have been accomplished.

16. You can now customize the page's appearance to make it look like other pages in your web. Use the techniques described throughout this book to do this. Be sure not to change the area beneath the text Form Submissions, which includes text boxes and buttons, as these are required to register users for the other web.

17. From the menu bar, select File ➢ Save As. The Save As dialog box appears.

18. In the URL text box, type a name for the form and click OK. The dialog box closes. The user registration page will be in view, with your changes apparent.

Before you take this thing live, remember that you need to go around the site and change any links that used to go to the now-protected area so that users must come here first and register. You can use a site-wide search and replace to do this; see Chapter 24, *Site Maintenance and Promotion*, for details.

Creating Effects across Multiple Pages

FrontPage allows you to create effects that are shared by many pages. This is a powerful feature known as *shared borders*. Shared borders allow you to add any graphic or HTML element around the top, bottom, and/or side of a page, making it, in effect, a border. For example, you can create a navigation bar (as described in an upcoming section) and then make it appear at the top or along the side of every page in a web by placing it in a shared border (a region set aside for this purpose) positioned at the top or along the side. You can enable shared borders for an entire web, so that the same border will appear on every page. You can make that so for any individual page within a web, or you can disable either of those options.

There are two basic steps to creating a shared border: First, you must specify where the item appearing in the border will be located. This is, in actuality, what you are doing when you use the shared borders technique—you are positioning a region in which something will appear. At first, something fairly generic and useless will appear there; so in the second big step of this process you have to place in the shared border whatever you actually do want to appear there—the graphic or piece of HTML or text or what have you. Let's take a look.

Enabling or Disabling Shared Borders for a Web

To enable or disable shared borders for an entire web, follow these steps:

1. With a web open in Page view, from the menu bar, select Format ➤ Shared Borders. The Shared Borders dialog box appears.

2. You can position a shared border along the top, left, right, and/or bottom edges of your web's pages. Select the appropriate checkboxes to do so. As you select the checkboxes, a preview showing the effects of your choice appears along the right side of the dialog box. Or, to disable shared borders, deselect all of the checkboxes.

3. Once you are done specifying the location of the shared borders, click OK. The dialog box closes.

Exactly what the page will look like depends on what shared borders you've enabled, but in general you'll see the shared borders there, with very generic comments in them (see Figure 15.15). To change the commentary to your own content, see "Adding Elements to a Shared Border."

FIGURE 15.15

You can place shared borders along the top, bottom, left, or right of your Web pages.

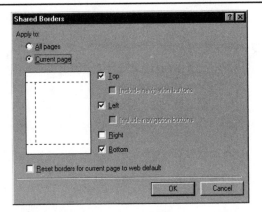

Enabling or Disabling Shared Borders for a Page

Just as you can enable or disable shared borders for an entire web, you can easily enable or disable shared borders for a single page. Try this:

1. With a page open in Page view, from the menu bar, select Format ➤ Shared Borders. The Shared Borders dialog box appears.

2. If you want to specify different borders (or no borders at all) for this particular page, click the Current Page button.

3. To specify borders for this page, now select the checkboxes that correspond to where you want them to appear. Your choices are top, left, right, and/or bottom. (A combination is quite possible.) Or, to disable shared borders, deselect all of the checkboxes.

4. Click OK. The dialog box closes and the Page view window reappears, with the page and its newly defined borders in view.

The shared borders themselves will appear on the page with generic commentary in them; these are just placeholders, really. It's time to add real content to the borders that you just defined. See the next section for details.

Adding Elements to a Shared Border

Okay, so you've enabled shared borders in your web or on a given page, and that put into position a placeholder, but now you need to add the content. You can place text, graphics, or some other HTML element in a shared border. Whatever you place in a shared border will then appear on every page that's been enabled for that shared border. This can be a handy way to place a page banner on all pages in a web, for example, or to put a copyright notice at the bottom of every page.

 NOTE If you have enabled shared borders for a whole web, you have specified which pages in that web will include what shared borders. (You may also have specified which pages will not.) Because of this, if you are dealing with the whole web, you can accomplish this next procedure by starting with any of the web's pages open. If, however, you are dealing with a single page for which you've enabled shared borders, you must have that specific page open.

To add elements to a shared border:

1. With a page open in Page view, place the cursor within the border area you want to modify.

2. Now use the tools (as described in Part I of this book) to place whatever image, text, or HTML you like in the border.

3. From the menu bar, select File ➤ Save to save your work. You will be returned to the Page view window with your page in view and the stuff you placed in the shared border quite evident.

You can also preview the page via the Preview tab, or view the page in a Web browser, and whatever you placed in any shared borders will appear.

Adding a Navigation Bar

Navigation bars (or *nav bars*) are a common element to most Web sites. They usually consist of a set of buttons or text links that appear along the top or side of every page in the site. Their purpose is to provide users with a way to get around. A good, easy-to-use nav bar is a complete boon to any site. Creating one can be a complex matter that involves site architects, designers, and so on; but with FrontPage, creating a nav bar becomes very simple indeed.

The nav bar created here will be based on the site's navigational structure. It will not be a single nav bar that is then applied identically to every page. Instead, a nav bar that appears on a given page will contain different links depending on where the page falls in the site's structure.

NOTE By placing the navigation bar within a shared border, you can quickly add a navigation bar to your entire site without having to open and edit every single page.

To add a navigation bar to a page, follow these steps:

1. With the page of interest open, place the cursor where you want to insert the nav bar. (If you are placing it within a shared border, click there.)

2. From the menu bar, select Insert ➢ Navigation Bar. The Navigation Bar Properties dialog box appears, as shown in Figure 15.16.

FIGURE 15.16

The Navigation Bar Properties dialog box is your gateway to controlling which links appear on the nav bar.

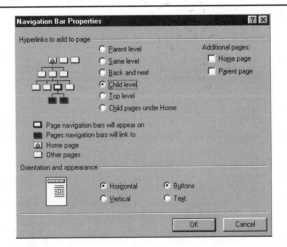

3. Here you'll specify which links to other pages will be included in the navigation bar. The dialog box does an excellent job of showing you the effects of your choices; click around and you'll see the results of your settings illustrated in the dialog box's diagram. Then select the button that corresponds to your intentions.

4. You can include two pages in addition to those you chose in step 3: the Home Page and the Parent Page. Select either or both by clicking their checkboxes.

5. The navigation bar can be positioned horizontally (length-wise) or vertically (height-wise); make your choice by selecting the appropriate button. (You can see a preview of your choice in the sample page along the left side of the dialog box.)

6. Now choose whether the links that appear on the nav bar will be graphical buttons (Button) or simple text links (Text).

 NOTE If you choose graphical buttons, the graphics will be created automatically by the FrontPage Server Extensions. You don't have to provide art—nor can you.

7. Click OK. The dialog box closes, and you'll see a text representation of your newly defined navigation bar on screen.

To see the actual nav bar, you'll have to preview the page in a Web browser.

 TIP You can use the FrontPage Web Setting dialog box to change the text on the labels generated by the Navigation Bar component. See Chapter 24 for details.

Building a Discussion Web

According to common wisdom, one of the best ways to get visitors to return to your Web site again and again is to build a sense of community. And one of the most effective ways to build a sense of community is to provide your visitors a place where they can visit others with similar interests—kind of like the electronic version of the office water cooler or a hobby circle. FrontPage allows you to create an easy discussion group. This discussion group will resemble a newsgroup; it's a public forum for discussion around a central topic.

TIP A discussion group must have a central theme or topic to be compelling and to attract participants. Make sure the theme or topic you select is appropriate to the goals of your site; for example, while a discussion group about bird watching may be compelling to bird enthusiasts, it's not very useful on a site that's about how to use computers.

 NOTE Unlike other components discussed in this chapter, all of which are integrated into your existing web, a discussion web is a FrontPage web unto itself. To set one up, you create a special web that holds only your discussion group, then you create links to it from your other web(s).

Follow these steps to get your group up and running:

1. From the FrontPage menu, select File ➤ New ➤ Web. The New FrontPage Web dialog box appears.

2. From the list of Web Sites, select Discussion Web Wizard.

3. Click OK. In a few seconds, the Discussion Web Wizard dialog box appears.

4. Click Finish and a basic, generic discussion group is created. Or, click Next to customize the discussion web, and then follow the instructions that appear on screen. You can customize a variety of options:

   • Whether the discussion web will include a search page to allow users to quickly search previously posted articles

   • Whether a user's message to the group will include a subject line or a product name line (including a product name line might be a gem of an option for a customer support discussion web)

   • Whether the discussion web will be protected by a user registration form (see "Registering Users")

   • Whether messages will be listed newest to oldest, or vice-versa

   • Whether a theme should be applied to the web, and if so, which one (see Chapter 4 for more about using themes)

   • What style your discussion will appear in (frames or no frames)

After you customize your discussion web and click OK, the Discussion Web Wizard dialog box closes and the Page view window reappears with the new web's pages visible. The files you see listed in the window are the Web pages that make up the discussion web. They include:

- A page that acts as the main page people see when they use the discussion group, which lists all the messages users have posted
- A page users will enter a new message into
- A page that facilitates searching for previously posted messages
- A page that appears after a user posts a message, to confirm receipt

To maintain continuity and professional polish, you should give the Discussion web a similar look and feel as the rest of your site. To do so, use the techniques described in Part I of this book. If the other webs in your site use a theme, for example, you can go ahead and apply that theme to this new web. You'll also want to link to the new discussion web from other parts of your site; see Chapter 4 to learn how.

Up Next

At this point, you should feel quite empowered by the various applications FrontPage has allowed you to add to your Web site. Banner ads, hit counters, user registration, and discussion groups are all examples of advanced technologies that, without Front-Page and its extensions, would be expensive and complicated to set up and manage. These components and techniques have added a level of sophistication to your work, and you've incorporated them with relative ease.

Before we leave our discussion of sophisticated techniques and move on to scripting technologies such as DHTML and JavaScript, we have to study one very important factor in Web design. Designing across the variety of browsers is a challenge that all designers wish there was an easy answer to. It's a complex issue, but one that demands exploration so that you can make informed choices as to what kinds of technologies will be most appropriate for your audience. In Chapter 16 we'll take a close look at these issues, and work with you to make the best decisions—rendering your sites to be truly sophisticated in both thought *and* design.

PART

II

Creating
Sophisticated
Designs

CHAPTER 16

Cross-Browser Design

The average visitor coming to your Web site is probably surfing the Web using a PC with a 28.8 or 36.6 modem. He's probably in the middle-class, a man who can afford a decent computer, probably a Pentium, although possibly not the fastest one on the market. He most likely has his screen resolution set to 640×480 or 800×600 (whichever resolution was set at the factory), with 24-bit color. He's probably using some version of Netscape Navigator, although it might not be the very latest one. The hip sister of this fellow is just as likely to drop by, using a Pentium with Windows 98, 1024×768 screen resolution, millions of colors, and using Internet Explorer, version 4—or possibly 5—sliding on in using a 56K modem.

There's a 50-50 chance that the next visitor to your site will be very much like one of these individuals, but the makeup of the rest of your audience could be anything else. Your next visitor could be a teenager surfing on her older brother's abandoned black-and-white Mac Plus, with a 9600 baud modem, using Lynx or an old version of Mosaic. The visitor after that could be an Internet security expert chugging coffee while she visits your site from a decked-out SGI workstation, using dual T3 lines to download your site lightning fast, and using a browser that just became available for download this morning. Or your next visitor could be an 80-year-old physicist and great-grandfather who has his browser read him your site aloud while he waters the plants.

Once you've designed your pages and put them online, it would be a shame if a large sector of the Internet population wasn't able to see them. You already know that your audience is one of the most important considerations to keep in mind during the design process, and your audience is comprised of not just people, but people with a huge variety of computing platforms and browser software. These differences in hardware and software will affect—in both large and small ways—what people see when they visit your site. In this chapter, we'll look at the ways you can massage your pages' design to create pages that look the best to the most people.

Of course, it's much easier to keep the variety of browsers (and users) in mind *during* the course of your site's design, rather than having to go back and fix incompatibilities later. In this chapter, we're going to cover what the different browsers do, what the differences between them are, and how to decide who to design for. Some browsers support proprietary features that other browsers don't support, and we'll make clear what those features are. We'll tell you what to do if you want to design for the lowest common denominator, and we'll also take a look at designing for text-only browsers. And we'll delve into one of the hidden drawbacks of FrontPage: the Internet Explorer-only tags that FrontPage doesn't warn you about.

NOTE   At the time of this writing, Internet Explorer's 5 version is nearly complete, and Netscape Navigator is working toward its own 5 release. By the time you read this book, both should be available. Since both Netscape and IE versions up to 4 have fairly solid statistics, we'll be relying on those for the purpose of this chapter. However, you'll want to check with the latest information available.

What to Design For?

When you're deciding how to plan your Web site, you should be aware of what the browser market looks like, so that you'll know what features to include and exclude from your site. Your design decisions will probably be based, for the most part, on what kind of audience you're trying to attract, and how niche-y that audience is. If you're trying to attract the cutting-edge technocrats who decide what's hot and what's not, you'll probably care less about the little people who surf the Web with outmoded software. On the other hand, if you're designing a site for an audience with a lot of die-hard Macintosh users (teachers and graphic designers, for instance), you'll want to make sure that it looks good in a Macintosh browser.

There are a few instances in which you can be pretty sure about the makeup of your audience. If you're designing for your company's Intranet, for instance, you should be (or can be) aware of the software that the staff uses to access the Intranet, and you may even have some say in what browsers are chosen, either now or during the next upgrade. If you're designing channel content, you're probably aiming for either the Internet Explorer 5 audience or the Netscape NetCaster audience, and you don't need to worry about backwards compatibility, since people with older software won't be looking at channels in the first place.

Other than the few instances in which you're designing for a limited or narrowly targeted audience, you'll get a wide range of people visiting your site, each of whom can have a slightly different combination of software and hardware on their desks. It's unlikely that every person who visits your page will be using the exact same platform, monitor resolution, color depth, browser version, and browser settings that you use.

PART

II

Creating
Sophisticated
Designs

NOTE Who uses what kind of software is not simply a computer-savviness indication, but a socio-economic one. Many, many people access the Web using public computer labs in schools, universities, and libraries, or live in remote areas where computer technology advances are prohibitive. Some machines in use are outdated, with little RAM and disk space available to accommodate every new software toy that comes down the pike. People generally can't choose—or modify—the software available to them through public terminals, including those in "cybercafés."

The following figures show the differences that browsers exhibit when viewing the same page. Note in particular the differences in how the tables and fonts are displayed in the first two browsers, and the unfortunate results when viewed in a text-only browser.

All of the following figures were shot on a PC with a screen resolution of 800×600. Figure 16.1 shows the page in Navigator 4; Figure 16.2 shows the same page in Internet Explorer 4. Figure 16.3 is the attempted view according to Lynx.

FIGURE 16.1

This page as seen in Navigator 4

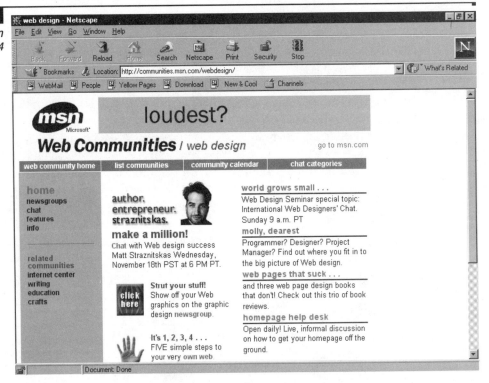

FIGURE 16.2

The same page viewed with Internet Explorer 4

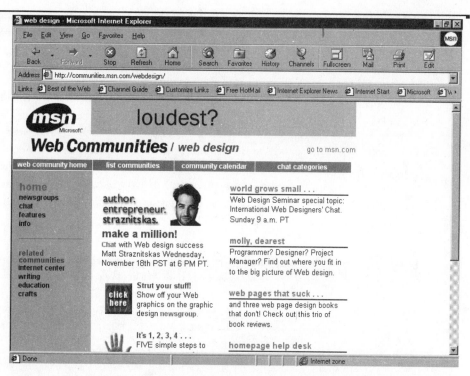

FIGURE 16.3

The same page, inaccessible via Lynx

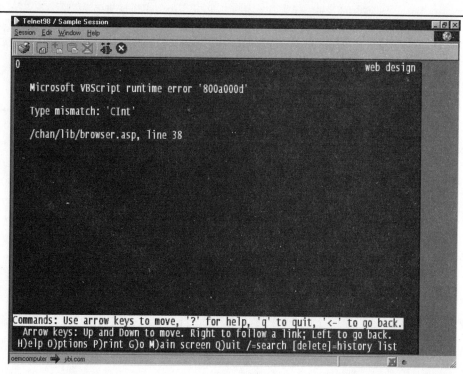

Who Has What? (And What to Do about It)

But what kind of software *do* people have?

According to BrowserWatch, a site that tracks browser software usage and popularity, approximately 90 percent of the people who surf the Web use either Netscape Navigator (51 percent) or Microsoft Internet Explorer (36 percent), with the other 13 percent being made up of other browsers including Lynx and Mosaic.

However, at last count there were at least *60 different versions of Navigator alone* floating around the Web, as well as 36 versions of Internet Explorer, and 50-odd other browsers besides. If you count international (foreign-language) versions of Navigator, and the beta versions that haven't yet expired, you approach 200 versions of Navigator alone. All of those versions of all of those different browsers have slightly different views of the Web, and that's not the half of it.

MASTERING WHAT'S ONLINE

BrowserWatch collects data only from people who visit BrowserWatch's home page, so it's not a scientific survey by any means, although it is a popular benchmark. You can visit this site at `browserwatch.internet.com/`.

There are many other different surveys of what browsers are in use, and you can visit a number of these by starting at the Yahoo! Index of them, at `www.yahoo.com/Computers_and_Internet/Software/Internet/World_Wide_Web/Browsers/Browser_Usage_Statistics/`.

There are five major ways that pages can look different on your audience's computers than on your own machine:

Resolution Most computers are 640×480, many 800×600, others 1024×768, and some 1280×1024, while some Unix workstations use much higher resolutions. Handheld computers, laptops, or very old computers use lower resolutions.

Color depth Some computers and most printers are black and white, most Windows 3.1 computers use 256 colors, and newer computers use 16-bit (thousands of colors), or 24-bit (millions of colors).

Platform Macintosh browsers do look slightly different from their Windows counterparts; graphics are much brighter and tend to dither better, but the font sizes are much smaller.

Browser types Each browser has its own ideas about what the Web should look like. There are many other browsers (aside from Navigator and Internet Explorer), including Opera, udiWWW, Arena, Amaya, GNUscape, AOL's browser, Lynx, and Mosaic, to name just a few. Also, there's the realm of text-to-speech browsers, Braille readers, telephone-based browsers (they exist!), and people using Lynx across a Telnet connection.

Individual preferences All browsers are customizable. People can change the font face and size for text (and sometimes even headings), their preferred background color, whether or not images are displayed, and so forth.

With all these different browsers, software platforms, and other variables churning up the idea of a single view of the Web, what (and who) do you design for? You have these basic options:

- Create a lowest common denominator site that everyone can see fine.
- Create a site that's compatible with most versions of Navigator and Internet Explorer, and let the rest eat cake.
- Create a site that uses the newest, fanciest features you can come up with, and ignore the majority of Web visitors.
- Use JavaScript to "sniff" out which browser is visiting your site, and deliver any one of numerous styles for each type.

There's another option, too. This option is a nice middle of the road option that offers you greater flexibility and makes sure all people visiting your site can indulge in the information therein. You can create a design to your tastes and make an accessible main page where people can choose to download a text version of the site—kind of a "high potency" and "lite site" option.

In upcoming sections, we'll look at which features are available to which browsers, so that once you decide who you're targeting, you'll know what you can (and can't) include for your general designs.

Creating Multiple Versions of Pages

It's a good idea to create two versions of your pages, one for the "next generation browsers" (such as Internet Explorer and Navigator version 4 and above) and one for the rest. The lowest common denominator pages would not include ActiveX, style sheets, plug-ins, Java, JavaScript, DHTML, or any of the newer tags and features, while the high-tech pages could include just about anything you wanted to load them down with.

If you decide to produce two versions, consider implementing a custom script that detects the user's browser and sends it the page it can read. For example, many sites use browser-detection scripts to decide whether or not to send heavy-duty, high-tech versions of their sites. The script runs ahead and finds out what version of which browser (called *client software*) is requesting the page. Then it sends down the appropriate version of the page.

How these scripts are written and handled depends on the server software you're running and what it is you want to do with your site. Some of these scripts can be implemented with JavaScript, some with CGI scripts. Of course, these scripts aren't foolproof. Some browsers send no information about themselves, and some versions of Internet Explorer identify themselves as Navigator.

MASTERING WHAT'S ONLINE

If you're looking for scripts, Matt's Script Archive is a good place to start. His scripts are popular and work well, and the collection includes a browser detection script and links to similar scripts. Point your browser toward www.worldwidemart.com/scripts/. To accomplish something similar with style sheets, pay a visit to www.verso.com/agitprop/css/.

Browser Wars: Who Does What

By now, we hope you've downloaded the *other* browser—if your favorite is Navigator, get a copy of Internet Explorer, and vice versa. Looking at your pages in each browser can help you consider things like table offset, image alignment, and text size. On the other hand, if you're planning to design a low-end site (or an alternate, low-end version of your site), you'll need to know exactly what you can and can't have on your pages.

When you're making a site (or a version of it) that can be used by as many people as possible, it helps to know exactly what the older (and still popular) browsers are capable of. The following sections discuss many features you may consider using on your pages, and tell you which browsers support them.

Netscape Navigator Features

Before Netscape Navigator, most people used either a text-only Web browser or a version of Mosaic, which was the first browser to support inline images. Netscape Navigator version 1.1 introduced a wealth of "Netscapisms"—nonstandard tags whose use had been proposed, but which had not yet been accepted into the standard HTML specifications. These features included centered text, blinking elements, tables, and changes to the way font sizes were handled.

As Table 16.1 shows, each edition of Navigator greatly expanded the browser's capabilities. The second edition's improvements included frames, Java, JavaScript, animated GIFs, and the introduction of browser plug-ins. It's still the only major commercial Web browser to include inline support for VRML, and version 4 supports such design innovations as style sheets and layers.

TABLE 16.1: FRONTPAGE FEATURES SUPPORTED BY POPULAR WEB BROWSERS

Feature	Popular Web Browsers									
	AOL1	AOL3	NN1.1	NN2	NN3	NN4+	IE1	IE2	IE3	IE4+
Absolute Positioning						✔				✔
ActiveX Controls									✔	✔
Animated GIFs				✔	✔	✔			✔	✔
Background Colors		✔	✔	✔	✔	✔	✔	✔	✔	✔
Background Images		✔	✔	✔	✔	✔	✔	✔	✔	✔
Banner Ad Manager				✔	✔	✔			✔	✔
Browser Plug-ins				✔	✔	✔			✔	✔
Channels										✔
Comments	✔	✔	✔	✔	✔	✔	✔	✔	✔	✔
Custom Font Colors		✔		✔	✔	✔	✔	✔	✔	✔
Custom Font Sizes		✔	✔	✔	✔	✔	✔	✔	✔	✔
Custom Font Faces				✔	✔	✔	✔	✔	✔	✔
Forms		✔	✔	✔	✔	✔	✔	✔	✔	✔
Frames		✔		✔	✔	✔			✔	✔
Hover Buttons				✔	✔	✔			✔	✔
Inline Audio/Video					✔	✔			✔	✔
Java				✔	✔	✔			✔	✔
JavaScript				✔	✔	✔			✔	✔
Marquee								✔	✔	✔
Page Transitions										✔
Style Sheets						✔			✔	✔
Tables		✔	✔	✔	✔	✔		✔	✔	✔

Designing pages that work for the latest version of Navigator (or Internet Explorer) means that you'll reach a cutting edge audience, but a lot of educational and public markets still use a version of Navigator 1.1, which doesn't support frames or most high-end gizmos.

 NOTE Many of Netscape's other innovations, such as those in its mail and news programs, don't affect the way your pages will look. Others, such as security features, may affect the way your pages act, and security is one reason why many merchant sites advocate using Netscape secure servers and Netscape browsers. Internet Explorer has caught up with Navigator's security features, so non-beta versions of either browser are generally safe for Internet commerce and other secure transactions.

Microsoft Internet Explorer Features

Microsoft Internet Explorer seemed to be just another Navigator until version 3, which introduced such special effects as ActiveX, designing with font faces and style sheets, and the use of inline frames (also called *floating* frames or *borderless* frames). Microsoft put in more of a browser presence than anyone expected, because free copies of Internet Explorer version 1 shipped with most versions of Windows 95; later versions of the software have shipped with Windows 95 and 98, the Office suite of software, and various other Microsoft CDs.

 NOTE An alliance between Microsoft and Apple, which included the bundling of Microsoft Internet Explorer with new Apple System Software, and the widely ballyhooed appearance of Internet Explorer as an integral part of Windows 98, have people even more convinced that the software giant is taking control of the browser market. In other words, the battle for market share isn't over, so designing for the proprietary features of one browser or another generally isn't your best bet.

Users with old software who hit Microsoft's (fully customizable) Microsoft Network home page after a new version of Internet Explorer is released are instructed that they need to download new software. The upgrade message is much stronger from Microsoft than it is from Netscape, although both companies' home pages are good examples of designing for both new and old software.

After version 3, Microsoft earned new respect from people who thought that the mammoth company had gotten too late a start to be competitive in the browser market. Some of this respect was also tied to the close compatibility of Internet Explorer with FrontPage.

Navigator vs. Internet Explorer: What to Do?

While Navigator remains the more popular browser, Internet Explorer's fans are utterly convinced that it's the better choice. The capabilities of the two browsers are pretty similar these days, but the way they display data—particularly in tables—is different enough that a pretty, well-designed page can look pretty ugly in the "other" browser, if you're not careful.

When you're designing a site that's "optimized" for one browser or the other, rest assured that most folks are not going to shut down their browser and launch a different browser just to view your site. They're going to mumble to themselves that it probably looks just as dumb in the other browser, look at the content you're offering to decide whether to continue, and keep surfing as usual.

Be sure to check your design in both Navigator *and* Internet Explorer before you launch it. Generally, a little fine-tuning to margins, table settings, and colors will make the display differences negligible, at which point you're free to advocate whatever browser you choose.

Generally, though, you'll have to give up the idea of total control endorsed by some of the more vocal big-deal Web designers. Your pages are going to look different in different environments; you just need to aim for them looking decent as often as possible.

If you'd like more details about margin differences between Macintosh and Windows platforms, and Navigator and Internet Explorer browsers, see David Siegel's page about Browser Offsets, at www.dsiegel.com/tips/wonk14/.

Just as Netscape pioneered such things as tables, frames, and plug-ins without so much as a by-your-leave from the standards committees, Microsoft is just as guilty for introducing extensions ("IEisms"?) as Netscape, with greater negative effect. Netscape's introduction of the BLINK tag was merely annoying, and if you couldn't see the blinking words, you probably weren't missing out on anything. On the other hand, Internet Explorer 2 introduced several extensions that were incompatible with other browsers, and which the World Wide Web Consortium had no intention of adopting. Of these, <MARQUEE>, <BGSOUND>, and page margins are the most notorious. (Other introductions by Microsoft, like the OBJECT element for embedding different types of information, and the IFRAME element for inline frames, work fine in newer non-Microsoft browsers and are totally supported by the W3C.)

PART

II

Creating
Sophisticated
Designs

Other Browsers (Including Lynx)

Dozens of other Web browsers are on the market. One relatively popular browser is Cyberdog, which works with the Macintosh. AmigaVoyager, for the Amiga platform, still has a steadfast following, and a handful of others, including Ibrowse, IBM Web-Explorer, and Opera, still haven't fallen off the map.

Most important of all, however, is the fact that Lynx, the text-only browser that's available for nearly every platform under the sun, is still more popular than one might think. People with very low modem speeds (less than 14.4Kbps) can happily wander the Web using Lynx, as can people in countries scattered around the world whose bandwidth scares them away from the graphical Web. Many public terminals in libraries and cyber-cafes support Lynx—which incidentally is one of the best choices for anyone with a VGA or other black-and-white monitor. Newer versions of Lynx do support both tables and frames (although not everyone has the very latest version of Lynx installed, either).

MASTERING WHAT'S ONLINE

Mastering What's Online

If you'd like to see a text-only view of the Web, read the Lynx Users Guide, at www.cc.ukans.edu/lynx_help/Lynx_users_guide.html, or use the Lynx Viewer at www.miranova.com/~steve/Lynx-View.html—it works in any Web browser. To get a copy of the software for yourself, try lynx.browser.org/.

What People Might Miss

So, people have different machines, and different software, and somewhere in Minnesota is a cranky old man surfing the Web at 2400bps with a Web browser built out of twigs, kite string, and gum wrappers. But what does it mean, exactly, when people can't "see" your pages? Do their Web browsers send back a message that says, "That's too high tech for me?" Not exactly. Do their computers freeze up and die? Yes, sometimes—particularly if your pages are infested with Java and other high-tech gizmos.

Mostly, though, your pages just look different from what you intended. What's so bad about that? Well, suppose your entire site is designed with tables, and Bob in Boise doesn't have a browser that supports tables. He'll see the data scattered all over his page. Or suppose your entire site depends on the background image (please consider adding more content than that to your pages). Some browsers don't load images at all, much less background images, and many people with slow connections have turned off auto-image loading. You need to decide how to present your content in the best-looking way possible to the majority of your target audience.

Tables, Frames, and Style Sheets

Tables have improved flexibility in page design more than any other HTML extension. While some browsers still have problems displaying them properly, you can generally assume that your visitors have access to tables.

So many designers construct poorly executed frames-based pages that a lot of Web surfers hate frames passionately—not to mention the many people who don't have a newer version of Navigator or Internet Explorer handy. Some folks find frames just plain confusing—if you don't know your way around frames intimately, you might have problems linking to or bookmarking the parts of the frameset you want.

If you're going to make a frames-based site, it's almost always a good idea to make a nonframes version available as well. If a user tries to visit your frames-only site with an older browser or text-only browser, a message will appear saying something like, "This page uses frames, but your browser doesn't support them."

You can easily create a nonframes page that will include links to all the files in the frameset, which people can click and read one at a time—the old fashioned way.

Also, if you're going to use style sheets—which boost your speed in designing an entire good-looking site—you need to grab some old browsers to view your site, to ensure it won't look anemic in the many browsers that don't support them.

Active Content

Users without new browsers won't be able to view active content such as Java, JavaScript, ActiveX, DHTML, plug-ins, inline multimedia, and the like. So many plug-ins and helper apps are flooding the market that the initial fervor most people had to load up their browsers with every plug-in around has significantly cooled. Many people will maintain their versions of Shockwave, RealAudio, and QuickTime, but few people bother to download every new media item that comes down the pike.

As with frames, it's a good idea to make versions of your site available that don't necessarily depend on Java, JavaScript, or multimedia to get the job done.

FrontPage's Internet Explorer-Only Features

While FrontPage makes it easy to add almost any available feature to your Web pages, it doesn't point out which of these features work only with Microsoft's own browser, Internet Explorer.

Keep in mind that FrontPage features are not necessarily Internet Explorer-only features. Some elements that you can add with FrontPage work only with servers that have the FrontPage Server Extensions installed, but they'll work with most any browser. These include many of the FrontPage components, such as scheduled images and page inclusions; form handling and script confirmation fields, and hit counters. (FrontPage components are covered in Chapter 15, and forms are covered in Chapter 14.) These features, as well as themes, will run properly only on FrontPage servers, but they work fine with most browsers. See Table 8.1 for a list of features that require the FrontPage Server Extensions.

Other features that only FrontPage can supply, however, can be viewed properly only with Microsoft Internet Explorer. These currently include all ActiveX/Active Platform components and most of the DHTML effects. While Navigator 4 can handle some ActiveX (if users install a plug-in) and manage its own brand of DHTML, earlier versions of Navigator (and Internet Explorer) can't play or view ActiveX controls or IE-style DHTML at all.

JavaScript and VBScript create other interesting browser-specific problems. JavaScript was developed by Netscape, and VBScript was written by Microsoft. Either browser can theoretically handle either language, but code that was written and tested only on one browser often performs erratically when used by the other. In other words, if you create a page that uses JavaScript and test it only with Internet Explorer, Navigator users may find their browser crashing or their machine's performance slowed down by nonstandard or buggy code that worked fine in your version of Internet Explorer. (The reverse is also true.)

 NOTE It's important to keep in mind that JavaScript doesn't work at all for browsers other than Navigator and Internet Explorer, or older versions of those browsers (Navigator 2 and Internet Explorer 3 are the oldest versions that support it). Also, JavaScript has better backward support in Navigator versions—IE's support for JavaScript didn't fully mature until version 4.

Java, too, only works with newer browsers (Navigator version 2 or later, and Internet Explorer version 3 or later). The FrontPage Insert ➢ Components ➢ Hover Buttons command inserts a Java applet onto your page. You may not be able to check and see if it works at all until you load your site onto the Web, but if you use this feature, you should check its performance (and download time) in both Internet Explorer and Navigator. (That goes for any Java applet, of course.)

 NOTE In general, Web developers are getting away from using Java on their pages. Java applets typically take time to download, and there are more elegant, cross-browser methods of delivering animations and other effects such as with JavaScript or DHTML.

Problems with the Marquee Tag

In online forums about FrontPage, the most common "problem" people ask about is why their MARQUEE tags don't work with Netscape Navigator. The answer to this is not a problem with Navigator, but with the MARQUEE tag itself. Microsoft introduced the MARQUEE tag as an answer to the scrolling text found in the status bar in early Netscape JavaScript and to the marquee boxes created with simple Java applets.

In Internet Explorer, the marquee text scrolls across the screen. In other browsers, it just sits there—no harm done really, but not very exciting. The detriment of the MARQUEE tag not scrolling isn't much greater than the BLINK tag not blinking, but it still frustrates people who go to the trouble to put it on the page.

To see what we mean, try this out:

1. With a page open in Page view, from the menu bar, select Insert ➤ Component ➤ Marquee. The Marquee Properties dialog box appears.

2. Type some text—any old text will do for this demo—in the Text text box.

3. Feel free to play with the properties, including speed, background color, and whatnot.

4. Click OK. The Marquee dialog box closes, and the window reappears, with some text sitting there.

5. Preview the page in Internet Explorer. (See the section "Previewing in Different Browsers" to find out how). The text scrolls merrily along.

6. Preview the page in Navigator or any other browser. The text languishes like a cat on a hot afternoon.

7. You can delete the Marquee by selecting it with your mouse and pressing Delete.

As you can see, using the MARQUEE tag isn't fatal, but for many folks it isn't very exciting either, and it isn't standard. A lot of people get very frustrated because their special effects don't work, and that shows that it's worthwhile to take the time to find out what browsers can do before you get set on special effects that don't work.

Testing, Testing, One, Two, Three

As we've said throughout this book, it's imperative that you test your pages before, during, and after putting them up on the Web (or on your corporate intranet). Aside from making sure that your links work, your images are in place, and your pages do what you think they're going to do, you need to test your pages in different environments than the one you designed them on to make sure they perform consistently well.

Previewing in Different Browsers

When you press the Preview button in FrontPage for the first time, the *default browser* launches. Generally, this is the browser that you first installed on your computer or one that you've since chosen as your default.

FrontPage allows you to select Internet Explorer, Navigator, or any other browser installed on your system to preview your site. At the very least, use both Internet Explorer and Navigator to preview each page. Previewing with Lynx isn't a bad idea, either.

The Preview In Browser Dialog Box

If you generally use the Preview button on the Standard toolbar to load your pages into the browser window, you may not be aware of all the available options. The Preview button generally launches your default Web browser; after you've used other browsers to preview pages, the Preview button loads the selected page into the last browser used, rather than the system default browser.

Previewing your pages in more than one browser is easy. Just follow these steps:

1. Open a page, or save the page you're currently working on.

2. From the menu bar, select File ➤ Preview In Browser. The Preview In Browser dialog box appears, as shown in Figure 16.4.

3. Choose a browser from the Browser list. Click Preview. The Preview In Browser dialog box closes and the selected browser window appears, with your pride and joy on display in its window.

Get in the habit of previewing your pages in at least Navigator and Internet Explorer on a regular basis.

FIGURE 16.4

Use the Preview In Browser dialog box to look at your pages in several different Web clients.

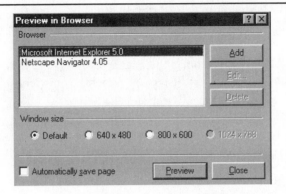

 TIP   You can set the window size of the browser window before you hit that Preview button. In the Window Size area of the Preview In Browser dialog box, click one of the buttons labeled 640×480, 800×600, or 1024×728 to emulate the window size for those screen resolutions. Selecting Default will leave your browser window size the way your browser remembers it from the past.

Getting Other Browsers into FrontPage

The easiest way to help FrontPage detect the browsers on your system is to install them *before* you install FrontPage. Now, you're probably reading this *after* you've installed FrontPage, so you'll be relieved to hear that you can also add browsers to FrontPage's preview list after installation.

After you've installed an additional browser on your system, just follow these steps to get FrontPage to recognize it as a preview option:

1. Open FrontPage, if it's not open already.

2. From the menu bar, select File ➢ Preview In Browser. The Preview In Browser dialog box appears.

3. Click Add. The Add Browser dialog box appears:

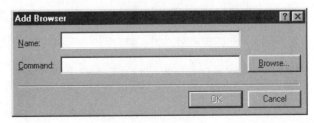

4. Click Browse. Another dialog box called Add Browser appears; this one's an awful lot like the Open dialog box you've used a million times in hundreds of Windows programs.

5. Browse through the files and folders on your computer until you locate the browser you want to use. Select the browser executable (.exe) file by clicking it.

6. Click Open. The Add Browser dialog box closes, and the initial Add Browser dialog box reappears. You'll see the pathname of the browser you chose displayed in the Command text box.

7. Type the name of your browser (i.e., Lynx, Mosaic) in the Name text box.

8. Click OK to close the Add Browser dialog box. The Preview In Browser dialog box reappears, and you'll see the name of the new browser displayed in the Browser text box.

9. Click Preview if you want to go ahead and preview a page in the selected browser, or click Close to close the Preview In Browser dialog box.

You can keep adding browsers as you see fit. When you delete a browser or upgrade from one version of a browser to another, FrontPage will *probably* detect the changes, although you might want to double-check by doing a quick preview after you upgrade. If FrontPage doesn't get it, you can repeat the steps above to select the new version of your browser.

NOTE   If you'd like to remove a browser from FrontPage's list of available browsers, open the Preview In Browser dialog box, click the name of the browser to be removed, and click Delete. To change the name or location of a browser in the Preview In Browser dialog box, open the Preview In Browser dialog box, click the name of the browser in question, and then click Edit. The Add Browser dialog box appears, where you can make changes to the name or command line (path name) of the browser. Unfortunately, you cannot edit or delete browsers automatically detected by FrontPage during the install.

WARNING   While Internet Explorer 1, 2, and 3 can coexist on the same computer, Internet Explorer 3, 4, and 5 cannot. Two or more different versions of Navigator can coexist on the same computer, but it's tricky to set them up and co-habitation can cause problems. Even so, there's nothing wrong with having Internet Explorer, Navigator, Mosaic, and Lynx on the same computer, along with any other browsers you feel like installing.

You may have an older version of Internet Explorer on your computer that was automatically installed by either Windows 95 or another version of Internet Explorer itself. Search your hard drive (Start ➢ Find ➢ Files or Folders) for files called `iexplore.exe` (Internet Explorer 1) or `ie20.exe` (Internet Explorer 2). If these browsers are still on your drive, you may as well add them to your preview list so you can check for backward compatibility.

Testing in Other Environments

Even if you have access to only one computer, you can certainly ask your friends to look at your pages using theirs. This can be especially helpful if you're designing a site from inside the comfort of a high-speed direct connection. You might never know that your page takes an hour to download unless you talk to someone who has done just that over a 14.4Kbps modem.

Here's a checklist of test environments. This checklist describes how to create an ideally accessible Web site. If you know your audience, you may not need to consider all of these items:

- Load your entire site using a 14.4Kbps modem. Would *you* wait that long to see your site?

- Check the number in the lower-right corner of the window—it is an estimate of how long this page will take to download using a 28.8 modem. Is the time shown acceptable?

- Test your design against as many browsers as possible. Do the tables break? Are the images okay? How are the fonts?

- Resize your browser window a half dozen times. Does the site look okay in small windows? How fast do the images refresh?

- Look at your home page on a PC, a Mac, and a Unix (or Linux) workstation, using either Navigator or Internet Explorer (or both). How are the colors? Is anything horribly out of whack?

- Run all your Java and JavaScript past both Internet Explorer and Navigator. Does it all function smoothly? Did the browser crash or freeze? Now try it again on the *other* platform, either Mac or PC.

- If you have alternate pages (such as a no-frames or text-only version of your site), make sure that they work, too.

- View a sampling of your pages with Lynx. Can you follow all the links? Do all the buttons have ALT tags?

- Visit your site at least once from a computer other than the one you designed it on. Are all the images still there? Do all the links still work? Do the forms respond properly?
- Try out your site on a gray-scale monitor. Is it legible?

Even if you don't get a chance to test every single option on this list, make sure you pay special attention to older browsers, text browsers, and the "other" platform. Your users surely will. And if you pass the test, your users will thank you for putting the effort into remembering that they exist.

Up Next

This chapter has helped refine your sense of what is and isn't supported in the variety of Web browsers your site visitors might be using. While some of the guidelines in this chapter might appear to be tedious because they add more work to your already busy schedule, they make the right sense if you want to have a more sophisticated brand of Web site out there.

Now it's time to shift gears from technology and challenge your creativity for a bit by delving into Part III, *Advanced Web Graphic Design*. Chapter 17, *Understanding Advanced Web Design*, looks at the basics of visual design and how they apply to the Web—helping you create Web sites that are not just technically interesting and cross-platform, cross-browser compatible, but that look great, too! The subsequent chapters in Part III introduce you to professional graphics programs and show you how to combine your advanced design skills with FrontPage to build a site from start to finish.

PART III

Advanced Web Graphic Design

LEARN TO:

- **Understand advanced graphic design concepts**

- **Use professional graphics programs**

- **Organize a site production schedule**

- **Create advanced Web sites with FrontPage 2000**

CHAPTER 17

Understanding Advanced Web Design

Many people come to FrontPage with little or no design experience. While FrontPage can address your needs by providing great themes and helpful wizards, you need to understand design concepts if you want to create custom, professional sites.

We've already looked at the basics. In Chapter 1, *Introduction to Web Design*, we gave you some design guidelines and took you on a site tour showing how design elements are used on the Web. In other chapters, such as Chapter 6, *Fantastic Fonts*, and Chapter 9, *Designing Graphics for the Web*, we examined how to use basic type principles and how to work with graphics.

But this chapter and the following chapters in Part IV of this book depart from the basics of design and lead you into the realm of the designer. The idea here is to challenge you to think about the elements of design—such as space, shape, and color—and understand how to manage these elements within the context of FrontPage.

Space

What is space? In our day-to-day lives, it is both the physical and emotional perception of room. In design, space is the absence of visual elements such as text or graphics. This absence is referred to as *white space*.

 NOTE Don't let the term *white space* confuse you. It doesn't mean that the space in question is literally white. It can be black, or green, or purple, or even a texture. It is what is left when no graphic or text element is there.

We need space. We use it as a cushion upon which to rest our eyes. It's necessary to help lead us to another element, or to help separate elements logically and attractively from other elements. Space is part of what makes a section of text readable; a graphic interesting within the larger design; a design flow naturally, without restriction.

Here is an interesting paradox: While space is the absence of certain visual elements, it is an element in and of itself. What this means in simple terms is that you need to think about, and use, space just as you would *any other element* on your pages.

Managing Space in FrontPage 2000

There are several helpful methods of adding space to your pages. While you should plan for this space in advance in your layout (see Chapter 19, *Creating Advanced Sites with FrontPage*), the next few sections show you how to gain the space you need.

Margins

Margins pull text and objects away from the virtual walls of your page. This gives you white space to the left, right, top, and bottom of a page—all necessary to help your page look more friendly and approachable.

If you're creating a site that does not use tables as a primary layout method, you'll want to ensure that margins are set. You can do this in a number of ways.

Blockquote   The *blockquote* is a tag that offsets your text from the edge of the browser. This is an effective way of gaining precious margin space and is particularly useful on pages that are text-heavy, such as reports, research articles, and long FAQs.

 NOTE   The blockquote element is not part of the HTML 4 strict standard. It has been set aside in favor of style sheets, which create very effective margins, as you'll soon see. However, style sheets are unpredictable even in contemporary HTML 4 and later browser versions. Using the blockquote will give your standard HTML pages the margins they need, and all current and most past popular browsers will have no trouble interpreting them.

We advise using blockquotes to manage text margins whenever you don't use tables. Figure 17.1 shows a standard HTML page without blockquotes. Note how the text runs from one end of the visual field to the other. In Figure 17.2, the blockquote is in use, giving a nice margin on either side of the text, and making the page not only look better, but easier to read, too.

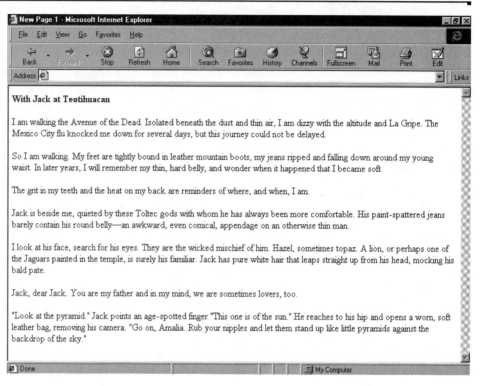

To add blockquotes to your text:

1. Open the page you'd like to edit in Page view.

2. Switch to HTML mode by clicking the HTML tab at the bottom of the Page view window.

3. Go to the top of the page, where your text begins. Type in the HTML tag **<blockquote>**.

4. Now go to the end of your text, and close off by typing the HTML tag **</block-quote>**.

5. Select File ➢ Save.

6. Preview your work by clicking the Preview tab in Page view.

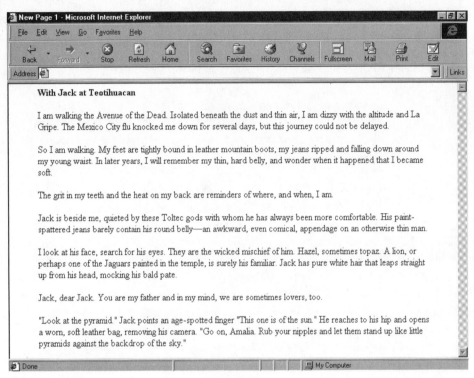

Your page now has defined space to the right and left of the text. This looks a *lot* better!

Here's an example of FrontPage code with the added blockquotes:

```
<html>
<head>
<meta http-equiv="Content-Type" content="text/html; charset=windows-252">
<meta name="GENERATOR" content="Microsoft FrontPage 4.0">
<meta name="ProgId" content="FrontPage.Editor.Document">
<title>New Page 1</title>
</head>
<body>
<blockquote>
<h3>Web Graphic Formats</h3>

<p>
```

> There are two dominant and useful file types used on the Web, the GIF, and the JPG (also known as JPEG). Understanding the difference in how these file formats compress data is extremely key in ensuring that the end product is speedy and attractive. Furthermore, there are special considerations regarding each format.</p>
>
> <p>
>
> For example GIFs can be transparent, interlaced, or used to create animations. JPGs can be progressively rendered, and enjoy the distinction of using a compression method that does not reduce the number of colors in an image.</p>
>
> <p>
>
> <i>Are there other file formats that can be used on the Web? The answer is yes, but they are either limited in that they require a plug-in to view with the browser, or only a few browsers support them inline. One such file, the PNG, has received some attention in recent months. But PNG is Not-ready-for-prime-time.</i>
>
> </p>
>
> <p>How and when to use each of these types of files is critical to optimization, as you will soon see.</p>

```
</blockquote>
</body>
</html>
```

Now what happens if you'd like to further offset text within a blockquoted section of text? You can *nest* the tags. This simply means that you place another set of open and close tags around any section of text within the blockquote. Take a look at this code:

```
<html>
<head>
<meta http-equiv="Content-Type" content="text/html; charset=windows-252">
<meta name="GENERATOR" content="Microsoft FrontPage 4.0">
<meta name="ProgId" content="FrontPage.Editor.Document">
<title>New Page 1</title>
</head>
<body>
```

```
<blockquote>
<h3>Web Graphic Formats</h3>

<p>
There are two dominant and useful file types used on the Web, the GIF, and
the JPG (also known as JPEG). Understanding the difference in how these file
formats compress data is extremely key in ensuring that the end product is
speedy and attractive. Furthermore, there are special considerations
regarding each format.</p>
<p>
For example GIFs can be transparent, interlaced, or used to create
animations. JPGs can be progressively rendered, and enjoy the distinction of
using a compression method that does not reduce the number of colors in an
image.</p>

<blockquote>
<p>
<i>Are there other file formats that can be used on the Web? The answer is
yes, but they are either limited in that they require a plug-in to view with
the browser, or only a few browsers support them inline. One such file, the
PNG, has received some attention in recent months. But PNG is Not-ready-for-
prime-time.</i>
</p>
</blockquote>

<p>How and when to use each of these types of files is critical to
optimization, as you will soon see.</p>
</blockquote>
</body>
</html>
```

Now the center paragraph has deeper margins than the rest of the text (see Figure 17.3). Lots of nice white space here, adding to the visual interest of the page. This is exactly what you're after when formatting pages that are text-heavy. However, don't overuse the blockquote. You can apply it once to the primary text area, and then use it sparingly to emphasize specific passages of text.

PART

III

Advanced Web
Graphic Design

FIGURE 17.3

Both the standard and indented margins in this example were created with the blockquote.

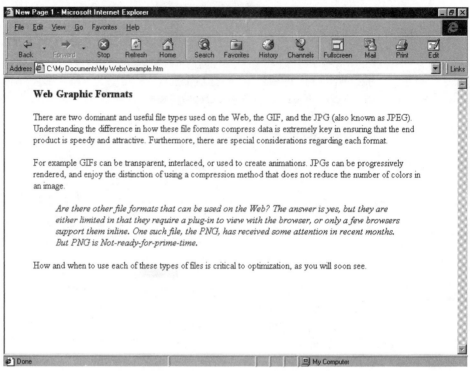

Margin Attributes   There are Internet Explorer–specific attributes that allow you to set margin controls within the <BODY> tag. This is a nice option when you know your audience is only using IE. A good example of this would be within a corporate intranet, where the software is consistent across the network.

NOTE   If you're designing for Netscape or other browsers, these attributes will not work.

One of the best aspects of margin attributes is that they can be used to set top margins as well as margins to the left and right of the page. This means that even if you're using tables for layout, you can control margins around the table.

There are four of these IE-specific attributes:

- `bottommargin`: This attribute allows you to fix a certain amount of white space, in pixels, to the bottom of a page.

- `topmargin`: Using this attribute, you can set the margin to the top of the page.

- `leftmargin`: This attribute gives you margin space to the left.

- `rightmargin`: This attribute provides margin space to the right.

Interestingly, FrontPage 2000 only provides a tool to add `topmargin` and `leftmargin`. If you want to use `bottommargin` or `rightmargin`, you'll have to add them manually.

To add top and left margins to a page:

1. Open the page of interest in Page view.

2. Right-click in the Page view window. From the menu that appears, select Page Properties.

3. The Page Properties dialog box appears. Click the Margins tab (see Figure 17.4).

4. Check both boxes and add a numeric value in pixels for your top and left margins, respectively.

5. Click OK.

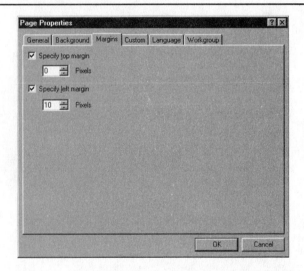

FrontPage adds the following information to your opening `<BODY>` tag:

```
<body topmargin="100" leftmargin="100">
```

Now, if you'd like to add a bottom or right margin, follow these steps:

1. With the page of interest open in Page view, click the HTML tab at the bottom of the window. You'll now see the HTML code for your page.

2. Find the opening `BODY` tag. Position your cursor next to the last margin attribute and value, and click once to add a space.

3. Type in the `bottommargin="value"` attribute, where *value* is a numeric value in pixels.

4. Follow this with another space, and add the `rightmargin="value"` attribute, including the desired numeric value in pixels within the quotes.

Your results should look similar to this:

```
<body topmargin="100" leftmargin="100" rightmargin="100" bottommargin="100">
```

Now, if you used 100 as your pixel value, the entire page will have a 100-pixel margin of white space around it when viewed in Internet Explorer (see Figure 17.5).

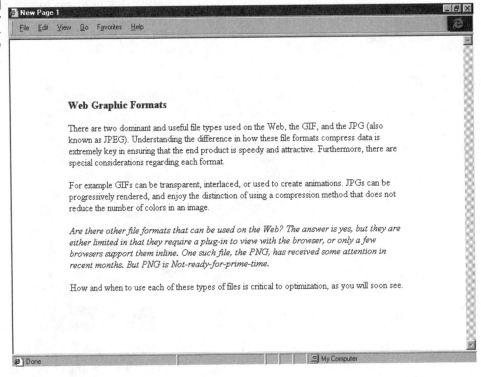

Style Sheets   *Style sheets* are a way to add margins to a page, and they're growing in popularity because they offer the ultimate control! Not only can you add values for top, bottom, right, and left margins, but you can also choose between different measurement types for those values, such as pixels, points, inches, and even centimeters.

NOTE The default measurement type for style sheets is pixels. FrontPage doesn't add a measurement type, but you can do this manually. We'll show you how in just a few moments.

In Chapter 13, *Getting in Style with Cascading Style Sheets*, we took a look at the types of style sheets that are available in FrontPage. The two types that we'll focus on here are *embedded* and *external* (or *linked*). We'll do a quick review of these approaches, and then we'll add margins to a page using style sheets.

To control the appearance of every element on a particular page, you can use *embedded style sheets*, which are stored in a special HTML tag at the beginning of a page. Use the FrontPage menu bar's Format ➤ Style command to create or edit an embedded style sheet. This manages style for a single page.

To use a single file to control the appearance of your site, you'll use *external* (also known as *linked*) *style sheets*, which are style sheets stored in separate files. The joy of an external style sheet is that you can update your Web site by changing just one file. An external style sheet must be linked to some or all of the pages on your site so that its effects are applied to those pages.

 TIP Should you require more familiarity with the syntax and process of using style sheets in general, review the information in Chapter 13.

Whether you are using embedded or external style sheets, there are three style sheet properties that are used to manage margins:

- `margin-left`: To set a left margin, use a distance in points (pt), inches (in), centimeters (cm), or pixels (px). The following sets a left margin to 3/4 of an inch: `{margin-left: .75in;}`
- `margin-right`: For a right margin, select an options measurement and value: `{margin-right: 50pt;}`
- `margin-top`: Top margins can be set using the same measurement values as for other margin attributes: `{margin-top: 20pt;}`

NOTE FrontPage offers easy access support to the left- and right-margin properties and values. However, it leaves out an easy way to add the `margin-top` property, so you'll have to add it manually if you want to use it. Furthermore, FrontPage assumes you want the measurement to be in pixels. If you want to use another measurement, simply change it manually.

Now, let's create an embedded style sheet with margins using FrontPage. To do so:

1. Have the page to be formatted open in Page view. From the menu bar, select Format ➤ Style. The Style dialog box appears.

2. Choose the selector you want to modify. In this case, BODY is an excellent choice, as margins will then be applied to the entire body of the page.

3. Click the Modify button in the Style dialog box. The Modify Style dialog box appears (see Figure 17.6).

4. Click Format. You'll get a drop-down menu with five options: Font, Paragraph, Border, Numbering, and Position. Select Paragraph. The Paragraph dialog box appears.

5. In the Before Text and After Text text boxes, add the number, in pixels, of your intended right and left margins.

6. Click OK. The Modify Style dialog box reappears.

7. Click OK, and the Style dialog box appears.

8. Click OK to save your changes.

FIGURE 17.6

Make style decisions in the Modify Style dialog box.

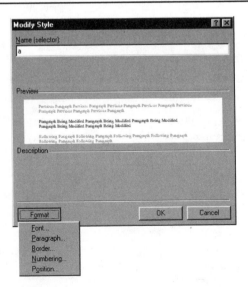

Here's the style sheet code that FrontPage has added to your work:

```
<style>
<!–
body        { margin-left: 100; margin-right: 100 }
–>
</style>
```

Note that this has been added into the HEAD section of your page.

Now, if you'd like to add the `margin-top` property, or just change the value type, follow these steps:

1. With the page you just modified open in Page view, click the HTML tab. You'll now see the HTML code.

2. Place your cursor right after the opening curly quote in the style rule.

3. Type in the property and value you want.

4. Select File ➢ Save to save your file.

You now have an embedded style sheet controlling the margins of your page. Now, let's take a look at how to create an external style sheet that you can use to control the margins of countless pages within a site.

1. Within FrontPage Page view, select File ➢ New ➢ Page. The New dialog box appears, as shown here:

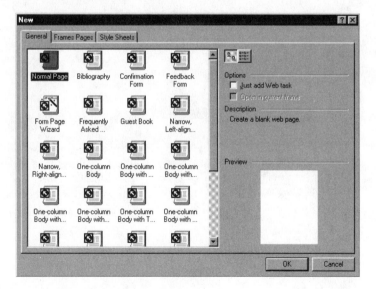

2. Highlight Normal Page and click OK.

PART

III

Advanced Web
Graphic Design

3. Manually type in the rulesets.

4. Save the file with a .CSS extension. From the menu bar, select File ➤ Save As. Name the style sheet, such as margin_style.css.

Your style sheet should look similar to this:

```
body      { margin-top: 0; margin-left: 100; margin-right: 100 }
```

 NOTE You can add many style sheet rules (syntax modifying a selector such as a paragraph, division, or spanned section of a page) to a single style sheet. We're focusing on the single rule controlling margins right now, but know that any style you want to add to the sheet can be added at any time.

Now, you'll want to link to the page any pages in your site that require this margin style. To do so:

1. Open the page or web to which you'd like to apply the style sheet.

2. From the main menu, select Format ➤ Style Sheet Links. The Link Style Sheet dialog box opens:

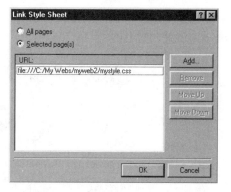

3. You'll see two radio buttons at the very top of the dialog. If you want the sheet applied to all of the pages in your web, select All Pages. If you only want certain pages to be affected by the style sheet, choose Selected Page(s) and use the Add button to add those pages. Each page you select appears in the Link Style Sheet dialog box.

4. Click OK. FrontPage now automatically links the style sheet to the pages you've chosen.

At this point, it's always a good idea to check your pages in the browsers you have available to make sure the results you're getting match your intentions!

Graphics and Space

There are several ways to ensure a nice balance of space beyond margins. For example, whenever you have a graphic, it's always wise to add space above, below, or to the side(s) of it. Figure 17.7 shows an example of text and a graphic being too close together. The results are difficult to read, as well as unprofessional.

FIGURE 17.7

Too close! The proximity of these page elements disturbs the eye.

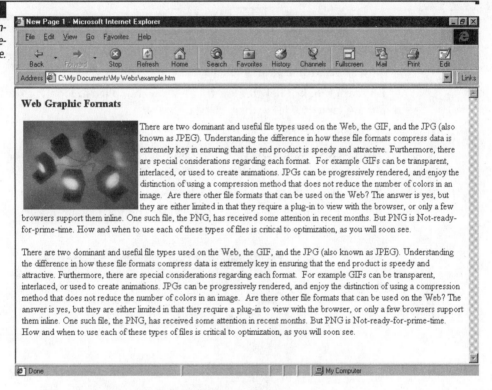

Web Graphic Formats

There are two dominant and useful file types used on the Web, the GIF, and the JPG (also known as JPEG). Understanding the difference in how these file formats compress data is extremely key in ensuring that the end product is speedy and attractive. Furthermore, there are special considerations regarding each format. For example GIFs can be transparent, interlaced, or used to create animations. JPGs can be progressively rendered, and enjoy the distinction of using a compression method that does not reduce the number of colors in an image. Are there other file formats that can be used on the Web? The answer is yes, but they are either limited in that they require a plug-in to view with the browser, or only a few browsers support them inline. One such file, the PNG, has received some attention in recent months. But PNG is Not-ready-for-prime-time. How and when to use each of these types of files is critical to optimization, as you will soon see.

There are two dominant and useful file types used on the Web, the GIF, and the JPG (also known as JPEG). Understanding the difference in how these file formats compress data is extremely key in ensuring that the end product is speedy and attractive. Furthermore, there are special considerations regarding each format. For example GIFs can be transparent, interlaced, or used to create animations. JPGs can be progressively rendered, and enjoy the distinction of using a compression method that does not reduce the number of colors in an image. Are there other file formats that can be used on the Web? The answer is yes, but they are either limited in that they require a plug-in to view with the browser, or only a few browsers support them inline. One such file, the PNG, has received some attention in recent months. But PNG is Not-ready-for-prime-time. How and when to use each of these types of files is critical to optimization, as you will soon see.

Small sections of text can be forced to the left or right of a graphic using HTML. Similarly, text can wrap around a graphic, creating a flow of three elements of interest to the eye: type, image, and space.

Text that wraps around a graphic is referred to as *dynamic text*. This term shouldn't be confused with other uses of the word "dynamic." In this case, it simply means that the text will wrap around the graphic when called to do so. How it looks at a variety of resolutions will be somewhat different—it's not a fixed method of getting space. To fix graphics, space, and type, refer to the upcoming "Tables and Space" section.

PART

III

Advanced Web Graphic Design

To ensure that text flows well around a graphic, you'll want to focus on three image tag (IMG) attributes and a variety of related values for each attribute. These attributes and values are as follows:

- `align=""`: In this case, alignment values relate to vertical or horizontal alignment. Since you can choose only one type of alignment per image, we encourage you to be most concerned with the horizontal values of left and right. (See Appendix E, *HTML Reference*, for complete alignment options.)

- `hspace=""`: This is *horizontal space* and takes a numeric value in pixels. Typically, you'll use somewhere from 5–10 pixels to gain the desired effect.

- `vspace=""`: Vertical space corresponds to the image's placement on the vertical axis. As with `hspace`, it takes a value in pixels.

Let's take a look at how these attributes can be applied in FrontPage and what results are gained by using them. To start:

1. Select File ➤ New from the FrontPage menu.

2. In Page view, add the text you'll want for the page by typing it in, or by cutting and pasting from another document.

3. Place your cursor at the point where you want to place your image.

4. Select Insert ➤ Picture. Select From File and locate your image file in the Select File dialog box:

5. Click OK. FrontPage now inserts your image, placing it at the left margin.

6. To work with alignment and space, right-click the image and select Picture Properties. The Picture Properties dialog box opens.

7. Click the Appearance tab (see Figure 17.8).

8. In the Layout section, you'll see a drop-down menu for Alignment. Choose the alignment style you want. Note that you will see a number of options beyond the scope of left and right. However, for text flow and space management, you'll want to choose either right or left.

9. In the Horizontal Spacing box, place the value, in pixels, of the horizontal space you desire. This sets up the hspace attribute.

10. Directly underneath the Horizontal Spacing box is option for Vertical Spacing. Enter the value of your choice to add vertical spacing. Set borders at 0 to eliminate any disruption between the image and the text.

11. Click OK.

FIGURE 17.8

Picture Properties dialog box with Appearance tab selected

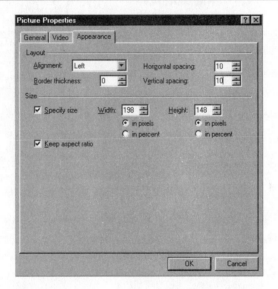

The image has now been placed into the text, with ample white space. This technique creates a sophisticated look and is easy on the eye (see Figure 17.9).

PART

III

Advanced Web Graphic Design

FIGURE 17.9

Whew! More space, much easier to look at.

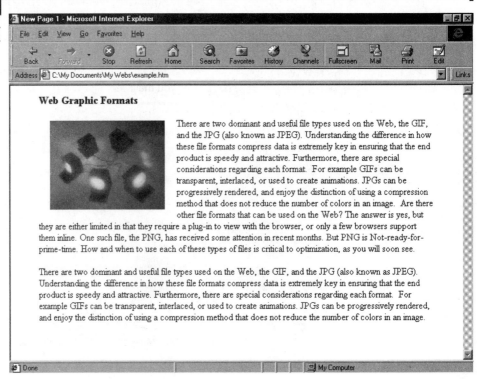

NOTE Once you've added an image, you can actually drag it to the location where you'd like it to reside on your web. This is a handy feature for quick layouts or to see if you like the look. However, you gain much more control by managing the position of the image yourself.

Tables and Space

Tables are especially handy when you're interested in controlling a variety of elements on a page. Across browsers and platforms, tables are currently the most effective method for specifically adding space around your text and images, or for precisely positioning images.

Cell Padding and Spacing   *Cell padding* is the addition of space around the fixed parameters of a given table cell. *Cell spacing* determines the amount of space appearing between cells. Using cell padding and spacing can add white space between information contained in individual table cells.

 NOTE Is it necessary to use both cell padding and spacing? Of course not! Depending upon your individual needs, the choices you make will vary.

To create a table with cell padding and spacing values, follow these steps:

1. Select File ➤ New ➤ Page from the FrontPage menu. The New dialog box appears. Select Normal Page and click OK.

2. From the FrontPage menu, choose Table ➤ Draw Table. The Tables menu appears.

3. Using the pencil tool, draw the outline of your table:

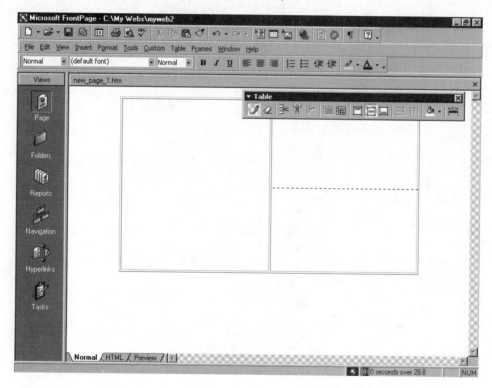

4. You can now add as many cells and rows as you'd like using the Tables menu options.

5. Once you've drawn the table to your tastes, right-click any table cell. From the menu, select Table Properties. The Table Properties dialog box appears:

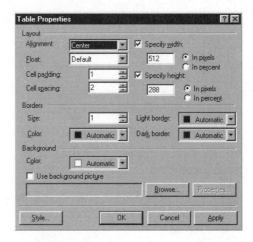

6. In the Layout section of the dialog box, you'll see options for cell padding and spacing. As with standard spacing, you're required to set the numeric value in pixels.

7. Type in the values of your choice.

8. Modify the table in any other way necessary to suit your design (see Chapter 11, *Using Tables for Advanced Layout*, for details).

9. Click OK.

You can now add text and images to individual cells. The cell padding will control the space between the elements in your cell and the table cell perimeter, and the cell spacing will add space between cells.

 TIP If you're using borderless tables (and in most cases of layout design, you should be), you can always set the border to a value of 1 when you're working. This gives you an idea of exactly where your elements, space, and table perimeters are. Using the Table Properties dialog box, simply switch back to 0 when you're finished.

Single-Pixel GIFs for Width and Height   The good thing about using cell padding and spacing is that it's a fast way to get white space for your page. The bad thing is that you don't have complete control over each individual area. The only way to get this kind of precision is to fix every cell element on a page. This is achieved in Web design by fixing both the width of the table and the width of every individual cell. No padding or spacing is used, and of course, there are no borders.

To gain precise space between elements, a single-pixel GIF is added to a table cell and spread out to the desired width. This fixes the element and the cells, ensuring that no collapsing of the table occurs. This technique requires a lot of planning—and a little bit of math.

First, you need to decide exactly how many pixels wide your table is going to be. For full-page layout, tables are typically set at 595 pixels. That's the recommended width to accommodate as many browsers and platforms as possible. Then you're going to have to look at what elements you want to include on your page: graphics, text, and/or any other media. What exact widths are they going to require? It's a good idea to write all of this information down.

Let's walk through a simple example. If we have an image that is 200 pixels wide and want that image placed to the right of any text, we have to subtract 200 from 595 to know what remaining space we have to work with. That leaves us with 395 total pixels. But say we want to have some space between the text and the image, maybe 15 pixels. Subtracting that from 395, we're left with 380 pixels for our text.

At this point, we know we need three table cells, too. One in which to place the text (this cell is 380 pixels wide), another for the space (15 pixels), and finally, another to hold the 200-pixel-wide image.

In FrontPage, we can draw this table by following these steps:

1. Select File ➤ New ➤ Page from the FrontPage menu. The New dialog box appears. Select Normal Page and click OK.

2. From the FrontPage menu, choose Table ➤ Draw Table. The Tables menu appears.

3. Using the pencil tool, draw the outline of your table.

4. Click the Insert Cells button on the Tables menu twice. This gives you a total of three columns.

5. Right-click anywhere in the table. From the menu, choose Table Properties. The Table Properties dialog appears.

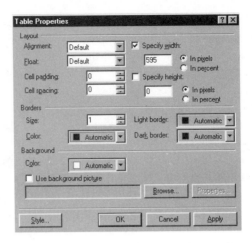

6. In the Layout section of the dialog, you'll see the Specify Width checkbox. Check the box if it's not already checked.

7. Directly beneath the checkbox is a box where you can input a specific number. Type in **595**.

8. Next to the number, there are two radio buttons offering percent and pixel values. It is *very important* that you make sure the In Pixels button is checked.

9. Click OK.

Your table is now be fixed at 595 pixels. To set the individual cell widths, follow this process:

1. Right-click in the first cell. From the menu, select Cell Properties. The Cell Properties dialog box appears.

2. You'll notice that the Cell Properties dialog box is very similar to the Table Properties dialog box. In the top-right corner is a Specify Width checkbox. Check this box.

3. Type in the numeric value of the cell in pixels. For our right cell, we know we want 380 pixels.

4. Check the In Pixels radio button.

5. Click OK.

Repeat this process with each of the cells, specifying the exact width, in pixels, that we predetermined as being necessary for the layout of this page.

WARNING In both the Table and Cell Properties dialog boxes, you'll notice a Specify Height option. In any case where you are using text on a page, you do *not* want to specify the table or table cell's height. Reserve this option for those occasions when all of your cells within a table contain graphics, and then be sure both the width and the height of the graphics match the width and height specifications of a given cell, and combined total of a given table—*exactly*. In all other instances, you'll want to be sure that the Table and Cell Height checkboxes are unchecked.

Following our example, you can now add the text to the first cell and the graphic to the final cell. But what about the middle cell? This is where the single-pixel GIF comes in.

Using a transparent, single-pixel (1 × 1) image, you can invisibly fix the width of the empty cell so it doesn't collapse. Some browser types and versions are very fastidious with table cells—if they see a fixed-width cell, they'll respect it! But others are not so precise and may collapse the cell if there's nothing in it to hold it up.

 NOTE To learn how to make a transparent GIF image, use your favorite image editor (see Chapter 9, *Designing Graphics for the Web*, and Chapter 18, *Working with Professional Graphics Programs*). In the editor, create a new single-pixel image. Fill the image with a single color (black or white is good) and export it as a transparent GIF. Your image file should be completely clear on any background or color. Typically, designers name this file `clear.gif` or `spacer.gif`.

You'll use this transparent GIF to hold the empty cell in place. In our example, the cell is 15 pixels wide, but the GIF is only one pixel. So, you'll have to modify the width of the image within the image tag. To do so:

1. In Page view, click once in the cell where you'd like to add the single-pixel GIF.

2. From the FrontPage menu, select Insert ➢ Picture ➢ From File. The Picture dialog box opens.

3. Find the GIF file and click OK. FrontPage inserts the GIF into the cell.

4. Right-click the GIF.

5. Select Picture Properties. The Picture Properties dialog box appears.

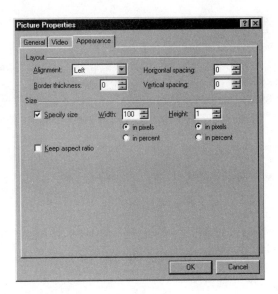

6. Choose the Appearance tab.

7. In the Size section of the dialog box, check the Specify Size checkbox.

8. To the immediate right of the checkbox, you'll notice that the width and height values are filled in and read 1 and 1, respectively. Change the width *only* to read 15 (or whatever the width of your spacing cell requires). Leave the height value at 1, and be sure that the In Pixels radio button is selected.

9. Click OK.

You now have a table with fixed cells that will not shift or collapse. You've got text, an image, and your desired goal: space! You can use this technique to lay out almost any design, and we highly encourage you to plan, fix, and lay out your advanced designs in this way.

Style Sheet Positioning

Another way of working with space is to position elements using style sheets. The specific technique is referred to as *Style Sheet Positioning*. Eventually, it is thought that this method will supercede the use of tables as a layout device with HTML. However, due to browser differences and version incompatibilities, this method is currently the least desirable way of achieving space on a Web page. As of this writing, we don't recommend it. Yet we do recommend that you read up on the technique, as you very well may need to use it at some point in the foreseeable future.

MASTERING WHAT'S ONLINE

To learn more about positioning elements using style sheets, visit the helpful style sheet tutorial at `www.builder.com/Authoring/CSS/`.

Color

Color is as important to a design as any other aspect of that design: text, graphics, space. Color creates a mood; it makes us think and feel at a deeper level than we might be aware.

Color has undeniable psychological and social impact. If you want to think like a designer, you need to think about color in terms of how it will represent your site in an appropriate fashion. Here's a quote from color expert J.L. Morton that sums up the importance of using correct color on the Web:

> Color plays a powerful role in that critical first impression—those first 5–10 seconds that either capture the viewer's attention and successfully communicate your message or fail miserably. Background colors and all link colors will either reinforce and enhance the site's theme or contradict it.

Let's say you are creating a site for your home-based resume and reports business. Your clients are in need of a professional, timely, precise, and neat service.

So how does color help or harm? Well, if you want to express precision and professionalism, you're going to require a sedate palette, such as muted earth tones or subtle blues. If you go with something too wild, such as neon green and yellow, or too soft, such as pastels, you won't project the neat and accurate image of your business.

When considering color, not only will you have to think about it carefully, but you'll also need to understand how color really works on the Web from a technical standpoint. FrontPage offers helpful utilities, and these will save you a lot of time and trouble. However, without the knowledge behind you, you can conceivably run into problems.

PART

III

Advanced Web Graphic Design

MASTERING WHAT'S ONLINE

Want to conjure up powerful responses to your Web sites? Visit J.L. Morton's Color Voodoo at www.jiffyart.com/cvoodoo.html.

About Web Color

As with most aspects of Web design, it is the limitations faced by the designer that make good design so challenging. With color, we're faced with thinking about significant variables, including our site visitor's hardware (computer, video card, monitor, and settings) and software (operating system and Web browser).

It's important to know that Web color is derived from computer color. Computer displays manage color using a technology known as *additive synthesis*. Think of your monitor as having three little paint guns. One of these paint guns fires red, another shoots blue, and the other, green. Depending upon the needed color, the guns fire a certain amount of each at the screen, where the color is then displayed. Think about it: The computer is *adding* color from its base of red, green, and blue (RGB) to create any number of colors.

Depending upon an individual's hardware, there can be anywhere from a handful to millions of colors capable of being displayed on the screen. Software such as operating systems and browsers can reduce or alter the way screen color is viewed. HTML also requires specific information to properly manage color.

In order to deal with all of these variables, the Web designer needs to know several important things. First, an awareness of the way computer color—and the resulting Web color—works is helpful. Then, understanding the way HTML interprets color and how to best work with that is imperative. Finally, because we are working with the restrictions born of the varied operating systems and browsers, understanding *Web-safe* color will ensure that all your color designs are as stable as possible.

RGB and Hexadecimal Color

RGB, as described earlier, stands for the red, green, and blue colors used by a computer monitor to deliver color to the screen. The amount of each color used to create a single color is based on math, and the result is a number relating to each of the three. So, for the screen, we might have 255 for green, 102 for red, and 0 for blue.

Web browsers require a standard way of measuring these colors so that HTML will recognize the numeric values and display the results to your site visitors. The numeric system used by browsers is known as *Hexadecimal* (or just *Hex*).

NOTE Recent browser versions do read RGB values without Hex conversion. When working with Cascading Style Sheets, many designers use RBG values instead of Hex, confident that if the browser can read the sheet, it can also interpret the Hex code. See "Controlling Color with Style Sheets" later in this chapter for an example of this approach.

Hexadecimal is the base 16 number system. Base 16 is an *alphanumeric* system, meaning that it uses both numbers and letters to represent a given color. Hexadecimal uses the numbers 0–9 and the letters A–F. You should always end up with a pair of three combinations (a total of six characters) for Hex-based color.

You can figure out all RGB colors by converting each individual color from our standard decimal system to the Hexadecimal system using a scientific calculator. Simply enter each individual red, green, and blue value and switch from standard decimal to Hexadecimal. For example, I can enter 255 for my green, and switch to Hex mode. My results will be FF. I then follow through for the red, then the blue. If my red is 102, my Hex will be 66. My blue is 0, and the corresponding Hex number is also 0. Since I'm required to have a total of six letters, I will use the value of 00 for my blue. My Hexadecimal color is FF6600. Incidentally, that's a bright red-orange.

WARNING In some cases, you've probably seen colors written out within HTML. For example, I could ask that my text color be "black" and my background color be "white." While many browsers have no trouble reading the name value of colors, others do not understand it. Another problem is that the name values are limited, whereas there are 216 Web-safe Hex values. Use Hex for professional results.

Using Safe Color

Before you put all of this knowledge to use, it's important to discuss the Web-safe palette. While computers can read RGB, and browsers read Hexadecimal values best, there is a limitation on the number of colors that are really, truly safe to use from browser to browser, across platforms, and with different monitor color capacities

PART

III

Advanced Web
Graphic Design

(assuming 256 is the least number of colors available and good systems offer millions of colors).

The safe palette is made up of 216 colors. These colors have been determined to be the most stable colors across browsers, platforms, and the range of computer monitor and video hardware available. It's important to use the safe palette in almost all instances, preventing your soft pastel yellow from becoming neon yellow on some poor soul's system.

FrontPage is somewhat helpful in providing you with easy access to Web-safe, Hexadecimal color. Its palette can be viewed as both limited or extreme, depending upon your take. To understand what we mean, right-click any Web page open in Page view. Select Page Properties, and when the Page Properties dialog box appears, click the Background tab.

If you select any of the options from the drop-down menus available in the Colors section, you'll notice that you have several different choices (see Figure 17.10). You can choose from a standard palette, a custom palette, or you can choose More Colors and pull up a new dialog box, as discussed in a moment.

FIGURE 17.10

Drop-down menus in the Colors section of Page Properties

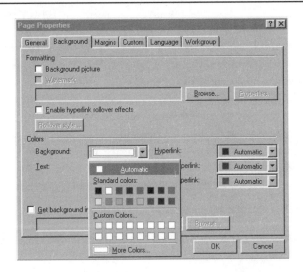

With any of these choices you run the risk of using unsafe color, because FrontPage doesn't pay close attention to safe color in most cases. So, if you click one of the colors from the standard palette, you'll likely end up with an unsafe color. The same is true when you use the custom palette. So in this sense, the palette is too extreme—giving you many choices, but little control.

If you choose More Colors, a dialog box pops up that has a palette of safe colors (see Figure 17.11). This is good! However, not all 216 colors are available. This is bad—it means you have to put the lessons learned about RGB and Hexadecimal color in this chapter to work rather than rely on FrontPage's utility.

FIGURE 17.11

While incomplete, the More Colors dialog box offers Web-safe options.

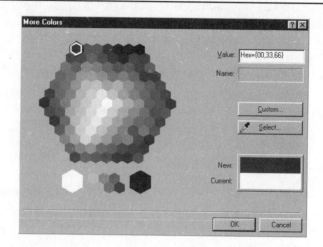

Once you know the colors you want to use on your page, you can set up the page using the More Colors dialog box. For each color option available to you, simply type the desired value in Hex directly into the Value text box.

Using Color Intelligently

So you're aware that color has psychological impact. You also know that you have to be very selective when you choose color for use on the Web (using the 216-color safe palette). This may seem as though it limits what you can do with color. But the truth is that it empowers you, like any good designer, to think in precise terms.

First, you'll want to think carefully about your goals. Are you creating a home page for yourself, or are you building a client site? Either way, you want to think about how colors best represent the expression you're after. If your client has a pre-set selection of colors, you'll want to work from those colors to match a look and feel that is

PART

III

Advanced Web
Graphic Design

consistent with your client's goals. If you don't have much to go on, use your instincts and any information you've gathered from analysis (see Chapters 1 and 3) to make choices appropriate for your intent. A conservative organization is going to want a conservative look—not neon greens and reds! Similarly, if you want a site that is energetic and on the edge, color can help you achieve that goal.

Once you've got a firm idea as to what you want to do with color, it's very helpful to create a custom palette for the site in question. To do this, simply choose up to seven colors you intend to use for background, text, links, and accents on the page. Then, either create a swatch of these colors using your favorite image editor, or make a list of each color along with its name, its RGB, and its Hex value. This will come in handy as you build the site.

Of course, follow general design guidelines (see Chapter 1) and make sure that you have enough contrast for your colors to be readable. Also, be consistent! Keep the same background, text, and link styles throughout your site, with only subtle modifications where absolutely necessary.

Controlling Color with Style Sheets

As with space, style sheets offer ways of including color information on a site. You can control everything from backgrounds to links using a basic style sheet. If you're new to style sheets, we recommend you look at one of FrontPage 2000's style templates. You can use them intact, or you can make modifications to customize the look.

Working with style templates in FrontPage is easy. Follow these steps:

1. From the main FrontPage window, select File ➤ New ➤ Page. The New dialog box appears.

2. Click the Style Sheets tab. You'll see a variety of templates.

3. Choose the template of your choice.

4. The style sheet appears on your screen.

You can now modify the style sheet, changing colors, removing undesired properties, or altering typographic elements. In the following section of code (a modification of the "arcs" style template), note how the style sheet uses RGB values to apply color to links and headers:

```
a:link
{
  color: rgb(51,153,255);
}
a:visited
{
```

```
    color: rgb(51,102,204);
}
a:active
{
    color: rgb(255,153,0);
}

h1
{
    font-family: Times New Roman, Times;
    color: rgb(153,153,51);
}
h2
{
    font-family: Times New Roman, Times;
    color: rgb(204,153,0);
}
```

It's important to point out that you can also opt to use Hex code instead of RGB in style sheets. Instead of RGB values in the a:link ruleset of the previous code, the Hexadecimal style should look like this:

```
a:link
{
    color: #3399FF;
}
```

Deciding which method to use is up to you; use whichever you prefer. We like to use Hexadecimal color, as we believe it is ultimately safer across multiple browsers. However, FrontPage uses RGB, so if you're working in a FrontPage- and Internet Explorer–dominant environment, using the RGB method is a reasonable choice.

 NOTE Be sure to revisit Chapter 13 for helpful instructions on modifying style sheets and adding them to your Web pages.

Shape

Wander around the Web for a while, and you'll probably be exposed to a variety of shapes. But if you watch carefully, you'll notice that one shape dominates the Web. Take a guess!

If you said rectangle, you're right on. The very nature of the Web is rectangular. We view the Web through a computer monitor, which is a rectangle. The browser window is rectangular. The shapes we can create with HTML using tables or frames are all rectangles. So it makes sense that rectangles will dominate.

This is precisely the reason you want to think about other shapes! Using shape to create visual impact can really help set your site apart from the standard look of the Web, making it a memorable experience for the user.

Shape, like color, has psychological impact. Here's a brief look at what primary shapes represent to our deeper selves:

Rectangle The rectangle represents stability, reliability, and longevity. If you're looking for a way to impress upon your site visitors that your product or company is there for the long-term, rectangles can help you do that.

Circle Circles evoke a sense of community, warmth, and wholeness. Circles are also considered feminine. If you're looking to make people feel at home, express a sense of strong ties, family, security, and safety, circles are the way to go.

Triangle Energy, movement, and intensity are suggested by triangles. They are related with the masculine. Triangles are a great choice when you're suggesting progress and movement.

Want to mix your messages? Mix your shapes!

MASTERING THE OPPORTUNITIES

Playing with Shape

Have some fun with shape! Open your favorite image editor (see Chapters 9 and 18) and make shapes. Combine shapes. Fill shapes with color.

Another cool exercise is to take a piece of paper and cut a particular shape out of it. For example, cut a triangle out of a paper. Now, walk around your house, office, even an outdoor area, and look through the shape at the view. Move the shape close to an object, then far away. You'll begin to see how shape alters the way we see things. This exercise can help you gain a designer's eye view of the world.

Using Graphics to Add Shape

So just how do you get shape onto a Web page? Primarily, this will be through the use of graphics. HTML can't handle shapes, although there are some unofficial DHTML methods of adding dimension or special treatments to page elements. For the most sure-fire method of adding shape to pages, use graphics.

Also, you need to start seeing the shapes that appear as the result of various images, including items from nature (a leaf, a cat's face) as well as items from the imagination. Any time you blend such an image with the flow of space, you end up with shapes!

So don't be limited—really get in there and work out your ideas. There are ways to combine the straight, flat edges of standard designs with interesting shapes. Figure 17.12 is a student project that combines the familiar left-margin navigation bar with the imaginative head of a dragon. Note how the resulting design is much more interesting to look at than a plain margin.

FIGURE 17.12

Student Sean D'Addamio's work demonstrates shape through the use of standard and creative Web graphics.

Type Tour

In Chapter 6, we introduced you to the important elements of Web typography. But now that you're beginning to think like a designer, it's important to mention how type plays a role in creating interesting space and shape on a page. What's more, you can use color to add impact or interest to your typographic designs.

In the following visual examples from real Web sites, we demonstrate exactly how type can work to create designs with punch. What's more, type can become a fine art—and depending upon your goals, you may just want to employ type as a method of going beyond the simplistic into the realm of cutting-edge design.

Tiro Typeworks (see Figure 17.13) has a simple but effective approach to their home page's type design. There's nothing particularly overwhelming or difficult in what they've done—in fact, it's the simplicity of the design that makes it so effective! The beautiful headline text is in and of itself interesting to look at, creating a variety of visual shapes. The body font, which is standard Times New Roman, works well to provide a simple but compelling look.

FIGURE 17.13

Tiro Typeworks: understated and effective

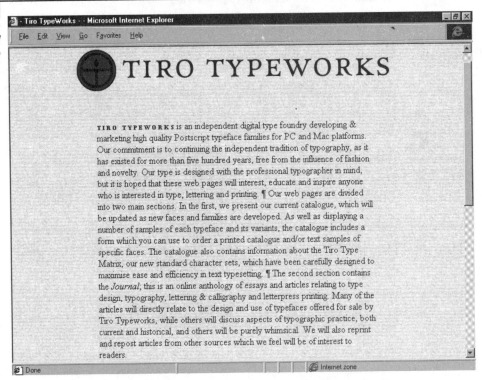

The designers had a little fun here—adding paragraph marks instead of actual paragraph breaks within the body text. This is not only clever, but an appropriate method of expressing the message of the Web page. It's about type, after all. Use this example as clean inspiration as to what can be done with a little bit of simplicity and a whole lot of imagination.

Matthew George (see Figure 17.14), a personal branding firm out of Oakland, California, approaches type, shape, and color in a confident and secure fashion. Pay special attention to the combination of serif and sans-serif titles.

FIGURE 17.14

Matthew George: type
direction at work

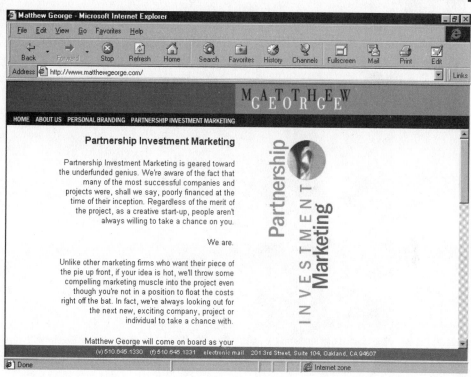

Especially important is the way the site uses direction to make the space, as well as the type, very exciting. The combination of confidence and movement are very appropriate for the site's intent: to market marketing! Potential clients feel that if they need rock-solid representation, it's there. But if they want to be more progressive, that option is available, too! Think about this design as a way to expand your options when designing with type.

Joel Neelen, a Belgian graphic designer, uses a great deal of edgy color, positioning, and type to achieve a very eclectic effect for his home page (see Figure 17.15).

PART

III

Advanced Web
Graphic Design

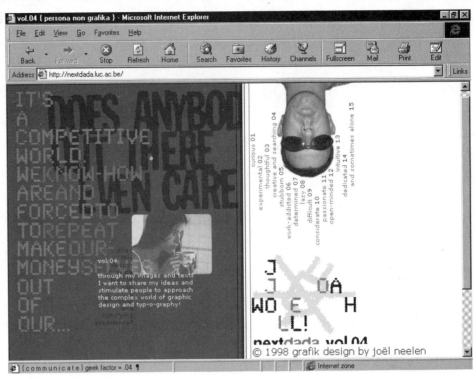

This example demonstrates how designers can, in certain instances, take elements of design to the cutting edge and still manage to express ideas effectively.

Up Next

Now you're thinking like a designer! You have an understanding of what shape, space, color, and type mean to professional design, and you're ready to apply your ideas. Moreover, you're beginning to see how they each work together to create *design*.

While FrontPage 2000 helps you add these elements to your sites, developing an awareness of how these design elements work together takes your Web pages from the ordinary to the extraordinary.

To be truly professional in your approach, you'll also need to work in tandem with a variety of sophisticated graphic programs to gain the impact you're after. Chapter 18, *Working with Professional Graphics Programs*, surveys both the imaging and imaging-support applications that you'll need to make your design ideas real.

CHAPTER **18**

Working with Professional Graphics Programs

I n Chapter 9, *Designing Graphics for the Web*, we introduced you to the accessible programs Microsoft offers along with FrontPage and the Office suite. Photo-Draw and Image Composer are solid tools in their own right, and we encourage you to get familiar with them.

Yet if you're looking for power and design on par with professional graphic designers, you'll want to explore a variety of other imaging, illustration, and optimization programs and related tools. Furthermore, you'll want the opportunity to work with these tools step-by-step so you can gain familiarity with how they are used.

Is it necessary to have professional tools to output high-quality graphics? Of course not! Tools don't make the designer. But newcomers to Web page design—especially those interested in taking their sites to the professional level—need to know how the pros do what they do.

If you're an experienced designer, much of the information in this chapter will be familiar. However, you may run across some gems that you'd not been aware of, so we encourage you to read it, and enjoy!

Understanding Imaging and Illustration Programs

To best understand the features of the programs mentioned throughout this chapter, it's good to know the difference between two important types of graphics: vector and raster.

Vector graphics are created mathematically in such a way that each plotted point in the illustration relates to quantity and direction at the same time. So if you create a vector graphic and save it for future editing in vector format (native format to a vector program, such as Illustrator), you can re-open and modify that file in terms of quantity and direction. Simplified: Within the vector application, you can make a vector graphic larger and smaller without losing quality, because you are simply altering the math involved.

In order to be portable across platforms—and readable by Web browsers—vector files have to be rasterized. *Raster graphics* are *bitmapped* files. You're probably familiar with these—they include BMPs, GIFs, and JPEGs. They use the x/y axes to create a pre-defined grid of information. This means that the space in which they are created is specific in terms of quantity and direction, and therefore can't be as elegantly modified as vector graphics.

Think about a grid. Color and information is placed in each of the little squares within that grid. It's a map of bits! Because they don't use the more complex mathematical statements of quantity and direction, raster graphics are fixed in quantity and direction. For that reason, they're larger, and they're harder to modify. You can make them smaller without losing quality, but make them larger and you force each bit to stretch out, resulting in blurry, blotchy graphics.

So, programs that output and edit proprietary or popular bitmapped images are raster programs. Vector programs are more mathematically complex—the graphic results are much smaller than raster graphics, but the applications that generate them take up a lot more RAM typically—and are reserved for high-end typographic, illustration, 3D, and animation designs.

Imaging and Illustration Programs for the Professional

If you want a career as a Web professional, it's very likely you'll be expected to be familiar with Photoshop and Illustrator. They are the graphic-design industry standards for imaging and are used by most top Web design groups world-over. Photoshop, incidentally, is a raster program, whereas Illustrator is vector-based. As we describe their unique features, you'll see why this distinction is important.

Along with the esteem of these two programs comes a steep learning curve. While the interfaces are intuitive, to use Photoshop and Illustrator with speed and power takes time and care to learn. There's also the high price tag—around $500 per program for a single license. Yet there are ways of getting software at a discount; if you are an educator or a student, you'll find very affordable alternatives to shelf-priced software. Also, you can download demos of the programs in order to find out if you want to make a longer-term commitment to them; see the "What's on the CD" page in the back of this book for the list of demos and other products available in the accompanying CD-ROM. We'll provide plenty of links and resources for you to find the appropriate demo software.

A turn of events is taking place with Web design graphic creation and manipulation. High-end software developers such as Adobe and Macromedia recognize that some of their offerings are not needed by Web designers. So, in order to focus the applications environment and specific tools for Web design, new programs are being developed that are both more sensible for the individual working on the Web and for the budget-wise purchaser of these programs. The end result is a happy one: great new software that has the power and professional flexibility of their foreparents, but with a price tag and learning curve that is much more attractive.

Adobe Photoshop

Adobe Photoshop is both a general graphic-design and Web-design industry standard. What this means is that if you plan on looking for employment in the design profession, you'll want to have Photoshop skills to be most attractive to your potential employers.

Photoshop is extremely powerful—far beyond the scope of what is needed for the Web. However, a good user can quickly learn how to use Photoshop to maximize his or her design work.

 TIP   Want to get the most Web knowledge from Photoshop? Check out *Mastering Photoshop 5.5 for the Web* by Matt Straznitskas (Sybex; Fall, 1999).

There are many reasons why Photoshop is appealing and why you'll want to seriously consider it as a tool to demo yourself, with the intent to eventually purchase. First of all, being an industry standard, there's plenty of support for Photoshop—and plug-ins galore!

Second, Photoshop is a raster-graphics program, which makes it easy to output Web-ready graphics. No need to mess with a vector program first, although you may want to use Photoshop in tandem with a vector program in order to get better control over shapes and type—which naturally can be altered much more easily without quality loss in a vector environment.

Layering

Another key component of Photoshop is the ability to work in layers (see Figure 18.1). While Image Composer has a similar feature, called *sprites* (see Chapter 9), and other programs such as Jasc's Paint Shop Pro have included layer functions in their imaging software, Photoshop has the most power and control. Essentially, you can create a file in Photoshop that contains different information on each layer, and save that file in native Photoshop format. Later, when you want to make a change to only one aspect of the design, you can simply go to the layer and change it! No need to re-do the entire graphic.

Layering is one of the reasons Photoshop is so extremely useful in professional design! Many times a client will want a color or text style altered. Using Photoshop, you simply go back to your initial files and make the change in the appropriate image layer. In Chapter 19, *Creating Advanced Sites with FrontPage*, we'll look at some layout techniques that put you through your paces using Photoshop layers to maximize your work.

FIGURE 18.1

Working in Photoshop layers

Specialty Features

With Photoshop, as with many raster-graphic programs, you can create transparent and interlaced GIFs. No need for extra tools—it's all right there in the software. Another feature that exists right within the application (versions 4 and above) is that the Web-safe palette we discussed in Chapter 17, *Understanding Advanced Web Design*, ships with the program and requires no additional filters or plug-ins to work.

Not only can you create all kinds of standard graphics such as buttons and backgrounds with Photoshop, but you can scan art, photos, and objects directly into the program and use Photoshop to enhance and manipulate your work.

Photoshop 5 offers a variety of powerful type options and filter features that allow you to quickly enhance your graphics with effects applied to the edges such as bevels, drop shadows, inner shadows, and light sources (see Figure 18.2).

PART

III

Advanced Web Graphic Design

FIGURE 18.2

Adding a drop shadow using Photoshop 5

MASTERING WHAT'S ONLINE

If you're looking for Photoshop demos, support, and/or help, visit www.adobe.com/. You might want to check out other layer-based programs, such as Jasc's Paint Shop Pro, available at www.jasc.com/, and Image Composer, available at www.microsoft.com/imagecomposer.

Adobe Illustrator

Illustrator is another Adobe program used by graphic design professionals that has an important place in the creation of professional Web graphics.

Unlike Photoshop, Illustrator is a vector-based program. This means that while it's not the most efficient tool for outputting Web-ready graphics, it allows you to create and work with graphics.

Remember, vector graphics work on a mathematical principle that allows for changes in quantity and direction simultaneously. What this means in real terms is that if we want to take type and vary its direction with finer precision than using a raster program, we can do it in Illustrator (see Figure 18.3). Using advanced intelligence within the program, we can create lines in the vector program and direct our type along those lines. We can't do this with raster-based graphic applications.

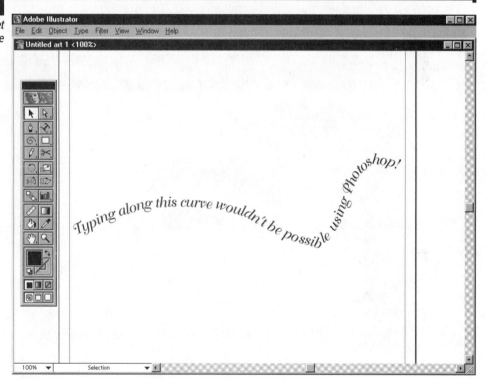

MASTERING WHAT'S ONLINE

Demos, support, and information about Adobe Illustrator can be found at www.adobe.com/.

Because Illustrator is a drawing program, shapes are much more easily created and manipulated in Illustrator (see Figure 18.4). Illustrator allows you to draw shapes using the intelligence of vector graphics. You can create your own lines for the shape to follow or use several pre-set shapes that Illustrator provides.

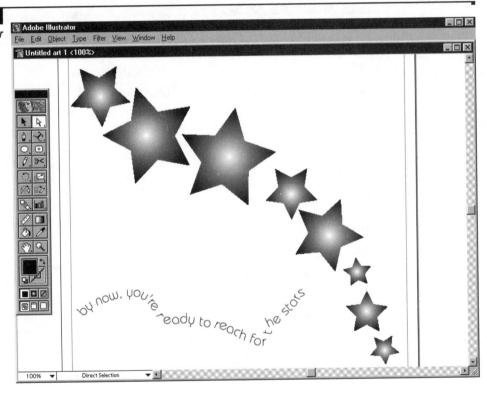

FIGURE 18.4

Shapes in Illustrator

MASTERING THE OPPORTUNITIES

Other Vector Programs

There are a variety of other popular vector-drawing programs. The two most common are Corel Draw (www.corel.com/) and Macromedia Freehand (www.macromedia.com). Interestingly, the multimedia program Flash, included on this CD, is vector-based. That's one of the reasons it requires a special plug-in—because the vector graphics have to be interpreted in order to be visible within supporting browsers. You can find more information on Flash at the Macromedia Web site.

Macromedia Fireworks

Fireworks is our first example of a multimedia program designed with the Web in mind. It was specifically developed to give Web designers an easy interface to create Web-ready graphics, as well as provide specialty tools necessary to create great looking Web sites.

Brand new from Macromedia, Fireworks allows you to create image maps, slice graphics for positioning within tables (see Chapter 11, *Using Tables for Advanced Layout*, and Chapter 17, *Understanding Advanced Web Design*). What's particularly impressive about Fireworks is that not only does it slice up your graphics, but it generates the appropriate table code! This makes your life with FrontPage 2000 so much easier, because you can combine the code generated from Fireworks with the page design you're working on in FrontPage.

 NOTE An interesting fact about Fireworks: While you're working in it, you're working in vector format! However, since you will use Fireworks to export files to GIF or JPEG formats (which are raster graphics), in the end, Fireworks is really a raster program.

Let's say you have Fireworks and want to use it to splice up a graphic so it fits properly on your page. Here's how you can begin to incorporate the Fireworks code into the FrontPage code:

1. Use Fireworks to create your graphic. To slice your graphic, select the Slice tool from the Fireworks toolbar.

PART

III

Advanced Web
Graphic Design

2. Draw over an area you want to slice. Remember, slice wherever it makes sense to slice. Are you going to update a portion of the graphic? That should be a separate slice. Is another portion fitting precisely over a background? Fireworks helps you slice the page after you make your initial selection, creating a grid from your design (see Figure 18.5).

3. Select File ➤ Slice Defaults. Select the default file types for the slices.

4. Click Save And Close.

5. From the main Fireworks menu, choose File ➤ Export Slices. Fireworks now exports the slices to a specific HTML file. It also saves the individual GIF files to a folder that you can specify—be sure it's the one where you're keeping the graphics for the FrontPage web you're working on.

FIGURE 18.5

Sliced areas in Fireworks

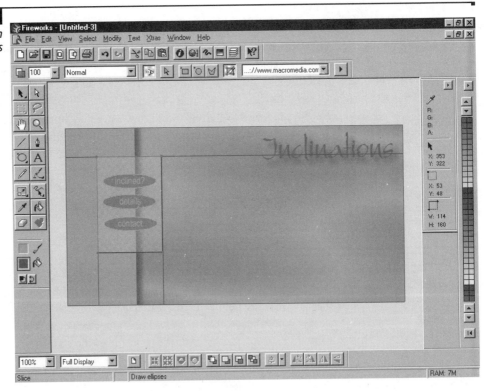

Now that Fireworks has generated the necessary graphics and the HTML for you to copy into your FrontPage web, follow these steps:

1. Open the FrontPage web to which you'd like to add the table and associated graphics.

2. In Page view, open the specific HTML page where the table and graphics will go.

3. Select the HTML tab so you can see the code of the page.

4. Load the Fireworks HTML page into your Web browser.

5. From the browser menu, select View ➣ Source. The source code appears (see the following "Viewing the Code from Fireworks" sidebar).

6. Look for the table section generated by Fireworks. Select the code with your mouse, and press Ctrl+C to copy to the Clipboard.

7. Switch back to FrontPage. With the HTML code of your Web page open in Page view, paste the Fireworks code right into your FrontPage code.

8. Save your work.

MASTERING THE OPPORTUNITIES

Viewing the Code from Fireworks

You'll notice that the following code uses comment tags (tags that are hidden from the browser) to help you work with it easily:

```
<!----- BEGIN COPYING THE TABLE HERE --------------->
<!- Image with table ->
<table border="0" cellpadding="0" cellspacing="0" width="297">
<tr><!- spacing row, 0 height. ->
  <td><img src="images/test_00.gif" width="6" height="1" border="0"></td>
  <td><img src="images/test_00.gif" width="141" height="1"
border="0"></td>
  <td><img src="images/test_00.gif" width="150" height="1"
border="0"></td>
</tr>
<tr><!- row 01 ->
```

PART

III

Advanced Web
Graphic Design

MASTERING THE OPPORTUNITIES CONTINUED

```
  <td rowspan="2" colspan="1"><a href="http://www.macromedia.com"><img
name="Ntest_01_01" src="images/test_01_01.gif" width="6" height="137"
border="0"></a></td>
  <td rowspan="2" colspan="1"><a href="http://www.macromedia.com"><img
name="Ntest_01_02" src="images/test_01_02.gif" width="141" height="137"
border="0"></a></td>
  <td rowspan="1" colspan="1"><a href="http://www.macromedia.com"><img
name="Ntest_01_03" src="images/test_01_03.gif" width="150" height="77"
border="0"></a></td>
  <td><img src="images/test_00.gif" width="1" height="77"
border="0"></td>
</tr>
<tr><!- row 02 ->
  <td rowspan="1" colspan="1"><a href="http://www.macromedia.com"><img
name="Ntest_02_03" src="images/test_02_03.gif" width="150" height="60"
border="0"></a></td>
  <td><img src="images/test_00.gif" width="1" height="60"
border="0"></td>
</tr>
</table>


<!- This table was automatically created with Macromedia Fireworks 1.0  -
>


<!- http://www.macromedia.com ->
<!----- STOP COPYING THE TABLE HERE --------------->
```

If you've been careful to save the graphics to the correct directory, you should now be able to view your Web page, complete with the new graphics and code generated by Fireworks.

Other special features of Fireworks include the ability to create bevels and drop shadows with ease, as well as creating mouseover images—and the JavaScript to go with them!

MASTERING THE OPPORTUNITIES

More from Macromedia

Aside from Fireworks, Flash, and Freehand, Macromedia makes several other programs that Web page enthusiasts are sure to want to learn more about. They include:

Macromedia Director   The Director 7 Shockwave Internet Studio is the professional standard for creating and delivering powerful multimedia for the Internet, CD-ROMs, and DVD-ROMs. Rather than serving simple graphics and text such as you would find in a simple Web page, Director lets you combine graphics, sound, animation, text, and video into compelling content. For the Web, these presentations are delivered using the Shockwave player. Shockwave Web sites are highly interactive.

Macromedia Authorware   Authorware Attain is a visually rich multimedia authoring tool for creating Web and online learning applications. It's especially useful for training developers, instructional designers, and subject matter experts to develop trackable learning applications and deploy them across the Web and on CDs.

Macromedia Dreamweaver   If you like FrontPage, you might want to take a look at Dreamweaver. It's also a Web design WYSIWYG interface. As with FrontPage, Dreamweaver integrates with other products in its family to create dynamic and interesting Web content.

Demo software of Authorware, Dreamweaver, Fireworks, and Flash are available on the CD-ROM accompanying this book.

Adobe ImageStyler

As with Fireworks, Adobe ImageStyler is another answer to the need for Web-specific tools. Like Fireworks, ImageStyler can create a wide range of Web graphics *and* generate the HTML or JavaScript code necessary to carry out the task.

ImageStyler has the advantage of maintaining the Adobe standard interface. As a result, users of other Adobe products such as Photoshop and Illustrator will find ImageStyler very easy to use (see Figure 18.6). You'll notice that the menus are laid out in the same way, and the individual palettes and toolbar help give you easy access to the application tools. This familiar environment reduces the time those familiar with Adobe products will spend trying to learn the program.

PART

III

Advanced Web Graphic Design

FIGURE 18.6

Working within the
Adobe ImageStyler's
interface

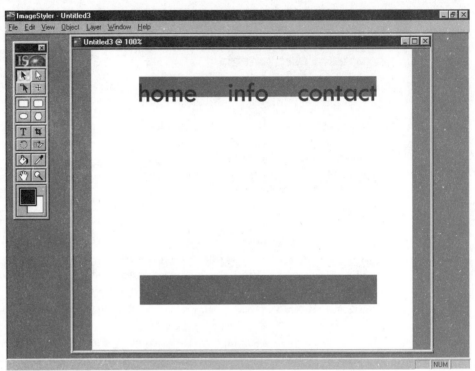

ImageStyler can slice graphics, just like Fireworks can. Since we showed you how to slice graphics with Fireworks, though, this time we thought you'd like to see how ImageStyler can be used to create mouseover graphics and the related JavaScript code with efficiency and ease.

Let's say you want to create a button with mouseover effects. Using ImageStyler, you can create the image and generate the JavaScript which you'll later add to your Web page using FrontPage. To create an image and set it up for JavaScript coding:

1. Create the image you want in ImageStyler. The image appears in the ImageStyler JavaScript palette:

2. Click the New icon to create another instance of the image in the onMouseOver layer. The modifications you make to this layer appear when a mouse passes over the original image.

3. Now modify the image attributes for the mouseover action (shape, color, type). Once you're satisfied, click the New icon again to create another instance of the original image for the onMouseDown layer.

4. You can leave this layer the same (common) or make it different in some way (less common but potentially fun!). Your modifications, if any, are seen when the mouse is clicked over the image.

5. Once again, click the New icon to create another instance of the image, this time for the onMouseOut layer. As the mouse leaves the image, the modifications you make to this layer are what appear on the screen.

6. To attach a URL to any layer (usually onMouseOut), select that layer. Then, in the Web palette, type in the associated URL:

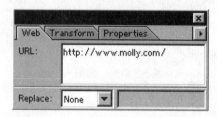

7. Select File ➤ Export As. The AutoLayout dialog appears. In the Filename text box, name your file for HTML export and click Save.

ImageStyler now creates the necessary JavaScript to the HTML file and the necessary images to an images directory underneath the directory where you've placed the HTML file.

Now you can modify the resulting script to match your needs—rename the buttons, change the link information, and so on. To do this:

1. Open the ImageReady HTML file in Notepad.

2. Open the FrontPage file you want to add the image and script to in FrontPage.

3. In Page view, select the HTML tab so you can modify the HTML.

4. Copy the area from the opening <SCRIPT> tag to the closing </SCRIPT> tag from the ImageReady HTML into the <HEAD> section of your FrontPage HTML document.

5. Copy the area that manages the images (denoted by comment tags) into the appropriate section of your FrontPage HTML document.

6. Save your FrontPage file.

Working with ImageStyler JavaScript

The JavaScript created by ImageStyler will appear as a complete HTML page. For best results, you'll need to place appropriate parts of the script within your FrontPage HTML. Here's the raw code generated by ImageStyler:

```
<Html>
<Head>
<Title>
Untitled1
</Title>
<Script Language="JavaScript">
<!-Adobe(R) ImageStyler(TM) 1.0 Generated JavaScript. Please do not edit.
isamap = new Object();
isamap[0] = "_df"
isamap[1] = "_ov"
isamap[2] = "_ot"
isamap[3] = "_dn"


function isimgact(id, act)
{
   if(document.images) document.images[id].src = eval( "isimages." + id +
isamap[act] + ".src");
}


if (document.images) { // ensure browser can do JavaScript rollovers.
isimages = new Object();
isimages.Untitled1_df = new Image();
isimages.Untitled1_df.src = "images/untitled1image.gif";
```

MASTERING THE OPPORTUNITIES CONTINUED

```
isimages.Untitled1_ov = new Image();
isimages.Untitled1_ov.src = "images/untitled1imageov.gif";


isimages.Untitled1_ot = new Image();
isimages.Untitled1_ot.src = "images/untitled1imageot.gif";


isimages.Untitled1_dn = new Image();
isimages.Untitled1_dn.src = "images/untitled1imagedn.gif";


}
// end generated JavaScript. ->
</Script>
</Head>
<Body BGcolor="#ffffff">


<!- The table is not formatted nicely because some browsers cannot join
images in table cells if there are any hard carriage returns in a TD. ->


<Table Border="0" CellSpacing="0" CellPadding="0" >
   <Tr>
           <Td Width="116" Height="166"></Td>
           <Td Width="88" Height="166"></Td>
   </Tr>
   <Tr>
           <Td Width="116" Height="73"></Td>
           <Td Width="88" Height="73"><a Href="http://www.molly.com/"
OnMouseOver="isimgact( 'Untitled1',1)" OnMouseOut="isimgact(
'Untitled1',2)" OnMouseDown="isimgact( 'Untitled1',3)" ><Img
Src="images/untitled1image.gif" Border="0" Height="73" Width="88"
Name="Untitled1" Alt=""></a></Td>
   </Tr>
```

MASTERING THE OPPORTUNITIES CONTINUED

```
    <Tr>
            <Td><Img Src="images/is_single_pixel_gif.gif" Alt=""
Width="116" Height="1"></Td>
            <Td><Img Src="images/is_single_pixel_gif.gif" Alt=""
Width="88" Height="1"></Td>
    </Tr>
</Table>



<!-Adobe(R) ImageStyler(TM) DataMap1.0 DO NOT EDIT
end DataMap ->
</Body>
</Html>
```

You'll see that the graphics are unnamed, and there's HTML code that won't be necessary when you copy and paste to FrontPage. You can now rename your buttons (be sure to rename the actual graphics as well as the buttons in the code). If the original script code is "untitled1," simply use FrontPage's search and replace feature to change the name to its proper name, such as "arrow."

Now copy and paste as described in the exercise above, and your JavaScript will be ready to go.

If all of the necessary images are appropriately named and placed in the proper images subdirectory, your mouseover JavaScript will work beautifully (see Figure 18.7).

MASTERING WHAT'S ONLINE

Imaging and Illustration Applications

You can learn more about the applications discussed in this section by visiting the program developer's home sites. For Adobe products, visit www.adobe.com. Macromedia products can be found at www.macromedia.com.

FIGURE 18.7

*Different mouse states
of an image*

noAction

onMouseOver

onMouseDown

onMouseOut

Helpful Utilities

Whether as plug-ins compatible with your imaging and illustration software or as stand-alone applications, there are two kinds of utilities you will find very, very helpful: compression utilities and filters. This section talks about some of the best compression utilities and filters available, where to get them, and what kind of results you can expect when using them.

Compression Utilities

Compression utilities allow you to make very specific decisions about how to optimize your graphics. These utilities will look at the best way to make your files smaller for the Web, while keeping the best visual integrity possible. While you can use any raster imaging program to create GIFs or JPEGs, it takes a fine hand to do so with the best compression results. What's more, it's time consuming!

Compression software can often make comparisons for you and help you decide which file format is best for the look you want. Furthermore, compression applications can batch-process numerous files at a time, making large jobs easy to manage.

DeBabelizer Pro

Used in a variety of media applications including TV and multimedia presentations, DeBabelizer Pro is a very sophisticated optimization program that can be used to optimize and batch-process graphics for the Web.

PART

III

**Advanced Web
Graphic Design**

Because DeBabelizer is such a high-end program, it's expensive. If you already have it, great! You can use it to optimize your Web graphics. But, if you don't have it, we recommend first looking to some of the other easy-to-use and affordable options below. However, be aware that if you are looking for employment as a professional designer, you may be expected to have or learn DeBabelizer Pro skills.

Adobe ImageReady

Another excellent Adobe application, ImageReady is designed specifically to optimize graphics for Web use. As with ImageStyler, the ImageReady interface is a lot like Photoshop, so it's easy for Photoshop users to use ImageReady.

ImageReady offers real-time compression and batch processing, as well as tools for animating images.

Ulead SmartSaver

Ulead creates impressive products at very cost-effective prices. SmartSaver lets you do everything DeBabelizer Pro does for the Web but eliminates the overhead. In Figure 18.8, you can compare images to see which results will be most effective for your needs, and you can output batches of optimized files, too.

FIGURE 18.8

Comparing images in Ulead's SmartSaver

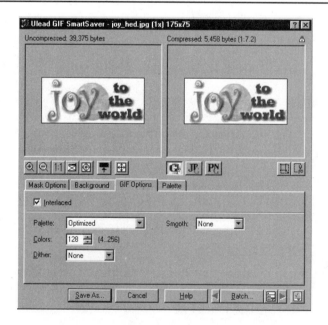

MASTERING WHAT'S ONLINE

Optimization Tools

Downloads, tutorials, and support for our favorite optimization tools can be found at these Web sites:

DeBabelizer Pro: www.debabelizer.com

Adobe ImageReady: www.adobe.com/prodindex/imageready/main.html

Ulead SmartSaver: www.webutilities.com

DeBabelizer is also available on this book's accompanying CD-ROM.

Filters

The way you present a graphic is as important as the graphic's quality itself. A well-processed image, while strong on its own, is rendered even more classy when enhanced with drop shadows, feathered edges, and geometric edge designs, just to name a few.

A *filter* is a small program, usually run right within your graphics program, that will help add these and innumerable other special effects to your page. Special effects can be achieved through the use of plug-ins to Photoshop or Photoshop-style imaging programs.

Alien Skin Software

A very popular suite of plug-ins, Alien Skin offers some cool filters including its Eye Candy and Xenofex packages. You can use Eye Candy with Photoshop and related raster-based programs to add shadows, glows, motion trails, jiggles, weaves, and water drops to your images. Examples of Xenofex's Baked Earth and Puzzle effects are shown in Figures 18.9 and 18.10, respectively; Figure 18.11 shows Eye Candy's Chrome effect.

FIGURE 18.9

Xenofex Baked Earth effect

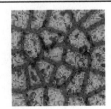

PART

III

Advanced Web Graphic Design

FIGURE 18.10

Xenofex Puzzle Effect

FIGURE 18.11

Eye Candy Chrome Effect

Auto F/X

One of the best ways to make a Web site look polished is to enhance images with professional edges (see Figure 18.12). Auto F/X offers three wonderful packages of edge effects for photos. You can also create interesting type effects with Auto F/X's Typographic Edges feature.

FIGURE 18.12

Adding an edge effect with Auto F/X

Kai's Power Tools

Perhaps the most popular of all filter packages, Kai's Power Tools can help you create Web buttons and complex color blends. Other filters include a "page curl" effect, twirls, and visual noise. One of the handiest features for Web designers is the Seamless Welder. This filter enables you to make tiles that are completely smooth, without unwanted edges or repetitions—perfect for Web backgrounds.

MASTERING WHAT'S ONLINE

Where to Get Graphic Filters

Use these helpful Web sites to get graphic filters and learn how to apply filter techniques:

Alien Skin: www.alienskin.com (You'll also find Alien Skin demos on this book's accompanying CD-ROM.)

Auto F/X: www.autofx.com

Kai's Power Tools: www.metacreations.com/kpt/

Scanning Techniques

Undoubtedly, you're going to want to scan photos, art, or objects at some point. Ideally, you'll be equipped with a good color flatbed scanner. They're very reasonably priced these days, and you should have no trouble finding one that will meet your needs.

And what might those needs be? Well, to start off with, scanners are excellent ways to get images from the everyday world into digital format. For the Web, this simply means good quality at low resolution. That's good news on your pocketbook, and on the demanding learning curve necessary to become a power user of Adobe products.

Scanning is simple, but scanning carefully means your results will be clearer, crisper, and more professional looking. Here are a few basic scanning rules you should follow to help make your scans the best possible quality:

- Begin with your imaging software. Photoshop, PhotoDraw, Image Composer, ImageReady, ImageStyler, and Fireworks all allow you to scan images.
- Ever seen the acronym GIGO? It means "Garbage-in, Garbage-out." Ideally, all of your source materials will be of high quality to begin with! If your photo is

PART

III

Advanced Web
Graphic Design

blurry or your drawing has a coffee stain on it, these elements will be picked up by the scanner and make your job much more difficult.

- Your scanner bed should be free from dust and dirt. Clean it according to your manufacturer's directions.

- Similarly, your source material should be clean. Use any commercial canned air pack (available at office supply and most art stores) to dust photos without touching them directly.

- Graphics for the Web will always end up at 72 dots per inch (DPI). Many people like to scan at 300 DPI and then reduce, claiming that this helps with quality. We're not convinced this is true, but try it and see if it doesn't work best. Either way, you should scan at 72 or 300 DPI and make sure your output image is set to 72 DPI.

- Once you've scanned your image, crop and size it accordingly. Use interesting cropping—perhaps a close-up of the face or eye is more interesting than the whole image itself.

- Add shadows, textures, edge effects, and other styles using filters for professional results.

- Always optimize your graphics properly. To do so, follow the guidelines in Chapter 9, or use one of the optimization applications discussed in this chapter.

Finding Stock Materials on the Web

Professional designers work from an assortment of stock photos, clip art, and type faces, and there are many resources on the Web geared toward helping you achieve your goals of great-looking design. Whether you need professional-quality materials or are looking for good clip art for a personal site, you can always find what you need, right online.

 TIP If you're closer to the professional end of the spectrum, think about beginning a library of stock materials. For each project you do, write in the cost of a necessary typeface or photo set. Your client will foot the bill, and you can keep the materials for future use. If this sounds a bit awkward, remember that this is standard operating procedure for graphic designers—just be legitimate in your purchases!

Here are some recommended resources for your professional stock photos, art, and typographic needs:

- Adobe offers excellent typefaces at www.adobe.com.

- Eyewire houses an excellent line of quality stock materials including great clip art and fonts. You can get a regular paper catalog delivered via snail mail, or you can browse and purchase stock materials online at www.eyewire.com.

- Photodisc provides some of the cleanest, sharpest photographic images available. A visit to their Web site, www.photodisc.com, will provide you with a shopping source for plenty of stock photos, backgrounds, and links to other sites of interest. Free membership entitles you to downloads of comp art and photos; you can also order a standard mail catalog.

- For an inexpensive (albeit less professional-quality) alternative, check out Art-Today. For a very reasonable membership fee, ArtToday gives you unlimited downloads at www.arttoday.com.

If you're looking for casual, fun clip art, photos, backgrounds, and animations, here are a few of our favorite starting points:

- The Internet Baglady has searched for (and found!) a wide number of inexpensive and free ways to get art for and information about building a Web site: www.dumpsterdive.com

- Caboodles of Clip Art is a perfect starting place for those new to design: www.caboodles.com

- Microsoft Images Gallery offers a great selection of images from Microsoft: www.microsoft.com/gallery/images/default.asp

---

 NOTE As with scanning, digital type and art demand that you work with the best images available; color, crop, and modify to suit your needs, and export at 72 DPI.

GIF Animation Programs

GIF animations are extremely useful for a variety of reasons. Whether you're looking to spice up a page with a bit of visual intrigue or you need an animation for an online ad, you'll want to explore a variety of imaging programs that allow you to make GIF animations.

PART

III

Advanced Web Graphic Design

A few tips about working with animations:

- If you're considering using an animation on a page, stop and think first. What purpose does it serve? Is it really necessary?

- Too many items on a page that blink and move detract from rather than enhance a design. Stick to one animation per page, at most!

- GIF animations should still conform to small file size requirements. This means paying close attention to each individual cell of the animation.

- One way to avoid large file size is to restrict the number of colors down to a handful and keep movement simple.

If you plan, design, and apply animations with care, you're bound to have excellent results. Of course, you'll need to have a great GIF animation program. Here's a few popular programs that you'll want to check out.

- GIF Movie Gear is an award-winning animation tool that has powerful palette control. This allows you to optimize each individual cell for maximum file optimization. Furthermore, it will throw out any repetitive colors or information.

- Ulead GIF Animator is another of Ulead's excellent, low-cost PC Web solutions. You can use this program to create sweeps, fades, and fills with very little learning curve.

- Microsoft's GIF Animator program works with Microsoft's Image Composer. Features include drag and drop directly from Image Composer; addition of special effects such as loops, spins, and fades; and automatic as well as custom palette optimization.

- GIF Construction Set is a popular shareware tool will allow you to create animated GIFs using a wizard that walks you through the simplified process of creating an animated image. Advanced users can build individual images themselves.

MASTERING WHAT'S ONLINE

Where to Get GIF Animation Tools

Use these Web sites to download GIF animation tools:

GIF Movie Gear: www.gamani.com

Ulead GIF Animator: www.ulead.com

Microsoft GIF Animator: www.microsoft.com/imagecomposer/gifanimatior/gifanin.htm

GIF Construction Set: www.mindworkshop.com/alchemy/gifcon.html

Up Next

Now you're not only thinking like a designer, but you've got the tools to create professional quality design work. But how do you put this all together in the context of FrontPage? Not to worry—we'll show you how in the next chapter, *Creating Advanced Sites with FrontPage*.

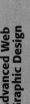

PART

III

**Advanced Web
Graphic Design**

CHAPTER 19

Creating Advanced Sites with FrontPage

In the past several chapters, you've focused on understanding advanced design concepts and learning about a variety of tools that can help you turn those concepts into reality. This chapter combines the lessons recently learned with the FrontPage knowledge you have gathered throughout this book and teaches you a process by which you can build your sites from start-to-finish.

At this point in your learning process, it's important to look at the professional approach to site production. Even though some of this information is going to be familiar—we started you out with some of the same tips and tricks mentioned in this chapter—this time around we're going to give you the information in the context of all the things you already know, moving you from the creation of more basic page creation to the development and management of Web sites on a refined level.

There's nothing particularly startling or new about the information in this chapter. Anyone who has ever worked in project management or in a production setting will be familiar with the basic steps, which include:

- Pre-production planning
- Production techniques
- Publication
- Post-production concerns

Many people who are either looking into Web design for the first time or wanting to find professional solutions overlook the time-honored production process. Whether this is a result of enthusiasm to get to the end result or simply an oversight, it's hard to say.

Fortunately, FrontPage 2000 has a variety of built-in tools to help you manage site development. These tools, combined with a clear vision of the road from site start to site launch, the development process is sure to be much more standardized and well-managed, and the result invariably more professional.

Pre-Production

The strategizing you'll do before actually sitting down to create graphics and use FrontPage to make your site come to life is possibly the most determining factor in the success of your Web site. It is here that critical issues of site intent, audience demographic, scheduling, procuring content, working with clients, creating a look and feel, planning technology, and building your site map happen.

Yes, that's a long list—as well it should be. It's very dangerous to go out into the wilds of the Web without understanding the reason you're doing a site and managing the procedural aspects of that site. This is true of all Web sites, but it is *especially* true of any site that has commercial or promotional intent. If you fail to plan properly, there is no infrastructure upon which to build. Without that structure, the site is going to be more costly, time consuming, and possibly more geared toward failure than success.

The best way to minimize risk is to *plan well*. We cannot emphasize the importance of this phase enough! We've seen many instances where developers rush into the job, only to find themselves spending a lot of time and money to go back and do it right. And, in all honesty, we've learned the importance of this by making the mistake of poor planning ourselves. Hopefully, our experience will help you avoid making logistical errors and create a smoother development approach.

Understanding Your Web Site

As with any project, an understanding of the project's long and short term goals, general intent, and audience is necessary. Furthermore, there are issues surrounding scheduling and how to work with clients. In this section, we'll look at each of these issues in detail and give you some inside tips on how to manage these first important steps in advanced site management.

Site Intent and Goals

What is your site's intent? In other words, what purpose does your site serve? We're sure you've seen as many sites as we have that, when arriving at the main page, have no definite communication of purpose.

From the get-go, you need to let your audience know who you are, what the site visitor will find on your site, and of course, give ample information about how to get from one place to the next with ease.

One of the reasons why intent is often missing from a site is the developers of that site failed to clarify their own goals before embarking on the design of the site. Developing a Web site takes time, and many people are in a rush to just get the site up and running. But whether you're designing a site for commercial purposes or for sharing pictures of your newborn baby with the world, clearly understanding your specific intent is going to help you build a clear, concise site.

A good exercise is to take time out and brainstorm your site intent. If you're working with a group of people, schedule a few hours of meeting time—order lunch in and get a white board where someone can write down ideas as they are introduced into the conversation.

TIP   If you are working in a company setting, refer to your existing business plan for guidance in terms of short- and long-term goals. Your company business plan is a powerful guide for your Web site intent—and in turn, plans for your Web site can affect the company plan.

If you're working alone, take some old-fashioned tools (we like yellow legal pads and fine point pens) to your favorite spot—a coffee house or quiet outdoor area is perfect! The idea is to be somewhere you are comfortable and *away* from the computer—you want to be creative here, letting ideas flow.

Begin to talk or think about what it is you really want to *do* with your site. Begin with the short-term. Do you have a specific product you want to sell? Maybe you have some ultrasound pictures of your baby or audio tapes of the baby's heartbeat. Think about what you want and what you have right now. Write down everything that comes to mind, without thinking in orderly terms—there's time for that later.

Take a little break before moving on to the next phase: brainstorming long-term goals. The break is important because it will clear your head, and the long-term goals list is sure to serve you well. The information you gather regarding longer-term vision will help you determine how to prepare your site for future growth.

 MASTERING THE OPPORTUNITIES

Sample Goal List

Here's a sample list of short- and long-term goals for a small company that sells hand-made greeting cards and gifts.

Short-Term Goals:

- To showcase cards and gifts in our current inventory
- To add new real-time venues for our cards and gift items
- To sell inventory direct to online site visitors

Long-Term Goals:

- Add more artists and styles to our inventory
- Expand inventory to include other items including t-shirts and hats
- Showcase the affiliated artwork of our contributing artists

> ◀ **MASTERING THE OPPORTUNITIES CONTINUED**
>
> From these simple lists, you can begin to see how this practice can clarify your site intent and plan. For the short term, you may find that you will need to have space to show off current inventory, include a way to directly communicate with potential outlets for product, and include secure, online shopping for your site-based customers.
>
> When you examine the long-term goals, you will see that you'll need to easily expand the existing Web site to include more inventory, diverse inventory, and finally, add an entire gallery section to show off the related work of contributing artists.
>
> Consideration of short- and long-term goals not only helps visitors because your communicated intent is clear, but it helps you know how to design your site well from today's needs through to tomorrow's vision.

Knowing Your Audience

Another critical step in the pre-production process is knowing who your audience is. We've made mention of this throughout the book, but now we're going to express in very clear terms just why this is so important.

Knowledge of audience, combined with site intent, creates the baseline from which *all decisions* you make about the look and feel, design, structure, and technology grow. Without this knowledge, the risk for failure is very high. This becomes especially true in team environments working under deadlines—at that point the risk is actually magnified rather than distributed. (See Chapter 28, *Using FrontPage with Microsoft's Visual InterDev*, for more information about risk management.)

Getting to know your audience is a complicated process and often is a recipe of existing statistical data mixed with one part guessing and one part post-launch tracking. But even just getting close to an idea using similar brainstorming methods described in the prior section can help avoid serious problems.

So just how do you get to know your audience? Begin with what you have and what you know. Many businesses keep information about who their customer base is. If you're working in a situation like this, it's a great place to start—get out those statistics and write down exactly who has been buying or using your products and services. If your site is more geared toward a personal page, it's still important to think about audience in general. Are children going to visit? Who do you really think is most interested in the site's information? Who definitely will *not* be visiting your site, at least intentionally?

Now, begin to question whether there are natural additions you can make to this existing group of people. For example, if your company has traditionally sold specialty auto parts to young males, it is possible that there are women online who might have need for or want to purchase these specialty parts? If the answer is yes, expand your demographic audience to include those women! Similarly, if you are putting up a site dedicated to your local bowling league, you might want to include information for bowlers outside of your geographical area too. Any time you can expand your audience without straining your budget, you potentially add a new site visitor, client, or customer.

Finally, you'll want to consider a demographics management program for your Web site. This is particularly important if you are doing electronic business, managing an online community, or are in any way concerned about tracking where your site visitors are geographically, what kinds of browsers and technology they are using, and how often they visit your site. Keeping statistical information like this helps you to modify your site as the demographic changes, maximizing your Web efforts.

MASTERING WHAT'S ONLINE

For a comprehensive review on commerce tools including statistical tracking software, check out `builder.com/Business/Affordable/index.html`.

Setting Up a Schedule

Scheduling the construction of your site is important if you have a deadline to meet. You'll want to fairly address time concerns and allow for adjustments, changes in direction, team members getting sick—planning for risky situations can help minimize the problems you might encounter when under heavy deadlines. And, even if you're on your own, setting up a schedule can sometimes help keep you organized and on-track when setting about building a Web site.

Schedules should be committed to—if you're working with a client, that schedule and dated milestones should appear within your service agreement or contract. If you're planning for yourself, set your own goals and stick to them as best as you can.

There are many software products on the market that manage schedules. Users of FrontPage most likely have Microsoft Outlook installed as well. Outlook has excellent calendar management capabilities. You can also use FrontPage's Task view to set up and manage tasks in a timely fashion, which we'll discuss later in this chapter.

Working with Clients

For those of you designing sites for others, working with your client(s) can be either a joy or a headache! Here are some general tips for client management that might help you out:

- *Always* treat clients with respect—and expect the same in return.

- Always keep the lines of communication open.

- Professional sites should be backed by a service agreement or formal contract.

- Be clear and specific about your goals and timeline.

- Be precise about milestone dates and payment—on both ends! The client will need to know what he or she must provide to you in terms of content, and you will need to turn that content into a product in a timely fashion. Billing statements should be sent out as previously agreed upon, and your client should pay on time.

- Always let a client know what you provide and what they will have to go elsewhere to get. For example, you should be happy to incorporate a pre-existing logo into a Web design, but you shouldn't design that logo unless you are getting paid appropriately and unless this is a service you are willing to provide.

- Provide clients with ample information and time to address needs. However, if a client is taking an unusual amount of time, clearly communicate boundaries in a supportive way.

- Know that sometimes the client is going to want to include design elements that you know are out-of-line or problematic. If a client wants you to do something that doesn't make good design sense, explain that in respectful terms to the client. If he or she still wants you to comply, try for a compromise. If all else fails, defer to your client.

- Never sell yourself short. Clients who pay less for professional work are often the ones who complain the most. Offer quality, honest, professional work in turn for fair and timely compensation.

- Meet your deadlines! If you see a problem with a deadline, be sure to communicate this to the client immediately, and make appropriate arrangements.

Good luck! If you have trouble with a client, or if you hire a company to work with you that is problematic, remember that you may have contractual rights allowing for the termination of the business agreement. In the best-case scenario, your project will run smoothly, because both the client and you, the designer, understand exactly what is expected of each of you every step of the way.

PART

III

Advanced Web Graphic Design

Designing Content

Once you have your groundwork done—a clear idea of your site's intent, your site goals, and the site audience— it's time to use this information as a means of determining how the site content will be designed.

What is content? It's a Web designer's term used to describe the elements of your site, including text, images, and technology. *Designing content* means organizing your content in such a way that it works logically and esthetically.

To design content, you'll need to examine how the site will be formally structured, how it will look, and what technology it will require in order to function properly.

Building the Site's Structure

Later in this chapter, we'll examine how to use FrontPage to set up your site. But first, you need to organize your content into logical groups.

Begin by collecting your content. Assemble all the materials you'll be using for the site. You should gather up printed and electronic text, photographic materials, digital artwork, and any other information you require to make the site work.

Using the research you've done regarding intent and audience to guide you, study the content. You'll want to set up areas of your site—list each relevant area by topic. Let's say your son has asked you to do a site for his alternative rock band, Cat's Eye. In this case, you might include main topics such as member bios, tour dates, audio files, video clips, fan club information, and a guestbook for site visitors to sign.

Once you have the main areas figured out, make a list of the content you will want within each area including the text, graphics, other media, and any necessary technology. Here's a sample table:

Member Bios	Tour Dates	Audio	Video	Fan Club Info	Guestbook
Charlie's bio	East Coast	All Too True	Cat's Eye	Special deals	
Demi's bio	West Coast	This Moment	In the Heat	Posters, hats, t-shirts	
Alicia's bio	Pacific Northwest	Now and Then			
Steph's bio	Europe	Get it Goin'			
Marcus's bio	Asia				

Study this table for a moment, and you'll see how a site structure begins to evolve. All of the main topic headers become your primary level of navigation. Within those main topics, you might either have a page, or several pages, creating a second tier.

For example, each of the member bios can form a second tier of information, as can the tour dates and fan club info, with each sub-topic becoming a separate page. In the case of audio and video, there's not too much available at this point, so a single page should suffice. However, depending upon the short- and long-term goals of the site, you may anticipate adding sections as more information becomes available, and as the audience demands it.

Now that your information is organized, it's time to think about how the site will be visually designed.

Creating a Look and Feel

Just what *is* "look and feel?" Well, this is a design term used to describe the visual sense of a site. It encompasses the many issues discussed in Chapter 17, *Understanding Advanced Web Design*, including color, shape, space, layout, and type—and how all of these things look together to send a visually-based message to your audience.

Because you have critical information from your intent and audience analysis, you're in a good position to begin determining what your site should look like. At this point, you're still in the brainstorming phase—nothing is being committed to hard graphics or HTML yet.

What you want to do now is seriously consider your audience and intent in the context of what look and feel is appropriate and effective. This can take an experienced visual designer, or it at least demands that you do some serious looking into the way professional sites are managed.

 NOTE Refer back to the lessons in Chapter 17. Visual design including shapes, typefaces, and color should all match what you know about your audience and intent.

Let's say you're working with a conservative church to help create a Web site. Your primary short-term goal is to offer information on clergy, schedules, and special events. Your long-term goal is to add a discussion forum where church members can seek support, discuss church directions, and ask questions on religious matters. The audience is the church's existing membership, but you want to make other local, potential members feel welcome. When your community is built, you want to encourage affiliate churches to become involved, creating a non-geographical community with input from a wide range of members and clergy.

Because the church is conservative, we think a neutral color scheme is going to be important. We'd keep our use of shape to a minimum, with religious symbolism being the exception. Navigation would be simple, as many of the members might be older and not as computer-savvy as the younger members. Further, contrast would be high—probably black type on a white background to accommodate everyone's eyesight. From a technology perspective, a light hand is probably best—adding supportive technology where necessary, such as to create the community forum. There should be no other media such as animation or JavaScript. If you do choose to use some subtle mouseover techniques to add a bit of color, just be sure to keep it very simple. All told, this site should be very easy to use and functional, not distracting.

 TIP Want inspiration? Go surfing! Start at your favorite search site, such as Yahoo! (www.yahoo.com) or Infoseek (www.infoseek.com), and look for other sites that are similar in content and purpose to your own. Browse through them and jot down notes. Which sites are strong? Which are confusing, and why? This experience will help you strengthen your ideas and avoid pitfalls.

Now, if your 19-year-old tattoo-loving, pierced son wants that Web site for his alternative rock band and comes to your for help, you've got a different story on your hands! A conservative, quiet, and mainly functional Web site isn't going to go over well with the audience here. You're going to want to have some fun—be a bit wild in your color scheme, more liberal in your use of technology, more creative and inventive in terms of interface.

But does this mean that you won't approach the site with a process? Of course not! After all, this site could mean the launch of your son's successful music career. Sit down and go over the short- and long-term goals with him. Have him brainstorm with you—what is the site's intent? Who is the obvious audience? What about secondary audiences? Working through this process will ensure that your colorful and even edgy site will have the strong foundation it needs.

Sketching and Mocking Up Your Site

With the research you've gathered regarding site intent and audience, you can now begin to sketch out ideas that will bring your Web site concept into page-by-page reality.

Gather your materials and study them hard. Now, instead of jumping right to the computer, it's helpful to the creative process that you pick up a sketch pad and begin drawing out the various sections of your site.

Many Web sites use a main page that serves as the gateway through with all navigation of the site will occur. The *splash page*—a visual first page that sets the tone of the site but contains little, if any, textual information—is not necessary, but it is often helpful in establishing the look and purpose of the site. If you decide you want a splash page, begin by sketching out ideas for it. Be sure to include navigation related to each main topic area. Try out different ideas for this page before moving on to sketches for subsidiary pages. Don't worry about perfection here—the idea is to get your creative juices flowing and come up with some general ideas.

Once you have a sketch that you really like, you can move to the imaging program of your choice (see Chapter 18, *Working with Professional Graphics Programs*). For this sophisticated level of design, we prefer using Photoshop, because we can place each element on a layer. However, other programs including Paint Shop Pro, ImageReady, Fireworks, and ImageStyler allow you to work in layers.

Since the concept is a global one, we'll use Photoshop as our example, and you can adapt to your preferred image editor's unique tools. To begin mocking up your site:

1. In your image editor, select File ➢ New. The New dialog box appears.

2. Create an image size that is no more than 595 pixels wide and at least 295 pixels high (the height will depend upon how long you expect the page to be; 295 is one screen) with a resolution of 72 in RGB mode. Be sure to select the Transparent button. (Note: This setup will vary from image program to image program.)

3. Click OK. Your work area is now set to the first layer.

PART

III

Advanced Web
Graphic Design

4. To this layer, add your background color or design your background graphic look:

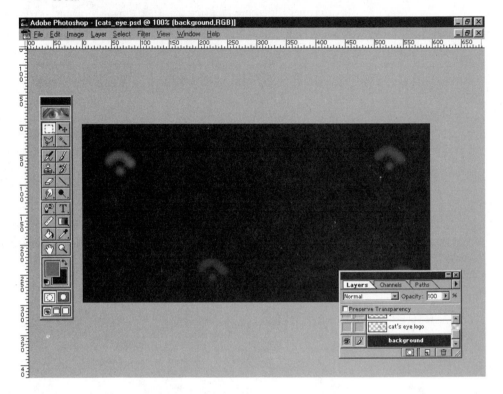

5. Now create a new layer by selecting Layer ➢ New ➢ Layer. On this layer, create the main logo or title, as shown next.

 TIP In Photoshop, you can double-click a layer in the Layers window and give the layer an identifiable name. For example, the background can be named "background," and the layer with your title or logo should be called "logo." This gives you quick access to your individual element information later on.

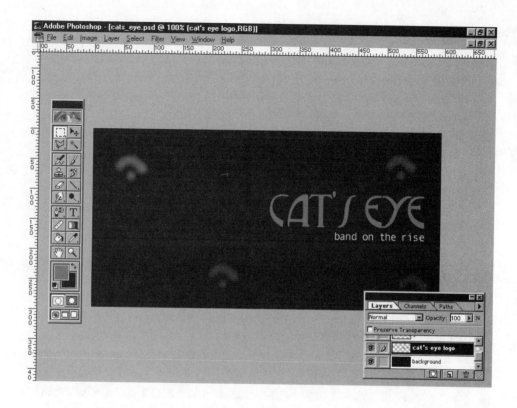

6. Add any navigation you'd like for this page. Typically, each button should be on its own layer (see Figure 19.1)—this allows you more control later on. For example, if you want to duplicate the buttons but use a different color for mouseover effects, keeping each button on a separate layer allows you to do that.

7. Once you've added all the elements you want for this page, save the file by selecting File ➢ Save As. The Save As dialog box appears. Name the file and save it in the native layer format of your imaging program.

FIGURE 19.1

Each of the navigation elements are on their own, individual layer.

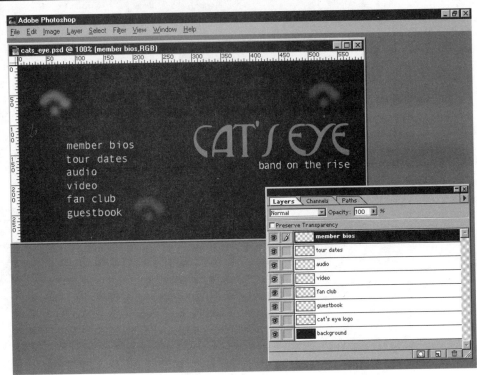

 WARNING Do not flatten your layered image. If you do, you will not be able to go back and access the individual layers later on.

Try a variety of designs, and when you find one that satisfies you and your client's needs, go ahead and build the images using the technique just described.

Planning Necessary Technology

Another excellent point in the process of designing content is to list any particular technology you're going to need for the site. It allows you to anticipate what you'll need to add to your production schedule, and it helps you ensure that both your front- and back-end technology is in place.

If we examine the rock band example, we know immediately that we're going to need to support a variety of technologies including:

- Animation or JavaScript to add lively, interactive components to the site
- Support for audio
- Support for video
- A guestbook

While the church example is less technology-laden, it is still important to note that eventually a forum will be necessary to manage the community discussions. If FrontPage is the desired format for this, you'll to ensure that the host server offers Front-Page extensions. If another method, such as CGI, is desired, it's important to make that decision *right now*. If the site is built and then hosted on a server that doesn't support the technology you wish to add down the road, this could wind up costing extra money as well as placing time demands on everyone involved: site developers, site managers, and site participants.

Production

The production phase of creating a site is where you roll up your sleeves and go to work. You'll be working back and forth between applications, including FrontPage and your imaging program. Depending upon your site needs, you'll also be working on the server-side to set up any scripts or other required elements (see Chapter 25, *Understanding CGI*).

Production work is all the labor that gears you up to actually publish your Web site on the Internet. The following sections will walk you through exactly what you need to do to make a site move from the planning phase, through production, and on out to the Web itself.

Setting Up Directories, Files, and Tasks

As you've worked through the planning of your site, you've collected a lot of important data and set up a powerful structure upon which to build your pages. Now it's a good time to turn to FrontPage and create the physical structure of your site. This will generate a site map, which you can use as your guide for the future of the site's life.

To set up directories for your site:

1. Open FrontPage.
2. Select File ➤ New ➤ Web. The New dialog box appears.

Advanced Web
Graphic Design

3. Highlight One Page Web and click OK. FrontPage creates the necessary Front-Page and images directories and open up a blank, untitled page within the root directory so you can begin working.

To add additional directories:

1. Select Folders view. You'll see the Folder List with your directories and files:

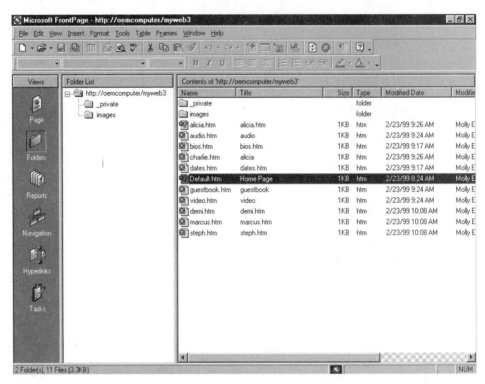

2. Highlight the root directory.

3. Select File ➢ New ➢ Folder. FrontPage adds an untitled folder.

4. Name the folder appropriately.

You now have all the directories for your web.

 TIP You can delete folders that you do not want by right-clicking the folder and selecting Delete from the menu.

Now that you have the map pretty much laid out, you need to set up individual files. To do so:

1. In Folders view, right-click anywhere in the interface. A menu appears.

2. Select New Page from the menu:

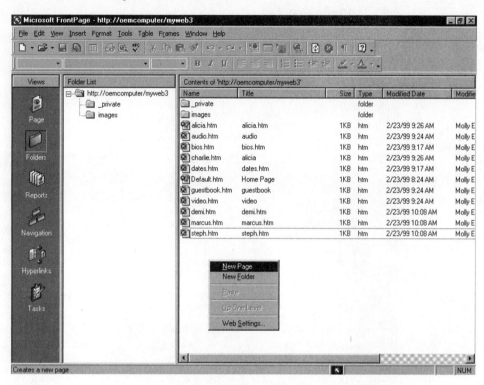

3. A new page appears in the root directory. Name the page appropriately.

Repeat this process until you have created all the pages you have planned for your site. You can always add or delete pages as necessary.

At this point, it's an excellent idea to set your work schedule. To do this, you can associate each file with a task. To set up tasks:

1. In Folders view, highlight the file you want to associate with a task.

2. Right-click and choose Add Task from the menu.

3. The New Task dialog box appears. Fill in the task name, priority, and a description.

4. Click OK.

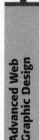

PART

III

Advanced Web
Graphic Design

You can also set up tasks that are not associated with a page. These tasks will help you remember various stages of the production process. To set up a task without a page association:

1. Select Tasks view and click anywhere in the FrontPage interface. A menu appears.

2. Select New Task. The New Task dialog box opens.

3. Fill in the task name, the task priority, and a description.

You'll want to set up as many tasks as necessary to complete the production phase of each page. In Figure 19.2, you can see the types of tasks we've set up for our model site.

FIGURE 19.2

Tasks guide the pro-duction process

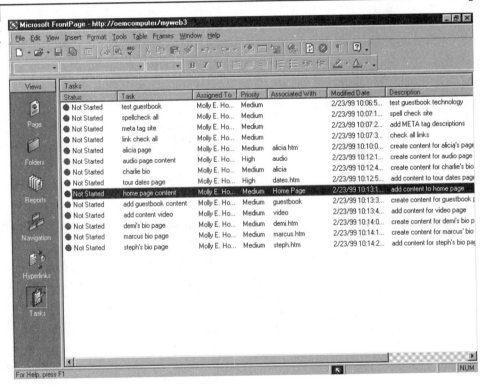

Generating Site Graphics

Now let's move back to the image editor. If you've been able to work in layers, it'll be fairly easy to begin generating the various graphics for your site.

Let's say you developed the splash page for the band Cat's Eye during mock-up. Following the layer techniques, you've set various elements on individual layers. Now all you have to do is isolate those elements and optimize them accordingly. To do this, follow these steps:

1. Open up the layered file in your imaging program.

2. Highlight the layer that has the image you want to process (see Figure 19.3).

3. Using the marquee or selection tool (it will vary depending upon your program), draw a selection around the part of the image you want to keep, making sure you're on the correct layer.

4. Copy and paste the section into a new file.

5. Add any background or transparency color you wish and flatten the file.

FIGURE 19.3

Optimizing image elements layer by layer

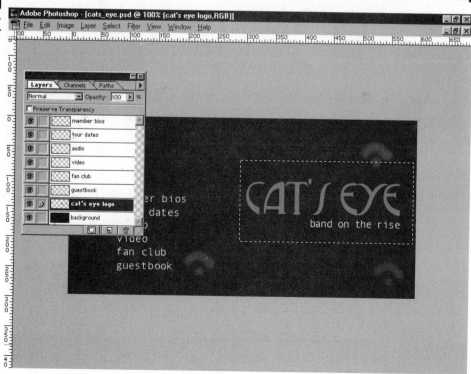

Follow optimization techniques (see Chapter 9, *Designing Graphics for the Web*, and Chapter 18, *Working with Professional Graphics Programs*) to manage your graphics appropriately. Name the graphic you just created and save it to the folder you've set up for your site images.

You'll need to repeat this process for all of your site graphics. If you haven't mocked up all the pages, you may need to do so now, or create individual graphics. You may also need to scan and size photos, and then optimize them for the Web. If that's the case, now's the time to do so! Be sure to add interesting and appropriate design elements to spot art (see Chapter 18) and create any additional graphics you'll need for JavaScript mouseovers, backgrounds, and headers.

Once you've got all the graphics you need, place them in the appropriate folder. Typically, this will be the /images directory off of the root you created earlier.

Page-by-Page Design

You may be wondering why we're working page-by-page rather than with a Web wizard. If this seems a bit tedious, it's simply because you, rather than the software, are responsible for most of the work! For the many readers interested in creating a simple Web site, this may not be the right approach. However, for those interested in really taking sites *over* the top, this is how to gain absolute control of a site's integrity: one page at a time.

Here is the real meat of the production—adding the fun to your site, one page at a time:

1. In Folders view, highlight the file you want to work on.

2. Right-click and select Open from the menu. The page opens in Page view.

3. You can now begin to add the text, graphics, and technology you've prepared for this page.

When you're finished working in a page, be sure to return to Tasks view to either mark the task as complete or modify the task if more work needs to be done.

NOTE   Keeping track of tasks is *very* important, especially if you're working in a team setting. This allows others working on the site to quickly see what's been done— and what needs to be done. For more information on how to use tasks to your advantage, visit Chapter 7, *Managing Tasks*.

Continue working on your pages until you've completed all the text and graphic work for each page. This process is the heart of Web site production—it will take the most time. If you've done your preparation well, the work will go much more smoothly than if you had just opened FrontPage and randomly went to work.

Preparing Your Site for Publication

Once your text, graphics, and technology have been properly added to each individual page, you'll want to take several more steps before publishing your site to the Web.

Copyedit and spell check all pages.   This is an *extremely* important step and should be done for *every* Web site you design. FrontPage will help; it has a built-in spell checker that you can use to ensure proper spelling (see Chapter 24, *Site Maintenance and Promotion*). For high-end professional sites, it's a good idea to have a copyeditor on staff or hire a copyeditor to oversee your content and ensure that your text is well-written and consistent.

Test all links.   It's crucial to be sure that all of your links—whether within your site or to other sites on the Web—are working properly. Chapter 24 gives you step-by-step instructions on using FrontPage to check links.

Add META tags where appropriate.   META tagging is a process by which you can aid your site in getting properly promoted on search engines. Adding META tag keywords and descriptions is commonplace for all commercial and hobbyist Web sites, although they may not be necessary in the case of private intranet and extranet publications. See Chapter 24 for more information on how to properly tag your pages for identification purposes.

Test Your Pages.   Using different browsers and platforms, check to be sure that all of your pages for Internet publication look good—no matter the screen resolution, the browser type and version, or the operating system.

 NOTE See Chapter 16, *Cross-Browser Design*, for details on how to properly plan and test your site for a variety of browsers.

If you pass all of these milestones, you can confidently move on to publishing your Web site. Publication is the movement of all of your produced work onto the server where the site will reside. See Chapter 8, *Publishing Your Pages*, for a comprehensive look at the publishing process.

PART

III

Advanced Web
Graphic Design

Post-Production

Once your site is published, all of the hard work you've done preparing for it will have paid off. Your site will be well-organized with clear intent, appropriate content for your audience, and attractive design. You'll also have tested the site locally for spelling, grammar, link integrity, and cross-browser concerns.

But now that the site resides on your server, live for the Internet audience, it's important to not forget that the site still requires your attention. Here are some issues you should address after your site has been produced and published:

Check content live.   Be sure all your graphics, links, and technology are working properly on the server, and check these regularly.

Follow maintenance and promotion guidelines.   In order to boost your potential success, you'll want to efficiently maintain and promote your site (see Chapter 24).

Prepare for the future.   Using your long-term goals as a guide, decide when and how it will be necessary and appropriate to add content to your site, expand the site, and even redesign the site to keep it contemporary and interesting.

Up Next

This chapter has set you up with a process you can apply to any Web site project for management success. With this strong methodology behind you, you can now move on to setting the stage for fully maximizing your Web sites with Microsoft Office integration and a variety of programming, maintenance, and development techniques.

PART IV

Taking Your Webs to the Top

LEARN TO:

- *Use other Microsoft Office applications in tandem with FrontPage*

- *Apply JavaScript and DHTML to your pages*

- *Add ActiveX and Java components*

- *Work with databases*

- *Successfully promote and maintain your site*

CHAPTER 20

Integrating Sites with Microsoft Office

Because FrontPage is part of the Microsoft Office family, it is highly integrated with its sibling members. This means that you can use existing Office programs that allow you to save your Office documents as HTML files and to integrate your Office programs with your Web browser.

There are many ways you can use Office to enhance your Web building experience. You can convert tables you've made with Word or spreadsheets created with Excel into HTML tables at the drop of a hat. Anything you can make with Office, you can turn into a Web page: databases, annual reports, personal or company schedules, and multimedia presentations. In this chapter, we'll show you how to use FrontPage's officemates including Word, Excel, PowerPoint, Publisher, and Access to create content for your Web site or company intranet.

 TIP You can also copy text and spreadsheets from within Word or Excel and paste them right into FrontPage, where they will appear with all of their existing Word or Excel formatting.

Most of the Office 2000 programs include a Web toolbar you can use to integrate your Web browser with your Office programs. This is true for Word, Excel, PowerPoint, Publisher, and Access. Furthermore, any URLs typed into an Office program will automatically be embedded as live links—making your entire Office suite completely joined with the Internet.

 NOTE See the sidebar "Word versus FrontPage" for tips on opening Office documents with FrontPage, cutting and pasting text between Word and FrontPage, and using Word's HTML templates.

Making Office 2000 Work with Your Web Browser

You can use the Web toolbar in Excel, PowerPoint, and Access to work with your Web browser; Word has the same toolbar, too. Generally, you'll want to use your "real" Web browser to wander the Internet, but the Office 2000 Web toolbar that comes with these programs acts like a browser and is especially useful when you're working with Office documents that you're in the process of exporting to HTML.

To view the Web toolbar from an Office 2000 program's menu bar, select View ➤ Toolbars ➤ Web, and it'll pop onto the window, directly below the Standard toolbar.

You might notice that the buttons on the Web toolbar are the same as those you'd find on Internet Explorer's toolbar. You can use these buttons to control the behavior of your browser from the Office program's window. (This is true even if your default Web browser is Netscape Navigator instead of Internet Explorer.) Using Access as an example, you can type a Web page URL in the Address text box and press Enter, and Access will launch your Web browser and open that page. The rest of the buttons also work as standard browser buttons, with the added feature that you can designate a Start Page and Favorites pages that are different from those you normally use with your Web browser.

Using Word to Create HTML Documents

Microsoft Word converts your Word documents into HTML pages automatically, so you don't even have to worry about coding them or opening them in FrontPage and applying all the formatting with FrontPage editing tools. This is especially convenient for tables, lists, and text formatting you've created in Microsoft Word—you can readily convert them into HTML tables and lists, so you don't have to start from scratch.

NOTE While it's possible to use Word as an HTML editor, Word is not nearly as robust or flawless an editor as FrontPage, so we're going to focus on converting content from Word format to HTML format.

Converting Word Files to HTML

You can convert your existing files to HTML in a snap. To convert a Microsoft Word file to HTML, just follow these steps:

1. From the Microsoft Word menu bar, select File ➤ Open, and use the Open dialog box that appears to open the file you want to convert to HTML.

2. From Word's menu bar, select File ➤ Save As A Web Page. The Save As A Web Page dialog box appears.

3. Be sure to give your HTML file a name that's Web-friendly; spaces and punctuation aren't generally allowed in the filenames of Web pages, although you can include underscores, and the filenames can be as long as you like (or as long as you are willing to type them out).

4. Click Save, and the Save As dialog box closes, returning you to the Word window.

You'll see your new Web page displayed in the Word window.

After you save a file as an HTML document, you can use the View menu to toggle between the HTML code and the WYSIWYG, MS Word view of the document. To view the source code, from Word's menu bar, select View ➢ HTML Source.

Once you've converted your Word document to HTML, you have several options:

- Continue to work with the document in Microsoft Word.

- Import the document into FrontPage, and work with it there (See Chapter 2 for more on importing files).

- Open the document in your Web browser to double-check its appearance.

Adding Hyperlinks to Word Files

You can also create Web pages from scratch using Word. Just create your Word document as you normally would, and when you save it, follow the steps outlined in the section titled "Converting Word Files to HTML" to save it as an HTML file.

It's easy to add hyperlinks and other HTML elements to your documents, too. To do so, follow these steps:

1. With Word open and a page in view, highlight the text you want to use as a link.

2. From Word's menu bar, select Insert ➢ Hyperlink. The Insert Hyperlink dialog box appears.

3. In the Type The File or Web Page Name text box, type the URL for the document to which you want to link. You can link to a full URL on the Web or to the URL of a file in your FrontPage web.

4. Click OK to close the Hyperlink dialog box and return to the Word window, where you'll see your link underlined in blue. It is now a live link.

That's all there is to it. To unlink text, right-click the hyperlink. From the menu, choose Remove Hyperlink, and Word unlinks your selection.

MASTERING THE OPPORTUNITIES

Word versus FrontPage

There's plenty more you can do with Word as an HTML editor; most of the commands should be familiar to you if you've used FrontPage. Speaking of FrontPage, it'll generally do a much better job of creating HTML files than Word does. Briefly, however, there are some things you should note about Word as an HTML editor:

- In Word, when you select File ➤ New from the menu bar, one of the tabs in the New dialog box is called Web Pages. The templates available from this panel include a blank Web page, a Web Page Wizard, and some demonstrations of other Web tricks you can perform with Word. This process will look astonishingly familiar, since you can do the very same thing in FrontPage!

- One way to create a Web page with Word is to use the HTML.DOT template. Just select File ➤ New from Word's menu bar. You'll see a selection called "Web Page." Select this, click the Template radio button on the lower right hand side, and begin working.

- When you open or save an HTML file with Word, the HTML toolbar will become visible automatically. The functions on the Formatting toolbar will change to become HTML functions; for example, text styles such as bold and italic will be applied as HTML formatting, and the lists and alignment buttons will perform their functions with HTML as well.

Generally, you'll want to open any HTML files you create with Word in Page view to make sure they look and act as they're supposed to. FrontPage's automatic HTML debugging functions will fix a lot of sloppy code that Word can create—as we mentioned, FrontPage is much more sophisticated and specialized for the job of creating Web pages!

In addition to creating and saving Word files as HTML, there are other ways to get your information into FrontPage. The simplest is to cut and paste your information from the Word window directly into the Page view window. While this isn't foolproof, it can definitely be handy. Font specifications will not move from one editor to the other, but formatting such as lists, text formatting, and most importantly tables, transfer back and forth with ease.

One last thing you'll probably want to know is that you can open Word and Excel files with FrontPage itself. Just follow these steps:

1. From the FrontPage menu bar, select File ➤ Open. The Open dialog box appears.

2. Click the Files Of Type list box, and select either All Files or the option for your particular version of Microsoft Word.

3. Browse through the files and folders on your computer until you find the Word or Excel file you want to open in FrontPage.

4. Click Open to close the Open dialog box. The Page view window reappears, where you'll see your document, formatting intact, in the window. Excel spreadsheets will be converted to tables.

This technique works because of the high level of integration Microsoft has created in its Office family. This is undoubtedly one of the reasons that FrontPage, along with its officemates, makes for such an effective team.

Using Excel to Create Web Pages

Suppose you have an Excel spreadsheet file for the budget for an upcoming project. With Office 2000, you can save this spreadsheet as an HTML table and post it to your company's intranet, where the project staff will be able to review it. They'll have access to the HTML files and can prepare their comments, which can save a lot of time during meetings.

You can also use Excel to create a new Web page from an existing spreadsheet, or to place HTML tables into existing pages. In this section, we're going to create brand new HTML files. In the next section, we'll cover adding a table to an existing Web page.

Using Excel to create a new page from an Excel spreadsheet is a snap. Just follow these steps:

1. In the Excel window, open a file.

2. From the Excel menu bar, select File ➢ Save As A Web Page.

3. Now, decide whether you want to save the entire Workbook or a Selection. To save the entire workbook, click the Entire Workbook button. Or, choose the Selection button to save only highlighted items you wish to save.

4. Now, title your page and save it (see Figure 20.1).

 NOTE To preview the way your page will look in Internet Explorer, select File ➢ Web Page Preview.

PART

IV

FIGURE 20.1

Excel allows you to save your spreadsheets as elegant HTML tables.

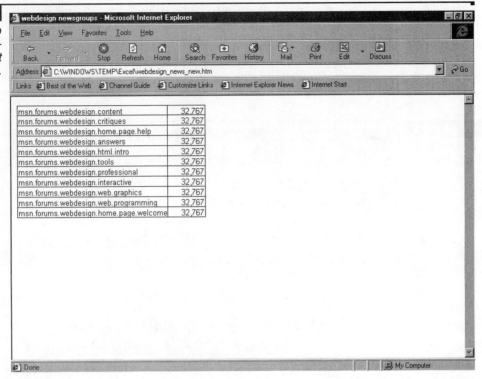

Now you can open this file in FrontPage, view it in your Web browser, or upload it to your FrontPage web. See Chapter 4, *Creating Basic Pages*, for more details on editing your page, and Chapter 2, *Exploring FrontPage 2000*, to find out about adding it to your FrontPage web. You can also refer to Chapter 11, *Using Tables for Advanced Layouts*, for details on adjusting the look and functionality of your table.

Inserting an Excel Spreadsheet into Existing FrontPage Documents

You can use FrontPage to insert an Excel spreadsheet into an HTML page. Follow these simple steps:

1. Open the page into which you want to insert a spreadsheet.

2. Place your cursor where you'd like the spreadsheet to appear.

3. From the main FrontPage menu, select Insert ➢ Component ➢ Office Spreadsheet.

4. The spreadsheet appears on the page (see Figure 20.2). You can now add information directly into the spreadsheet.

5. When you've completed working with the spreadsheet, save your file.

Now you can open this file with Internet Explorer to see what your spreadsheet looks like.

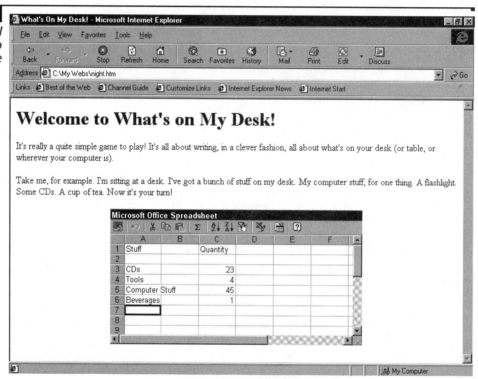

FIGURE 20.2

Adding an Excel spreadsheet to your Web page

NOTE Because this process uses an ActiveX component (see Chapter 22, *Specialty Programming Techniques*), it's Internet Explorer–specific. This makes the component especially useful in intranet situations, or whenever you know your audience is using the IE browser.

MASTERING THE OPPORTUNITIES

Linking in Excel Documents

You can use Excel 2000 to insert hyperlinks into Excel documents just as you can in Word and Access documents. With a worksheet open in Excel, just click in the cell to which you want to add a hyperlink, and from the Excel menu bar, select Insert ➢ Hyperlink. You'll be prompted to save the file, if you haven't already, then the Insert Hyperlink dialog box will appear. Type your URL in the Link To File Or URL text box, and then click OK. You'll see your real, live link underlined in blue in the cell where you placed it.

Any links you insert this way are live links; click them, and your browser will launch and load the target page. Then, when you export your spreadsheets to HTML, the links will be clickable there, too. You can also click the Browse button in the Insert Hyperlink dialog box to link to other files on your computer or intranet. You can link spreadsheets together, link Excel documents to Word files, or just about anything else—have a ball!

Working with PowerPoint

Converting your PowerPoint presentations into Web pages can be a great way to mobilize your office. You won't have to mess with bringing disks or overheads with you when visiting clients, because you'll be able to access your presentations through the Internet. You won't have to worry about the cost of fixing transparencies or slides that need revisions, because you'll simply be able to change the page digitally and upload it to the Web, rather than reprinting an overhead. And you'll be able to give colleagues and prospective clients previews of your presentations by simply sending them a URL. You can even do remote presentations!

 NOTE   Of course, before you visit your clients armed only with a URL, you need to be sure that their office has Internet access, and that your site is accessible to them. Check with your system administrator to learn where to post your Web files so they are not hidden behind a firewall, and give your presentation a test run from outside the office to make sure that loading the files isn't a painstakingly slow process.

Embedding Links in a Presentation

You can use PowerPoint to embed links in your slides, which effectively can turn objects into buttons or images into image maps. Just follow these steps:

1. With your PowerPoint slide show open in the PowerPoint window, click an object (an image or a block of text) that you'd like to make clickable.

2. From PowerPoint's menu bar, select Insert ➤ Hyperlink. The Insert Hyperlink dialog opens, looking like Figure 20.3.

FIGURE 20.3

The Insert Hyperlink dialog box lets you link objects in your slides to other slides, documents, programs, or Internet addresses.

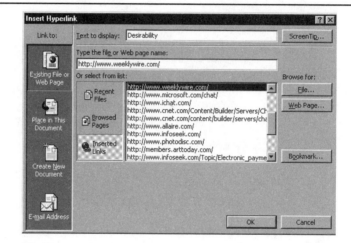

3. To have your object link to another file, type the file name and location into the Type The File Or Web Page Name text box, or click the File button and from the menu, select the file you'd like to link to. Or, to have your object link to an Internet URL (a Web page, e-mail address, FTP address, or any other Internet address), simply type the URL into the Type The File Or Web Page Name text box, or select from the available list.

4. When you're finished, click OK to close the dialog box and return to the PowerPoint window.

TIP If you'd like text to display in a tool-tip style box as a mouse passes over the link, simply type the text you'd like to display into the Text To Display text box at the top of the Edit Hyperlink dialog box.

Repeat this process as often as necessary to link objects and text within Power-Point. You won't notice your changes right away, but they'll be evident when you run the slide show, either in PowerPoint or after exporting the presentation to HTML and viewing it in a Web browser. Let's find out how to do just that.

Exporting Your Presentation to HTML

PowerPoint lets you save a single page, or publish your entire presentation in HTML. To save a single slide within your PowerPoint presentation, follow these steps:

1. With the page you want to put on the Web open in the PowerPoint window, from the PowerPoint menu bar, select File ➢ Save As Web Page. The Save As dialog box appears, as shown in Figure 20.4.

FIGURE 20.4

The Save As dialog box will help you save individual PowerPoint pages as HTML.

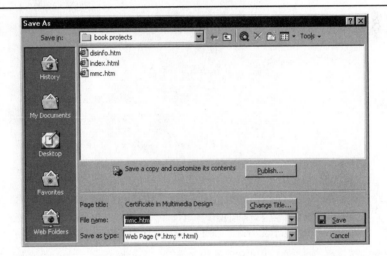

2. If you wish to change the page name, click the Change Title button and rename your page.

3. You may also rename your file by simply typing the new name into the File Name text box.

4. You'll notice that PowerPoint already has the HTML extensions selected. At this point, simply click OK to have PowerPoint export the page as HTML.

To save your entire presentation:

1. Open the presentation.

2. From the PowerPoint menu bar, select File ➢ Save As Web Page.

3. Click the Publish button. The Publish As Web Page dialog box appears (see Figure 20.5).

FIGURE 20.5

The Publish As Web page dialog box allows you to export all, or part of, a PowerPoint presentation into a Web page.

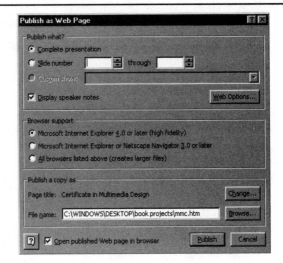

4. You can choose to save the entire presentation by making sure the Complete Presentation button is selected. If you'd like to save only a specific number of slides, click the Slide Number button and fill in the slide numbers.

5. You can choose the type of browser support you want by clicking the radio button next to the selection most appropriate for your presentation. Options include Microsoft Internet Explorer 4 Or Later, Microsoft Internet Explorer Or Netscape Navigator 3 Or Higher, and All Browsers Listed Above.

6. Click Publish to let PowerPoint publish your presentation using its built-in default settings.

To view your presentation in the browser of your choice, simply follow these steps:

1. From your Web browser's menu bar, select File ➢ Open to locate the file you created. Click the opening file's name (it will likely be index.htm unless you renamed it).

2. Click the links on the Index page to browse through your documents by using their titles, or use the arrow buttons to proceed from slide to slide.

3. Be sure to check all the links!

Customizing Your PowerPoint Presentation

If you'd rather take control over the appearance of your PowerPoint export, you can use the Web options button in the Publish As Web Page dialog. Here's how:

1. Open your PowerPoint presentation.

2. From the PowerPoint menu bar, select File ➢ Save As Web Page.

3. Click the Publish button. The Publish As Web Page dialog box appears.

4. Choose the presentation or slide range you'd like to save.

5. Select your browser preferences.

6. Now, click the Web options button. The Web Options dialog box appears. Notice that you have four tabs to select from: General, Files, Pictures, and Encoding. Each of these tabs controls a different aspect of your presentation.

7. Click the General tab. Here, you can deselect the Add Slide Navigation Controls checkbox if you *do not* want your presentation's navigation to be processed as links. To select presentation colors, use the drop-down menu next to the Colors option. You can opt to have the slide show continue animating as you browse—the default is to leave this option off, and that's probably the most convenient for you. Similarly, you'll probably want to keep the Resize Graphics To Fit Browser Window checkbox checked.

8. Click the Files tab. Here, you can optimize the way in which your files are managed and saved. In most situations, you'll want to leave these at the default; however, your needs might differ according to the options here.

9. Click the Pictures tab. In this area, you can optimize your graphics according to browser type. For example, if you'll be running Internet Explorer 5.0 or later, you can check the Rely On VML checkbox, as well as the Allow PNG As An Output Format checkbox.

 WARNING Both of these options will enable PowerPoint to optimize your images so they are very small. However, support for VML (Vector Markup Language) and PNG (Portable Network Graphic file format) is very limited, so be sure you know that the browser you'll be using for your presentation supports them.

10. In the Target Monitor drop down menu, select the screen size for the monitor on which you'll be using your PowerPoint presentation. If you're unsure, you can set it to 640×480, as that is the lowest common denominator monitor size. Reserve monitor settings higher than 800×600 for those situations when you are absolutely sure of the monitor size available.

11. Click the Encoding tab. Use this box whenever you're setting up a presentation that uses lettering other than that used for standard English. In most cases, you'll leave this section as is.

12. Click OK.

13. Click Publish to have PowerPoint process your presentation as a Web site—with your settings intact!

You are now free to use FrontPage to edit these files and add any elements you'd like to spruce up the pages. When you're satisfied with your presentation, upload all the HTML documents and images to your Web site (as described in Chapter 8, *Publishing Your Pages*), and double-check the links and image locations before you announce your URL to the world.

MASTERING WHAT'S ONLINE

For more information on PowerPoint, be sure to drop by www.microsoft.com/powerpoint/. There you'll find news, demos, special offerings, and other resources to help you maximize your PowerPoint experience.

Using Access

You can create HTML versions of Access datasheets, database reports based on the information in your Microsoft Access databases, and management documents. For example, you can create a list of all your employees from your payroll database, a table of clients and their contact information from an accounts database, or even an online catalog from an inventory database. Any kind of information suitable for a database can be put onto an Access HTML datasheet.

Exporting Access Data into Web Pages

Before you can export Access data to HTML, you will need to have an HTML file available so that you can provide document and style information to your data. You can use *any* HTML file to fulfill this need—just be sure you have an HTML file that has the background, text, link colors, and any images or other information you want included within the Access data. If you don't have a file you'd like to use on hand, you can easily create one in FrontPage, and save it to a folder.

 TIP If you plan on using the HTML file to format your Access data in the future, you can save the HTML file in a convenient location, such as within the Microsoft Office templates folder.

To output Access data as HTML, you need to use both the File ➤ Save As, and File ➤ Export options. These options let you create an HTML-based page from your Access database. Follow these steps:

1. With your database open in the Access window, from the menu bar, select File ➤ Save As.

2. The Save As dialog box appears (see Figure 20.6). Name the file and select whether you want it to be a table, form, or report.

FIGURE 20.6

The Save As dialog will help you choose the type of file you'd like the database saved as.

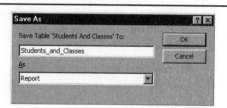

3. Access opens the file in the format you've selected (see Figure 20.7). Check to make sure this is how you want your information organized.

FIGURE 20.7

The format that you select—in this case, a report—will appear on the screen.

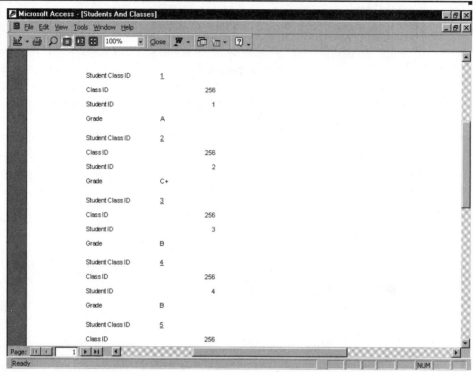

4. With the file open, select File ➤ Export. The Export To dialog box appears (see Figure 20.8).

FIGURE 20.8

The Export To dialog box allows you to export your Access data to HTML.

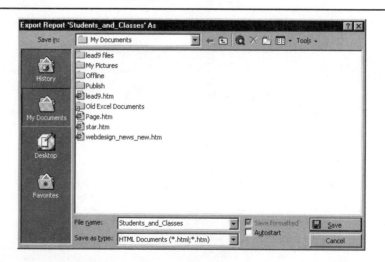

5. In the File Name text box, you'll see the name of your file. You can modify this name to be more HTML-friendly. For example, if your database name is Students and Classes, you can give it a short name (such as **sc.htm**) or a long name, using underscores to link the words: **students_and_classes.htm**.

6. In the Save As Type area, select HTML Documents.

7. Click Save. The HTML Output Options dialog box appears (see Figure 20.9).

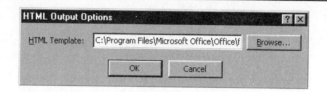

FIGURE 20.9

The HTML Output Options dialog box lets you select the HTML template you've designated for your Access database.

8. Click the Browse button and find the HTML file you've designated as a template for your Access data.

9. Click OK.

10. Access now converts the data into HTML form.

You won't see your new HTML file right away—you'll have to open it with your Web browser to see the product of your export. To do this, open your Web browser. From your Web browser's menu bar, select File ➤ Open to locate the file you created. Click the opening file's name (it will likely be index.htm unless you renamed it). The file will now appear within the browser window (see Figure 20.10).

Do you like the results? If so, great! If not, you can open this file in FrontPage and edit it any way you like, using the techniques described throughout this book.

 MASTERING TROUBLESHOOTING

Missing Images and Backgrounds

You can use any HTML file for a profile, but the images—including the background image, if any—won't appear unless they are in the same directory as the HTML files. All the images for the standard Access templates, including the background images and the Made with Microsoft Access button, are stored in the Access templates folder, whose path is probably something like \Program Files\Microsoft Office\Templates\Access. However, if you save your HTML files in another location, such as \My Documents\, the images won't show up.

Continued

MASTERING TROUBLESHOOTING CONTINUED

You can fix all this by viewing the source code of the HTML file (with either your Web browser or FrontPage) to find out the names of the images, and then copying the images from the Access templates folder to the location of your HTML pages. You should always double-check image pathnames in your pages before you post them to the Web; FrontPage makes this easier for you, because it always asks if you want to copy images to your FrontPage web when you save a file.

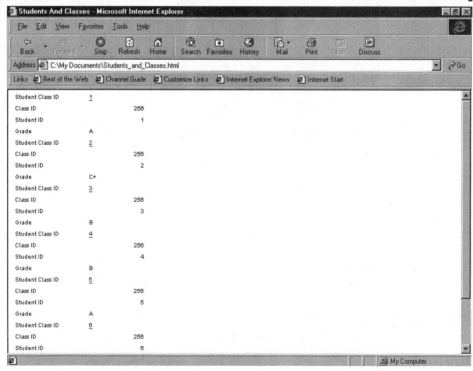

Inserting Hyperlinks into Your Access Database

You can insert hyperlinks to Web pages into tables in your Access database; then if you export those tables into HTML, a click on a hyperlink field will take you to another Web page. For example, suppose you have a client database that includes contact information; you can establish links to your clients' Web sites from your Access-created contact pages.

NOTE You can use Access to insert links to objects within this database or within other databases. These procedures are a bit complex, and out of the scope of this chapter, but you can find information about all kinds of hyperlinks in the Access Help files. From Access's menu bar, just select Help ➢ Contents And Index, and search for "hyperlink" as a keyword.

Before you can insert a hyperlink, you must define the data type for that field as *hyperlink*. To define an existing field as a hyperlink field in an Access table, just follow these steps:

1. With your database open in the Access window, view the table to which you want to add a hyperlink field.

2. If you're not already in Design view, from the Access menu bar, select View ➢ Design View. The window changes to show you the Design view of your table, rather than the Datasheet view.

3. Click in the field's Data Type column, and then click the list box button at the right of the field. From the drop-down menu that appears, select Hyperlink. The Data Type field now displays Hyperlink as the data type.

Now you can enter hyperlinks into that field. Follow these steps:

1. With your table still visible in the Access window, from the Access menu bar, select View ➢ Datasheet View. The window changes to show you the Datasheet view of your table, rather than the Design view. (You may be prompted to save your changes, if you haven't done so already.)

2. Click in the field you just defined as a hyperlink field (you can start from any row in your table).

3. On the Access toolbar, the Insert Hyperlink button is now available. Click this button, and the Insert Hyperlink dialog box appears (see Figure 20.11).

FIGURE 20.11

The Insert Hyperlink dialog box lets you drop links to Web pages into your Access tables.

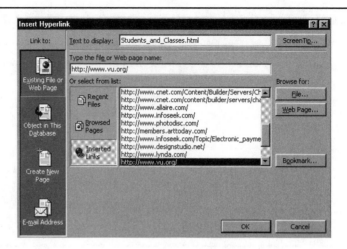

FIGURE 20.11

The Insert Hyperlink dialog box lets you drop links to Web pages into your Access tables.

4. In the text box labeled Type The File Or Web Page Name, type (or paste) the location of the file to which you'd like to link. This can be a location on your computer, on your corporate intranet, or on the World Wide Web. Alternatively, select a URL from the list. You can also click the Web Page button or the File button to find a Web page or file for your link.

5. Click OK to close the Edit Hyperlink dialog box. The Access window appears, and your selection is properly linked.

Now, if you export your table into HTML, you'll be able to click the hyperlinks you inserted into your table. If you click a hyperlink to a Web page within the Access window, your default Web browser will launch and open the page.

MASTERING WHAT'S ONLINE

Want more information on Access? Visit www.microsoft.com/access/ for updates, troubleshooting, downloads, and product support.

Microsoft Publisher and HTML

Publisher is Microsoft's desktop publishing software. It allows you to design professional publications such as newsletters, brochures, business reports, business stationery, business cards, and menus.

Publisher allows you to both export publications you build in the program to HTML, and build quick Web pages, as well as use HTML to link to local files or Internet Web sites.

 NOTE Using a Web page wizard, Microsoft Publisher lets you create entire Web sites from scratch. While Publisher is useful in helping you build a Web page, it has nowhere near the power that FrontPage does! For this reason, we recommend using it as a desktop publishing tool, and saving your documents to HTML. At that point, you can always use FrontPage to enhance your pages in any way you see fit.

Exporting Existing Publisher Files to HTML

Exporting a Microsoft Publisher publication to HTML is very easy! Simply follow these steps:

1. With your publication open in Publisher, from the menu bar, select File ➢ Save As A Web Page.

2. The Save As A Web Page dialog box appears (see Figure 20.12). In the Folder Name text box, type the name of the folder you'd like to save your publication to.

3. Click OK.

4. Publisher will now publish your publication to HTML.

You can now view your page(s) within a Web browser. Simply open your browser, select File ➢ Open, and find the location of the publication. The first page will have been named index.htm.

FIGURE 20.12

The Save As A Web Page dialog box

Using Publisher to Create Quick Web Pages

If you'd like to create a page quickly, you can set up a page in Publisher and then immediately export it as a Web page. To do so:

1. Open Publisher.

2. Using any one of the available wizards, design a page. Figure 20.13 shows one we've created.

3. Don't save your file in Publisher format! Instead, select File ➤ Create Web Site From Current Publication.

4. A warning pops up, letting you know that you are about to publish unsaved content to a Web format. To publish directly to a Web format, click No.

5. Publisher now lets you run a series of design checks to ensure that your page is within Web site guidelines. It's wise to click Yes to this option, and let Publisher run through the checks.

6. Once your pages have been checked and modified and reappear on the Publisher screen, select File ➤ Save As A Web Page.

7. The Save As A Web Page dialog appears. In the Folder Name text box, type the name of the folder where you'd like to save your publication.

8. Click OK.

Publisher now publishes your publication to HTML. Figure 20.14 shows the page we created saved as a Web page and viewed within the Internet Explorer browser.

FIGURE 20.13

*A Publisher document
we've built using a
Publisher wizard*

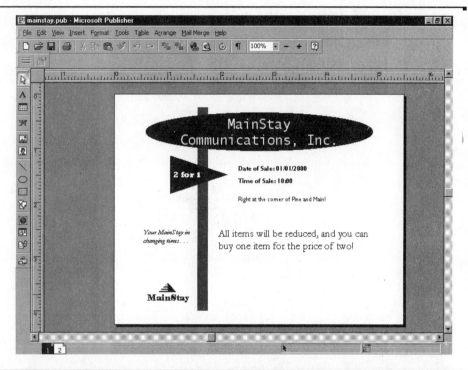

FIGURE 20.14

*The same document
now published as a
Web page and viewed
in Internet Explorer*

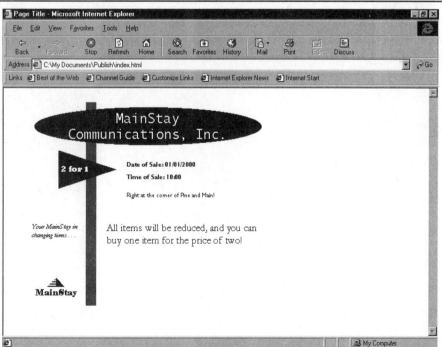

Creating Hyperlinks within Publisher

If you'd like to link to files or Web sites from within your Publisher documents, you can easily do so:

1. With your Publisher document open in the main Publisher window, find the text or object you'd like to make into a link.

2. Highlight the text or object.

3. From the main Publisher menu, select Insert ➤ Hyperlink.

4. Publisher's Hyperlink dialog appears (see Figure 20.15).

5. Click the button most appropriate for your hyperlink. Your choices include A Web Site Or File On The Internet, An Internet E-Mail Address, Another Page In Your Web Site, or A File On Your Hard Disk.

6. In the Hyperlink Information area, you can type (or paste) the name of the file or URL, add one from the existing drop-down menu, or select the Favorites button to add one from your Internet Explorer Favorites.

7. Click OK.

You now have a link! Be sure to test it before saving your file with the updated information.

FIGURE 20.15

Publisher's Hyperlink dialog box

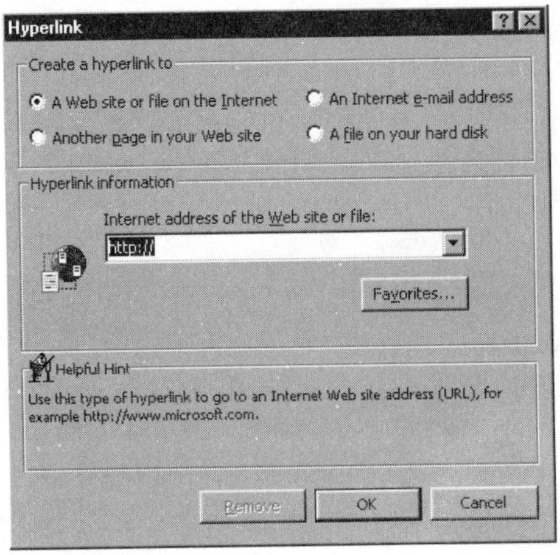

MASTERING WHAT'S ONLINE

You can get updates, information, support, and find great add-on downloads for Microsoft Publisher at www.microsoft.com/publisher/.

Linking to Office Documents

Instead of converting your Office Documents to Web pages, you can simply provide links to the Office files themselves (DOC, XLS, PPT, and MDB files, in other words). In a corporate environment that uses Microsoft Office and has an intranet, it's likely that your colleagues will have the programs necessary to view your Office documents. Even on the Internet, however, you can distribute Office documents that anyone can read using a free Office viewer. (A *viewer* is a very small piece of software that can be used to open documents, but not edit or change them.) If you'd like to make your Office documents available to your users, you can point them to the Office Internet page to download the free viewers for Word, Excel, and PowerPoint.

 NOTE Version 3 or later of both Netscape Navigator and Microsoft Internet Explorer are capable of viewing—and even editing—Office documents within the browser window.

Linking to an Office document is the same as linking to any other document. Post it to your Web site as you would any other document, and make sure that links to it end in .doc (Word), .xls (Excel), or .ppt (PowerPoint), rather than the .htm or .html extensions you use for regular Web pages. (Chapter 2 discusses importing Web pages; the same process works here.)

 TIP It's a good idea to let people know that you're linking to an Office document rather than to a regular Web page. Your link and the surrounding text might read something like this: *Download our 1998 Annual Report (MS Excel format).*

When a user clicks a link to an Office document, one of three things might happen:

- If the user's Web browser is capable of opening Office documents, the document will appear in the browser window.

- If the user has the appropriate Office program, and his or her browser is configured to open Office documents, the document will be saved to disk, and the Office program will open and load the document.

- If the user's browser is configured to save Office documents to disk (the default for most people), he or she will be prompted to save the document to disk, and can then open it at a convenient time.

It might be handy to tell your users that they can get free Office viewers to read these files, and to provide a link to Microsoft's Office Internet page.

MASTERING TROUBLESHOOTING

Don't Let Your Computer Get Sick!

You've got yourself some up-to-date anti-virus software, right? A certain type of virus, called a macro virus, inhabits Microsoft Office documents exclusively. Virus protection programs that do not specifically state that they detect macro viruses probably don't. Most of these viruses fall into the annoying category, rather than the deadly one, but you should always be prepared to run regular virus checks to stamp them out.

Office programs include an automatic macro virus scanning feature, but it isn't foolproof; the scanning software simply detects macro code created by a user other than yourself and warns you of its presence, but it doesn't destroy virus code. Earlier versions of the software do not have scanning included.

For information about macro viruses and how to detect and destroy them, visit the Microsoft Office Anti-Virus page at www.microsoft.com/office/antivirus/. You'll find virus protection for Word templates, recommendations regarding other anti-virus software, and updates on virus solutions.

Up Next

In this chapter, you've learned a lot about how to make pages interactive. Office 2000 allows all of your Office documents to be linked to one another, as well as linked to, or from, a Web page. You've also seen how you can use Office programs to make or enhance your Web pages, which can then be improved upon using Microsoft FrontPage.

Our next step will be to take a look at JavaScript and Dynamic HTML. These technologies allow for a much broader spectrum of interactivity to be added to your pages, as well as offering a variety of management tools and cool special effects.

CHAPTER **21**

JavaScript and Dynamic HTML

S o, you've got a fantastic looking Web site. You're happy with the code, you're pleased with the look and feel, and the graphics are positively beautiful. You've even got some interactivity, such as forms and permissions. Perhaps you've gone so far as to add some features drawing from Office 2000's suite of powerful tools. But you still feel you're missing something. Whether it's as simple as a mouseover effect, a pop-up window to aid in navigation, or a page transition, you can just sense that your site needs something more.

JavaScript is a powerful scripting language that not only allows you to add interesting effects to your pages, but also gives you a realm of administrative and function-oriented tools that serve to empower your site in both design and behavior. *Dynamic HTML*, or *DHTML*, is an umbrella name for a combination of technologies that include JavaScript and work together to create powerful design options for your sites.

In this chapter, you will learn what JavaScript and DHTML are—and where they fit into the big picture of Web programming technologies. We'll also show you how you can begin using JavaScript and DHTML with FrontPage, and add that much-desired missing element to your pages right away.

About JavaScript

JavaScript is a small-scale, easy to learn scripting language that allows you to add event-driven interactivity to your Web pages.

In the early days of the Web, common interactive Web elements such as fill-in forms, image maps, and automatic elements like the "Last Modified on" line at the bottom of pages had to be added by the Web server. These *server-side* elements are still in use by many sites. But as you can imagine, the more work a Web server has to do in creating and serving these elements, the more bogged down it gets and the slower the entire site becomes. Luckily, JavaScript can help because it is a *client-side* application. This means it is downloaded to the browser right away, and then does its magic within the browser—it doesn't have to make a return visit to the server to get any more information after the initial handshake.

Let's say you have a form on your Web site that allows children to practice their multiplication tables. One way to evaluate the child's answers would be to use CGI—that is, the child would click the Submit button, and all of the answers he or she typed would travel back to the Web server. The server would run a little program to evaluate the answers, and then it would send back a Web page that showed how many were correct. That's three trips to the server—one for the child to get the page in the first place, one to send the answers in for grading, and one to send back the score.

If, however, you create the multiplication test with JavaScript, the user would communicate with the server only *once* to get the initial Web page. Contained on this initial page is the JavaScript program, which is actually run on the user's computer. The program itself collects the answers, evaluates them, and shows how many are correct. Because the user doesn't have to send data back to the server to get the results, the response is much, much quicker. And, as we all know, the faster your Web pages appear, the better.

Of course, JavaScript isn't always the appropriate choice for all applications. It does have its limitations. Because it is a script rather than a fully executable program, you can only get so fancy! Some of the things you can use JavaScript for include:

- Launching a new browser window. This script application allows you to construct a link that actually opens a second browser window to display the linked Web page. Some sites use this feature to avoid sending their users to another site; others use it as a convenience. If, for example, you have a list of links to related topics, launching a new browser window for each topic means the user doesn't have to keep navigating back to the page with the original list.

- Validating the input from HTML forms without sending the data off to the server.

- Placing the current date and time on your page.

- Displaying the date that the page was last updated.

- Detecting which browser the user is running. You might use this feature for users whose browsers don't support a feature you want to use on your Web site (like frames, for example). Scripts can detect users who have older browsers and show them a version of your Web site without the advanced features.

- Playing sounds or displaying images when the mouse enters a certain part of the Web page.

- Navigating and generating pages in a frames environment. One example of this feature is an expanding navigation bar—similar to the Windows Explorer or the Macintosh Finder—on the left side of a two-frame Web page. You could use scripts to redraw the bar when a user asks for another level of detail, resulting in an instant change in the available nav bar's links.

MASTERING THE OPPORTUNITIES

Understanding the Difference between JavaScript, Java, and JScript

A common misconception about JavaScript is that it is an easier-to-use, scaled-down version of Java. This can't be farther from the truth. The reason the two have a similar name has more to do with history than any common features found within the languages.

JavaScript has its origins in a Netscape language known as LiveScript. Sun Microsystems, who is the developer of the Java language, teamed with Netscape to help bring LiveScript to sophistication. The name "JavaScript" was given to the end product to create a unity and familiarity between two products being developed with the Web in mind.

JavaScript runs inline, on the client-side. Java is a full-fledged programming language that must be compiled in order to run. This is a world of difference, and the confusion about similarities between the two has come about largely due to the similarity in their names.

Interestingly, JavaScript has become a mainstay in the Web design world, used regularly to control a variety of features on Web sites. Java, on the other hand, has receded from the Web as a tool of choice. With the exception of a few small Java *applets* (mini applications), Java as a full programming language is simply too cumbersome to be as effective as the fast client-side JavaScript. Java itself has become more useful for general programming purposes—but its use as a tool to add design features to Web pages is fast going out of style.

So what about *JScript*? This is another name you'll run across, and you may wonder what the heck it means. Remember, we've told you that Sun Microsystems is heavily involved in the development of both JavaScript and Java. Well, Sun and Microsoft have had legal battles, and in that unfortunate process, Microsoft has had to accommodate legal and competitive concerns. JScript *is* JavaScript, with a Microsoft naming convention. There is essentially no difference in the language, but the browser support is somewhat different.

Naturally, because the origins of JavaScript lie with Netscape, browser support from the Navigator realm is very explicit and stable. Microsoft's earlier versions of Internet Explorer were faulty in their adoption of JavaScript, but by the 4 generation of IE, most of the problems were solved. Where Microsoft has gained its competitive edge is with DHTML, as you'll see later in this chapter.

Ultimately, the most powerful aspect of JavaScript in terms of today's browser technology is that it addresses the need for cross-platform, multibrowser support. Both Netscape Navigator and Microsoft Internet Explorer now support JavaScript, so if your audience uses both, JavaScript is your best choice as a scripting language. In addition, JavaScript is fully supported on Windows 95, 98, and NT, Macintosh, and Unix machines.

NOTE In your Web design travels, you will undoubtedly run across another scripting language known as *VBScript*, or *Visual Basic Script*. This powerful scripting language is related to Microsoft's Visual Basic. It was originally Microsoft's competitive product to JavaScript, but it has long since lost its ability to compete in the client-side arena. Where VBScript comes in very handy is behind the scenes. VBScript is quite often used along with databases, Microsoft Web-server configurations, and back-end products.

Inserting a Script

So, now that you know a bit about JavaScript, you will quickly understand why Front-Page 2000 has chosen to minimize support for the product. DHTML effects are the rage as well as being the Microsoft edge, so when FrontPage 2000 was redesigned from earlier versions, the Script Wizard—which allowed you to add your own scripts—was taken out!

Does this mean you can't use any script you want? Of course not! In fact, one way that FrontPage ensures that you *can* use any JavaScript of your choice is that it does not alter any code you choose to enter by hand. This means you can add anything you want and FrontPage won't get in your way.

So, if you want to use a script, you'll add it like this:

1. Download and save the script of your choice and any of its components. Open this file (you can open it right in FrontPage, if you like) and copy the script to the clipboard by choosing Edit ➢ Select All ➢ Edit ➢ Copy.

2. In FrontPage, open the Web page into which you want to insert the script.

3. Place the cursor where you want to insert the script (typically this will go in the HEAD section of the document).

TIP JavaScript is usually placed at the top of the Web page to make it easier to locate and edit. In general, if the script should display content when the page is first loaded, the script must be at the top of the Web page or embedded within the page where the script output should be displayed.

4. Paste the script into your Web page by selecting Edit ➤ Paste (or Ctrl+V). (See Figure 21.1.)

FIGURE 21.1

Inserting a script into a Web page with the Script dialog box

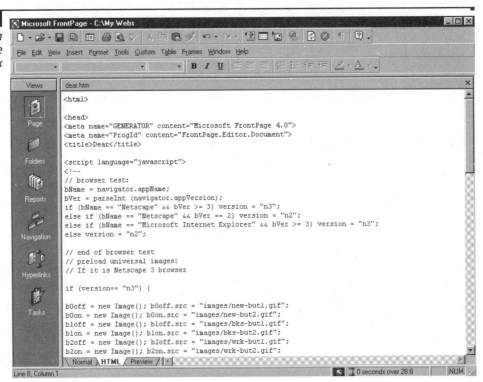

5. Save the file.

Be sure to test your page in a JavaScript-compliant browser to ensure that it works!

MASTERING THE OPPORTUNITIES

Where to Get JavaScript Help

If this section on JavaScript feels like a bit of a tease, it is! We encourage you to go out and find fun and functional JavaScripts to use on your pages. There are numerous JavaScript archives and help sources on the Web. Here are a few favorites:

Want to learn JavaScript from the ground up? Check out Voodoo's JavaScript introduction, at www.webteacher.com/javatour/framehol.htm.

JavaScript World: Articles, scripts, and discussion forums, at www.jsworld.com/.

Doc JavaScript: Improve your scripting health, at www.webreference.com/js/.

JavaScript Developer Central: Netscape's resource center for JavaScript developers, at developer.netscape.com/tech/javascript/index.html.

JScript Tutorial: Microsoft's overview of JScript from basics to advanced scripting, at msdn.microsoft.com/scripting/default.htm?/scripting/jscript/beta/doc/jstutor.htm.

Dynamic HTML

Dynamic HTML actually refers to using JavaScript, Cascading Style Sheets (CSS), and internal browser technology to make pages more vibrant and active. Normally, in order to create Dynamic HTML pages, you'd have to understand each of these technologies, and write scripts for each of your pages to perform tasks such as moving blocks of text around or changing images when the user points at them. But as luck would have it, FrontPage 2000 includes Dynamic HTML effects that you can incorporate into your pages without having to do any programming at all.

WARNING Unfortunately, Internet Explorer 4 and Netscape Navigator 4 use two different forms of Dynamic HTML; you can probably guess which version FrontPage supports. If you use Dynamic HTML in FrontPage 2000, your pages will load in Netscape Navigator, but any special effects you created using FrontPage's Dynamic HTML features simply will not appear on them. For more advanced programmers, you can learn about DHTML from the ground up. See the DHTML resource sidebar later in this chapter.

DHTML in FrontPage 2000 is controlled from a special toolbar. You can get to this toolbar by selecting View ➣ Toolbars ➣ DHTML Effects.

Using DHTML, you can actively modify just about any element on your Web pages—text, images, links, you name it.

Animating Text

To animate text, follow these steps:

1. With the page of interest open, select the text you want to animate.

2. On the DHTML toolbar, you'll see an arrow to the right of the On text box. Click the arrow to display a drop-down list.

3. You now have several options, including:

- Click makes the animation occur when you click the text in question.
- Double Click makes the animation occur only upon double-clicking the text.
- Mouseover makes the animation occur when your mouse passes over the text.
- Page Load makes the animation occur immediately upon page load.

Choose an option to place it in the On text box and close the drop-down list.

4. The neighboring Apply text box also has a drop-down list, where you can now select the type of action you want to apply to the object. With text, you have two options:

- Fly Out will give you options to make the text move in a specified way across the page.
- Formatting will allow you to add borders or font changes to the selected text.

5. If you want to make your text fly, highlight Fly Out on the drop-down list, and a secondary drop-down list appears. Choose one of the following to occur upon the action you specified (click, double-click, mouseover, or page load) in the On text box:

- To Left will cause the selected text to slide to the left.
- To Top will cause the selected item to move to the top.
- To Bottom-Left causes the selection to move diagonally to the bottom left of the page.

- To Bottom-Right makes the text move diagonally to the bottom right of the page.

- To Top-Right causes the selected text to move diagonally to the top right of the page.

- To Top-Left makes the text move diagonally to the top left of the page.

- To Top-Right By Word moves the selection diagonally to the top right of the page, one word at a time.

- To Bottom-Right By Word causes the text to move diagonally to the bottom right of the page, one word at a time.

6. If you want to add a formatting change to your text upon the action specified in the On text box, highlight Formatting on the Apply drop-down list, and a secondary drop-down list appears. Now you can choose from the following:

- Font allows you to have the text change font face, color, size, or style.

- Borders And Shading displays the Borders And Shading dialog box (see Figure 21.2), which allows a variety of borders and shading effects to be displayed.

FIGURE 21.2

Selecting borders for DHTML effects

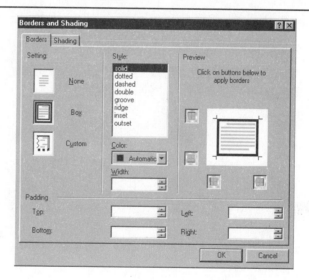

Alternately, to turn off any previously selected animation, simply select Off.

7. Save your page.

You won't see any change on the editing screen itself, but if you select the Preview tab, the selected object will appear on screen and you can view the animation. For example, if you select a header (see Figure 21.3) and set it to fly to the bottom right, the header will fly from the bottom-right side of the Preview window right off the page (see Figure 21.4)!

FIGURE 21.3

A text header in its normal state

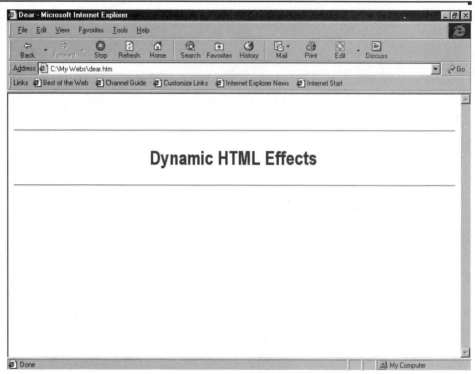

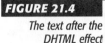

FIGURE 21.4

*The text after the
DHTML effect*

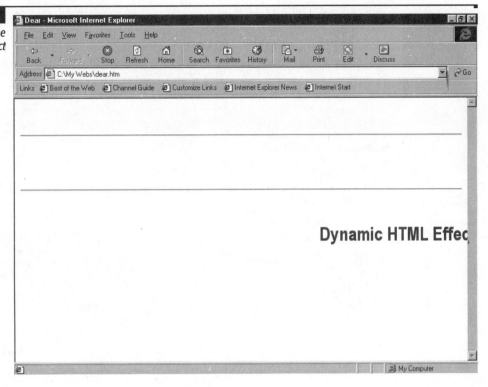

Animating Images

You can animate images, too! Your options are the same as for text—you can fly an image or have its border change color and style.

In this example, we're going to make our lion fly to the top when you click his face.

1. With a page open, select the image you want to animate.

2. On the DHTML toolbar, you'll see an arrow to the right of the On text box. Click the arrow to display a drop-down list.

3. You now have several options:

- Click makes the animation occur when you click the text in question.

- Double Click makes the animation occur only upon double-clicking the text.

- Mouseover makes the animation occur when your mouse passes over the text.

- Page Load makes the animation occur immediately upon page load.

Choose an option to place it in the On text box and close the drop-down list. For this demo, we chose Click.

4. In the neighboring Apply drop-down list, select Fly Out, and a secondary drop-down list appears.

5. Choose a direction and style for flying the image, upon the action specified in the On text box. We chose To Top.

6. Save the page.

7. View the page in your browser, and you'll see the original image (see Figure 21.5) fly in the direction you specified (see Figure 21.6).

FIGURE 21.5

The original image

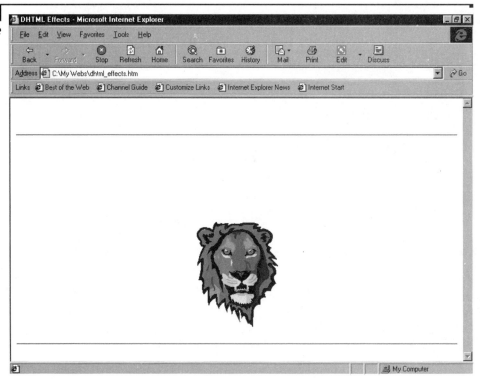

FIGURE 21.6

*The image flies
upward after the
DHTML effect is
invoked.*

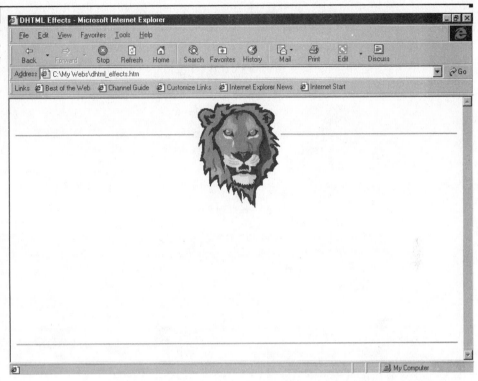

Are there other cool animation effects for DHTML? Absolutely! See the Mastering What's Online sidebar a bit later in this chapter, where we offer up some very helpful resources on using DHTML.

Setting Transitions between Pages

You can also use FrontPage's Dynamic HTML features to set the transitions that occur between pages. For example, you might want one page to dissolve as another appears. Other options are available, too—we've come a long way from simply jumping from link to link. To set the transition from one page to another, do this:

1. With a page open in Page view, from the menu bar, select Format ➢ Page Transition. The Page Transition dialog box appears.

2. In the dialog box's Event drop-down list, select the transition for which you want to set a special effect. The transitions you can assign effects to are:

- Page Enter, which occurs when the page is loaded by a user
- Page Exit, which occurs when a user replaces the page with another page
- Site Enter, which occurs the first time a user accesses a page from your site
- Site Exit, which occurs when a user loads a page that is not part of your site

3. In the Transition Effect list box, select the effect that appeals to you. (The best way to learn about the effects is to try them all out.)

4. In the text box labeled Duration (Sec), type the number of seconds you want the effect to last.

5. Click OK. The dialog box closes.

You won't see any indication of that spanking new Dynamic HTML when you first return to the Page view window. However, when you preview the page by selecting the Preview tab, or view the page in Internet Explorer itself, you'll see the page transition in all its glory.

MASTERING WHAT'S ONLINE

As with JavaScript, you can add DHTML to pages on your own—you don't have to feel restricted to what FrontPage offers. Furthermore, if you're interested in setting up DHTML that works across browsers, you'll need to spend time reading up on the subject. Here are some helpful Web sites for you to get started:

The DHTML Zone. This is Macromedia's site dedicated to all things DHTML, such as articles, tutorials, and a discussion group, at www.dhtmlzone.com/.

DHTML Lab. Internet.Com's entrance, with tools, demos, articles, and discussion, at www.webreference.com/dhtml/.

WebCoder. Ready-to-Use DHTML scripts, at www.webcoder.com/.

Dynamic HTML in Netscape Communicator, at developer.netscape.com/docs/manuals/communicator/dynhtml/index.htm.

Dynamic HTML in IE, at www.microsoft.com/workshop/c-frame.htm#/workshop/author/default.asp.

Up Next

Knowing when and why to use programming on your Web site is a big challenge for Web designers. Some of you are designing for the pure creative joy of it; others have a professional need. Each case is going to dictate how you use techniques such as JavaScript and DHTML.

But, now that you've got a taste of Web programming, it's time to dish up some more! This way, you'll have plenty of choices when it comes to planning and weighing what is appropriate for your site needs.

In Chapter 22, *Specialty Programming Techniques*, we'll take a look at the way Front-Page manages Java applets and ActiveX—two programming techniques that are powerful, yet highly specialized.

CHAPTER 22

Specialty Programming Techniques

I n addition to client-side techniques such as those discussed in Chapter 21, *JavaScript and Dynamic HTML*, there are methods for inserting actual, executable programs into your pages. As warned in the previous chapter, however, these techniques can add to download time. The bottom line is that with the types of programming we're going to look at here—ActiveX and Java applets—you're given maximum choice when you sit down to enhance your Web pages.

While FrontPage comes with some ActiveX and Java applets that anyone—even a nonprogrammer—can use (see Chapter 15, *Special Effects*), it is also possible to use many others in FrontPage webs. It is even possible (if you are a programmer) to create original ActiveX controls and Java applets for use in Web pages. This chapter is a quick introduction to all those possibilities.

About ActiveX

ActiveX is a technology designed by Microsoft that enables software developers to create applications using *components*. Each component is a small piece of computer code that encompasses one part—or function—of the program. A number of components are then assembled into one big application, called a *container* application. By combining a bunch of components, in other words, one ends up with a real application. The most widely used application yet developed with this technology is (yes, you heard it here) Internet Explorer itself.

Internet Explorer consists of a container application and a bunch of ActiveX controls that perform such specific tasks as actually displaying Web pages. When all the components within the container application work together, you end up with (in this case) a Web browser. Similarly, one can use controls as parts of a Web page. ActiveX can be used by programmers to create controls (known, logically enough, as ActiveX controls) that you can then embed into your Web pages—whether you yourself are a programmer or not.

 NOTE When we talk about *active content* in this chapter, we are referring to compact computer programs you can incorporate into your Web pages. These are most often implemented to facilitate user interaction–typical examples might be an image that changes its look when the user moves a mouse pointer over it, or a calculator into which a user can enter numbers and from which a result is returned.

Remember, when a user experiences an ActiveX control on a Web page, the control is actually made up of both what the user sees and some computer code that causes something to happen in response to the user's action.

Finding ActiveX Controls

The best place to find ActiveX controls for your use is on the Web itself. Microsoft's Sitebuilder Network, for example, is a popular site that offers tutorials on how to build and implement components such as ActiveX.

1. With Internet Explorer (version 3 or newer) running, from the menu bar, select File ➤ Open. The Open dialog box appears.

2. In the Open dialog box's text box, type the URL of an ActiveX gallery listing. See the Mastering What's Online sidebar in this section for some ActiveX gallery locations.

3. Review the ActiveX gallery pages and locate an ActiveX control you want to incorporate into one of your pages.

4. Follow the directions on the site for downloading the control to your computer. The instructions vary from one site—and one control—to another. Also, note any copyright or other restrictions on the control's use before you simply assume you can use it as you will.

5. Once the control has been downloaded, select File ➤ Exit to exit Internet Explorer. The Internet Explorer window closes.

You now have the control on your computer, and you can incorporate it into your Web page. Turn to the section in this chapter titled "Placing ActiveX Controls" to find out how.

MASTERING WHAT'S ONLINE

To locate ActiveX controls you can incorporate into your own Web pages, visit:

BrowserWatch's ActiveX Arena at www.browserwatch.com/activex.html.

CNET's dedicated ActiveX site at www.activex.com.

Microsoft's Component Development site at www.microsoft.com/workshop/ c-frame.htm?911867875960#/workshop/components/default.asp.

Creating ActiveX Controls

While getting and using controls may be a fairly simple matter, actually creating an original ActiveX control is true programming, and best done by experienced programmers. If you are a programmer, you can use any of a number of languages to write code to create the control. Although how to turn your original idea into a new ActiveX control is beyond the scope of this book, we can offer a few words of advice about the popular programming environments used for this: Visual Basic and Visual C++. These tools were originally designed for writing Windows programs, so they are familiar to many programmers.

Visual Basic Control Creation Edition is a special version of Microsoft's highly popular Visual Basic software development system, modified for the sole purpose of creating ActiveX controls. Visual Basic is simple to use (again, assuming you are a programmer), and millions of people—even novice programmers—are familiar enough with it to succeed in writing controls.

While Visual Basic's strength is that it's no sweat to use, Visual C++'s strength is that it is complicated and powerful. It takes a lot longer to get up to speed in creating original controls using Visual C++, and novice programmers will find it a big challenge; but in general, it affords a broader range of possibilities.

The component development site from Microsoft offers resources for programmers, so take a run by it for more information and directions should you be interested in the idea of component development.

Placing ActiveX Controls

Having downloaded the ActiveX control you want to place into your Web page, as described earlier in "Finding ActiveX Controls," you're ready to go. With the target Web page open in FrontPage:

1. Position the cursor at the point in the document where you want the control to appear.

2. From the menu bar, select Insert ➢ Advanced ➢ ActiveX Control. The Insert ActiveX Control dialog box appears, as shown in Figure 22.1.

3. Click OK. The ActiveX Control Properties dialog box closes, and the Page view window reappears, with an icon representing the ActiveX control you just inserted.

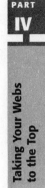

FIGURE 22.1

*The Insert ActiveX
Control dialog box*

That's all there is to inserting an ActiveX control into your Web page. You can now preview your page and the control you've added to it by clicking the Preview tab at the bottom of the Page view window.

 TIP You can also use Internet Explorer to preview the ActiveX control as it will be seen in an actual browser window. With the page open in FrontPage, select File ➢ Preview In Browser. In the dialog box that appears, select Internet Explorer and click the Preview button. Internet Explorer will launch and you'll see the page with the control in place.

About Java

Using Java (developed by Sun Microsystems), developers can create little applications called *applets*, which can be embedded into HTML documents or launched to run alongside your Web browser.

So how can you put Java to use? Let's say a programmer makes a Java calculator and you want to use it. Once you've downloaded the calculator *applet*, you can punch in numbers and the calculator doesn't have to ask the main server what the answer to "2 + 2" is; all the information it needs is right there in that little tiny program. The potential of Java applets is almost boundless, especially given the fact that Java is also theoretically *platform-independent*. This means that a Windows user, a Macintosh user, and a Unix user can all use the same applet and its appearance and performance will be *exactly* the same for all of those users.

Using Java, programmers can create other dazzling effects, like animation that might be used in games or for illustrations; ticker tape feeds for news, sports, and stock data; real-time interactivity that can be used in the creation of crossword puzzles, programs for the sharing of medical data, or even others that allow users to select airline seats; and handy gadgets such as mouse pointers that change shape, size, or color when you drag them over something.

As mentioned in Chapter 21, Java is retreating as a programming method of choice on the Web. The primary reason is time—applets typically take longer to load, and often require a conversation between the browser and the server beyond the initial handshake. Java does have some good applications, so it's important to learn a bit about how to use it, but keep in mind its limitations, and most especially, its differences from JavaScript.

 NOTE   FrontPage is not a Java-authoring tool, so it does not facilitate the actual writing of applets. FrontPage does allow you to embed existing applets into your Web pages. These can be original applets that you have written (see the following section, "Creating Java Applets") or applets you've acquired from other sources (see "Finding Java Applets," later in this chapter).

Creating Java Applets

As mentioned, Java applets are actually computer programs written in Java, which is a programming language. Java is much like those other popular languages, C and C++, but with "extensions" that make it adaptable to the Web.

When it comes to actually creating Java applets, you can use a programming environment that is designed specifically to create Java applets, or you can use one of a number of "point-and-click" tools that allow you to assemble applets out of existing components even if you are not a programmer. Let's look briefly at each of these options.

Java Development Environments

Working with a Java development environment is not for the faint of heart (or for those who want to quickly gain programming experience). Java development environments, such as Microsoft's Visual J++ and Symantec's Visual Café, are industrial-strength software development packages. If you are a programmer, for example, you'll find in them all the features you'd find in development packages aimed at developing Windows applications. When you use them, you'll bring into play a combination of existing Java elements—buttons and forms and more—along with original Java code you'll write yourself. In using one of these packages, there is no way to get around actual programming. That is, in fact, exactly what Java development environments are for—programming.

"Point-and-Click" Tools

As an alternative to developing your own Java code, you can build Java applets using so-called "point-and-click" tools, such as Jamba. For this you need not be a programmer. You are initially presented with a canvas on which you can draw your Java applet. You are then given a choice of elements to place onto the canvas—a container to hold a GIF file, a button, a drop-down list, and things like that. Everything is basically done for you, so all you really have to do is select which elements you want to use, point, and click. No programming is necessary. You can control some interaction between the elements you place on the canvas (for example, you can make it so that when a user clicks a given button, a specified image will appear). All this is done by entering information into a dialog box or two, without the need to actually write any Java code.

Once you have thus "described" the applet you want to create, you then select a menu option to actually generate the Java applet. The drawback in using these point-and-click tools is that they are very limited—they allow you little creativity as compared to actual programming. However, for the programming-impaired, they can be a very handy alternative.

MASTERING WHAT'S ONLINE

Check out Jamba's Web site at www.jamba.com/ for demos and applets, too!

Finding Java Applets

As we've said, you needn't actually write original Java applets in order to incorporate them into your Web site. Many existing applets are available for you to download from the Web and use. Some of these are freeware—meaning that you can nab them and use them as you like, without having to pay for them. Other applets are shareware—meaning you'll have to pay a specified licensing fee before you can use them. Still others are demos of commercial applets that you must purchase from their creators.

MASTERING WHAT'S ONLINE

You can find Java applets galore at Gamelan (www.gamelan.com). Sun Microsystems (the creator of Java) also offers applets for consumption at www.javasoft.com/applets/js-applets.html.

Every Java applet exists as a file with the extension .class. To use an applet you find on Gamelan (or on any other online source of Java applets), you'll have to download the .class file for that applet. Once you have downloaded the .class file, you must copy it into the folder that contains the FrontPage web you'll be using it in. The following section discusses how to incorporate a Java applet into a page on your web.

Inserting Java Applets

You can insert Java applets into your Web pages very quickly and easily; to do so, you must have downloaded or otherwise procured the applet, and placed it into the folder that contains the web you plan to use it in. Then follow these steps:

1. With the target Web page open in FrontPage, from the menu bar, select Insert ➢ Advanced ➢ Java Applet. The Java Applet Properties dialog box appears, as shown in Figure 22.2.

2. In the dialog box's Applet Source text box, type the Java applet's name. For example, for an applet called ticker.class, type **ticker.class**.

3. In the Applet Base URL text box, type the URL that leads to the location of the Java applet. If the Java applet is located in the same directory as the rest of your web's stuff (the HTML file and images for the page), you can leave this field blank.

4. Some Web browsers do not recognize Java. For users of those browsers, you can specify a message that will appear in place of the Java applet. In the text box labeled Message For Browsers Without Java Support, type an appropriate message.

5. You can control the size of the applet as it will appear on screen. In the Size area, you'll see two text fields, labeled Width and Height. Specify the width and height (in pixels) you prefer.

FIGURE 22.2

You can easily insert Java applets into your Web pages, or make changes to the settings for applets you've already inserted.

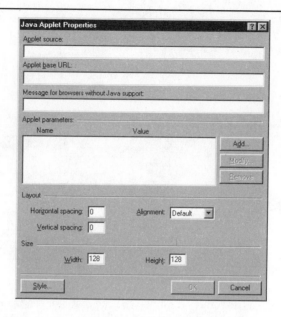

6. In the Vertical Spacing text box of the Layout area, enter the amount of space, in pixels, you'd like to appear between the Java applet and any other elements to the left or right side of it.

7. In the Horizontal Spacing text box of the Layout area, enter the amount of space, in pixels, you'd like to appear between the Java applet and any other elements above or below it.

8. Finally, you can specify the applet's alignment as compared to other elements. In the Alignment drop-down list, select the alignment you prefer.

9. Click OK. The dialog box closes and the Page view window reappears, containing a small box representing the Java applet you inserted.

Setting Parameters

Some applets require you to specify parameters to indicate how the applet will work. For example, a tickertape applet would require a parameter to specify what text will appear in the tickertape as the applet runs. If you use an existing applet, such as one downloaded from Gamelan or elsewhere, it will come with some documentation telling you what parameters must be set.

To set parameters for an applet:

1. With the page that contains the applet open in FrontPage, double-click the applet. The Java Applet Properties dialog box appears.

2. Click the Add button. The Set Attribute Value dialog box appears, as shown in Figure 22.3.

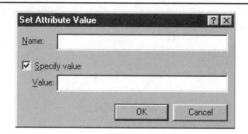

3. In the Name text box, type the name of the parameter you want to set. (Get this info from the applet's documentation.)

4. In the dialog box's Value text box, type the specific information needed. (Again, find out your options from the applet's documentation.)

5. Click OK. The dialog box closes and the Java Applet Properties dialog box reappears. The parameter you just set will be visible in the middle of the dialog box.

6. If additional parameters are required, repeat steps 2 through 5 as needed.

7. Click OK. The dialog box closes.

You won't see any visible changes resulting from the parameters you just entered—parameters affect applets only while they are actually running in a Web browser. If you switch to HTML view (by clicking the HTML tab along the bottom of the Page view window), you will, however, see the <PARAM> tags you just (unknowingly) added.

Changing Applet Properties

Having inserted a Java applet into one of your Web pages, you can then make changes to the applet's properties. You may want to do this, for example, if you want to change the amount of screen space or the alignment of the applet.

Follow these steps:

1. With a Web page open, double-click the applet. The Java Applet Properties dialog box appears.

2. You're home free. This dialog box is the same one you used originally to insert the applet. (See the earlier section, "Inserting Java Applets.") Make changes as you like.

3. When you've finished, click OK. The dialog box closes.

The changes you made will take effect immediately; if you've changed the size of the applet or its alignment, you'll see those results right away. However, some other changes may become apparent only when you view the page in a Web browser that supports Java, so if you don't see what you expect to see right away, check your page using a browser.

 TIP You can use Internet Explorer to preview an applet as it will be seen in a browser window. With a page open in FrontPage, select File ➤ Preview In Browser. In the dialog box that appears, select Internet Explorer and click Preview. Internet Explorer will launch and you'll see the page with the applet.

Up Next

ActiveX components and Java Applets are often fun, and sometimes functional. As with any Web programming technique, it's important to think about your audience—can they see the effect, or will they end up reading a message that tells them their browser doesn't support it? Or will they find that the effect simply takes too long to download to be of real use? These questions are left to you—the designer—to answer. You've got the options now, and can make an educated choice regarding how these techniques are employed.

The next chapter shifts focus a bit to a growing and important area of Web development—databases. While we've focused a lot on the front-end of Web sites, databases are the heart and soul of what goes on behind the scenes to add function and driving power to your webs.

CHAPTER 23

Adding Databases for Maximum Impact

When it comes to rich content on the World Wide Web, there's never too much of a good thing. You can ride the top of the technology curve by adding scripts, applets, and animated logos to your site, but there's no substitute for providing useful, solid information—and lots of it! As Web developers, we understand the value of content, but we find that as we add more and more content to a Web site, it becomes increasingly difficult to keep everything current and well organized. Whether you start small by collecting user input or begin your Web project with a thousand-page catalog, you'll soon find you need a better way than static Web pages to keep everything organized and accessible to users. If you want to make a large amount of related data available on the Web, you'll need the power and versatility of a database.

How can you be sure that you need a database? To help you decide if your site could benefit from the addition of a database, we'll talk about how other Web sites are using databases right now. We'll also discuss some database theory and explore some database jargon to help you understand what databases are all about. Finally, to assist you in adding the power of a database to your Web site, we'll give you step-by-step instructions for using FrontPage to create Web pages that will dynamically interact with your database.

 TIP You can also use Microsoft Access to publish your database. See Chapter 20, *Integrating Sites with Microsoft Office*, for details.

 NOTE This chapter covers the basics about incorporating databases into your Web sites. To learn more about professional aproaches to database design, dive into Chapter 27, *Databases in Detail*.

About Databases and Web Sites

Many Web sites use databases to organize and present all kinds of information. For example, sites that let you book travel arrangements, including Expedia and Travelocity, use databases to store and retrieve massive amounts of flight information.

Another common Web database application is the online catalog. Amazon.com, an online bookstore that lists several million titles, lets users access its database to find the books they want to buy.

In addition to providing travel or book title information, all of these sites let you purchase online. Online purchasing requires storing users' order information, billing information, and preferences. Once such a site gains popularity, you can imagine how quickly the size of these databases can grow!

Finally, there is the granddaddy of database applications: the Web-wide search engines. All of the key players—AltaVista, Yahoo!, Excite, Infoseek, and others—rely on powerful databases to provide those quick keyword searches on millions of Web sites.

As you can see, databases are essential for offering users convenient access to large amounts of data. Without them, many online projects would simply be impossible to create or maintain.

 MASTERING TROUBLESHOOTING

Can Your Web Server and Database Software Share the Same Machine?

As long as your Web server fulfills the requirements for the software, you can run both your Web server and database software. However, if you expect your Web site and database to get a lot of use, you should consider running these two services on separate machines. Remember, "a lot of use" can mean different things, since how much a processor can handle before the whole machine slows down—or even crashes—varies according to operating system and processor type. If you're unfamiliar with your server's general beefiness, consult your system administrator for a realistic idea of how much traffic your machines can take.

Whether you choose one server or several, make sure the machine you plan to put your database on exceeds the requirements for disk drive space and RAM. Plan for future expansion and newer versions of the product you choose, since software tends to be more resource-intensive with each new release.

As a general rule, it's always a good idea to include your system administrator in discussions regarding new software and services you plan to make available for your Web site. He or she will often have good suggestions and practical experience that can help you avoid problems down the line.

What Is a Database?

We've heard of them, we've talked about them, we use them—sometimes unknowingly—every day, but what is a database, really? Let's start by taking a look at the individual parts of a database. Like most other areas of computer technology, each part comes with its own set of descriptive jargon.

Learning More Database Lingo

A *database* is a system that lets you organize and store pieces of related information so that they're easier to find and use. Sounds simple, but what does it really mean? In the real world, we use systems to organize and store information all the time. For example, you may have a stack of business cards from associates or clients. The business cards usually hold the same information from card to card: the person's name, company name, office address, phone number, and e-mail address.

 NOTE In normal conversation, the words *data* and *information* can be easily interchanged. However, in the world of database jargon, data and information do not refer to the same thing. In database lingo, *data* is broken down bits of stuff. *Information* is what happens to data when you organize it into a meaningful structure. Data would be a list of first names: Pete, Jill, Fred. Information would be a list of the first name followed by the last name: Pete McGill, Jill Greene, Fred Forrest. Without the context of a last name or a familiar face, a list of first names doesn't really mean very much to anyone. You must organize this data into information—in this case, by adding the last name—for it to be useful.

Information is what is contained on each business card. That information is organized into several *fields*—in our example, the fields might be name, phone number, address, e-mail, and company name. Each single business card, with its fields of information, would be called a *record*. For a database to work properly, each record in it must contain exactly the same fields. Organize the records—business cards—alphabetically in a Rolodex and you have a *database*. The Rolodex full of business cards is a database because it fits our definition of a database—it is a bunch of information broken down into discrete pieces and organized in a way that's easy to use. Other real-life examples of databases include library card catalogs, dictionaries, and phone books.

Databases are extremely useful tools because organized information makes it easier to find a specific item in a search. A database search request is called a *query*. A database query is much more efficient than searching through random, unorganized data. For example, if you carry all of your customers' business cards around in a plastic baggy, you must sift through *all* the cards each time you need to find John Smith's phone number. If, however, you've alphabetized those cards in your Rolodex, you know you can go directly to the *S* section to find John's information right at your fingertips.

Relational Database Basics

Computer databases have been around just about as long as computers themselves, and several different types of databases have evolved. Today, the *relational database* is one of the most popular. Its counterpart is the *flat file database*. To understand the difference between these two, and why relational databases are more powerful, we'll need to define still more database jargon.

Suppose you work for a company that supplies computer components. Your client database—represented by your stack of business cards—is a *table* that you use on a regular basis.

But your company also has to keep track of who ordered what and when. So you also have access to a database of computerized invoice sheets that list each customer's name and their order.

Now, one of your customers wants you to check on the status of an order. You take that company name from your Rolodex of business cards and compare it against invoice sheets to see if the order has shipped yet. You've just used relational database theory, relating two different databases (the Rolodex and the invoicing system) based on a shared field (the company name). By linking tables with shared fields, you can create some very complex and elegant database queries to get information into and out of the database in any way you need.

When a Database Is What You Need

So how do you decide when a Web-based database is needed? When you have a lot of related information that changes frequently, you should think about organizing that data into a database. You'll know you should consider using a database if:

You collect data using surveys or contests. While you probably won't want visitors to your site to peruse this kind of data, you may find that several departments in your company want to access and search this data. Sending the survey or contest data directly into a searchable database can save you time and effort in the long run.

You have a catalog. To let your users browse through a selection of items or products, you'll want to use a database.

You plan to implement online shopping. You'll need a way to take shipping and payment information from your users, and you'll probably want to save their information so that they don't have to enter it each time they order from your site.

Your company already uses databases. If you're developing an intranet, or maybe you simply want to make company resources available to the public, you may want to access your company's existing database through a Web interface.

Once you've identified your database application, it's time to move on to implementation. If you already have a database up and running, you won't need to pay much attention to the next two sections. However, if you are starting your database project from scratch, read on for some background information and design tips.

TIP The Database Connection Wizard lets you pull data out of a database; it does not help you in entering data. You can use custom ASP scripts to create a form for data entry; however, doing that is beyond the scope of this book. You can then use FrontPage's Form Page Wizard to store the data collected via such forms in a comma delimited text file, which is perfectly suited for importing into a database package. See Chapter 14, *Making Interactive Pages with Forms*, for more on forms.

Adding Database Information to Your Page

FrontPage includes a wizard that allows you to incorporate data from a database right into your Web pages. Before you can begin integrating your database and Web site, however, you'll need to create a database. The first step is to choose a database product that is ODBC-compliant. *ODBC*, short for *Open Database Connectivity*, is a standard way to access different database systems. FrontPage uses ODBC to shuttle information between your database and Web site. ODBC-compliant databases include Microsoft Access, Microsoft SQL Server, Oracle, and others.

NOTE Most ISPs prefer that you not develop your data-centric Web pages on their database server—they'd rather you do development elsewhere and then place your finished database on their machine. If you find this is the case for you, make sure the ODBC data sources on both of those machines use the exact same name.

Step 1: Obtaining a Database

If you don't already have a database, you'll need to create one. Microsoft Access, which is integrated into the Office 2000 family of applications, is the perfect tool to do this. It offers a variety of Wizards that should address most general database needs. See Chapter 20 for more information on Microsoft Access.

For the examples in this chapter, we created a database called "Orders" (see Figure 23.1). This database contains information about several simulated customers.

FIGURE 23.1

Order database created with Microsoft Access

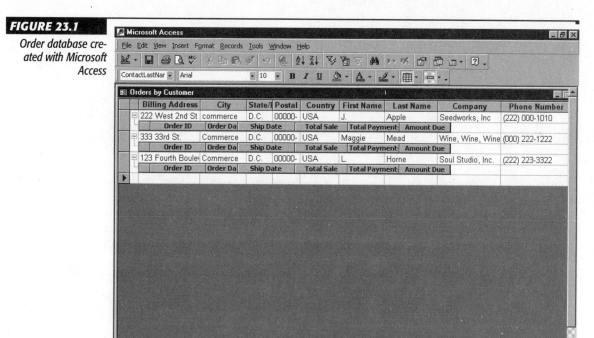

Step 2: Obtain or Create a Data Source Name

The ODBC Data Source Name (DSN) points to your database file—it's what allows your Web pages and database to share information. If your Web server is administered by someone else, you may need to contact your system administrator to obtain the DSN and an optional login and password for your database.

TIP Be sure to close the database in any other applications such as Access before you follow these procedures.

If you're setting up the database yourself on Windows 95, 98, or NT, you can take these simple steps to create a DSN:

1. From the Windows Start menu, choose Settings ➢ Control Panel. The Control Panel Window appears.

2. Double-click the 32-bit ODBC icon. The ODBC Data Source Administrator dialog box appears.

3. Select the User DSN tab. A list of the current user DSNs appears, as shown in Figure 23.2.

 NOTE As you work through the steps in this section, you'll notice that there are several different kinds of Data Source Names (DSNs). The one that's most important to you at this stage of the game is the User DSN. However, so you'll understand the difference between the different kinds, a System DSN is available to all users, whereas a User DSN is only available to the user who creates it. All the details that are created when you set up system or user DSNs are stored in the system registry. File DSNs are a bit more complex—instead of the Registry, information is stored in a file with a .dsn extension. The database then must look for the file in order to understand how to run. File DSNs are usually reserved for administrators and very advanced users with highly specific needs.

FIGURE 23.2

The User DSN tab lists all current DSNs on your system.

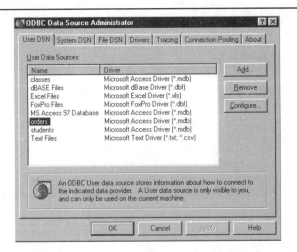

4. Click Add to add a new DSN. The Create New Data Source dialog box appears, as shown in Figure 23.3.

FIGURE 23.3

*Use the Create
New Data Source
dialog box to create
a new DSN.*

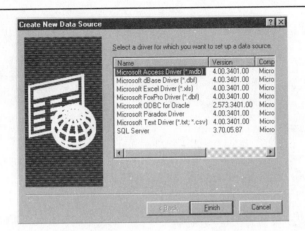

5. From the list, select the driver for the database software that you're using. For our Access example, we'll choose Microsoft Access Driver (*.mdb). You should choose the driver for the specific ODBC-compliant database software that you're using. Then click Finish. The ODBC Microsoft Access Setup dialog box appears.

6. In the Data Source Name text box, type in a name for your DSN. For our example, we'll choose *orders*. It's a good idea to use something descriptive, short, and easy to remember, since you'll have to retype it exactly later on. You can also add a description of the new DSN in the Description text box. You'll have to type in this description later to identify the source of the data you are incorporating into your page.

7. Now you must associate your database file with the DSN. To do this, in the Database area, click Select. In the dialog box that appears, double-click your database file.

 WARNING The DSN is dependent on the location of the database data file, so if your server administrator tells you where to put the data file, be sure to put it there. If you're setting up your own DSN, put your data file some place where you expect it to stay, and don't move the file around. In either case, if you move your database file to a different directory than your DSN expects it to be in, the DSN won't work and the Web pages that access the database will be broken.

8. Some databases are set up to require a username and password. If the database you are using requires this, click Advanced. In the dialog box that appears, fill in the login and password fields and click OK. The ODBC Microsoft Access Setup dialog box reappears.

9. Click OK to close the ODBC Microsoft Access Setup dialog box and return to the ODBC Data Source Administrator dialog box. You should see the name of your new DSN listed in the User DSN tab.

10. Click OK to close the ODBC Data Source Administrator dialog box. The Control Panel window reappears.

Now you're ready to use the Database Results Wizard in Microsoft FrontPage.

Using the Database Results Wizard

The Database Results Wizard allows you to do one of three things:

- Set up a sample database connection, using a pre-existing database named "Northwind."

- Set up an existing database connection.

- Link to the database connection you just created.

The sample database connection is helpful to you if you'd like to make a dry run through the process, and is especially useful when you've never worked with a database before.

To use the sample database:

1. In FrontPage, open the HTML file where you'd like the database to go.

2. Select Insert ➤ Database ➤ Results.

3. The Database Results Wizard appears (see Figure 23.4). Click the Use A Sample Database Connection (Northwind) button.

4. Follow the wizard's directions, leaving all settings at the default unless you know what various options you'd like to enter. When the wizard is finished, the database will appear on your page.

FIGURE 23.4

*The Database Results
Wizard*

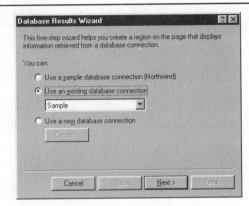

To use an existing database connection:

1. In FrontPage, open the HTML file where you'd like the database to go.

2. Select Insert ➤ Database ➤ Results.

3. Select the Use An Existing Database connection button.

4. Choose one of the databases that appear in the box.

5. Click OK.

FrontPage now links the data.

While you should be familiar with each of these options, the one most critical to your needs at this time is linking to the database connection that you've created.

1. In FrontPage, open the page where you want to insert your database data, and place your cursor where you want the database results to appear. Be sure to select an area that allows for plenty of room to accommodate your database.

2. From the menu bar, select Insert ➤ Database ➤ Results. The Database Results Wizard appears (see Figure 23.4).

3. Click the button at the bottom, Use A New Database Connection.

4. Click Create.

5. The Web Settings dialog box appears (see Figure 23.5). The Database tab should already be selected, but if it's not, go ahead and click it.

FIGURE 23.5

The Web Settings
dialog box

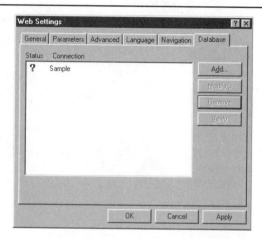

6. To add your database, click Add. The New Database Connection dialog box appears (see Figure 23.6).

FIGURE 23.6

The New Database
Connection dialog box

7. Type the name of your database in the Name text box. (We typed in **orders**.) Then click one of the Location Of Database buttons. You will most likely be linking to a file or folder in the current Web. However, if you are trying to connect to a data source on a Web server, click that button. Similarly, if you are looking for a file that resides elsewhere on the network, click the Other Database Server On The Network button.

8. Click Browse and locate the database file of your choice.

9. Click OK. You'll return to the New Database Connection dialog box. If your database requires a user ID and password, click the Advanced button and enter the appropriate information. Click OK to close the New Database Connection dialog box.

10. When you return to the Web Settings dialog box, you'll now see the name of your database and its status. Click OK to return to FrontPage.

 NOTE Like any other HTML text, you can change the font of the database section, make it bold, or increase the type size. For more on changing the look of text on a Web page, see Chapter 5.

Your database is now linked, and you can modify it to your design tastes using the techniques learned elsewhere in this book. However, in order to make this database fully operational, you must save your HTML file with an .asp (Active Server Pages) extension, and upload all of the information, including the database, to your ASP-compliant server.

Saving Your Page

It's important to pay special attention when saving files that contain database regions. When the Database Results Wizard is applied to a Web page, it actually turns that page into an Active Server Page. Active Server Pages are different from regular HTML pages in that they contain special scripts that must be processed by the Web server before they can be sent out to the user. To indicate to the Web server that these pages require special processing, you must do two things:

- Save the file in a folder that allows scripts to run.
- Change your file's extension to .asp.

Create an Executable Folder in Your FrontPage Web

Web pages that contain Database Results Wizard additions (or any other ASP pages, for that matter) must be stored in a folder that allows scripts or programs to be run. This is not the default setting for FrontPage web folders.

Continued

CONTINUED

If you do not already have an executable folder in your FrontPage web, it's easy to create one:

1. From the FrontPage menu bar, select File ➢ New ➢ Folder.

2. Give the new folder a name. Web folders that allow scripts or programs to run are usually called *cgi*, *cgi-bin*, or *scripts*, but you can choose any name you like.

3. Right-click the folder you just renamed and choose Properties from the menu that appears. The folder's Properties dialog box appears.

4. At the bottom of the folder's Properties dialog box, select the checkbox labeled Allow Scripts Or Programs To Be Run.

5. Click OK. The Properties dialog box closes and your new folder will now allow any scripts and ASPs it contains to be run.

Front Page will attempt to remind you to save your ASP files correctly by showing you some alert boxes (see Figure 23.7).

FIGURE 23.7

FrontPage will alert you to save your file as an ASP file.

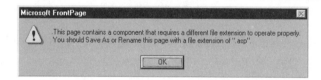

You can follow these simple steps to save your file properly:

1. The file you're preparing to save should be open in Page view.

2. From the menu bar, select File ➢ Save As. The Save As dialog box appears.

3. In the Save As dialog box's list of directories, select the directory you created to hold scripts. (See "Create an Executable Folder in Your FrontPage Web," earlier in this chapter.) In the URL text box, type a filename. The name you give the file should end with the extension .asp (for example, whatever.asp).

4. Click OK. The dialog box closes and the file is saved to the location you specified. The Page view reappears.

ISP Issues

It's important to consider who's supporting your Web site when you're planning and implementing any interactive Web pages, including adding database interaction—especially if your Web site is hosted by an ISP. There are several issues to consider regarding a Web site hosted by an ISP:

- Your ISP may not be using the right operating system or Web server to support ASPs.
- For security reasons, your ISP may not routinely allow users to post Web pages that contain scripts—including ASPs.
- Your ISP may not allow you to use a database as part of your Web, or it may allow only certain database products.

It all comes down to this: If an ISP hosts your Web site, you absolutely must check with (and perhaps make special arrangements with) your ISP *before* you begin adding or uploading databases or ASPs.

Changing Database Properties

You've created this great new interactive database Web page, but nobody's perfect. What if you want to make a change to a database region once you've left the Database Results Wizard? Fortunately, FrontPage makes it easy to go back and edit the database you've added to your pages. Here's how:

1. In FrontPage, open the Web page containing the database templates. You'll see sections demarcating the beginning and end of the database regions (see Figure 23.8).
2. Right-click within the database area. A menu appears, as shown in Figure 23.8.
3. From the menu that appears, select Database Results Properties. The Database Results Wizard dialog box appears. All the values you typed in when you last used the wizard will still be in place.
4. You can now make any modifications to your database that you'd like.

Once you are done with the Database Results Wizard, you'll be returned to Page view, where you'll see the changes you made to the database.

FIGURE 23.8

Right-clicking the database gives you a menu of options.

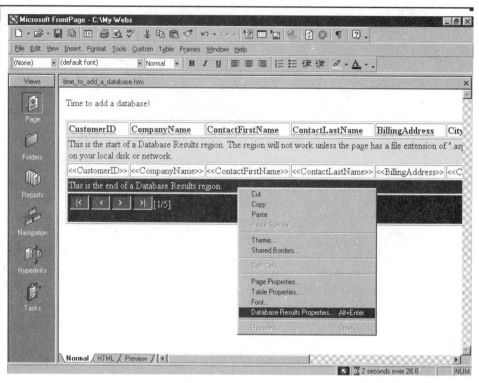

Viewing Your Page

After you've saved your database-enabled Web page, you can view it. One option is to view the page by selecting the Preview tab along the bottom of the window. You'll notice that the database values do not appear on the page as they should.

NOTE Database values do not appear in the FrontPage Preview window because the Web page must be served by a Web server.

It's easy to view your page as a user would see it. Follow these steps:

1. Make sure your Web page has been properly saved as an ASP file in a folder that allows scripts to be run.

2. Open the database-enabled page in Page view.

3. From the menu bar, select File ➤ Preview In Browser. The Preview In Browser dialog box appears.

4. Click the Preview button. The page appears in a Web browser window.

The resulting page looks quite different from the preview you looked at in Page view. Instead of placeholder text appearing where data from the database should appear, the actual data appears.

Notes on Database Maintenance

You've defined the project, organized the data, chosen a database product, and implemented the solution. But you're not done yet! Getting the most out of your database requires that you maintain the database and the information contained within it.

You or your staff can perform some of the regular maintenance that your database requires, but some changes may require calling in a *database administrator* (*DBA*) or consultant. Here are some items you can manage yourself, once the database is up and running:

- Adding new records to the database
- Editing existing records
- Deleting old or outdated records
- Making regular backups

Maintenance items that may require the assistance of a DBA or consultant include:

- Creating new kinds of queries
- Adding new fields or new tables to an existing database
- Upgrading the database software
- Upgrading the hardware of the machine on which the database software runs

Up Next

Databases add functionality in a variety of ways, and entire books have been written that describe how databases can be used to enhance Web sites. While we can't address such a vast technology in one short chapter, we have given you the basics to get you started.

As mentioned, databases, like any advanced or interactive Web application, demand updates and maintenance.

In Chapter 24, *Site Maintenance and Promotion*, we'll take a look at how you can apply professional techniques to help you get the most mileage out of your databases and webs in general. We'll show you how to keep track of changes, make updates, and keep links fresh, as well as how to promote your site once it's on the Web.

CHAPTER 24

Site Maintenance and Promotion

Congratulations! You have successfully constructed a well–thought-out, well-designed, robust FrontPage web. You've linked it up, brought it live, and taken your team out to lunch to celebrate. Now you find yourself charged with keeping your creation current and working like new. You'll need to be sure that your site's content is visually, textually, and technically up-to-date, and that your fellow Webmasters and favorite search engines are paying attention. This chapter takes you through the basics of site maintenance and promotion, assuring that your site will get the airtime it deserves.

Managing Maintenance of Your Web Site

Keeping a Web site going is a constant challenge, not unlike maintaining a house. A house can't keep itself in good repair; you have to scoop leaves out of drains and gutters, fix leaks in the roof, insulate the pipes to prevent freezing in the winter, and that sort of thing. Similarly, a Web site needs basic maintenance on a regular basis.

Some tasks are pretty obvious. You have to check the links that go from your site out into the Web world (to make sure they're still live), fix the odd script or database query here or there that breaks at random, and refine navigational elements as you add new pages and areas to your site. You also have to do a certain amount of routine server maintenance, which basically consists of reading log files and dealing with what comes up. Luckily, FrontPage offers some handy tools that make site maintenance quite a bit easier than it might be otherwise; rather than a major time sink, it's now simply a matter of delegation.

 TIP Don't forget to use the handy Tasks view feature described in Chapter 7, *Managing Tasks*, to organize and track your maintenance tasks.

Organizing and Assigning Maintenance Tasks

Maintenance doesn't tend to be at the top of a Web team's list of things to do. You'll find that Web site maintenance will happen only if the tasks involved in it are specifically detailed and then assigned to particular people. Almost everyone we know would rather have fun than clean their rooms, and it's really easy for Web site managers and worker bees alike to get caught up in the glamour tasks (like creating new pages or adding zippy features). Site maintenance can turn into a low priority until something breaks or users start to complain.

 TIP Keep in mind that if one person takes the time to complain about a broken link, half a dozen more probably didn't bother and just left your site instead, carrying along with them a bad impression. Don't wait for complaints. Find broken items on your site before visitors do, and fix them immediately.

Make yourself or your group an organized list—a *chore chart* of sorts—showing what maintenance needs to be done and who will do it. You might even consider keeping a log and having each person jot in his or her initials when a task is complete, along with any notes for others who might do that task in the future. (Often you'll find it easier to trace the source of some special problem if you have a good history of events to consult.)

Basic Web site maintenance includes:

Verifying that links work. The section titled "Verifying Hyperlinks" later in this chapter shows you how to use FrontPage's Verify Hyperlink Status feature to painlessly locate and fix any links that may have died or otherwise gone sour on your site.

Replacing outdated text and images. FrontPage's search-and-replace function enables you to easily substitute new text for outdated content. (To replace images, you must find and replace them manually. See Chapter 4, *Creating Basic Pages*.)

Improving organization and navigation as needed, especially when new material is added to the site or old material is deleted. You'll need to change both your navigation bars (see Chapter 15, *Special Effects*) and your button text.

Repairing broken queries or scripts. See Chapter 21, *JavaScript and Dynamic HTML*, Chapter 22, *Specialty Programming Techniques*, and Chapter 23, *Adding Databases for Maximum Impact*, for more on databases and scripts.

Conducting server maintenance. This is a matter of reading and responding to log files, identifying broken scripts, monitoring disk and memory usage, predicting load levels, and generally taking steps to ensure that your Web site doesn't cause the server to crash.

Depending on the size, goals, and mission-critical status (or lack thereof) of your site, these tasks might be done often or rarely; the point is to do them *regularly*. The allocation of maintenance responsibilities among your team members depends on how your team is configured. The point is this: To ensure that maintenance tasks are performed on schedule, those tasks must be assigned to specific people who will be accountable for getting them done.

Your graphically inclined team members, for example, will be the obvious nominees for keeping your Web site's imagery up-to-date. Copywriters can be tasked with periodic content revision. Programmers can be relied on to parse server logs and regularly offer the reassurance that your site is (or will immediately be) bug-free. As for "grunge work" like checking retroactive links and search engine placement: taking turns doing it is one option, but you may also want to consider hiring a willing high school or college intern to support your team. You'll appreciate the labor; they'll appreciate the good reference on their resume. All of these services can also be outsourced to independent consultants if your budget permits, and if it seems to be the best alternative for your company.

 MASTERING THE OPPORTUNITIES

Managing Style

With multiple people handling various parts of your Web site, you need a way to communicate to all members of the group what's been decided about matters of *style*. (Even if it's just you, you're better off jotting these things down for your own reference than trying to remember from one month to the next.) This is an important part of maintaining the look, feel, and general content integrity of your site. For example, you'll want to communicate exactly which colors comprise your site's palette, and which fonts are used for what elements. You should even document such nit-picky matters as how to spell certain words that have more than one commonly used spelling (like *e-mail* or *email*) and how to punctuate things (like whether to say *U.S.* or *US* when abbreviating *United States*). Nothing looks more unprofessional than random inconsistency, and the best way to maintain consistency is to create, maintain, and consult a *style guide*.

Your style guide can be an online document, a printed document, or both. It should include information about:

- The site's *mission*—for example, a brief statement describing the product or service the site offers or the goal it will accomplish, along with the style in which it will do so, the audience it will reach, and how its success might be assessed in the context of the goals set out for the site.

- The site's *look and feel*—including color and font choices, guidelines regarding placement of art on the pages, where banners and nav bars go, and even records

Continued

MASTERING THE OPPORTUNITIES CONTINUED

of how certain design decisions were reached and who did the actual design work (so you can later reference that information instead of reinventing the wheel).

- Conventions you've established for *use of HTML*—for example, the screen size (in pixels) you design for, how and when to use META, ALT, and other tags, what types of headings go where, which browsers are supported and how, how tables are used (with specifics of cell size, and so on), how to lay out tabular matter, and how to use art, captions, sidebars, pull quotes, and footers.

- Policies for *linking and crosslinking*—for example, how many links can appear on a page or in a paragraph, and which sorts of words or phrases to link on (hint: linking on Click here is nowhere near as useful as linking on a word describing what the user will actually find behind the link).

- Standards for *editorial tone and conventions*—for example, whether the site's written text has a hip, playful, or "professional" tone, and whether to style certain phrases certain ways (again, will it be email or e-mail? What about P.M., PM, or p.m.?).

- Guidelines regarding *navigation and architecture*—for example, how the directory structure is organized and where things go in it, as well as (generally speaking) how the user is expected to make his or her way around.

- Conditions for using the company *logo and copyright notices*, as well as any other pertinent legal information—for example, what colors the logo is allowed to appear in and where it may be placed, as well as where copyright notices and other legalese must appear and what they must say.

- Processes and procedures you've established for *review and posting* of material—for example, who has the final say on which content is posted, how long will they have to offer feedback or consent, who decides which feedback to incorporate and how, and who may do the actual posting to the site.

You can see some examples of style guides on the Web; some of these give certain matters more coverage than others, and some are easier to navigate or more attractively designed than others. Take a look at several and you'll get ideas about what should be in your own style guide.

MASTERING WHAT'S ONLINE

A great example of a Web site style guide is the Yale C/AIM Style Guide at `info.med.yale.edu/caim/manual/index.html`. Contrast its navigation and content with the Ball State guide at `www.bsu.edu/handbook`. Check out Lincoln University's University Outreach style guide at `outreach.missouri.edu/webteam/style`; for another example, see West Virginia University's guide (which offers at least some editorial information) at `www.wvu.edu/~telecom/wwwinit/guidelines.html`. For a look at a big, complex style guide, wind up your tour at Sun's: `www.sun.com/styleguide`.

Verifying Hyperlinks

Dead links can kill your site's interest level. Links "die" when the page or site at the other end of the link goes down or its URL changes. You can't control that, and all too often, you know about it only because your users complain. Few things will chase users off your site faster than a lot of links that go nowhere. And yet, finding and eliminating dead links on a big site is a big chore—in days of old, it involved a tedious process of clicking one link after another to be sure they all worked. Now FrontPage automates this process, making link maintenance so easy that there's just no excuse for not doing it.

Checking Link Status

Before you can fix broken links, you must track them down. Checking links is a snap with FrontPage; the process is very automatic and results in an easy-to-use list showing the status of all the links in your web. You can then move on to the more entertaining part—fixing them.

TIP If you use a dial-up connection to the Internet rather than connecting via a LAN, you'll have to be connected before you can verify the links in your site. Otherwise, when you verify the links, all the links that go outside your site will appear to be bad. (The pages they point to were inaccessible, and so they appeared to FrontPage to be dead.)

To check links on your site, follow these steps:

1. With a web open in the FrontPage Reports view, open the Reporting toolbar by selecting View ➤ Toolbars ➤ Reporting. The Reporting Toolbar appears (see Figure 24.1).

FIGURE 24.1

The Reporting Toolbar allows you to perform a variety of site checks, including link verification.

2. Click the Verify Hyperlinks button.

3. The Verify Hyperlinks dialog box appears (see Figure 24.2).

FIGURE 24.2

The Verify Hyperlinks dialog box

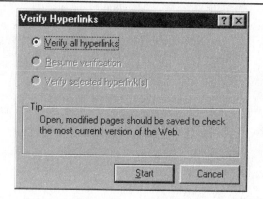

3. Click one of the following buttons:

- Verify All Hyperlinks to verify all the links in the current FrontPage web.
- Resume Verification to resume an interrupted check.
- Verify Selected Hyperlink(s) to verify links in selected pages.

To check all links in the current web, which is our current purpose, click the Verify All Hyperlinks button.

4. Click Start. The dialog box closes and the window returns to the FrontPage Reports view. In this report, every single link in your web appears in a list, along with the URL associated with that link and the link's status. At first, the status of

all of the links will be *Unknown*. This is because the window appears immediately, before the check is begun.

5. One by one, the status of all the links is updated in the Broken Hyperlinks report view. Each link's status is described with one of the following indicators:

This Status...	Means...
OK	The link works.
Broken	The link is broken.
Unknown	The link has not yet been verified.
Verifying	The link is currently being verified.

Now you can move on to fixing those broken links that you've discovered. Read on.

MASTERING WHAT'S ONLINE

If you're checking links from a computer where FrontPage isn't installed, you may want to try the venerated Doctor HTML. The Doc verifies links and HTML tags and even checks spelling; it also provides further information in the course of doing so beyond what FrontPage tells you. For example, Dr. HTML calculates how long the page will take for a user to load using a 14.4 modem. Consult Doctor HTML at `imagiware.com/RxHTML.cgi`.

Another site you'll enjoy is NetMechanic at `www.netmechanic.com`. If these sites don't suit you, or you want to find others, do a search for HTML validators on your favorite search engine. There are many great sites that evaluate your Web sites at no charge to you.

Fixing Broken Links

Okay, so you've checked the links on your site and found a few that were, to your dismay, broken. (If you didn't, good job! But don't forget to check again next week.) FrontPage offers two ways to deal with broken links. You can change a particular URL (whether it appears in one instance or throughout the site), or you can edit a page that contains a bad URL. Changing links is a convenient technique in many instances, but if you have other work to do on a single page or if you want to delete the broken link instead of changing it, editing is the preferred route. Let's take a look.

NOTE Yet a third way to replace links is to simply find and replace them using the techniques described in the section "Finding Text and Replacing It Globally," later in this chapter. This is sometimes not the most convenient method, but it is an available method.

Changing Broken Links

Perhaps only one link showed up as broken. Or, perhaps you found that a lot of links on your site were a problem. A handy FrontPage feature enables you to change that link once and have the change instantly propagate throughout the site–a big time saver. (You can actually use this method for a single broken link as well; this might be preferable to editing the page because it is such an easy operation.) To fix one broken link or many, follow these steps:

1. In Reports view, double-click Hyperlinks. The Broken Hyperlinks report appears.

2. Double-click the link you want to change. The Edit Hyperlink dialog box appears, as shown in Figure 24.3.

FIGURE 24.3

Whether you want to fix a single broken link or many instances of that broken link, here's the place to do it.

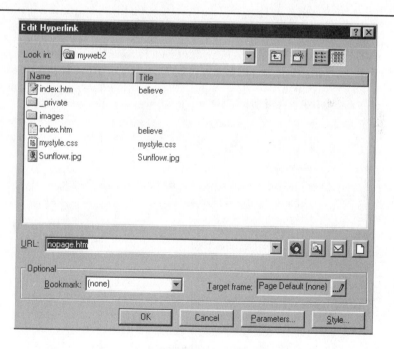

3. In the URL text box, type in a new, good link to replace the old one. For example, if you made a typo when you typed in the old link, `http://www.acompany.cm`, and the new, good link is `http://www.acompany.com`, type the correct link into the URL text box.

4. You can elect to change all of the occurrences of the URL or just selected occurrences. To change all of the occurrences, click the button labeled Change In All Pages. (To change the URL only in selected pages, highlight the pages in the list of pages and click the Change In Selected Pages button.)

 TIP If you don't want to fix a given URL right now, you can add this task to your Task list as a reminder to do it in the future. Just right-click the URL in question and, from the menu that appears, select Add Task. The New Task dialog box will appear. See Chapter 7 for information about managing and completing tasks.

5. Click the Replace button. The dialog box closes and the FrontPage window reappears. In it, the new, good link will appear in the list in place of the old one; the status of the new link will be shown as Unknown (because it hasn't been checked in the most recent round of checking).

The link is fixed. You can continue to fix other broken links, or you can perform other tasks simply by switching views.

Editing Broken Links

To edit links, follow these steps:

1. In the Broken Hyperlink report view, right-click the link you want to edit. A menu appears.

2. From the menu, select Edit Page. FrontPage opens the page containing the selected URL in the Page view.

Edit the page using the standard page-editing techniques we covered earlier in the book. You can edit as much of the page as you like, including changing or deleting the URL at will.

 TIP In some cases, you might want to make other changes to a page in addition to fixing a broken link; alternatively, you might want to simply remove the broken link. In those cases, editing the page is a good practice.

Finding Text and Replacing It Globally

As you build bigger and more complex Web sites, you'll find yourself wanting to make a single change across many, many pages. Maybe you want to change a name every time it appears on the site, or simply make a quick fix to a link. (A link is, after all, simply a piece of text.) The global search and replace features of FrontPage will save you a lot of time in doing this. They allow you to search—and make changes to—all of the pages that make up any given webs in your Web site using a simple two-step process.

Finding Text

Searching your entire web for a specified piece of text is just as easy as searching a single page for text:

1. With the FrontPage web open, if you want to search an entire web, from the menu bar, select Edit ➤ Find *or* Replace. The Find dialog box appears, as shown below.

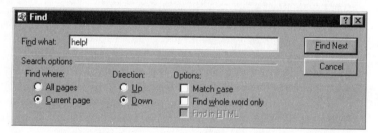

2. In the Find What text box, type the text you seek.

3. If you want the sought-after text to be found only when it appears as a whole word (as opposed to a fragment of a word), click the checkbox labeled Find Whole Word Only.

4. If you'd like to find the text only in cases where its capitalization matches what you entered in step 2, click the checkbox labeled Match Case.

5. If the text you're looking for is HTML code, click the checkbox labeled Find In HTML.

6. To search the entire Web site, click the button labeled Entire Web. To search only the pages you specified in step 1, click the button labeled Selected Pages.

7. Click the Find In Web button. The search begins, and when it is completed, a text window appears in the bottom portion of the Find dialog box listing all the occurrences of the text you've just sought out.

8. To open one of the pages listed, double-click it in the dialog box. The view shifts to the Page view, and the page you selected opens. Your search text appears in the Find dialog box.

9. Click Find and the search begins. As FrontPage finds instances of the specified text, it highlights them in the page.

10. Make any changes you like using the editing methods described in Part I of this book.

11. Repeat steps 8 through 10 to edit other pages if you like, or click Close to close the dialog box and return to the FrontPage window.

If you want to make changes to the found text globally (throughout the web), you'll use the Replace function. More on that in a moment.

 TIP You may want to simply identify the changes you'd like to make, and add them to your Task list to be done later. To do this, highlight the page in question and click the Add Task button. For more information about using the Task list, turn to Chapter 7.

Replacing Text

You can quite easily find and replace a specified piece of text in all of the pages that make up a web. This is an obvious convenience; when the company changes the official spelling of the name of a product, you don't have to track down all instances of it on the site and edit them one by one; you can easily change them globally and save yourself the effort.

 WARNING Watch out. We've seen it happen and done it ourselves. You make what you think should be a simple global change, and sometime later, in casually viewing your site, you see unexpected consequences. For example, the seemingly innocent change of *hat* to *coat* can inadvertently give you occurrences of *that* changed to *tcoat*. Just be sure the apparent wisdom of making a global change is not a false friend.

Here's how to make a global change to text:

1. With the FrontPage web open, if you want to make replacements across an entire web, from the menu bar, select Edit ➤ Replace. The Replace dialog box appears.

2. In the Find What text box, type the text you want to find.

3. In the Replace With text box, type the replacement text.

4. If you want the text to be found only when it appears as a whole word (as opposed to a part of a word—see the example in the note in this section), click the Match Whole Word Only checkbox.

5. If you'd like to find the text only in cases where its capitalization matches what you entered in step 2, click the Match Case checkbox.

6. To make replacements across the entire web, click the Entire Web button. To make replacements only in the pages you specified in step 1, click the Selected Pages button.

7. Click the Find In Web button. The search begins, and when it is completed, the Find Occurrences dialog box appears, listing all the pages that contain the search term.

8. Now, to actually make the replacements in a given page, double-click that page in the list. (You have to make the actual changes one page at a time.) The page opens in Page view and the Replace dialog box is visible, with both the *find* and *replace* text you specified in steps 2 and 3 all filled in.

9. Click the Replace All button. All occurrences in the page are replaced, and a dialog box appears, offering to save and close the current page.

10. If you want to make the global change on additional pages, repeat steps 8 and 9 for each page.

11. When you've finished, click the Cancel button. The dialog box closes and the Page view reappears.

Now you can resume other tasks, take a walk, or get a cup of coffee.

Promoting Your Site and Building Traffic

If there are no links to your site, you will get no hits. This is a law of physics on the Web. You will want many entry points to your site. You want *retroactive links* (links from other sites to yours), and you want prominent listings in directories and search engine databases. You want your site to get all the attention it deserves—and if no one knows it's there, how will they visit? It's your job to get out there and tell people your site exists. You want lots of people visiting, lots of hits, consistent *traffic*.

TIP The best way to get publicity for your Web site is to make it such a whiz-bang piece of genius that no one can ignore it. Make sure your site includes outstanding original content presented in an appropriate style, with great design, easy navigation, and a healthy dose of wit. The combination of all of these elements will make your site appealing to those in the know who see so many and recommend so few. These individuals, when satisfied, are the best visitors to any site.

The stuff of real world publicity includes press releases; newsletters; print advertising; direct mail or other distribution of flyers, postcards, or letters; public appearances; gala events; and so on. You may be surprised to find out how many of these common real-world publicity techniques transfer directly to the Net. A press release can easily go to selected online venues via e-mail; an electronic "mailing list" can be an avenue to distribute newsletters to your circle of associates; a chat might be thought of as an "event," and so on. Effective use of these techniques requires a combination of diligence and creativity.

The most important caveat in using online publicity techniques is basic: *respect the culture within which you're moving*. Online culture is not a grab-and-run environment and does not suffer a deluge of junk mail lightly. It's important to avoid "spamming," or flooding people with e-mail they're not interested in reading. Your goal is to center your online publicity on the values Netizens hold dear—choice, privacy, and content over form. Before we launch into specific techniques for publicizing your site, let's look at how to identify your target audience and how to choose which venues to use in your campaign.

Finding Your Target Audience

When marketing a product, you can go either *broad* or *deep*. You usually don't want to slam your message at everyone on the Internet (that's *broad*) unless your site is of overall interest to everyone. A search engine site or other online directory is one example of a site that has very broad appeal and would especially benefit from broad exposure; another example might be a site devoted to some piece of Internet software. For most topics, however, you'll do better to focus your efforts on reaching those who are most likely to respond to the topic of your site. That's *deep*—meaning that you deeply penetrate a narrower market. If your site is about cars, for example, you want to reach people with an interest in cars.

The content of your site will help you decide whether to go broad or deep. If you're going broad, look for venues that will reach a large number of people. If deep is the route you choose, look for venues that are trafficked by the folks you want to reach. Be creative about your target audience—if your site is about lunch boxes, your audience might be kids, pop culture fans, memorabilia collectors, and even fans of some celebrities who appear on lunch boxes. If your site is about rose gardening, your audience will be not only garden hobbyists, but also decorators, landscape architects, florists, and Valentine's Day gift-givers.

Take a minute to think through the topic of your site and brainstorm about what types of people might be interested in it. This preliminary demographic study will help you choose the best means of locating the audience you want to communicate with.

Planning Your Campaign

Organizing and carrying out a promotional campaign for your Web site is much like conducting promotional efforts for any other product, service, or company. Of course you need to know what your site is about and who your target audience is. To create your own campaign, you'll also need to get your message in order. Planning your promotional campaign will include:

- Gathering materials. For example, you'll want to have your site's mission statement and goals on hand, as well as any logos and other visual elements you can use in your marketing efforts.

- Writing up some key points (*talking points*) and a brief summary of your site's content (a *blurb*). These are, in a sense, just friendlier versions of your list of goals and mission statement.

- Researching how your site compares to others of its type, and what differentiates it or sets it apart from those competitors. (Be sure to cover this in your talking points and blurb.) You may also have to research what individual promotional options cost, who's who at a print venue you want to target, and so on.

- Considering your budget. You always want to get the biggest bang for your buck; how to accomplish the most economical and *effective* promotion is the name of the game.

- Targeting the venues most likely to reach your audience and reel them in.

The rest of this chapter offers pointers to addressing these action items. Let's start by looking at how people—most people, that is—locate Web sites they might find of interest. Most folks find what they're looking for on the Internet through just a few venues. The most common are:

- Search tools
- Retroactive Links
- Newsgroups
- The press (magazines and newspapers)

Signature (sig) files ("from a friend") and books are less common venues. However, don't write off these options—they are often the least expensive venues and sometimes reach extremely specific audiences; they also carry the weight of great authority—recommendations from a friend or a book, for example, are very persuasive, aren't they?

In considering which venues to tackle, your goal is to determine which are best for you and which will reach the largest percentage of your target audience.

 TIP You can choose to pursue any combination of venues—for example, you can pursue a presence in newsgroups that are appropriate to your topic, *and* in the press, *and* in search tools, and so on. Don't overlook the "smaller" venue of placing a small notice of your site in a sig file that will appear at the bottom of every e-mail you send out. More on each of these options as we go along.

Your campaign should be as extensive as your time and resources allow. But it should also take into account which venues will be most likely to reach your target audience, and which are most cost effective. For example, many people find out about Web sites via newsgroups. While frequenting newsgroups to evangelize your site seems easy enough, it is also time-consuming for you to do it, and it's not cheap to pay someone to sit around shuffling through Usenet, either. Should you choose to go the seemingly free newsgroups route (described in an upcoming section), consider the hidden costs involved, and rather than spreading your efforts around many newsgroups, *target those most likely to lead to success* given how you've envisioned your audience.

To focus your campaign, start by thinking about the benefits your site offers (not just the features, but the *benefits*)—what will people get from a visit to your site? Will they get fast solutions to specific problems or challenges? Easy access to other Web sites? The product or service they've been looking for? A quality entertainment experience? Jot down a few talking points so you'll remember what features you really want to emphasize when writing the copy of your announcements and messages. Write up perhaps five phrases or sentences that describe the benefits of your site and/or the product you deliver via your site. Do this in a bulleted list, not paragraphs. Hone these phrases—your talking points—until they describe exactly what you want people to know at a glance about your site.

Keep your talking points near you or in a folder with records of your promotional efforts and how they panned out. These talking points can form the basis of any press releases you send out and ads you create. They can also help you in focusing the design or redesign of your site, since they are a sort of shorthand definition of your mission.

Remember to keep in mind the goals you've set for your site as you write up your talking points and focus your promotional campaign and the audience you plan to reach.

To actually plan your campaign, you will need to weigh the cost versus benefit of each potential venue you consider. Among the benefits to consider are:

- Will your message be intensely targeted (deep) or reach a wide variety of people (broad)? Which is more appropriate to your product, service, or site?

- How many users will you reach?

- What will it cost to reach each user? (If it costs you $1 to reach a single user, that's probably not very cost effective.) You usually want to spend, at most, a few pennies per user. Generally speaking, the less you spend to reach a single user, the better.

- What hidden costs are involved? (Adding a sig file to the end of every e-mail message sent out by every employee in the company is obviously free, but the seemingly free venture of trading ads with another site may involve hidden costs. Think of the time it takes one employee to rustle up those ad trades as well as the time needed to create the ads.)

Consider these items carefully as you put together your promotional budget and your overall publicity campaign. Now, let's take a look at the most commonly accessed venues—those that users say they most often employ to find what they seek. Then you can determine which venues are right for you and attack those first.

Getting Listed with Directories and Search Engines

You can get your page listed in many big directories such as Yahoo! or Excite quite easily by submitting your URL via a handy form that you'll find at the directory's site. Or you can go to a central location (like "Pointers to Pointers" or "Submit It!"—see the sidebar in this section for more information on these sites) that lists a lot of different directories. Select as many or as few directories as you'd like your site to appear in, click an oh-so-easy-to-use Submit button, and—wham-o! An announcement of your site's birth will be blasted off to all the appropriate places in cyberspace in no time flat. Many of the Submit-It! type of announcement services used to be free but now charge a fee for making announcements to the major venues like Yahoo! and AltaVista, so you may just want to do the work yourself. It's quick and easy.

TIP As always, consider your target audience when choosing where to list your site. For example, while Submit It! and other services list hundreds of search sites you *could* list with, will it really be an effective means of reaching your target audience if you list a site about lunchboxes in a medical research directory or search engine?

Just go, or send your intern, to the directories of interest to your site. These will all prominently feature a link that will allow you to register your site in that directory. Keep in mind, however, that it is up to a given search engine or directory whether it will list your Web site. It also can take some time to get listed in these venues, which are overwhelmed with requests—you cannot expect to submit your site for consideration on Tuesday and see it listed on Friday. It actually may take weeks, so remember that patience is a virtue!

TIP Part of your site's continuing maintenance consists of keeping sure that you're where you need to be in the search engine rankings. Many engines, directories, and link databases are updated every 24 hours. You don't want to look back a week later and find that your site has been eclipsed by your competitor's! More on optimizing your search engine ranking in the next section.

MASTERING WHAT'S ONLINE

Pointers to Pointers is at www.homecom.com/global/pointers.html; Submit It! is at www.submit-it.com/. To check out other places to promote your page, visit Yahoo!'s list of Announcement Services at www.yahoo.com/Computers_and_Internet/ Internet/World_Wide_Web/Announcement_Services. If your site is commercial, try the LinkStar commercial directory at www.linkstar.com.

Optimizing Your Standing

Most Internet search tools—like AltaVista, Infoseek, Lycos, and Excite—use small automated code-searchers called "spiders" to find your site. These spiders are released out into the Net, follow links, and index every site they find in the databases they service. Often they'll use the first few lines of text on your Web page as a description or as the basis of keywords to attach to your site. When a user searches for a given topic, the search tool usually lists whatever matches that search according to *relevancy*. So why does the spider think things are relevant that, to you, might not necessarily be so? Keep in mind that all the spider knows about your site is the description and keywords it "figured out" after running its automated processes on the beginning text of your Web pages.

You can control this all-important description and keyword list. Most of the big-gun search engines recognize the contents of a META tag—an HTML tag that resides in the HEAD area of a Web page and describes the page to spiders—which will aid in indexing Web sites in the database. You can use this tag and a few others to control the relevancy ranking of your site. Note that you ought to complete this exercise before listing your site with search engines. They don't come around looking for changes very often once they list you, so you want your house clean the first time they visit.

There are several types of META tags you can (and should) use. For example, you can specify a "title" META tag, which will identify the title of your page, a "keywords" META tag, which will allow you to specify keywords that describe your site more precisely than the automated Web crawlers will, as well as a "description" META tag.

You can easily insert META tags into your Web pages using the Page Properties dialog box. To start, write down a few items that describe your page:

- A couple of words that correspond to the topic of your page (place these in the title of the page, too)

- Some keywords (10 or 12 of them) that also correspond to the topic

- One short sentence (not two) that clearly describes the page

Having done that, you're ready to roll. Follow these steps:

1. Open the page in Page view. From the menu bar, select File ➤ Properties. The Page Properties dialog box appears.

2. In the dialog box's Title text box, type the "title" words you targeted. Note that the title must be understandable as well as include as many keywords as possible. Here's an example: **Horse Care and Riding**.

3. Now click the Custom tab. The contents of the dialog box change to reflect your choice.

4. In the lower part of the dialog box, locate the User Variable area. This area displays a list of all the META tags in the current page. To add a new META tag to the page, which is what you want to do, click the Add button. The User META Variable dialog box appears.

5. In the Name text box, you need to identify the type of META tag you want to add. For example, type **keywords** now, so you can specify some keywords.

6. Now, in the User META Variable dialog box's Value text box, type the keywords you think best describe your site. For our example site about horse care and riding, you'd type keywords such as *horse, riding, horse care, dressage, saddle, bridle, horsemanship, thoroughbred, horses, rider,* and *horse riding.* Because not all search engines are case-sensitive, always make your keywords lowercase, even if they are proper nouns. Also, remember to think up synonyms to include among your keywords. Finally, do not stack words—pages containing repeated keywords like *horse, horse, horse* will be tossed out or otherwise penalized.

7. Click OK, and the dialog box closes. The Page Properties dialog box reappears, with the information you specified for your keywords META tag now visible.

8. Now repeat steps 5 through 7, this time typing **description** in the Name text box (instead of **keywords**) and then adding the description you think best. In our example, this might be *Horse care and riding information for the serious amateur.* In your description, avoid using "I" (as in "I teach horse care"). Instead, when necessary, use the third person ("horse care expert"). This will allow you to squeeze in additional references to keywords; it will also help users to understand what the site is about. A good description runs about twenty-five words or less, although you should be sure to check with search engines for their specific requirements.

9. Click OK, and the Page Properties dialog box closes. The Page view window reappears, displaying your Web page. While visible signs of the META tags you just added won't be evident (META tags have no visible effect on a Web page), rest assured that they are now part of the HTML that defines your page.

10. Your META tags alone won't boost your relevancy score as much as you'd like. You also need to repeat the words you targeted for your title and keywords (*horse* and *riding,* for example) in the page's text at least once and preferably more than once. Make these mentions as close as possible to the top of the page. Then repeat them a few more times elsewhere in the page.

Your Web site is now enhanced in ways that will help it receive the ranking it deserves in search engine and Internet directory databases. This will be a big help to users in search of sites like yours.

MASTERING WHAT'S ONLINE

Search Engine Watch, by Calafia Consulting, offers good background information and tips for getting listed with the major search engines. It also offers a mailing list that announces major changes in search sites. Swing by `searchenginewatch.com` and sign up.

Retroactive Linking

Trust us, there are lots of other folks on the planet with businesses or hobbies that have things in common with the subject of your Web site. You can find sister Web sites by conducting a simple search via AltaVista, Yahoo!, Lycos, or Excite, then contact those Webmasters by e-mail and offer to trade links. Having links to your Web site from other sites not only provides Web surfers with additional ways to reach your site, it also makes your site more visible to Web directories. Many Web spiders follow links from site to site, and the more often your site shows up, the higher it will be rated on the database.

If you're feeling creative, use a paint program or Image Composer to create a nifty little button or logo you can offer to Webmasters to use as a link to your site. Try to make the look of the button similar enough to the look of your site to create a connection in the minds of users. Try, too, to make the button or logo a size that is both small enough to be acceptable for others to place on their sites without your logo overwhelming everything else on their page, and large enough to be legible to users. Keep the size of the file for the button or logo small—don't use too many colors, avoid dithering, and stick to simple colors. (See Chapter 9, *Designing Graphics for the Web*, to learn more about how to do this using Microsoft PhotoDraw and Image Composer.)

MASTERING THE OPPORTUNITIES

Finding Out About Retroactive Links to Your Site

AltaVista offers a quick and easy way to investigate whether your site has retroactive links. You can actually use this method to find out quite a bit about your retroactive links; in fact, you can learn just which domains and sites are backlinking to you. To find out what retroactive links lead to your site, follow these steps:

1. Open AltaVista (www.altavista.com) using your favorite Web browser.
2. In AltaVista's search box, where you would usually type a word or phrase to search on, instead type (in lowercase) **link:http://www.*yourdomain*.com/-host:your-domain.com**.

Note that "**-**" here is a hyphen; also, replace *yourdomain* with (what else?) your own domain name. A list of retroactive links to your site will be returned.

Announcing Your Site in Selected Newsgroups

You can announce your site in various newsgroups and mailing lists via announcement services; just be sure to choose appropriate venues based on whether their topics are related to the topic of your page. Remember your Net value system here, though, and be discreet: no one wants to get junk mail in newsgroups any more than in real life. Make sure your announcement is timely, relevant, to the point, and respectful of a particular newsgroup's culture.

TIP To find newsgroups that are related to your site's topic, you can search using a newsreader, such as Microsoft Outlook Express or Netscape Collabra. (These products come with Internet Explorer and Communicator, respectively.)

MASTERING TROUBLESHOOTING

Avoid Spamming, but Get Your Message Out

Spamming—sending unwanted e-mail messages to multiple recipients—is the electronic counterpart to junk mail. Indiscriminately sending duplicate messages to every newsgroup and mailing list you can find is considered very bad form. Your Web site will not be well received if your promotional efforts are perceived as spam. But this doesn't mean you can't promote your site. You just need to use judgment and discretion in your electronic promotions. Here are some guidelines:

- Be selective. Post announcements only on newsgroups and mailing lists where the members are likely to have a genuine interest in your site.

- Before posting an announcement of your Web site on a Usenet newsgroup or a mailing list, monitor the group to get a feel for its tone and culture. Then tailor your announcement to the group.

- Check and respect the rules of the newsgroup or mailing list to which you plan to post an announcement. Some allow brief announcements; others explicitly forbid them. There is usually a FAQ file or charter available that spells out the rules for a given list or newsgroup.

- Be brief. Keep any announcements short and to the point, and give your message an appropriate subject that identifies its purpose.

- Include your Web site URL in a short signature at the bottom of each e-mail message you send. This subtle form of promotion is generally accepted by most places on the Net.

- Participate in relevant newsgroups and mailing lists. A little low-key self-promotion by a group regular is often accepted when the same behavior by a newcomer would be met with angry flames.

- Be helpful. Answer a question or suggest a solution to a problem being discussed on a mailing list or newsgroup, and refer the reader to your Web site for more information. If your Web site actually contains such helpful information, this is an excellent way to get the word out.

Getting Listed in Magazines and Newspapers

Your press release may not be greeted with overwhelming excitement. The sad truth is that each and every magazine and newspaper must constantly sift through thousands of unsolicited press releases. Some companies keep people or even whole departments on their staffs just to manage the company's relationship with the press and to get notice in the press for both the company's products and the company. Getting that notice often involves lots and lots of persuasion, cajoling, schmoozing, and sending of knick-knacks—if you've got the budget, go for it. Even magazines as diverse as *People* and *The New Yorker* now have columns devoted to recommending Web sites.

MASTERING WHAT'S ONLINE

There are a number of magazines devoted primarily to showing people what's online and how to get there, notably:

Yahoo! Internet Life (www.yil.com)

NetGuide (www.netguidemag.com)

Internet World (www.iw.com)

Internet User (www.internetuser.com)

The Web (www.webmagazine.com)

The Net (www.thenet-usa.com)

Your best bet in contacting any of these magazines is to take a look at their *mastheads* (the listing of information including who works at the magazine). Find the name of some person whose title includes the noun *editor* along with some other phrase suggesting that he or she handles listings, and send your press release to that person. (Don't go for the managing editor or anyone else too high up; they are busy people who throw lots of press releases right in the trash.) And before you write your press release, pick up a good book on the topic.

But remember—these magazines are in the business of making money, after all, and are usually twice as happy to notice paying advertisers as unsolicited press releases in search of attention. Unless you give them money to promote your site, you may find that the print press is largely uninterested in you. Here's where it comes in handy to flaunt an incredibly original, high-concept killer app—sexy things catch editors' eyes far more effectively than a niche market product or a message unlikely to be understood outside your target audience.

MASTERING THE OPPORTUNITIES

Get Listed with What's New or Purchase Premium Listings

Your page is new—and some special pages post links to other pages that have just launched. The criteria for acceptance vary; some are choosy, while others list anybody who's new. Anything goes at Internet Magazine's What's New page (www.whatsnew.com). What's New Too is at newtoo.manifest.com/WhatsNewToo. Stop by to have a look at their latest set of criteria for acceptance and to find out how to get listed.

If you've got a big-ticket budget for promoting your page, you may want to invest in premium listings. Getting listed on Netscape's What's New page may be the priciest option; check their site for details. You can spend upwards of $1,000 to have your site appear in Yahoo!'s Web Launch (www.yahoo.com/docs/pr/launchform.html) or Lycos' New2Net (www.lycos.com/new2net.html) for one week. Other commercial announcement services, like WebPromote (www.webpromote.com/) or PostMaster (www.netcreations.com/postmaster/), are also not for low-budget amateurs, but if this option is within your means, check those sites for further details.

Taking Advantage of E-Mail Publicity

E-mail publicity is free and easy. You can use every e-mail message you send to publicize your site—this may well be the simplest way to get publicity. (If your site represents your company, make sure every employee includes the company URL in his or her e-mail sig file.) You can also set up a mailing list or take advantage of existing mailing lists to announce your site and what's new on it.

TIP Basically, you can and should treat your Web site's URL as part of your extended address—much like your telephone and fax numbers. Any place where you list information for customers, contacts, and friends is a potential place to promote your Web site.

Using a Signature File

Place your site address (URL) in a very brief signature file (in Netspeak, your "sig") that appears at the conclusion of all your e-mail messages. This will get the word out to those with whom you correspond on any topic. Your sig might look something like this:

```
Julie P. Ciamporcero, Yale '96
http://pantheon.yale.edu/~ciampor
ciampor@pantheon.yale.edu
```

Some e-mail programs provide menu options for creating a signature file within the program. Most e-mail programs can use any plain-text file as a sig. To create a text file to use as a signature file, first open your word processor and write a brief signature file for yourself. (Be sure to include your site's URL.) Keep in mind as you do this that it is generally considered bad form for your signature to be more than four lines long. Also, no single line of your signature should be more than 64 characters long—shorter lines are preferable, so that the text wrapping in different browsers doesn't leave your signature formatted oddly. Save the file (as a plain text file, of course) with a filename you'll remember (such as SIGFILE.TXT). Then open your e-mail program and follow its procedure for specifying a signature file. This should all take only a few mouse clicks to accomplish. (If the procedure to use for your e-mail program is not obvious, you can search the program's online help system for *signature*.)

Sigs, especially short ones, are perfectly acceptable in Net culture. From this moment forward, whenever you send out an e-mail message, your Web site will be announced discreetly to the person with whom you're communicating. (And, if you subscribe to any e-mail mailing lists, it'll be announced publicly there, but *politely*, as well.)

 TIP Bonus! When you create a sig file this way and send messages using any of several popular e-mail programs (such as Microsoft Outlook Express, Netscape Messenger, or Eudora Pro), your URL will appear as a live link. When the recipient of your message clicks the link, a Web browser window opens and your Web page appears.

Creating a Mailing List

Another option is to create an e-mail *mailing list* so you can send out announcements to interested parties whenever you launch or update your page. Creating a mailing list is not difficult, but it does take some work. You can either create one just for occasional announcements, or create one that offers people interested in a given topic a place for discussion of that topic. A simple form page on your site will enable visitors to subscribe to your mailing list.

MASTERING WHAT'S ONLINE

To learn how to set up a mailing list, look into the article "How to Set Up and Run Your Own Internet Mailing List," by Asha Dornfest, in the "how to" section of the popular CNET site (www.cnet.com).

NOTE If you create a mailing list just for sending out announcements, be sure to offer people on the list a means by which to get off the list—a very prominent and easy to use "unsubscribe" option. No one wants to be bombarded with what they consider junk mail, and if you send out announcements they don't want, your desire for their interest in your site might backfire.

A very interesting way to build traffic for your Web site is to sponsor a mailing list discussion group on a particular topic. Subscribers to this sort of mailing list will get copies of all the messages distributed to the list. Some mailing lists are one-way affairs with announcements going out from the mailing list owner (you) to the list of subscribers. Some provide a forum for lively discussions by automatically forwarding all messages and replies addressed to the list to all members of the list.

WARNING Don't send e-mail to every e-mail address you run across. As we mentioned before, it's important to avoid the very rude practice known as *spamming*—the unnecessary junking up of newsgroups or people's e-mail inboxes with messages of no interest to them.

Announcing via Other Mailing Lists

You can also announce your page via Internet mailing lists like the venerable Net Happenings. Net Happenings, by the way, is also a wonderful way to stay current with what's happening on the Internet. To subscribe to Net Happenings, send e-mail to majordomo@lists.internic.net; in the body of your message, type **subscribe <net-happenings>**. The good people there will help you learn how to use Net Happenings to announce your site.

There are many, many mailing lists around on many topics. To find a topical mailing list likely to be frequented by your target audience, the best directory to search is at www.lsoft.com/lists/listref.html. As always, check the culture of a mailing list you've targeted before you barge in and start doing what is, in effect, "advertising"— some mailing lists allow it, and some don't.

Publicity through Your Plan File

A popular means of site (and personal) promotion commonly used in the programming culture is a plan file. Email users who log in through Unix-based shell accounts have access to a program called "finger." When you "finger" a user, you retrieve information on that user that's stored on his or her computer. This package of retrievable information can be customized by altering a file called "plan":

```
> finger ciampor@pantheon.yale.edu
[pantheon.yale.edu]

Login name: ciampor                      In Real Life: Julie Ciamporcero
Directory: /home02/c7/ciampor      Shell: /usr/bin/tcsh
Last login: [minerva/pts:75] Tues Nov 23 1998 09:16:25 from 130.132.160.105

-Plan-

The design team at Sapiens Concepts is pleased to announce the launch of the
Rachmaninoff Page v3.0! Check it out at http://www.rachmaninoff.net !
```

Savvy users will take advantage of every means available to promote their web sites for minimal dollars. Plan files are one of these options. Using a plan file to communicate web site or product updates is popular among game designers, for example. Check with your Internet service provider to see if you have a shell account with a functioning finger service. (Note: it's possible for an ISP to support both Unix features, like finger service, and Microsoft features, like FrontPage extensions. There's no reason why we all can't just get along.) If your ISP offers finger service, spend some time talking to their technical support staff about how to get your plan file up and running.

Buying and Trading Banner Ads

Whether your budget is big or small, you, too, can advertise on other Web sites. You can either buy ad space—which doesn't *have* to cost an arm and a leg—or you can trade ad space. Ad rates are set based on how much traffic a site gets—before you buy ad space from a site, you'll need to know a bit about this. We'll get to it in a minute, but first let's look at some other basics.

Banner ads are typically long rectangles, about 468 pixels by 60 pixels in size (see Figure 24.4). Many sites, however, specify different sizes, including smaller ones and different shapes. What you really want from a banner ad is for a user to see it and click it, so as to go to your site and get more of whatever you offer. Banner ads often include the same design elements as print ads, though they are more compact and have to get to the point and catch a user's attention in a heartbeat. They can also be animated, which seems to inspire more clicking through.

FIGURE 24.4

A typical banner ad

the web design community

Placing your ad will require procuring the space in which to run it. On the home pages of many sites, you'll find a link that says something like (guess what) Advertising or About Our Site. Go there, and what you will *not* find is an ad rate card. That's because they want you to talk to an actual person, who will try to sell you ad space—if they simply tell you the rates, you aren't as lured in, or so the thinking goes. When you do get through to this salesperson, you should know a few things so you can ask smart questions and not seem like a yokel.

Banner ad space is generally sold in batches of one thousand *impressions* (an impression occurs every time a viewer sees a single Web page), at rates ranging from less than a penny per impression to thousands of dollars, depending on how much traffic that site gets.

NOTE Remember, a *hit* is not the same as an impression. A hit occurs every time a server serves up a file. A given Web page, as you know, can consist of many files, so when a single viewer sees one Web page, many hits can be generated, though only one impression has occurred.

The most highly trafficked portal sites—Netscape Netcenter, Yahoo!, Microsoft—charge in the millions for space on their most prominent pages; and thousands for less-trafficked sections of the site or less prestigious placements. Less highly trafficked sites, obviously, charge far, far less. There is no rule saying that you must advertise only on expensive, highly trafficked sites, or that they are the best venue for you. Go back to your promotional plan, your talking points, your mission statement, and your *budget*, and figure out what's going to be most cost effective.

Ads are also sometimes sold per *click-through*. This is not the preference of the sites selling ads, but has been demanded by some big-time advertisers, who want to pay only if they actually get the bang they expected out of their buck. (A click-through happens when someone who sees the ad clicks on it to visit the advertiser's site.)

While it is easy to count hits and click-throughs, it is very difficult to count impressions—you'll often have to take a host site on their word. The print, radio, and TV advertising industries all have an established way of auditing the claims of those selling ad space. For example, in print media, ad space is sold based on a publication's circulation. In the Web world, such a standard system has yet to be organized and adopted. Like print publications, Web sites that charge for ad space base their rates on a guaranteed number—usually impressions.

However, it is then up to them to simply keep their word that the specified number of impressions occurred. They base their numbers on their own log files, which account for traffic on their Web servers as part of regular server maintenance. These files are great at telling the number of hits, but cannot count impressions; what's more, the reporting of the number is up to people who have a vested interest in the numbers being high. If and when you buy ad space, look carefully at how the company from which you're buying verifies that you've received what you paid for. An external audit by a respected company is preferred, especially if you are paying through the nose for the ad space.

Another option, as mentioned, is to trade ad space. To do this, you will have to arrive at some rates yourself; the best way to do this is to inquire into rates at sites similar to yours and get a bead on what the market will bear. Note that in most cases ad rates are *soft*, meaning that the price is always negotiable. Put on your bargaining hat both when you buy ad space and when you trade it.

For the very cost-conscious, "link exchanges" (the largest of which can be found at www.linkexchange.com) file your banner ad in a database of thousands of similar ads. In exchange, you post a piece of code on your site that displays a random image from the database every time your page receives an impression. With the requisite willful suspension of disbelief, you can see how your banner ad might be pulled up on hundreds or thousands of other sites. However, since there's no guarantee of such, you're most likely better off paying a little money for the assurance that your ad will be seen.

Using Assorted Other Media to Support Your Online Efforts

A relatively short time ago, a URL appearing on a business card or letterhead was a novelty, and many viewers might not have even recognized the strange-looking string of characters punctuated with periods. Now, Web site addresses are almost universally recognized and are commonplace on most business (and many personal) communications. In addition to business cards, stationery, brochures, and other printed pieces, URLs regularly show up on TV commercials. We've seen URLs on the sides of delivery trucks and have even heard announcements of Web site addresses while waiting on hold during telephone calls!

Some magazines list the addresses of Web sites, sometimes for a small fee—this is a different business than those magazines like *Yahoo! Internet Life* that review or recommend sites. In this case, we're referring to magazines that simply *list* sites.

 TIP In some areas, you can get your Web address listed in the telephone book. It costs about the same as getting an additional listing. Also, if you have a display ad in the yellow pages, you'll want to include your Web address there.

The bottom line in publicizing your Web site is to be creative, seek opportunities, and weigh which venues are most cost effective and suitable for your company, product, or site.

Up Next

Site maintenance and promotion is one of the most important means of getting your site in ship-shape and out into the public for the enjoyment of your site visitors. Whether your interests lie in self-expression or advertising, the information in this chapter will help you keep your sites fresh and gain plenty of exposure.

In the next part of this book, *Back-End Applications and Professional Management*, we begin an in-depth journey into the back-end, professional management concerns of Web sites. Chapter 25, *Understanding CGI*, gives us an understanding of the Common Gateway Interface (CGI) and a powerful Web programming language known as Perl. This chapter, oriented toward readers interested in having a broader understanding of the way Web sites function on the server side, begins a series of chapters that are specifically geared to help move you from standard site development into the realm of the professional.

PART V

Back-End Applications and Professional Management

LEARN TO:

- *Use CGI and scripting languages to power your Web sites*

- *Tap into the power of Active Server Pages*

- *Work with database technology on the professional level*

CHAPTER <u>25</u>

Understanding CGI

FrontPage can do a lot, but there are some things you'll want to do that work with FrontPage but extend beyond its WYSIWYG support. One example of this is the *Common Gateway Interface*, or *CGI*.

CGI has been around longer than FrontPage, and longer even than many of the servers and related technologies that Microsoft has brought to the Web. This means that CGI can be used by a much wider range of servers, and it can be understood by almost all browsers. This aspect of CGI is critical to today's Web designer concerned with portability and backward compatibility.

There are instances where FrontPage uses CGI, such as with forms. When you create a form with FrontPage, you are, in most instances, working with CGI. Yet while Microsoft has created powerful technologies that are quite stable (see Chapter 26, *Using Active Server Pages*), there are aspects of FrontPage that simply are either not accessible to other browsers or impossible to use without the right server supporting the correct FrontPage extensions.

CGI transcends these concerns gracefully. In this chapter, we explore what CGI is (and what it's not), how it works, what it can do for your FrontPage webs, how and where to find valuable scripts and resources, and last—but most definitely not least—how to add CGI scripts to your FrontPage sites.

What Is CGI?

The answer is in the name: Common Gateway Interface. CGI is a method of getting a variety of Internet servers, software applications (such as a browser), and languages (including HTML and Perl) to be able to speak with one another. No matter the platform, the operating system, or the editing environment, the goal of CGI is to create a stable, multi-platform method of receipt and delivery of many Web-related events. CGI is necessary to allow information to move freely between HTTP via the browser, the Web server, and the script program(s) involved in a given Web event.

Contrary to what many might believe, CGI is not in and of itself a programming language. It *relies* on a variety of languages to work. But you cannot build applications with CGI, nor can you use CGI to create Web pages and events alone.

With CGI and related scripts, you can add a variety of powerful functions and features to your Web sites. While some of these functions can be handled by FrontPage, remember that you'll be required in most cases to use FrontPage extensions in order for them to work. This isn't always the best route! However, the entire purpose of this chapter—and of this premium edition of *Mastering FrontPage 2000*—is to take your Web knowledge into the realm of the Internet professional.

Imagine these features on your Web sites, working with stability, portability, and cross-browser consistency:

Forms   Probably the most familiar of all CGI processes, the standard, interactive form is a long-standing and important player in CGI-related technologies.

Time and date stamping   Using a time and date stamp on a page makes that page appear current and personal. Using CGI and related scripts, time and date stamping is an easy, attractive method of keeping sites looking fresh.

Page update comments   Another method of keeping sites current is allowing a page to reflect a *"page last updated on"* comment. CGI and its companion scripts can do this for you—you don't have to think about adding it by hand.

Timed updates   Instead of setting your alarm clock to make sure Monday's information is available across time zones, you can prepare the material in advance and rely on CGI, along with server-side scripts, to deliver the material to your site visitors while you get that precious extra hour of sleep!

Randomization   Undoubtedly, you've been to a site where content or images change upon a new visit, reload, or refresh. This is often delivered using CGI-based randomization scripts. You prepare a list of graphics and text options, and a discussion occurs between browser, server, and script to send back a random set of information upon the next viewing of the page in question.

Sequential events   If you want to set up changes that happen in a particular sequence rather than randomly, you can use CGI and related scripts to have your pre-determined graphics, text, and Web elements sequentially delivered to the Web pages of your choice.

Navigation   Tired of standard navigation? If you want to try some new methods of getting your site visitors from here to there, you can use CGI and scripts to create drop-down menus and other alternative methods of navigation.

Customization of pages   Site visitors really like customizing favorite Web sites to behave in a way that best suits their needs. Take a weather site for example. Even though an individual lives in a given area—say, California—he or she might also be interested in the weather where family, friends, and business colleagues reside and work. You can allow your site visitors to make choices about what kind of information appears on a page by setting up custom scripts via CGI.

Games and fun features   Using CGI and related technologies, you can please your Web surfers by providing a wide range of games and fun features such as mad libs, community story telling—even online painting and coloring (see Figure 25.1).

Search engines Sophisticated search engines rely on technologies that work to get you information that you need, fast. CGI is frequently the power behind effective search engines.

Web community Bulletin boards and forums can be delivered using CGI, without the worry and portability concerns that FrontPage extensions can create.

Shopping carts Pile on those CD and book purchases! The best, most secure, and most effective shopping carts are made available courtesy of CGI.

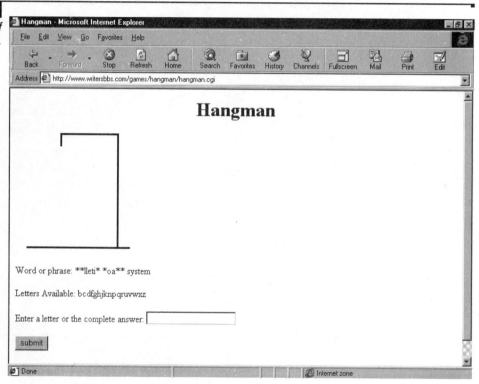

Impressive? No doubt! How on earth can CGI be so diverse and powerful, yet so platform-dependent and browser independent at the same time? The primary reason is that CGI is server-sided—meaning that it does not rely on the browser to make many decisions as to what it should do.

Furthermore, unlike FrontPage extensions, CGI has been around for a long time and is very flexible in terms of what kinds of scripts can be used. This means that there are more server and programming choices available. CGI takes the sting out of proprietary technologies and makes a lot of power available to the Web professional at a lower cost, and sometimes at a lower pain threshold, than FrontPage's proprietary and often browser-centric technologies.

NOTE Does this mean you should choose CGI and its script companions over Front-Page extensions? Not at all! You are going to perform more professionally if you understand your choices and *why* you would choose an individual technology over another. If you have a desire to be as portable, as browser-independent, and as varied in your applications as possible, CGI is probably going to be your best bet.

To understand where CGI gets its power and how to tap into it, let's look at how servers and browsers relate to one another.

Web Servers and Browsers

The server-browser relationship is a critical one. Without it, no Web page can successfully function on public or private networks. With CGI, this relationship is somewhat complex, so let's take a step back for a moment and look at the relationship in simple terms.

At the most elementary level, the server is where the HTML and graphic files for a basic Web page reside. When a site visitor types in a Web address, the browser will request that the server deliver those files to the visitor via Hypertext Transfer Protocol (HTTP). The server does so, and the files appear within the visitor's browser window.

As the demand for a variety of file types and diverse Web events has grown, two methods of managing programmed events stepped forward to address that demand: server-side programming and inline scripting.

Server-side programming allows for data management and processing using the resources of the server. The visitor gets to a Web page containing information that can be simple, as in our earlier description of graphics and HTML, or information that can be more complex—for example, requesting the server to run a server-side program written in a language such as Perl or C. Once the program is run and the results are ready, the server sends it back to the browser via HTTP. Note that CGI orchestrates this entire process!

The other method for managing programmed events, what we call *inline scripting*, lies on the side of the browser. A perfect example of this is JavaScript, which as many

PART

V

Back-End Applications and Professional Management

of you are aware, is entirely included *within* HTML documents. This means that the visitor gets to a page with JavaScript, and presuming that he or she can support JavaScript and has it enabled, the browser will retrieve the HTML (including the script). Once retrieved, the programmed event is carried out by the browser, using the software and hardware resources found on the visitor's machine.

Historically, server-side programming was really the only existing method of managing programmed events. Browsers were the interface through which a Web page was viewed, and nothing more. But now browsers are more sophisticated and can easily manage a variety of programming events on the client side of the virtual fence.

In fact, over the past three years or so, the major changes in Web technology have taken place with the browser as the matrix. It makes sense! The general public wants exciting features, the browser developers are undeniably involved in a one-upmanship the likes of which may never have been seen before, and Web developers are seeking new opportunities for their Web sites.

Which is better, server-side programming or inline scripting? Even with the inconsistencies in browsers, that's a tough question to answer. Each technology boasts a set of features that make it attractive. We think that what's really best about all of this is that there's finally some choice in how programmed Web events can be delivered to audiences. Whether you choose proprietary FrontPage technology, ASP (see Chapter 26), CGI, JavaScript, or DHTML, the fact that you have a choice and a way of best solving the needs of your audience is very empowering.

 NOTE In some cases, developers mix server-side and browser-side technologies for maximum effect.

Here are some server-side features worthy of note:

- Server-side programs rarely, if ever, cause problems. Because certain browsers do not support JavaScript or DHTML, and the browsers that do often allow users to turn those features off, many browser-side events will be lost on site visitors. Server-side programs are going to deliver the goods, consistently, to almost every browser in existence.

- Use server-side scripts to work with databases and local files. Many times, you'll want to save information about your visitors, enable them to work with databases (such as with search), and customize their pages. Browser technologies do not currently address these types of applications.

- Server-side programs do not rely on browser type and version to work. This is perhaps the most powerful aspect of server-side programming. Regardless of the browser—whether Microsoft Internet Explorer or Netscape Navigator; whether version 1.2 or 4.5, whether for Mac or for PC—CGI will work.

Of course, working on the server-side is not for everyone. As you'll find out later in this chapter, there's a lot involved with getting even a simple script up and running. For the experienced Web developer or programmer, it won't be a big deal. To the novice, it might seem terribly overwhelming. There are so many variables regarding CGI that it's difficult to teach it step-by-step without writing an entire book! If you're a newcomer to the Web and dedicated to accessing the power that CGI scripting allows, we encourage you to stick with it and use the resources provided in this chapter to get additional help.

 MASTERING WHAT'S ONLINE

CGI Resources

Use these selected CGI sites if you'd like to learn more about CGI—we've included some Web-based listings of books and articles, too.

The Common Gateway Interface Overview:

hoohoo.ncsa.uiuc.edu/cgi/intro.html (introduction)

hoohoo.ncsa.uiuc.edu/cgi/primer.html (primer)

CGI City:

icthus.net/CGI-City/references.shtml (references)

icthus.net/CGI-City/books.shtml (books)

CGI Resources.com:

www.cgi-resources.com/Documentation/ (tutorials and help)

www.cgi-resources.com/Books/ (books)

www.cgi-resources.com/Magazine_Articles/ (helpful articles)

So far, we've discussed the relation of server to browser, and we know that the information must get back and forth between these two key players in order to make a Web page real. But CGI must also work with scripts to process the requested information. It's the scripts that perform the seemingly magical feat of making your input information appear in a distant individual's mailbox, neatly formatted. It's scripts that allow you to add another CD or book to your virtual shopping cart and enable you to pass through with all of your items intact upon check-out.

In the following sections, we'll look at the specific languages that help create these server-side processes.

CGI and Programming

Let's revisit the familiar concept of forms. As mentioned, forms very frequently use CGI to manage the shuttling of information from one place to the next. Once CGI has seen a request to send some specific information along to a forms processing script, it will do so.

What kind of process happens when the script goes into action? Well, in the case of a form, it's possible that the Web developer has expressed a desire that the name, address, phone number, and geographical location of the site visitor are organized into a sensible, line-by-line list. The script is tailored to do just that.

Once the information is properly organized, the Web developer wants it delivered to a specific e-mail address. Furthermore, the developer has asked his or her programmer to ensure that once the visitor has clicked the Submit button, the visitor is sent a proper thank you for submitting the information.

So, while the script is organizing the information and handing it back to the CGI to get passed along to an e-mail address (in this case using an e-mail protocol such as SMTP), it's also pulling up a special "thank you" HTML Web page to have the CGI deliver back to the visitor, via HTTP.

What kind of scripts can do such efficient multitasking? Perl is one, C is another. Other languages used with CGI include C++, TcL, and AppleScript. Most programmers will agree that Perl is the most common, flexible, and easy-to-use option.

Perl

Perl is the favored server-side language used to script events that CGI manages. It is a democratic language with no proprietary regulations. In simple terms, there's a lot of great, free Perl scripts that—with a little skill—you can quickly and easily put to work on your Web sites.

Perl has an interesting history. It was originally developed by Larry Wall in an effort to solve problems inherent to Unix programming. Wall posted his nascent language to Usenet groups on the Internet, opening up the language for discussion and comment. Since that time, Perl has been expanded to include the numerous suggestions offered up by enthusiastic programmers. Although Wall retains the copyright on the language, it is distributed for free.

 NOTE While today's Web is served up by a wide range of servers, Unix Web servers still remain prevalent and, according to some statistics, dominant.

In addition to the program language and many of its scripts being free, Perl resources and help files are widely available. Whether you're only interested in specific Perl script for your CGI needs or you really want to play around with the language, the info is all out there in substantial quantities.

Surpassed only by the fanaticism of Macintosh users, Perl programmers have an extremely dedicated community, with an entire culture surrounding the language. It's a little difficult to fathom that a programming language can inspire such intensity, but it happens. That's to the Web developer's benefit, really, since the books, resources, free script sites, and helpful newsgroups provide immediate support for newcomers and experienced Perl programmers alike.

 NOTE Perl, of course, relies on CGI to be delivered to the Web in usable form.

Here's a look at Perl code. Note that this is just a snippet to give you a feel for the way a Perl script looks. For the full script, visit www.writersbbs.com/cgi-src/.

```perl
#!/usr/bin/perl5

require "cgi-lib.pl";

 MAIN:
 {

  $data_directory="/games/hangman/";
  $image_directory="/games/hangman/";
  $cgi_name="hangman.cgi";.
  # Print the header
  print "Content-type: text/html\n";
  print "Pragma: no-cache\n\n";
  print "<HTML><HEAD><TITLE>Hangman</TITLE></HEAD>
```

```
<BODY BGCOLOR=\"#FFFFFF\">";
 print "<H1 ALIGN=CENTER>Hangman</H1>";

# Read in all the variables set by the form
 if (&ReadParse(*input) && $input{'reset'} == 0)
 {
  &ProcessForm;
 }
 else
 {
  $tries_left=10;
  $word=&GetRandomWord;
  $stars = $word;
  $stars =~ s/\w/\*/g;
  $letters_left = "abcdefghijklmnopqrstuvwxyz";
  &PrintForm;
 }
}

sub GetRandomWord
{

   $data_file=$data_directory . "hangman.dat";
   open (FILE, $data_file);
   @LINES=<FILE>; #Read in the entire data file
   close(FILE);
   $count=@LINES; #Get the number of entries
   srand; #seed the random number generator with the current time
   $word_number = int rand($count); #pick a random nuber between 0 #and
$count
   $current_line = $LINES[$word_number]; # get the randomly chosen #word
   chop $current_line; # chop off the CR/LF
   return $current_line;
 }

sub RandomReset
{
   # the following "reset=rand" bit is a hack to be sure the browser
won't use
```

```
# a cached copy of the form

srand; #seed the random number generator with the current time
$random_number=int rand(9999999)+1;

    return "You can <A HREF=\"$cgi_name?reset=$random_number\">Play Again</A>
or <A HREF=\"http://www.writersbbs.com\">Return to The Writer's BBS</A>";
}

sub YouWon
{
  print "<H1>You got it!</H1>\n";
  print "The answer was: $word<P>\n";
  print &RandomReset;
}
```

MASTERING WHAT'S ONLINE

Perl Resources

Learn more about Perl with a trip to these Web sites:

What is Perl?: www.tpj.com/whatisperl.html

The Virtues of Perl: webreview.com/wr/pub/97/02/28/feature/index.html

Perl's Past and Future: www.colorado.edu/infs/jcb/sinewave/technology/perl/intro.html

Perl.com: www.perl.com (the name says it all!)

Other Programming Languages

While Perl is extremely popular, CGI works with other programming languages, too. Here's a selection of them, with brief descriptions:

C   C is widely used with, and for, operating systems. Like Perl, C is very compatible with the Unix environment and therefore is a natural for CGI processes.

C++   Considered a "superset" of C, C++ is distinct in that it is an object-oriented programming language. This means the programming itself is focused on objects and data instead of procedural logic. If that sounds confusing to you, don't worry. What you really need to know is that it's widely used to develop software, and Java is based on C++, but optimized for Web use. It's not the most popular of scripting options for CGI, but some C++ scripts are available for this kind of application.

TcL   An interpreted script language, TcL is considered to be similar to Perl, JavaScript, and Visual Basic Script (VBScript). It's occasionally used with CGI.

AppleScript   Developed for Macintosh systems, AppleScript is also occasionally used for CGI.

In most instances, you'll be working with Perl. However, there may be times when you find a script written in a language other than Perl that really appeals to you. As long as the server you're working on supports the language in question, you should be fine.

Getting the Right Server

At this point, you should have a good, basic understanding of CGI and how it works. More importantly, in the context of this book, you know why you might want to choose it over options such as FrontPage server extensions.

As with those extensions, you need the right server to run CGI. The servers that support it are numerous and vast. Where you can run into trouble is whether or not your Internet service provider will allow you to run scripts that you find on the Web or that you build yourself. For that reason, we've provided some guidelines to help you know what to look for when you're shopping around for the right server to support your CGI-driven sites.

 NOTE   If your current ISP isn't able to provide access to CGI and Perl or other languages, you may need to consider switching providers. Some options are provided later in this section.

To find the right server, start by finding out what Web server and operating system(s) your ISP offers. Most CGI and Perl scripts are fully supported on any Unix-based system such as Apache, Windows NT, and IIS, among others. Ask specifically what is being run and if CGI and Perl (or the languages your particular script calls for) are supported. Also find out what version of the language or languages are running.

Next, and perhaps most critical, you must find out whether the provider in question will allow you to run *your own CGI programs and scripts* with the account you currently have. While some ISPs do offer CGI, they only allow you to select from a few scripts that they have pre-approved. It's important to respect the ISP's choice, because usually these kinds of rules stem from past problems with abusive users. However, you'll ideally have full compliance to run whatever scripts you feel are appropriate for your site.

 NOTE Some ISPs have a hard rule that says they will not accept user scripts. However, *if you ask*, you might find that your ISP will allow you to submit your script for review and, if it looks OK to them to use it. Of course, if you have to constantly run scripts by the ISP, you might end up spending a lot more time and energy than is reasonable.

Once you've got a compliant ISP, you'll need to grab a pen and paper, or pop open Notepad, and jot down some important information, including:

- What's the path to the CGI? Most servers have a specific directory set aside for CGI programs, normally /cgi-bin/ or /htbin/.

- What's the path to Perl (or your preferred language)? It should look somewhat like /usr/bin/perl/.

- Are there any naming conventions of which you should be aware? Most CGI programs use .cgi as their extension, and Perl uses .pl. Make sure your ISP is using these conventions, and if not, find out what the convention is. Also, any other type of programming language you use will require a specific extension, so if you're not using Perl, check out naming conventions for the script in question.

 WARNING Unix servers tend to be case sensitive. This means that your script must appear in the appropriate case in all instances (on the server, within your HTML) in order to run.

Once you acquire this information, put it in a safe place. It will be very helpful to you as you work with CGI, and having the information nearby will prevent unnecessary calls to your service provider.

MASTERING THE OPPORTUNITIES

Finding Supportive ISPs

Before seeking out any and all ISPs who will meet your needs, check with your local service providers first, or with the service provider you're already using. Failing that, check out these ISPs for CGI and user-script support:

ProHosting Virtual Web Hosting (www.prohosting.com)   This provider is very helpful; they even offer an online CGI FAQ that tells you everything you need to know about where scripts are located, what kinds of scripts are supported, extension names, and what to do in case of problems.

U2ME3 (www.u2me3.net)   In this case, you can get both FrontPage extensions *and* CGI script access. The best of both worlds! You'll also find plenty of Web-based FAQs and support on how to use various available technologies like FrontPage extensions and scripting to get the most from your pages.

Host Me! (www.hostme.com)   This host also supports both FrontPage extensions and CGI. Technical support offers some limited free help when working on scripts, and should your needs exceed that, you can get additional CGI scripting support for a fee. Host Me! goes out of its way to make sure that you are a satisfied customer, with plenty of online help, tutorials, and resources.

DigitalNation (www.dn.net/hosting.html)   If you're looking to manage an entire Internet server, digitalNation will set you up with a virtual server. This means you can have a variety of custom features, run at high speed, and have tailored account access. This option is best for the very large Internet site, or if you're considering running your own Web design business and want plenty of server space.

Jumpline.net (www.jumpline.net)   Featuring FrontPage extensions and CGI, as well as a wide range of other attractive and affordable features, Jumpline.net is a good choice for anyone interested in quality service for a very reasonable price.

Pair Networks (www.pair.com)   This host offers FrontPage, limited CGI on certain plans, full service CGI on other plans, shopping cart, and database technologies.

Pegasus Web Technologies (www.pwebtech.com)   CGI, FrontPage extensions, commerce solutions. An excellent choice for both novices and experienced developers,

Note that this list is provided at your own risk—call or e-mail several on the list and be sure you go with the one that sounds most compatible with your individual needs.

Finding Scripts

The Web is rich with CGI and related scripts. Many are free; some of the more advanced are not. If you're just getting started with CGI, your best bet is to start with free scripts until you get the hang of working with them.

Once you feel confident, and your needs suggest it's time for a more advanced script, you can consider purchasing scripts if necessary. But before you do that, look around and compare—many of the free scripts are just as good, if not downright better, than the ones you pay for.

Here's a look at some of our favorite script repositories, with a description of what's available and the URLs that will take you there when you're ready to get started:

CGI Resources (www.cgi-resources.com)   Our all-time favorite CGI script site. This Web site offers several thousand scripts in a variety of languages including Perl, C, C++, TcL, and AppleScript. Scripts are organized first by language, and then by function. You can find scripts ranging from simple counters and utilities to complex shopping carts and auction software. Scripts also range in price—most are free, some are inexpensive, and some are for the higher-end developer. Aside from excellent scripts, CGI Resources is also home to a wide range of supportive resources including tutorials, books, magazine articles, and access to programmers—there's even a job database where skilled CGI programmers can find listings for work (see Figure 25.2).

Matt's Script Archive (www.worldwidemart.com/scripts/)   This site is another helpful stop along your CGI travels. Find Perl and C++ scripts written by 18-year-old book author and programmer Matt Wright, as well as contributions from other CGI enthusiasts.

CGI-World Professional Scripts (www.cgi-world.com)   This archive is a bit on the high-end, offering professional CGI scripts for surveys, real estate Web software, search, discussion forums, and image management. Some of the scripts are pricey, but all are considered high-quality, and all have demos available.

CGI Script Center (www.cgiscriptcenter.com)   Scripts on this site are free and for-purchase for business. The CGI Script Center keeps technical support representatives available, so when you run into problems, you can get personal troubleshooting help.

PART

V

Back-End Applications and Professional Management

FIGURE 25.2

CGI Resources is an excellent place to look for scripts.

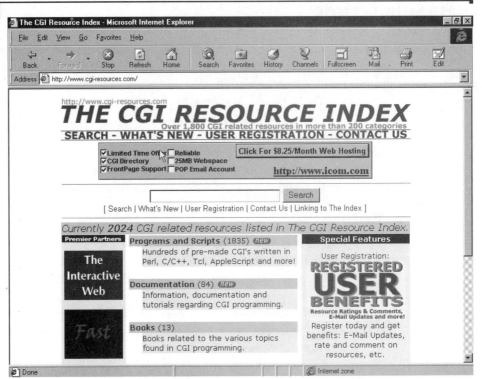

 NOTE These resources will start you off well—all of the individual sites have links to other, related resources.

Getting Ready to Work with Scripts

If you've followed the advice in this chapter, you have a good idea of what you need before you start to work. Here's a quick checklist:

- A server that allows you CGI access
- A script or scripts that you'd like to add to your Web site
- An understanding of where your CGI and script information is housed on the server

NOTE Adding CGI to your FrontPage web typically requires some information that we can't cover in this book, since it requires a working knowledge of your server. However, we can get you started by helping you get all of the pieces in place.

Because working with CGI is largely external from FrontPage, you'll need some additional tools to help you transfer files and set permissions. The two most popular tools for accessing servers from a desktop, remote PC is an FTP client and Telnet software.

FTP Client

FTP stands for *File Transfer Protocol*. An *FTP client* is a software interface that allows you to send and receive files from your computer to a remote computer. Since FrontPage handles your web transfers for you when you select File ➤ Publish Web (see Chapter 8, *Publishing Your Pages*, for more details), you might not have had a chance to work with FTP software directly. However, the professional Web developer or the hobbyist aspiring to diverse applications should have, and know how to use, an FTP client.

There are many FTP clients available for PCs. The one we like best is Ws_Ftp from Ipswitch, at `www.ipswitch.com` (see Figure 25.3). Ws_Ftp is a very powerful, low-cost tool that we have used daily for years, and we find it incomparable.

PART

V

Back-End Applications
and Professional
Management

FIGURE 25.3

Ws_Ftp is a powerful FTP client.

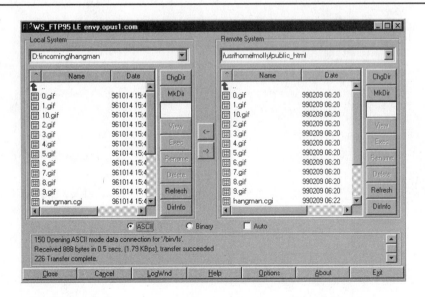

NOTE   There are many other reliable FTP clients. If you have another client that you'd like to use, note that the directions in this section will apply in general terms to that client. You can also find other FTP clients for your system by visiting www.download.com and looking through what's available.

To use Ws_Ftp, you'll need to set it up. Here's what you need to do:

1. Open Ws_Ftp. The Session Properties dialog box opens:

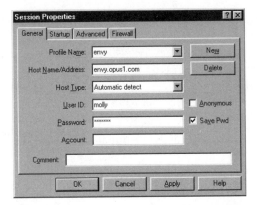

2. In the Profile Name text box, type in the general name of your Internet server. For example, if your server is called "greed.com," simply type in **greed**.

3. In the Host Name/Address text box, type in the specific address to your server, such as **ftp.greed.com**. Be sure to check with your service provider for exact details.

4. In the Host Type text box, leave Automatic Detect selected (the default). If you know exactly what kind of server you are connecting to, use the drop-down menu to find it.

5. Type your user ID into the User ID text box.

6. In the Password area, type in your password. Note that it will echo back stars rather than distinct characters.

7. Click the Save Pwd checkbox, so Ws_Ftp will keep the password information for you. Leave the Anonymous checkbox unchecked.

8. Click OK. The client now connects you to your server.

TIP When you get to your server, you may have to click over to the correct directory. If you usually connect to the same directory on the server, simply type the path to the directory into the Account text box in the Session Properties dialog box. Your directory information will be saved, and you'll be able to connect immediately to that directory.

At this point, you can highlight the files you want to send or retrieve, and then click the arrow button to transfer the files.

WARNING Be sure that all plain-text (ASCII) documents are transferred using ASCII, and all binary data is transferred using binary. Plain-text documents include HTML files, Perl, and CGI scripts. Binary files include GIFs, JPEGs, zipped files, and executable programs. It's very important that you do this correctly! If you send ASCII data via binary, you can end up with a script that will not run.

Telnet

Telnet is a protocol on the Internet that, like FTP, allows you remote access to a server. You might need a Telnet client in order to access your server in command-line mode. The best example of this is when you want to change permissions of scripts—a necessary step in the process of adding CGI power to your FrontPage webs.

Fortunately, Ws_Ftp allows you to change permissions on files—a necessary step in setting up CGI scripts—using the FTP interface. This is a good thing, because working from the command-line using Telnet usually means dealing with Unix, which is a bit challenging for many newcomers and even some old-hats at Web design. It's much more technical than a graphical user interface, demanding that you work with some confusing commands in order to make your changes.

If it turns out that you do require Telnet, or if you want extra options when working with your scripts that FTP can't provide, simply go to the Windows Start menu and select Run. In the text box, type **Telnet**, and the native Windows Telnet client will open (see Figure 25.4). You can use this to log on to your server and perform the required tasks.

FIGURE 25.4

*Accessing a server with
Windows Telnet*

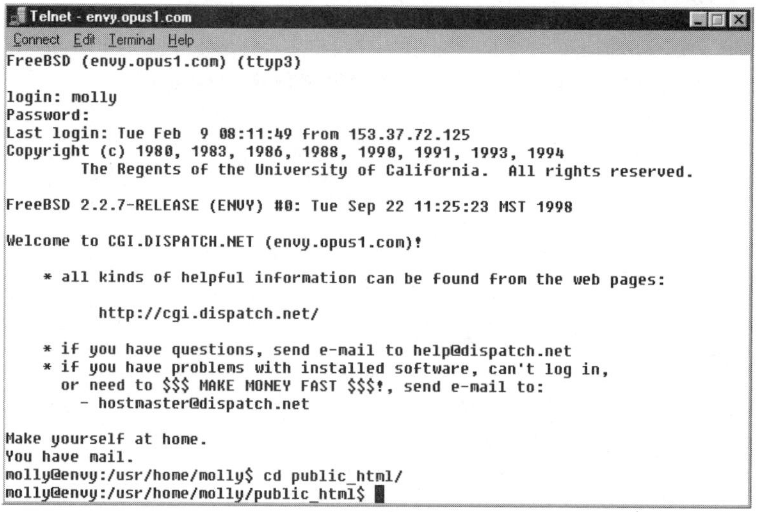

```
Telnet - envy.opus1.com                                          _ □ X
Connect  Edit  Terminal  Help
FreeBSD (envy.opus1.com) (ttyp3)

login: molly
Password:
Last login: Tue Feb  9 08:11:49 from 153.37.72.125
Copyright (c) 1980, 1983, 1986, 1988, 1990, 1991, 1993, 1994
          The Regents of the University of California.  All rights reserved.

FreeBSD 2.2.7-RELEASE (ENVY) #0: Tue Sep 22 11:25:23 MST 1998

Welcome to CGI.DISPATCH.NET (envy.opus1.com)!

    * all kinds of helpful information can be found from the web pages:

          http://cgi.dispatch.net/

    * if you have questions, send e-mail to help@dispatch.net
    * if you have problems with installed software, can't log in,
      or need to $$$ MAKE MONEY FAST $$$!, send e-mail to:
        - hostmaster@dispatch.net

Make yourself at home.
You have mail.
molly@envy:/usr/home/molly$ cd public_html/
molly@envy:/usr/home/molly/public_html$ █
```

 NOTE   As with FTP, other Telnet clients are available and can be found at software repositories around the Web. If you already have one installed that you want to use, the stepped directions in the "Changing Permissions (CHMOD)" section below will apply, in general, to how you'll use other Telnet software.

Adding Scripts to FrontPage Webs

With the script you want to use close at hand, you'll need to follow a series of steps to get the script working with FrontPage. Here's a quick overview:

- Place the script on the server.
- Change the permissions of the script (using the CHMOD command).
- Point to the script from a page within your FrontPage web.
- Place the page on the server.
- Test your work.

Let's get down to it!

Placing Your Script on the Server

To place your desired script on your server, you'll need your FTP client and the script. Once you're set, follow these steps:

1. Open your FTP client.

2. Connect to your server.

3. Find the appropriate directory for your CGI script (check with your system administrator if you're unsure).

4. Locate the script you've saved to your local drive.

5. Checking to make sure the ASCII radio button on the Ws_Ftp interface is marked, transfer the file to the server.

When the file transfer is complete, Ws_Ftp will let you know by giving you a "transfer complete" message within the status window:

```
150 Opening ASCII mode data connection for '/bin/ls'.
Received 888 bytes in 0.4 secs. (2.45 KBps), transfer succeeded
226 Transfer complete.
```

Changing Permissions (CHMOD)

The next immediate task is to ensure that the correct permissions are set on the script. On Unix servers, this is done with the CHMOD (change mode) command. If you're using another server, such as Microsoft NT or Microsoft IIS, check with the systems administrator for information relating to permissions.

To set permissions using Ws_Ftp:

1. If you're no longer connected to your server, connect now using Ws_Ftp.

2. Locate the script file on the server. Highlight the file and right-click. A menu appears.

3. Click chmod (Unix). The Remote file permissions dialog appears:

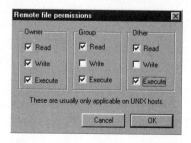

4. Under Owner, be sure the Read, Write, and Execute checkboxes are marked.

5. Under Group, check the Read and Execute boxes only.

6. Under Other, check the Read and Execute boxes, leaving the Write box unchecked.

7. Click OK. Ws_Ftp provides you with a "command successful" note in the status window.

If you want to be sure your CHMOD command has worked, click the DirInfo button to the lower-right of your Ws_Ftp interface. A list of all the files will pop open in Notepad, with a series of letters and dashes at the onset of each file entry. The proper permission setting for most CGI scripts will look like this: -rwxr-xr-x.

To change mode using Telnet:

1. From your Windows Start button, select Run.

2. In the Open dialog box, type **telnet** and click OK. The Windows telnet client opens.

3. Select Connect ➤ Remote System. The Connect dialog box appears:

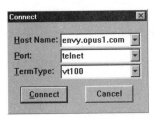

4. In the Host Name box, type the name of your server.

5. Click Connect. Telnet connects to your server.

6. Your server will probably ask for your login name and your password. Type these in to access your server.

7. Once you're in the server, at a command line, you'll need to change directories to the directory in which your CGI script resides. On most Unix systems, this means typing **cd** and then the directory name.

8. When you're at the appropriate directory, if you type **ls** on most Unix systems, you'll get a directory listing. You should, at this point, see your file.

9. From the command prompt of the directory containing your file, type **CHMOD 755** followed by the filename. In *most* cases, this is the correct command. If you're unsure, check with your system administrator.

Your file permissions should now be properly set.

Pointing to the CGI from Your HTML

At this point, the server-side work is done. It's now time to point to the CGI from your HTML. This way, when a visitor gets to the particular page on which your script is to run, the CGI will initiate, and the discussion between the browser, the server, and the script can ensue.

There are a variety of ways you can point to a script within your HTML. In many cases, it will depend on the script, and we encourage you to consult the documentation that comes along with the script, or visit one of the resources in the "Getting Help" sidebar later in this section.

Often, you'll point to a script using the <FORM> tag—particularly when the CGI script requires some direct input from the visitor. For example, a game or a standard form requires that you click Submit, and it is through that action that your CGI script is located and executed using a variety of HTML attributes, including:

> action   This attribute allows you to point directly to the script. Let's say it's a Perl script, residing in the cgi-bin of greedy.com. Here's what the action attribute will look like within the <FORM> tag:

```
<form action="http://www.greedy.com/cgi-bin/myscript.pl">
```

> method   As its name suggests, this attribute controls the way in which information is sent to a server. There are two values for this attribute, GET and POST.

So what do you use—ACTION or METHOD, GET or POST? The syntax you'll choose will depend upon the script, the server, and your specific needs. There is really no way to globally tell you which is correct for your environment and circumstances. What you can do is check with the script author, ask the system administrator, or look to one of the help newsgroups included in the "Getting Help" sidebar later in this section.

Once you know what syntax is necessary to operate your script, here's what you do:

1. Open FrontPage.

2. Select File ➢ New ➢ Page to begin with a fresh page. Or, to work on a file that contains a form ready to be pointed at your script, select File ➢ Open.

3. If you're working on a new page, use the Insert ➢ Form option and create a new form (see Chapter 14, *Making Interactive Pages with Forms*).

4. From Page view, click the HTML tab. The HTML code is now on-screen.

5. Locate the <FORM> tag. Add the attribute or attributes necessary to process your form, and add the path to the form on your server (check with the script author or your system administrator for the syntax relevant to your script).

PART

V

Back-End Applications
and Professional
Management

6. Save the file.

7. Select File ➢ Publish To Web. FrontPage now sends the updated HTML to your server. If you've done everything properly, your script is ready to run.

MASTERING TROUBLESHOOTING

Getting Help

If you're working with a script and don't know what to do, you can get help by posting a message to one of these helpful newsgroups and Web sites:

`comp.infosystems.www.authoring.cgi`   This newsgroup covers all topics related to writing and working with CGI scripts.

`comp.lang.perl.misc`   Here you'll find miscellaneous questions related to Perl scripts.

`comp.infosystems.www.servers.unix`   If you have problems with Unix servers, check here.

`microsoft.public.inetserver.misc`   This is a helpful resource for CGI and scripting questions related to Microsoft Internet servers.

`comp.infosystems.www.servers.misc`   This site includes general questions related to World Wide Web servers.

`www.microsoft.com/workshop/languages/fp/`   This site has a list of Peer-to-Peer newsgroups covering a wide range of FrontPage and related issues.

`communities.msn.com/webdesign/`   This Web design community offers plenty of support for FrontPage and programming. It is an excellent starting point for newcomers to FrontPage and Web design.

Testing Your Script

To find out if your script is operating properly, simply open your browser, type in the URL of your site, and open the specific page you've just updated. Does the script run, or do you get an error? If the script runs, congratulations! If you get an error, don't despair. Start by going over these important questions:

• Is your server properly set up to handle the script you chose?

• Did you name your script with the right extension and the correct case?

- When you transferred your script, did you make sure it was transferred using ASCII rather than binary?
- Did you place your script in the correct directory?
- Were the permissions for the script set accurately?
- Is the HTML pointing to your script using the syntax necessary to make it run?

If you've answered yes to all of these questions, and your script still isn't running, it's time to get help! Check the script's documentation for any special concerns or instructions, contact your systems administrator, or visit one of the newsgroups listed in the "Getting Help" sidebar.

Up Next

CGI is an extremely stable, portable, and powerful method of adding interactive and interesting events to your Web pages. While it demands knowledge and patience, the rewards are worth it: cross-browser, cross-platform Web events that perform consistently well.

As with CGI, Active Server Pages (ASPs) can add power to your Web sites. Whether it's a matter of interactivity or database connectivity, ASP is a potent Microsoft technology worth understanding. In Chapter 26, *Using Active Server Pages*, we introduce you to ASP, give you a look at how it works, and show you how to use it to add professional functions to your FrontPage webs.

PART

V

Back-End Applications and Professional Management

CHAPTER **26**

Using Active
Server Pages

As you make the move from relying on FrontPage technologies to advanced technologies that will take your Web sites to new levels, you will undoubtedly hear about *Active Server Pages*, referred to simply as *ASP*. The Web, as you probably know, is changing from a static environment to one of greater dynamism and interactivity. ASP is one of the technologies that developers are using to achieve these goals.

As one of the most prevalent Web technologies for dynamic application development, ASP is another Microsoft brain child. However, as with its non-Microsoft distant cousin, CGI, ASP requires a base of knowledge beyond the scope of this book. Yet we want to give you an introduction to what ASP is, how it's used, why it's used, and where it's used. This chapter gives you enough preliminary information to make some technological decisions about your Web site or to move into more aggressive areas of Web development, should you so choose.

ASP Overview

Like CGI, ASP is a server-oriented process. It works by combining HTML and scripting code to access databases and create on-the-fly Web pages, or parts of Web pages. For example, if you want to have a new welcome page, a header, a footer, or an advertising area updated regularly without doing it manually, you can use ASP. You can also combine browser- and server-side processes with ASP to bring about your dynamic design needs.

 NOTE If ASP and Dynamic HTML seem alike to you, you're correct. They work in a similar *conceptual* fashion to create dynamic pages. However, remember that ASP is a server-side technology, and DHTML is interpreted by the browser. It's interesting to note that they can be used together for maximum results.

At their most simple, ASP pages are HTML pages with some added code that will have a conversation with the server. You'll save this HTML page with an extension of .asp rather than .htm, however, and you'll save it as a plain text (ASCII) file.

Here's a very simple look at ASP code that, when run on an ASP server, will return a greeting depending upon the time of day. Note that ASP combines standard HTML, text, and programming code:

```
<html>
<head>
<title>My Site</title>
```

```
</head>
<body>
<%If Time >= #08:00:00 PM# And Time < #12:00:00 AM# Then%>
Good Evening!
<%Else%>
Good Day!
<%End If%>
</body>
</html>
```

Scripting is the heart and soul of what makes ASP so interactive. As mentioned earlier in relation to DHTML, there's a real difference between what happens on the server and what happens within the browser. ASP is interesting because it asks for a script to exist within the HTML page; but because it is the server, not the browser, that parses that code and makes it work, ASP is a server-side scripting application.

 NOTE Many application developers consider ASP simple to learn. This is especially true if you take well to scripting and programming. If not, there are a few tools that can help you out. While no specialty tools are required to create ASP files, you need to have access to a server that supports ASP. Many servers do; check with your Internet service provider to be certain *before* selecting ASP as a method of delivering dynamic pages. ASP is native to Windows NT, and as mentioned, now runs on a variety of servers including Unix, giving it portability (see Chapter 25, *Understanding CGI*).

MASTERING THE OPPORTUNITIES

ASP and Web Browsers

The browser situation has evolved into two camps: Internet Explorer and everyone else. IE has about 50 percent of the marketplace. The real issue is support of VBScript and ActiveX technology in the browser.

With the large base of developers who know VB and use ActiveX technology, this is something that needs attention. There are many environments to consider, like most intranet applications that need the added functionality of VB and ActiveX. In a controlled environment, the browser selection is easier to manage.

If you need real browser independence, then stick to Java for your scripting. Remember that you can use Java in ASP and can call Java servlets from an ASP.

ASP Structure

ASP uses an object model in order to work. An object model is a collection of data concepts that are the foundation of a given application. Many programming languages including C++ and Java work on this model. ASP uses a set of built-in objects as well as installable objects.

The built-in objects used to make an ASP page work are:

Request object   A request object works to get information from the user, such as information that is inputted into a form, or data about who the user is and what browser is being used.

Response object   The response object takes the information from the user, packages it, and uses that information to send a response. Using the response object, you can create a cookie to redirect a user to a different page or terminate a given process, such as a form.

Session object   The session object stores information about a single session in a cookie. This cookie can then keep track of each subsequent user session.

Application object   Session objects relate to one user, but an application object shares information such as specific settings to all users throughout the life of the application (not the life of the session).

Server object   These objects control the relationship between a browser and the server's various components. The server object is the interface to Active Server Components—the pieces of ASP that make it work.

Installable objects come packaged with specific servers or can be obtained from third-party vendors (see the "ASP Resources" sidebar at the end of this chapter). For example, Microsoft IIS comes with a variety of very handy objects including an ad rotator and detailed browser sniffing information.

 NOTE   ASP often works in tandem with databases. A good example of this is an ASP-driven discussion forum. The information must be saved in a database. The ASP, with its embedded script, pulls that information from the database and sends it to the site visitor's Web page. For more information on creating databases, see Chapter 23, *Adding Databases for Maximum Impact*. If you'd like to learn more about database concepts, visit Chapter 27, *Databases in Detail*.

Scripting Choices in ASP

ASP is referred to as a *language-independent* application. This means that you can conceivably write the accompanying code in just about any language with which you are familiar. To choose a language, simply include the one you'd like to use in the language tag:

```
<script language="javascript">
```

You can use Perl (see Chapter 25) if you'd like, but most people use VBScript, which is a natural for ASP, or JavaScript, which works well too. But which languages you use to work with ASP will depend upon your given requirements for each individual project and environment.

Because JavaScript is widely supported, it is the language of choice any time a process is started on the browser side. VBScript is only supported by Microsoft browsers. However, any language can be used on the server side as long as the resulting information is readable by the widest range of browsers.

Obviously, because VBScript is a Microsoft technology, as is ASP and most of the servers with the best ASP support, using VBScript offers a variety of enhancements to ASP applications. Using a combination of VBScript and ActiveX controls, your server can carry on discussions with the site visitor's operating system via the browser.

Here's an example of JavaScript code in an ASP page. The point of this code is to manage the branding, advertising, and general header information on the Microsoft Network's Web Design Community Home page.

```
<script language="javascript">
<!-
var rgblt=new Array("autos","business","computing","communities","consumer
guide","entertainment","games","homes");
var rgblb=new Array("msn central","net events","news","personal
finance","shopping","sports","travel","women");
var rgbqc1=new Array("air tickets","downloads","stock quotes");
var rgbqc2=new Array("buy books","maps","tv listings");
var rgbqc3=new Array("buy music","reference","weather");
var rgbqc4=new Array("chat","movies","white pages");
var rgbqc5=new Array("classifieds","scoreboards","yellow pages");
function wbl(rgbl){
var iMax = rgbl.length;
for (i=0;i<iMax;i++){document.write('<a href="/chan/gbl/'+rgbl[i]+'.asp"
class=bl>'+rgbl[i]+'</a>  ')};
}
```

PART

V

Back-End Applications
and Professional
Management

```
function wbls(){
document.write('<nobr>');
wbl(rgblt);
document.write('</nobr><BR><nobr>');
wbl(rgblb);
document.write('</nobr>');
}
function wbql(rgbql){
var iMax = rgbql.length;
for (i=0;i<iMax;i++){document.write('<a href="/chan/gql/'+rgbql[i]+'.asp"
class=bql>'+rgbql[i]+'</a><BR>')};
}
function wbqls(){
wbql(rgbqc1);
document.write('</TD><TD CLASS="bql">');
wbql(rgbqc2);
document.write('</TD><TD CLASS="bql">');
wbql(rgbqc3);
document.write('</TD><TD CLASS="bql">');
wbql(rgbqc4);
document.write('</TD><TD CLASS="bql">');
wbql(rgbqc5);
}
// ->
</script>
```

Here's the resulting HTML code:

```
<SCRIPT SRC="/chan/chan.js" language="Javascript"></SCRIPT>

<LINK REL=STYLESHEET TYPE="text/css" HREF="/chan/home/chan.css">
<A NAME=TopOfPage></A>
<table bgcolor=white cellpadding=0 cellspacing=0 border=0 width=100%>
<tr>
<td>
<TABLE BORDER=0 CELLSPACING=0 CELLPADDING=0 WIDTH=608>
```

```
<TR><TD><A HREF="http://go.msn.com/npl/msnt.asp" target="_top"><IMG
SRC="/chan/home/logo.gif" WIDTH=140 HEIGHT=60 BORDER=0 ALT="go to
msn.com"></A></TD><TD><A
HREF="http://ads.msn.com/ads/redirect.dll/CID=0002f0752eef19d000000000/AREA=
IMGWCM?image=http://ads.msn.com/ads/IMGWCM/HD030002_LG.GIF"
target="_top"><IMG SRC="http://ads.msn.com/ads/IMGWCM/HD030002_LG.GIF"
ALT="Click here for MS HomeAdvisor!" BORDER=0></A></TD>
</TR>
</TABLE>
<TABLE BORDER=0 CELLSPACING=0 CELLPADDING=0 WIDTH=608>
<TR><TD ALIGN=LEFT WIDTH=280>
<IMG SRC="/chan/home/title.gif" WIDTH=280 HEIGHT=40 BORDER=0>
</TD>
<TD WIDTH=188 ALIGN=LEFT><FONT face=arial COLOR="#669999" SIZE=5
class="headerSml"><B>/ <I>web design</I></B></FONT></TD>
<TD ALIGN=RIGHT WIDTH="140">

<A HREF="http://go.msn.com/npl/msnp.asp" CLASS="msn"
TARGET="_top">go to msn.com</A>

</TD>
</TR>
</TABLE>

</td>
</tr>
</table>
<table width="600" border="0" cellspacing="0" cellpadding="0">
<tr>
<td width="600" bgcolor="#ffffff" height="1"><img src="/images/spacer.gif"
width="600" height="1"></td>
</tr>
</table>
<table width="600" border="0" cellspacing="0" cellpadding="0">
<tr>
```

PART

V

Back-End Applications
and Professional
Management

```
<td width="1" bgcolor="#ffffff"><img src="/images/spacer.gif" width="1"
height="18"></td>
<td width="142" bgcolor="#669999" align=center valign="middle"><font
face="Arial" size=-1 color="#669999"><a href="/home/default.asp"
class="horBar"><nobr>web community home</nobr></a></font></td>
<td width="1" bgcolor="#ffffff"><img src="/images/spacer.gif" width="1"
height="18"></td>
<td width="142" bgcolor="#669999" align=center valign="middle"><font
face="Arial" size=-1 color="#669999"><a href="/home/community.asp"
class="horBar"><nobr>list communities</nobr></a></font></td>
<td width="1" bgcolor="#ffffff"><img src="/images/spacer.gif" width="1"
height="18"></td>
<td width="142" bgcolor="#669999" align=center valign="middle"><font
face="Arial" size=-1 color="#669999"><a href="/calendar/default.asp"
class="horBar"><nobr>community calendar</nobr></a></font></td>
<td width="1" bgcolor="#ffffff"><img src="/images/spacer.gif" width="1"
height="18"></td>
<td width="170" bgcolor="#669999" align=center valign="middle"><font
face="Arial" size=-1 color="#669999"><a href="/chat/default.asp"
class="horBar"><nobr>chat categories</nobr></a></font></td>
</tr>
</table>
<table width="600" border="0" cellspacing="0" cellpadding="0">
<tr>
<td width="600" bgcolor="ffffff" height="1"><img src="/images/spacer.gif"
width="600" height="1"></td>
</tr>
</table>
```

Figure 26.1 shows the page before the script is run. In this image, you'll see graphics, advertising, and header information culled from the local computer. Figure 26.2 shows the page after it's been converted to ASP and is running live with regularly updated ads, graphics, and information.

PART

V

Back-End Applications
and Professional
Management

FIGURE 26.1

The page before being converted and run on a server with ASP support

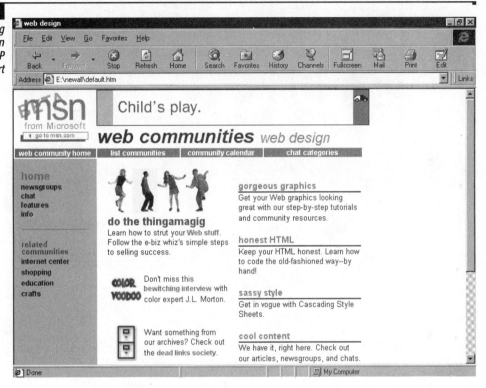

FIGURE 26.2

The page after being run on the supportive server

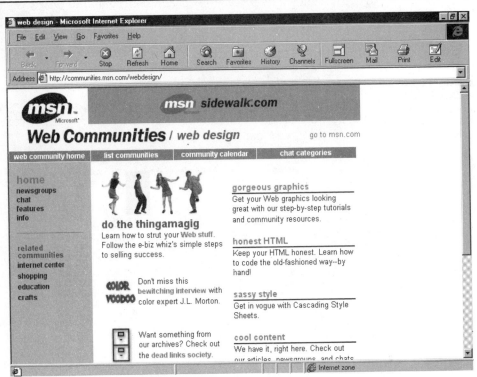

This example is a VBScript ASP calendar. Note how the script and HTML are integrated within the code:

```
<%@ LANGUAGE="VBScript" %>
<%
Option Explicit

Dim dtToday
dtToday = Date()

Dim dtCurViewMonth ' First day of the currently viewed month
Dim dtCurViewDay ' Current day of the currently viewed month

%>
```

```
<% REM This section defines functions to be used later on. %>
<% REM This sets the Previous Sunday and the Current Month %>
<%

'_____

  Function DtPrevSunday(ByVal dt)
   Do While WeekDay(dt) > vbSunday
     dt = DateAdd("d", -1, dt)
   Loop
  DtPrevSunday = dt
  End Function
'_____


%>


<%REM Set current view month from posted CURDATE, or
' the current date as appropriate.


' if posted from the form
' if prev button was hit on the form
  If InStr(1, Request.Form, "subPrev", 1) > 0 Then
   dtCurViewMonth = DateAdd("m", -1, Request.Form("CURDATE"))
' if next button was hit on the form
  ElseIf InStr(1, Request.Form, "subNext", 1) > 0 Then
   dtCurViewMonth = DateAdd("m", 1, Request.Form("CURDATE"))
' anyother time
  Else
     dtCurViewMonth = DateSerial(Year(dtToday), Month(dtToday), 1)
  End If
%>



<% REM ----BEGINNING OF DRAW CALENDAR SECTION---- %>
<% REM This section executes the event query and draws a matching calendar.
%>
<%
  Dim iDay, iWeek, sFontColor
%>
```

```
<HTML>
<HEAD>
</HEAD>
<BODY>

    <BR>

      <CENTER>
    <FORM NAME="fmNextPrev" ACTION="calendar.asp" METHOD=POST>
    <TABLE CELLPADDING=3 CELLSPACING=0 WIDTH="95%" BORDER=2
BGCOLOR="#99CCFF" BORDERCOLORDARK="#003399" BORDERCOLORLIGHT="#FFFFFF">
      <TR VALIGN=MIDDLE ALIGN=CENTER>
        <TD COLSPAN=7>
        <TABLE CELLPADDING=0 CELLSPACING=0 WIDTH="100%" BORDER=0>
         <TR VALIGN=MIDDLE ALIGN=CENTER>
           <TD WIDTH="30%" ALIGN=RIGHT>
            <INPUT TYPE=IMAGE NAME="subPrev" SRC="Left.gif" BORDER=0 WIDTH=18
HEIGHT=20 HSPACE=0 VSPACE=0>
           </TD>
           <TD WIDTH="40%">
           <FONT FACE="Arial" COLOR="#000000">
           <B><%=MonthName(Month(dtCurViewMonth)) & " " &
Year(dtCurViewMonth)%></B>
            </FONT>
           </TD>
           <TD WIDTH="30%" ALIGN=LEFT>
            <INPUT TYPE=IMAGE NAME="subNext" SRC="Right.gif" BORDER=0
WIDTH=18 HEIGHT=20 HSPACE=0 VSPACE=0>
           </TD>
         </TR>
        </TABLE>
        </TD>
      </TR>

      <TR VALIGN=TOP ALIGN=CENTER BGCOLOR="#000099">

      <% For iDay = vbSunday To vbSaturday %>
        <TH WIDTH="14%"><FONT FACE="Arial" SIZE="-2"
COLOR="#FFFFFF"><%=WeekDayName(iDay)%></FONT></TH>
```

```
          <%Next %>

          </TR>

<%
   dtCurViewDay = DtPrevSunday(dtCurViewMonth)

   For iWeek = 0 To 5
    Response.Write "<TR VALIGN=TOP>" & vbCrLf

    For iDay = 0 To 6
      Response.Write "<TD HEIGHT=50>"

      If Month(dtCurViewDay) = Month(dtCurViewMonth) Then
       If dtCurViewDay = dtToday Then
         sFontColor = "#FF3300"

       Else
         sFontColor = "#000000"
       End If

      '-- Write day of month

       Response.Write "<FONT FACE=""Arial"" SIZE=""-2"" COLOR=""" &
sFontColor & """><B>"
       Response.Write Day(dtCurViewDay) & "</B></FONT><BR>"

       '--Else
        '--Response.Write " "
       End If

      Response.Write "</TD>" & vbCrLf
      dtCurViewDay = DateAdd("d", 1, dtCurViewDay)
    Next
    Response.Write "</TR>" & vbCrLf
   Next
%>
<%REM -----END OF DRAW CALENDAR SECTION----- %>
</TABLE>
```

```
<INPUT TYPE=HIDDEN NAME="CURDATE" VALUE="<%=dtCurViewMonth%>">
</FORM>
</CENTER>
</BODY>
</HTML>
```

MASTERING WHAT'S ONLINE

In-Depth ASP

For in-depth documentation on ASP, visit msdn.microsoft.com/library/tools/asp-doc/iiwawelc.htm.

ASP Tools

A few tools exist to help people create Active Server Pages. One excellent application tool is Microsoft's Visual InterDev, a visual environment that will empower anyone building ASP pages. Figure 26.3 shows the InterDev interface.

Not only will Visual InterDev assist in programming, but it has a wide range of integrated uses, including integration with FrontPage (see Chapter 28, *Using FrontPage with Microsoft's Visual InterDev*).

Another useful ASP tool is the ASP Table Wizard. This wizard prompts you though each step of making an ASP page (see Figure 26.4).

FIGURE 26.3

The Visual InterDev environment

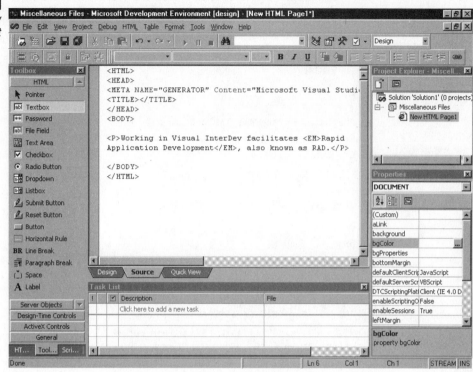

FIGURE 26.4

Using the ASP Table Wizard

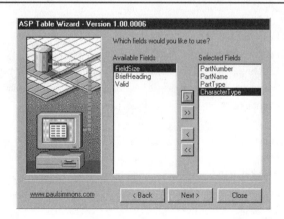

Here's an example created by the program's developer that creates a formatted table, a section of which is shown in Figure 26.5:

```
<%

Option Explicit


'----------------------
'-- Generated by the ASP Table Wizard --
'-- http://www.paulsimmons.com --
'----------------------


Dim iCount
Dim sRowColor
Dim objDB
Dim objRS
Dim sDBName

'TODO: Verify database path...
sDBName = "driver={Microsoft Access Driver
(*.mdb)};dbq=D:\websites\fp\PaulSimmons\db\Northwind.mdb"
Set objDB = Server.CreateObject("ADODB.Connection")
objDB.Open sDBName

'TODO: Modify the next line to only return the records you want...
Set objRS = objDB.Execute("select * from Products")

Response.Write("<html>")
Response.Write("<head>")
Response.Write("<title>Paul Simmons Dot Com</title>")
Response.Write("</head>")
Response.Write("<body bgcolor=white>")

Response.Write("<h3>ASP Table Wizard</h3>")
Response.Write("<a href=codebrws.asp?source=tablewiz.asp><div
class=tiny>Steal this code</div></a><p>")

If objRS.EOF Then
    Response.Write("<b>No matching records found.</b>")
```

```
        objRS.Close
        objDB.Close
        Set objRS = Nothing
        Set objDB = Nothing
        Response.End
    End If


    Response.Write("<table border=0 cellpadding=2 cellspacing=2>")
    Response.Write("<tr bgcolor=silver>")

    'COOL TIP: the <filter> tag is used by Excel 97
    'if your users save this file from the browser and open it in XL 97, XL will
    'parse all the table cells into XL ranges and turn on filtering...

    Response.Write("<th filter=ALL>Productid</th>")
    Response.Write("<th filter=ALL>Productname</th>")
    Response.Write("<th filter=ALL>Supplierid</th>")
    Response.Write("<th filter=ALL>Categoryid</th>")
    Response.Write("<th filter=ALL>Quantityperunit</th>")
    Response.Write("</tr>")

    Do While Not objRS.EOF
        'this code alternates the color of the table rows...
        iCount = iCount + 1
        If iCount Mod 2 = 0 Then
            sRowColor = "skyblue"
        Else
            sRowColor = "#C4CEE5"
        End If

        Response.Write("<tr bgcolor=" & sRowColor & ">")
        Response.Write("<td align=right>" & objRS("Productid") & "</td>")
        Response.Write("<td>" & objRS("Productname") & "</td>")
        Response.Write("<td align=right>" & objRS("Supplierid") & "</td>")
        Response.Write("<td align=right>" & objRS("Categoryid") & "</td>")
        Response.Write("<td>" & objRS("Quantityperunit") & "</td>")
        Response.Write("</tr>")
        objRS.MoveNext
```

```
Loop

Response.Write("</table>")
Response.Write("</body>")
Response.Write("</html>")

objRS.Close
objDB.Close
Set objRS = Nothing
Set objDB = Nothing


%>
```

FIGURE 26.5

A portion of the table created with ASP Table Wizard

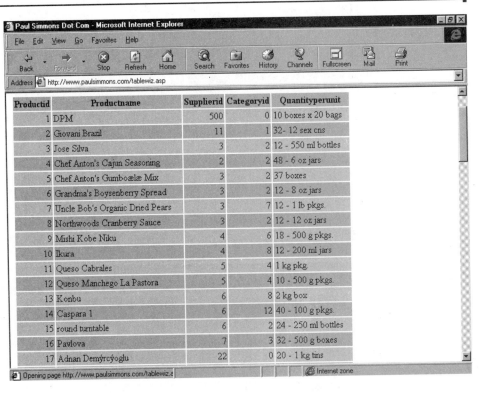

MASTERING WHAT'S ONLINE

ASP Tools

For more information on how to purchase Microsoft Visual InterDev, visit `msdn.microsoft.com/vinterdev/`. To download the ASP Table Wizard, check out `www.paulsimmons.com/business.html`.

Adding a Script to a Page

As you've seen with the code examples in this chapter, you can add your ASP-related script directly into your HTML page. Then, to save the file in ASP format, all you need to do is save with the `.asp` extension.

> **NOTE** You'll need to use scripts that are appropriate for use with your needs, audience, and server, and you must have an ASP supported server in order to run them. This information can be obtained from your Internet service provider.

Here is an exercise that walks you through adding and saving your ASP file:

1. Create an executable folder in your FrontPage web. This allows scripts to run.

> **NOTE** Since the default for a folder is not set to executable for security purposes (see the "Security Issues" sidebar later in this section), you'll have to set the permissions yourself.

2. From the FrontPage menu bar, select File ➤ New ➤ Folder.

3. Give the new folder a name. For ASP files, you can use the name *scripts* for your ASP-related script files.

4. Right-click the folder you just renamed and choose Properties from the menu that appears. The folder's Properties dialog box appears.

5. At the bottom of the folder's Properties dialog box, select the Allow Scripts Or Programs To Be Run checkbox.

PART

V

Back-End Applications
and Professional
Management

6. Click OK. The Properties dialog box closes and your new folder allows any scripts and ASP it contains to be run.

Now you need to open the page where you want to add your ASP scripts. To do so:

1. Add the script to the page by typing it in, or copy-and-paste it from another application.

2. From the menu bar, select File ➤ Save As. The Save As dialog box appears.

3. In the Save As dialog box's list of directories, select the directory you created to hold scripts. Type a filename in the URL text box. The name you give the file should end with the extension .asp.

4. Click OK. The dialog box closes, and the file is saved to the location you specified.

MASTERING TROUBLESHOOTING

Security Issues

Security is a major concern for all developers. Security measures must be taken on *all* aspects of server-side applications.

All of your hardware and software will come with extensive security information. Be sure to follow guidelines to ensure that every tier of your servers, operating systems, and databases are free from holes. If you are purchasing server service from an ISP, ask your customer service representative to describe, in detail, what security options are available and what security measures are taken to ensure the safety of your documents.

Here are a few guidelines to help you ensure a secure server environment:

- Use Secure Sockets Layer (SSL) security where you can. Most contemporary Web servers offer this technology.

- If you are running an electronic commerce site, look into Secure Electronic Transaction (SET) technology. This provides specific security measures for online transactions.

- Set up certificates for Internet Explorer. Certificates alert the site visitor when he or she is entering an area or attempting to download information that might be insecure.

- Where you can, set ASP pages to read and write only. This disallows any execution of programs, prohibiting potential hackers from entering your system.

If you have further questions, check with your systems administrator or service provider. Another avenue of security support is to visit the Web site of your server's manufacturer.

Now that you have some of the basics of ASP down, we'd like to offer some good online resources so you can expand your knowledge. There are also many excellent books on ASP and related scripting technologies, such as JavaScript, VBScript, and Perl.

 MASTERING WHAT'S ONLINE

ASP Resources

Microsoft Site Builder Network (www.microsoft.com/sitebuilder/) Full of great information, tutorials and samples

Active Server Pages.Com (www.activeserverpages.com) Tutorials, advice columns, and code

The ASP Developer's Site (www.genusa.com/asp/) Extensive site with ASP developer information, breaking news, and scripts

ASP Developer Network (www.aspdeveloper.net) A helpful network for ASP developers

The ASP Hole (www.asphole.com) Code, FAQs, consultants, demos, and book recommendations for ASP developers

CNET Builder.com (www.builder.com) A great resource for all Web technologies

Ziff-Davis University (www.zdu.com) Free information as well as many low-cost interactive training classes

Sybex Publishing (www.sybex.com) A wide range of supportive computer titles

PART

V

Back-End Applications and Professional Management

Up Next

ASP is an important Microsoft technology that is sure to appeal to you if you are interested in managing dynamic, data-driven sites. While it demands programming know-how, there are some good tools, such as Microsoft's Visual InterDev, that can get you started. More information on ASP is widely available should you find that you need to delve into it in more detail.

Up next is a look at databases—in detail. While we showed you how to work with databases in the context of FrontPage in Chapter 20, in the following chapter we'll help you learn a bit of the foundational concepts that go into data management on a large scale. We'll also provide you with plenty of resources so that you can follow up any interest in databases with quality information.

CHAPTER 27

Databases in Detail

Databases are the heart and soul of high-performance Web sites. Without them, we couldn't be making airline reservations through our favorite online travel agency, managing an online stock portfolio, or working with our company's intranet to stay on top of customer, manufacturer, or purchasing information.

Databases work with numerous other technologies discussed in this book, including CGI, ASP, Java, and other programming languages. A database is primarily a server-side operation, but it involves complex relationships between the browser and the server in order to make a given process occur.

High-end databases are not for everyone—while you can create a simple database with FrontPage and Access (see Chapter 23, *Adding Databases for Maximum Impact*), database technology is a specialty field. This chapter looks at databases in detail and introduces you to important concepts that you'll want to have as you think about your personal and company needs. You'll get you familiar with what databases are, what their internal structure looks like, and what they can do.

About Databases

The many brands of databases on the market fall into two categories: *File Server* and *RDBMS* (*Relational Database Management System*). Each of these databases has specific aspects that make it attractive to developers. Ultimately, you will have to choose your database using your desired goals and specific environment as your guides.

If your database is fairly small and is servicing a limited number of users on an individual server, you can choose from one of the File Server databases, which include Access, FoxPro, Dbase, Clarion, Paradox, and Filemaker Pro.

Larger databases with a large number of users and intensive application demands such as electronic commerce support are better served by an RDBMS database. Products from Oracle, Sybase, SQL, and Informix are RDBMS databases.

The primary difference between File Server databases and RDBMS databases is that a File Server database shares resources while RDMBS is the isolated child of database systems—it works alone and handles data from within its own set of tools. Another significant difference is that File Server systems are widely available for desktop machines but may lose their power when asked to work in high-end environments. RDBMS products, on the other hand, are completely scalable, able to shift from the desktop level right on up through mainframe systems. In fact, they are the preferred database for major industry, used for the back-end systems of most large online Internet services with heavy database needs.

WARNING Manufacturers of File Server databases often offer products that will help you scale your File Server database to a relational database system. Serious developers caution against using this type of product if you can avoid it, and they recommend choosing the right database for your needs from the start.

To help you make the right decision when planning for backend operation purchases, here is a list of some advantages and disadvantages of File Server and RDBMS databases.

File Server Database

Advantages	Disadvantages
User-friendly	Limited data storage
Affordable	Not primed for high-end transactions
Available on all popular OSs	Stores but does not manage data with advanced programming
Available as part of a suite of complementary tools	Limited management tools
Lower demand on system resources	
Easy to find support and information	

Relational Database Management System

Advantages	Disadvantages
Can be used on a wide range of system types	Greater cost
Manages high traffic situations easily	Poses a significant learning curve
Easy access to support and tools	Demands advanced hardware
Highly configurable	Demands extensive human resources
Supports advanced technologies and programming languages	
Built-in or add-on Web-related services	
Excellent security	

PART

V

Back-End Applications
and Professional
Management

TIP Manufacturers eager to sell their wares are typically happy to provide you with demonstration software, white papers, and support information. Try before you buy!

Popular Database Products

There are a wide range of databases in the marketplace today. The most common File Server and RDBMS databases used by Web developers are looked at here.

File Server Databases

Two of the most popular database products in this class include Microsoft Access and Sybase Adaptive Server Anywhere.

Microsoft Access

For those readers new to databases, Access may be your best choice in terms of a starting point, as you probably have the software and can take advantage of Office 2000 documentation to learn a bit about the program.

What's even more appealing to new and general audiences is that Access is equipped with Wizards that will take you step-by-step through a variety of database development procedures (see Figure 27.1). This makes your job less stressful, as the learning curve is smaller than what you'll face with a RDBMS option.

Also, as we pointed out in Chapter 20, *Integrating Sites with Microsoft Office*, Access allows you to save documents directly to HTML for further editing in FrontPage. This is part of the powerful suite integration offered by Office, and it saves you a lot of steps when offering information culled from your database onto your Web site.

 NOTE Typically, you'll want to use the Microsoft Information Server or Microsoft NT to manage your Office-based data processes.

FIGURE 27.1

*Using Microsoft Access
2000's Table Wizard*

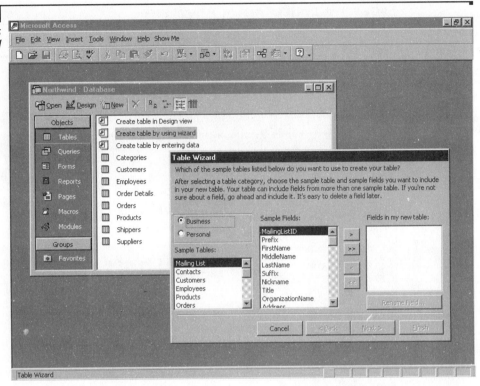

Of course, Access might not suit your needs should they be more demanding than
File Server applications can manage. Still, it's a great place to start learning about how
data is managed in the context of databases and Web-based applications.

MASTERING WHAT'S ONLINE

Microsoft Access

General information on Microsoft Access is available at www.microsoft.com/access.

For Access training in your area, visit www.microsoft.com/train_cert/.

You can get questions answered by looking for Office- and Access-related newsgroups
at support.microsoft.com/support/news/.

Sybase Adaptive Server Anywhere

Adaptive Server Anywhere from Sybase is especially popular due to its user-friendly installation and administration features (see Figure 27.2). It's also pretty powerful for a File Server database, as it includes transaction processing. This feature is always of interest to individuals wanting to add online shopping to their Web sites.

FIGURE 27.2

Adaptive Server Anywhere's home page

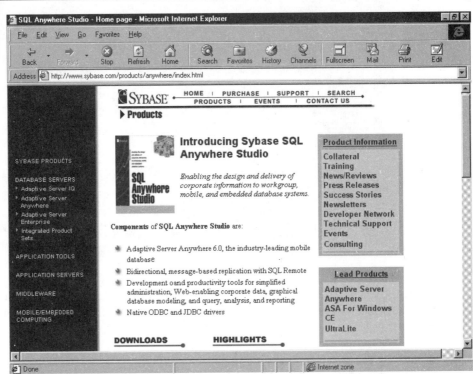

Another feature of Sybase Adaptive Server Anywhere is that it has a bit more programming support than Access and most of the other File Server databases. For example, developers can use Java (see Chapter 22, *Specialty Programming Techniques*) for maximum Web-oriented, cross-platform power.

MASTERING WHAT'S ONLINE

Sybase Adaptive Server Anywhere

For more information on the Adaptive Server Anywhere product, free demos, and updates to software, visit Sybase on the Web at www.sybase.com.

RDBMS

Let's move from the more simple but user-friendly realm of File Server database systems into the more complex environment of the Relational Database Management System. There are many contenders in this arena, and we've chosen to discuss those that best address Web-based applications and that are favored by Web-oriented developers.

Oracle8*i*

Oracle has been very involved in the development of advanced RDBM systems. Of the various Oracle products, Oracle8*i* (see Figure 27.3) offers very high performance along with tools that enable you to create databases from within a logical interface.

With Oracle8*i*'s special, Web-oriented features including a Publishing Assistant, developers don't need to manage their data output to the Web hands-on if they don't want to. Of course, if you're using FrontPage, you'll probably find that you can use tools to manage Web-based files processed by Oracle8*i* with ease.

MASTERING WHAT'S ONLINE

Oracle Databases

Check out news, tools, community, and troubleshooting tips at Oracle's helpful Web site, www.oracle.com.

PART

V

Back-End Applications and Professional Management

FIGURE 27.3

Oracle8i's home page

Informix

Informix has consistently added more Web-related applications to its database management systems. Along with Informix's database software, complementary applications for the Web including electronic commerce and Web content management solutions (see Figure 27.4) provide a range of choices for the Web-savvy database developer.

FIGURE 27.4

Informix offers electronic commerce and Web content management solutions.

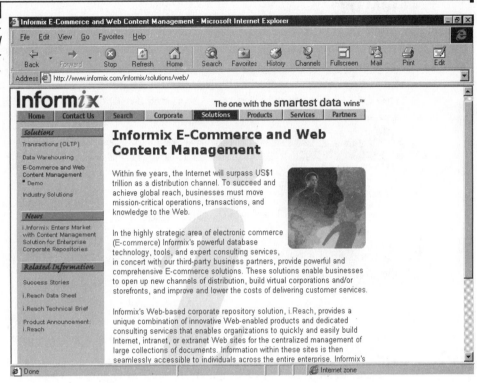

Informix is also well known for having security support services, auditing, managing high-end memory demands with ease, and offering programmable aspects via the Java language.

MASTERING WHAT'S ONLINE

Informix

You can find out what Informix is doing for Web-oriented database systems at www.informix.com.

IBM DB2

IBM is making a big play for market share in the electronic commerce industry. With excellent cross-platform support including Windows, Linux, and Unix systems, DB2 is extremely portable.

With a variety of extended applications for the Web, DB2 sports very stable technology, including backup and recovery as well as replication options.

MASTERING WHAT'S ONLINE

IBM DB2

Learn more about DB2 at the IBM Web site, www.ibm.com. You can even download a free trial of the software from www.software.ibm.com/data/db2/.

An independent DB2 users group offers online information as well as training and seminars at www.idug.org/.

Sybase Adaptive Server Enterprise

This is Sybase's entry into the realm of relational systems. Along with the features available in its File Server system, extremely secure online transactions make Adaptive Server Enterprise a favorite for developers managing large e-commerce systems.

Database Structure

No matter the database you end up using, you'll find that there is a common structure and language applied to both the type of database and the brand. Let's examine a few of the concepts that make up database structures.

Database   As the term implies, this is the central brain of a data-driven system. It is the file, or combination of files, where the primary intelligence is stored.

Schema   All of the basic components of a database (see below).

Database schema   All of the components of a database viewed as a unified, single package.

In order to use databases effectively, you'll need to know more about how the components of a database, or the *schema*, work. The following list defines database schema components:

Tables   Don't confuse database tables with HTML-based tables, although their information is similar in that it is a structural method of organizing information. Database tables contain the meat-and-potato details of a database. Let's say you're tracking a list of stock buyers on your stockbroker Web site. A database table might include the stock buyer identification number, stock buyer name, stock identification, current pricing, and purchase number. In a database table, this information is organized into columns, and each column relates to one type of information.

Keys   This is a method of identifying information within a table. In our example, the key might be the stock buyer identification number.

Tablespaces   The most basic of database information, tablespaces are the areas where database components, including tables, are stored. Depending upon the way a database is built, a given tablespace might be stored on separate drives within the hardware system.

Indexes   As with any method of cataloging information, a database index is used to help find records or other information within the database with speed and accuracy.

Columns   Part of a table, a column is the specific information within a table. In our earlier description of tables, we discussed how a column might relate to a topic. If we are monitoring patients in a hospital, a column could be the patient number, another column would be the patient name, and still another might be the patient's medical status.

Triggers   This is a block of code within a database that orders a specific operation to execute automatically upon a given command or action. Let's say a nurse updates his patient record. A trigger would be a block of code that commands the database to update all the information for that patient upon the completion of the nurse's update.

Stored procedures   Similar to triggers, stored procedures are blocks of code that order specific actions to occur. However, stored procedures are independent of user input and are related more to the function of the database and database performance.

Sequences   Sequences are aspects of database code that allow a database developer to organize an automatic increment in a given value. For example, if a customer record begins with 001, a sequence can be written to automatically add each subsequent customer record with the next logical increment.

Rollback segments   Rollback segments can be though of as data safety valves. Let's say you get to a Web site, decide to purchase a CD, enter your credit information, and invoke the transaction. At that point, the transaction is submitted for processing. If all goes well, that transaction is permanently added to the database. However, if something goes wrong, a rollback segment will hold the information and resubmit it until it is permanently committed to the database.

Let's take a look at some actual code used to create a database that is used to track patients in a hospital. First, we'll show a tablespace example, show the actual table, and demonstrate what a trigger looks like. Here is the tablespace example:

```
CREATE TABLESPACE INDEXES
DATAFILE 'E:\Data\Indexes\IndxRMS.Dbf' SIZE 500M REUSE
DEFAULT
 STORAGE(
 INITIAL 10240
 NEXT 10240
 PCTINCREASE 50
 MINEXTENTS 1
 MAXEXTENTS 121);
CREATE TABLESPACE DATA
DATAFILE 'D:\Data\RMS\DataRMS.dbf' SIZE 800M REUSE
DEFAULT
STORAGE(
 INITIAL 10240
 NEXT 10240
 PCTINCREASE 50
 MINEXTENTS 1
 MAXEXTENTS 121);
```

And here is a table example:

```
CREATE TABLE PATIENT-Column definitions first
 (ID VARCHAR2(16) NOT NULL-this is the key
 ,ALTERNATEID VARCHAR2(16)
 ,ACCOUNTNUMBER VARCHAR2(16)
 ,SSN VARCHAR2(16)
 ,FIRSTNAME VARCHAR2(30)
 ,MIDDLEINITIAL CHAR(1)
 ,LASTNAME VARCHAR2(30)
```

```
,NAMESUFFIX VARCHAR2(3)
,ALIASNAME VARCHAR2(30)
,ISALIAS CHAR(1) DEFAULT 'N' NOT NULL—set a default value and add a
,ISACTIVE CHAR(1) DEFAULT 'Y' NOT NULL            "not null" constraint
,BIRTHDATE DATE
,SEX CHAR(1)
,RACE CHAR(1)
,ETHNICGROUP CHAR(1)
,LANGUAGE VARCHAR2(30)
,MARITALSTATUS CHAR(1)
,RELIGION VARCHAR2(3)
,WEIGHT NUMBER(7,2)
,WEIGHTUOM VARCHAR2(3)
,HEIGHT NUMBER(7,2)
,HEIGHTUOM VARCHAR2(3)
,SURFACE NUMBER(5,0)
,SURFACEUOM VARCHAR2(3)
,WARD VARCHAR2(6)
,ROOM VARCHAR2(5)
,BED VARCHAR2(2)
,CART NUMBER(3,0)
,ALLERGIES VARCHAR2(2000)
,NOTES VARCHAR2(2000)
,NEXTDOSE DATE
,NEXTCRITICAL DATE
,WITHIN CHAR(1)
,CRITICALITY NUMBER(3,0)
,NEXTOUTCOME DATE
,NUMCHARTINGREQ NUMBER(4,0) DEFAULT 0 NOT NULL
,LASTADMIN DATE DEFAULT SysDate NOT NULL
,NUMADMIN NUMBER(7,0) DEFAULT 0 NOT NULL
,LASTMODIFIED DATE DEFAULT SysDate NOT NULL
,REVIEWWITHIN NUMBER(3,0) DEFAULT 0 NOT NULL
,NEXTHUMANREVIEW DATE
,LASTHUMANREVIEW DATE
,NUMUNVERIFIED NUMBER(3,0) DEFAULT 0
,NUMSTAT NUMBER(3,0) DEFAULT 0
,CHANGEDBY VARCHAR2(2) DEFAULT 'M' NOT NULL
)
```

```
PCTUSED 40-define table parameters such as size and growth
PCTFREE 10
INITRANS 1
MAXTRANS 255
TABLESPACE DATA
STORAGE(
INITIAL 10240
NEXT 10240
PCTINCREASE 50
MINEXTENTS 1
MAXEXTENTS 121);
```

The following trigger example is used to check the status and update the record in question:

```
CREATE OR REPLACE TRIGGER EMARDELETE BEFORE DELETE
 ON EMAR
 REFERENCING OLD AS OLD NEW AS NEW FOR EACH ROW
BEGIN
 /* Check the status of the EMAR and update the Patient table */
 IF ( :old.Status = 1) THEN
  /* Decrement NumChartingReq on the Patient table */
  UPDATE Patient SET NumChartingReq = NumChartingReq - 1 WHERE Patient.Id =
:old.Patient;
 END IF;
 EXCEPTION
  WHEN OTHERS THEN
   NULL;
 END;
 /
```

It's possible that you'll understand these examples, but if you don't, worry not. The idea here is to get familiar with the way database-related code looks. Does it make you curious? Great! You might be a perfect candidate to learn more about back-end operations and database management. If the code isn't something that interests you, but you know you need the power of databases to run your Web site needs, it's time to contact a professional database developer or company.

Database Modeling

Modeling a database is essentially defining the business process, selecting the data elements, and generating the database codes. In a way, this process is similar to working using a specific production method as described in Chapter 19, *Creating Advanced Sites with FrontPage*. The concept of modeling and production methods (see Chapter 28, *Using FrontPage with Microsoft's Visual InterDev*) is extremely helpful when working in environments where rapid development is necessary. Beyond saving time, modeling can help you or your client save money, too.

There are a variety of tools and languages that can assist with database modeling. Some are free, others are very expensive. As with anything in computer technology, evaluating your needs and knowing your budget limitations will help you make the best choice.

Unified Modeling Language

The *Unified Modeling Language*, or *UML*, is considered the standard database modeling tool. It approaches the database development process from a software engineering perspective, making a "blueprint" of the application in development.

The brainchild of Rational Software (see Figure 27.5), UML has been built into a number of products including Rational Rose. This product is especially effective because not only can a developer use it to map out the application, but it is highly visual, making it completely accessible to team members and clients.

Rational Rose generates database schema and offers multi-language support including Java, a friendly user interface, and even an HTML development component.

That's the good news. The challenging news is the price tag. Rational Software products run between $2,000 and $4,000 U.S. per license. For the high-end developer, Rational Rose is the industry standard, but be sure it's something you need and want before making the financial commitment to the product.

PART

V

Back-End Applications
and Professional
Management

FIGURE 27.5

Rational Software uses the language they developed, UML, for modeling applications.

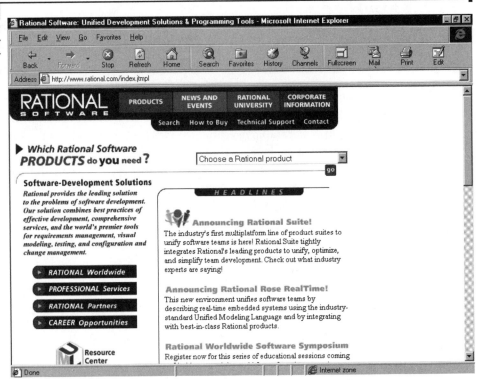

MASTERING WHAT'S ONLINE

Rational Software

For detailed information on Rational Software products including Rational Rose and related applications, visit the Rational Software Web site at www.rational.com.

Microsoft Visual Modeler

Microsoft Visual Modeler (MVM) is a visual modeling tool that you'll find to be helpful and affordable—in fact, it's free! Integrated with Microsoft's developer environment, Visual Studio, MVM breaks up development into components (FrontPage users will be familiar with this concept; see Chapter 15, *Special Effects*). The advantage of MVM components over those created with other development modules is that they are smaller, more manageable, and can be used within related software programs.

In the MVM environment, there is a very handy three-tiered service model that shows the database in a highly visual environment. The three tiers are:

User Services   This tier is the interface where the developer inputs client side scripting information to ultimately receive data from the database.

Business Services   The Business Services tier acts as the bridge between user and data services. The user inputs information, and the Business Services then accept the data and apply certain rules to it, such as protecting the server from the user's input for security purposes.

Data Services   These are the database components where data is inputted, updated, maintained, and managed. Data Services can receive data via the Business Services and return data to the user via the connecting Business Services pipe. This separation is helpful because using this model, developers can make changes on the data end without modifying the other tiers.

Other Modeling Options

There are a variety of other modeling software applications. One example is Oracle Designer, which generates a variety of database models and can also create DHTML, Java, and Visual Basic code. For more information, visit the Oracle Web site, www.oracle.com.

Applying Database Concepts: A Closer Look

Partitioning information in the way that MVM does is also referred to as *N-tier architecture*. What happens within this type of architecture is that a relationship is set up between the client and the server. When we discuss *client* in this case, we're referring to one thing only: the Web browser. It doesn't matter what browser brand or version, or what platform the browser runs on.

However, when discussing a *server* (just as with an Operating System), we're looking at two distinct issues. The first is the hardware that is being used, and the second is the software.

Software runs on hardware, and in the case of the server, different software can run on the same hardware platform. Similarly, in very large systems, a single software application might be running on numerous, individual computers. So what you end up with is a rather complex relationship where the client, or browser, needs to receive information. In the case of a database, that information resides somewhere on a computer, making use of a variety of software to make it work.

The tier concept helps manage all of this information more clearly:

- In the User Services tier, the developer will use scripting languages such as HTML, JavaScript, and Dynamic HTML. This is the information that manages the visual appearance of the data to the site visitor—who is using the client, a Web browser.

- In the Business Services tier, server-based software applications such as secure transactions and ASP (see Chapter 26, *Using Active Server Pages*) are stored.

- The Data Services tier is where the database and all of its components reside. Since database systems are a combination of software and hardware, both play a role in this area.

This tier concept keeps the client and the server separate but equal partners in the database process.

Normalization of Data

De-normalized environments have information stored in duplicate areas. For example, there might be a patient name in several areas of a database. But what happens when a change is made to one of the records? Without extra programming and accounting for the data, all of the records might not be globally updated.

Normalizing databases is the process by which data is stored in a simple, error-free manner. Typically, this means storing given data *one time only*. If there are more instances of the same data, there is a higher risk for error, more demand on developers to manage each copy of the data, and more resources required from the software and hardware to manage the data.

Both environments have their place. Sometimes it's necessary to have multiple instances of a record, but if you can avoid this and normalize your data, you're likely to have a smoother running system.

Data Relationships

RDBMS is based on relationships, hence the name *relational*. The concept is that the relationship between information creates the core technology beneath database management and design.

Data relationships work in normalized database environments to keep data organized. The following relationships are key to database creation:

One-to-One This refers to the relationship between data elements. In a hospital setting, there might be a main table comprising of all the segments of the hospital (cardiac, surgery, neo-natal) and another table where the patients are listed. Each table will have a relationship to the other, because each section of the hospital contains individual patients, and each patient is placed in a specific location within the hospital.

One-to-Many Imagine two tables; one is a list of patients, the other, a list of medications. Each individual patient requires a relationship with the list of medications, although each medication on the list does not necessarily correspond to an individual patient.

Many-to-One This is the reverse of a One-to-Many relationship. Let's say there's a list of patients, and a table that relates to nurses. Only one nurse is assigned to a certain group of patients.

Optimizing Database Performance

In order to make databases perform better, there are several steps developers take. This process is referred to as *optimizing* performance.

In the "Database Structure" section of this chapter, we looked at various aspects of a database. One such aspect is the *index*. An index is especially helpful in allowing databases to find and retrieve information with speed and accuracy. Well-written indexes can fully optimize the way a database performs.

Another aspect of optimization is called *caching*. This is similar in concept to what your Web browser does with Web information. If you visit a site with relative frequency, chances are your browser has cached, or stored, graphics and HTML-based information from that page in its cache, or memory. This allows for faster load times. Similarly, database caches can hold stored procedures, triggers, and components that are used frequently, improving the speed of the database.

Advanced database management allows developers to put sections of data onto different drives. A database developer might opt to put data on one drive, indexes on another, and components on still another. For high-demand systems, this reduces the load on a single machine's resources by balancing the demand across different machines.

PART

V

Back-End Applications and Professional Management

NOTE   Database software typically offer a suite of tools to help developers fine-tune performance. There are also a number of excellent books and resources to assist you in learning how to maximize your database's performance potential.

Reducing Traffic on a Network

Reducing the load on the network helps keep a database operating smoothly. Some of the things that can be done to reduce traffic include:

- Relying on stored procedures and triggers within the database to do the "heavy" work
- Using Dynamic HTML (DHTML) to manage data
- Using ASP (see Chapter 26)

Here's an ASP sample that is helping to reduce network traffic with the aid of the Structured Query Language (SQL), which works to get information from and update information to a given database:

```
' First create command and recordset objects
Set Cm = Server.CreateObject("ADODB.Command")
Set Rs = Server.CreateObject("ADODB.RecordSet")

' Set the ActiveConnection property of command object to the
' ODBC source you will use
Cm.ActiveConnection = "Your_ODBC_Source"

' Now, create the SQL statement
sSQL = "SELECT * FROM tbl_patient WHERE zip='54123' "

' The CommandText property of Command object should contain
' this SQL statement
Cm.CommandText = sSQL

' Since we are using a SQL Statement in Command object, the
CommandType
' Property should be adCmdText which has a value of 1
Cm.CommandType = 1
```

```
' Execute the command, and set the recordset object to the result
' of this execution. We obtain the resulting records in Rs object
Set Rs = Cm.Execute
```

Configuring Hardware

There are two important concepts to put to use when configuring database hardware:

RAID   No, it's not a bug spray! In this case, it's *Redundant Array of Independent Disks*. Essentially, this is a much-used method of saving data. RAID relies on saving the same information to a number of disks on a system at the same time. This way, if one drive becomes unavailable, the data is immediately available elsewhere.

Parallelism   In this case, RDBM systems break up the work between multiple computer systems. Though similar to RAID in a sense, the main difference between RDBM systems and RAID systems is that the information is not only stored on separate disks, but on separate computers as well.

MASTERING WHAT'S ONLINE

Database Resources

Enjoy these resources to help you understand more about the power of databases for Web development:

Put Your Database on the Web (builder.cnet.com/Programming/Databases/index.html)   A helpful article from Builder.Com about how to get a database up and running on the Web

Datamation Magazine (www.datamation.com)   A site rich with news, tutorials, and resources for those interested in databases

Database Resources (www.unifx.com/links.html)   A long list of compiled links about databases including manufacturers

Up Next

As you've seen in this chapter, databases are complex but powerful tools that can address big issues in high-end site development. Whether you're working on a site such as a customer service center that requires the storage, retrieval, and updating of data or working internally on an intranet or extranet and keeping track of clients, patients, or the progress of a corporate project, databases are the tool for helping you manage this information.

In the next chapter, we look at another important tool in Web site development related to the back-end of sophisticated Web sites: Microsoft's Visual InterDev. This is a development environment specifically geared toward team-oriented, rapid development of powerful Web sites.

CHAPTER 28

Using FrontPage with Microsoft's Visual InterDev

rontPage is undeniably a powerful product, and FrontPage 2000 has specifically added team-oriented tools to take it from being a hobbyist's tool into the realm of professional development. You've seen how FrontPage is well-integrated into the Microsoft Office suite of tools (see Chapter 20, *Integrating Sites with Microsoft Office*). But FrontPage is also part of another group of tools specifically geared toward a higher development level than this book has covered thus far. Included in this group is Microsoft's Visual InterDev.

Visual InterDev is the visual interface tool that can not only create Web sites in a similar way to FrontPage—using a WYSIWYG page design tool and themes reminiscent of those in FrontPage—but can help the developer create and debug server-side technologies such as advanced scripting with ASP, Visual Basic, Java, and database applications.

Visual InterDev might sound like the big-brother to FrontPage, and in many ways it is. But in the true spirit of software integration, Visual InterDev and FrontPage have been optimized to work together in a team environment with powerful results.

In this chapter, we'll introduce you to the features of Visual InterDev, giving you an overview of why it exists, what it does, and how it integrates with FrontPage to create a work model for advanced Web site development.

Rapid Application Development (RAD)

In order to properly describe the features of Visual InterDev, we first need to look at an important concept in project management that drives the rationale for using Visual InterDev and FrontPage together. This concept is known as *Rapid Application Development*, or *RAD*.

For those readers who have a background in software development, the concept of RAD is likely to be very familiar. This complex system was specifically designed to address the high-pressure needs of the software industry: short deadlines, multiple platform concerns, user demand, and constantly shifting technologies.

The Web development environment is no different. The challenges are the same, and the argument could be made that Web sites are software products. Many features are indeed similar, and applying a management system to the development of Web sites makes complete sense (see Chapter 19, *Creating Advanced Sites with FrontPage*).

The idea here is to create a streamlined production environment that effectively manages the job of a Web site in an organized fashion with precision and, ultimately, great expediency and meeting of deadlines.

RAD is often described as having three main themes that drive the system:

- Avoiding known mistakes
- Following good development practices
- Managing risk

Let's take a closer look at what each of these themes mean and how they pertain to working within the Web development industry.

Avoiding Mistakes

In an ideal production setting, each stage of the process would be handled without a glitch (see Chapter 19). But as everyone knows, that's not a very accurate state of affairs when it comes to real life.

RAD looks to common, or *classic*, mistakes for avoidance. These are the mistakes of hard-won experience. Just as the child must put her hand on a hot stove in order to fully understand what it means to be burned, so must we all learn from experience what *not* to do in order to protect ourselves. If we're very fortunate—and very wise— we'll listen to our elders and not make the same mistakes they did, helping us to avoid the common problems that can turn a development process into a stressful, even impossible situation. Some of the classic mistakes to avoid include:

No planning or ineffective planning   As mentioned in Chapter 19, planning is an essential part of Web site production. If you fail at this level, the conse- quences, particularly for large projects, could be disastrous. In order to accom- plish the goals of RAD, a strong, effective plan must be in place.

Forgetting to include necessary tasks in the production plan   It's easy to forget tasks necessary for a large project, and obviously you cannot anticipate every step you'll need from start to finish. However, if you are comprehensive at get- ting this phase done, potential problems will be minimized.

Adding inappropriate technology to a project   Every time a technology is added to a given site, the amount of testing and potential failure rises accord- ingly. While it's fun to add Java applets, interactive forms, animations, guest- books, and advanced scripts to Web pages, in professional development you must have a very strong rationale for having them there. Every component of a page must serve a specific purpose. Be sure that when you do your planning, you are extremely honest about what you need and, perhaps more importantly, about what you do *not* need on the site.

Changing tools mid-project   If you know your tools going in to a project, there will be little need to change them later on. Changing a tool means loss in time and design control—you and team members are faced with having to learn or adapt to a new development environment. The time that this takes and the frustration factor can conceivably ruin a well-run production.

Selecting team members haphazardly   When you're working in a team, it's imperative that fast, clear, and effective communication takes place. Any known problems with colleagues should guide you to think carefully about selecting those individuals for rapid, team-oriented Web site development.

Not resolving team conflicts early on   Despite our best intentions, conflicts do arise. When they aren't resolved early on, they can become very serious risks to the maintenance of production flow.

Unsatisfactory working environments   No matter our personal work habits, the fact is that clutter leads to disorganization. Moreover, if we as individuals feel stressed because we don't have adequately lit, comfortable, and quiet environments to work in, our work will suffer.

Poor relations between Web development team and client   One of the most critical problems that can come up during the production of a Web site is a major change in the climate between the Web team and the client. If communications fail or if the needs and responsibilities were unclear from the beginning, potential difficulties that affect the project's ability to survive can ensue.

Setting expectations that are unrealistic   All of us run the risk of being overly optimistic about scheduling and skill levels—particularly in the exciting, early stages of a project's life. This can lead us to set expectations both of ourselves, and others, that are unrealistic.

Is it always possible to avoid mistakes? Of course not. After all, they're inevitable by-products of both humans and their technologies. However, as everyone knows, mistakes can help us learn how to be more effective in how we approach our work.

Following Good Development Practices

To address many of the classic production mistakes, employ these solid development practices:

Understand the complete nature of your Web site—intent, audience, and long- and short-term goals.   In Chapter 19, we explained the importance of planning. We'll say it again: Planning your site from birth to adulthood and beyond is your strongest ally in reducing problems.

Plan your production effectively and thoroughly.   Not only should the concept of your site be well-planned, but the individual tasks that you'll need to take each step of the way should be included in the production plan.

TIP　Map out your master plan on a large whiteboard. Leave this in a prominent place and mark off tasks as they are completed. Individuals on the project will then know exactly where in the project they are and where they need to go.

Determine all necessary tools before beginning production.　One of the concerns this chapter addresses is planning your site and site production. This includes choosing the tools you're going to use to plan, build, and maintain the site. Obviously, your primary tool is FrontPage and an imaging program. In a large site development experience, there are going to be other software tools necessary to carry out the job: other Office suite members such as Word and Access, graphic utilities including specialty filters and optimizing programs, technical utilities such as Telnet or FTP, a plain text editor, database applications, programming interfaces, and even Visual InterDev.

 TIP　Develop a tools list and ensure that everyone on the team has the necessary skills to use those tools effectively. Keep the list public and provide it as part of a documentation set for the project. If your team has an intranet site, make sure it's available there, too.

Know the technological needs and direction of your site.　Understand what technology you need going in. This should be documented and clearly outlined in technical terms at critical points within the planning of the site, as well as in the master task list.

In a team environment, an efficient project manager is key.　Whether you are that individual or you are a member of a team run by a project manager, knowing the role of such a manager is imperative. The project manager is the conductor—he or she takes the plan and ensures that each member of the team plays his or her part correctly, in a timely fashion, and with enthusiasm.

Select team members with care.　Team members should be chosen equally for their skills as well as their ability to effectively meet deadlines and work well in the team environment. Individuals who do not fit this profile should be left out of projects that require rapid development and deployment.

Resolve conflicts quickly.　Despite your best intentions, conflicts can, and will, arise. Use any effective conflict-resolution strategy (there are many books on this subject—check the business section of your favorite bookseller) to resolve conflicts as soon as you see them come up. If left alone, such conflicts can rise to a boiling point, eating up precious time and emotional energy while adding unnecessary stress to your team members.

Ensure positive working environments.   Keep your work area free of clutter and recommend others do the same. This makes it easy to find reference materials and provides a psychological aid to smooth work habits—clutter can make people tense! Wherever possible, encourage members to take breaks with relative frequency. Small, frequent breaks can help refresh the mind and body, actually reducing stress-related problems or illness over the course of the site's development.

Guarantee that relations between the Web development team and the client are managed properly.   Keep the communication with the client between the fewest amount of development members as possible. The project manager should really be the only individual who is deeply involved in the client relationship. Ensure that proper contracts are written, clearly defining the responsibilities and milestone dates that both parties have to upload (see Chapter 19).

Set realistic expectations.   Think optimistically but realistically! Team members get sick, delays occur, conflicts happen. When strategically positioning your site tasks within a schedule, allow for some leeway should problems come up.

Risk Management

Managing risk is such an important element that schools teaching computer science and information technology have at least one, if not several, courses dedicated to this area alone.

Risk management means exactly what it says. If you've avoided mistakes and followed good development practices, there's still going to be a potential for risk. That's life, after all—stuff happens! So once a situation becomes critical, it's necessary to manage that risk.

Following is a list of ways to effectively address risk. Each suggestion here can help you know what to do in case of a problem:

Assess a project's potential risks.   This is a process by which the entire site's life is assessed in terms of what problems it potentially contains. This includes everything from a general awareness of classic mistakes to a specific personality challenge with a team member.

Create a plan to address each individual risk.   If you think you've exhaustively planned for your site, guess what? Your planning and assessment will clarify risk potential. For each of these potential problems, have a plan ready to go *should it become necessary*.

If problems should occur, prioritize them. Let's say one week you have a team member out of the office due to illness, the client calls up and wants to add something to the site right away, and there are problems with the computer network you're using to develop the site. Prioritize your problems by determining which problem will cause the most critical delay.

Resolve individual risks in terms of priority. In the case above, the priority order might be: fix the computer network, address client need, have a willing team member temporarily manage the sick team member's responsibilities.

Track the resolution and monitor it closely for any new risk potentials. Once a problem is resolved, don't turn away just yet—watch the situation to ensure that new problems don't come up.

Use all risks and solutions found in an individual production as a reference for future risk management. Keep a daily log of problems and effective solutions. For a professional development company, this practice will become invaluable. Each time you go through a project, you'll have new experiences and come up with new solutions. These experiences will help you prevent mistakes, improve development practices, and learn to manage risk more effectively.

By adequately planning your site's production, developing and following good production techniques, and successfully managing risk, you will create as smooth a production schedule and environment as possible.

 NOTE If you're very lucky, the RAD approach as applied to Web development environments will work on first-take. However, that's optimistic! RAD obviously becomes a more potent approach over time, when a given production team catalogs risk and learns from prior mistakes.

MASTERING WHAT'S ONLINE

RAD Resources

Use these Web sites to gain a deeper understanding of RAD and to learn how to use it to effectively manage your Web development teams:

RADtdg—Rapid Application Development Technologies Design Group (www.bluemtn.com/radtdg.html) Resources and discussion about RAD

A Quality Approach to RAD (www.avnet.co.uk/tesseract/QiC/articles/Stapleton/25.html) An interesting article about the British perspective on RAD

RAD Overview (web.cs.bgsu.edu/maner/domains/RAD.htm) An article examining RAD and why it should be used

Visual InterDev Close-Up

As you now are aware, RAD is a powerful method aimed at planning, organizing, and deploying projects. So how does Visual InterDev fit into the picture? Well, as a visual interface for Web site project management, it can give an eagle-eye view of a project in its entirety as well as of provided tools and integrated applications to facilitate the production process in an organized fashion (see Figure 28.1).

FIGURE 28.1

The Visual InterDev Interface, main view

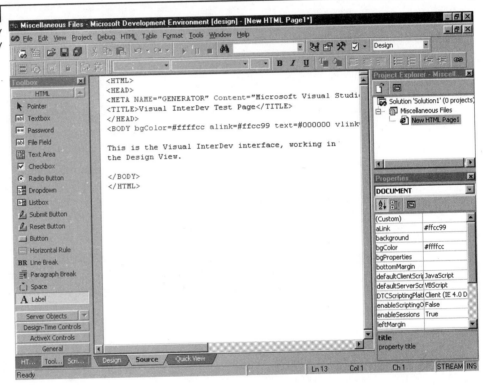

Visual InterDev is not only helpful to the Web development team using RAD as a management method; the software itself was developed to facilitate rapid deployment of integrated technologies. Think of the way your human team works: A project manager oversees team members and uses production techniques to ensure quality and timeliness. Visual InterDev is akin to the project manager—it oversees other applications, such as FrontPage, as well as its own internal facilities, to produce a good product within a set schedule.

Visual InterDev aids the RAD process from a conceptual point of view by:

Tracking tasks   Using a task manager, Visual InterDev can keep lists of what needs to be done as well as track tasks that are finished:

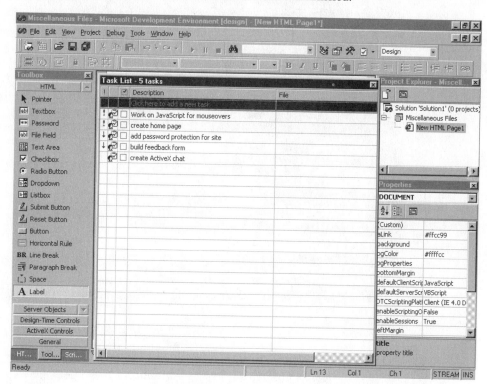

Working in tandem with related applications such as FrontPage   In the spirit of teamwork, Visual InterDev plays a major role in combining the efforts of multiple workstations and servers during production (see "The Development Team Model" section later in this chapter).

Providing a built-in interface to all aspects of the development process including:

- HTML and page design: While Visual InterDev is completely set up to work with FrontPage, it has a WYSIWYG page designer for those who use it as their primary interface to the team environment (as seen in the following screen shot).

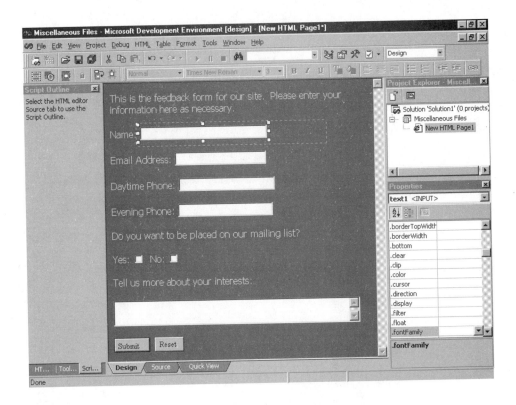

- ASP development: Using Active Server Page technology (see Chapter 22, *Specialty Programming Techniques*, and Chapter 26, *Using Active Server Pages*), Visual InterDev can help developers create server-side routines for on-the-fly Web site updates and changes, and advanced processes.

- Databases: Developers can use Visual InterDev to develop and maintain complex databases (see Figure 28.2).

- Advanced programming: Using a variety of programming languages (see the "Programming Model for Web Developers" section later in this chapter), Web site developers use Visual InterDev to manage programming tasks related to site production.

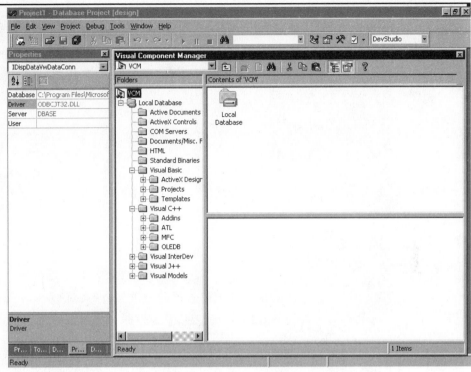

FIGURE 28.2

Visual InterDev's Visual Component Manager

Managing activities directly on remote Web servers. Visual InterDev has modules that allow developers to carry out debugging and other events on remote machines.

Visual InterDev has these practical elements embedded in the tool itself that assists in the ability of its users to work in a highly effective manner by:

- Allowing for drag-and-drop between applications

- Using a system known as Intellisense to complete programming statements from within the visual interface (see Figure 28.3)

- Employing modes such as Master mode, which allows team access to all project files—regardless of where they are on the network

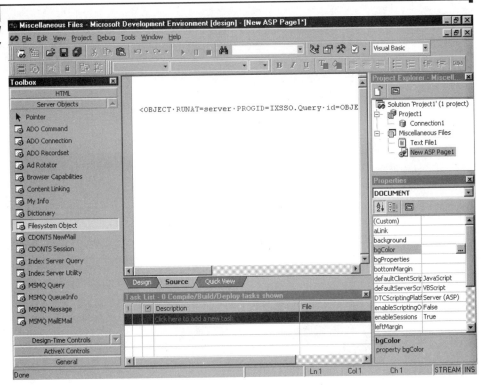

Now let's look at some of the ways in which Visual InterDev approaches the management of Web sites.

Database Design

Database design is a critical piece of today's professional Web site. Visual InterDev allows for the same variety of approaches to database development as FrontPage offers to the Web page designer. Features include:

Database Designer   This is akin to Page view, where a range of controls are available to the user to design and develop databases.

Database wizards   Use these wizards for help creating various aspects of databases quickly and with ease.

FrontPage is fairly limited in what it can do database-wise, so this level of support is extremely helpful, particularly in environments where speed is essential. Supported database servers include Microsoft SQL and Oracle servers.

Programming Model for Web Developers

Where FrontPage offers some support for programming, it's not an advanced programmer's tool. Visual InterDev, on the other hand, lets Web programmers work within its interface to develop with a variety of languages including:

- HTML
- CSS
- DHTML
- JavaScript
- VBScript
- ActiveX
- Java

We should also mention that support for ASP is a major focus of Visual InterDev. Since ASP uses a combination of the above programming languages, and since ASP is also a Microsoft product, it's a natural fit.

 NOTE   Unfortunately, CGI and Perl are not well supported by Visual InterDev. For more information on using these technologies with FrontPage, see Chapter 25, *Understanding CGI*.

 MASTERING WHAT'S ONLINE

Visual InterDev Resources

The following online resources will provide you with technical support, developer insight, and additional references for working with Visual InterDev:

Microsoft Developer's Network (msdn.microsoft.com)   Full range of support for developers using Microsoft products

Microsoft Visual InterDev (msdn.microsoft.com/vinterdev/)   Articles and resources for Visual InterDev users

Developer Community (msdn.microsoft.com/vinterdev/community/)   Events, training, chats, and newsgroups for Visual InterDev developers

PART

V

Back-End Applications
and Professional
Management

The Development Team Model

The heart and soul of Visual InterDev lie in its deep integration. Not only is the tool itself powerfully integrated with other Microsoft Web development tools such as FrontPage, but it works as the management center for a project. In order to understand how FrontPage fully works with Visual InterDev, it's necessary to describe the way Microsoft has used this product integration to assist developers.

Imagine that you're the project manager of a Web development team. You have a variety of very skilled individuals working with you. The team will likely include a content developer, a graphic designer, a database developer, and a Web programmer. Each is responsible for a very different but necessary aspect of the Web site.

Along with the people, you have the technology. At this level, you're probably designing on a network. Finished production will go to a propping (also referred to as *staging* server) for testing before it's placed at its final publication destination: the Internet, intranet, or extranet server environment. Then, the project is delivered over wide or local area networks to individuals via their Web browsers.

This process is a complex one, and it involves the ability of both people and technology to successfully communicate and create relationships with each other. While individual team members will have specialty areas, the project manager oversees those areas to combine to a greater whole.

Herein lies the relationship of Visual InterDev and FrontPage! (Figure 28.4 shows this relationship in detail.) Earlier in this chapter, we described how Visual InterDev is the software equivalent of a project manager. If you are the project manager, you will likely be using management skills such as RAD to organize and maintain a smooth production schedule. But you'll also be ensuring that application production goes smoothly, relying on management software within FrontPage *and* Visual InterDev to track tasks and production milestones.

Your graphic designer will be using design theory to guide the thought behind a design, but will use a program such as Photoshop to render the graphics and FrontPage to render the design. Content developers will use tools including plain text editors, Microsoft Word and Excel, and Microsoft FrontPage to develop copy and manage content. Database engineers and programmers are using Visual InterDev and other programming tools to work their magic.

FIGURE 28.4

The Visual InterDev team model

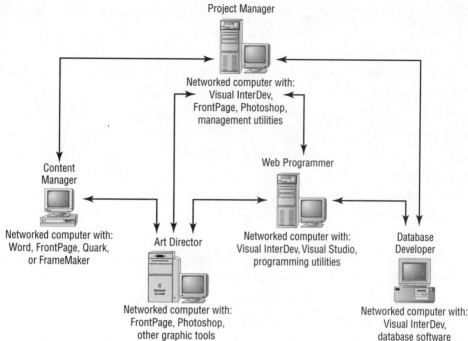

Visual InterDev, then, is the application that pulls together all of the parts of the team, and provides all the tools necessary to develop high-end Web sites within the concept of RAD: avoiding mistakes, working efficiently, using integrated tools, managing risk, and meeting deadlines.

Up Next

You've now seen FrontPage perform a very wide range of esthetic and functional tasks. Whether it's the design of a personal home page or the advanced, integrated model discussed in this chapter, the scope of the application is very broad—and very flexible.

The next part of this book focuses on using FrontPage to create Web sites from start to finish. Using the production techniques you've learned in Chapter 19 in combination with the rest of the information in this book, the next four chapters walk you through the development process of four Web sites including a personal Web page, a small business Web site, a community site, and a large-scale site.

PART VI

Step-by-Step FrontPage Sites

LEARN TO:

- Create a personal Web page

- Design a small business Web site

- Build a community Web site

- Build and manage a large-scale site

CHAPTER **29**

Creating A Personal Web Page

I n this and upcoming chapters, we look at how FrontPage webs actually get produced. Using the method-based production concepts introduced in Chapter 19, *Creating Advanced Sites with FrontPage*, we walk you page-by-page through a variety of site types that you'll probably be designing: personal Web pages, small business Web sites, community sites, and large-scale sites.

We also share helpful tips and guidance throughout the process, enabling you to create powerful pages that are effective, stylish, and unique.

What Is a Personal Web Page?

A *personal Web page*, or *home page*, is a site where people share information about themselves, their families and pets, their interests, and their activities. Personal Web pages make up a significant portion of what kind of sites are on the Internet. It's the perfect place for self-expression, and many people enjoy having and visiting them.

 NOTE A "home page" can also refer to the welcome page of a commercial or private site. Both uses are accurate, but the meaning will depend upon the context in which the term is being used. Another term, "splash page," is also often used to refer to the first page of a Web site, particularly if the page is mostly graphical.

What's more, building home pages is the perfect way to exercise your skills as you learn about Web design. Many of today's Web site designers started out designing their own personal pages and became enamored of the technology, art, and Web environment. Making a home page is probably your best opportunity to decide whether Web design is really for you! In fact, before moving on to creating more advanced sites, it's advisable that you try out a home page first.

Remember, though, that once you've published your page, it's there for the whole world to see! That means you're going to want to do some thinking before setting out on the creation of your own page. Here are some general guidelines to help you out:

- Only share those things about yourself that you feel safe sharing. If something is very personal and private, the Web is *not* a good place for it.

- Potential employers may find your site, so be sure that anything you put up about yourself is acceptable to share with them.

- Using the Web as an expression of personal beliefs and opinions is an exercise in freedom of speech. However, be careful that you do not slander or libel anyone (this protects *you*) or say anything that you are not willing to say in person.

- Be sure that any graphics, multimedia, or written content that you put on a Web site belong to you or are in the public domain. Otherwise, without express permission of the original author to use it, you may be violating copyright laws.

- Avoid putting personal addresses and phone numbers on the Web. This can put you and your family in danger.

Expressing yourself can be fun, but along with it comes responsibility. The Web can certainly be about freedom for many people, but with all freedom there comes the important need to think before you act.

 TIP A good way to learn more about home pages is to visit a wide variety of those done by other people. See what you like, what you dislike, and find guidance and inspiration from those sites that have succeeded in doing something along the lines of what you'd like to do.

In this chapter, we're going to work on a site called "Hallie's Horse Crazy." The fictitious young woman, Hallie, wants a home page that looks good and helps provide information about herself as well as her favorite thing in the world: horses!

Planning the Site

It's always important to plan out your site. You've got to think about audience, site intent, and site goals. From this information you can get ideas about what kind of a design you want to create.

Audience and Intent

Audience is always important—even in the construction of a personal page! This is something people often overlook, and it's a dangerous thing to miss. Why have a page if you don't want to share it with others? So you have to think carefully about who those others are going to be.

In Hallie's case, the audience will typically be made up of young women who share her interests. Other groups she'll need to prepare for include:

- Family and friends
- Horse lovers of all ages
- Individuals within her age group

Hallie's site is intended to share information about herself, her horses, her horse-related art and photo collection, and a great selection of horse-related links, as well as to provide a method for folks to get feedback to her regarding her site.

Short- and Long-Term Goals

Initially, Hallie wants a small site with a variety of information, but down the road she hopes to expand the links and have us possibly even add a forum for horse lovers to discuss their horses, display photos, and share favorite Web sites.

Knowing what we do about Hallie's audience, intent, and goals, we sketch out the actual structure of her Web site. This will be our guide as we set up the structure of her Web site:

SPLASH PAGE

Me   Hallie's bio and some photos

My Horses   Stories and pictures about Hallie's horses

Horse Pics   Photos and drawings of horses

Horse Links   Favorite links to horse sites on the Web

Awards   Hallie's awards and Hallie's horse's awards

Guestbook   A place where people can say hello

Preparing for Production

Based on the audience and topic of your site, you want to create a look and feel that work as well as make great graphics that download quickly but look good, too.

Creating a Look and Feel

One of the first things to look at is color. For Hallie's site, we want to convey a sense of warmth, friendliness, and earth. So we created a palette of color to express these things:

Color Name	RGB Value	Hex Value	Expression
Deep gold	102 51 0	CC6633	Warmth
Dark brown	204 102 51	663300	Horses, earth
Light gold	255 204 102	FFCC66	A youthful, happy, upbeat color

We also included black for text and white for any accents.

Next, we worked with the typefaces that are used in the company logo to determine a nice method of displaying the information. We wanted something fun and decided to mimic this approach in the way we laid out the Web page's type:

Type Family	Typeface	Expression/Use
Decorative	Whimsy ICG Heavy	Fun, playful look for headers
Decorative	Trackpad Letraset	Light, handwritten-style font for navigation and smaller headers
Sans serif	Arial	Easy to read for body text

We then examined the way to approach graphic accents. We decided that header text would have a drop shadow to add some depth to the pages. We created a similar drop shadow for the photos as well, adding interest to the page. The final decision was that navigation buttons would be graphic-based, flat text.

Preparing for Technology

We want to keep technology limited on this page, because typically a personal page is the first Web site a person does. The idea is to have fun, but keep it simple as you learn the Web-site-design ropes.

In order to technologically challenge ourselves a little bit, as well as provide an opportunity for Hallie's visitors to send in feedback, we chose to use FrontPage's Guestbook. This means we'll need to make sure the Internet service provider we are using will support the guestbook with the appropriate FrontPage extensions. To find this out for your site, you'll need to give the ISP you're working with a call or drop an e-mail and ask.

Production

With the planning of the site complete, we entered the hard-work phase. This means laying out the pages in our image editor, generating the site graphics, and using FrontPage to design the individual pages. We'll also be using FrontPage to help us manage our tasks as we work through the process and to set up the guestbook.

Laying Out the Pages

Photoshop is our primary choice for page layout, but of course you may use the image editor of your choice. We do recommend you use an image editor with layering capabilities (see Chapter 18, *Working with Professional Graphics Programs*).

To lay out the splash page:

1. In your image editor, select File ➤ New. The New dialog box appears.

2. Create an image that is 595 pixels wide by 295 pixels high.

3. Click OK. You now have your work area set to the first layer.

4. Add your background color to this layer. We selected Deep Gold (see the color chart earlier in this chapter).

5. Create a new layer by selecting Layer ➤ New ➤ Layer. On this layer, we added the page name:

6. Add the buttons one by one. They should be done on individual layers so that you can easily move, change, remove, or add to them in the future.

7. Once you've added all the elements you want for this page, save the file by selecting File ➢ Save As. The Save As dialog box appears. Name the file and save it in the native layer format of your imaging program.

Figure 29.1 shows the completed splash page design.

Next, create the layout for an internal page by following these steps:

1. In your image editor, select File ➢ New. The New dialog box appears.

2. Create an image that is 595 pixels wide by 600 pixels high (longer if the page content needs to be more than two screens in height).

3. Click OK.

4. You now have your work area set to the first layer. To this layer, add your background color.

5. Create a new layer by selecting Layer ➤ New ➤ Layer. On this layer, create the header:

6. Layer by layer, add the graphic components of the page, including design elements such as sub-headers, navigation, and photos:

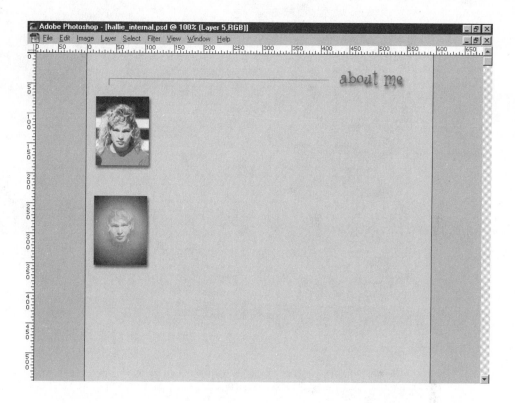

7. Once you've added all the elements you want for this page, save the file by selecting File ➢ Save As. The Save As dialog box appears. Name the file and save it in the native layer format of your imaging program.

Figure 29.2 shows a completed inner page design.

You'll repeat this process for each and every page you've designed for the site.

FIGURE 29.2

*The completed internal
page design*

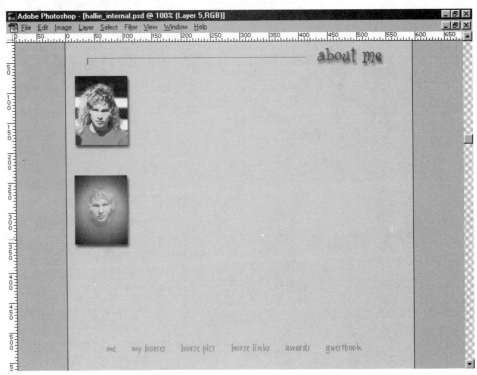

To generate the actual graphics for your site, move back to your imaging program and follow these steps:

1. Open up the layered file in your imaging program.

2. Highlight the layer that has the image you want to process.

3. Using the marquee or selection tool (it will vary depending upon your program), draw a selection around the part of the image you want to keep, making sure you're on the correct layer.

4. Copy and paste the section into a new file.

5. Optimize the file as a GIF or JPEG, depending upon the graphic.

6. Name the graphic and save it directly to the images folder within your Front-Page web.

Repeat the process for all of the buttons, headers, backgrounds, and spot art that you'll require.

NOTE For detailed help optimizing and working with graphics, see Chapter 9, *Designing Graphics for the Web*, and Chapter 18, *Working with Professional Graphics Programs*.

Working with FrontPage

At this point, we turn to the wisdom of FrontPage to help us set up directories, tasks, and begin the actual design of our Web pages. Begin by setting up your directories:

1. Select File ➤ New ➤ Web. The New dialog box appears.

2. Highlight One Page Web and click OK. FrontPage creates the necessary Front-Page directory and images directory, and opens up a blank, untitled page within the root directory so you can begin working.

Since Hallie's is a small, manageable site, we use the root directory for all of the HTML pages and the images directory for all graphics.

To set up individual files in your root directory:

1. In Folders view, right-click anywhere in the interface. A menu appears.

2. Select New Page.

3. A new page appears in the root directory. Name this page **default.htm**.

4. Repeat this process until you have created all the pages planned for the site, using the chart prepared in the planning phase as a guide. You can always add or delete pages as necessary.

To add the guestbook:

1. Select File ➤ New ➤ Page. The New dialog box appears.

2. Highlight Guestbook and click OK. FrontPage will add the guestbook and its companion files.

3. Save the file to the web. You'll customize it in just a bit.

Tasks are one of FrontPage's most helpful tools to guide you through building your Web site. To set up tasks using Folders view:

1. In Folders view, highlight the file you want to associate with a task.

2. Right-click and choose Add Task from the menu.

3. The New Task dialog box appears. Fill in the task name, priority, and a description.

4. Click OK.

PART

VI

Step-by-Step
FrontPage Sites

TIP Whether associating a task with a page or without it, be sure to include as many tasks as you'll need to complete the production and post-production processes. For more information on tasks, see Chapter 7, *Managing Tasks*.

You can also set up tasks that are not associated with a page. To set up tasks using the Tasks view:

1. Select Tasks view, and click anywhere in the FrontPage interface. A menu appears.

2. Select New Task. The New Task dialog opens.

3. Fill in the task name, the task priority, and a description.

Creating the Splash Page

Now it's time to design the pages! Start with the splash (or home) page, as this will set the tone for the rest of the site.

1. In Folders view, highlight the default.htm file that you created earlier.

2. Right-click and select Open from the menu. The default page will open in Page view.

3. Set the background color and links. To do this, right-click the empty page and select Page Properties from the menu that appears.

4. The Page Properties dialog appears. In the Colors section, find Background and click the arrow to activate the drop-down menu.

5. Choose More Colors. The More Colors dialog box appears.

6. In the Value text box, type in the hexadecimal color you want for the background. Refer to the list you made in pre-production when you developed the look and feel of the Web site. In our example, we chose the Medium Gold, hex value CC6633, for the background.

7. Click OK. You'll be returned to the More Colors dialog box. From here, continue adding colors for each of the available selections: Text, Hyperlink, Visited Hyperlink, and Active Hyperlink. When you're finished, click OK in the Page Properties dialog box.

Your page will now appear in Page view, with the color and link information added to the page.

Now you're ready to add the first graphic. To do this:

1. Place the cursor where you'd like to insert the graphic.

2. From the FrontPage menu, select Insert ➢ Picture ➢ From File.

3. The Picture dialog box appears. Select the image you'd like to place on the page by highlighting it.

4. Click OK.

FrontPage will insert the file into your page. You can now place the image where you like by dragging it to the location where you want it to reside.

 NOTE If you've set up a task list for this first page, you'll want to mark the task completed.

You can check the results of your work by saving the pages and selecting File Preview In Browser. In Figure 29.3, you'll see the results of our page design within the browser window.

FIGURE 29.3

The completed splash page design

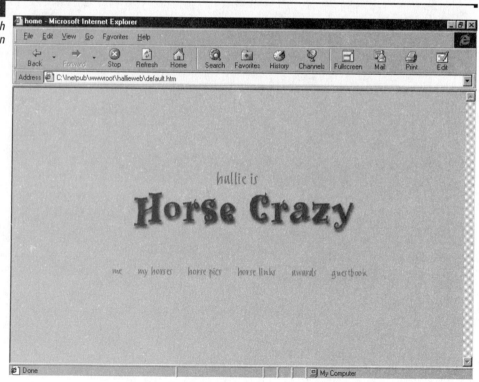

PART

VI

NOTE Any time you're using consistent navigation from page to page, you have the option of using FrontPage's shared borders. For more information on this topic, see Chapter 15, *Special Effects*.

Designing an Internal Page

Typically, tables are needed to lay out most pages. Hallie's internal pages are no exception.

In Figure 29.4, you can see the page layout we did using our image editor. We set up some guides to show how we'd like to map out our table grid. Based on this information, we can turn to FrontPage and begin creating the actual table.

FIGURE 29.4

Planning the table

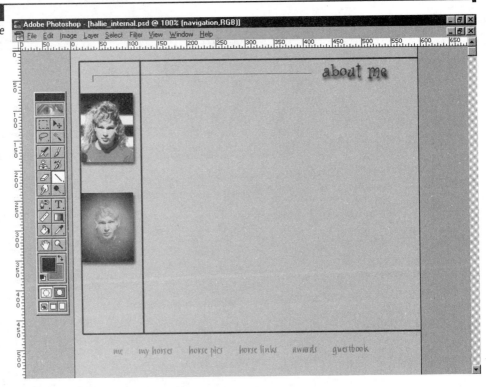

When planning a table, begin with vertical columns, only adding rows where necessary. Be sure to revisit Chapter 11, *Using Tables for Advanced Layout*, for more information.

With your table in mind, follow these steps to lay out the page:

1. With the page open in Page view, select Insert ➤ Table. The Insert Table dialog box appears:

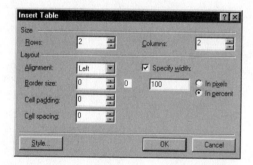

2. Enter the number of rows in the Rows text box (we entered 1).

3. Enter the number of columns (we entered 2) in the Columns text box.

4. In the Layout section, choose an alignment for your table. Typically, left alignment will be used.

5. Set the Border, Cell Padding, and Cell Spacing to 0.

6. Check Specify Width.

7. Add a numeric value for fixed-width tables and a percentage for dynamic. In an example such as this one, we want to fix the width so that all the content including images and graphics is neatly managed. We entered a total width of 595 pixels.

8. Click OK. The table appears on your page.

9. Add images and text using the techniques you learned in related chapters of this book to refine the page's look. Be sure to adjust table and table cell properties where necessary (see Chapter 11).

10. When you're finished adding images and text, save the page. Continue adding pages in this fashion until you've completed the full content of your site.

PART

VI

Step-by-Step
FrontPage Sites

You can preview your new page(s) externally, or internally using the Preview tab to see the way the page(s) will appear (see Figure 29.5).

FIGURE 29.5

The completed page in Preview mode

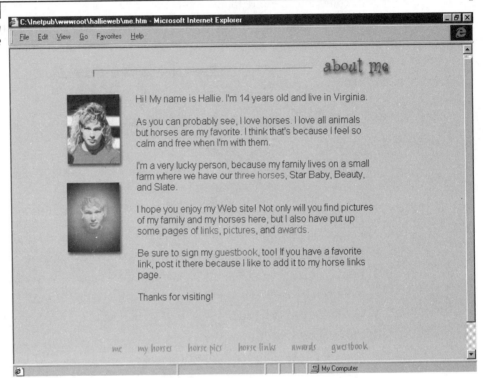

NOTE When working with navigation, be sure to remember that you can use shared borders on appropriate pages if you will be using a server supporting FrontPage extensions. Check Chapter 15 for details, and be sure to ask your ISP if you have access to FrontPage.

Customizing the Guestbook

Since we want the guestbook to match our design rather than the prefabricated look that FrontPage uses, we'll want to customize the form using our own colors and graphics. Here's how!

1. In Folders View, double-click guestbook.htm. The file opens in Page view.

2. Add the background and link colors to the page by following the directions we discussed in the "Creating the Splash Page" section.

3. Delete the comment and the horizontal rule from the top of the page.

4. Add your graphic header by selecting Insert ≻ Picture ≻ From File and choosing the appropriate header image for your page.

5. Customize the comments within the form field. Simply click within the field where you'd like to change the text and type in the new text.

6. If you'd like to change the text on the form buttons, simply right-click the button. From the menu that appears, choose Form Field Properties. The Push Button Properties dialog box appears.

7. In the Value/label text box, type in the word or words you'd like to have appear on the button.

8. Click OK, and repeat the process for the Reset button if you'd like to change that, too.

9. Customize any remaining text on the page, and be sure that the page is included in the shared borders if you are taking that approach to navigation.

10. Save your file to the web.

Your results should be similar to those in Figure 29.6.

 NOTE Have you marked off your tasks? If not, and you are confident the work for a given task is finished, go into Tasks view and mark the task as complete.

PART

VI

Step-by-Step
FrontPage Sites

FIGURE 29.6

Hallie's Guestbook

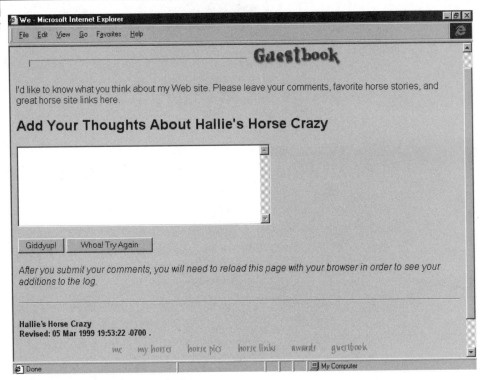

Preparing Your Site for Publication

Once you've got all your pages designed, you're almost ready to upload them to the server so they can be live on the Internet. But there are a few things you should to do before showing your creation to the world!

First, you'll want to spell check all of the pages. To do this:

1. From the Views toolbar, select Folders view.

2. From the folder list, highlight the root directory of the web.

3. From the main FrontPage menu, select Tools ➤ Spelling. The Spelling dialog box appears.

4. Choose the Entire Web button. You can also check the Add A Task For Each Page With Misspellings option, if you'd like.

5. Click Start.

FrontPage will now spell check all of the pages and report back any misspellings. At this point, be sure to go back and change any misspelled words. Once you've made your corrections, repeat the process until you receive a No Spelling Errors Were Found message at the bottom of the Spelling dialog box.

Now, check all of the links on your site. To do so, follow these steps:

1. With the web open, open the Reports toolbar by selecting View ➤ Toolbars ➤ Reports.

2. Click the Verify Hyperlinks button. The Verify Hyperlinks dialog box appears.

3. Select Verify All Hyperlinks to verify all the links in the current FrontPage web.

4. Click the Start button. The dialog box will close and the window will return to the FrontPage Reports view.

One by one, the status of all the links will be updated in the Broken Hyperlinks Report view. Each link's status will be described with a particular indicator. (See Chapter 24, *Site Maintenance and Promotion*, for a full list of these indicators.)

If one of the links on your web is no longer valid, or *broken*, you'll need to replace it with an updated one. To change your broken link:

1. In the Broken Hyperlinks Report view, double-click the link you want to change. The Edit Hyperlink dialog box appears.

2. In the Replace Hyperlink With text box, type in a new, good link to replace the old one. For example, if the old link is `http://www.products.cm` and the new, good link is `http://www.products.com`, type **`http://www.products.com`**:

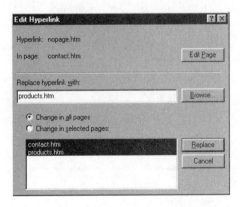

3. You can elect to change all of the occurrences of the URL or just selected occurrences. To change all of the occurrences, select the Change In All Pages button. To change the URL only in selected pages, highlight the pages in the list of pages and select the Change In Selected Pages button.

4. Click the Replace button. The repaired link appears in the list in place of the old one.

Continue to repair links as necessary. When you're finished, run through the process again to ensure no broken links remain.

The next step in the process is to add META-tag descriptions and keywords to the pages. To do this:

1. Open the page in Page view. From the FrontPage menu bar, select File ➤ Properties. The Page Properties dialog box appears.

2. In the dialog box's Title text box, type the "title" words you targeted. Note that the title must be understandable as well as include these words. In our example, we used "Hallie's Horse Crazy."

3. Click the Custom tab. The contents of the dialog box change to reflect your choice.

4. In the lower part of the dialog box, locate the User Variable area. This area displays a list of all the META tags in the current page. To add a new META tag to the page, which is what you want to do, click the Add button. The User Meta Variable dialog box appears.

5. In the Name field, you need to identify the type of META tag you want to add. For example, type **keywords** now, so you can specify some keywords.

6. In the User Meta Variable dialog box's Value text box, type the keywords you think best for your site. For Hallie's site, try keywords and keyword combinations such as horse, horses, horse pictures, horse links, horse photos, hallie, hallie's horses, and so forth.

7. Click the OK button; the dialog box closes. The Page Properties dialog box reappears with the information you specified for your keywords META tag now visible.

8. Now repeat steps 5 through 7, this time typing **description** (instead of **keywords)** and adding the description you think best. In our example, this would be: "Hallie's Horse Crazy is for all people who love horses. Links, guestbook, great horse pics!"

9. Click OK. Your site is now properly META tagged.

 NOTE Be sure to test the site using different browsers, platforms, and screen resolutions to ensure that you've done a good job at making the site cross-browser compatible (see Chapter 16, *Cross-Browser Design*).

Now that all the planning and fancy footwork is done, you're ready to publish your site to the Web!

Publication

The first thing you need to do to get your site live on the Web is make sure your computer is connected to the Internet and that you know the full URL for the machine to which you'll be publishing your web—the target server.

Once you have that info, follow these steps:

1. With the web you want to publish open in FrontPage, from the menu bar, select File ➤ Publish Web. The Publish dialog box appears.

2. If you have not previously published a web, the Publish FrontPage Web dialog box appears. In the dialog box's text field, type the name of the server and the location to which you want to upload the web.

3. Click OK, and FrontPage uploads the web to the Web!

Once your site is published, all of the hard work you've done preparing for it will have paid off. You've tested the site locally for spelling, grammar, link integrity, and cross-browser concerns. Further, your site is well organized with clear intent, appropriate content for your audience, and an attractive design scheme.

Post-Production

Now that the site resides on your server, live for the Internet audience, it's important not to forget that the site still requires your attention. Here are some issues you should address after your site has been produced and published:

Check content live.   Be sure all your graphics, links, and technology are working properly on the server.

Follow maintenance and promotion guidelines.   In order to boost your potential success, you'll want to efficiently maintain and promote your site (see Chapter 24).

Prepare for the future.   Using your long-term goals as a guide, decide when it will be necessary and appropriate to add content to your site, expand the site, and even re-design the site to keep it contemporary and interesting.

PART

VI

Step-by-Step
FrontPage Sites

Up Next

In this chapter, you became familiar with what it takes to make a personal Web page. The process is meant to be fun, and we hope you had fun doing it! Yes, there's work involved—planning, production, publication, and post-production techniques cannot be avoided if you want a strong site. However, the results are certainly worth it.

In Chapter 30, *Designing a Small Business Web Site*, we look at a site geared toward aiding a small business extend its sales and branding opportunities.

CHAPTER **30**

Designing a Small Business Web Site

Commerce on the Web is quite a deal. Major players such as MCI*Worldcom* and IBM are spending a great deal of money developing electronic commerce for high-end Web selling.

But what about the talented American Indian artisan who lives in a rural community in the Southwestern United States? There's an enormous market for Southwestern art, pottery, and jewelry—a global demand, in fact. This artisan can conceivably use the Web to reach that audience, and in turn tap into a great way to improve the economy within the immediate area of his or her geographic location.

There's also the consultant who wants to take his or her talents to a larger audience. By using a promotional Web site, this consultant can make a resume and specialty list available, include a photo, client feedback, and contact information, reaching a much greater client base than before.

Then, there's the small goods manufacturer who has a successful small company with numerous employees, but is looking at ways to expand its client base by placing a catalog online.

In our example, we're going to create an imaginary manufacturer, Zapaton, that specializes in a small, elegant selection of women's shoes and handbags made of the finest Spanish and Italian leather and natural fibers. Zapaton is looking to reach beyond its mom-and-pop style shop and into the international arena.

Understanding Site Intent and Demographic

In Chapter 29, *Creating a Personal Web Page*, we demonstrated how site intent and audience is important to the way a site is developed. This is especially true for the small business site. Whether the idea is to promote a person, service, or commodity—knowing your goals and audience is very important.

At first glance, we see that an example such as Zapaton should appeal to an audience of older, well-heeled women, who are interested in the quality and style of their shoes and handbags, and who have the finances to cover the cost. That's the natural audience, and it's an important one.

But Zapaton is also looking to position itself in several other areas, including:

- Making the competition aware of its existence
- Impressing potential corporate buyers and representatives in specialty boutiques world-over
- Expanding its client base to include younger women

Where does this information come from? Most businesses work from a detailed business plan. It is this plan that will guide and inspire the way you work day-to-day, as well as on the Web.

MASTERING THE OPPORTUNITIES

Think about Competitors!

One way to assist with market positioning is to check out what competitors are doing online. Visit Web sites of known competitors and do a more general search via your favorite search engine. Go to Web sites related to what you're doing, too. For example, if you sell women's shoes, see how companies specializing in men's footwear present their information. Take notes on the look and feel of sites, notice what is memorable and why, and think about how your site can make its own niche within the online marketplace.

Working the Business Plan

Why are you in business? What are your goals for quality, service, and financial growth?

This information should be readily available in your business plan. If you are in the early phases of thinking about your business, we heartily advise you not to jump in haphazardly as planning is the name of the game when it comes to a Web site. The same is true of any venture.

If you do not have a business plan, consider writing one. There are many helpful books in the business section of your favorite local and online bookstores. Check your favorite software source for helpful applications that can guide you through the task of creating such a plan.

If you already have a business plan, it's time to turn toward it for guidance and inspiration for what you are about to do on the Web. The business plan should tell you plenty about your product, your market, and the pathways to your audiences. You'll want to evaluate these issues in light of what the global perspective of a Web site can do for you. In a best-case scenario, you already have a Web marketing plan as part of your business plan; but, if you do not, you can easily add it as you go.

Use the following template to help guide you in making good Web site development decisions:

Describe the current product.   Your business plan should have a detailed description of your product.

Zapaton shoes and handbags are handcrafted with attention to detail. Zapaton uses only the finest leather from Spain and Italy, and all-natural fibers for its more casual line.

Are there plans to expand the product line?　Look to your business plan for guidance here. Sometimes expansion is part of the product line, and sometimes adherence to standards is the name of the game.

In Zapaton's case, the concern is not to expand, but rather to keep current with fashion trends. Each season, a new line is introduced.

How are products currently sold?　What avenues are you using for sales?

Zapaton sells direct to the customer from one location. A small distribution deal allows Zapaton to sell its products in three boutiques located in New York, Los Angeles, and Scottsdale, Arizona.

Describe your current competition.　A business plan will have exhaustively examined product and service competitors. One of the purposes of a business plan is to help position your products and services in a competitive environment, carving a niche market from a specific audience to enable yoursurvival and ultimate success.

Competitors for quality shoes and handbags are numerous and include almost all major fashion designers.

How will your product be different from the competition's?　Knowing the differences in your quality of product and service will help you find your distinct personality in the marketplace.

Zapaton spares no expense in terms of quality materials. Each shoe is hand-made, and each season sees an entirely new selection based on both style and comfort.

What is the current image of the business, and how can a Web site expand that image?　This is an important question that can be answered by looking at what your current business plan calls for, as well as what your hopes are to expand via a Web site.

Zapaton has a consistent but small clientele and distribution range. Within this environment, the image of the business is excellent, well branded, and respected. However, the need is to expand the type of clientele and the range of distribution.

It is upon this template, and upon your business plan, that you'll want to base your short- and long-term Web site goals. Also, be aware that your Web site plan should be incorporated into your primary business plan now, if it wasn't before.

Short- and Long-Term Goals

Time and money are key here. You'll save more of both if you set your goals realistically, and you'll spend more of each if you don't. You want a clear idea of what you need immediately, what you want in the next few months, and what you expect to have down the road. These goals should always work in tandem with your business goals in general, too, so keep that business plan and your site-planning templates handy.

Short-Term Goals for Zapaton

Some of us make to-do lists on a daily basis. But list writing is often a short-term goal. Short-term goals are those you want realized within a one- to six-month plan.

NOTE Immediate needs should be examined and met, certainly. But without looking at them in the context of short- and long-term goals, the results could be disastrous! For example, if an immediate need is to have a Web site up and running ASAP, and you spend a lot of money to develop a Web site in a week's time, it's highly likely that it will not be structured to meet your short- and long-term needs. This means scrapping what you paid for and starting over again! Remember that you can work in segments, deploying one aspect of a Web site for immediate needs, and later adding other areas that are important. This should not be done without incorporating *all* of your goals.

Using Zapaton as our guide, let's envision some short-term goals from what we know about the company:

- Create a good-looking site that appeals to potential partners and buyers.
- Ensure that buyers and partners know how to get in touch with you.
- Make your current line available online in terms of both description and visual expression through photos and graphics.

MASTERING THE OPPORTUNITIES

Do You *Really* Need a Web Site?

Some companies think they need a Web site just because everyone has one, too! That's not always a wise move—if you put up a Web site quickly, without thinking through your goals and needs, you could do yourself and your company a great disservice. Think carefully about logical reasons to have a Web site, and *be prepared* to have it updated and kept fresh in order for it to be of use to site visitors.

Mapping Long-Term Goals

Long-term goals should relate to the strategy your business plan sets to help grow your business. If you foresee an expansion in your products or services, or a shift from the storefront to a Web-based model, then address these issues immediately so your Web project can successfully manage the growth.

Zapaton eventually sees that the Web will be not only a primary point of sales to individual customers, but a showroom to demonstrate current products to larger buyers and distributors. Eventually a network of those distributors will discuss business strategies regarding Zapaton's positioning, and as the company grows, more information as to its activities—need for new employees, corporate success stories, and charitable activities—will help add to its favorable prestige.

Certainly your site will change over time, too. You will add technology, refresh the design, and expand the content. But the essential truth remains: If you create a model that is flexible and prepared for expansion, you'll have fewer limitations on expansion.

When building the site, not only will you want to look at areas of current need, but imagine ways of creating navigation to which you can easily add new areas. If you make an image map rather than buttons, you lock yourself into having to redesign an entire map every time you add or remove an area. However, if you use individual buttons, you simply add or remove a button. Furthermore, sensible categories enable you to grow a site logically (see Figure 30.1).

FIGURE 30.1

Using buttons rather than an image map

Your brand should be strong and consistent with print and other campaigns from the start (see "Branding a Product" later in this chapter). Don't try out a "new" look on the Web just yet—if you have plans to update your brand, do it in a different test market. In order to be effective, a Web site must carry your concept to the online audience seamlessly.

What about Domain Names?

Should your site have a domain name? Effective branding means having a domain name that is an extension of your product name or mark. If you're in the business of promoting a person, product, or service, a domain name helps to reinforce your brand.

You can get a domain name in a number of ways. First, you need to see if it's available, and you can do this yourself by visiting Network Solutions (`www.network-solutions.com`) and using the search features offered. Type in the desired name of the business with an appropriate suffix, such as:

- `.com`: relating to a commercial business
- `.org`: usually a non-profit or religious organization
- `.net`: a network of related content

NOTE There are other suffixes, such as `.edu` for education, `.mil` for military, and `.gov` for government organizations. For these suffixes, you will need to follow the guidelines of your organization for procuring the appropriate domain. Also, there are new proposed suffixes to be added to the mix at some point, since there are so many domains in use today.

So, the developer for Zapaton will visit Network Solutions, and, using the search system available, type in **zapaton.com**. The results are as follows:

`No match for "ZAPATON.COM".`

This indicates the domain name is probably available.

NOTE If the domain is not available, the results of the search will be a page including the registrant's name and contact information. You always have the right to query the owner about the use of the name, and a fair agreement may be worked out for the purchase of that name. However, no means no, so don't harass someone. If they got there first, you may be out of luck. If you own a trademark on the name, you might want to consult an attorney who has Web-related experience.

You can fashion a domain name with up to twenty-six characters (letters, numbers, and dashes—no spaces or extraneous characters are allowed). The name will then be followed by a dot (.) and the appropriate suffix. Depending on your ISP, you may or may not have a www in front of the name; you may have another word, such as the name of the server: `molly.annex.com`.

Branding a Product

If you hear the name Coca-Cola, no doubt an image comes to mind. A product's success often comes from its ability to remain at the forefront of an audience's mind. This image is not happenstance—it is the result of calculated marketing on the part of the company and its advertising partners.

To brand a product, a company should have:

- A unique company name
- An appropriate and memorable slogan
- A logo that is simple but strong

Other methods of enabling a company to create a lasting and important image include:

- Positioning the company with some positive feature related to service or product, such as quality, price, or reliability.
- Company involvement in community success: Does the company participate in outreach programs, provide training and education for employees, or give money and time to charitable or humanitarian causes? These types of activities reflect a favorable light upon a company.

Many readers might have heard the term *presence* applied to a Web site. In a sense, it is the benefit of presence—the establishment and extension of a company's brand—that is the most beneficial aspect of a Web site.

Think of a billboard. No doubt you've seen effective billboard campaigns. Do they make you go directly out and buy a specific product? Not necessarily. What they do is embed a sense of that company or product's existence into your mind by reminding you what their image is and what they can offer you. Ultimately, this affects sales, but it doesn't usually do it in an immediate and obvious way.

The same is usually true for Web sites. Only a handful of site types have seen overwhelming success in direct online sales. These include sites that offer adult content, sites that sell books and CDs, and sites that provide travel-related services. And, even if your product or service fits into one of these categories, you'll still want to be aware that *branding* and *presence* are the best benefit your site can help you gain.

MASTERING THE OPPORTUNITIES

Branding in Action

A company that has had enormous success in branding client products is Landor Associates, www.landor.com. Landor provides a detailed look at its branding strategies, www.landor.com/strategy/index.htm.

Developing the Look and Feel

In Chapter 29, we walked through the creation of a look and feel for a personal Web site. We're going to do that here, too. It's important to develop the look and feel of your site using your business plan, and in the case of a company with a pre-existing brand, the logo (see Figure 30.2) and other branding methods already in use.

FIGURE 30.2

The Zapaton logo

Let's examine the intent and audience of Zapaton in the context of design:

Assessing current demographic as wealthy women, aged 45 or older   The desire is to keep hold of this demographic. An elegant but somewhat sedate look is in order.

Making competition aware of their existence   The competition should see the site as a well-designed, well-positioned site with a brand consistent with known factors exist about the company.

Impressing potential corporate buyers and representatives in specialty boutiques world-over   This will be done using a sophisticated design, as well as ensuring that the products are attractively displayed and well described.

Expanding client base to include younger women   Adding fashionable accessories and creating designs that appeal to younger women will help expand the product to this market.

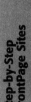

PART

VI

Step-by-Step FrontPage Sites

One of the first things to look at is color. We want to convey a sense of elegance and sophistication, and we want to draw from any existing colors and design that a company might have in current advertising media. So we created a palette of color to express that elegance. We chose to use what is known as a *monochromatic* scheme (a theme based on one basic color—in this case, olive green), because that helps convey consistency as well as a sense of calm.

Color Name	RGB Value	Hex Value	Expression
Light olive green	204 204 153	CCCC99	Light, youth, refreshment
Medium olive green	153 153 102	999966	Elegance, refinement
Deep olive green	102 102 0	666600	Consistency, depth

We also included black for text and white for any accents. Black is typically an elegant color, and white is known for clean and crisp results.

Next we worked with the typefaces that are used in the company logo to determine a nice method of displaying the information. The logo is done in Fritz Quadrata, and the sub-header of the logo uses Helvetica. We decided to mimic this approach in the way we laid out the Web page's type:

Type Family	Typeface	Expression/Use
Serif	Fritz Quadrata	Elegant, beautiful
Sans serif	Helvetica	Strong, easy to read

We then examined the way to approach graphic accents. We decided graphic text should be flat, so as not to compete with the product images. We created a crumpled-paper look for the product photos, which add some texture and intrigue to the design. Buttons are graphic-based text with a subtle JavaScript mouseover.

Preparing for Technology

While we've decided to keep technology somewhat limited on the Zapaton site, these are three areas of concern:

JavaScript mouseovers   While you could do mouseovers with a Java applet, we prefer to use JavaScript for this effect. The reason is that JavaScript is very fast, easy to use, and demands little resources from your server, or your visitor's hardware and software. While this means having to go in and add script, there are good copy-and-paste scripts available to make this process easy.

Feedback form   We definitely want a way for our prospective buyers and partners to get in touch. So we're going to ensure that a Feedback Form is made available, using FrontPage's Feedback Form template.

Ordering methods   This is an area that's less clear than the others. For larger product lines, a shopping cart would be put in place; however, this is a small product line. Instead of a shopping cart, we decided to rely on a secure commerce server to allow direct ordering of individual products off a single page. This keeps costs lower at the outset, and since there is *no expected expansion* of the number of products, but rather the product type, we felt it would be the best route. However, for those of you interested in shopping cart technologies, we've provided a helpful sidebar so you can investigate what's available to best suit your needs.

MASTERING THE OPPORTUNITIES

Shopping Cart Technologies

There are several helpful resources that will aid you in making good decisions regarding your shopping cart needs. Some are free, others inexpensive, and others can be very expensive. Be sure to research your needs well before jumping into a purchase.

For CGI scripts, see www.cgi-resources.com/.

Often, your ISP will be working with specialty backend programs such as Cold Fusion, which have built in functions allowing for commercial transactions. It's possible they have or can write a custom script for your purposes. Checking with your ISP first is always a good place to start!

Understanding Secure Transactions

Secure transactions are those communications that take place in an environment using special Internet technologies called *protocols* or *encryption systems*. The concept is an important one for a number of reasons. First, it creates a way to protect site visitors when they enter personal information such as home address, telephone number, and credit card numbers with a very high level of security. Second, the *sense* of security that is conveyed is incredibly important, too. All too many users are afraid of hackers and fraud, and while there is always the possibility that an unfortunate incident can occur, the reality of it occurring is truly very rare.

Secure systems use methods including:

SSL   Secure Sockets Layer was created by Netscape to manage secure transactions.

STT   This is Microsoft's Secure Transaction Technology.

PART

VI

Step-by-Step
FrontPage Sites

SET   This is Secure Electronic Transaction. SET uses digital certificates to "sign" secure data.

RSA   RSA is an encryption system typically used by SSL, STT, and SET to encode and authenticate digital data.

NOTE   One of the biggest issues in security isn't the fact that sites are insecure—but that people *perceive* them as being insecure. A note about your site's privacy can help site visitors feel more comfortable when making purchases online.

Laying Out the Pages

Once again, we turn to Photoshop as our primary choice for page layout. However, you may use the image editor of your choice. We do recommend you use an image editor with layering capabilities (see Chapter 18, *Working with Professional Graphics Programs*).

To start, you want to lay out the splash page. To do so:

1. In your image editor, select File ➤ New. The New dialog box appears.

2. Create an image size that is 595 pixels wide by 295 pixels high.

3. Click OK.

4. You now have your work area set to the first layer. To this layer, add your background color. We selected Medium Olive Green (see the color chart earlier in this chapter).

5. Now create a new layer by selecting Layer ➤ New ➤ Layer. On this layer, create or add the company logo (see Figure 30.3).

FIGURE 30.3

Adding the main logo

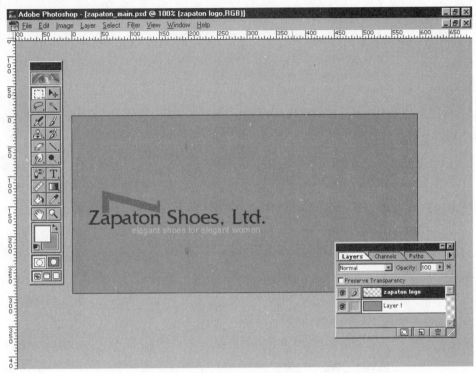

FIGURE 30.3

Adding the main logo

6. Once you've added all the elements you want for this page, save the file by selecting File ➢ Save As. The Save As dialog box appears.

7. Name the file and save it in the native layer format of your imaging program.

Now create the layout for an internal page by following these steps:

1. In your image editor, select File ➢ New. The New dialog box appears.

2. Create an image size that is 595 pixels wide by 600 pixels high (or higher if the page content needs to be more than two screens in height).

3. Click OK.

4. You now have your work area set to the first layer. To this layer, add your background color.

5. Now create a new layer by selecting Layer ➣ New ➣ Layer. On this layer, create the header:

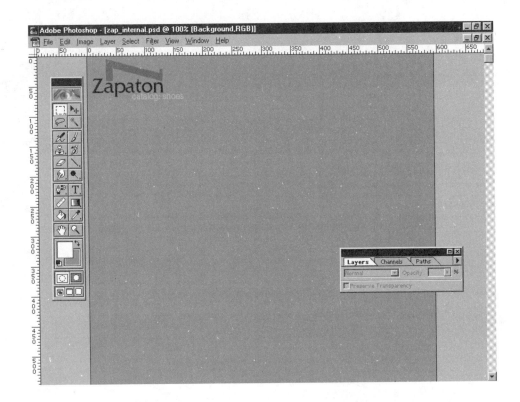

6. Layer by layer, add the graphic components of the page such as sub-headers, navigation, and photos:

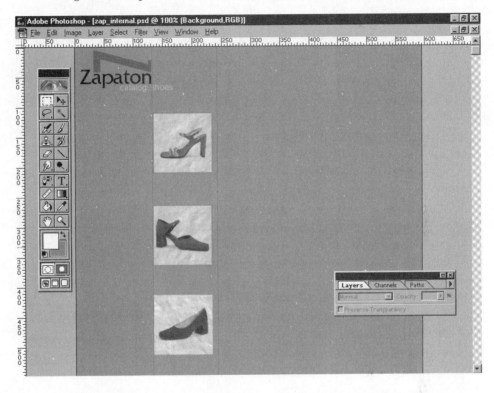

7. Once you've added all the elements you want for this page, save the file by selecting File ➤ Save As. The Save As dialog box appears.

8. Name the file and save it in the native layer format of your imaging program.

Figure 30.4 shows a completed inner page design. You'll now repeat this process for each and every page you've designed for the site.

FIGURE 30.4

The completed internal page design

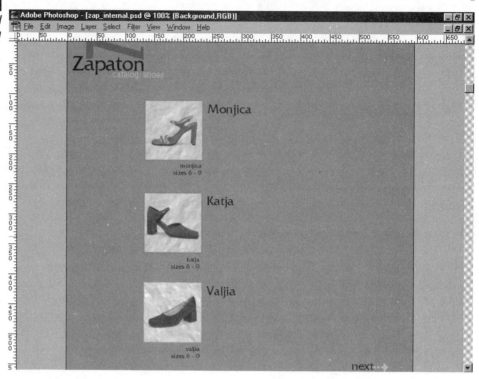

To generate the actual graphics, move back to your imaging program to produce the site graphics, and then follow these steps:

1. Open the layered file in your imaging program.

2. Highlight the layer that has the image you want to process.

3. Use the marquee or selection tool (it varies depending on your program) to draw a selection around the part of the image you want to keep, making sure you're on the correct layer.

4. Copy and paste the section into a new file.

5. Optimize the file as a GIF or JPEG, depending on the graphic.

6. Name the graphic and save it directly to the images folder within your Front-Page web.

Repeat the process for all buttons, headers, backgrounds, and spot art that you'll require.

NOTE For detailed help optimizing and working with graphics, see Chapter 9, *Designing Graphics for the Web,* and Chapter 18, *Working with Professional Graphics Programs.*

Working with FrontPage

Now that you've got the layout done, it's time to start working with FrontPage. We begin by setting up our directories in this way:

1. Select File ➢ New ➢ Web. The New dialog box appears.

2. Highlight One Page Web and click OK. FrontPage creates the necessary FrontPage directory and images directory, and then opens a blank, untitled page within the root directory so you can begin working.

Since ours is a manageable site, we use the root directory for all the HTML pages, and the images directory for all graphics.

Follow these steps to set up individual files in your root directory:

1. In Folders view, right-click anywhere in the interface. A menu appears.

2. Select New Page.

3. A new page appears in the root directory. Name this page `default.htm`.

Repeat the process until you have created all the pages planned for the site. You can always add or delete pages as necessary.

To add the Feedback Form:

1. Select File ➢ New ➢ Page. The New dialog box appears.

2. Highlight Feedback and click OK.

3. Save the file to your web as **feedback.htm**. We'll modify it later.

To set up tasks

1. In Folders view, highlight the file you want to associate with a task.

2. Right-click and choose Add Task from the menu.

3. The New Task dialog box appears. Fill in the task name, priority, and a description.

4. Click OK.

PART

VI

Step-by-Step
FrontPage Sites

You can also set up tasks that are not associated with a page. To do so:

1. Select Tasks view and click anywhere in the FrontPage interface. A menu appears.

2. Select New Task. The New Task dialog box opens.

3. Fill in the task name, the task priority, and a description.

 TIP Whether associating a task with a page or without it, be sure to include as many tasks as you'll need to complete the production and post-production process. Tasks are one of FrontPage's most helpful tools to guide you through building your Web site. For more information on tasks, see Chapter 7, *Managing Tasks*.

Designing the Splash Page

Now it's time to design the splash page for your site. We'll begin with the Zapaton splash page:

1. In Folders view, highlight the default.htm file that you created earlier.

2. Right-click and select Open from the menu. The default page opens in Page view.

3. Let's first set the background color and links. To do this, right-click the empty page and select Page Properties from the menu that appears.

4. The Page Properties dialog box appears. In the Colors section, find Background and activate the drop-down menu.

5. From the menu, choose More Colors. The More Colors dialog box appears.

6. In the Value text box, type in the hexadecimal color you want for the background. Refer to the list you made in pre-production when you developed the look and feel of the Web site. In our example, we've chosen the Medium Olive Green, hex value 999966, for the background.

7. Click OK. You return to the More Colors dialog box. From here, continue adding colors for each of the available selections: Text, Hyperlink, Visited Hyperlink, and Active Hyperlink. When you're finished, click OK in the Page Properties dialog box.

Your page will now appear in Page view with the color and link information added to the page.

Let's add the first graphic:

1. Place the cursor where you'd like to insert the graphic.

2. From the FrontPage menu, select Insert ➢ Picture ➢ From File. The Picture dialog box appears.

3. Select the image you'd like to place on the page by highlighting it. Then click OK. FrontPage inserts the file into your page. You can now place the image where you like by dragging it to the location where you want it to reside.

 NOTE If you've set up a task list for this first page, you'll want to mark the task completed.

You can check the results of your work by saving the pages and selecting File Preview In Browser. In Figure 30.5, you'll see the results of our page design within the browser window.

FIGURE 30.5

The completed splash design as shown in the browser

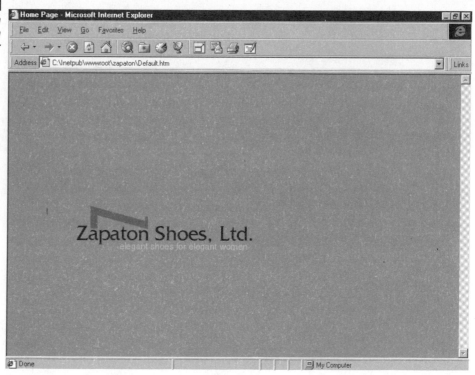

Designing an Internal Page

Typically, tables are needed to lay out most pages. The Zapaton catalog pages are no exception.

In Figure 30.6, you can see the page layout we did using our image editor. We've set up some guides to show how we'd like to map out our table grid. Based on this information, we can turn to FrontPage and begin creating the actual table.

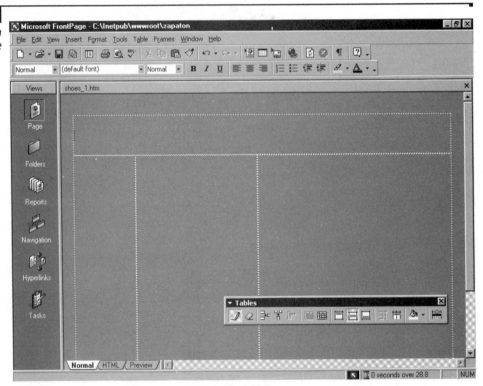

FIGURE 30.6

Planning the table in FrontPage

When planning a table, begin with vertical columns, only adding rows where necessary. Be sure to revisit Chapter 11, *Using Tables for Advanced Layout*, for more information.

With your table in mind, follow these steps to lay out the page:

1. With the page open in Page view, select Insert ➤ Table. The Insert Table dialog box appears.

2. Enter the number of rows in the Rows text box (we entered 1).

3. Enter the number of columns (we entered 4) in the Columns text box.

4. In the Layout section, choose an alignment for your table. Typically, left alignment will be used.

5. Set the Border, Cell Padding, and Cell Spacing to 0.

6. Check the Specify Width box.

7. Add a numeric value for fixed-width tables and a percentage for dynamic. In an example such as this one, we want to fix the width so all the content including images and graphics is neatly managed. We entered a total width of 595 pixels.

8. Click OK. The table appears on your page.

9. Add images and text using the techniques you learned in related chapters of this book to refine the page's look. Be sure to adjust table and table cell properties where necessary (see Chapter 11).

10. When you're finished, save the page. You can preview it externally, or internally using the Preview tab to see the way the page will appear (see Figure 30.7).

Continue adding pages in this fashion until you've completed the full content of your site.

FIGURE 30.7

The completed page in Preview mode

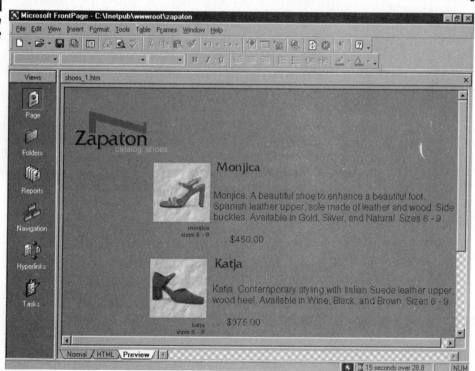

PART

VI

Step-by-Step
FrontPage Sites

NOTE When working with navigation, be sure to remember that you can use shared borders on appropriate pages if you are using a server supporting FrontPage extensions. Check Chapter 15, *Special Effects*, for details, and be sure to ask your ISP if in fact they are using the appropriate extensions for your needs.

Customizing the Feedback Form

Since we want the Feedback Form to match our design rather than the pre-fabricated look that FrontPage uses, we'll want to customize the form using our own colors and graphics. Here's how:

1. In Folders view, double-click feedback.htm. The file opens in Page view.

2. Add the background and link colors to the page by following the directions discussed in "Designing the Splash Page."

3. Delete the comment and horizontal rule from the top.

4. Add your graphic header by selecting Insert ➤ Picture ➤ From File and choosing the appropriate header image for your page.

5. Customize the comments within the form field. Simply click within the field where you'd like to change the text and type in the new text.

6. If you'd like to change the text on the form buttons, simply right-click the button. From the menu that appears, choose Form Field Properties. The Push Button Properties dialog box appears.

7. In the Value/label text box, type in the word or words you'd like to have appear on the button.

8. Click OK and repeat the process for the Reset button if you'd like to change that, too.

9. Customize any remaining text on the page, and be sure the page is included in the Shared Borders if you are taking that approach to navigation.

10. Save your file to the web.

Your results should be similar to those in Figure 30.8.

FIGURE 30.8

The Zapaton Feedback
Form

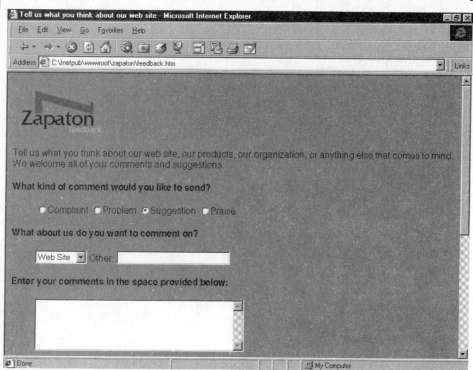

 NOTE Have you marked off your tasks? If not, and you are confident the work for a given task is finished, go into Tasks view and mark the task as complete.

Adding the JavaScript

To achieve the mouseover effect, you'll want to add JavaScript. Certainly, this can be done with other methods, such as Java hover buttons, which many FrontPage 1998 users will be familiar with. However, JavaScript is a much faster method, and it's also less demanding on resources both on the client and server side.

Since FrontPage doesn't offer JavaScripts, you'll have to find your own. We're going to show you a great mouseover script here, and we'll describe how to add it to your pages. Be sure to check Chapter 21, *JavaScript and Dynamic HTML,* for general guidelines and specific JavaScript resources.

PART

VI

Step-by-Step
FrontPage Sites

To work with this JavaScript, you'll need to create two graphics for the standard and mouseover states. In our example, we'll create two next buttons; one will be a standard button, and the other will have some modification such as a highlight. We'll also name the graphics logically so we know which is the standard and which is the mouseover state graphic.

 NOTE This script is written to sniff and pre-load images if a supportive browser visits. If the browser is an older version without JavaScript, the standard state button will function just fine.

Here's the main portion of the script *before* customization. Note that the bold items are what you'll need to change.

```
<script language="javascript">

<!-
// browser test:

bName = navigator.appName;

bVer = parseInt (navigator.appVersion);

if (bName == "Netscape" && bVer >= 3) version = "n3";

else if (bName == "Netscape" && bVer == 2) version = "n2";

else if (bName == "Microsoft Internet Explorer" && bVer >= 3) version =
"n3";

else version = "n2";


// end of browser test

// preload universal images:
```

```
// If it is Netscape 3 browser

if (version== "n3") {


bloff = new Image(); bloff.src = "path to standard image";

blon = new Image(); blon.src = "path to over image";

}

function hiLite(imgDocID,imgObjName) {

  if (version == "n3") {

    document.images[imgDocID].src = imgObjName;

    }

  }

function hiLiteOff(imgDocID,imgObjName) {

  if (version == "n3") {

    document.images[imgDocID].src = imgObjName;

    }

  }

//-->

</script>
```

To add the script to a page using FrontPage:

1. Open the page of interest in Page view.

2. Select the HTML tab. The HTML code will come into view.

3. Locate the opening <HEAD> tag. Below any META tag information and before the closing </HEAD> tag, copy the script *exactly* as it appears here.

4. In the first bold area, replace the comment with the path and name of your standard image:

```
b1off = new Image(); b1off.src = "path to standard image";
```

becomes

```
b1off = new Image(); b1off.src = "images/next.gif";
```

5. In the second bold area, replace the comment with the path and name of your mouseover image:

```
b1on = new Image(); b1on.src = "path to over image";
```

becomes

```
b1on = new Image(); b1off.src = "images/next_over.gif";
```

6. To add additional images, add image sets directly beneath each other and rename the numeric values:

```
b2off = new Image(); b2off.src = "path to second standard image";
b2on = new Image(); b2on.src = "path to second over image";
```

7. Continue this process until you've accounted for all images.

Save the file by pressing Ctl+S on your keyboard.

Now make these additional modifications to the image and the image link:

1. In Page view, select the HTML tab. The HTML code is now in view.

2. In the appropriate section of the body, add your image by selecting Insert ➢ Picture ➢ From File and selecting the *static* image file. The following code appears:

```
<img src="images/next.gif">
```

3. Highlight the code and right-click. Select Tag properties. The Picture Properties dialog appears.

4. Select the Appearance tab:

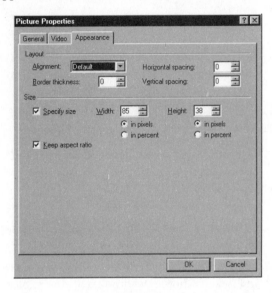

5. In the Layout section, make sure all settings are set to 0.

6. In the Size section, check Specify Size (FrontPage will automatically have entered the width and height; do *not* change these numbers), and be sure the In Pixels radio buttons are selected.

7. Check Keep Aspect Ratio.

8. Click the General tab. In the Alternative Representations section, add descriptive text into the Text area.

9. Click OK. Your code looks like this:

```
<img src="images/next.gif" alt="go to the next page" border="0"
width="32" height="32">
```

10. Now add the bolded information to the image:

```
<img src="images/next.gif" name="b1" alt="go to the next page"
border="0" width="32" height="32">
```

Continue adding images and corresponding names to your code until all your standard images are included.

Now add the proper link syntax and JavaScript code. We prefer you do this by hand. To do so:

1. In front of your first image, type everything that's in bold:

```
<a href="shoes_2.htm" onmouseover="hiLite('b1','images/next_over.gif')"
onmouseout="hiLiteOff('b1','images/next.gif')"> <img
src="images/next.gif" name="b1" alt="go to the next page" border="0"
width="32" height="32">
```

2. Now add the closing </a> tag after the image:

```
<a href="shoes_2.htm" onmouseover="hiLite('b1','images/next_over.gif')"
onmouseout="hiLiteOff('b1','images/next.gif')"> <img
src="images/next.gif" name="b1" alt="go to the next page" border="0"
width="32" height="32"></a>
```

3. Continue to add the information as necessary for each image. Be sure your image names and numeric values match!

4. Once you're finished, check your work in a browser by selecting File ➤ Preview In Browser. Choose the browser of your choice.

Your mouseover script should now be in perfect working order!

Ready? Set? Publish!

Now that we have all the pieces of the site together, it's time to prepare each page for publication. First, you'll want to spell check all pages. To do this:

1. Select Folders view.

2. From the folder list, highlight the root directory of the web.

3. From the main FrontPage menu, select Tools ➤ Spelling. The Spelling dialog box appears.

4. Choose the Entire Web button. You can also check the Add A Task For Each Page With Misspellings option if you'd like.

5. Click Start.

FrontPage now spell checks all pages and reports any misspellings. At this point, be sure to go back and change any misspelled words. Once you've made your corrections, repeat the process until you receive a No Spelling Errors Were Found message at the bottom of the Spelling dialog box.

Now it's time to check for invalid, or broken, links on your site. To do so:

1. With the web open, open the Reports toolbar by selecting View ➤ Toolbars ➤ Reports. The Reports Toolbar appears.

2. Click the Verify Hyperlinks button. The Verify Hyperlinks dialog box appears.

3. Select Verify All Hyperlinks To Verify All The Links In The Current FrontPage Web.

4. Click the Start button. The dialog box will close and the window will return to the FrontPage Reports view.

5. One by one, the status of all the links is updated in the Broken Hyperlinks report view. Each link's status is described with a particular indicator (see Chapter 24, *Site Maintenance and Promotion*, for a full list).

To change your broken links:

1. In the Broken Hyperlinks Report view, double-click the link you want to change. The Edit Hyperlink dialog box appears.

2. In the Replace Hyperlink With text box, type in a new, good link to replace the old one. For example, if the old link is http://www.acompany.cm and the new, good link is http://www.acompany.com, type **http://www.acompany.com**.

3. You can elect to change all occurrences of the URL or just selected occurrences. To change all occurrences, select the Change In All Pages button. To change the URL only in selected pages, highlight the pages in the list of pages and select the Change In Selected Pages button.

4. Click the Replace button. The repaired link appears in the list in place of the old one.

Continue to repair links as necessary. When you're finished, run through the process again to ensure no broken links remain.

The next step in the process is to add META-tag descriptions and keywords to the pages. To do this:

1. Open the page in the Page view. From the FrontPage menu bar, select File ➤ Properties. The Page Properties dialog box appears.

2. In the dialog box's Title text box, type the title words you targeted. Note that the title must be understandable as well as include these words. Here's our example: "Zapaton Shoes, Inc."

3. Now click the Custom tab. The contents of the dialog box changes to reflect your choice.

4. In the lower part of the dialog box, locate the User Variable area. This area displays a list of all the META tags in the current page. To add a new META tag to

the page, which is what you want to do, click the Add button. The User Meta Variable dialog box appears.

5. In the Name field, identify the type of META tag you want to add. Type **keywords** now so you can specify some keywords.

6. In the User Meta Variable dialog box's Value text box, type the keywords you think best for your site. For Zapaton's site, try keywords and keyword combinations such as *women, shoes, handbags, leather, leather goods,* and so forth.

7. Click the OK button to close the dialog box. The Page Properties dialog box reappears with the information you specified for your keywords META tag visible.

8. Repeat steps 5 through 7, this time typing **description** instead of **keywords**, and then add the description you think best—in our example, this would be: "Zapaton Shoes, Ltd. features handmade shoes and handbags of the finest Spanish and Italian leather and all natural fibers."

9. Click OK. Your site is now properly META tagged.

Now that all of the prep work is done, we're ready to publish the site to the Web!

 NOTE   Be sure to test the site using different browsers, platforms, and screen resolutions to ensure you've done a good job at making the site cross-browser compatible (see Chapter 16, *Cross-Browser Design*).

Publishing the Site

If your site has passed all the important spelling, link, and browser tests, it's time to upload your site to the server. FrontPage has a trouble-free method of doing this for you:

1. With your web open in Page view, select File ➢ Publish Web. The Publish Web dialog box appears.

2. In the Specify The Location To Publish Your Web To text box, type the path to your Web server (if you don't know this path, check with your system administrator).

3. Click the Options button to open the dialog box to its full size. You'll see some important information here including which files to publish, and how to pub-

lish them. Since this is the first time we're publishing the Web, we are going to click the Publish All Pages button.

4. Now click Publish. If you're not connected to the Internet, your computer connects you and establishes communication with the server. The transfer begins after you input your user ID and password.

FrontPage does the rest. When you have finished, be sure the web has successfully transferred and perform some post-publication testing.

Post-Production Needs

A Web site should always be kept fresh. If you're not seeing changes and growth on at least a quarterly basis, it reflects to visitors that your own business isn't dynamic. Continue to develop your site as your business develops. If you have a new product, or new job listing, or are offering an incentive or special—put it online!

Of course, this translates to human power. Many people make the mistake of thinking they can put a Web site up and the job is done—that's all that will ever be needed or necessary. This is like saying you'll put a sign up over the front door and the rest will take care of itself! It doesn't happen that way: effort and attention must be paid.

Whether you, someone in your organization, someone that you have come in on a part-time basis, or a Web design firm do the updates and maintenance, the reality is that *someone* will have to do it. It might be cost-effective to train someone within your organization to manage updates, particularly if you don't expect too many changes over time. FrontPage can help you manage maintenance using tasks.

In any case, you should have a good idea of what it really means to be a "Webmaster." The following list includes qualities of a good Webmaster:

- Understands the business at hand. This way, the Webmaster can not only add to the site, but be alert for potential problems, and come up with helpful ideas, as well.

- Works with the technology. The Webmaster must be proficient in HTML and be able to use FrontPage and image editing programs.

- Understands the mechanisms by which to publish Web sites.

- Has good communications skills and an ability to discuss issues with the Web Service provider.

- Has a basic knowledge of branding and marketing concepts.

Sounds demanding? It is! Be confident that you can use this book and the resources within it, as well as many other books and Web sites, to supplement the education of your Webmaster.

PART

VI

Step-by-Step
FrontPage Sites

TIP Just because you have a Web site doesn't mean people are going to show up and suddenly start participating in your offerings. You've got to get the word out on the virtual street as well as within your preexisting marketing circles. Be sure to visit Chapter 24 for helpful guidance in this regard.

Up Next

In this chapter, you've not only extended your knowledge and practice of a process-oriented method of developing Web sites, but you've focused on how these practices apply specifically to the small business. Issues such as branding and identity were carefully demonstrated, and resources for additional ways to grow and manage your site have been provided.

In the next chapter, we take a look at how a community site is built and maintained. Communities are a powerful and growing force on the Web, and if you have interest in providing the ultimate user experience by building a community, be sure to read beyond the structural elements we've included, particularly the conceptual and management-oriented community issues also covered.

CHAPTER 31

Building a Community Site

In this chapter, we take a close look at what goes into the planning, production, and management of an online community. Community sites are popular, can offer opportunities for developers interested in building potential revenue sources, and are a great way to get people on the Web involved in special interests. Stretching beyond the standard offerings of a personal or small business Web page, a community site places significant demands on developer resources, technology, and human resources. An idea of what those demands are can help you decide if a community is in order and how to best manage a community once you decide to launch one.

What Is Online Community?

Many readers will remember Bulletin Board Services, fondly referred to as BBSs. These typically single-line (although sometimes multiple-line) community boards allowed people to use their computers and modems to dial into and engage in communication, file downloads, and games.

Coupled with BBSs were commercial online services. You might remember GEnie, at one time the most popular online service. Other such services still in existence include Prodigy, Compuserve, and the still-thriving America Online (AOL).

BBSs and commercial online services were the first widely available online communities. Until the early 1990s, the Internet was restricted in its scope and access. So the home computer user interested in online life used these boards and services to find information and communicate with others who had shared interests.

When access to the Internet expanded, newsgroups became the focus of special interest communities, and Internet Relay Chat (IRC) became the free venue for chat-oriented folks to enjoy real-time community. The Web quickly became a locale for personal expression as well as business-oriented sites.

But creating a Web-based community has been challenging. This is largely due to the technology. Inline newsgroups and chats are inconsistent and difficult, and linking to existing resources from the Web often involves plug-ins and multiple software interfaces. Luckily, the technology is getting easier. And, as the technology becomes more accessible, Web-based communities are rising up with rapid force.

Why an Online Community?

The advantages of creating an online community are many. In some cases, online communities can extend a business. A great example of this is Saturn Cars, a company that has very effectively used a community-oriented concept in all of its advertising. This has extended to its Web site, where community thrives.

Sometimes community is more utilitarian. You provide forums and chats as a way of handling outreach to company members who are out in the field. Or you may have an online fan club and provide forums and chats to talk about your favorite actor, musical group, or game.

Community sites are often funded by sponsors and advertisers. Larger communities can offer advertisers a pool of collected individuals with a specific demographic. This allows advertising to be more targeted and direct, and ultimately, more effective.

Planning the Community

Community sites are typically a combination of Internet and Web technologies that focus on human rather than technological activity. People meet in chat rooms to discuss issues in real-time; use newsgroups to discuss projects, ask questions, and share art; or visit community Web sites for collected information on their favorite topics.

As a developer, you need to have a firm vision of what you want your community to be—both in structure and in content.

First, let's look at the components of a community. Then we'll take an example and walk you through the familiar preproduction activities of planning a site—defining intent, goals, and technology needs. While much of the process is similar to what you'll be doing in other chapters in Part VI of this book, the content is geared more specifically toward the specific subject of community sites. So this chapter will walk you through a familiar process, but with the individual look and feel, technologies, and production needs of a community site.

Community Structure

Communities can be made up of a variety of components, but they must have a common, central point. For a Web-based community, this is naturally the community Web site. Let's look at the aspects of a community in detail:

Web content   Web content refers to articles, interviews, FAQs, and other information placed on a Web site. Typically, Web content will grow, with older articles getting archived and newer features moving to the front of the community.

Newsgroups and forums   Much like BBSs, a newsgroup (also called a *forum*) is often the primary place where people choose to meet. A visitor leaves a message, and subsequent visitors respond to that message. The banter can be humorous, informative, and sometimes downright fiery! Newsgroups are best streamlined in their topical areas of interest. If your community is about women, your newsgroups might focus on women's health, romance, women and money, and so forth.

Chats   While the majority of chats are populated by younger Internet users, chats within specialized communities are popular with more mature audiences, too. Special guests, specific topics, and chat hosts who can remove troublemakers all help to make chatting a very interesting real-time experience for visitors.

Ancillary content   Depending upon the type of community you're developing, you might have a variety of related content. Some communities offer Web-based e-mail, games, and postcards for their visitors. This type of content can keep a community colorful and lively.

Figure 31.1 shows how these community components are structured within a Web site.

FIGURE 31.1

Components of a community Web site

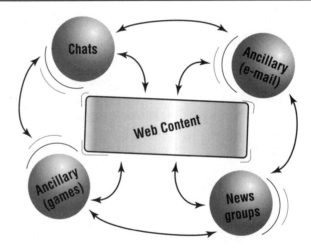

Audience and Intent

When creating communities, these familiar issues are especially important. Communities can be broad in topical interest, such as automobiles, or they can be very specialized, such as The Mustang Convertible Club.

You might be developing a community as a hobbyist, in which case it's likely that you'll have a specialized audience. However, if you're building a community for commercial purposes, the community structure is likely going to be much bigger.

Defining how broad or specific you are going to be is critical to every aspect of site production and management. Knowing ahead of time how many newsgroups and chats (you may only have one of each, or you may have hundreds) and what kind of Web and ancillary content you want to have will help you make better site-design decisions. Also, the amount of potential traffic will help you and your Internet service provider choose the best technology in a given case.

We're going to use the example of Web Answers for Everyone, a community based on Web building. We want to be very broad in our scope, including design, programming, marketing, and other development interests, as well as appealing to a variety of audiences, including newcomers and professionals. We don't want to be technology-specific.

What all of this means is that we're planning a *big* community. However, for the purposes of this chapter, we're going to stick to the basic areas of development and show how FrontPage can help you produce the community in question.

 TIP For specialized information on the management of large Web sites, see Chapter 32, *Constructing and Managing a Large-Scale Site.*

Short- and Long-Term Goals

Our short-term goal for our Web Answers for Everyone site is to provide a content-rich, community-oriented environment for Web developers of all skill levels. Information will be completely free. For the long term, we want to amass members to draw the interest of advertisers and sponsors so the community can grow revenue, and eventually we'd like to create an online school where community members can get training in Web design and related topics.

We've sketched out the concept of our community, which you can see in Figure 31.2.

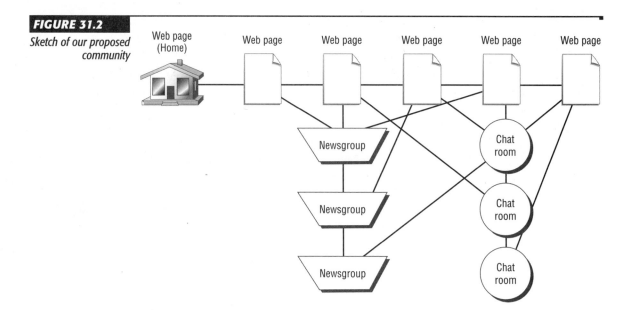

FIGURE 31.2

Sketch of our proposed community

Getting Ready for Production

While we've abbreviated the planning phase in terms of scope, once you have your community well planned in terms of intent, goals, and structure, it's time to get ready for production by creating the look and feel of your community and determining what technologies will be necessary.

Creating a Visual Design

Community look and feel should be fun, gregarious, bright, and welcoming. We first looked to color and shape to help us create the tone of the site:

Color Name	RGB Value	Hex Value	Expression
Dark orange	204 102 0	CC6600	Bright and warm
Light orange	255 153 0	FF9900	Fun and energetic
Dark blue	51 51 102	333366	Intelligent
Medium blue	0 102 153	006699	Another energetic color conveying "cool"
White	255 255 255	FFFFFF	Clean, crisp, easy on the eyes

We also included black for text and white for any accents.

Next, we worked with the typefaces that are used in the company logo to determine a nice method of displaying the information. We wanted something fun, and we decided to mimic this approach in the way we laid out the Web page's type:

Type Family	Typeface	Expression/Use
Decorative	Vienna Black	Chunky, humorous font for headers
Decorative	Architeqtura	Slender, decorative typeface for sub-headers
Serif	Times Roman	Common, cross-platform serif font good for body text

We then examined the way to approach graphic accents. We decided that header text would have a drop shadow to add some depth to the pages. We created a similar drop shadow for photos and illustrations, as well, and we employed a JavaScript mouse-over animation for navigation (see Chapter 30, *Designing a Small Business Web Site*).

Community Technology

When it comes to community sites, technology plays a critical role in how the site is managed and how needed functions are delivered. While we can't possibly demonstrate all of the ways community technology can be used in one small chapter, we will discuss the basics and help you see where FrontPage can be especially of use.

The following technologies are often used to create and enhance online communities:

Advertising banners Since your site will likely be supported by sponsors and advertisers, planning for ad banners is a good thing. FrontPage offers an Ad Banner component, which you can learn to use in Chapter 15, *Special Effects*.

Forums FrontPage allows you to create interactive forums. This is very helpful, but for very big communities, FrontPage might not be sufficient for the kind of control or scope of forums you'll want to have. For our example, we'll walk you through how to set up forums effectively using FrontPage.

ASP Active Server Pages can help keep your Web content pages dynamic. For more information about ASP, see Chapter 26, *Using Active Server Pages*.

Chats Unfortunately, Microsoft FrontPage doesn't have a built-in chat component. However, there are a variety of ActiveX components and Java applets that you can use to create chats. Another method of chat creation is running your own chat server, or arranging with your ISP to let you have access to a chat server running on IRC technology. Then you can allow people to access the chat rooms using the software of their choice.

PART

VI

Step-by-Step
FrontPage Sites

Technologies for ancillary services Web-based e-mail, postcards, and games all have their uses. Many of these ancillary services are available in the form of free or low-cost scripts. Check resource sites made available in the Mastering What's Online sidebars of Chapter 21, *JavaScript and Dynamic HTML*, Chapter 25, *Understanding CGI*, Chapter 26, *Using Active Server Pages*, and Chapter 27, *Databases in Detail*.

Producing the Site

As with the previous two chapters in this section, we're going to walk through aspects of producing the community site. First, we're going to create the design using our image editor, and then we're going to move on to FrontPage itself where, using a combination of wizards and templates, we get the community site going.

Laying Out the Pages

For this site, we decided not to have a splash page. We felt that a community site should have a sense of immediacy—where people can get to the information and interaction they want without a progression of visual and navigational information. So the first page we designed is our welcome page.

To lay out a welcome page:

1. In your image editor, select File ➢ New. The New dialog box appears.

2. Create an image that is 595 pixels wide by 600 pixels high.

3. Click OK. You will now have your work area set to the first layer.

4. To this layer, add your background color. We selected white (see color chart earlier in this chapter).

5. Create a new layer by selecting Layer ➢ New ➢ Layer. Here, you'll add the areas of color and shape to create the unusual feel. In our example, we build the arcs using Adobe Illustrator (see Chapter 18, *Working with Professional Graphics Programs*), a vector-based drawing tool, and then import them into Photoshop.

6. On subsequent layers, add the page title, navigation, and sub-headers.

7. Once you've added all the elements you want for this page, save the file by selecting File ➢ Save As. The Save As dialog box appears. Name the file and save in the native layer format of your imaging program.

Figure 31.3 shows the completed welcome page design.

FIGURE 31.3

The completed welcome page layout

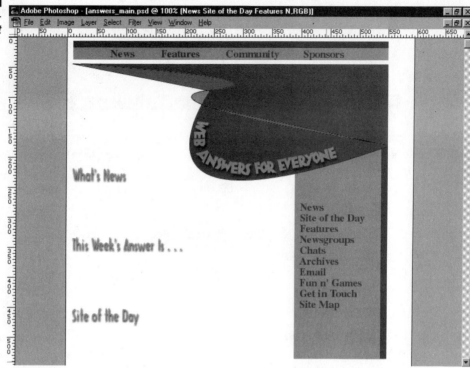

To generate the actual graphics for your welcome page, move back to your imaging program and follow these steps:

1. Open up the layered file in your imaging program.

2. Highlight the layer that has the image you want to process.

3. Using the marquee or selection tool (it will vary depending upon your program), draw a selection around the part of the image you want to keep, making sure you're on the correct layer.

4. Copy and paste the section into a new file.

5. Optimize the file as a GIF or JPEG, depending upon the graphic. Name the graphic and save it directly to the images folder within your FrontPage web.

Repeat this process for all of the buttons, headers, backgrounds, and spot art that you'll require.

PART

VI

Step-by-Step
FrontPage Sites

NOTE For detailed help optimizing and working with graphics, see Chapter 9, *Designing Graphics for the Web*, and Chapter 18, *Working with Professional Graphics Programs*.

Using FrontPage to Create the Community Site

We'll use the Discussion Web Wizard to set up our discussion web, because the wizard easily sets up the initial forums necessary for our site. From there, we can use templates to add the pages that will link to the discussion.

To set up your site using the Discussion Web Wizard:

1. Open FrontPage.

2. Select File ➢ New Web. The New dialog box appears.

3. Highlight Discussion Web Wizard.

4. In the Specify The Location Of The New Web text box, enter the local path to your new web.

5. Click OK.

6. The Create New Web pop-up menu will appear and set up the web. Once the wizard is finished initializing the process, the wizard will open to its main page. Read the information and when you're ready, click Next.

7. The first question you'll be asked is to determine the main features of your discussion:

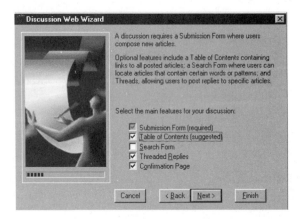

Go ahead and check the features that you want, then click Next.

8. The next dialog box will ask you for your discussion name. Type it into the appropriate text box. You'll also be asked to name the folder. FrontPage may have already filled these fields in for you; you can leave them as is or customize them by simply changing the information within the text boxes. When you're finished, click Next.

9. Now set up the input fields. We chose Subject, Category, and Comments, but you should use what is best for your site. You can always add fields by hand later in the game. When done, click Next.

10. Now you are given the choice to let only members access your discussion or to make it open to all. Use what is best for you. We chose members only. When you've completed this choice, click Next.

11. Now you are asked how you want the Table of Contents to sort messages. We chose Newest To Oldest. When you're ready, click Next.

12. The wizard will now ask if you want the Table of Contents to be the home page. We don't, so we selected the No button. Once you've made your choice, click Next.

13. Now you can choose to use a Web theme or not. Since we are designing our own page, we simply clicked Next to move on to the next dialog box in the wizard.

14. The wizard offers configuration options. Choose what you feel is best for your site. We chose a dual interface using frames if available. When you have made your choice, click Next.

15. You'll see a synopsis of pages. Click Finish, and FrontPage will set up the pages as you've requested them.

Once FrontPage is finished with the discussion portions of the web, you'll want to go ahead and set up individual files in the root directory. To do this:

1. In Folders view, right-click anywhere in the interface.

2. Select New Page in the menu that appears.

3. A new page appears in the root directory. Name this page **default.htm**.

4. Repeat the process until you have created all the pages planned for the site, using the chart prepared in the planning phase as a guide. You can always add or delete pages as necessary.

PART

VI

Step-by-Step
FrontPage Sites

Tasks are one of FrontPage's most helpful tools to guide you through building your Web site. To set up tasks:

1. In Folders view, highlight the file you want to associate with a task.

2. Right-click and choose Add Task from the menu.

3. The New Task dialog box appears. Fill in the task name, priority, and a description

4. Click OK.

You can also set up tasks that are not associated with a page. To do so:

1. Select Tasks view and click anywhere in the FrontPage interface.

2. Select New Task from the menu that appears. The New Task dialog box opens.

3. Fill in the task name, the task priority, and a description and click OK.

TIP   For more information on tasks, see Chapter 7, *Managing Tasks*.

Creating the Welcome Page

Now that you have your site set up, it's time to lay out the Welcome page. Since tables are needed to lay out most pages, we'll walk you through the process of building them.

In Figure 31.4, you can see the page we laid out with our image editor. We've set up some guides to show how we'd like to map out our table grid. Based on our information, we can turn to FrontPage and begin creating the actual tables necessary.

NOTE   When planning a table, begin with vertical columns, only adding rows where necessary. Be sure to revisit Chapter 11, *Using Tables for Advanced Layout*, for more information.

FIGURE 31.4

Planning the table

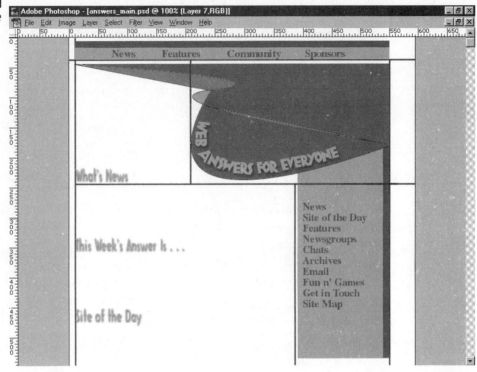

With your table in mind, follow these steps to lay out the page:

1. With the page open in Page view, select Insert ➤ Table. The Insert Table dialog box appears.

2. Enter the number of rows in the Rows text box.

3. Enter the number of columns in the Columns text box.

4. In the Layout section, choose an alignment for your table. Typically, left alignment will be used.

5. Set the Border, Cell Padding, and Cell Spacing to 0.

6. Check the Specify Width box.

7. Add a numeric value for fixed-width tables and a percentage for dynamic. In our example, we want to fix the width so that all the content including images and graphics is neatly managed, so we entered a total width of 595 pixels.

8. Click OK. The table now appears on your page. If you need to stack or nest a table, go ahead and draw those tables as well (see Chapter 11).

9. Add images and text using the techniques you learned in related chapters of this book to refine the page's look. Be sure to adjust table and table cell properties where necessary (see Chapter 11).

10. When you're finished, save the page. You can preview it externally, or internally using the Preview tab.

Continue adding pages in this fashion until you've completed the full content of your site.

Customizing the Forum and the Table of Contents

Since we want the Forum pages to match our design rather than the prefabricated look that FrontPage uses, we'll want to customize each of the Forum pages using our own colors and graphics.

To customize the Forum pages:

1. In Folders View, double-click one of the Forum pages (we began with the discussion welcome page, `discl_welc.htm`). The file opens in Page view.

2. Add background and link colors to the page.

3. Add your graphic header by selecting Insert ➢ Picture ➢ From File and choosing the appropriate header image for your page.

4. Customize the comments within the page. Simply highlight the text you want to change and type in the new text.

5. Save your file to the web.

You'll want to repeat this process for each of the individual discussion pages. Your results should be similar to those in Figure 31.5.

 NOTE Have you marked off your tasks? If not, and you are confident the work for a given task is finished, go into Tasks view and mark the task as complete.

FIGURE 31.5

*Sample discussion
welcome*

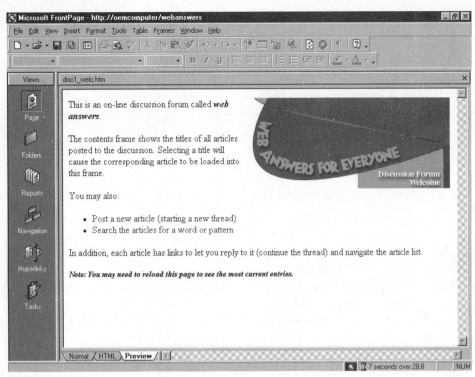

Adding Chats

There are a variety of ways to add a chat to a community site. First, you'll need to decide which method you want to use. The most common are ActiveX components, Java applets, and actual links to chat servers.

For the best compatibility for inline chats (*inline* refers to the fact that the chat runs in the browser and requires no extra software), Java applets are a good choice. ActiveX is an excellent choice if you're running chats to a private audience with Microsoft browsers. Relying on a chat server can be a daunting task—the server has to be maintained around the clock. This means human resources. However, if you are interested in very large community creation, it's a good option, as it gives people the most choice.

Depending upon your choice of chat, you can refer to Chapter 22, *Specialty Programming Techniques*, which discusses Java and ActiveX, or take the discussion up with an Internet administration specialist.

Preparing Your Site for Publication

Now that you've figured out all of the logistics and have everything from planning to design completed, it's time to prepare your site for production. This process, which includes spell checking your pages, looking for and repairing broken links, and ensuring that your site is cross-browser compatible, is discussed at length in Chapter 29.

Managing Community

Ideal online communities are well organized and well managed in order to run smoothly. This means human resources to help with the many day-to-day functions of the community.

Think about your online community just as you would your local, real-time community. People get along well most of the time, but there are problems that arise. Sometimes these problems are as simple as straying from the topic when there's business at hand, or as complex as people abusing others.

Managing a community is no easy task, but depending upon the resources you have and the general interest of people within your community, you might be able to hire or recruit volunteers to help keep things in order.

Moderated Forums

Because forums are subject to specific types of problems, moderating them is in order. Common problems include:

Topic drift   This is when conversation moves off of the specified topic. For example, if the newsgroup is about HTML, and people start talking about their children, the topic has drifted!

Unsolicited advertising   Unwelcome advertisers will often post their products, get-rich-quick schemes, and adult site advertisements on your forums. These can be very disruptive to the flow of conversation.

Inappropriate posts   Sometimes members get angry at an issue and will use language that is inappropriate or a tone that is argumentative.

Flame wars   Arguments can break out between community members. These can escalate into members taking sides and one attacking the other.

You can approach these problems in several ways. First, you or community member volunteer moderators can work with topic drift to gently get it back on course. Unsolicited advertising should be removed from the forum quickly, and the same is true of inappropriate posts. When such a post is made by a regular member, typically the moderator will remove the post and write a short e-mail note to the member explaining why the post was removed.

Chat Hosts

Because of their real-time nature, chats are vulnerable to specific types of abuse including:

Scrolling   This is when a malicious user sends a script that scrolls messages too rapidly, overtaking the normal conversation.

Inappropriate comments   Common offenses include sexual comments where they are not welcome, use of foul language, and harassment of other visitors.

Take-over scripts   These are scripts that actually take over the room, removing powers from moderators and chat hosts.

As with newsgroups, it's very helpful to have a moderator and tools that can help manage such incidents. Check with your chat software documentation or ISP for more information on management techniques appropriate to your type of chat environment.

Content Managers

Web content management is a big job! You may want to consider working with others to help develop and manage content. Here are some helpful tips:

- Generate content relating to conversations taking place in forums and chats.
- Recruit interested individuals to find or write content for the community site.
- Match content to calendar events such as holidays.
- Contests tend to generate excitement and involvement.
- Cross-promote activities in one area of a community with another.
- Cross-promote with other, related communities.

PART

VI

Step-by-Step
FrontPage Sites

TIP Another way to get ideas is to visit other community sites. What are they doing with their content? You may find a lot of inspiration from what other communities are doing—even if the community focus is very different from your own.

 MASTERING THE OPPORTUNITIES

Creating Community Rules

The following is a bona fide community rule page taken from the Senior's Community on the Microsoft Network (MSN). Use this as a guideline to building your own community regulations.

Senior's Community Rules

In order to take full advantage of this Community, you must read and understand the following rules and operating procedures of the community and agree to abide by the rules and operating procedures in their entirety. This community was created and is administered by a Community Manager, an entity which is separate and apart from MSN. As such, rules and operating procedures of this community must also be followed. Your access to this community is a privilege, not a right. The act of joining the community and your use of the community constitutes your acceptance of and agreement to be bound by these Community Membership Rules.

These rules will be enforced and violators may, at the sole discretion of the Community Manager, be suspended or "Locked Out" of the Community. Certain behavior carries potential risks to the Community Manager and cannot be allowed.

Members are invited to call a community manager or assistants attention to a potentially problematic message.

While there is nothing wrong with a healthy argument, you must not use offensive language or engage in personal attacks on members (or nonmembers) or the staff of this Community. Personal attacks may subject you and the Community Manager to potential liability for defamation, contribute nothing to the free flow of ideas, and tend to inhibit rational discussion of the issues. The Community Manager is not limited in any way in deciding whether a particular message may be offensive to a particular member or the Community in general. Examples of potentially offensive messages include, but are not limited to, messages that denigrate, insult or ridicule another person, or that contain negative comments on the integrity, personality, honesty, character, intelligence, methods or motives of any person.

MASTERING THE OPPORTUNITIES CONTINUED

In addition, you must respect the privacy of the members (and non-members) of the Community. Do not publish private messages or e-mail messages without the permission of the sender (unless you feel a Community rule has been broken; if so, forward the message privately to a Community Manager for evaluation). Do not publish facts, rumors, or innuendo regarding anyone's personal life.

Members may not use profanity or sexually explicit language in the Community. Although these terms are not easy to define, the Community Manager and sysop staff may use its discretion to make this Community comfortable for members who may be sensitive to profane or sexually explicit language.

You may not use the community to promote or facilitate illegal activities.

Planning, inciting, promoting or facilitating illegal activities through the Community is strictly prohibited.

You may not post copyrighted, trademarked, or other proprietary material without the express permission of the owner.

Library uploads will be reviewed prior to posting in a relevant Library section to determine whether, in the sole discretion of the Community Manager, copyrighted, trademarked, or other proprietary material is included in the upload. The Community Manager cannot review messages prior to posting in the Message section. Reproduction and/or publication, whether knowing or inadvertent, of copyrighted, trademarked, or other proprietary material may result in liability to the Community Manager and/or the posting member and therefore cannot be tolerated. Your upload or posting of any material constitutes a certification by you to the Community Manager that the material does not make use of or infringe on any copyright, trademark, or other proprietary material of others. If you have any question as to whether your upload or post contains copyrighted, trademarked, or other proprietary material, please e-mail the Community Manager, prior to posting or uploading the material.

Because it is important that this Community is useful and enjoyable to all its members, we will take appropriate action, which may be a warning, a suspension, or a termination of membership rights in the Community, if a member breaks these Rules, or threatens the security or order of this Community. We don't plan on doing these things, but we will do them if we judge that we must.

PART

VI

Step-by-Step
FrontPage Sites

MASTERING THE OPPORTUNITIES CONTINUED

Indemnification

Operation of this Community carries inherent risks to the Community Manager because the Community Manager literally cannot control all aspects of the Community at all times. Accordingly, by joining the Community, you agree to indemnify the Community Manager for any damages, costs, and expenses, including reasonable attorneys fees, that accrue to the Community Manager as a result of or arising out of your activities on the Community, including, but not limited to, any claims for violation of any copyright, trademark, or protected material, or any claim of defamation, slander, libel, disparagement, or the like.

Limitation of Liability

You join and participate in this community at your own risk. The Community Manager shall not be liable for any damages or losses which result to you from your use of or participation in this community.

Choice of Law and Community

In joining this Community, you agree that any disputes between you and the Community Manager will be governed by the law of the State of California for all disputes arising out of or related to your membership or participation in the Community.

Any and all actions and proceedings relating to this Community or activities on this Community shall take place in courts located in the State of California.

No Warranties

The Community Manager makes no warranty, express or implied, that access to the community will be available at any particular time; that operation of the community will be uninterrupted or error-free; or that any particular result or information will be obtained. Membership in the community is offered on a "AS IS" Basis without warranties of any kind, other than warranties which are incapable of exclusion, waiver, or restriction under the law applicable hereto.

Entire Agreement

The operating rules and procedures of this Community as described here constitute the entire agreement between you and the Community Manager concerning your participation in this Community. The operating rules and procedures of the Community may change from time to time and such changes will be posted in this Announcement. Only the Community Manager or MSN can change a rule or policy of this Community.

> ### MASTERING THE OPPORTUNITIES CONTINUED
>
> #### Severability
>
> If any of the rules, promises, conditions or agreements described here are held to be void, invalid, or unenforceable it shall not affect the enforceability, effectiveness, or validity of any of the other rules, promises, conditions or agreements.
>
> *If you have read and agree to the terms of the foregoing rules and operating procedures, you may use the Senior's Community.*

Obviously, you will tailor the rules to your own needs. While many people will ignore your rules, it protects *you* to make them clear. Ultimately, the rules are in existence to help your community run smoothly and effectively. Be sure that any and all volunteers or staff members are familiar with the rules of conduct, too.

Up Next

Community sites are often fraught with challenges born of both the technological limitations of forum and chat applications and the management of people. In this chapter, we looked at some of the options available for dealing with these issues, as well as stepped through a mock site design to get you going conceptually.

Chapter 32, *Constructing and Managing a Large-Scale Site,* moves away from the page-by-page approach and examines site structure, advanced management, and what tools and technologies can be used to work with very large Web sites.

PART

VI

Step-by-Step
FrontPage Sites

CHAPTER <u>32</u>

Constructing and Managing a Large-Scale Site

By now, it will be evident to you that the more you add to a Web site, the more critical the planning stages become. And, the more content you have to manage, the more demands this places on resources, be they technological or human.

Big sites take constant vigilance on the part of the Web teams that run them. Imagine what goes into the management of Microsoft, Yahoo, or CNET! Even managing a daily paper can be strategically challenging and require exhaustive resources.

While FrontPage is a terrific tool for building smaller sites, you have undoubtedly seen that the larger a site becomes, or the more technology that is added to it, the more FrontPage is moved from a central tool to an ancillary one. A perfect example of this was demonstrated in Chapter 28, *Using FrontPage with Microsoft's Visual InterDev*. There, we discussed how FrontPage becomes a part of a team of tools in order to manage more demanding sites. In reality, FrontPage will *probably not* be the central tool to any large-scale site. It can, and often does, however, play a role in the design and management of such sites.

In this chapter, we discuss some of the ways large-scale sites are managed. We begin with details about Web site structure, then look at management of data, and then move on to demonstrate how FrontPage becomes the prototyping tool to manage and design individual pages within the site.

 MASTERING WHAT'S ONLINE

Great Big Web Sites!

Check out these sites to see how large sites are managed and designed:

Microsoft (www.microsoft.com): Microsoft's is an enormous site comprising all of the faces of the software giant. From individual applications to developer support to an extensive knowledge base, magazines, news, press releases, and communities, Microsoft is one of the largest sites on the Web.

Yahoo (www.yahoo.com): This ever-popular site started as a catalog of Web sites and grew into a vast Web event with community, news, shopping, services, electronic mail—the list goes on and on.

CNET is the premier Web site for technology-oriented individuals. It is broken into a series of individual sites such as www.download.com, where individuals can find thousands of files for download, www.builder.com, CNET's vast developer center, and www.cnet.com, where technology news is the buzz; there are also community events, special reports, and even a career center.

Web Site Structure

In order to create successful Web sites—particularly very large ones—an understanding of the medium from the technological ground up is necessary. While this knowledge can be very helpful when building a personal page, it's much less important in that context. However, when you have multiple sections with hundreds or even thousands of documents to manage—and new documents being added regularly—understanding the Web's infrastructure becomes paramount.

With this understanding, you gain control over the way documents are managed within the structure. And, with that understanding, you can plan not only how your site visitors will interact with your web, but how backend technology will work behind the scenes to make the process a powerful and effective one.

Historically, the Web was never specifically intended to be a graphical medium. The idea was to create a fast way to connect text-based documents for easy access. For example, if a doctor publishes the finding of a medical research study with references, she could, in the pure hypertext environment, link those references directly to her primary study.

Of course, today's Web might seem very different with its commercial sites, personal fan magazines, and online games, but essentially, the structure has not changed. It is to this structure that we go to gain our foothold when designing very large sites.

MASTERING WHAT'S ONLINE

History of Hypertext

If you'd like to explore the history of the Web and hypertext a bit more, read the original proposal for the Web prepared by Tim Berners-Lee. Find it on the Web at www.w3.org/History/1989/proposal.html.

When you create a link, you're grabbing hold of the Web's structural power. This is the element upon which Web sites are built. Seem too simple? Well, the reality is that with all of the cool things we can do on the Web these days, we've easily overlooked that it is this simple concept that makes the Web a very different medium than almost any other which with contemporary individuals are familiar. And this linking is what brings the concept of *interactivity* to the Web.

PART

VI

Step-by-Step FrontPage Sites

This doesn't mean a page cannot be *static*. In fact, in many cases, static Web sites are necessary or even preferred. A static site is one that has very simplistic options and really is an extension of a printed page. It contains limited information, isn't updated, and offers no interactive opportunities for the site visitor. As with a TV program, the only real options for the visitor is to go somewhere else—to change the virtual channel.

Interactive sites are dynamic, moving content. If you can set aside what you've learned so far about dynamic this and interactive that and think of the most essential aspect of what makes a site interactive, you come up with one element: the hyperlink. Of course, we build from that, and the farther away we move technologically from just the link as an interactive element, the more compelling and visually interesting design can become. Unfortunately, this growth away from the essential can also make it difficult to explain how simple and fundamental the hypertext structure of the Web really is.

 NOTE Interactive media has been called "New" media. Essentially, it is this interactivity that separates it from familiar, static media such as newspapers, magazines, books, radio, standard animation and video, and even film.

The Web, and with it—hypertext—soon moved away from the purely textual and into the realm of the graphical. As soon as graphic file formats were supported inline using graphical Web browsers, the text link became the graphical link. Nowadays, that link might have all kinds of options added to it via HTML and Style Sheets, JavaScript, and Dynamic HTML. The options are growing, but we remind you that the *essential structure has remained the same*.

Linearity

What we can do with hypermedia—be it text-based, graphic-enhanced, or technologically dynamic—is pretty amazing. Not only can we present static information if we want to, but we can present information in varying degrees of what is known as *linearity*.

In the contemporary, dominant cultures of the Western world, we think of time in terms of a linear structure; 12:00 P.M. is followed by 1:00 P.M., Monday by Tuesday, January by February, and so forth. We also perceive life as being a line—beginning with birth and ending with death. It's interesting to note that this is not the way much of the world thinks! American Indian tribes have been described as having a spiral view of life, and many Eastern philosophies relate to time as a circular event, with birth and death simultaneously representing a beginning and an ending. Spirals, circles, and other conceptual or physical structures that move beyond the horizontal and vertical axes are referred to as *non-linear*.

Another comparison of linear and non-linear would be a prepared monologue versus a relaxed conversation. In a prepared monologue, the speaker is discussing an issue, followed by a sub-issue, and so forth. He or she is speaking in one direction: to the audience.

In a natural, relaxed conversation, people talk about different topics, and the topics can suddenly tangent and become something else. You might begin discussing the movie you saw last night and end up supporting a friend through his emotional challenges with an ill parent. And, in conversations, people talk at different intervals, and sometimes all at once!

The Web, interestingly enough, encapsulates all of these things. You can have a completely linear presentation, with one page following another following another and yet another. Or, another linear form common in the West is the *hierarchy*, which is essentially levels of lines. On the Web, you can have linear structures with some non-linearity, or you can have completely non-linear sites.

Knowing that these structures are possible empowers you to create powerful and appropriate data when working within them. Is there an ideal way to go about this? Well, there are certainly choices, and we are convinced that the only way to make the best choice is to go back to that all-important determinant of what drives your site: your audience. If the audience wants very flat information, a linear site is in order. If the audience wants a wild ride, lots of linking and randomization will give them just the thrill they're after.

But in most cases, you want to create a balance. The more data you're working with, the truer this becomes! Usually you want to work with a familiar linear structure and only add tangential information where it is necessary and appropriate.

In order to achieve this balance when planning your sites, you can follow these steps:

1. Begin with a simple, tier-based structure (see next section).

2. Add links within that site that are logical: navigation, references, indexes.

3. Add links to external but complementary sites where appropriate and where it won't distract from your primary information.

Let's begin by examining tier-based models. This will help you begin conceptualizing how to structure your large-scale Web site within the infrastructure of the Web itself.

Tier-Based Models

A *tier-based model* is really a familiar hierarchy; information is structured on levels, or tiers. Simple tier models lean toward the linear, complex models add links that are based on logic, and shared-tier models begin to lean toward the more non-linear in that they add a wide variety of pathways within the site. Let's take a look at these model types in detail.

A Simple Tier Model

The simple tier model in Figure 32.1 shows two levels. The first is a point-of-entry, or home page, and the second is the page's content. If you refer back to Hallie's site in Chapter 29, *Creating a Personal Web Page*, and the Zapaton site in Chapter 30, *Designing a Small Business Web Site*, you'll see that they are both models based on simple tiers.

FIGURE 32.1

A simple tier model

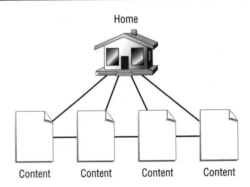

A Complex Tier Model

The model in Figure 32.2 demonstrates three levels with multiple pages. Note how pages are linked to one another, creating a logical but slightly less linear set of navigational pathways.

FIGURE 32.2

A complex tier model

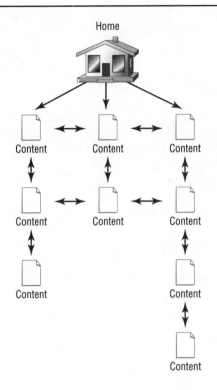

With complex tier models, it's important to provide some frame of reference for site navigation. This helps people re-orient themselves should they become lost within the site (see Figure 32.3). Typically, this task is carried out by the addition of a site map, table of contents, or index that defines the various elements of the sites and links directly to them individually.

 TIP As sites become more complex, *orientation* becomes paramount. A site map can help with this, so be sure to include a link to it on every page of the site. Another important issue is that individual pages must be clearly identified. Use titles, headers, and footers to help reinforce where in a site a visitor is.

FIGURE 32.3

*A table of contents or
a site map can anchor
a site by providing
links to all areas*

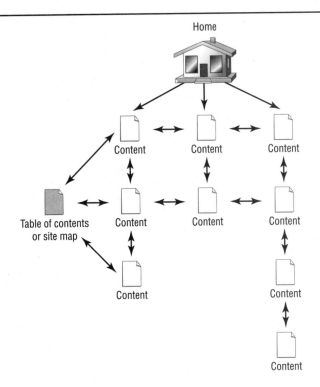

Shared, Complex Tiers

Where we begin moving away from the linear and into the more tangential, complicated structure is when we create sites using shared tiers. Figure 32.4 shows how a
shared tier works. Essentially, it looks like a complex tier, but instead of having
sequential pages for every page on a given tier, pages are shared and cross-referenced.

Not only does the shared-tier model provide a more interactive, choice-driven
experience for site visitors, but it is often very helpful when managing large sites. For
example, if you run a feature article and there are other, related articles to that feature, you'll provide links to those pages within the site, creating new pathways and
corridors for people to travel.

FIGURE 32.4

Shared tiers cross-reference multiple pages

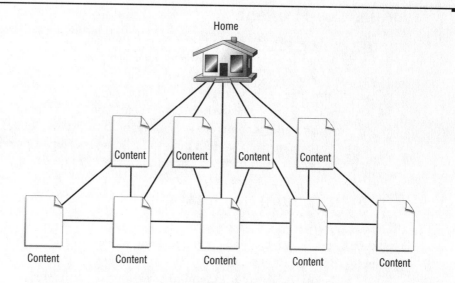

At this stage, it also may become important to create *sub-sites*. This is true when a main site has so many sub-sections that each is in and of itself a Web site with related areas of information. We'll take a look at this in our chapter model, which we begin discussing in detail in the next section.

Planning a Large-Scale Site

So what is a large-scale site, really? We look at a large site as anything beyond 25 pages that is updated on a regular basis. Typically, large-scale sites will range from corporate sites to e-commerce sites, and even to information or personal promotion sites.

The example used in this chapter is taken from real life. One of the authors of this book, Molly E. Holzschlag, often repeats the old saying "a painter never paints his house." She feels that her site is never up-to-date enough, nor does it offer enough information to site visitors who want details on books including code and graphics, access to articles, activities, Web design information, news, and personal information.

So Molly set about drawing up a site that fits into the large-scale model. The idea is to ensure that a lot of information is offered to site visitors and that a shared, tier-based model will enable cross-referencing where appropriate and keep information fresh.

The following sections detail Molly's progress in building her site. The first step, of course, is to define audience, intent, and goals. Then, we'll show how her site structure was sketched out and walk you through the actual building of some of the site's areas.

PART

VI

**Step-by-Step
FrontPage Sites**

Audience and Intent

Both the audience and intent of Molly's first site related to individuals interested in her books and design services. However, over time, audience needs have grown to include requests for support and FAQs for individual books, Web design tutorials, listings of upcoming courses, and personal information.

So, the intent and audience have broadened. In order to accommodate these needs, it began to appear as if numerous sites would need to be developed. And, in a way, that's what is being planned right now—a main site encompassing several sub-sites that focus on specific content concerns for each of these needs.

Short- and Long-Term Goals

Molly's short-term goal is to provide a content-rich, easy-to-navigate, personable yet useful site that can help individuals find current events, ancillary information, and personal information surrounding Molly's activities.

Long-term goals include expanding the resources on the site, adding community elements (see Chapter 31, *Building a Community Site*), and even adding online classes in Web design.

Site Structure

Based on the knowledge of audience, intent, and goals, as well as on a study of the Web's structure, Molly developed a site map showing the tier-based environment. Take a look at the aspects of the site in detail to gain an idea of the actual impact of each of the planned site elements:

News   This section is geared to highlight anything that is newsworthy for the month in question. The concept here is to point to other areas on the site for extrapolated information on activities. This makes good use of the shared-tier concept. News will highlight new Web site clients, new books, public appearances, classes, articles, and online events.

Books   This is a site unto itself but makes good use of the cross-referencing elements of shared-tier structures by linking to related areas such Web design and courses. The book area includes a section highlighting all books and provides ordering details. A book resource area offers code, errata, and other support information for readers. The reader's section has reader mail and a FAQ about which books might best suit an individual's needs.

Courses   The course section offers information on current and upcoming courses and appearances. There will also be a student gallery of selected student works.

Web Design   In this area, the focus is on all things Web design. There will be tutorials in areas such as HTML, Web graphics, user interface design, and other Web-related technologies and resources. Also included is a site design portfolio.

Professional   This area encompasses professional and public information. Included will be a resume, publications list, publicity photos, and a summary of radio and television appearances.

Personal   The "home page" section of the site will include biographical information, photos, essays, poetry, music, and other items of a more personal nature.

Contact   This area can be used to provide feedback about the Web site or to write a personal e-mail.

While the News and Contact pages will likely be no more than one page, most of the primary areas of this site will contain at least 25 and possibly hundreds of pages, with new pages being added over time.

Preparing for Production

With the infrastructure firmly managed and a strong idea of what will be necessary to get this site rolling, the next major step is gathering the information and organizing it into appropriate areas.

At this point in the process, many site designers will use a white board or other large, erasable drawing area upon which they will begin sketching out how individual groups of content will relate to other groups of content on the site. This process is a fluid one and, in large-site production, is often subject to change. Feel good about your primary areas before moving on to creating a design appropriate to the site.

Creating a Look and Feel

Because the most significant aspect of this site is promotion of an individual's collected works and ideas, the site is going to be personal and warm, but express the bold and inventive nature of its creator. To accomplish this on her site, Molly chose a variety of warm, vibrant colors.

Color Name	RGB Value	Hex Value	Expression
Dark orange	255 102 0	FF6600	Deep and warm
Light orange	255 153 51	FF9933	Fun and energetic
Bright yellow	255 255 153	FFFF99	Vibrant
Light yellow	255 255 204	FFFFCC	Bright, warm, inviting

Molly also included black for text and white for background color and accents.

Next, Molly worked with typefaces. She wanted to ensure that information was readable and basic but still had a fun, bold appearance.

Type Family	Typeface	Expression/Use
Sans serif	Helvetica Bold	Thick, clean typeface for headers
Sans serif	Helvetica	Standard weight for sub-headers
Serif	Times Roman	Common, cross-platform serif font good for body text

Molly then examined the way to approach graphic accents. She decided that flat patches of bright color would give the site its visual impact. Playing off of that, she used color photos and spot art. She employed JavaScript mouseover animation for navigation, using a fiery design with a lot of movement to add excitement and vivacity to the pages (see Figure 32.5)

FIGURE 32.5

Mouseover buttons in static and over states

 NOTE For more information about adding JavaScript to a page, see Chapter 30.

Preparing for Technology

Technology plays an important role in large-scale sites. Molly's example uses the following:

JavaScript   A JavaScript mouseover effect is used for navigation.

Feedback Form   Molly uses a standard set of feedback forms so individuals can get more information or write personal letters.

TIP   To learn more about working with forms, see Chapter 14, *Making Interactive Pages with Forms*, and Chapter 25, *Understanding CGI*.

Site Search   Because of the scope of the site, Molly used a Web site search. This will allow people to enter a keyword and find information on the site.

It's important to know that aside from commonly used technologies like these, large sites will often place large demands on back-end technologies including:

Active Server Pages   APS helps keep a site dynamic and helps Webmasters manage updates and interactive aspects on a site. ASP is a natural extension of FrontPage, as it is a Microsoft product and is well integrated into Microsoft's suite of Web-server and -design applications. (For more an ASP, see Chapter 26, *Using Active Server Pages*.)

Common Gateway Interface   CGI programming is extremely helpful when managing large amounts of data. It can help manage updates and interactivity on a site as well as perform a wide range of Webmaster functions. (For more on CGI, see Chapter 25.)

Databases   Databases help Web developers store, retrieve, and manage all kinds of information about a site. Databases can help developers search, track site visitors, archive information, and enable electronic commerce events on a site. (For more on databases, see Chapter 27, *Databases in Detail*.)

Advertising banners   FrontPage has an Ad Banner rotator, which can be used to handle advertising on a large site. Other advertising methods are available, too. (Check out Chapter 24, *Site Maintenance and Promotion*, to learn more about advertising-related techniques.)

No matter the technology you choose, large sites are demanding! You'll want to take special care in the planning stages that you think clearly about what you want to do with your site so that you can make good selections when it comes to technology.

TIP   You'll always be matching site intent, audience, and site goals with budget and availability. Be sure to research your options before settling on options that might be too time consuming for your resources, or too under budget for your true needs.

Production

As in the previous three chapters in this part of the book, we're going to walk through aspects of the large-scale site. First, Molly creates the design using her image editor, and then she moves on to FrontPage itself, where, using a combination of wizards and templates, she gets the large-scale site going.

Laying Out the Pages

As with the community site in the previous chapter, Molly decided not to use a splash page for this site. She felt that a personality- and information-oriented site should have a sense of immediacy—people can get to the information and interaction they want without a progression of visual and navigational information. So, the first page she designed is her welcome page.

To lay out your welcome page:

1. In your image editor, select File ➢ New. The New dialog box appears.

2. Create an image size that is 595 pixels wide by 600 pixels high.

3. Click OK. You will now have your work area set to the first layer.

4. To this layer, add your background color. Molly selected white (see color chart earlier in this chapter).

5. Create a new layer by selecting Layer ➢ New ➢ Layer. Here, you'll add the areas of color and shape to create the unusual feel. Molly built the arcs using Adobe Illustrator (see Chapter 18, *Working with Professional Graphics Programs*), a vector-based drawing tool, and then imported them into Photoshop to be optimized.

6. On subsequent layers, add the page title, navigation, and sub-headers.

7. Once you've added all the elements you want for this page, save the file by selecting File ➢ Save As. The Save As dialog box appears. Name the file and save it in the native layer format of your imaging program.

Figure 32.6 shows the completed welcome page design.

FIGURE 32.6

The completed welcome page layout

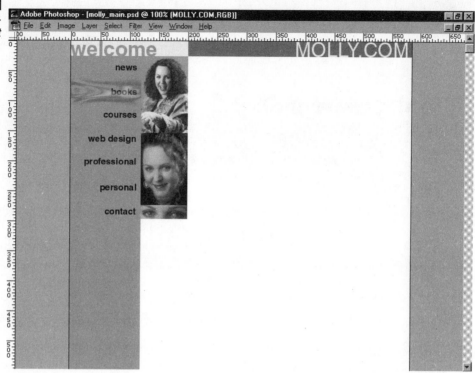

You'll need to repeat this process for each and every page you've designed for the site. To generate the actual graphics for your site, move back to your imaging program and follow these steps:

1. Open up the layered file in your imaging program.

2. Highlight the layer that has the image you want to process.

3. Using the marquee or selection tool (it will vary depending upon your program), draw a selection around the part of the image you want to keep, making sure you're on the correct layer.

4. Copy and paste the section into a new file.

5. Optimize the file as a GIF or JPEG, depending upon the graphic.

6. Name the graphic and save it directly to the images folder within your FrontPage web.

Repeat the process for all of the buttons, headers, backgrounds, and spot art that you'll require.

NOTE For detailed help optimizing and working with graphics, see Chapter 9, *Designing Graphics for the Web*, and Chapter 18, *Working with Professional Graphics Programs*.

Working with FrontPage

As mentioned earlier, with very large Web sites, you may find yourself using a range of development tools. Chapter 28 discussed how designers and content managers can use FrontPage in tandem with other team members to develop and maintain large sites. For the purposes of this chapter, we're going to use FrontPage to set up the site prototype. Depending upon how large a given site is, other members might use Front-Page, Visual InterDev, or other development tools to design and manage the site.

In the prototype for her site, Molly began by setting up a single-page Web and then added folders and files by hand. This gives her the ability to first demonstrate if the site looks good and behaves well. Eventually she'll set up a more detailed series of directories. For example, all of the sections discussed earlier will likely have their own directories, and it's possible that these directories will have sub-directories, and so forth.

 NOTE When beginning to build your prototype, always look to your site structure in order to include all of the various aspects of your site.

To set up the web:

1. Select File ➤ New ➤ Web. The New dialog box appears.

2. Highlight One Page Web and click OK. FrontPage will create the necessary FrontPage directory and images directory, and open up a blank, untitled page within the root directory so you can begin working.

Once FrontPage is finished building the web, you'll want to add folders and files as necessary. Molly used the root directory for top-tier HTML pages, but created sub-directories for the data that will go into those areas. She'll have one images directory for all graphics.

To set up individual files in your root directory:

1. In Folders view (see Figure 32.7), right-click anywhere in the interface. A menu appears.

2. Select New Folder.

3. A new folder appears in the root directory. Name this folder accordingly.

4. Repeat the process until you have created all the pages planned for the site, using the chart prepared in the planning phase as a guide. You can always add or delete pages as necessary.

FIGURE 32.7

Using Folders view to add individual site folders

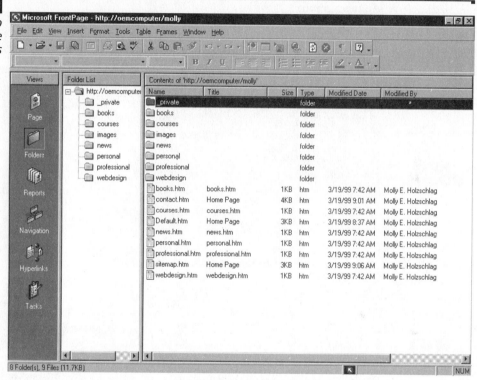

Your next step is to set up individual pages. To do so:

1. In Folders view, right-click anywhere in the interface. A menu appears.

2. Select New Page.

3. A new page appears in the root directory. Name this page **default.htm**.

4. Repeat the process until you have created all the pages planned for the site, using the chart prepared in the planning phase as a guide. You can always add or delete pages as necessary.

At this point, you'll want to get organized and allow FrontPage to help you manage the various production steps you'll be following. To set up tasks:

1. In Folders view, highlight the file you want to associate with a task.

2. Right-click and choose Add Task from the menu.

3. The New Task dialog box appears. Fill in the task name, priority, and a description.

4. Click OK.

You can also set up tasks that are not associated with a page. To do so:

1. Select Tasks view and right-click anywhere in the FrontPage interface. A menu appears.

2. Select New Task. The New Task dialog box opens.

3. Fill in the task name, the task priority, and a description.

In a large-scale site scenario, Task view is your friend! While this view is helpful in any site's development, it is invaluable when managing large sites. Task view can help you keep track of the project and allow different people to work on the project, start and stop at specific tasks, and even leave detailed messages for other team members as to the status of a given task.

Creating the Welcome Page in FrontPage

The welcome page of any site is a critical one. It sets the tone for the entire site and gives people an idea of what's to come. We'll begin by laying out the welcome page. Typically, tables are going to be needed to lay out most pages.

To build your tables, begin with vertical columns, only adding rows where necessary. Be sure to revisit Chapter 11, *Using Tables for Advanced Layout*, for more information.

With your table in mind, follow these steps to set up your grid for the page's layout:

1. With the page open in Page view, select Insert ➤ Table. The Insert Table dialog box appears.

2. Enter the number of rows in the Rows text box.

3. Enter the number of columns in the Columns text box.

4. In the Layout section, choose an alignment for your table. Typically, left alignment will be used.

5. Set the Border, Cell Padding, and Cell Spacing to 0.

6. Check the Specify Width box.

7. Add a numeric value for fixed-width tables and a percentage for dynamic. In Molly's example, she wanted to fix the width so that all the content including images and graphics is neatly managed. She entered a total width of 595 pixels.

8. Click OK. The table appears on your page. If you need to stack or nest a table, go ahead and draw those tables as well (see Chapter 11).

9. Add images and text using the techniques you learned in related chapters of this book to refine the page's look. Be sure to adjust table and table cell properties where necessary (see Chapter 11).

10. When you're finished adding images and text, save the page. You can preview it externally, or internally using the Preview tab to see how the page will appear.

Continue adding pages in this fashion until you've completed the full content of your site.

In Figure 32.8, you can see the page grids we've set up using FrontPage's table building tools.

FIGURE 32.8

Table grid in FrontPage

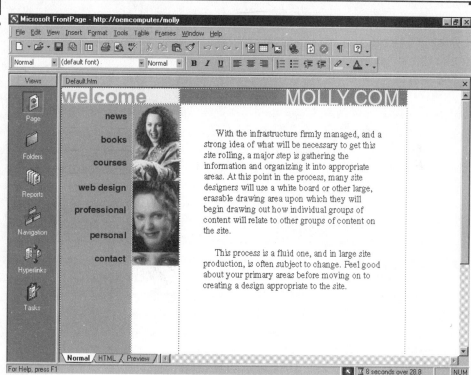

Creating and Customizing a Site Map

The easiest way to do this using FrontPage is to put the Table of Contents template to work for you. The template not only makes life easier for you by providing you with a simple but effective outline, but it is also structured so that it will automatically update any pages added to the site if you are using FrontPage extensions.

To use the Table of Contents template:

1. With your Web open in Page view, select File ➤ New ➤ Page. The New dialog box appears.

2. Find the Table of Contents template and highlight it by clicking it once (see Figure 32.9).

3. Click OK. The Table of Contents page appears.

FIGURE 32.9

Highlighting the Table of Contents template

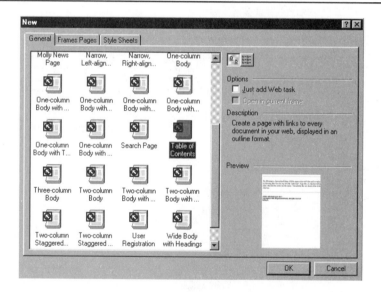

Now, let's tap in to the automatic updating power of the Table of Contents template. To customize the Table of Contents page to meet your individual needs:

1. Add background and link colors to the page.

2. Add any tables or design features to match the layout of the page.

3. Customize the comments within the page by simply highlighting the text you want to change and typing in the new text.

4. Save your file to the web.

NOTE Your Table of Contents page relies on FrontPage extensions to supply the information to the page. You'll need to publish the page in order for the Table of Contents to display with the appropriate information.

Adding a Feedback Page

If you've planned a Contact page for people to use as a method of getting in touch, you'll want to create it using the Feedback Form template. To do so:

1. With your Web open in Page view, select File ➤ New ➤ Page. The New dialog box appears.

2. Find the Feedback Form template and highlight it by clicking it once.

3. Click OK. The Feedback page appears.

Molly wanted her Form to match her design rather than the prefabricated look that FrontPage uses, so she customized the form using her own colors and graphics.

To do this:

1. With the feedback template open in Page view, add the background and link colors to the page.

2. Delete the comment and horizontal rule from the top.

3. Add any tables or graphic headers to your page.

4. Customize the comments within the form field. Simply click within the field where you'd like to change the text and type in the new text.

5. If you'd like to change the text on the form buttons, simply right-click the button. From the menu that appears, choose Form Field Properties. The Push Button Properties dialog box appears.

6. In the Value/label text box, type in the word or words you'd like to have appear on the button.

7. Click OK. Repeat the process for the Reset button if you'd like to change that, too.

8. Customize any remaining text on the page.

9. Save your file to the web with the appropriate filename.

Your results should be similar to those in Figure 32.10.

FIGURE 32.10

A customized feedback form

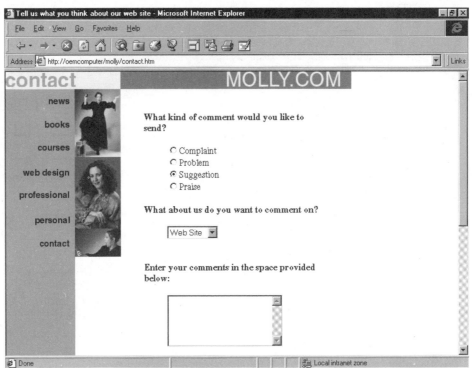

FIGURE 32.10

A customized feedback form

 NOTE Just a reminder! Have you marked off your tasks? If not, and you are confident the work for a given task is finished, go into Tasks view and mark the task as complete.

Preparing Your Site for Publication

Now that you've figured out all of the logistics and have everything from planning to design completed, it's time to prepare your site for production. This process, which includes spell checking your pages, looking for and repairing broken links, and ensuring that your site is cross-browser compatible, is discussed at length in Chapter 29.

Managing Growth

A critical issue with large publications is how to successfully and easily manage growth. This relates to the swell of content on your site, as well as to the growth in interest that your site can generate.

Managing your growth involves looking carefully at what you have today, what you're planning to have tomorrow, and what you'll need to accommodate down the road. You want to think about archiving articles and keeping that information readily available by linking to it from current articles of interest.

It's helpful to organize your growth plans into current, past, and future areas. For example:

Current: News	Past: Archived News	Future: Upcoming Events
Recent book	All books	Books to be published and planned books
Design feature and site of the week	All articles and sites	Upcoming sites and planned design projects
Current course list	All courses, student gallery, relevant course materials	Planned courses and related materials
Up-to-date resume and publicity information	Archived press releases and publicity	Planned area for new professional items of interest
Personal bio, creative writing, photos	Essays, poems, songs, and photos	New writing and photos

This table will be very valuable as your site expands. You can refer to it and modify it as necessary. Using it as a guide, decisions as to what you need to accommodate all of your current and past information, as well as how to manage future additions to the site, can be assessed.

Up Next: Your Future

As you've worked through this book, the exercises and knowledge have become increasingly complex. You've gained a solid base of FrontPage skills and have become aware of the wide range of technologies that are available to you.

Assessing your own needs is going to help you look to your future with FrontPage. If you're involved in the creation of an ongoing personal project, FrontPage will be an extremely valuable tool. Small businesses will benefit from using FrontPage to create and update sites. Communities can be built and maintained with FrontPage, and even large-scale, team-based sites can benefit from the prototyping power of the application.

But are you sticking with the program for all your needs, or are you examining a future in Web development? For those of you who are or who want to become professional developers, there's a lot of information yet to be learned. It will help a great deal to define your own interest and desired role in the Web design world. Here's an overview of the variety of positions available to those interested in pursuing professional design options, and a rundown of the skills you might consider researching in order to achieve your goals.

Web Project Manager   If you want to manage Web projects, you'll need to know at least a little about a whole lot of Web-related technologies. Having a good foundation in management, human resources, and information technology is essential. Then, you'll want to know a bit about all aspects of Web development—applications such as FrontPage and Visual InterDev, Photoshop, and backend technologies such as ASP, as well as general concepts involving site structure and user interface design.

Web Content Developer   A Web content developer is responsible for the collection and creation of Web site content. Typically, a content developer has a background in writing, with excellent communication skills, editorial knowledge, and an awareness of what kind of content works well on the Web. Content developers will need to be familiar with a variety of applications and technologies, including HTML, FrontPage, Word, and other members of the Microsoft Office suite.

Web Graphic Designer   Typically, the Web graphic designer will have a serious background in design. He or she will have studied the elements of design such as space, shape, typography, and color. The Web graphic designer also will be versed in multimedia development and have a good understanding of how to create useable, attractive, and appropriate visual interfaces. Graphic designers will be proficient in a range of design-oriented applications including Photoshop, Illustrator, and broad-spectrum utilities and tools related to Web imaging.

Web Programmer   Web programmers are interested in multiple languages. The Web programmer is fluent in HTML and aware of trends and standards. He or she will be familiar with a variety of technologies related to programming including JavaScript, Perl, CGI, and ASP, and will probably have a good understanding of various operating systems. Applications of interest to the programmer will include Visual InterDev and Visual Studio when working from the Microsoft family of software.

Web Database Engineer   A database engineer is not only skilled with a range of database types, but is likely to be a skilled programmer, employing C, C++, Perl, Java, JavaScript, Visual Basic, and VBScript in his or her daily tasks.

Systems Administrator   If you're interested in operating and maintaining Web servers and Internet systems, you'll undoubtedly want strong familiarity with operating systems and related server software. Networking, from the standpoint of both hardware and software, will be the heart-and-soul of your work.

Obviously, the Web profession has grown from a fairly simple, one-person operation to a wide and deep field with numerous specialties. However, there are many opportunities, and if you have been inspired by this book to pursue Web development as a serious career, we are certain you will find an area of interest that is both suitable and personally gratifying.

 MASTERING WHAT'S ONLINE

Certification

If you're interested in pursuing certification in any of these Web design fields, visit Microsoft's Training and Certification Web site at www.microsoft.com/train_cert/.

PART

VI

Step-by-Step
FrontPage Sites

Appendices

- *Customizing FrontPage 2000*

- *Setting up Web servers*

- *FrontPage Server Extensions*

- *Installing and testing network connections*

- *HTML Reference*

APPENDIX <u>A</u>

Customizing
FrontPage 2000

S ince Microsoft FrontPage is now shipped as part of Microsoft Office 2000, it's possible that you are installing it either as part of the entire Microsoft Office package or as a stand-alone program. In either instance, the program installs quite easily—and on its own—unless you decide to make custom decisions about install. These decisions are typically for advanced users. We recommend you follow the instructions that come with your version of FrontPage 2000.

Once you've installed FrontPage on your computer, you probably want to get started right away. But wait! You can customize FrontPage to make it better suit your needs. For example, you can modify general settings to control the overall way FrontPage works, modify proxy settings to allow FrontPage to work along with a proxy server on your local area network, and modify settings to allow you to integrate other programs into the FrontPage environment.

To set these options, you must have FrontPage running. If FrontPage is not running, start it now. From the Windows taskbar, select Start ➢ Programs ➢ Microsoft FrontPage. FrontPage starts and its title window appears.

You can continue setting FrontPage options by following the steps outlined in the next sections.

General Customization

You can set a number of general FrontPage options, including options for modifying the interface, receiving warnings when your content needs updating, and receiving warnings when you apply a theme such that permanent changes throughout your site will occur. (You need not opt to set all of these; pick and choose, as you prefer.) Here's how:

1. From the FrontPage menu bar, select Tools ➢ Options. The Options dialog box appears, as shown in Figure A.1.

2. Click the General Tab. The contents of the dialog box change to reflect your choice.

3. In the dialog box, you can control the following options by clicking the appropriate checkboxes:

   - Open Last Web Automatically When FrontPage Starts allows you to decide whether FrontPage will automatically start exactly where you left off.

   - Check If Office Is The Default Editor For Pages Created In Office determines which Office program created the page and whether it should be used to continue editing the page.

   - Check If FrontPage Is The Default Editor For Pages checks to see if FrontPage is the appropriate editor for Web pages.

FIGURE A.1

*The FrontPage Options
dialog box: your door
to customizing
FrontPage*

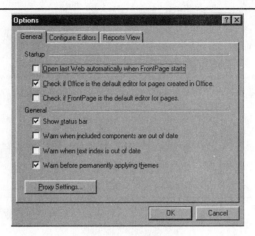

- Show Status Bar allows you to customize the interface to include the helpful status bar along the bottom of FrontPage, or to remove it to maximize your space.
- Warn When Included Components Are Out Of Date controls whether a warning appears when you open a page that includes out-of-date content.
- Warn When Text Index Is Out Of Date controls whether a warning appears when you open a page that includes out-of-date links.
- Warn Before Permanently Applying Themes controls whether a warning appears when you attempt to apply a theme that makes permanent changes.

You can turn any of these options on or off by clicking its checkbox.

4. Once you have made your selections, click OK. The dialog box closes and Front-Page window reappears.

The changes you just made take effect immediately. To continue setting other options, read on.

Configuring FrontPage 2000 for Your Proxy Server

If your computer is on a local area network (LAN) that requires you to use a proxy server to access the Internet, you'll have to configure FrontPage to accommodate this. You can complete this process in a few short minutes.

TIP You need to enter proxy information *only* if your computer is on a network that uses a proxy server *and* you are going to be publishing FrontPage webs to Web servers that are not part of your LAN.

1. From the FrontPage menu bar, select Tools ➤ Options. The Options dialog box appears.
2. Click the Proxies button. The Internet Properties dialog box appears, as shown in Figure A.2.

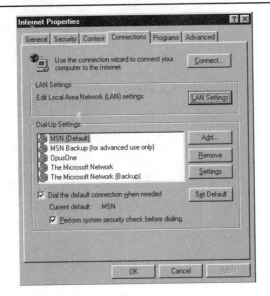

3. All of the connections available to you appear within this dialog box. If you want to enter a new proxy server, click LAN Settings. Click the Use A Proxy Server checkbox, and type the server location (you can get this from your system administrator).
4. For advanced configurations, click the Advanced tab. (For example, if you commonly access machines on your local network and do not want to list them, add those servers in the Exceptions text box.)
5. When you're done, close all open dialog boxes and the FrontPage window reappears.

The changes you made take effect immediately. FrontPage is now set up to use your network's proxy server and is able to access computers on your local network as well as on the Internet.

Configuring FrontPage 2000 to Use Other Editors

FrontPage allows you to customize which editors will be used to edit different types of files. This is very handy if you want to edit JPEG files with PhotoShop, for example, instead of with Microsoft Image Composer. To change the editor that's associated with a specific type of file, just follow these instructions:

1. From the FrontPage menu bar, select Tools ➢ Options. The Options dialog box appears.

2. Click the Configure Editors tab. The contents of the dialog box change to reflect your choice (see Figure A.3).

FIGURE A.3

You can easily specify which editor will be used to edit different types of files.

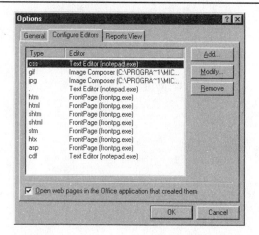

3. In the dialog box's list of file types, highlight the file type you want to work with (JPEG images, for example). Click the Modify button. The Modify Editor Association dialog box appears. Or, if you don't see the file type for which you want to specify an editor, click the Add button. The Add Editor Association dialog box appears.

4. Regardless of whether you are modifying an existing association or creating a new one, a dialog box similar to the one displayed in Figure A.4 appears. Fill in or modify the following text boxes as appropriate:

- File Type is the file extension for the type of file you wish to edit.
- Editor Name is the name of the editor you are setting up.
- Command is the command to start the editor you are setting up.

FIGURE A.4

The Add Editor Association dialog box

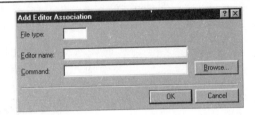

5. Once you have filled in the above information, click OK. The dialog box closes and the FrontPage window reappears.

The next time you edit a file of the type you just changed, the editor you specified will be used.

Now you have FrontPage 2000 all set up the way you like it. Turn to Chapter 1, *Introduction to Web Design*, to begin the experience of creating, editing, and managing Web pages and entire Web sites.

APPENDIX **B**

Setting Up Web Servers

You are probably running FrontPage either on a stand-alone machine with a dial-up connection (via modem) or on a machine that's part of a corporate network (which implies that a firewall is involved). In the first case, your connection is neither powerful enough nor round-the-clock enough for a real Web server; in the other case, the firewall poses security issues that make it impractical for your machine to function as a real Web server.

 NOTE To run a publicly accessible Web server, you need to dedicate a powerful machine with a high-speed Internet connection (a T1 line) to that purpose. That means you have to post the live, publicly accessible site to such a dedicated server at your ISP or at your company, if your company hosts its own Web server.

FrontPage is designed to work as an authoring tool in tandem with different types of Web servers. To address your local needs, you'll want to set up the Personal Web Server that is automatically offered with FrontPage 2000 to help make the process of building Web sites and/or pages easy. Having the server running on your machine will also, by the way, allow you to offer access to your FrontPage Web site to others on the same local network. You can use the server for a small intranet, or allow workgroups to access the site and work on different parts of it. Just don't expect to make it into a viable public Web server.

 WARNING It is possible for other people on the Internet to access data on your computer using the Web server that is installed on your machine along with FrontPage 2000. To minimize the likelihood of this happening, limit and closely guard access to the Web server using the procedures outlined in Chapter 24, *Site Maintenance and Promotion*.

However, if you want maximum power for full-fledged intranet or Internet server support with FrontPage, you'll want to use a suitable server, such as the Microsoft Peer Web Server.

Using Peer Web Services for Windows NT

If you plan on reaching beyond developing your webs for local use and offering them to others across a private intranet, or even right on the Internet itself, you'll need a much more powerful server. Microsoft Peer Web Services is a stripped-down version of Microsoft's workhorse Web server (Internet Information Server) for Windows NT Server. As you may know, Windows NT actually comes in two flavors: NT Workstation is the more user-oriented, desktop operating system, while NT Server is designed to act as a network server.

Microsoft Peer Web Services (which works with NT Workstation) allows you to build sites on your local machine using FrontPage 2000. It can also act as a fully functional Web server. In this section, we'll talk about Microsoft Peer Web Services and how you can configure and use its features.

TIP Windows NT Server comes with Internet Information Server (IIS), which is a full-scale Web server you can use to host your Web site. If by chance you are running Windows NT Server on your computer rather than NT Workstation, go ahead and use IIS as your server software for developing webs with FrontPage.

MASTERING WHAT'S ONLINE

You can learn all about Microsoft's heavy-duty Web server, Internet Information Server, at www.microsoft.com/iis.

Microsoft Peer Web Services is very powerful; combined with the reliability of Windows NT Workstation, it actually affords you the *oomph* to host a public Web site on your machine. Of course, you'd still have to have a high-speed connection, and you pretty much have to hand over your machine to the serving of your site, but it is an option given the power of the server software we're describing here.

Microsoft Peer Web Services is also more than just a Web server; it actually consists of *three* Internet servers: the Web server, an FTP server, and a Gopher server. We'll discuss in depth the first two types of servers. But because Gopher has been almost totally eclipsed by the Web, we're going to skip that one.

Starting and Stopping Servers

A server, like any other program, can be running or not running, although they generally run all the time. (There are exceptions to this, but don't worry about them now.) You do have to start a server up, and you may want to stop one sometimes, for maintenance or some other reason. You can start and stop any of the three Microsoft Peer Web Services servers (the Web, FTP, or Gopher server) by following these steps:

1. From the Windows taskbar, select Start ➢ Programs ➢ Microsoft Peer Web Services ➢ Internet Service Manager. The Microsoft Internet Service Manager window appears.

2. In this window, you'll see a list of the Internet services provided by Peer Web Services: WWW, Gopher, and FTP. To the right of the Service list is the State column, which shows the current "state" of the service: Running, Stopped, or Paused. Highlight the service whose state you want to change.

3. With that service highlighted, from the window's menu bar, select one of the following:

Select This	To Do This
Properties ➢ Start Service	To start the highlighted server
Properties ➢ Stop Service	To stop the highlighted server
Properties ➢ Pause Service	To pause the highlighted server

The change you make takes effect and appears immediately in the State column.

Configuring the Web Server

You can control a number of aspects of the Peer Web Services Web server, including which port the Web server listens to and the number of simultaneous connections that the server will handle.

Web Server Settings

To configure the Peer Web Services Web server, follow these steps:

1. With the Microsoft Internet Service Manager window still open, double-click the entry for WWW. The WWW Service Properties dialog box appears.

2. In the TCP Port text box, you can change the port number the Web server listens to. This option is used to host multiple sites on a single server when that is necessary. The standard port for Web servers is 80, so you should leave this alone unless you have a good reason to change it and know what you're up to.

TIP Changing the port number will affect the URL used to access material shared with the Web server. For example, if you change the port number from the default of 80 to 8080, you'll have to add :8080 to the URL (after your machine's name) used to access the server.

3. In the Connection Timeout text box, you can change the *timeout*—or how long the server will wait for a Web browser to receive a file. The default value of 900 seconds is a perfectly good choice. If people access your machine's Web server over a very slow connection, then increasing this value will increase the number of files the server can successfully serve. On the other hand, a large timeout number means your computer has to work harder and can slow down the whole process of serving Web pages (not to mention anything else you're doing with it while you're running FrontPage).

4. Each file request made of the Web server uses memory and can slow down the computer. To limit the number of files that can be requested at one time (and thus speed up the serving of that number of files), in the Maximum Connections text box, enter the maximum number of connections your machine should handle at once. Once the server is handling the maximum number of requests that you specify, all additional requests will be refused. (Those people will generally know to come back at a less busy time.)

5. The Anonymous Logon section of the dialog box includes Username and Password text boxes, which are used to control access to the local machine. When Peer Web Services was installed, it created a default user on the machine and called that user IUSR_*machine*, where *machine* is the name of the computer on which you installed Peer Web Services. If you want Peer Web Services to use a different username and password than the default to access the local machine, type the preferred username and password into the appropriate text boxes here.

 TIP Having an easily identifiable username or password is generally a bad idea—it opens up a security hole as big as leaving the keys in your car. This is especially true if your machine is accessible from the public Internet. (Then it's like leaving the door unlocked, too!) If your machine is on the Internet, for heaven's sake, create a unique username and apply it as described in step 5.

APP

B

Setting Up
Web Servers

6. You can control the method by which the server will *authenticate*—or identify—users who access content on the server. Your choices are described below:

- Allow Anonymous lets users access content without identifying themselves.

- Basic (Clear Text) allows users to identify themselves using a nonsecure password mechanism. This is supported by all Web browsers.

- Windows NT Challenge/Response allows users to identify themselves based on the username they used to log into the Windows NT network. This is the most secure method to identify users, but it only works when they're using Internet Explorer and they are logged into the local network.

7. Finally, in the Comment text box, you can type a comment—usually something that describes the machine on which the server is running. The description you enter here will appear in the Microsoft Internet Service Manager window's Comments column.

 NOTE Comments can be very handy if you have to administer multiple servers running on multiple machines. It's quite possible to view and configure all of the servers running on different machines from one copy of Microsoft Internet Service Manager, and through the use of comments, you can distinguish among those different computers quickly.

8. Having changed what you must in the WWW Service Properties dialog box, click OK. The dialog box closes and the Microsoft Internet Service Manager window reappears. The changes you made take effect immediately.

Sharing Folders with the Web Server

Once you have Peer Web Services' Web server running, you can publish any folder on your machine, making it available to other users via their Web browsers.

To publish a folder, follow these steps:

1. With the Microsoft Internet Service Manager window open, double-click the entry for the WWW service. The WWW Service Properties dialog box appears.

2. Click the Directories tab. The contents of the dialog box change to reflect your choice.

3. The Directories tab displays a list of all of the folders on your computer that are accessible from the Web server, along with the *alias* (or URL) used to access them. To add a new folder to those available, click the Add button. The Directory Properties dialog box appears.

4. In the Directory Properties dialog box's Directory text box, type the path for the folder you wish to share. For example, to make the folder C:\HOME available, type **C:\Home**.

 TIP If you want this folder to correspond to your server's root directory, click the Home Directory button and skip ahead to step 6.

5. Click the Virtual Directory button and, in the Alias text box, type the URL that should be used to access the folder.

6. To restrict the type of access allowed to the folder to read-only, click the Read button. Also, if the folder contains ASP scripts, click the Execute button.

7. Click OK. The dialog box closes and the WWW Service Properties dialog box reappears, with a new entry in the dialog box for the folder you just shared. You're almost done sharing the folder—you have two more options to set.

8. In the list box, locate and highlight the entry for the folder you just shared. (The list is alphabetical.)

9. The server is able to serve a *default document* or file when the folder is requested. If you'd like a file to be served even when no individual file is specified, click the Enable Default Document checkbox, and, in the Default Document text box, type the name of that file. The default filename is default.htm and, unless you know what you're doing, you should leave this alone.

10. When a user accesses a URL that points to a directory (as opposed to a specific file), if the directory does not contain a default file, the user should be notified; you, the Webmaster, can choose whether this notification will be via an error message or via the appearance of a directory listing. To enable directory listings, click the checkbox labeled Directory Browsing Allowed. Otherwise, an error message will appear.

11. Click OK. The WWW Service Properties dialog box closes and the Microsoft Internet Service Manager window reappears.

The changes you made take effect immediately. If one of the changes was to share a folder (for example, C:\HOME as MyHome), you can check your work by using a Web browser on your local machine to load http://localhost/MyHome; you'll see a list of files in the folder.

APP

B

Setting Up
Web Servers

Stopping the Sharing of a Folder

So, what do you do if you want to *stop* using the Web server to share a folder on your machine? Well, that's easy enough. Just follow these steps:

1. In the Microsoft Internet Service Manager window, double-click the WWW entry. The WWW Service Properties dialog box appears.

2. Click the Directories tab. The contents of the dialog box change to reflect your choice.

3. In the list of folders, highlight the folder you no longer want to share.

4. Click the Remove button. The highlighted folder will be removed from the list of shared folders.

5. Click OK. The WWW Service Properties dialog box closes and the Microsoft Internet Service Manager window reappears. The change you made takes effect immediately.

 NOTE Peer Web Services also includes a Gopher server. Gopher is a protocol used to distribute documents—text files and graphics, for example—over the Internet. It was very popular before the Web overshadowed it; now Gophers are scarcer than the Moa bird.

Configuring the FTP Server

Microsoft Peer Web Services also provides an FTP server. This server works with an FTP program to allow the transfer of files to and from your computer.

FTP Server Settings

To set options for the FTP server, follow these steps:

1. With the Microsoft Internet Service Manager window still open, double-click the entry for FTP. The FTP Service Properties dialog box appears.

 WARNING Although you can change the port used by the FTP server, doing so will only cause you trouble. Port 21 is the universally used port for this service. If you feel weirdly compelled to change the port number, well, don't say we didn't warn you.

2. In the Maximum Connections text box, enter the maximum number of connections the FTP server should handle at one time. Again, this allows you to limit the number of people who access data on your server at one time and can help improve the machine's performance.

3. To allow that mainstay of "anonymous FTP," *anonymous connections* (that is, to allow access to people without accounts on your local machine), click the checkbox labeled Allow Anonymous Connections.

4. If you are allowing anonymous connections, you have to specify a username and password the server will recognize when the anonymous connection occurs. This username and password can be the same ones used by the Web and Gopher servers; for expediency's sake, they should be the same ones you specified when you installed the server. (Don't go making up new ones.) Type the username and password in the appropriate text boxes.

5. If you want to allow *anonymous FTP* only to the machine (in other words, you want people who actually do have accounts on the machine not to be able to use their own usernames and passwords to access the machine), click the checkbox labeled Allow Only Anonymous Connections. (You actually may want to require people with accounts on the machine to use their own usernames and passwords so you'll know who's who and who's done what, but if it doesn't matter to you, use the anonymous FTP option.)

6. In the Comment text box, you can type a descriptive comment—usually this will be something that describes the server machine. This description will appear in the Microsoft Internet Service Manager window's Comments column.

7. Click OK. The dialog box closes and the Microsoft Internet Service Manager window reappears. The changes you made take effect immediately.

Setting a Welcome Message

When a user connects to an FTP server using an FTP program, a message appears; usually the message conveys information about the company or organization that runs the FTP server. Sometimes, it includes legalese that restricts the use of the FTP site. You can determine what this message will say by following these steps:

1. In the Microsoft Internet Service Manager window, double-click the entry for the FTP server. The FTP Service Properties dialog box appears.

2. Click the Messages tab. The contents of the dialog box change to reflect your choice.

3. In the Welcome Message text box, type the welcome message you prefer.

4. In the Exit Message text box, type a farewell message; it will appear when a user ends the FTP connection.

5. In the Maximum Connections Message text box, type a message that will appear to warn users that the FTP server is already servicing the maximum number of simultaneous users. (You might want this message to suggest that they come back in a while.)

6. Click OK. The dialog box closes and the Microsoft Internet Service Manager window reappears.

The changes you made take effect immediately, though you won't see any evidence of that unless you test the FTP server using an FTP transfer.

Sharing Folders with the FTP Server

Sharing folders via the FTP server is very much like sharing folders via the Web server. To share a folder, follow these simple steps:

1. With the Microsoft Internet Service Manager window open, double-click the entry for the FTP service. The FTP Service Properties dialog box appears.

2. Click the Directories tab. The contents of the dialog box change to reflect your choice.

3. Click the Add button. The Directory Properties dialog box appears.

4. In the Directory text box, type the path for the folder you plan to share. For example, to share the folder C:\PROJECT\FILES, type **C:\PROJECT\FILES**.

5. Click the Virtual Directorybutton, and in the Alias text box, type the path that should be used to access the folder. For example, if you want users to access the folder you are sharing as \PROJECTFILES, type **\PROJECTFILES** here.

6. You can control the type of access allowed to the folder. Your options are:

   - Read to allow read access, which allows people to download files from the folder

   - Write to allow write access, which also allows them to change the contents of the folder

   Or you can select both, which allows people to have total access.

7. Click OK. The FTP Service Properties dialog box reappears. The folder you elected to share is now visible in the list of shared directories.

8. Click OK to close the FTP Service Properties dialog box and return to the Microsoft Internet Service Manager window.

The folder you just shared will be available via the FTP server immediately.

Stopping the Sharing of a Folder

So, you say you've had enough of sharing and want to keep things to yourself now? You can stop sharing a folder on your FTP server easily. Follow these steps:

1. In the Microsoft Internet Service Manager window, double-click the entry for the FTP server. The FTP Service Properties dialog box appears.

2. Click the Directories tab. The contents of the dialog box change to reflect your choice.

3. Click the Remove button. The highlighted folder is removed from the list of shared directories.

4. Click OK. The FTP Service Properties dialog box closes and the Microsoft Internet Services Manager window reappears.

The changes you made take effect immediately. The folder will no longer be available via the FTP server.

Logging Access to the Servers

The final area of Peer Web Services that deserves your attention is *logging*. Logging is the process of recording all requests the server receives. These can include requests for a Web page, requests to upload a file via FTP, or requests to view files via Gopher. Although each Peer Web Services server maintains its own log files, configuring the options you have for each is the same, so we'll cover all of 'em right here in one fell swoop. Follow these steps:

1. In the Microsoft Internet Service Manager window, double-click the entry of the server to be configured. The Properties dialog box for the chosen service appears.

2. Click the Logging tab. The contents of the dialog box change to reflect your choice.

3. To enable logging, click the Enable Logging button.

 TIP You can totally disable logging by deselecting the Enable Logging button and clicking OK to close the dialog box. This stops all logging on your machine.

4. In the Log Format drop-down list, you can choose a format for the log files. If you are using special third-party software to analyze your log files, select the format required by that software. (The software's documentation or its tech support

folks will tell you which choice to make.) Otherwise, leave this option set to Standard Format.

5. You can use a single log file forever—it will grow longer and longer as time marches on—or you can specify that new log files will open at predetermined intervals of time. To have new logs files start at predetermined intervals, click the checkbox labeled Automatically Open New Log and then click one of these buttons:

- Daily to start a new log file at the beginning of each day.
- Weekly to start a new log file at the beginning of each week.
- Monthly to start a new log file at the beginning of each month.
- When File Size Reaches to start a new log file when the current log file reaches the specified size. (You should enter the size at which you want a new file to start into the supplied text box.)

6. In the text box labeled Log File Directory, type the path of the folder in which the log file should be created, or accept the default folder of `C:\WINNT\ SYSTEM32\LOGFILES`.

7. Click OK. The dialog box closes and you are returned to the Properties dialog box. Although you won't be able to see any visible sign of it, the changes you made take effect immediately.

You can now, at last, close the Microsoft Internet Services window and return to the Windows Desktop. To do so, from the menu bar, select Properties ➢ Exit, and you'll be on your way.

APPENDIX C

The FrontPage
Server Extensions

FrontPage asks a lot more of Web servers than most other HTML authoring tools do. FrontPage lets you upload and download files to and from Web servers directly instead of FTPing around; it also lets you incorporate active elements such as discussion groups, indexes, and search pages into a Web page instead of just standard HTML. This sort of thing goes well beyond what most Web servers are created to handle; because of this, the Web server on which the site resides needs special *extensions* or programs that extend its capabilities. That's where the FrontPage Server Extensions come in. They add to almost any Web server the functionality needed by FrontPage to do its thing.

What Are Server Extensions?

The FrontPage Server Extensions consist of a suite of programs that can be installed on the Web server. (The extensions are included in the servers that come with Front-Page; to use them with other servers, you'd have to install them.) FrontPage, running on your computer, communicates with the extensions using standard Web protocols, and they, in doing what they are designed to do, provide the extra Web server functionality needed by FrontPage. Think of the function of the FrontPage Server Extensions as split into three general categories:

Authoring extensions allow you to save files to the Web server directly instead of FTPing them over there.

Administrating extensions allow you to assign Web team members the appropriate access to read or modify various parts of your site. Once access is allowed, that person can use FrontPage to make changes to the assigned portion of the site right from his or her desktop. These extensions also track what's what in the Tasks view, which is stored, logically enough, on the server. This gives all team members access to the Tasks view.

Browsing extensions allow you to include in your site such nifty elements as discussion groups, search pages, site indexes, and more—without these extensions, many of the more advanced features of your site simply would not work.

If you're simply building FrontPage webs on your local machine (and even if you're uploading them to your ISP), a lot of this is handled for you and you'll generally be unaware of the fact that the extensions are operating. If you have overall responsibility for a server, how to use the extensions will vary depending on your server. Here we offer a brief introduction; refer to bigger books on servers for more detail.

MASTERING WHAT'S ONLINE

As part of its FrontPage site, Microsoft offers information for Web site administrators at www.microsoft.com/frontpage/wpp. There you'll find plenty of detailed information about running the extensions in general, along with information for ISPs that want to support the extensions, and all sorts of useful tips.

NOTE The FrontPage Server Extensions as included on the FrontPage 2000 CD are presented in a choice of languages: English, German, and French, for example. This is mainly because the dialog boxes and messages you'll encounter in installing and using the extensions must appear in a language you'll understand. If the language you need is not on the CD, check for it on Microsoft's FrontPage Web site (www.microsoft.com/frontpage).

Which Servers Are Supported?

You'll probably never have to deal with installing the FrontPage Server Extensions. When you installed FrontPage, they were automatically installed on your computer. If your site is hosted by an ISP, it will be up to the ISP's system administrator to install the extensions on their Web server. Only if you host your site on your own in-house server will you have to install the server extensions. In any case, you ought to know a bit about them, if only to have intelligent conversations with your ISP.

The FrontPage Server Extensions are available in Unix and Windows versions. The Unix version works with the following types of Unix:

- Digital Unix
- BSDI Unix
- Linux
- HP/UX
- IRIX
- Solaris
- SunOS

You can use the FrontPage Extensions for Unix with any of the following Web servers:

- Apache
- CERN
- NCSA
- Netscape Commerce Server
- Netscape Communications Server
- Netscape Enterprise Server
- Netscape FastTrack Server

You can use the FrontPage Server Extensions for Windows with the following Web servers, running under Windows 95, Windows 98, or Windows NT:

- Microsoft Peer Web Service
- Netscape Commerce Server
- Netscape Communications Server
- Netscape Enterprise Server
- Netscape FastTrack Server
- O'Reilly WebSite
- Microsoft Personal Web Server

 TIP Microsoft is constantly working on the FrontPage Server Extensions. If your particular variant of Unix or your Web server is not listed, check to see if it's available online at the FrontPage home page (www.microsoft.com/frontpage).

Installing the FrontPage Server Extensions for Windows

The FrontPage Server Extensions are included with FrontPage on the CD-ROM. From there, you can install either the FrontPage Server Extensions for Windows or for Unix.

TIP Unless you're responsible for running a Web server—such as your corporate Web site's server—you won't have to deal with installing the FrontPage Server Extensions. When you installed FrontPage, a Web server was installed on your local machine automatically, along with the FrontPage Server Extensions.

You'll find the FrontPage Server Extensions for Windows in the FrontPage CD-ROM's SERVEXT directory. In that directory, you'll find the following files:

Select This File...	If You're Installing This...
FP98_EXT_ALPHA_ENU.EXE	English FrontPage Server Extensions for Alpha-based Windows NT
FP98_EXT_X86_DEU.EXE	German FrontPage Server Extensions for Windows 95, Windows 98, or Windows NT
FP98_EXT_X86_ENU.EXE	English FrontPage Server Extensions for Windows 95, Windows 98, or Windows NT
FP98_EXT_X86_ESP.EXE	Spanish FrontPage Server Extensions for Windows 95, Windows 98, or Windows NT
FP98_EXT_X86_FRA.EXE	French FrontPage Server Extensions for Windows 95, Windows 98, or Windows NT
FP98_EXT_X86_IRA.EXE	Italian FrontPage Server Extensions for Windows 95, Windows 98, or Windows NT
FP98_EXT_X86_JPN.EXE	Japanese FrontPage Server Extensions for Windows 95, Windows 98, or Windows NT

To install the FrontPage Server Extensions, simply run the appropriate program on the machine that's designated as your Web server. You'll be presented with a series of dialog boxes and files that will be copied to your local machine. Which dialog boxes actually appear will depend on the Web server you are running on your computer.

Configuring the FrontPage Server Extensions for Windows

Once you have the FrontPage Server Extensions for Windows installed on your computer, you can use the FrontPage Server Administrator to configure one or more of them. To run the FrontPage Server Administrator, follow these steps:

1. On the Windows Desktop, double-click the My Computer icon. The My Computer window appears.

2. In the My Computer window, double-click the C: icon. The contents of the window change to reflect your choice.

3. Now, in order, double-click Program Files, then Microsoft FrontPage, then Version 3.0, then Bin. The contents of the BIN directory now appear in the window.

4. Double-click FPSRVWIN.EXE. The FrontPage Server Administrator window appears, as shown in Figure C.1.

FIGURE C.1

The FrontPage Server Administrator window

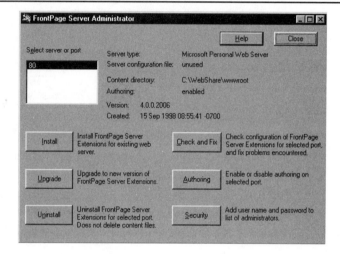

Now you can administer the FrontPage Server Extensions on your local machine. To learn more about administering the FrontPage Server Extensions, click the Help button. A Windows Help window appears, with online help for the FrontPage Server Administrator in view.

APPENDIX D

Installing and Testing Network Connections

For FrontPage to function properly, you must have IP (the *Internet Protocol*) running properly; if you're connected successfully to the Internet, it probably is. There may be cases, however, where some trouble has occurred. For the sake of helping you out of such a quandary, we've provided this appendix, which is like one long "Mastering Troubleshooting" sidebar.

In this appendix, we discuss how to get TCP/IP running on a Windows 95 or 98 machine, how to run the FrontPage TCP/IP test application, and how to test your machine's interaction with other machines on an intranet. Then we finish off by demonstrating how, when your computer is connected to the Internet, anyone else on the Internet can access the Web server on it. Let's take a look.

Installing TCP/IP

Installing TCP/IP correctly can be challenging. If you're lucky, you'll have access to a highly skilled network administrator who can install it on your computer for you.

 NOTE *TCP/IP* stands for the *Transport Control Protocol/Internet Protocol*, which is the method used to send information between computers on the Internet. Every computer that's connected to the Internet must be able to use TCP/IP. Windows includes TCP/IP, although it's not necessarily installed by default. Instead, TCP/IP is installed when you set up your Dial-Up Networking connection to your ISP, or by the person who sets up your network connection on your computer.

Sometimes, however, you might have to go it alone and install (or reinstall) TCP/IP yourself. If so, you'll need a few things:

- Your Windows 95 or 98 installation CD or floppy disks
- The IP addresses for two or three DNS servers
- The IP address of a gateway computer, if one is available (you can get this information from your ISP or from your network administrator)
- The IP address that has been assigned to your computer (if your computer is part of an intranet with a full-time connection to the Internet)

Now, if you've got your propeller beanie on and you're ready to give network installation a try, follow these steps:

1. No matter what you're working on, close all programs (saving your work if necessary). The Windows Desktop should be clear and visible.

2. From the Windows Start menu, select Settings ➤ Control Panel. The Control Panel window appears, with a list of various control panels.

3. Double-click the Network icon. The Network dialog box appears.

4. Read through the list of network components that are installed. You should see Client For Microsoft Networks, Dial-Up Adapter (if you have a modem), and the brand of your network card (if you have one). If the word TCP/IP appears anywhere here, skip ahead to step 9.

5. Click the Add button. The Select Network Component Type dialog box appears, with a list of four different types of components: Client, Adapter, Protocol, and Service.

6. Double-click Protocol. The Select Network Protocol dialog box appears. Manufacturers are listed on the left side; network protocols are listed on the right.

7. In the list of manufacturers, click Microsoft. Several different protocols appear on the right side of the dialog box. One of these should be TCP/IP.

8. Click TCP/IP, then click OK. You'll return to the Network dialog box. Newly listed should be one or two entries for TCP/IP. (It might say simply "TCP/IP"; if you have both a modem and a network card, you'll see "TCP/IP -> Dial-Up Adapter," and "TCP/IP -> NE2000," or whatever type of network card you have.)

9. Double-click the first TCP/IP entry. The TCP/IP Properties dialog box appears.

10. Click the IP Address tab. The dialog box changes accordingly.

11. If you are dialing up to the Internet, then it's 99 percent likely that you don't have a permanent IP address. Click the checkbox labeled Obtain An IP Address Automatically. Or, if you know your computer's permanent IP address, then click Specify An IP Address. Type the four numbers of your IP address in the four text boxes. Leave the subnet mask area blank unless your network or ISP requires one.

12. Click the WINS Configuration tab. The dialog box changes accordingly. Click the button labeled Disable WINS Resolution.

13. Click the Gateway tab. The Gateway panel appears. If you know your gateway's IP address, type the four numbers in the New Gateway area's four blanks. Click Add and the gateway's IP address appears in the Installed Gateways area.

14. Click the DNS Configuration tab. The DNS Configuration panel appears. Click the button labeled Enable DNS.

15. In the Host text box, type the name you want to use for your computer. (Remember this name, since you'll use it again in step 20.) Leave the Domain text box blank unless your intranet has a registered domain name and a full-time Internet connection.

16. In the DNS Server Search Order area, type the four numbers of the first DNS server's IP address. Click the Add button. The IP address of the first DNS server appears in the box below. Type the four numbers of the second DNS server in the same box. When you click the Add button a second time, it appears listed above the first DNS server. (If you have a third DNS server, you can enter its IP address in the same way.)

17. Click OK. The Network dialog box reappears.

18. Repeat steps 9 through 17 if more than one TCP/IP option is listed. The network card TCP/IP options might use different IP addresses for the DNS servers and gateway computer; check with your network administrator for the proper values. (If you're setting up your own small network, you may not need TCP/IP for your network card; you could use a different protocol like IPX/SPX or NetBEUI instead.)

19. Click the Identification tab. The dialog box changes accordingly.

20. In the Computer Name text box, type the same name that you used in step 15.

21. In the Workgroup text box, type the workgroup you want to join. (If your intranet doesn't have workgroups set up, then just make sure that every computer has the same workgroup, or use a generic name such as **mygroup**.)

22. In the Computer Description text box, you may optionally describe your computer (such as what type of computer it is, where it's located, or who uses it; for example, you could type **Anne's Pentium in Accounting**).

23. At this point, you may optionally click the Access Control tab. Two access control options appear on the panel. You may choose Share-level or User-level access control.

24. Click OK. Windows installs the network options that you have requested. A dialog box is displayed to indicate the installation's progress. You may be prompted to insert your Windows installation CD or floppy disks. A dialog box may appear asking you whether you want to keep files that are newer than the files now being installed. If this dialog box appears, click Yes. When Windows is finished, a dialog box appears telling you to reboot your computer.

25. Click Yes to reboot now. Your computer restarts.

Once the computer restarts, a new dialog box—the Windows Login dialog box—will appear every time you start Windows. You should type a username and password into the dialog box.

At this point, TCP/IP should be installed. You should run the FrontPage TCP/IP test as described in the next section.

Running the FrontPage TCP/IP Test Program

Every time you use FrontPage, it refers to your computer by its URL (which is simply http:// followed by your computer's name or address). While computer names are easier to type and remember, you'll usually have to use the *IP address* if you're accessing your computer remotely, across the Internet.

NOTE An *IP address* is a series of four numbers separated by periods (each number ranges from 0 to 255). Every computer on the Internet has an IP address. While we're all used to referring to Web sites by name (such as http://www.yahoo.com/), we could refer to them by IP address instead (such as http://204.71.200.66/).

The first time you run FrontPage, it detects the name and IP address of your computer. Every time you run FrontPage after that, it verifies that your computer's name and IP address are still valid. To see your computer's name and IP address, you can run the FrontPage TCP/IP test.

To run the FrontPage TCP/IP test, follow these steps:

1. From the FrontPage menu bar, select Help ➤ About Microsoft FrontPage. The About Microsoft FrontPage dialog box appears.

2. Click the Network Test button. The FrontPage TCP/IP Test dialog box appears.

3. Click the Start Test button. After a few seconds (or perhaps a few minutes, if your computer has an unusual configuration or if you're not connected to the Internet), the test results and information appear (see Figure D.1).

4. When you're finished looking at the results of the test, click the Exit button to return to the previous dialog box. Then click OK to return to FrontPage. The dialog box closes and you'll see the normal FrontPage window again.

As shown in Figure D.1, FrontPage's TCP/IP test performs five tests, and the word *Yes* should appear next to all five. (If any of the tests fail, you'll need to check your Windows Network control panel and make sure that all of the networking protocols are installed correctly; we'll give you some troubleshooting tips after describing the tests.)

In addition to verifying that the networking options are installed correctly, the TCP/IP test gives you valuable information about the name and IP address of your computer.

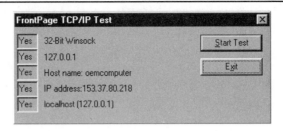

Here's an explanation of each of the five tests:

- The first test makes sure that a 32-bit Winsock is correctly installed. Winsock (Windows Socket) is the interface used by applications on your computer to work with TCP/IP. Windows provides a 32-bit version of Winsock (usually installed along with TCP/IP), but some computers may have an older, 16-bit version (designed for Windows 3.1). FrontPage requires a 32-bit Winsock to work correctly. If you have a 16-bit Winsock, you'll need to uninstall it and install the Windows 95 or 98 Winsock instead.

- The second test makes sure that the default IP address is working. The special *loopback* address 127.0.0.1 is shorthand for referring to the current computer, no matter what computer you're working on. FrontPage must be able to use 127.0.0.1 to refer to the computer it's installed on. If this test fails, there is a serious problem with the way TCP/IP was installed on your computer. You'll need to reinstall TCP/IP in the Windows Network control panel.

- The third test determines the host name of the current computer (established in the Windows Network control panel under the Identification tab). If this test fails, then your computer's network protocols are installed incorrectly.

- The fourth test determines the IP address for this computer. In general, every computer has to have its own unique IP address; no two computers on the entire Internet can share the same IP address. A computer may have two IP addresses: one for its Internet IP connection, and another for its Windows network address. FrontPage shows you the Internet IP address, if you're connected. Disconnect from the Internet to find out your network IP address. If this test fails, then your computer is not permanently connected to the Internet and does not have a network IP address.

- Finally, the fifth test makes sure that the special name *localhost* is working. Localhost, just like 127.0.0.1, should always refer to the current computer. If this test fails, then there is a serious problem with your TCP/IP installation.

By default, FrontPage uses your computer's name when you create FrontPage webs. Whenever you save a web, FrontPage saves the web to your local computer's Web server. Whenever you open a FrontPage web, you'll see your computer's name listed in the URL below the web.

You should also verify that your computer is accessible by its name and that your local Web server is running properly. Follow these steps:

1. From the Windows Start menu, choose your usual Web browser (such as Internet Explorer or Netscape Navigator). The browser window appears.

2. Now that you've fired up your browser, in the browser's location box, type **http://localhost** and press Enter. The default web, referred to by FrontPage as <Root Web> (local), should appear in the browser, as shown in Figure D.2.

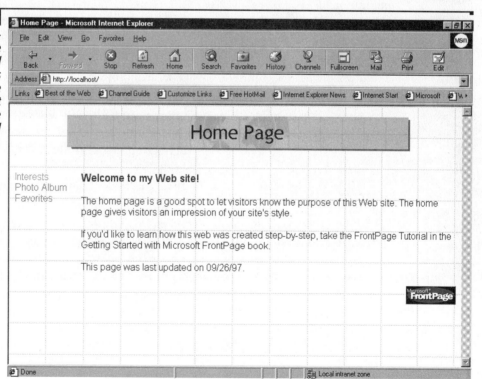

FIGURE D.2

Internet Explorer displays the default home page for the local computer, known as "localhost." This page is installed by default along with the Microsoft Personal Web Server.

3. Close your browser as you normally would (for example, by using the menu bar's File ➢ Exit command). You'll return to whatever you were doing before.

If this test was successful, great! You're well on your way to posting your FrontPage web. But if the test was not successful, you'll need to make sure that TCP/IP is installed correctly. You should review the installation instructions in Appendix A and verify that one of the Web servers that come with FrontPage was installed on your computer.

Testing Your Intranet Connection

Now for the tricky part: If your computer is part of an intranet, you'll need to test your connections on another computer located on the same intranet. When you run a browser on that remote computer, you should be able to reach your computer by using its IP address (not the localhost name or 127.0.0.1 address; those refer to *your* computer). You may also be able to reach it using its name; that depends on the way your intranet is set up.

For example, to see your computer's FrontPage webs from another computer on the intranet, follow these steps:

1. "Borrow" another computer on your intranet (your co-worker won't mind an extra coffee break) and start up its resident browser.

2. In the browser's location bar, type **http://** followed by your computer's IP address. For example, if the machine named has the IP address of 10.0.0.1, we would type **http://10.0.0.1** in the location box to see the root web for your computer (named "fargo" in this example) and press Enter. Your root web should appear.

3. Now in the browser's location bar, type in **http://** followed by your computer's name (for example, we would type **http://fargo**). If the root web of your machine loads in the browser window, you know that your intranet is set up to use machine names as well as IP addresses. If you receive an error message, then you know that other people will have to use your machine's IP address to access the Web server on your computer, not your machine's name.

4. Once you've verified that you can access your computer's FrontPage webs, close the browser as you normally would. The browser disappears and your co-worker can return to whatever he or she was doing before. (And be sure to thank him or her for loaning you the computer.)

Accessing Your Web Server across the Internet

If your computer has an Internet connection, then your computer is on the Internet. That means that anyone can actually see your computer's FrontPage webs, from anywhere on the Internet—if they know your IP address.

 WARNING If you're worried about potential security problems, check out FrontPage's Permissions feature; it's discussed in detail in Chapter 24, *Site Maintenance and Promotion*.

Before you get excited about this possibility, however, note that there are a few limitations to having your computer be a Web server. First, your computer must be turned on 24 hours a day and connected 24 hours a day to act as a permanent Web server. Second, your connection to the Internet must be fast. Don't even think about trying to host your Web site if your connection is through a modem. Third, any time that someone accesses your home page, your computer has to do work. If you're only getting a few visitors, you won't notice much of a slowdown. But if your site has lots of visitors, your computer may become too slow for you to use it. Fourth, your computer must be powerful and have lots of memory to be able to serve lots of visitors.

To prevent these problems, most people use a different computer for their staging server and their live Web server, and they don't use their local machines as public Web servers.

If, after all our cautionary notes, you're still interested, try it out. Connect to the Internet (if you're not connected already), and follow the steps we listed earlier in "Running the FrontPage TCP/IP Test Program" to find out your computer's IP address using the FrontPage TCP/IP test.

Now call up a friend and have them browse to your computer. They'll simply use the URL of http:// followed by the four numbers of your IP address. After a few seconds, they should see your root web.

 NOTE If they can't see your root web, it's probably because your computer is protected by your corporate firewall. A *firewall* is a barrier that prevents outside access to an intranet.

If you're part of an intranet that is permanently connected to the Internet and has its own domain name, then other people outside the company, on the Internet, might also be able to use your computer's name along with the domain name to reach it. For example, suppose you work for HappyFunCo, and your company's domain name is happyfunco.com. If your computer's name is fred, then people on the Internet may be able to see your computer's home page by using the URL of `http://fred.happyfunco.com/`.

 WARNING For this to work, your network administrator must have set up your network properly, enabling it to resolve names on your intranet. In addition, he or she must place your computer on a special list of computers that are allowed to be accessed by the Internet. Most network administrators will not allow access for security reasons.

APPENDIX <u>E</u>

HTML Reference

This HTML reference includes relevant tags and attributes for Web designers. It has been arranged alphabetically for convenient reference.

HTML Tags and Attributes

Tags	Attributes	Description
<!-- ... -->		SGML comment
<!DOCTYPE>		Public declaration
	HTML PUBLIC...	DTD conformance
<A>...</A>		Anchor
	ACCESSKEY=	Keyboard shortcut
	CHARSET=	Character encoding of link
	CLASS= ID= STYLE= TITLE=	Class(es), unique ID, style information, title
	COORDS=	Object coordinates of anchor
	DIR= LANG=	Text direction and language ID
	HREF=	Hypertext link
	NAME=	Name of hypertext link
	REL=	Forward link type
	REV=	Reverse link type
	SHAPE="rect | circle | poly | default"	Object shape of described anchor
	TABINDEX=	Explicit tabbing order
	TARGET=	Target frame name for rendering
	[events]	Core intrinsic events
<ACRONYM>...</ACRONYM>		Acronym content
	CLASS= ID= STYLE= TITLE=	Class(es), unique ID, style information, title
	DIR= LANG=	Text direction and language ID
	[events]	Core intrinsic events
<ADDRESS>...</ADDRESS>		Address content
	CLASS= ID= STYLE= TITLE=	Class(es), unique ID, style information, title
	DIR= LANG=	Text direction and language ID
	[events]	Core intrinsic events
<APPLET>...</APPLET>		Java applet
	ALIGN=	Alignment of applet
	ALT=	Alternate text description
	CODE=	Java applet name
	CODEBASE=	Location of applet
	DOWNLOAD=	Order of applet download

Tags	Attributes	Description
`<APPLET>...</APPLET>`	HEIGHT=	Height of object
	HSPACE=	Horizontal space
	NAME=	Name of applet
	VSPACE=	Vertical space
	WIDTH=	Width of object
`<AREA>`		Client-side image map area description
	ALT=	Alternate text description
	COORDS=	Coordinates
	HREF=	Hypertext link
	NOHREF	No hypertext link
	SHAPE="rect | circle | poly | default"	Shape of described area
	TABINDEX=	Explicit tabbing order
	TARGET=	Target frame name for rendering
	[events]	Core intrinsic events
`<B>...</B>`		Bold text
	CLASS= ID= STYLE= TITLE=	Class(es), unique ID, style information, title
	DIR= LANG=	Text direction and language ID
	[events]	Core intrinsic events
`<BASE>`		Base URL
	HREF=	Hypertext link
	TARGET=	Target frame name for rendering
`<BASEFONT>`		Font setting for document
	COLOR=	Color of basefont
	FACE=	Typeface of basefont
	SIZE=	Size of basefont
`<BDO>`		Bi-directional override
	DIR=	Text direction required
	LANG=	Language ID
`<BGSOUND>`		Background sound
	LOOP=	Number of times sound repeats
	SRC=	Address of sound file
`<BIG>...</BIG>`		Big text
	CLASS= ID= STYLE= TITLE=	Class(es), unique ID, style information, title
	DIR= LANG=	Text direction and language ID
	[events]	Core intrinsic events
`<BLOCKQUOTE>...</BLOCKQUOTE>`		Block quote
	CLASS= ID= STYLE= TITLE=	Class(es), unique ID, style information, title
	DIR= LANG=	Text direction and language ID
	[events]	Core intrinsic events
`<BODY>...</BODY>`		Body of document
	ALINK=	Active link color

Tags	Attributes	Description
	BACKGROUND=	Location of background image
	BGCOLOR=	Background color
	CLASS= ID= STYLE= TITLE=	Class(es), unique ID, style information, title
	DIR= LANG=	Text direction and language ID
	LEFTMARGIN=	Create left margin
	LINK=	Link color
	TEXT=	Text color
	TOPMARGIN=	Create top margin
	VLINK=	Visited link color
	[events] onload, onunload	Core intrinsic events
 		Break
	CLASS= ID= STYLE= TITLE=	Class(es), unique ID, style information, title
	CLEAR=	Fixes text beside or below image
<BUTTON>...</BUTTON>		Form button
	CLASS= ID= STYLE= TITLE=	Class(es), unique ID, style information, title
	DIR= LANG=	Text direction and language ID
	DISABLED	Disables button
	NAME=	Name of button
	TABINDEX=	Explicit tabbing order
	TYPE=	Type of button
	VALUE=	Action desired
	[events] onfocus, onblur	Core intrinsic events
<CAPTION>...</CAPTION>		Table caption
	ALIGN=	Alignment of table caption
	CLASS= ID= STYLE= TITLE=	Class(es), unique ID, style information, title
	DIR= LANG=	Text direction and language ID
	VALIGN=	Vertical alignment
	[events]	Core intrinsic events
<CENTER>...</CENTER>		Centers text
	CLASS= ID= STYLE= TITLE=	Class(es), unique ID, style information, title
	DIR= LANG=	Text direction and language ID
	[events]	Core intrinsic events
<CITE>...</CITE>		Citation content
	CLASS= ID= STYLE= TITLE=	Class(es), unique ID, style information, title
	DIR= LANG=	Text direction and language ID
	[events]	Core intrinsic events
<CODE>...</CODE>		Code content
	CLASS= ID= STYLE= TITLE=	Class(es), unique ID, style information, title
	DIR= LANG=	Text direction and language ID
	[events]	Core intrinsic events

Tags	Attributes	Description
<COL>...</COL>		Column
	ALIGN=	Alignment of column
	CLASS= ID= STYLE= TITLE=	Class(es), unique ID, style information, title
	DIR= LANG=	Text direction and language ID
	SPAN=	Number of columns spanned
	VALIGN=	Vertical alignment
	WIDTH=	Width of column
	[events]	Core intrinsic events
<COLGROUP>		Column grouping
	ALIGN=	Alignment of column grouping
	CLASS= ID= STYLE= TITLE=	Class(es), unique ID, style information, title
	SPAN=	Number of column groupings spanned
	VALIGN=	Vertical alignment
	WIDTH=	Width of column grouping
<DD>		Definition data
	ALIGN=	Alignment of data
	CLASS= ID= STYLE= TITLE=	Class(es), unique ID, style information, title
	DIR= LANG=	Text direction and language ID
	[events]	Core intrinsic events
<DEL>...</DEL>		Deleted text
	CITE=	Change data
	CLASS= ID= STYLE= TITLE=	Class(es), unique ID, style information, title
	DATETIME=	ISO change date
	DIR= LANG=	Text direction and language ID
	[events]	Core intrinsic events
<DFN>...<DFN>		Definition content
	CLASS= ID= STYLE= TITLE=	Class(es), unique ID, style information, title
	DIR= LANG=	Text direction and language ID
	[events]	Core intrinsic events
<DIR>...<DIR>		Directory list
	CLASS= ID= STYLE= TITLE=	Class(es), unique ID, style information, title
	COMPACT	Compact representation
	DIR= LANG=	Text direction and language ID
	[events]	Core intrinsic events
<DIV>		Document division
	ALIGN=	Alignment of text section
	CLASS= ID= STYLE= TITLE=	Class(es), unique ID, style information, title
	DIR= LANG=	Text direction and language ID
	[events]	Core intrinsic events

Tags	Attributes	Description
<DL>...</DL>		Definition list
	ALIGN=	Alignment of list
	CLASS= ID= STYLE= TITLE=	Class(es), unique ID, style information, title
	CLEAR=	Clears list
	COMPACT	Compact representation
	DIR= LANG=	Text direction and language ID
	[events]	Core intrinsic events
<DT>		Definition term
	ALIGN=	Alignment of term
	CLASS= ID= STYLE= TITLE=	Class(es), unique ID, style information, title
	DIR= LANG=	Text direction and language ID
	[events]	Core intrinsic events
<EM>...</EM>		Emphasized text
	CLASS= ID= STYLE= TITLE=	Class(es), unique ID, style information, title
	DIR= LANG=	Text direction and language ID
	[events]	Core intrinsic events
<EMBED>...</EMBED>		Embedded object
	ALIGN=	Alignment of object
	HEIGHT=	Height of object
	HIDDEN=	Hides object
	PALETTE=	Sets color palette
	PLUGINSPAGE=	Sets plug-ins source link
	SRC=	Location of object source
	WIDTH=	Width of object
	[events]	Core intrinsic events
<FIELDSET>...</FIELDSET>		Form fieldset
	CLASS= ID= STYLE= TITLE=	Class(es), unique ID, style information, title
	DIR= LANG=	Text direction and language ID
	[events]	Core intrinsic events
<FONT>...</FONT>		Font
	COLOR=	Color of font
	FACE=	Typeface of font
	SIZE=	Size of font
<FORM>...</FORM>		Form
	ACCEPT-CHARSET=	List of supported character sets
	ACTION=	Server-side form handler
	CLASS= ID= STYLE= TITLE=	Class(es), unique ID, style information, title
	DIR= LANG=	Text direction and language ID
	ENCTYPE=	Encryption type
	METHOD="get | post"	Form data sent to server

Tags	Attributes	Description
	NAME=	Name of form
	TARGET=	Target frame name for rendering
	[events] onsubmit, onreset	Core intrinsic events
<FRAME>...</FRAME>		Frame within frameset
	BORDERCOLOR=	Color of border
	FRAMEBORDER=	Width of border
	HEIGHT=	Height of frame
	MARGINHEIGHT=	Height of margin
	MARGINWIDTH=	Width of margin
	NAME=	Name of frame
	NORESIZE	Prohibits resize
	SCROLLING="yes | no | auto"	Sets scroll
	SRC=	Location of frame source
	WIDTH=	Width of frame
<FRAMESET>...</FRAMESET>		Frameset
	BORDER=	Width of border
	BORDERCOLOR=	Color of border
	COLS=	Number of columns
	FRAMEBORDER=	Width of border
	FRAMESPACING=	Space between frames
	ROWS=	Number of rows
	[events] onload, onunload	Intrinsic events
<HEAD>...</HEAD>		Document head
	DIR= LANG=	Text direction and language ID
	PROFILE=	URL of metadata
<H1>...</H1>		Heading 1
	ALIGN=	Alignment of heading
	CLASS= ID= STYLE= TITLE=	Class(es), unique ID, style information, title
	CLEAR=	Fixes text beside or below image
	COLOR=	Color of text
	DINGBAT=	Adds defined dingbat
	DIR= LANG=	Text direction and language ID
<H2>, <H3>, <H4>, <H5>, <H6>	Same as <H1>	Headings 2 through 6
<HR>		Horizontal rule
	ALIGN=	Alignment of rule
	CLASS= ID= STYLE= TITLE=	Class(es), unique ID, style information, title
	CLEAR=	Fixes text beside or below image
	COLOR=	Color of rule
	NOSHADE=	No shading on rule
	NOWRAP	No wrapping of rule

Tags	Attributes	Description
	SIZE=	Height of rule
	WIDTH=	Width of rule
	[events]	Core intrinsic events
<HTML>...</HTML>		Document container
	DIR= LANG=	Text direction and language ID
	VERSION=	HTML standard version used
<I>...</I>		Italic text
	CLASS= ID= STYLE= TITLE=	Class(es), unique ID, style information, title
	DIR= LANG=	Text direction and language ID
	[events]	Core intrinsic events
<IFRAME>...</IFRAME>		Inline frame
	ALIGN=	Alignment of inline frame
	BORDER=	Size of border
	BORDERCOLOR=	Color of border
	FRAMEBORDER=	Width of border
	FRAMESPACING=	Space between frames
	HEIGHT=	Height of frame
	HSPACE=	Horizontal space
	MARGINHEIGHT=	Height of margin
	MARGINWIDTH=	Width of margin
	NAME=	Name of inline frame
	NORESIZE=	Prohibits resize of frame
	SCROLLING="yes | no | auto"	Sets scroll
	SRC=	Location of inline frame source
	VSPACE=	Vertical space
	WIDTH=	Width of frame
<ILAYER>...</ILAYER>	(same as LAYER tag)	Inline layer positioning (behaves like text element)
<IMG>		Image
	ALIGN=	Alignment of image
	ALT=	Alternate text description
	BORDER=	Size of image border
	CLASS= ID= STYLE= TITLE=	Class(es), unique ID, style information, title
	DIR= LANG=	Text direction and language ID
	DYNSRC=	Dynamic source
	HEIGHT=	Height of image
	HSPACE=	Horizontal space
	ISMAP	Server-side image map
	LOOP=	Number of repetitions
	LOWSRC=	Location of low-resolution image

Tags	Attributes	Description
	NAME=	Name of image
	SRC=	Location of image source
	USEMAP=	Client-side image map
	VSPACE=	Vertical space
	WIDTH=	Width of image
	[events]	Core intrinsic events
<INPUT>...</INPUT>		Form input
	ACCEPT=	Accept input
	ALT=	Alternate text description
	CHECKED	Loads checkboxes already selected
	CLASS= ID= STYLE= TITLE=	Class(es), unique ID, style information, title
	DIR= LANG=	Text direction and language ID
	DISABLED	Disables input
	MAX=	Maximum number of input characters
	MAXLENGTH=	Maximum length of field
	NAME=	Name of form
	SIZE=	Size of field
	SRC=	Location of added images
	TABINDEX=	Explicit tabbing order
	TYPE=" button | checkbox | file | hidden | image | password | radio | reset | submit | text"	Type of input method
	USEMAP=	Client-side image map
	VALUE=	Sets default value
	[events] onfocus, onblur, onselect, onchange Core intrinsic events	
<INS>...</INS>		Inserted text
	CITE=	Change data
	CLASS= ID= STYLE= TITLE=	Class(es), unique ID, style information, title
	DATETIME=	ISO change date
	DIR= LANG=	Text direction and language ID
	[events]	Core intrinsic events
<ISINDEX>		Document is a searchable index—Obsolete, use <FORM> instead
	ACTION=	URL
	CLASS= ID= STYLE= TITLE=	Class(es), unique ID, style information, title
	DIR= LANG=	Text direction and language ID
	PROMPT=	Prompt text
<KBD>...</KBD>		Keyboard
	CLASS= ID= STYLE= TITLE=	Class(es), unique ID, style information, title

Tags	Attributes	Description
	DIR= LANG=	Text direction and language ID
	[events]	Core intrinsic events
<KEYGEN>...</KEYGEN>		Form-generated security key
	NAME=	Required
	CHALLENGE=	Public key challenge string
<LABEL>...</LABEL>		Form field label
	ACCESSKEY=	Keyboard shortcut
	CLASS= ID= STYLE= TITLE=	Class(es), unique ID, style information, title
	DIR= LANG=	Text direction and language ID
	DISABLED	Disables labeling
	FOR=	Field ID
	[events] onfocus, onblur	Core intrinsic events
<LAYER>...</LAYER>		Layer positioning element (behaves like structure)
	Note: Style sheets can also be used to control positioning of layer elements ina manner similar to but not the same as the W3C DOM and CSS-Positioning methods.	
	ABOVE=	Relative stacking order
	BACKGROUND=	Background image
	BELOW=	Relative stacking order
	BGCOLOR=	Background color
	CLIP="n,n,n,n"	Coordinates of viewable area
	HEIGHT=	Height of layer
	LEFT=	Horizontal position of layer in layer
	PAGEX=	Horizontal position of layer in page
	PAGEY=	Vertical position of layer in page
	SRC=	Source of content
	TOP=	Vertical position of layer in layer
	VIEW="hidden | inherit | show"	Define layer visibility
	WIDTH=	Horizontal size of layer
	Z-INDEX=	Absolute stacking order
	onmouseover, onmouseout, onfocus, onblur, onload	Intrinsic events
<LEGEND>		Form fieldset legend
	ACCESSKEY=	Keyboard shortcut
	ALIGN=	Alignment of legend
	CLASS= ID= STYLE= TITLE=	Class(es), unique ID, style information, title
	DIR= LANG=	Text direction and language ID
	[events]	Core intrinsic events

Tags	Attributes	Description
<LI>...</LI>		List item
	ALIGN=	Alignment of items
	CLASS= ID= STYLE= TITLE=	Class(es), unique ID, style information, title
	DIR= LANG=	Text direction and language ID
	TYPE=	Numbering or bullet style
	VALUE="number"	Reset sequence number
	[events]	Core intrinsic events
<LINK>		Link
	CLASS= ID= STYLE= TITLE=	Class(es), unique ID, style information, title
	DIR= LANG=	Text direction and language ID
	HREF=	Hypertext link
	MEDIA=	Supported media list
	NAME=	Name of link
	REL=	Forward link type (application dependent)
	REV=	Reverse link type (application dependent)
	TARGET=	Target frame name for rendering
	TYPE=	Media type
<MAP>...</MAP>		Client-side image map
	CLASS= ID= STYLE= TITLE=	Class(es), unique ID, style information, title
	NAME=	Name of image map
<MENU>...</MENU>		Menu list
	COMPACT	Compact representation
	CLASS= ID= STYLE= TITLE=	Class(es), unique ID, style information, title
	DIR= LANG=	Text direction and language ID
	[events]	Core intrinsic events
<META>		Metadata
	CONTENT=	Content description
	DIR= LANG=	Text direction and language ID
	HTTP-EQUIV=	Server response
	NAME=	Name of document
	TITLE=	Title of document
	URL=	URL of document
<NOBR>...</NOBR>		Inhibits line breaking
<NOEMBED>		Inhibits embedding
<NOFRAMES>...</NOFRAMES>		No frames alternate document body
<NOLAYER>...</NOLAYER>		Inhibits layers
<NOSCRIPT>...</NOSCRIPT>		Noscript data
<OBJECT>...</OBJECT>		Object
	ALIGN=	Alignment of object

APP
E

HTML Reference

Tags	Attributes	Description
	BORDER=	Width of border
	CLASS= ID= STYLE= TITLE=	Class(es), unique ID, style information, title
	CLASSID=	Class identifier
	CODE=	Type of script
	CODEBASE=	Object code base
	CODETYPE=	Media type
	DATA=	Data type
	DECLARE=	References object name
	DIR= LANG=	Text direction and language ID
	DISABLED	Disables object
	HEIGHT=	Height of object
	HSPACE=	Horizontal space
	NAME=	Name of object
	SHAPES=	Name of shaped hyperlink
	STANDBY=	Standby message
	TABINDEX=	Explicit tabbing order
	TYPE=	Media type
	USEMAP=	Image map
	VSPACE=	Vertical space
	WIDTH=	Width of image
	[events]	Core intrinsic events
<OL>...</OL>		Ordered list
	ALIGN=	Alignment of list
	CLASS= ID= STYLE= TITLE=	Class(es), unique ID, style information, title
	COMPACT	Compact representation
	DIR= LANG=	Text direction and language ID
	START=	Starting number
	TYPE=	Numbering style
	[events]	Core intrinsic events
<OPTION>...</OPTION>		Form option
	CLASS= ID= STYLE= TITLE=	Class(es), unique ID, style information, title
	DIR= LANG=	Text direction and language ID
	DISABLED	Disables option
	SELECTED=	Option selected at default
	VALUE=	Value to be returned
	[events]	Core intrinsic events
<P>...</P>		Paragraph
	ALIGN=	Alignment of paragraph
	CLASS= ID= STYLE= TITLE=	Class(es), unique ID, style information, title
	DIR= LANG=	Text direction and language ID

Tags	Attributes	Description
	WIDTH=	Width of paragraph
	[events]	Core intrinsic events
<PARAM>...</PARAM>		Parameter
	NAME=	Name of parameter
	TYPE=	Internet media type
	VALUE=	Sets value
	VALUETYPE=	Interprets value
<PRE>...</PRE>		Preformatted text
<Q>...</Q>		Inline quote
	CLASS= ID= STYLE= TITLE=	Class(es), unique ID, style information, title
	DIR= LANG=	Text direction and language ID
	[events]	Core intrinsic events
<S>...</S>		Strikeout text
	CLASS= ID= STYLE= TITLE=	Class(es), unique ID, style information, title
	DIR= LANG=	Text direction and language ID
	[events]	Core intrinsic events
<SAMP>...<SAMP>		Sample text
	CLASS= ID= STYLE= TITLE=	Class(es), unique ID, style information, title
	DIR= LANG=	Text direction and language ID
	[events]	Core intrinsic events
<SCRIPT>...</SCRIPT>		Script data
	LANGUAGE=	Script language
	SRC=	URL of script source
	TYPE=	Internet content type
	[events]	Core intrinsic events
<SELECT>...</SELECT>		Form selection list
	ALIGN=	Alignment of list
	CLASS= ID= STYLE= TITLE=	Class(es), unique ID, style information, title
	DIR= LANG=	Text direction and language ID
	DISABLED	Disables list
	HEIGHT=	Height of object
	NAME=	Names of object
	SIZE=	Size of object
	TABINDEX=	Explicit tabbing order
	WIDTH=	Width of object
	[events] onfocus, onblur, onselect, onchange	Core intrinsic events
<SMALL>...</SMALL>		Small text
	CLASS= ID= STYLE= TITLE=	Class(es), unique ID, style information, title

Tags	Attributes	Description
	DIR= LANG=	Text direction and language ID
	[events]	Core intrinsic events
<SPAN>...</SPAN>		Generic text container
	ALIGN=	Alignment of container
	CLASS= ID= STYLE= TITLE=	Class(es), unique ID, style information, title
	DIR= LANG=	Text direction and language ID
	[events]	Core intrinsic events
<STRIKE>...</STRIKE>		Strikeout text
	CLASS= ID= STYLE= TITLE=	Class(es), unique ID, style information, title
	DIR= LANG=	Text direction and language ID
	[events]	Core intrinsic events
<STRONG>...</STRONG>		Strong text
	CLASS= ID= STYLE= TITLE=	Class(es), unique ID, style information, title
	DIR= LANG=	Text direction and language ID
	[events]	Core intrinsic events
<STYLE>...</STYLE>		Style sheet definition
	DIR= LANG=	Text direction and language ID
	MEDIA=	Supported media list
	TYPE=	Internet content type
_{...}		Subscript text
	CLASS= ID= STYLE= TITLE=	Class(es), unique ID, style information, title
	DIR= LANG=	Text direction and language ID
	[events]	Core intrinsic events
^{...}		Superscript text
	CLASS= ID= STYLE= TITLE=	Class(es), unique ID, style information, title
	DIR= LANG=	Text direction and language ID
	[events]	Core intrinsic events
<TAB>		Tab value
	ALIGN=	Alignment of tab
	INDENT=	
<TABLE>...</TABLE>		Table
	ALIGN=	Alignment of table
	BACKGROUND=	Location of background image
	BGCOLOR=	Background color
	BORDER=	Size of border
	BORDERCOLOR=	Color of border
	BORDERCOLORDARK=	Dark color for 3-D border
	BORDERCOLORLIGHT=	Light color for 3-D border
	CELLPADDING=	Space between table cell edge and content

Tags	Attributes	Description
	CELLSPACING=	Space between cell borders
	CLASS= ID= STYLE= TITLE=	Class(es), unique ID, style information, title
	COLS=	Number of columns
	DIR= LANG=	Text direction and language ID
	FRAME=	External border around table
	HEIGHT=	Height of table
	NOWRAP	Prohibits text wrapping
	WIDTH=	Width of table
	[events]	Core intrinsic events
<TBODY>...</TBODY>		Table body
	ALIGN=	Alignment of table body
	BGCOLOR=	Background color
	CLASS= ID= STYLE= TITLE=	Class(es), unique ID, style information, title
	DIR= LANG=	Text direction and language ID
	VALIGN=	Vertical alignment
	[events]	Core intrinsic events
<TD>...</TD>		Table cell
	ALIGN=	Alignment of table cell
	AXIS=	Abbreviated cell name
	AXES=	AXIS values
	BACKGROUND=	Location of background image
	BGCOLOR=	Background color
	BORDERCOLOR=	Border color
	BORDERCOLORDARK=	Dark color for 3-D border
	BORDERCOLORLIGHT=	Light color for 3-D border
	CLASS= ID= STYLE= TITLE=	Class(es), unique ID, style information, title
	COLSPAN=	Number of columns spanned
	DIR= LANG=	Text direction and language ID
	HEIGHT=	Height of table cell
	NOWRAP	Prohibits text wrap
	ROWSPAN=	Number of rows spanned
	VALIGN=	Vertical alignment
	WIDTH=	Width of table cell
	[events]	Core intrinsic events
<TEXTAREA>...</TEXTAREA>		Form input text area
	ALIGN=	Alignment of text field
	CLASS= ID= STYLE= TITLE=	Class(es), unique ID, style information, title
	COLS=	Width of text input field
	DATAFLD=	Field of data
	DATASRC=	Location of data source

Tags	Attributes	Description
	DIR= LANG=	Text direction and language ID
	DISABLED	Disables text field
	ERROR=	Error message
	NAME=	Name of text field
	READONLY	Read-only
	ROWS=	Height of text input field
	TABINDEX=	Explicit tabbing order
	WRAP=	Wrap text
	[events] onfocus, onblur, onselect, onchange	Core intrinsic events
<TFOOT>...</TFOOT>		Table footer
	ALIGN=	Alignment of footer
	BGCOLOR=	Background color
	CLASS= ID= STYLE= TITLE=	Class(es), unique ID, style information, title
	DIR= LANG=	Text direction and language ID
	VALIGN=	Vertical alignment
	[events]	Core intrinsic events
<TH>...</TH>		Table cell heading
	ALIGN=	Alignment of heading
	AXIS=	Abbreviated cell name
	AXES=	AXIS values
	BACKGROUND=	Location of background image
	BGCOLOR=	Background color
	BORDERCOLOR=	Border color
	BORDERCOLORDARK=	Dark color for 3-D border
	BORDERCOLORLIGHT=	Light color for 3-D border
	CLASS= ID= STYLE= TITLE=	Class(es), unique ID, style information, title
	COLSPAN=	Number of columns spanned
	DIR= LANG=	Text direction and language ID
	HEIGHT=	Height of table cell
	NOWRAP	Prohibits text wrap
	ROWSPAN=	Number of rows spanned
	VALIGN=	Vertical alignment
	WIDTH=	Width of table cell
	[events]	Core intrinsic events
<THEAD>...</THEAD>		Table header
	ALIGN=	Alignment of header
	BGCOLOR=	Background color
	CLASS= ID= STYLE= TITLE=	Class(es), unique ID, style information, title
	DIR= LANG=	Text direction and language ID

Tags	Attributes	Description
	VALIGN=	Vertical alignment
	[events]	Core intrinsic events
<TITLE>...</TITLE>		Document title
	DIR= LANG=	Text direction and language ID
<TR>...</TR>		Table row
	ALIGN=	Alignment of table row
	BGCOLOR=	Background color
	BORDERCOLOR=	Border color
	BORDERCOLORDARK=	Dark color for 3-D border
	BORDERCOLORLIGHT=	Light color for 3-D border
	CLASS= ID= STYLE= TITLE=	Class(es), unique ID, style information, title
	DIR= LANG=	Text direction and language ID
	HEIGHT=	Height of table row
	NOWRAP	Prohibits text wrap
	VALIGN=	Vertical alignment
	VSPACE=	Vertical space
	[events]	Core intrinsic events
<TT>...</TT>		Monospaced text
	CLASS= ID= STYLE= TITLE=	Class(es), unique ID, style information, title
	DIR= LANG=	Text direction and language ID
	[events]	Core intrinsic events
<U>...</U>		Underline text
	CLASS= ID= STYLE= TITLE=	Class(es), unique ID, style information, title
	DIR= LANG=	Text direction and language ID
	[events]	Core intrinsic events
<UL>...</UL>		Unordered list
	ALIGN=	Alignment of list
	CLASS= ID= STYLE= TITLE=	Class(es), unique ID, style information, title
	COMPACT	Compact representation
	DIR= LANG=	Text direction and language ID
	SRC=	Location of list source
	TYPE="disk|square|circle"	Bullet style
	WRAP=	Wrap text
	[events]	Core intrinsic events
<VAR>...</VAR>		Variable content
	CLASS= ID= STYLE= TITLE=	Class(es), unique ID, style information, title
	DIR= LANG=	Text direction and language ID
	[events]	Core intrinsic events
<WBR>		Conditional break

INDEX

Note to the Reader: Page numbers in **bold** indicate the principal discussion of a topic or the definition of a term. Page numbers in *italic* indicate illustrations.

C

G